The Hardball Times Baseball Annual 2007

Featuring contributions by THT's staff writers:

Brian Borawski • John Brattain • Chris Constancio

David Gassko • Aaron Gleeman • Brian Gunn

Ben Jacobs • Larry Mahnken • Jeff Sackmann

Dave Studenmund • Steve Treder • Bryan Tsao • John Walsh

With additional contributions by guest writers:

Rob Neyer • John Dewan • Will Leitch

Rich Lederer • Jon Weisman • John Burnson

Vince Gennaro • Greg Rybarczyk • Mac Thomason

Produced by Dave Studenmund

The Hardball Times Baseball Annual 2007

New articles daily at www.hardballtimes.com

Edited by Carolina Bolado, Ben Jacobs, Bryan Tsao and Greg Tamer
Stats developed by Dave Studenmund and Bryan Donovan
Cover design by Tom Wright
Typesetting by Dave Studenmund

Published by: ACTA Sports
                 5559 W. Howard Street
                 Skokie, IL 60077
                 1-800-397-2282
                 info@actasports.com
                 www.actasports.com

ISBN-10: 0-87946-312-0
ISBN-13: 978-0-87946-312-0
Printed in the United States of America
Year: 12 11 10 09 08 07 06
Printing: 10 9 8 7 6 5 4 3 2 1

What's Inside

What's Inside (cont.)

Welcome to Our Book

This book is the result of a lot of hard work. To pull together a review of the 2006 baseball season, The Hardball Times staff and our guest writers performed Herculean feats of baseball reporting and analysis all year long. How hard did we work? Let me count the ways.

We forced ourselves (forced, I tell you!) to watch hours and hours of live and recorded baseball, often to the exclusion of our loved ones and pet rocks. We spent every extra hour—lying in bed, driving to work, showering—thinking about baseball and what it all means, just so we can communicate it to you in this Annual.

Our friends at Baseball Info Solutions watched every game live and on video (more than once) and recorded the speed and location of every pitch, the type of every batted ball and where it landed, and a number of other things I'm afraid to ask about.

We used BIS's data to create new batted ball stats, available only in this Annual. And John Dewan, the owner of BIS and creator of the *Fielding Bible*, converted the stats into the "Team Defense" article you can read in these pages.

During the season, David Appelman of Fangraphs (www.fangraphs.com) processed stats every morning and posted the results on his site, including the revolutionary Win Probability Added included in this tome.

Greg Rybarczyk of Hit Tracker (www.hittrackeronline.com) watched video of every single home run every night, logged it in his amazing Excel spreadsheet, and calculated the exact distance of each one. You can find his insights in our Analysis section.

Chris Constancio and Jeff Sackmann both built minor league websites that are updated daily and provide projections, graphs and splits for minor league players. Some of the fruits of their labors are included herein. Chris's site is First Inning (www.firstinning.com) and Jeff's is Minor League Splits (www.minorleaguesplits.com).

David Gassko created his own system for ranking pitchers, presented for the very first time in this book. David has also contributed other groundbreaking research for your reading pleasure, such as the impact of Tommy John surgery on pitching careers.

John Burnson, as part of his job publishing *Heater Magazine*, tracked how often each player played in each position during the year. That's not such a big deal, but his graphical depictions of playing time (included in our Appendix) are a new addition to the best of baseball analysis.

Brian Borawski tracked the fiduciary side of the diamond all year long and has written a summary of baseball business news. Vince Gennaro, who has analyzed so many baseball income statements and balance sheets that he's about to publish a book about them, has contributed a piece about competitive balance in baseball.

Very few baseball fans have worked as hard at their craft as the folks who bring you Retrosheet (www.retrosheet.org). For the Annual, John Walsh cranked through their play-by-play files to uncover the best outfield arms of the past 50 years.

Tom M. Tango, co-author of *The Book*, has spent years researching new statistical techniques and lent his WPA and Leverage Index tables to this effort.

We logged the specifics of every player's contract, so we could tell you who got the best deal and who got hosed (financially, that is). We incorporated Bill James's entire Win Shares formulas into Excel spreadsheets so we could post them on our website (and in this book). We probably did a bunch of other things that I don't even remember.

Some of us work so hard at this baseball thing that we've turned it into a profession. Author Rob Neyer (as in *Rob Neyer's Big Book of Baseball Blunders*), Will Leitch of Deadspin (www.deadspin.com), and sports editor Ben Jacobs spent the entire season tracking everything that happened (on and off the field) so that they could give you their own takes on the good, the bad and the bizarre.

Finally, the guy who co-founded The Hardball Times, Aaron Gleeman, has joined the ranks of fully employed baseball writers by signing a contract with NBCSports.com. Given the constraints on his time, Aaron's contribution to this Annual may be his last official act for the website he created; not a one of us will be able to thank him enough for the opportunity and fun THT has provided.

And then we produced this book. It took four editors—Carolina Boldabo, Bryan Tsao, Ben Jacobs and Greg Tamer—to handle all the editing chores. Andrew Yankech and Charles Fiore of ACTA Publications provided invaluable assistance and Bryan Donovan, the man who makes the THT website stats work, also lent a vital hand.

And what do we ask in return from you, dear reader? Please turn the page.

Happy Baseball,
Dave Studenmund
The Guy Who Harassed Everyone Else to Work Really Hard

The 2006 Season

Ten Things I Learned This Year

by Dave Studenmund

Every baseball season has its own character. Some seasons are remembered for their great pennant races, others for their exceptional individual performances, while a few are just remembered for their oddities. 2006 is likely to go down in the record books as, well, an odd duck.

The drama of division races in the AL Central and NL West was diluted by the Wild Card safety valve. Barry Bonds's new National League home run record was diluted by the specter of steroid use. And even the Cardinals' World Series victory was considered less than significant because they had the worst regular season record of any World Champ ever.

Still, there was much that was new in 2006, much that we learned and enjoyed. Allow me to list 10 things that caught my eye.

It's not the National Pastime anymore.

We Americans used to call baseball the National Pastime, but that quaint, parochial label no longer fits. The World Baseball Classic, played in March before an enthusiastic international audience, proved that players and fans from countries around the world take a back seat to no one, including us "North Americaners."

In a way, you can't blame us for being confused. The Olympics kicked baseball and softball out in 2005, supposedly because they were too "American" for the world stage. The WBC, a concept that had been bandied about for many years, seemed like a weak response to the Olympic rejection. A lot of folks probably figured that it would be a humdrum affair. The games were being held in the middle of spring training, so it was natural to think of the WBC as a bunch of international exhibition games. We were wrong; they were much more.

What we didn't understand was how passionate many countries are about their baseball, and how a tournament that consists of the best major league players differs from past international competitions. When Japan and Cuba agreed to play, joining Latin American powerhouses such as Puerto Rico and the Dominican Republic, a great time was guaranteed for all.

Many of the games reached a fever pitch worthy of the World Series. Fans from countries such as the Dominican and Venezuela, with their national pride at stake, took to the games in huge, boisterous numbers. Their enthusiasm carried through to the product on the field.

In the end, the United States team didn't even make it to the semifinals. The final four teams—Japan, Korea, Cuba and the Dominican Republic—all made fine showings in the tournament, and the games proved to be a great draw in their home countries and in the U.S., where 126,000 fans turned out for the final three games in San Diego's PETCO Park.

The next WBC will be played in 2009 and every four years thereafter. They promise to be thrilling affairs. For more about this year's WBC, read Jeff Sackmann's coverage a little later in this Annual.

The American League is better than the National.

Once we moved onto the regular season, there was another revelation waiting for us: the American League is way better than the National League. How do we know? Because interleague play, which began as a marketing ploy in 1997, was a lopsided affair in 2006. The American League busted the National in interleague competition, 154-98, which was a full 18 wins better than the previous high win total.

The junior circuit's rout was thorough and embarrassing. Only one NL team—the Rockies—had a record substantially above .500 in Interleague Play (they were 11-4; the Giants had a 8-7 record and no other team was above .500). The AL scored almost a full run more per game (5.3 to 4.4) and dominated the close games (one- or two-run margins) with a 64-41 record.

> **Nice Start**
>
> On September 2, the Indians' Kevin Kouzmanoff hit a grand slam in his first major league at bat. That's happened twice before, but according to SABR's David Vincent, Kouzmanoff was the first player ever to hit a slam on his very first major league pitch.

Interleague play even played a role in the pennant races. The Red Sox had their best first-place run by going 16-2 against the NL (only to fall spectacularly against the Yankees in August), and the Twins seemed to pick up steam while playing against the other league, also going 16-2 and eventually overtaking the Tigers for first place on the very last day of the season.

The AL cemented its superior position with a win in the All-Star game, guaranteeing home field advantage for the league representative in the World Series. Never mind that the Midseason Classic was a close 3-2 victory, with the deciding hit a two-out, two-run double by Texas' Michael Young in the ninth inning. It still "counted."

The lopsided interleague tally cast a season-long pall over the NL division winners (no one believed an NL team would win the World Series), and even screwed up a number of individual performances. For instance, Washington's Alfonso Soriano, who had a spectacular year for the Nationals, batted only .182 against his old league. As Soriano shops for a new team this offseason, he'd be well advised to seek out a National League one.

I don't expect the balance between the two leagues to be so severe in 2007; but for one brief period, the AL was just plain better. Until the World Series, that is.

Youth has been served.

Gone are the days when older players like Barry Bonds, Randy Johnson and Curt Schilling dominated the field and headlines. A new generation of ballplayers officially took center stage this year.

Nearly every statistical or dramatic angle in 2006 had a player under 30 in the lead, and it was often a rookie or second-year player. 23-year-old catcher (catcher!) Joe Mauer led the majors in batting average. 26-year-old Ryan Howard led the majors in home runs and RBIs. Jered Weaver became the first American League rookie since Whitey Ford to win his first nine decisions. Francisco Liriano was only the second rookie to ever go into the All-Star break with an ERA under 2.00 and at least 10 wins (Jerry Koosman did it in 1968).

> **Not So Fast There, Son**
> On September 10, the Mets' Julio Franco was a "defensive substitute" for third baseman David Wright, who wasn't even born the last time Franco played third.

The Dodgers turned to youth to save their season. When players such as Eric Gagne, Dioner Navarro, Kenny Lofton and Bill Mueller were injured, their replacements weren't just adequate, they were better. Russell Martin, Andre Ethier and Jonathan Broxton were just some of the youngsters who made a splash in LA and helped propel the Dodgers to the playoffs.

The American League champion Detroit Tigers displayed some of the finest young arms in the game, including rookies Justin Verlander and Joel Zumaya. Two of the best players on the best regular-season National League team (the Mets) were also virtually kids: Jose Reyes and David Wright.

And the Florida Marlins seemingly played no one but youngsters who were born after Julio Franco first played in the major leagues. Their rookie starter (okay, one of many rookie starters) Anibal Sanchez, pitched a no-hitter against the Diamondbacks on September 6, more than two years since the last major league no-hitter. Even milestones were set by the kids.

> **Detroit Turnaround Facts**
> The American League champion Detroit Tigers, who finished 95-67, were 43-119 just three years ago. That's the biggest three-year turnaround in baseball history, eclipsing even the 1914 Miracle Braves.
>
> On August 2, the Tigers posted their 72nd win of the year. Detroit was 71-91 in 2005. That was the earliest date on which a team coming off a season of at least 60 wins surpassed its victory total from the prior year.

The cast of youth took on biblical proportions when Jered Weaver's ascendancy prompted the Angels to designate his brother, Jeff, for assignment. Jeff, of course, redeemed himself with an outstanding postseason for the Cardinals.

In Tampa Bay, the kids provided a different sort of drama. Delmon Young was suspended 50 games for throwing his bat at an umpire during a minor league game and B.J. Upton was arrested on suspicion of drunken driving. A *USA Today* article, on the first page of the sports section, highlighted the discontent of the Devil Rays' youth with Young saying "I don't know what they're waiting for. They're, what, 30 games out of first place? They think they're going to mess up their clubhouse chemistry. B.J. should be up there. What are they waiting for? They always have excuses."

Hey, Delmon, just because you're young doesn't mean you have to act immature.

What happened to the old guys? Nothing bad, really. They just continued to get old. Randy Johnson struggled in New York; Barry Bonds struggled with his knees but still had one of the best over-40 seasons in baseball history; Roger Clemens returned to the Astros again (this time for $22 million) and pitched very well, but not as well as in 2005; Julio Franco continued to be an ageless wonder but didn't match his production of 2005.

A few pages in, Rich Lederer covers the rookie class in more detail, but let's just say that 2006 will be viewed in history as the year in which a new breed of stars emerged. Book it.

Negro Leaguers (and pre-Negro Leaguers) who belong in Cooperstown.

Bruce Sutter was inducted into the Hall of Fame this year. As rightfully controversial as that selection was, it was nothing compared to the brouhaha that erupted when the Hall announced its Negro League selections earlier in the year.

To its credit, the Hall recognized that great players from the pre-integration era were still underrepresented in its ranks, and asked Negro League historians to fix the situation. A five-person committee chose an initial list of 39 potential candidates for the Hall, and then a 12-person committee, chaired by non-voting former commissioner Fay Vincent, met early in 2006 to vote for Hall inclusion. Seventeen of the 39 candidates received at least the 75% minimum required for induction into the Hall.

The result was an extraordinary list of early pioneers in baseball history; players and owners who would receive their just recognition in Cooperstown. But their moment in the sun was eclipsed by the omission of Buck O'Neill, who had become the face of Negro League baseball to many baseball fans.

In fact, this is what commentator Keith Olbermann had to say about O'Neill's snub:

Just to twist the knife a little further into Buck O'Neil, the special committee elected Alex Pompez, owner of the New York Cubans team... Also an organized crime figure... Part of the mob of the infamous '30s gangster Dutch Schultz... Indicted in this country and Mexico for racketeering.

He's in the Hall of Fame. For all time. Buck O'Neil is not. It is not merely indefensible. For all the many stupid things the Baseball Hall of Fame has ever done... This is the worst.

The situation isn't so clear to me. Based on his playing career alone, many Negro League experts feel that O'Neill wasn't qualified for the Hall. Presumably, Olbermann's outrage was based on the significant work O'Neill did to keep the memory of those times alive. Perhaps that sort of consideration was, or should have been, included in the committee's charge. But who knows?

Buck O'Neil spoke at the Hall of Fame ceremony, saying "This is quite an honor for me." He showed class every time someone asked him about the Hall, refusing to express any regret. But Buck O'Neil passed away two months later, losing a chance to see his own plaque in the Hall.

Unfortunately, the O'Neill controversy eclipsed the achievements of the 17 inductees, great historical figures who deserved more. Here is a partial list of those who were inducted:

- Jose Mendez, who played in Cuba and the Negro Leagues until 1926, was called "The Black Diamond" and was generally recognized as the greatest black pitcher of his era. Sometimes, people would stand and clap when he walked into a restaurant.
- Pete Hill, a star outfielder who played mostly before the Negro Leagues were organized, hit over .300 eight times and over .400 twice with Cuban teams and some of the loosely organized pre-Negro League teams.
- Ray Brown was an outstanding pitcher in the Negro Leagues, and one of five players recognized as major-league caliber in a 1938 Pittsburgh Pirates memo. The other four were Satchel Paige, Cool Papa Bell, Josh Gibson and Buck Leonard, all members of the Hall already.
- Cum Posey, an outfielder and then owner of the Homestead Grays, who was one of the most powerful executives of the Negro Leagues.

Space considerations force me to stop here, but I urge you to read about the newest Hall-of-Fame inductees at the Negro League Baseball Professional Association website (http://www.nlbpa.com/index.html).

It's not just steroids anymore.

Steroids continued to be the story that sizzled in 2006. Stronger drug testing was introduced. For the first time, testing could occur anytime during the season, not just during spring training. Tougher penalties were included (50 games for the first offense, 100 for the second and a lifetime ban for the third) and amphetamine testing was also included.

A book entitled *Game of Shadows*, by two *San Francisco Chronicle* reporters, chronicled alleged steroid use by Barry Bonds in great detail. Former Senator George Mitchell was asked by Bud Selig to conduct an independent investigation into steroid use and abuse in recent baseball history. And former Red Sox pitcher Paxton Crawford admitted in a story in *ESPN the Magazine* that he used steroids during his career.

> ### Recommended Reading
> There were a lot of baseball books published this year. We didn't read them all (not even close!), but we can recommend the following:
> - *Feeding the Monster* by Seth Mnookin
> - *John Dewan's Fielding Bible*
> - *Rob Neyer's Big Book of Baseball Blunders*
> - *The Echoing Green* by Joshua Prager
> - *Fantasyland* by Sam Walker
> - *The Only Game in Town* by Fay Vincent
> - *The Book* by Tom Tango, Mitchel Lichtman and Andy Dolphin

Well, it turns out that this focus on steroids may be a little bit shortsighted. In fact, someday we may fondly recall the days of Congressional investigations and grand jury leaks; Jose Canseco, Rafael Palmeiro and, um, Alex Sanchez.

The landscape shifted early in the season when Arizona pitcher Jason Grimsley was busted for receiving a package of Human Growth Hormone (HGH). Immediately, our umbrella of concern spread from just steroids to a host of potential performance-enhancing drugs, or PEDs. Because many of us don't really understand the difference between all of these chemicals and their effects, we may have to settle on PEDs (if you say it real fast, it sounds like Pez) as the description of everything we're likely to hear about in the future.

The upshot of these acronyms is that drug use and abuse is never going to go away. Current drug tests don't adequately test for HGH use, and players can be expected to continue to search for new chemical edges in their pursuit of athletic excellence and outrageous salaries.

Meanwhile, Barry Bonds's new National League home run record was greeted with suspicion and indifference everywhere but in San Francisco. And future feats of athletic derring-do, such as Ryan Howard's prodigious home run total this year (58, which used to be a really, really big number) will be forever tainted by unwarranted suspicion. And that may be the most damaging aspect of PED use of all.

Satire and reality. What's the diff?

The excellent satirical humor newspaper *The Onion* started a sports section this year, and there were times when it was hard to tell the difference between what was happening on the field and what the *Onion* was "reporting." Half of the following stories were real-life events this year, and the other half were Onion headlines. See if you can tell the difference:

- David Wright endorses faith healer in a TV ad: "Hi, I'm David Wright. I invite you to the 'Salvation Miracles Revival Crusade' with Dr. Jaerock Lee, at Madison Square Garden, July 27, 28 and 29."
- Alfonso Soriano regrets joining 40-40 club after meeting other members.
- Blue Jays forced to disinfect clubhouse after two players are placed on the DL.
- MLB to place asterisk, pound sign, exclamation point, letter 'F' next to Bonds' name in record books.
- Orioles return shipment of Brian Roberts bobble head dolls because Roberts isn't really black.
- Ozzie Guillen fined $10,000 for what he just thought.
- Pete Rose signs baseballs saying "I'm sorry I bet on baseball." When the purchaser sells them on eBay, Rose decides to sell his own on his website.
- Pete Rose caught trying to get inducted into Hall of Fame under assumed name.
- Giant frog mascot for the Class-A Greenville Drive arrested for fondling woman at game.

We've asked Will Leitch, the editor of the excellent baseball site ("with an edge") Deadspin (www.deadspin.com) to contribute his own take on 2006 in this year's Annual. All of the events in Will's article really happened.

Nothing works in the postseason. Nothing.

"My shit doesn't work in the postseason." Ever since Billy Beane famously muttered that self-assessment in Michael Lewis's *Moneyball*, baseball writers and analysts have spent a lot of time and energy looking for the keys to postseason success. Before this year's postseason run, some even felt they had found it, citing hot pitching, starting pitching and success against top pitching as the real keys to a championship run.

But all the head scratching and stat-adding didn't help predict this year's postseason. In fact, only one of the postseason series ended with the favorite actually winning—the Mets' win over San Diego in the first round—and the St. Louis Cardinals made history by having the worst regular-season record of any World Series winner ever (their 83-78/.516 record was worse than even that of the 1987 Twins, who were 85-77/.525). This was the year that commentators returned to that old saw, "The postseason is just a crapshoot."

Even the new fad of Wild Card teams winning the World Series didn't pan out. The Cardinals actually did finish first in the NL Central, despite being the first team to ever blow a five-run lead (or greater) three different times during the season and despite losing nine of their last 12 games and almost allowing the Astros to grab the division title at the last minute. There was nothing in a book or spreadsheet that would have led you to choose the Cardinals as the eventual World Series champion.

Yet win it they did. In the end, spreadsheets and theories mean nothing. Only head-to-head competition matters and the Cardinals, particularly their reborn starters and reconstructed bullpen, beat the best. The postseason isn't constructed to make baseball analysts feel better about their formulas. It's simple head-to-head competition between the teams. The Cardinals won that competition fair and square.

So if you're upset that the Cardinals won the World Series, I have three words for you: Get over it.

Maybe curses never really go away.

Imagine that you're lost on a desert island. You're a doctor, and you've helped your fellow survivors make it through many terrible ordeals. Unfortunately, you've been captured by The Others who want you to cooperate with them on something that's not yet quite clear.

How do you suppose they gain your cooperation? Do they threaten or torture you? Promise to make you rich? Not in the television show *Lost*. *Lost's* protagonist, a diehard Red Sox fan named Jack Shephard, was stuck on that island when the Sox won it all in 2004, so he never knew that the Sox had broken the "curse." So when The Others showed Jack the videotape of the Sox winning the Series and finally ridding themselves of the Curse of the Bambino, he fell apart, putty in their hands, realizing that he had missed the one thing of real meaning in his life.

Unfortunately, if Jack ever does return to Boston circa 2006, things will feel remarkably similar. The Sox had a typically great run in May and June (thanks partly to the interleague bloodbath) and were only a game and a half out of first when the division-leading, ever-reviled Yankees came to town for a five-game series in mid-August. Five-game series are rare in this day and age, and East Coast fans were ready for battle.

What they got was a massacre. The Boston Massacre, it was quickly called: a destructive five-game Yankee sweep by tremendously high scores (such as 12-4, 14-11, 13-5 and 8-5) and the Red Sox subsequently plummeted in the standings, eventually finishing as low as third place for the first time in nine years.

> **That's Just Eerie**
> On June 25, Baseball Musings (www.baseballmusings.com) noted that "after giving up six runs in four innings to the New York Mets, a pitcher named Towers owned an ERA of 9.11."

Everything went wrong for the Sox. Former Golden Boy Theo Epstein seemingly lost his Midas Touch when he traded Bronson Arroyo for Wily Mo Pena. That trade may eventually turn in Boston's favor, but Arroyo had a sensational year for the Reds and Pena was injured part of the year for the Sox.

Worse, the Sox had to trade for a catcher they initially traded away—Doug Mirabelli to and from the Padres. One of the principals they gave up to get Mirabelli back was the sensational rookie Cla Meredith, who was a key contributor to San Diego's pennant-winning season.

Then Jason Varitek had arthroscopic surgery on his knee in August, and the Sox acquired Javy Lopez from the Orioles to replace him. Lopez batted .191 in 18 games before being released just one month later. The transactions just didn't go Boston's way this year. Have I mentioned Coco Crisp?

Even worse, long-time Boston correspondent Peter Gammons suffered an aneurysm, promising rookie starter Jon Lester was diagnosed with cancer late in the year, and David Ortiz suffered heart palpitations. Yes, the Curse seemed to return in full force this year. But it didn't stop at the New England borders.

The curse turned fickle and also turned on its long-time beneficiary, the Yankees. Alex Rodriguez, the American League's Most Valuable Player in 2005, endured catcalls and media sniping as he slumped through several months of the season and hit his personal nadir in the postseason. In the first round of the playoffs against the Detroit Tigers, A-Rod went 1-for-14 and was dropped to eighth in the order.

And true tragedy struck the Yankee organization when pitcher Cory Lidle's plane crashed into a Manhattan apartment building—killing Lidle and his flight instructor—just days after the Yankees were eliminated from the postseason.

Obviously, this is a new curse with new victims. Perhaps we should call it The Curse of The Others.

Now we know who's probably winning

In 1970, Eldon and Harlan Mills published a little book called *Player Win Averages*. It was a review of the 1969 season using brand new computations spit out by new-fangled things called computers. It didn't provoke a revolution in baseball watching, but it should have.

We now call the Mills' brothers' approach Win Probability Added or Win Expectancy, and 2006 was the year it started to really seep into the public's consciousness. OK, I'm overstating the point. WPA may never really make it into the general public's eye or the mainstream media, but it did come a long way in 2006.

- It was highlighted in *The Book*, a fantastic mathematical review of baseball field strategy.
- Daily WPA updates for every player and game were made available at Fangraphs (www.fangraphs.com)
- The *Washington Post* posted live WP graphs of National games on its Internet site.
- Fan sites such as Soxwatch (http://soxwatch.blogspot.com/) and Lookout Landing (www.lookoutlanding.com/) posted daily WPA updates and game graphs.

WPA isn't so much a new baseball statistic as it is a new way of following the game. As such, it's different from any other recently introduced baseball calculation. I've got an in-depth look at 2006's Win Probability Added in the Analysis section of the book. As you read it, keep an open mind. You may not watch the game quite the same way again.

There will be no player strike for the next five years.

While the postseason was still being played, negotiators for Major League Baseball owners and the player's union were hammering out a new Collective Bargaining Agreement in the hopes of averting another long, drawn-out public spat. The good news is that they succeeded. There really isn't any bad news.

The new agreement tweaks the system in terms of revenue sharing, free agent and draft compensation and salaries.

> **Double Threat**
> Chad Cordero recorded the last defensive out of the season for the Nationals, and then in the bottom of the 9th he struck out, making the final offensive out of the season, too.

You can read about some of the key provisions in Brian Borawski's "Business of Baseball Report," and we'll report more details on our website as they become available during the offseason.

That they succeeded is a sign that owners and players have reached a point of relative equilibrium, at least for now. It's not as though things couldn't be better (Hello? World Series in the snow?), but things are pretty darn good right now, and no one wants to mess with success.

After the trauma of the 1980s and 1990s, we baseball fans deserve it.

American League East Review

by Larry Mahnken

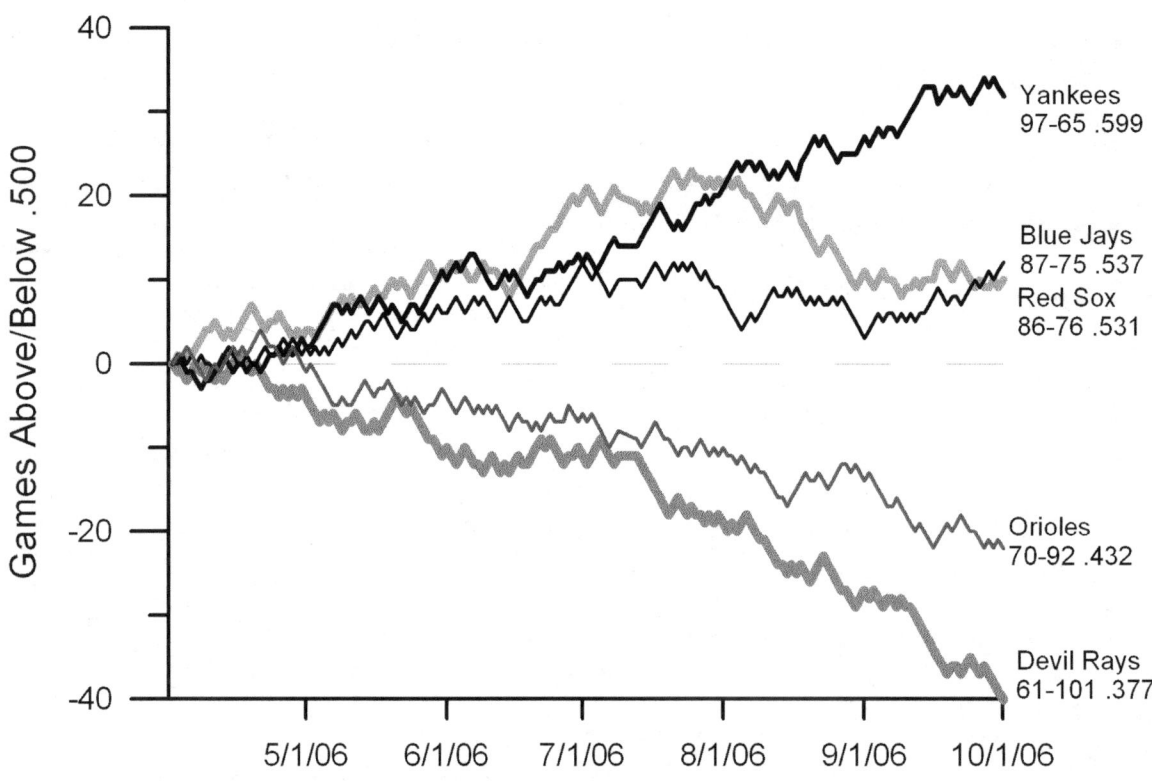

Year after year, while the main story and epilogue change, the denouement always remains the same in the AL East. Yankees win, Red Sox stick around for a while, and the Blue Jays, Orioles and Devil Rays are out of it before the games get meaningful. Is everyone other than the Yankees and Red Sox unlucky? Incompetent? Or is there something seriously wrong with the system? Is it designed in such a way that these three teams will never get a whiff of October glory, unless something seriously goes wrong both in Beantown and the Big Apple? Maybe a natural disaster of some sort could hit the Northeast and wipe those two teams out. But then, that would probably take out Baltimore, too. Oh well, sometimes you've got to crack a few eggs...

There were no Atlantic tsunamis this year, so it pretty much looked like New York and Boston again in 2006, though the Blue Jays had spent big in the winter hoping to make the leap from "everyone else" to "the team in the AL East people can root for." Leo Mazzone may have said that "The time is now, the place is now" when he was hired to work his Atlanta magic with the O's pitching staff, but this year wasn't the "place" it was going to happen. There were three teams in the division with better starters, better relievers and better hitters

than Baltimore, and the Orioles would have to pass all three to make the playoffs. The rest of the American League was too good for them to win the Wild Card with fewer than 90 wins, and they weren't going to win 90 games. As for the Devil Rays—come on.

Once the games started, things pretty much went as expected. The Orioles couldn't repeat their first-half surge of 2005, and they quickly settled into fourth between the good teams and the Devil Rays, who sank to last place just as quickly, despite Jonny Gomes's 11 April home runs. Boston's offense fell off considerably and Coco Crisp got injured right away, but Curt Schilling and Josh Beckett looked untouchable, while Jonathan Papelbon *was* untouchable. He didn't give up an earned run until May, and he didn't blow a save until June. The Yankees were scoring runs at a spectacular pace, but they struggled to win games in which they didn't score a bunch of runs. Mike Mussina was the team's only strong starter early, and Randy Johnson started getting torched regularly after a spectacular first half of April. At the end of April, the Yankees and Red Sox were separated by percentage points at the top of the standings, both three games over .500, with the Blue Jays only a game behind.

It was fortunate for the Blue Jays that the Yanks and Sox started slowly, because they did, too. While the line-up had been almost as good as New York's in the first month, the pitching was hideous. Roy Halladay was as good as you'd expect him to be, Ted Lilly was good—and that was it. A.J. Burnett didn't start until April 15 because of an injury, and after another injury in his second start, he didn't take the mound again for two months. The rest of the starters were giving up over seven runs per nine innings. With the bullpen leading up to B.J. Ryan posting an ERA of 5.63, it was a testament to how well they were hitting that they were still over .500.

And so it went through the summer. On May 11 in a home game against the Red Sox, the Yankees suffered a devastating loss when Hideki Matsui broke his wrist diving for a ball and was knocked out of the lineup for three months. Only a couple of weeks later, Gary Sheffield, who had been on and off the DL with a wrist injury, underwent surgery on his wrist that knocked him out for three months, too. Their great lineup was suddenly gutted, they had Bernie Williams and Melky Cabrera starting in the corners, and yet still they plugged away. At the end of May the Yankees and Sox were tied, with Toronto 2½ back. On June 15, the Yankees led by a game, with Boston and Toronto in a virtual tie for second, each a game behind.

Then Boston exploded. They swept the Braves in Atlanta, the Nats in D.C. and crushed the Mets at home to sweep Pedro Martinez's new team in his return to Fenway. It took late-inning heroics by David Ortiz two games in a row, but they extended their winning streak to 12 by sweeping the Phillies. After they were finally stopped by Dontrelle Willis, they won two more, and 14 of 15. On July 1, they had the Yankees and Jays on the brink, both four games out of the division lead.

By this time the Devil Rays, 15½ out, knew they weren't going anywhere in 2006 and started to sell off their spare parts. Joey Gathright was the first to go; they were able to get a good young arm in J.P. Howell from the Royals in exchange. Then they were able to pawn Mark Hendrickson, who was having a surprisingly good season, and Toby Hall, who was unsurprisingly not, off on the Dodgers, who sent Jae Seo and Dioner Navarro back—younger players with more potential (and smaller salaries). Before the trade deadline, they were also able to move Aubrey Huff to the Astros and Julio Lugo to the Dodgers.

But before they completely threw in the towel, the Devil Rays brought the Red Sox back down to earth. Scott Kazmir two-hit the Sox on July 3, and they scored six runs in the last two innings to beat Boston the next night, keeping the Yankees, who were getting

shellacked in Cleveland, from losing any more ground. They then won the third game before dropping the finale, but they weren't able to help Boston like they'd helped the Yankees—they lost the first two games of their weekend set against New York before salvaging the last game before the All-Star Break.

It was at this point that the Yankees and Blue Jays parted ways. The Yankees went into the break three back—Toronto, five back. Boston lost three of four to the A's at home coming out of the break, which gave the Yankees, who swept, and the Blue Jays, who won two of three from Seattle, an opening to get right back in. After beating the Rangers 10-1 on July 17, the Jays were just 3½ out, but they would never get any closer. Two days later, Shea Hillenbrand incited a confrontation with manager John Gibbons by writing "this is a sinking ship" on a dry-erase board in the clubhouse, which he followed by telling the press that he had been mistreated by the front office and expected to be traded. Sure enough, during the game he was designated for assignment. The team responded by winning three of four from the Yankees that weekend. And then, the ship sank. They dropped five of seven on a West Coast trip before getting swept in New York to fall 8½ games out on August 3. They had one more surge in them, going 18-9 to finish the season to take second place away from the Red Sox for the first time since 1997.

The Red Sox ended July in first place, but things were becoming a lot less cheery in Boston. Aside from Ramirez and Ortiz, the lineup lacked punch. Trot Nixon didn't hit at all in July and went on the DL at month's end; Jason Varitek hit terribly all year and would have knee surgery in early August. Coco Crisp had been expected to match Johnny Damon's production, but instead he was struggling to keep his OPS over .700. Josh Beckett was giving up home runs at an alarming rate, and his ERA was hovering around 5.00; the bullpen was in tatters, and outside of Schilling and rookie Jon Lester, nobody was pitching well.

And there was worse news coming out of—where else?—New York. Since losing Matsui and Sheffield, the Yankees had tried to replace their production without trading away their top prospects or the youngsters contributing to the team. Since everyone was insisting on getting one or two of those players in exchange for anyone useful, they were stuck with what they had, or could pick up on waivers. They did pretty well with that, but in late July the deal of a lifetime fell into their laps.

The Phillies were falling out of contention, and general manager Pat Gillick was eager to shed payroll. He preferred to move Pat Burrell, but when he couldn't find takers, he lowered his asking price for Bobby Abreu. Abreu's power numbers had dropped precipitously in 2006, but he was still an on-base machine, and he was perfect for the Yankees' lineup. With a hefty option for 2008 that would probably need to be picked up, Abreu was out of the price range of almost every team that could use him, except, of course, the Yankees. When Gillick stopped asking for top prospects, Brian Cashman swooped in and lifted Abreu away from Philly for B-level minor leaguers.

The Yankees lineup was suddenly a beast again, and the addition of Cory Lidle, also acquired in the trade, helped deepen a rotation in need of deepening. Chien-Ming Wang had stepped up to become the Yankees' ace, but no one else in the rotation was particularly reliable, except perhaps Mussina, who was nowhere near as good in midsummer as he'd been early on.

Boston needed two miracle ninth-inning comebacks in three days against the Indians to hold off the Yankees, but on August 3 they finally succumbed and fell a game behind New York for the first time since the start of their 12-game winning streak. They nearly collapsed there, losing two of three in Tampa Bay and getting swept by the Royals in Kansas City, but the Yankees couldn't take advantage. After expanding their lead to three games on August 15, the team stopped hitting and lost two straight. The Yankees headed into a five-games-in-four-days do-or-die series in Fenway just 1½ games up.

Both teams had reason to be worried. The Sox had been slumping, their lineup was beat up and their rotation was shoddy. The Yankees' bullpen was shot, they had been shut down by mediocre pitching the previous two days, and Sidney Ponson was starting the nightcap on the first day. Both teams feared losing four or five games; both would have been satisfied with two wins. Everyone knew that it was a crucial series, but nobody realized that it would end up comprising the last five games that would matter in the AL East in 2006.

The first game was close early on, but the Yankees finally broke through in the fifth against Jason Johnson, broke it open in the seventh, and went on to win 12-4. Neither starter escaped the fourth in the nightcap, and Boston was able to take a 10-7 lead into the seventh. But Craig Hansen and Mike Timlin couldn't hold the lead, and the Yankees exploded for seven runs, sweeping the Friday doubleheader with a 14-11 win.

Saturday, the Yankees took an early lead, but the Red Sox were able to break through against Randy Johnson in the fourth. But Josh Beckett gave the lead right back, and when Boston tied it again in the bottom of the fifth, Beckett exploded, giving up four more runs and sending

the Yankees on their way to their third straight victory, 13-5. Not only had the Yankees already won the series, they were conjuring up memories of the 1978 "Boston Massacre," only instead of erasing the last vestiges of a huge deficit, this massacre was opening one up.

The Sox appeared to be in position to stop the bleeding on Sunday night, when they took a 5-3 lead into the eighth inning behind Curt Schilling. But Terry Francona chose to go with Timlin and Javier Lopez instead of Papelbon for two innings, and the bases were quickly loaded with no outs. Papelbon came in to hold the Yankees to just one run, but in the ninth Derek Jeter dunked a two-out RBI single into right to tie the game, and in the 10th Jason Giambi and Jorge Posada homered to win the game 8-5, and essentially bury the Red Sox.

The finale was something of a formality. David Wells gave the Red Sox every chance, but Cory Lidle was untouchable, tossing six shutout innings to lead the Yankees to a 2-1 win and a 6½ game lead. Boston's slim chances at a comeback faded as they started suffering more injuries, losing Ortiz, Ramirez and Papelbon. Jon Lester was diagnosed with lymphoma in early September, putting not just his career, but his life in danger. Despite the sense of perspective that might have given, the season still had to be a disappointment, even for a team that was viewing 2006 as something of a retooling year.

That kind of "disappointment" would have been a success for the O's, though. The team took a major step backwards in 2006, losing 92 games and finishing near the bottom of the league in both offense and pitching. There were highlights: 22-year-old Nick Markakis stepped up to hit .291 with 16 homers, three of them on one night in August against the Twins. Chris Ray, 24, stepped into the closer role and excelled, and Erik Bedard became a 15-game winner and perhaps the cornerstone of a rotation that would lead the O's back to the top. And the man they hope will be the other cornerstone, Daniel Cabrera, gave them the highlight of the season, taking a no-hitter into the ninth inning against the Yankees in New York.

It was a sub-optimal lineup that Cabrera shut down that night, but a week later Kenny Rogers and Jeremy Bonderman were doing the same thing to the good one. The Yankees' postseason collapse made the season a failure from the perspective of each of the five teams in the East, but they can all look at their rosters for 2007 and see hope. They don't all have a hope of contending next year, but they should all have someone worth watching.

And you never know—there's apparently a big volcano off the coast of Africa just waiting to collapse into the Atlantic and send a big wave towards the US. That would make the pennant race real interesting.

American League Central Review

by Aaron Gleeman

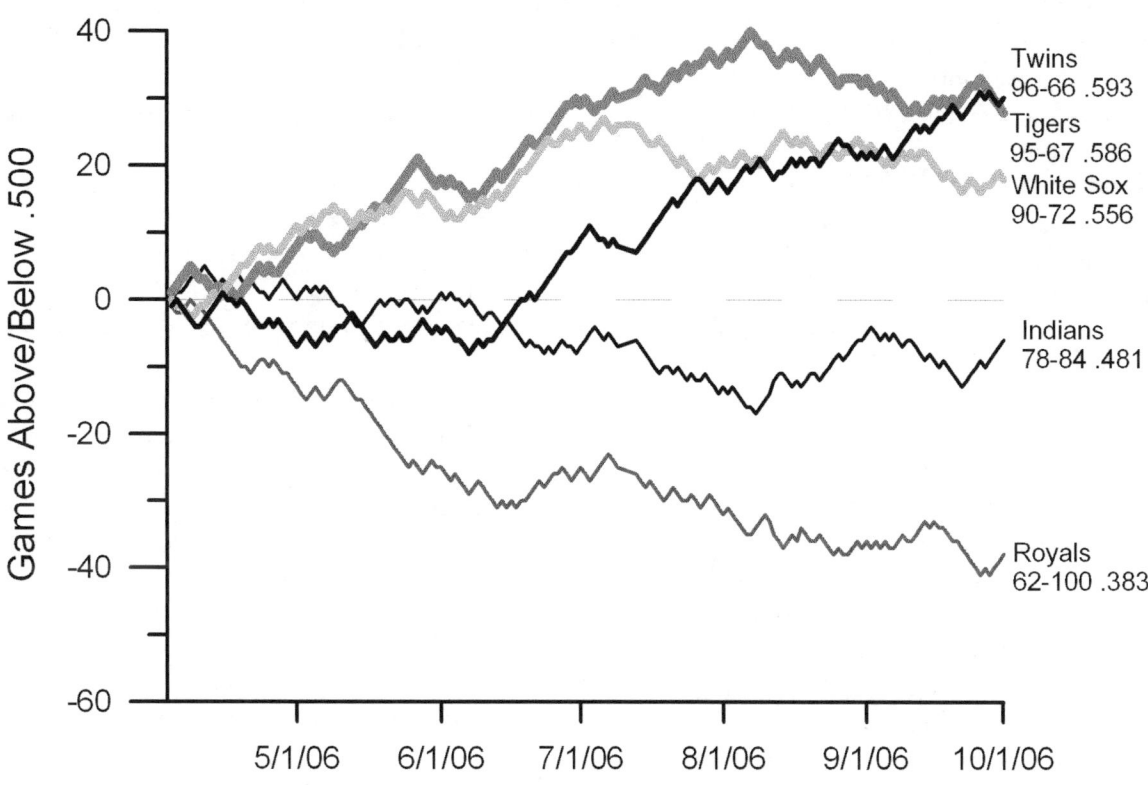

"Don't look back. Something might be gaining on you." – Satchel Paige

Take the script from the 2005 American League Central race. Now swap in "Detroit" for "Chicago" and "Minnesota" for Cleveland." Finally, just for fun, spruce up the ending a bit by changing it so that the big comeback attempt—the one that falls agonizingly short in the final week of the season—actually happens this time.

Congratulations, you've successfully penned the story of the 2006 American League Central.

In 2005, it was the White Sox who defied preseason expectations to jump out to an incredibly fast start, opening up a huge lead in the division before the other four teams even knew what hit them. In 2006, it was the Tigers who came out of nowhere by looking nearly unbeatable out of the gates, leaving the rest of the division gasping for air as they blitzed through the schedule and built up a huge early lead.

The '05 White Sox went 17-7 in April, 18-10 in May, 18-7 in June, and were sitting at an MLB-best 57-29 at the All-Star break. The '06 Tigers went 16-9 in April,

19-9 in May, 20-7 in June, and were sitting at an MLB-best 59-29 at the All-Star break. As Yogi Berra might say, it was déjà vu all over again.

Both teams continued their amazing run in the second half, with Chicago arguably reaching its 2005 high-water mark after sweeping a four-game series in Baltimore beginning the last weekend in July. After finishing off the sweep with a 6-3 win over the Orioles on August 1, the '05 White Sox were 69-35 and led the AL Central by 15 games over the Indians and 15½ games over the Twins, with just 58 games left to play.

Similarly, Detroit likely reached its high-water mark in early August, sweeping Cleveland in a three-game series and then blowing out Minnesota in a game that saw Francisco Liriano leave after four innings with elbow and shoulder problems that would eventually end his amazing rookie season. It was August 7, the Tigers were 76-36, they led the division by 10 games over the White Sox and 10½ games over the Twins, and there were just 50 games left to play.

Armed with baseball's best record, a double-digit lead, and only one-third of the season left on the schedule, both the '05 White Sox and '06 Tigers proceeded to steadily give away their cushion in the standings. Chicago did so by playing .500 baseball, going 28-28 between August 2 and the end of September, which allowed red-hot Cleveland to rapidly make up ground by going 38-16 over that same span.

In 2006, Detroit coughed up its huge lead the old-fashioned way and started losing games left and right. After dropping just 36 of their first 112 games, the Tigers finished August 3-9 and then went 12-15 in September. The Twins continued to plug away through it all, posting a 34-23 record between the two months.

Thanks to a game-tying homer from Joe Mauer in the bottom of the ninth and a walk-off, bases-loaded single from Jason Bartlett in extra innings, the Twins improbably moved into a first-place tie after defeating the Royals on Thursday, September 28. After trailing Detroit by a dozen games at the All-Star break and double digits in the middle of August, Minnesota merely had to win more games over the final 72 hours of the season to take home its fourth division title in five years (thanks to the Wild Card going to the loser and Detroit's edge in the tie-breaker, there would be no one-game playoff for the title).

Of course, even that looked unlikely. The Twins hosted a three-game series with the White Sox over the final weekend of the season and had committed to skipping Johan Santana's final start in order to keep him rested for Game 1 of the postseason. Meanwhile, the Tigers welcomed the last-place Royals to Comerica Park for a three-game set after having won 14 of their first 15 matchups with Kansas City.

And then something funny happened. Detroit lost Friday, and so did Minnesota. The Tigers dropped Saturday's game too, and so did the Twins. Suddenly neither team looked like they wanted the division championship, and a Twins comeback that seemed laughable in June and improbable well into September was now down to the final day of the season.

Minnesota finally took care of business, beating the White Sox 5-1 behind Carlos Silva early Sunday afternoon. The Twins then gathered in the dugout to watch the end of the Tigers-Royals game on the Metrodome JumboTron along with the 25,000 fans who stuck around to do the same. Looking like a bunch of little leaguers on a sugar-high—they were dancing around and pulling out all sorts of rally caps—the Twins looked on as the Royals came back from a 7-4 deficit, scoring four runs in the eighth inning to take an 8-7 lead.

Then, just because they're the Royals and anything else would have been anticlimactic, Scott Dohmann

served up a game-tying solo homer to Matt Stairs in the bottom of the inning. After a scoreless ninth inning, the game headed into extra frames as Kenny Rogers came out of the bullpen for the Tigers, making it clear that manager Jim Leyland wanted the division title (and a first-round matchup against the A's instead of the Yankees).

Rogers held the Royals off the board in the 10th, but loaded the bases with one out in the 11th and Esteban German at the plate. German—who had upset various AL Central foes throughout the season by exaggeratedly celebrating what seemed like an obscenely high number of key hits for someone on a horrible team—came through yet again with a single to right field, giving the Royals a 9-8 lead.

After getting David DeJesus to ground into a force out at home plate, Rogers then gave the Royals an added cushion by walking Emil Brown with the bases loaded (bringing up memories of his doing the same against Andruw Jones in the playoffs years ago). Armed with a two-run lead, Jimmy Gobble came out of the Royals' bullpen and slammed the door for Kansas City's 62nd win of the season. The Metrodome crowd erupted, and the Twins stormed the field for their second champagne-pouring, goggles-wearing celebration in a week.

If not for the fact that Detroit still advanced to the postseason via the Wild Card, it would have been one of the most improbable, dramatic, exciting comebacks in baseball history. And it was still pretty damn amazing, Wild Card or not. After beginning the season 25-33, the Twins finished with 71 wins over their final 104 games to win the division without ever leading prior to the season's final day.

Prior to that final Sunday, there was no single moment when the balance of power shifted, and the Twins didn't even deliver their own knockout blow, allowing the Royals to do it for them. It was like a boxing match that saw one fighter get knocked down five times in the first three rounds before getting up, quietly dominating the fight without knocking his opponent down, and then walking away with the victory on a judge's decision.

Rarely has the old cliché about baseball being a marathon rather than a sprint been truer, because the Twins were an absolute mess early on, owning the league's second-worst record after one-third of the season. Tony Batista and Juan Castro combined to form perhaps baseball's worst left side of the infield, single-handedly dragging the lineup down while turning a once-stout defense into a lethargic show of rangelessness.

Francisco Liriano was stuck dominating one inning at a time in the bullpen, Justin Morneau was putting together a second straight disappointing campaign, and the supposed strength of the team—starting pitching—was giving up runs in bunches. Realizing the team as currently constructed was going nowhere fast, general manager Terry Ryan and manager Ron Gardenhire decided to admit to their early mistakes and shake things up.

Liriano entered the starting rotation, going 11-3 with a 1.92 ERA in 16 starts to give the Twins an unmatched "pair of aces" along with Johan Santana. Liriano led the league in ERA before injuries eventually sidetracked his incredible rookie season. Morneau was reportedly given a strong "talking to" that resulted, whether directly or not, in his hitting .345/.396/.592 with 28 homers and 113 RBIs over the final 129 games of the year.

While perhaps not quite as dramatic, Castro and Batista were unceremoniously dispatched and replaced with Nick Punto and Jason Bartlett. Bartlett had been putting up big numbers at Triple-A for three seasons, yet had fallen out of favor with the coaching staff due to what was vaguely referred to as a "lack of leadership." His defense was an immediate improvement over Castro's—and Punto's an even bigger upgrade over Batista's—and a .309 batting average made everyone forget why he was stuck at Rochester again to begin with.

And, of course, the Twins also had arguably the two best players in the American League in Santana and Mauer. Santana was brilliant from start to finish, going 19-6 with a 2.77 ERA and 245 strikeouts in 233⅔ innings to become just the eighth pitcher in baseball history to win the MLB Triple Crown by leading both leagues in wins, ERA, and strikeouts. Had the voters not suffered a collective lapse in judgment by giving Bartolo Colon the 2005 Cy Young Award, Santana would have captured his third straight CYA in 2006.

His 23-year-old battery mate made history of his own by becoming the first catcher in baseball history to lead both leagues in batting average, hitting .347 and collecting a pair of hits on the season's final afternoon to hold off Derek Jeter for the AL batting title. Mauer threw out 38% of would-be basestealers, caught over 1,000 innings for a staff that ranked second in ERA, and batted a ridiculous .452 in June before putting an exclamation point on his season (and putting to rest talk of catchers having to tire down the stretch) with a .329 average in September.

Between Santana, Mauer, and Morneau, the Twins had three of the league's leading MVP candidates, and

it would have been four had Liriano's elbow not gotten in the way. Add closer Joe Nathan to the mix—he went 7-0 with a 1.58 ERA, 36 saves, 95 strikeouts, and a .158 opponent's batting average in 68⅓ innings—and no team in baseball could match the Twins in terms of top-heavy star power. The Twins' comeback was the story of the season, but their numerous MVP-caliber performances were the driving force behind it.

In fact, the AL Central was home to numerous outstanding individual performances in 2006, which led to what was once annually MLB's weakest division becoming its strongest. In the first dozen seasons of the AL Central's existence, the division combined for a better-than-.500 winning percentage just three times and had a cumulative mark of 325 games *below* .500 outside of division play.

That all changed in 2006, as Minnesota, Detroit, and Chicago all won at least 90 games, and even fourth-place Cleveland approached a break-even record. Kansas City went just 62-100, but still won 40% of its games outside of the division. In all, the AL Central went 421-389 in 2006, which was good for a .520 winning percentage that ranks as the division's best since its inaugural season in 1994. And, as Tigers fans will be quick to point out when hearing about the Twins' amazing comeback, the Central also produced the AL's Wild Card for the first time.

The division's great individual performances stretch beyond Minnesota's superstar quintet of Santana, Mauer, Morneau, Liriano, and Nathan. Detroit's unsung MVP was Carlos Guillen, who batted .320/.400/.519 with 100 runs at shortstop, but the Tigers were as deep as the Twins were top-heavy. Detroit got 15-plus homers from seven players—including 20-plus from Brandon Inge, Craig Monroe, Magglio Ordonez, and Marcus Thames—and Ivan Rodriguez batted .300 while gunning down 26-of-51 stolen-base attempts despite just missing the previous list with 13 homers.

Even with all that power, the pitching staff was the real story, as the Tigers sliced their ERA from 4.51 to a league-best 3.84. The rotation included 41-year-old Kenny Rogers, who went 17-8 with a 3.84 ERA, and 23-year-old flame-throwers Jeremy Bonderman and Justin Verlander, who combined to go 31-17.

Thirty-eight-year-old closer Todd Jones appeared on the verge of losing his job early on, but ended up converting 37 of his 43 saves chances and posting a 1.80 ERA in the second half. Jones racked up all the saves, but the real key to the bullpen was rookie Joel Zumaya, who lit up radar guns across the league with triple-digit readings while going 6-3 with a 1.94 ERA and 97 strike-outs in 83⅓ innings.

In Chicago, a disappointing title defense still led to 90 wins and huge numbers from the middle of the order. Holdovers Paul Konerko and Jermaine Dye combined to blast 79 homers while driving in 233 runs, with offseason acquisition Jim Thome delivering 42 bombs and 109 RBIs of his own. Maneuvering through the heart of Chicago's lineup was a nightmare for opposing teams, but the White Sox were ultimately done in by a pitching staff that was a different kind of nightmare.

The Indians were an even bigger disappointment after making serious noise in 2005, but Travis Hafner cemented his status as baseball's most underrated player by hitting .308/.439/.659 with 42 homers and 117 RBIs before injuries conspired again to keep him from playing a full season. Hafner was perhaps the league's most productive hitter prior to the injury, but had trouble matching teammate Grady Sizemore's all-around value. In his second full season, Sizemore batted .290/.375/.533 with 28 homers, played all 162 games, stole 22 bases while being caught just six times, played outstanding defense in center field, and led the league in doubles (52), extra-base hits (92), and runs scored (134).

Using Win Shares Above Bench (WSAB), the AL Central accounted for eight of the league's top dozen players in 2006, including three from Minnesota (Mauer, Santana, Morneau), two from Detroit (Guillen, Rodriguez), two from Chicago (Thome, Dye), and one from Cleveland (Sizemore). From an amazing comeback, two playoff participants, a second straight World Series team, and a number of amazing individual performances, it was a season to remember in the AL Central.

American League West Review

by Bryan Tsao

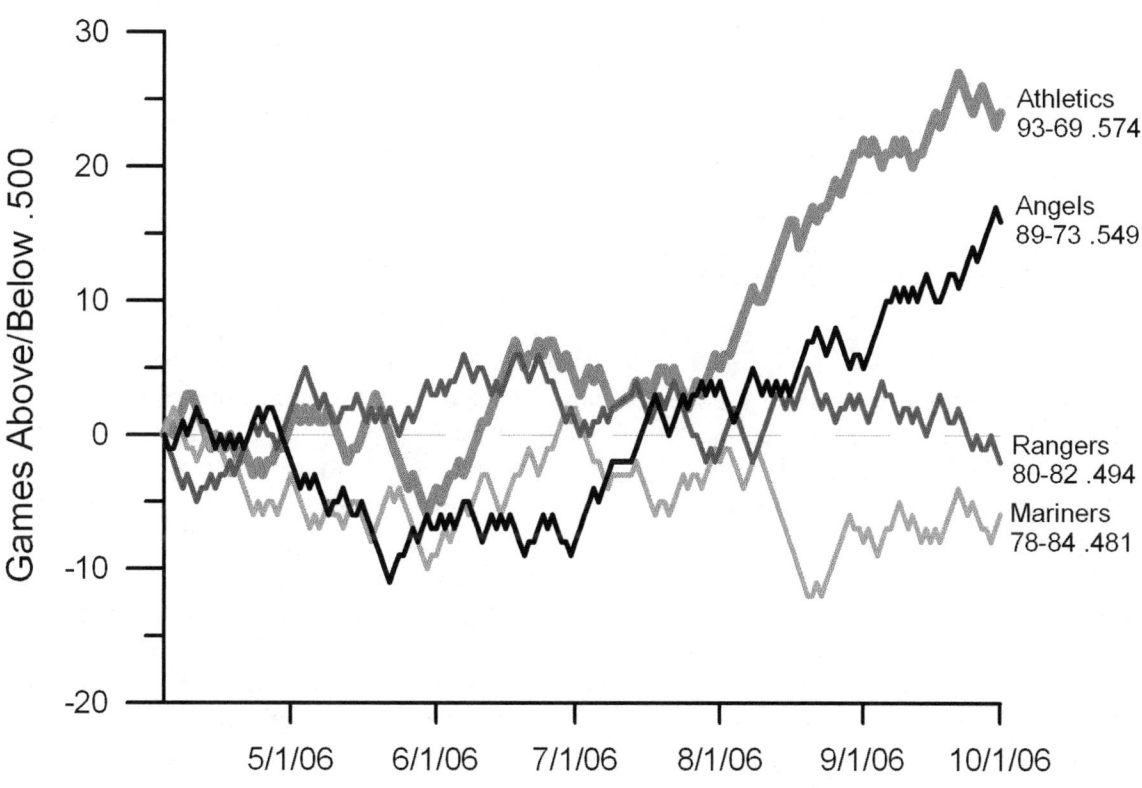

If a rivalry forms on the West Coast, and no one on the East Coast notices it, is it still a rivalry? Since 2001, the Oakland A's and the Los Angeles Angels of Anaheim have combined for the last five American League West titles, finishing 1-2 in every season except 2003. Coming into this season, most pundits had the A's and the Angels battling it out for the division (not to mention NorCal-SoCal bragging rights), and once again, they delivered (unlike, say, another more bally-hooed division rivalry).

On top of that, the division also featured a worthy third place team in the Texas Rangers, who led the division as late as mid-July, and a promising young team in the Seattle Mariners, who contended well into the summer. But those two teams couldn't flip the script on the best rivalry that happens after half the country goes to bed.

So what was the difference between the A's and the Angels this season? Many might point to the two teams' divergent records against the Mariners—the A's went 17-2 against Seattle, while the Angels went a more pedestrian 10-9. However, I would look at the underly-

ing reason the A's were able to win so many more games against an otherwise solid Mariners team: depth.

In 2005, the A's surged to the division lead in the second half, only to falter in September with Rich Harden, Bobby Crosby and Mark Kotsay all missing significant time in the second half. During the offseason, Athletics general manager Billy Beane addressed his team's propensity for the disabled list by adding veterans Frank Thomas, Milton Bradley, Esteban Loaiza and prospect Chad Gaudin without subtracting any significant players. As a result, the A's were able to weather the inevitable injuries and ineffectiveness from their young and injury-prone roster.

Due to injuries, the A's were only able to get a limited number of games and innings from erstwhile ace Rich Harden, Crosby, Loaiza, Bradley and Justin Duchscher-er. But thanks to their newfound depth, they were able to plug guys like Kirk Saarloos into the rotation and Jay Payton into the lineup, instead of throwing guys like Joe Kennedy, Seth Etherton and Matt Watson into the mix. Here's a quick look at how the A's main replace-ments this season fared compared to their counterparts in 2005:

Batters

Year	Player	Games	OPS
2005	Scott Hatteberg	134	.677
2005	Marco Scutaro	118	.710
2006	Marco Scutaro	117	.747
2006	Jay Payton	142	.743
2006	Bobby Kielty	81	.770

Pitchers

Year	Player	Games	ERA*
2005	Joe Kennedy	8	5.27
2006	Kirk Saarloos	16	4.88

*ERA in starts only

The A's depth also allowed them to cut bait on Dan Johnson quickly after he struggled coming out of the gate; he was replaced with Jay Payton, which upgraded the defense. All in all, the A's reinforcements allowed them to overcome far more troublesome injuries in 2006 than the ones that derailed their 2005 season.

And the A's needed every last bit of that depth to overcome an Angels team with which it was very evenly matched. Over 162 games, the A's won only four more games than the Angels (93-89), scored just five more runs (771-766), and allowed just five fewer runs (727-732). Both teams featured strong rotations despite losing their aces for most of the season, defenses that regressed from previous years, and offenses in the bottom half of the league.

Interestingly, many Angels observers have singled out defense as the difference between the two teams. At first glance, that seems reasonable, given that the Angels committed 124 errors, compared to 84 for the A's, and were subsequently charged with 80 unearned runs (48 for the A's). Given the slim five-run difference between the A's and the Angels' respective overall run prevention, it seems reasonable that a 32 unearned run difference would be responsible for a large amount of the difference between the two teams. High profile defensive miscues, such as booted balls by Vlad Guerrero, Adam Kennedy and Orlando Cabrera on June 3 against Cleveland that led to nine unearned runs and a 14-2 Indians blowout, certainly added to that perception.

But results from advanced defensive metrics, such as the plus/minus system described in the "Team Defense" chapter (which takes into account each player's performance on every single play of the 2006 season), show that the two defenses were more evenly matched than simple errors would suggest. According to the data,

both the A's and Angels had good corner infielders, making nine and four more plays on balls hit to first or third than the average defense. But their defenders up the middle and in the outfield made 45 and 55 *fewer* plays than the average defense would, respectively.

Add up those plays, and both defenses surprisingly finished in the bottom half of baseball, with the A's ranking 23rd and the Angels ranking 25th. So while the Angels' defense was something of an Achilles' heel, as suspected, it probably wasn't actually a disadvantage *vis a vis* the division race with the A's. The A's had an equally subpar defense. The A's poor showing, particularly in the middle infield, probably highlights the importance of Bobby Crosby. In last year's *Fielding Bible*, John Dewan had Bobby Crosby at eight plays above average, and the A's clearly missed his range and arm up the middle.

So if it wasn't the defense, and the offenses and pitching were pretty evenly matched, then what was the difference? In any close race—and despite a relatively uneventful September, the race was very close until the A's pulled away with a scorching 21-6 August—a number of individual moves can make a big difference, and I'd like to focus on two of them that helped swing the division: Frank Thomas and Jeff Weaver.

It's easy to see the impact that Frank Thomas had on the 2006 A's. A look at his performance compared to the A's designated hitters in 2005 quickly reveals how the A's were able to score nearly the same amount of runs despite major down years at the plate from Bobby Crosby, Mark Ellis and Eric Chavez.

Year	Player	PA	OPS
2005	Scott Hatteberg	515	.667
2005	Erubiel Durazo	166	.673
2006	Frank Thomas	547	.926

Weaver is a similarly interesting case, but his impact can be overstated. Signed to a one-year, $8.35 million contract in the offseason, Weaver was supposed to solidify the back of the Angels rotation (not to mention outpitch Esteban Loaiza). Instead, Weaver posted a 3-10 record in 16 starts with the Angels, and earned it with a 6.29 ERA and 1.52 WHIP. After being called up, Jered Weaver and Joe Saunders both posted much better numbers, combining for a 18-5 record with a 3.40 ERA in 190⅓ innings.

But on the other hand, if you look at the actual games that Jeff Weaver pitched in, the Angels' poor offense at the beginning of the season bears no small part of the responsibility for his poor record. In only six of his 16 starts did his offense score more than four runs, and the Angels actually won five of those six games. On the whole, the Angels offense only scored 3.75 runs per game in Weaver's starts in a league that averaged 4.97 runs per game on average. In fact, even the worst offense in the league, Tampa Bay, managed 4.25 runs per game overall.

So if Jeff Weaver didn't cost the Angels the division, Frank Thomas was only balancing out down years from other regulars, and the A's and Angels actually scored and allowed about the same number of runs, why did the A's win the division? *Einmal ist keinmal.* I'll leave it to brilliant novelist Milan Kundera to explain:

> *There is no means of testing which decision is better, because there is no basis for comparison. We live everything as it comes, without warning, like an actor going on cold. And what can life be worth if the first rehearsal for life is life itself? That is why life is always like a sketch. No, "sketch" is not quite the right word, because a sketch is an outline of something, the groundwork for a picture, whereas the sketch that is our life is a sketch for nothing, an outline with no picture.*
>
> *Einmal ist* keinmal, *says Tomas to himself. What happens but once, says the German adage, might as well not have happened at all. If we have only one life to live, we might as well have not lived at all.*

Kundera was writing about life, but his words apply aptly to baseball as well. Start the season with two evenly matched good teams, and one of them will usually win more games. It doesn't necessarily mean that the team was categorically a better team—play the season a thousand times and things might end up very differently, on balance. But that's why they play the games. This season, the A's ended up on top.

Of course, for long periods of the season, it didn't look like that would be the case at all. In fact, on May 31, with more than one third of the season in the books, the Texas Rangers led the division by four games over the struggling A's and five games over the third-place Angels. Both the A's and Angels were below .500, and it looked very possible that Texas, at 28-25 (only the sixth-best record in the AL at the time), would be the class of an otherwise weak division. So what went wrong?

In a nutshell, nothing. From that point until the rest of the season, the Rangers scored 564 runs and allowed 522, for a run differential of +42. Comparatively, the

A's went +52 and the Angels +72. The Rangers did the most to improve themselves at the trade deadline, adding Carlos Lee, who gave them 256 plate appearances of .322/.369/.525 offense after joining the team three days before the trade deadline.

While the Rangers did not have the run prevention that the A's and Angels sported, they did have the best offense in the division, even with park effects taken into account. Given the way things turned out, it's hard to blame their lost season on the Alfonso Soriano trade, despite his breakout in Washington, D.C. Soriano's .277/.351/.560 is not tremendously better than what the Rangers got from Lee after the trade deadline. Between Lee and Kevin Mench's not-terrible .284/.338/.459, it's hard to say that Soriano's extra offense would have pushed the Rangers over the 13-game hump they faced at the end of the season.

If anything, the move that I would take back if I were in charge of the Rangers would be the Chris Young and Adrian Gonzalez for Adam Eaton and Akinori Otsuka deal. Eaton, who was coming off an injury-plagued 2005, ended up pitching just 65 innings of 5.12 ERA ball, while Young broke out in San Diego, making 31 starts and posting a 3.46 ERA. Now, Arlington against the American League and PETCO against the National League are two completely different contexts, but any ERA below 5.00 would have been a welcome upgrade to the Texas rotation.

Still, the Rangers had a talented team that under-achieved last season. The same core of veterans that has gotten the team close in recent seasons should return. If one of the Rangers' vaunted trio of John Danks, Edinson Volquez and Thomas Diamond can overcome his control woes and harness his stuff, it wouldn't be out of the question to see a Detroit Tigers-esque rise to the playoffs.

Meanwhile, the 2006 Seattle Mariners will probably be remembered for gifting the division to the Athletics more than anything else, a fate that's not fair to a solid Mariners team, or the A's for that matter. Despite the offseason acquisitions of Kenji Johjima and Jarrod Washburn, the Mariners weren't expected to contend, but they nonetheless stayed within striking range for most of the first half of the season.

More importantly, they developed their core of young players at the major league level and showed that they have some promising pieces for the future, like middle infield duo Jose Lopez and Yuniesky Betancourt. Of course, none of those pieces is more important than King Felix Hernandez, hyped as the best pitching prospect this side of Doc Gooden. King Felix didn't appear to live up to expectations, posting a 4.52 ERA in a pitcher's park. But ERA doesn't always tell the full story. Here's a look at what Hernandez actually did, compared with another pretty decent pitcher's peripheral numbers:

Player	K/9	BB/9	HR/9	LD%	GB%
Player A	10.2	2.0	1.00	19.8	40.6
Hernandez	8.3	2.8	1.09	17.7	57.7

Player A is Johan Santana, who finished the season with a 2.77 ERA and will almost certainly be the AL Cy Young winner. Goes to show what a little timing and defense can do for you. To wit, the Twins' defense turned 73.1% of the balls in play allowed by Santana into outs, while the Mariners did the same for only 68.8% of Hernandez's. Sure, Santana gets more popups (not shown) and fly outs, but that shouldn't nearly account for a 4.3% difference. Add all of that up, and Hernandez actually finished second to Santana in the American League in Expected Fielding Independent Pitching, which adjusts a player's ERA to take into account defense and luck on balls in play.

So if you like intense regional rivalries and tightly contested divisions, live arms and big bashers, once and future kings and quality baseball between competitive teams, do yourself a favor next season and hold out for that late edition of Baseball Tonight or splurge on an MLB.tv subscription. You won't regret it.

The Continual Fall and Rise of the Oakland Athletics

For each of the past three years, the A's have followed virtually the same course: start the season around .500, go into a funk in May (well, except for 2004; somebody must have been improvising), turn on the jets in June and August (okay, the players got July and September reversed in 2005), and hold on for dear life in September. Perhaps the script hasn't been exactly the same each year, but putting them on one graph paints an intriguing picture.

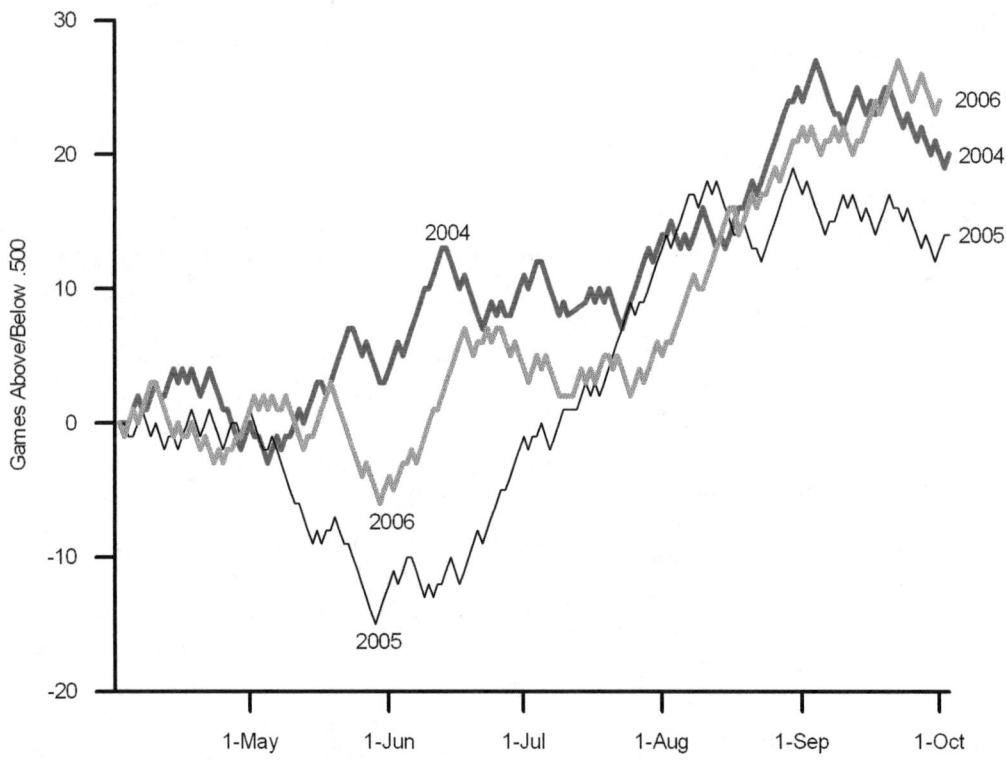

National League East Review

by John Walsh

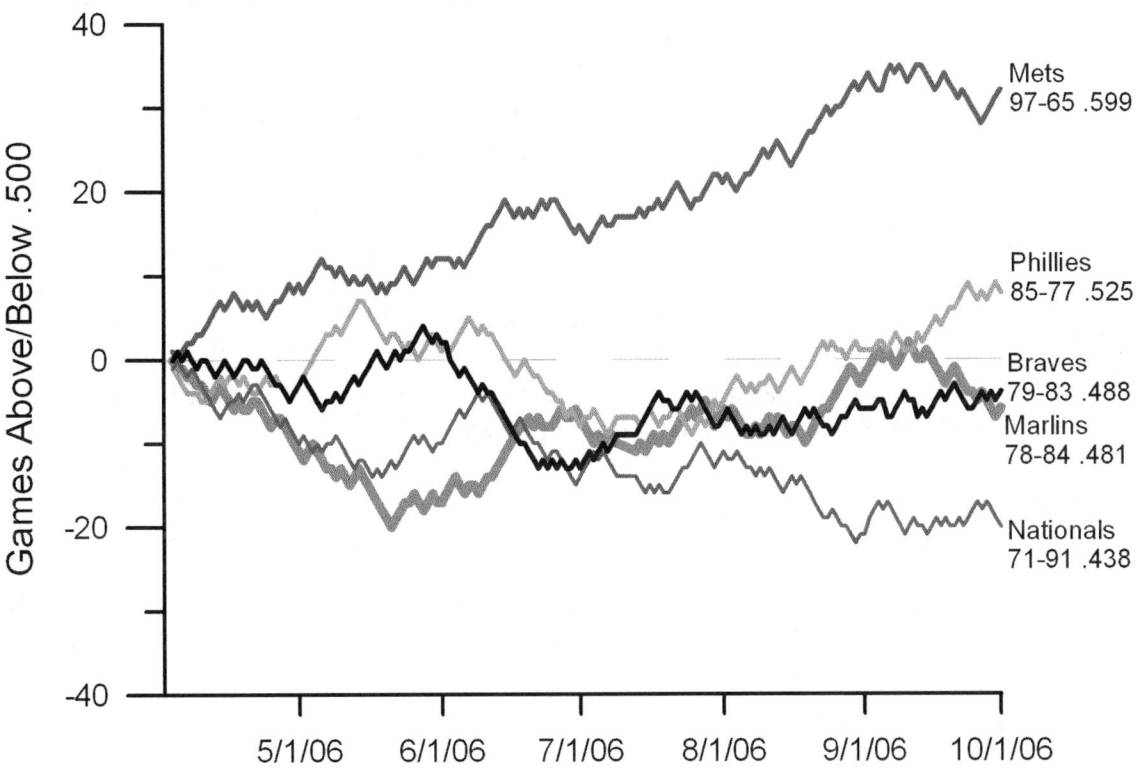

The National League East looked like it might be a pretty good race. It really did. The preseason consensus here at The Hardball Times favored the Braves, and we weren't the only ones to blow that call; the ESPN staff made the same mistake. Now, of course, it seems like the outcome of the division was never in doubt—the Mets went ahead to stay the very first week of the season. But things looked different six months earlier.

First of all, pundits and fans alike had learned from experience that it was a fool's game to pick against the Braves. Atlanta had won 14 straight NL East Division titles (excluding the 1994 strike year), including the previous three or four despite everyone thinking that they just couldn't do it again. On the other hand, there were reasons to think that 2006 might really be the year the Braves would finally fail to win the division. Pitching coach and guru Leo Mazzone left in the offseason, and there were serious questions about the Braves' bullpen. Rafael Furcal left as a free agent and was replaced by Edgar Renteria, who was coming off a miserable season with the Red Sox. So yeah, the Braves had holes, but they had been able to plug them many times before. Why not in 2006?

The Mets, on the other hand, continued to build by reaching into deep pockets. After signing Carlos Beltran and Pedro Martinez to enormous free agent contracts the previous year, Mets general manager Omar Minaya continued the spending spree this season by snagging Billy Wagner, Carlos Delgado and Paul Lo Duca. The Mets definitely seemed poised to contend in 2006.

And let's not forget the Phillies, who finished just two games behind the Braves in 2005. They traded slugger Jim Thome to make way for even-bigger-slugger Ryan Howard, obtaining Aaron Rowand to play center field. They also could reasonably expect improvements from their young middle infielders Jimmy Rollins and Chase Utley. They managed to plug the hole left by the departing Wagner with a comparable replacement, Tom Gordon.

While one could make the case that any of these teams had a decent shot at the postseason, it was hard to imagine either the Nationals or the Marlins doing much in 2006. The Marlins had a huge fire sale in the offsesason: they traded or let walk Lo Duca, Delgado, Luis Castillo, Mike Lowell, Alex Gonzalez, Juan Pierre and Juan Encarnacion. That's seven-eighths of their starting lineup. They also let go of two starting pitchers (A.J. Burnett and Josh Beckett) and essentially all of their bullpen. The last team to pull a stunt like this was, well, the Marlins, who cleaned house right after winning the World Series in 1997. The following season they went 54-108 and finished 52 games out of first. The Marlins were not expected to do much in 2006.

For their part, the Nationals did not inspire much hope going into the 2006 season. Although they finished their first year in the nation's capital a surprising 81-81, they stumbled badly in the second half. They did make several offseason moves, most notably acquiring Alfonso Soriano and making room for rookie Ryan Zimmerman at third base, finally ridding themselves of the carcass of Vinny Castilla.

So, you see, the race for the NL East pennant promised to be a close one. It didn't turn out that way. Here's what happened, and why.

On April 6, the Mets handily defeated the Nationals by a score of 10-5, thereby taking over first place in the division with a 2-1 record. The Mets banged out 15 hits against Nats starter Ramon Ortiz. Delgado and Beltran each hit home runs, David Wright went 3-for-4 with a walk and Jose Reyes had three hits, two runs scored and two RBIs. Pedro Martinez was nothing special; he surrendered five runs in six innings with six strikeouts and five walks. He got the win though, behind the Mets' thunderous bats. Well, that and the three innings of scoreless relief turned in by Duaner Sanchez and Chad Bradford.

Why am I harping on this one game? Because it's the perfect metaphor for the Mets' 2006 season: a hugely potent offense, average-ish starting pitching and a top-notch bullpen took the Mets to the division crown. Reyes, the Mets' shortstop and leadoff batter, showed great improvement in almost all offensive categories, including average, on-base percentage and slugging. He even grounded into fewer double plays. Wright didn't exactly improve on his 2005 season, but it's tough to improve on a line of .306/.388/.523. He put up virtually the same numbers in 2006. Beltran had a huge year after a surprisingly feeble debut season in New York. The Mets center fielder, despite playing in fewer games this season, saw his home run total jump from 16 to 41, his walk total go from 56 to 95 and his slugging average, which had dipped to a scary .414 in 2005, get back to Beltran-territory at .594 this year. Everything was going right for these guys.

The starting pitching was just average, but it was good enough. Martinez was hampered by injuries and was generally ineffective in his 132⅔ innings pitched, posting a very un-Pedro-like ERA of 4.48. This was the first

time in his career that Martinez's ERA came in worse than league average. Tom Glavine and Steve Trachsel were the only Mets starters to make 30 starts. Glavine did about as expected, pitching well (15-7, 3.82). Trachsel also met expectations; we expected him to be mediocre and he was: 15-8, 4.97. The rest of the rotation was filled out mostly by Orlando "El Duque" Hernandez (20 starts, 9-7, 4.09) and John Maine (15 starts, 6-5, 3.60).

The bullpen was nothing less than marvelous. A couple of early high-profile blown saves by Billy Wagner were quickly forgotten as the closer won over fans with a sterling season in his first year as the Mets closer. Duaner Sanchez (before being injured in a car accident), Chad Bradford, Aaron Heilman and Pedro Feliciano all had very fine seasons in the league's best bullpen.

Another key part of the Mets' success this year was their ability to get excellent production from fill-in players. When Kaz Matsui didn't work out, the Mets got above-average production (OPS+ 112) from Jose Valentin. Other guys like Endy Chavez and Shawn Green did very well plugging holes. The same thing can be said of Bradford, Feliciano and Roberto Hernandez in the bullpen. These role players were a key reason the Mets easily won the division crown.

If the April 6 win over the Nationals epitomizes the Mets' season, perhaps a 9-7 loss to the Yankees on June 20 symbolizes the Phillies' 2006 campaign. Ryan Howard drove in seven runs with two home runs and a triple, but the Phils still lost to the Yanks. Howard ended up being the brightest star in the Philly sky this season, bashing 58 home runs and driving in 149, leading the majors in both categories. Second baseman Chase Utley also had a superb season that included a 35-game hitting streak. He was the best-hitting second baseman in the National League this season and is also considered a plus fielder. If the Phillies could have found a warm body to play third base, they might have had the best-hitting infield in the league. Overall, the Phillies had a potent offense and led the National League in runs scored.

Unfortunately, the pitching was just bad. Phillies starters surrendered more runs than any other team's rotation. Only Brett Myers made at least 30 starts, and he actually missed three starts after being arrested for assaulting his wife. Of the other starters, only rookie Cole Hamels gave Phillies fans any cause for hope, as the 22-year-old posted an ERA of 4.08, while throwing 132⅓ innings. Jon Lieber, Cory Lidle and Ryan Madson were all disappointments, each posting ERAs well north of league average. The bullpen actually performed well, led by Gordon, who saved 34 games while striking out 68 batters in 58⅓ innings. Geoff Geary was the bullpen workhorse: he appeared in 81 games and posted a 2.91 ERA in 91⅓ relief innings, tied for second-most in the majors.

On July 30 the Phillies sported a 49-54 record, 5½ games and six teams away from a Wild Card berth. Apparently deciding that they were out of contention, the Phillies front office decided to save some money by trading Bobby Abreu and Cory Lidle for low-level prospects. The Phillies then got hot, going 36-22 the rest of the way, and were in the Wild Card hunt until the last weekend of the season. I'm not of the mind that the Phillies went on a tear because of the trade, but I wonder if Abreu and Lidle could have helped them make up the three games that ultimately separated them from the Dodgers in the Wild Card sweepstakes.

The Braves' amazing run of 14 straight division titles (excluding postseason-less 1994) finally came to an end this year, as widely predicted. Was it the loss of Leo Mazzone? Well, the Braves pitching staff did go from a 2005 ERA of 3.98, good for sixth in the NL, to an ERA of 4.60 this year, ranked 10th in the league. Of the six Braves pitchers who threw at least 50 innings in both 2005 and 2006, five of them saw their ERAs rise this year. Now, I don't believe all of that is due to Leo's departure, I'm just sayin'.

In any case, it was the pitching, historically Atlanta's strong suit, that sank the Braves in 2006. The offense was fine, scoring 849 runs, good for second in the NL. Andruw Jones had another solid season, hitting 41 homers, driving in 129 and posting an .894 OPS, all top-tier numbers for a center fielder. Chipper Jones also had a typical season: splendid numbers when he was healthy (1.005 OPS), but he wasn't that healthy (110 games played). Pop Quiz: who was the best-hitting catcher in baseball in 2006? Hint: he's 22 years old and his last name begins with "M." Right! It's Brian McCann. I guess one could argue about the relative merits of Joe Mauer and McCann, but the latter put up numbers that were just as good at less than half the publicity. Another nice surprise for the Braves was the breakout season of Adam LaRoche, who hit .285/.354/.561. Jeff Francoeur, on the other hand, regressed quite a bit from his excellent rookie season. His 29 homers and 103 RBIs camouflaged an unproductive campaign: he only managed an OPS+ of 89 and made 507 outs, third-most in baseball this season.

The Florida Marlins were expected to do a passable imitation of their 1998 forebears and lose 100 games or so. But a funny thing happened on the way to last place: the Marlins came up with some very talented rookies who played terrific baseball and kept things interesting all season. The Fish parted with two young, good starting pitchers in Beckett and Burnett, but they came up with four even younger and, arguably, better hurlers: Josh Johnson, Anibal Sanchez, Scott Olsen and Ricky Nolasco. Dontrelle Willis stuck around to show these guys how to shave.

Equally impressive was the gaggle of rookie position players the Marlins put on the field. Shortstop Hanley Ramirez, acquired along with Sanchez in the Beckett deal, was nothing short of astonishing, batting .292 in the leadoff spot, with 74 extra-base hits and 51 stolen bases. Second baseman Dan Uggla and left fielder Josh Willingham also were solid contributors in their rookie campaigns.

The Marlins actually looked like they might contend for the Wild Card, but they faded slightly in September. Still, they finished with a respectable 78-84 record, just five games behind their pre-fire sale 2005 record. It was a very positive season for the Marlins.

The year 2006 proved to be a difficult one in Washington—as well as for the city's baseball team, the Nationals. After their honeymoon year in 2005, the Nats took several steps back this season, winding up 71-91, good for last place in the division. Not only was the news bad on the field, it was also depressing at the gate: attendance fell to 2.2 million, down from 2.7 million in 2005.

The reason for the Nats' troubles this year can be easily found in their pitching ledger. They were last in the league in ERA, runs allowed, home runs allowed, walks and shutouts. Oh, and second-to-last in strikeouts. This was quite a comedown from 2005, when they ranked fourth in the NL in ERA. What happened? Esteban Loaiza and his 3.77 ERA departed via free agency, and John Patterson and his team-best 3.13 ERA made only eight (ineffectual) starts this season due to injuries. Newcomer Ramon Ortiz was, well, Ramon Ortiz (ERA 5.57) and Pedro Astacio threw 90 innings of 6.00 ERA ball. Since 1997—that's 10 years folks—Astacio has thrown 1,464 innings with an ERA of 5.21. Anybody can have a bad year, but 10 in a row? Why is anyone handing this guy the ball?

There were some bright spots on offense. Alfonso Soriano had a fine year, although the best hitter on the team was Nick Johnson, whose OPS+ of 146 topped Soriano's mark of 132. Ryan Zimmerman's rookie season was excellent: the 21-year-old hit .287/.351/.471 while playing, by most accounts, excellent defense. Speaking of defense, Soriano, who reluctantly took left field in the Nats' season opener, ended up thriving there. He showed above-average range and led all major league outfielders with 22 assists.

The story of the NL East in 2006 was mostly a story of "finally." Finally, the Braves were knocked from their perch atop the division standings, and finally, the Mets put their huge financial resources to good use, resulting in a division flag. We all knew this would happen, right? Sooner or later, anyway.

National League Central Review

by Brian Gunn

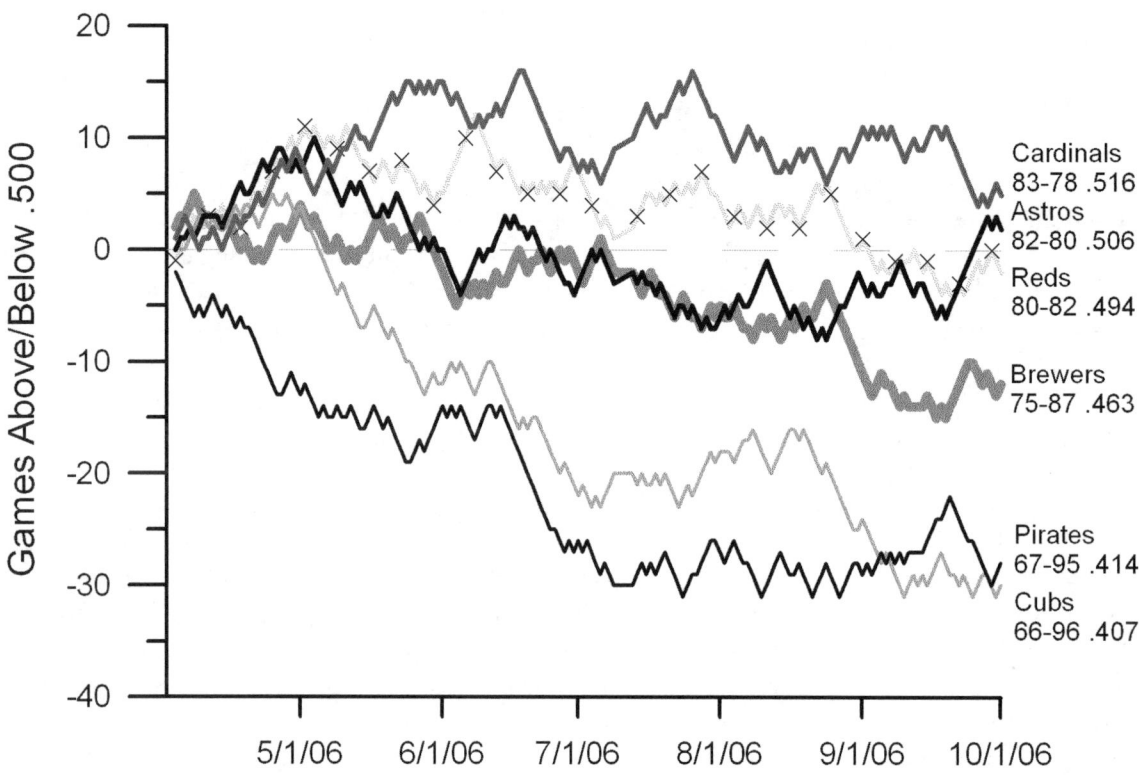

The record will show that the St. Louis Cardinals moved into first place in early June and stayed there for the rest of the year, just like they had in 2004 and 2005. But make no mistake: this was not the Cardinals juggernaut of years past. Like the rest of the NL Central, the Cards slipped and stumbled throughout most of the summer and, come autumn, found themselves locked in an impossibly thrilling climax with their perennial rivals, the Houston Astros.

But we're getting ahead of ourselves.

Let's start, as the Bible says, "in the big inning," back in April, with baseball's oldest franchise: the Cincinnati Reds. The Reds were basically written off by preseason pundits—of the 10 baseball experts on ESPN.com, only Eric Karabell picked them to finish better than last. He picked them to finish second-to-last.

But the Reds got off to a hot start, thanks to a number of new faces—not least of all Wayne Krivsky, who was named the team's general manager in February. Krivsky flipped Wily Mo Pena for Bronson Arroyo in the offseason, and Arroyo paid immediate dividends, sporting a 5-0 record and a 2.06 ERA a month into the season. Krivsky also found Brandon Phillips on the Indians' scrap heap, plugged him in at second base, and watched him slug .587

with 22 RBIs his first three weeks as a starter. Aaron Harang chipped in by winning five of his first six decisions, and two weeks into May the Redlegs were 11 games over .500 with the best record in the National League.

The Cardinals were right there with them in the early going, largely due to the heroics of (who else) Albert Pujols. Pujols turned the new Busch Stadium into his personal playground, setting a major league home run record for April and hitting 25 homers in his team's first 51 games. The highlight of his early season came on Easter Sunday, when Big Al went deep three times against the Reds' pitching staff. His first homer tied the game 4-4, his second gave the Cards a 6-4 lead, and his third was a two-run walkoff job to win it 8-7. Shortly before Memorial Day the Cards pole-vaulted the surprising Reds, took two of three from the Mets at home, grabbed the best record in the National League, and had sportswriters around the country prepping for another Cardinals cakewalk.

Meanwhile, the Pirates were headed in the opposite direction. They opened the season 0-6, and then, later in the month, dropped every game of a road trip against the Cards and 'Stros to see their record fall to 5-18. It was the Bucs' worst start since their historically bad 1952 squad (but this time they were without Joe Garagiola

28

to lighten things up). Believe it or not, things then got worse. At the end of June, the Black and Gold embarked on a 13-game losing streak, including a comical 15-7 loss to the Royals in which the Pirates issued seven walks, five unearned runs, and hit four opposing batters. It was around this time that new manager Jim Tracy all but threw his players under the bus, declaring that "as a manager there are only so many things I can do." *The Onion's* sports page had a funnier take on things with the following headline: "PNC Park Threatens To Leave Pittsburgh Unless Better Team Is Built."

Over in Chicago the Cubbies were holding their own in the early going—a credit to the mini-resurgence of future Hall of Famer Greg Maddux. Maddux twirled his way to a 5-0 start, including an eight-inning, 87-pitch three-hitter against the Dodgers on April 17 that hearkened back to his Cy Young years in Atlanta. At that point in the season the Cubs looked solid—just two nights later the Cubs finished a sweep of the eventual NL Wild Card winners when Ryan Dempster notched a club-record 23rd straight save.

Unfortunately that was the same night Cubs first baseman Derrek Lee stretched for an errant throw and found himself on the business end of Rafael Furcal, who was charging toward first base. Lee, the most productive hitter in baseball in 2005, broke his right wrist, sat out the next nine weeks, and was never the same. Even worse, Lee's injury seemed to unleash some kind of scourge on the rest of the team. The Cubs played miserably over the next five months, including separate stretches of 5-22 (most of May), 7-19 (most of June), and 8-22 (most of August). When all was said and done, Kerry Wood and Mark Prior combined for two wins and a 6.22 ERA, the Cubs bullpen got torched so many times it could be arrested for arson (Ryan Dempster went 1-9 and blew a staggering nine saves), and the roster was so fundamentally lopsided that the Cubs issued almost 300 more walks from the mound than they drew at the plate. Of course, Wrigley Field remained packed, but it was clear early on that the North Side faithful would have to wait, once again, 'til next year.

It was that kind of year in the NL Central. Throughout the summer, nearly every team suffered bouts of serious disappointment. Take the Houston Astros. Like last year, ace Roger Clemens flirted with retirement in the offseason. When he rejoined the team in late June, he was expected to be the savior of a team that was treading water, six games off pace. Instead the Astros promptly dropped seven of their first eight games with the Rocket. The only game the 'Stros won during that stretch was a wild Sunday night affair in U.S. Cellular Field, when the team squandered a 9-1 lead to the White Sox—the big blow was a two-out, game-tying grand slam by Tadahito Iguchi in the bottom

of the ninth off of closer Brad Lidge. Lidge was so hinky last summer that he eventually lost his closer's job to Dan Wheeler. The conventional wisdom around baseball was that Lidge was suffering from post-traumatic stress disorder since October '05, when Albert Pujols tagged him for a titanic home run in the NLCS.

After breaking even in the standings last year, the Brewers were a fashionable sleeper pick in the preseason. But they never made much of a charge, hovering near .500 until the All-Star Break. Part of the problem was Geoff Jenkins, who went all of June without a home run, and another part of the problem was Derrick Turnbow, who celebrated his berth on the All-Star team with a 21.32 ERA in July. But perhaps the biggest culprits were injuries. Ben Sheets (shoulder tendonitis), Tomo Ohka (rotator cuff), Corey Koskie (post-concussion syndrome), and J.J. Hardy (sprained ankle) all missed at least half the season. Rickie Weeks tore a tendon in his wrist while waggling his bat back and forth in the dugout. Jeff Cirillo sprained his ankle by leaping in frustration over a fly ball that died at the warning track. And reliever Matt Wise cut his finger on, of all things, a pair of salad tongs. It was as if the team was vying for a collective Darwin Award.

Even the Cardinals, the darlings of spring, short-circuited as the season wore on. Their low point was an eight-game losing streak to their counterparts in the AL Central at the end of June, which began when the White Sox blitzkrieged them 20-6 and 13-5 on successive nights. The Cards regrouped enough to build a four-game lead over Cincinnati at the All-Star break, but their pitching was just shaky enough (particularly Mark Mulder and Jason Marquis, who combined for a heinous 6.38 ERA) that the Reds decided to make a bold move to challenge them. Krivsky traded Austin Kearns, Felipe Lopez, and Ryan Wagner for Royce Clayton and a bevy of young relievers. The deal was widely jeered, especially in sabermetric circles—and indeed, afterwards the Reds' hitting went south: their offense went from five runs per game to 4.1. (Although in all fairness, the biggest offender here was Adam Dunn, who put up a grisly .176/.299/.346 line over the season's final two months.)

As August turned to September, the Brewers essentially dropped out of the race, suffering a disastrous 10-game losing streak, including seven in a row to the fledgling Marlins. Meanwhile the Reds endured a rough patch of their own, doomed by a miserable West Coast swing that saw them lose nine of 10 to the Giants, Dodgers and Padres. Mathematically speaking Cincinnati would hang in until the final weekend of the season—thanks largely to Arroyo and Harang, who combined for 30 wins and 475 innings pitched—but in the end the team's record was glumly familiar, as they finished below .500 for the sixth straight year.

Over in Steeltown, the Pirates merely played out the string, a few bright spots notwithstanding. They got decent starting pitching down the stretch, had a winning record after the All-Star break, and enjoyed a few huzzahs for infielder Freddy Sanchez, who won Pittsburgh's first batting title in 23 years. And despite their wretched start, they actually finished ahead of the reeling Cubs. As the season wound down, Chicago manager Dusty Baker fended off daily questions about his status for next season. Eventually the Tribune Company decided not to renew his contract, and Baker departed the same way 47 Cubbie managers had before him, without a World Series ring.

The Cardinals, on the other hand, saw themselves sitting pretty at the end of September. They opened up a seven-game lead in the NL Central with only a dozen games left, mostly due to lights-out pitching from reigning Cy Young Award winner Chris Carpenter, the emergence of rookie slugger Chris Duncan, and the continued excellence of (who else) Albert Pujols. In contrast, the Astros were left for dead, eulogized by local sportswriters who denounced an anemic offense that finished 12th in the league in runs.

But the worm turned on September 20, with an innocuous 7-2 win by the Astros over the Reds, in which the Rocket lowered his ERA to 2.37. Meanwhile, the Cards lost a 1-0 game to Milwaukee, which would usually qualify as a heartbreaker, except no one seemed especially broken up by it. After all, at that point St. Louis still led Houston by 7½ games.

That weekend the Astros squared off against the Cards for a four-game series in Houston. The 'Stros had to win all four games to have even a remote chance of capturing the division; Baseball Prospectus listed their odds of winning the NL Cenrral at roughly 152 to 1. In Game 1, the Redbirds opened up a 5-2 lead, but Lance Berkman tied a career high with his 42nd homer in the fifth, then corked a two-out two-run homer in the bottom of the eighth off Carpenter to seal the 6-5 victory.

Game 2 followed a similar script. Once again the Cardinals jumped out to a 5-2 lead, but the Astros battled back. This time the hero was Craig Biggio, who hit a two-run single in the eighth to cut the lead to 5-4, then smacked a two-out walk-off single to give his team yet another 6-5 win. It was a rare happy moment for the Houston second baseman, who endured his worst offensive season since his rookie year.

Game 3 was yet another nip/tuck affair, with left fielder Luke Scott providing the night's fireworks. Scott

had been the poster boy for the Astros' resurgence in the second half—a 28-year-old rookie recalled from Triple-A in July, he sported a .382/.470/.700 line after his first couple hundred plate appearances. And on the second-to-last Saturday of the season he downed the Cards with a walk-off blast into the right field stands, his second home run of the game.

The following night the Astros dispatched the Cards once again, completing a four-game sweep and closing the gap in the NL Central. Of course, the 'Stros still faced a serious uphill climb—3½ games out with but a week of road games to play. But people began to wonder if they were witnessing a repeat of '04 and '05, when the Astros played possum all summer long then rallied furiously down the stretch to sneak into the playoffs.

Sure enough, the Astros won their next game. And the game after that. And the game after that. And the game after that, to stretch their winning streak to nine. The Cards helped out by dropping seven straight, reviving ghosts of the 1964 Phillies. Despite a mammoth, game-saving home run from Pujols on Wednesday night, the Cards dropped the next game while Roy Oswalt (1.85 ERA in September) and the Astros swept the Pirates.

The stage was set for the final weekend. Cards vs. Brewers, Astros vs. Braves, only a half-game separating the two clubs. In the end the Cards managed to stave off a disaster of Hindenbergian proportions, taking two of three from the Brew Crew while the Astros dropped a pair of tight games in Atlanta. The big hit for the Cards came on Saturday afternoon, a two-out bases-clearing pinch-hit triple from Scott Spiezio that turned a 2-0 deficit into a 3-2 win. Meanwhile the Braves were getting revenge for last year's NLDS loss. "We didn't want [the Astros] to make the playoffs," Atlanta's Andruw Jones told the Atlanta Journal-Constitution. "We just wanted to go out there and hurt them." The race officially ended on the last day of the regular season, when the Astros lost 3-1 and fans at Busch Stadium (no joke) broke into a spontaneous Tomahawk Chop.

Some say the Cardinals won it with an MVP-worthy performance from Albert Pujols, while cynics will say that the real MVP of the Cardinals was the division in which they played. Consider that the Cards, who finished with the 13th-best record in baseball, lost 36 of their final 61 games, and had not one, not two, but three losing streaks of 7-plus games. Fortunately for them they played in a division that, as a whole, finished a whopping 65 games worse than the rest of baseball. As White Sox manager Ozzie Guillen put it, "If we played National League teams, the Central Division, we might win 150 games in that f---ing league."

National League West Review

by Steve Treder

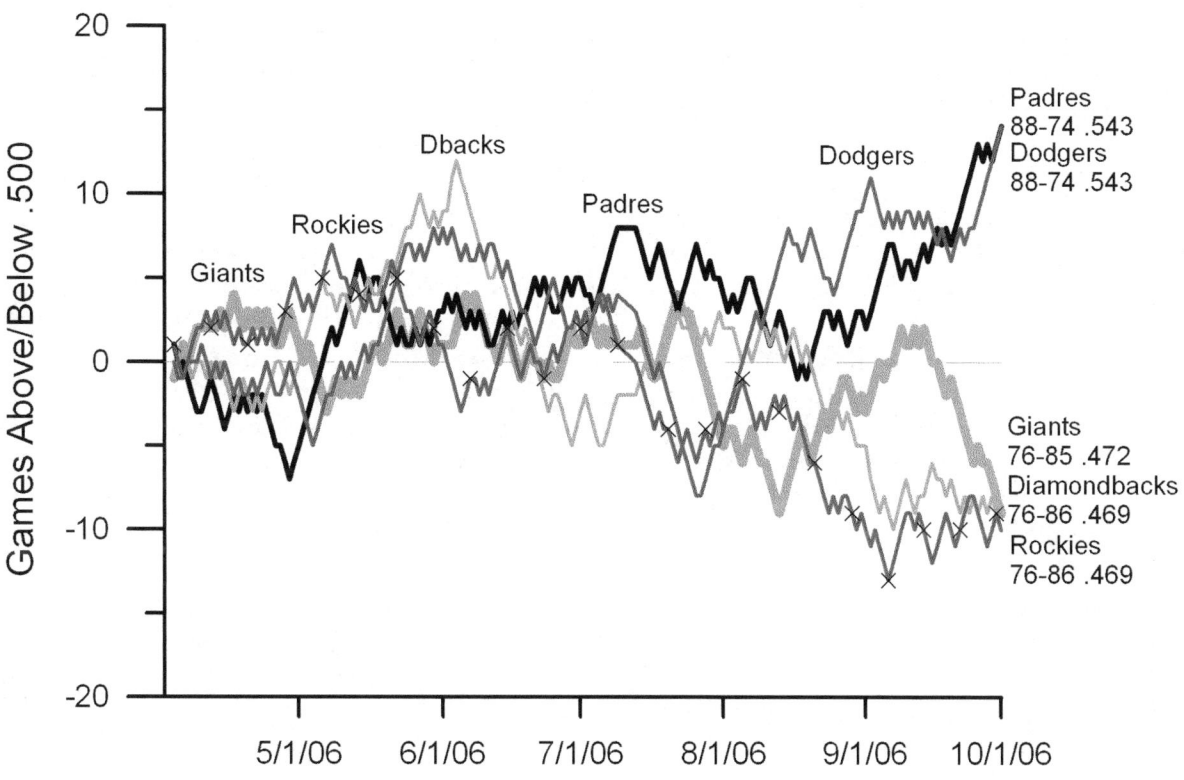

If the 2005 National League West Division was a 97-pound weakling, helplessly enduring taunts from the bullies and humiliation before the swimsuited gals—not to mention all that sand in the face—then the 2006 version apparently responded to the Charles Atlas ad on the back cover of the comic book. The '06 NL West hardly emerged as a strapping behemoth (you don't *really* believe those before-and-after pictures, do you?), but nevertheless seemed to have derived meaningful benefit from a crash program of isometrics and raw-egg milkshakes, and, if still not the envy of everyone on Muscle Beach, was no longer a pitiful runt.

The 2006 NL West, after all, displayed an aggregate win-loss record of 404-405 (.499), second among the three National League divisions, and fourth best among the six in the majors. That's right, fourth best among the six; not the best, but no longer the worst, and better not only than the NL Central, but also than that of the vaunted, preening, pomaded weightlifter from the "popular" end of the beach. That's right, American League East Division, we're talking about you.

Gosh. That sand stings the eyes a little bit there, doesn't it?

Sure, the '06 NL West wasn't a division that prompted admiring oohs and aahs, but neither was it a laughingstock this time around. And in its quiet, earnest little way, it provided an entertaining race.

For much of the season, all five NL West clubs were densely packed, and unlike 2005, this was the *good* kind of parity; for a few days in late May, all five were above .500. The extraordinary absence of daylight produced a delightful fluidity in the standings: every team spent time in both first place and last and all points in between, as the journey from top to bottom was very short and quickly traversed in both directions. Through the season's first four months, following the National League West was like watching socks in a tumble dryer, flopping up, over, and atop one another in a regularly rotating jumble. One got the feeling that the eventual division champ wouldn't be the team that pulled away from the pack, but rather whichever one would happen to be at the apex of the warm, fluffy little pile when the beep signaled "cycle complete."

That dynamic changed, at last, in late August, as the Los Angeles Dodgers and then the San Diego Padres finally put some distance between themselves and the rest. And those Dodgers and Padres put together a strong race to the wire, yielding—and this is definitely something no one anticipated—the National League's Wild Card champion. (Alas, both postseason qualifiers got bounced in the first round, shunted aside as easily as, you know, an AL East representative.)

That Wild Card circumstance drained some of the tension from the neck-and-neck stretch run by the southern California rivals, and dampened a bit of the thrill of a staggering epic they waged on September 18. In the finale of a four-game showdown series at Dodger Stadium, the home team fought back from two separate four-run deficits—the second by virtue of back-to-back-to-back-to-*back* home runs to open the bottom of the ninth (the final two on consecutive pitches from none other than Trevor Hoffman, who'd surrendered just two bombs in 56 innings)—before coming from behind yet again in the bottom of the 10th, winning it 11-10 on a two-run walkoff tater. Wild Card drama-drain notwithstanding, it was without exaggeration among the most scintillating and improbable contests in the history of major league baseball—another feather in the cap (or quarter-inch in the bicep) for the '06 NL West.

The Padres (crowned as division champs despite tying the Dodgers with an 88-74 record, thanks to that other dubious innovation, the tiebreaker) were perhaps the most fitting winner of this unassumingly respectable division, as the Padres bowled no one over, but presented a solid top-to-bottom roster. Under the calm, steady hand of veteran manager Bruce Bochy, the Padres' only hole was at third base (not filled until the late August acquisition of Russell Branyan), as seven other position regulars all had good years: center fielder Mike Cameron (28 Win Shares), right fielder Brian Giles, left fielder Dave Roberts, rookie second baseman Josh Barfield, catcher Mike Piazza, shortstop Khalil Greene (though, as usual, he battled injuries), and pleasant surprise 24-year-old first baseman Adrian Gonzalez.

Aided by their pitcher-friendly home park, San Diego allowed the fewest runs in the league (679) by a wide margin, leading the league as well in Defensive Efficiency (.714) and finishing third in Fielding Independent Pitching (4.22). Ace Jake Peavy had so-so results (11-14, 4.09), yet was third in the league in FIP at 3.42, and overall the Padres' staff, like the rest of their roster, wasn't overwhelming but was rich in depth. The bullpen was particularly strong, led by the ever-sterling Hoffman, and most intriguingly featuring a 23-year-old rookie named Cla Meredith—acquired from the Red Sox in May and brought up to the majors for good in July—who was utterly unhittable.

The Dodgers were a phoenix, rising from the smoking soot of their immolated 2005. Rookie general manager Ned Colletti undertook a clean sweep of the Dodgers roster; by August of 2006, he'd handed one-way tickets to outfielders Milton Bradley and Jayson Werth, infielders Cesar Izturis, Oscar Robles, Antonio Perez, Mike Edwards, Jose Valentin, and Willy Aybar, first baseman Hee Seop Choi, catchers Jason Phillips and Dioner Navarro, and pitchers Jeff Weaver, Odalis Perez, Yhency Brazoban, Duaner Sanchez and D.J. Houlton.

Not all of their replacements flourished, but most did. The best of the new Dodgers were Rafael Furcal (27 Win Shares), Nomar Garciaparra, rookie catcher Russell Martin, closer Takashi Saito, Kenny Lofton, rookie left fielder Andre Ethier, rookie starting pitcher Chad Billingsley and third baseman Wilson Betemit. A couple of late-season acquisitions were particularly helpful: Greg Maddux and Marlon Anderson.

There were a few holdovers amid the massive churn, and they too were keys to the team's success: J.D. Drew established career highs in games played, doubles and RBIs; Jeff Kent missed a few weeks with injuries but hit predictably well when in the lineup; Derek Lowe and Brad Penny won 16 games apiece. The Dodgers' bullpen overcame another lost-to-injury season from erstwhile closer Eric Gagne through the fine work of Saito, as well that of jumbo-sized 22-year-old sophomore Jonathan Broxton.

Among the most interesting of Colletti's many bold decisions was his choice of field manager: Grady Little, who'd been hooted out of Boston in 2003. Thrust into a tense, sour, high-profile media-frenzied situation, Little was handed a roster within which almost no one had previously played together, yet he forged an apparently harmonious clubhouse and an obviously well-performing on-field unit. The Dodgers withstood a disastrous stretch in July in which they lost 13 of 14 (while scoring just 26 runs), and fell into last place; they immediately rebounded to win 11 straight and 17 of 18 (a streak in which they only twice allowed as many as five runs), and under Little the team played its best baseball over the season's final couple of months.

Here's something that might be a rule of thumb for general managers: when things go just about as well as could be reasonably expected for an extremely veteran, built-to-win-now-or-never team, and still it winds up a 76-85 dud, that's probably a sign that the master plan is in need of refreshment. At the beginning of the 2006 season, San Francisco Giants general manager Brian

Sabean couldn't plausibly have anticipated much better than this:

- 39-year-old shortstop Omar Vizquel and 34-year-old second baseman Ray Durham would both deliver superb seasons.

- 39-year-old right fielder Moises Alou would hit wonderfully in his modulated availability.

- That most ultraveteran of all, Barry Bonds, would rebound from his injury-ruined 2005 with a robust 130-game performance.

- The hard-throwing 1-2 punch of veteran Jason Schmidt and youngster Matt Cain would be solidly effective.

- A season-ending injury to Mike Matheny wouldn't create a problem, as 27-year-old career minor leaguer Eliezer Alfonzo would step in and do just fine.

- Three other key players would contribute useful no-surprises seasons: Pedro Feliz, Randy Winn, and Steve Finley.

The things that went wrong for the Giants didn't go disastrously wrong, nor were they shocking: starters Matt Morris and Noah Lowry were disappointing, and neither Jamey Wright nor Brad Hennessey did very well in the fifth starter slot. Closer Armando Benitez had another injury-plagued, ineffectual season. First base, which looked as though it would be a hole, was a hole, as the first-half platoon of Mark Sweeney and Lance Niekro didn't get it done, and mid-season acquisition Shea Hillenbrand failed to solve the problem.

Certainly, the Giants' pitching might have been better than it was, but realistically not all *that* much better. All in all the 2006 Giants seemed like a once-excellent sitcom that might have bowed out gracefully while still close to the top of the Nielsens, but instead stuck around for a few seasons too many: the structural elements that made it a hit were still in evidence, but the absence of a couple of old favorite supporting characters was telling. Overall the spark was gone, the tired formula played out.

For the Arizona Diamondbacks, 2006 was encouraging. Even though their 76-86 record was a game below their 2005 mark, several things about the '06 performance represented progress: it was a consolidation of the 2005 26-win leap forward; it was, quite unlike '05, in line with (indeed slightly below) their run differential; and most significantly, the primary Arizona talents were young.

Quite like the 2005 edition, the 2006 D-backs were roller-coaster inconsistent. As of June 4, they were in first place at 34-22, but for the rest of the month they failed to win as many as two games in a row, and they dropped firmly into last. But soon they got hot again, climbing back into mid-summer contention, until encountering another deep slide from mid-August into early September.

Unquestionably the most lethal rattlesnake was Brandon Webb, who at age 27 emerged as one of the game's elite aces, at 16-8 with a 3.10 ERA, leading the league with a FIP of 3.20 and finishing third in Pitching Runs Created with 124. Other standouts were 28-year-old second baseman Orlando Hudson (.809 OPS and excellent defense), 26-year-old third baseman Chad Tracy, 24-year-old first baseman Conor Jackson, and two 23-year-old midseason call-ups: shortstop Stephen Drew and right fielder Carlos Quentin. The lone graybeard in the lineup was 38-year-old Luis Gonzalez, who contributed 52 doubles in what was almost certainly his final Arizona season. Journeymen Eric Byrnes and Johnny Estrada turned in solid performances at center field and catcher.

Beyond Webb, Arizona pitching was quite spotty. Starters Miguel Batista and midseason acquisition Livan Hernandez were so-so, while Claudio Vargas and Enrique Gonzalez were pretty bad, and big-contract Russ Ortiz was hideous, and was finally released in June. Jose Valverde and Jorge Julio alternated at closer, where both could be counted upon to rack up strikeouts but neither could be counted upon to nail down victories. The D-backs did get a useful swingman season from 27-year-old stringbean righthander Juan Cruz, who was acquired from the A's for Brad Halsey in the spring.

For few franchises would a 76-86 season stand as an unqualified success, but such a franchise is the Colorado Rockies. Not only did that degree of mediocrity represent the team's greatest achievement since 2000, it was a significant improvement upon their 2005 record, and moreover the '06 Rockies were also a youthful ball club.

Something further for the Rockies to cheer about was the terrific year they got from their humidor: in previous seasons the Rockies' ball-deadening program had yielded noticeable results in making mile-high baseball less cruel to pitchers, but in 2006, for some reason, Coors Field almost-sorta-somewhat resembled a neutral park. Playing half the schedule in an extreme offense-friendly environment is no excuse for a weak roster (though Rockies management often seems to have attempted to spin it that way over the years), but there's no question it presents a major challenge, particularly in developing pitchers, but also in simply assessing everyone's "true" talent level.

With the ball flying less readily than ever before this season, Colorado was able to recognize two 26-year-old regulars as legitimate breakout stars: third baseman Garrett Atkins (26 Win Shares) and left fielder Matt Holliday. In 27-year-old Jason Jennings, 25-year-old Jeff Francis, and 27-year-old Aaron Cook the Rockies presented three young, solid starting pitchers, a feat that few previous Colorado teams have achieved.

At 32, Todd Helton was no longer a premier slugger, but remained a distinct asset. Two other solid Rox were closer Brian Fuentes, who turned in his second straight good year, and right fielder Brad Hawpe, in his first season as a regular. Two more did well in late-season trials: 30-year-old infielder Kaz Matsui, scavenged from the Mets, and 25-year-old rookie power-hitting outfielder Jeff Baker. Second-year shortstop Clint Barmes was a huge disappointment, prompting manager Clint Hurdle to hand the job in September to 21-year-old rookie Troy Tulowitzki, who didn't hit well either, but showed some promise.

Thus the Rockies, like the Diamondbacks, weren't good yet but took real steps in that direction. This improvement ensured that their division, while presenting no powerhouses, neither provided any pushovers. The only NL West team that didn't finish the year in shape to become or remain a solid competitor was the Giants, and despite their many question marks, San Francisco is a franchise with ample economic muscle to avoid serious anemia, provided, of course, that might is wisely applied.

So the division that spent the summer of 2005 getting picked on and pushed around showed some mettle and stood its ground this time, and is now ready to confidently stride, head high, across the hotly competitive sands. Though few bikini-babe heads may turn, the knowing smirks and rude dismissals are *so* last year. Maybe there's something to that dynamic tension stuff after all.

The Game of the Year

On September 18, the Dodgers and Padres, battling for the NL West lead, engaged in a wild one, swapping leads and performing heroics at the plate and on the mound. In the end, the Dodgers won 11-10 on Nomar Garciaparra's two-run home run in the tenth inning, after the Padres had taken the lead in the top of the tenth. But the truly spectacular inning was the ninth, when the Dodgers improbably hit four solo home runs in a row to tie the game.

The game had many emotional ups and downs for Dodger and Padre fans alike, as this graph of the Dodgers' Win Probability demonstrates. LI stands for Leverage Index, which measures the criticality of each situation. You can read more about Win Probability in "WPA in the USA" in the Analysis section.

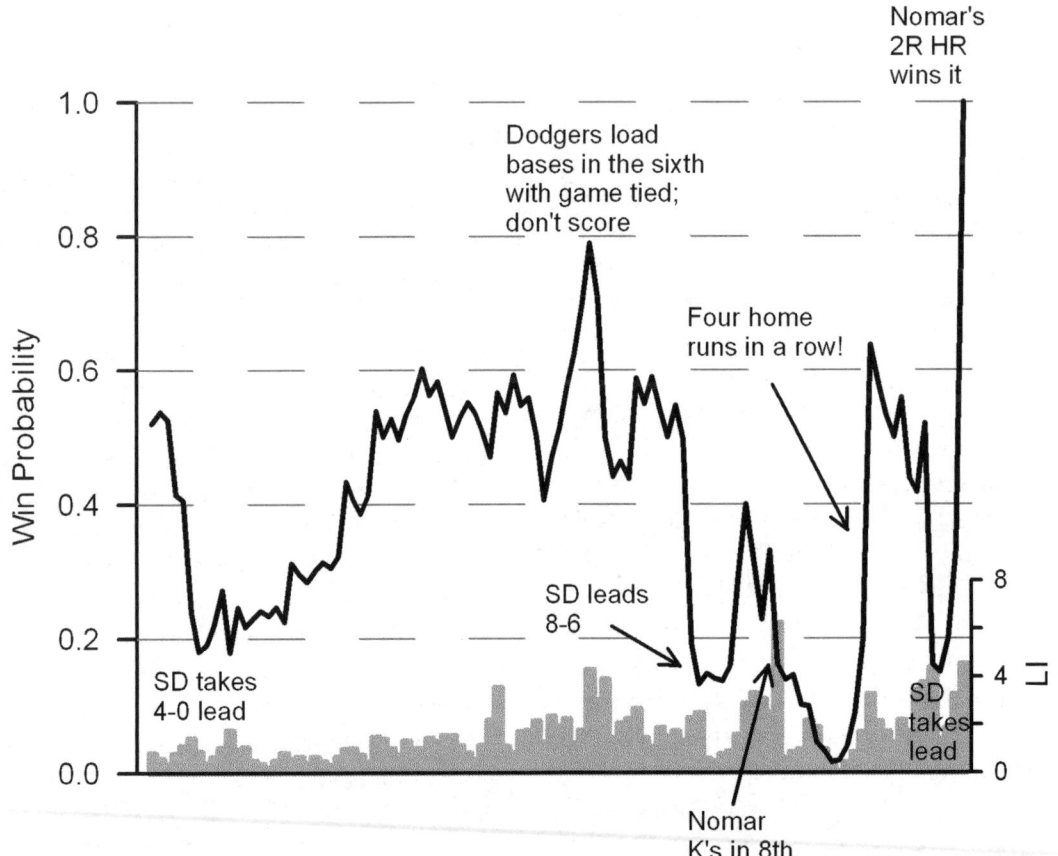

The Cardinals Win It All

by Jeff Sackmann and Jon Weisman

It has become popular in the last few years to say that the postseason is a crap shoot, that the results of a five- or seven-game series do not determine the better team, just the better team that week. There has been plenty of evidence along those lines in the 21st century so far: Several Wild Card teams, including the 2002 Angels, the 2003 Marlins, the 2004 Red Sox and the 2005 Astros, have advanced to the World Series, sometimes defeating the teams that edged them in their own division in the regular season.

The 2006 postseason was no different. While all four playoff teams from the American League were strong—each won at least 93 games, and the Wild Card winner won 95—the NL qualifiers were a strange mix of regular-season dominance and mediocrity. The Cardinals beat out their Central Division counterparts with a mere 83 wins, while the Dodgers and Padres tied with 88 wins in the West. Only the Mets, on paper, appeared to match up with the AL playoff teams. The stage was ripe for upsets.

ALDS: Oakland A's vs. Minnesota Twins

Oakland: The A's were built around defense and pitching and suffered from a startling lack of power. Even with Frank Thomas's huge comeback season, the A's were second-to-last among AL teams in slugging and just barely in the top half in OBP. Even in pitching and defense, the A's more obvious strengths, the team didn't dominate the AL—or even their division. They ranked fourth in runs allowed (the Angels were third) and seventh in defensive efficiency (behind the Angels and Mariners). With a starting three of Barry Zito, Dan Haren and a resurgent Esteban Loaiza, the A's looked competitive in a short series, but they were clearly outclassed by some of their potential opponents.

Minnesota: The Twins, on the other hand, had only one starting pitcher they could count on: Johan Santana. For much of the season, Minnesota fans watched in awe as Santana and Francisco Liriano mowed down opponents two games out of every five, but Liriano was lost to injury in August. Instead of the second half of the best one-two punch in baseball, Boof Bonser would get the ball in Game 2. Bonser, like nearly everyone on Minnesota's roster, had a strong second half, but not nearly enough of one to make him comparable to Liriano. Like Oakland, much of Minnesota's strength rested on its pitching (second in the AL), while its offense wasn't even in the top half of the league.

The Series: Santana was slated to pitch Games 1 and 5, meaning that if he defeated Zito in both of those games, the Twins would only have to manage one victory in between. As it turned out, they'd accomplish neither. In Game 1, Santana may have pitched better than his counterpart, but the results showed the opposite. Zito, who walked three and struck out just one in eight innings, allowed a single run, while Santana dominated the A's for eight innings except for a two-run homer to Frank Thomas. Both bullpens allowed a run in the ninth (Thomas hit another for the A's) and Oakland held on to win, 3-2.

In Game 2, Loaiza and Bonser proved to be well-matched, and the game turned on an uncharacteristic misplay by Twins center fielder Torii Hunter. Loaiza gave up two runs in five innings; Bonser allowed the same in six. The game's defining play came with Dennys Reyes on the mound for the Twins in the seventh. After Jason Kendall beat out a double play relay throw to keep the inning alive, Mark Kotsay hit a shallow line drive to Hunter in center. Hunter appeared to get a bad read on the ball, yet charged in an effort to make a diving catch. He missed, the ball skipped by him, and Kotsay circled the bases with a two-run, inside-the-park home run. Justin Duchscherer and Huston Street kept the Twins in check for three innings, and the A's moved within a single win of the ALCS.

Brad Radke's start in Game 3 would've made for a great story, had he not lost the game for the Twins in his first three innings. Radke, pitching with a torn labrum and possibly appearing for the last time in his career, gave up home runs to Eric Chavez and Milton Bradley and put the Twins in a 4-0 hole in the third inning. Despite scattering 12 hits against Dan Haren, Duchscherer and Street, the Twins never scored more than a run in any inning. The A's tacked on four more runs in the eighth, won the game 8-3 and moved on to the next round without having to face Santana a second time.

ALDS: Detroit Tigers vs. New York Yankees

Tigers: Detroit led the AL Central for nearly the entire season, but thanks to a September surge from the Twins and a swoon of their own, the Tigers ended up winning the Wild Card and facing the Yankees in the first round. However, they were no weak WC of the 88-win variety. These Tigers were a powerful team, with several starting pitchers who could dominate a game—Jeremy Bonderman, Justin Verlander, and Kenny Rogers among them—and a strong, balanced offense. While the Tigers had no player with 30 HRs and just one with more than 100 RBIs, eight of their nine starters hit double-digit HRs. Detroit ranked fifth in runs scored among AL teams (second among playoff teams) but allowed fewer runs than any other club in the junior circuit.

Yankees: New York didn't feature the pitching that made the Tigers a daunting opponent, but their hopes rested on an offense that scored nearly six runs per game. Led by Derek Jeter, Alex Rodriguez, Jason Giambi, Robinson Cano and midseason acquisition Bobby Abreu, this was a team that could make you forget their lack of intimidating pitching. Besides, the staff was far from dreadful: It allowed only 4.73 runs per game, good for sixth in the AL. That number was the worst among AL playoff teams, but sufficiently respectable to give their offense a chance.

The Series: Game 1 went according to script. Yankee starter Chien-Ming Wang gave up three runs in 6.2 innings while the New York offense destroyed Nate Robertson. The first six batters in the third inning reached base against Robertson, including Abreu's two-run double and Giambi's two-run homer. Four Yankee relievers combined to limit the Tigers to one run, while the offense tacked on two more against Robertson. Derek Jeter added a home run off of Jamie Walker en route to an 8-4 victory

The Yankees lost Game 2 by failing to capitalize on a potential big inning the way they did in Game 1. In the first inning, after a leadoff single by Johnny Damon, Jeter popped up a bunt. Gary Sheffield struck out with runners on first and second and Rodriguez struck out with the bases loaded. The same thing happened the following inning: After Hideki Matsui and Jorge Posada reached base to open the frame, the Yanks went down in order. Finally, a three-run Damon homer put them on the board in the fourth, but that was all the scoring they'd manage against Justin Verlander. Meanwhile, the

Tigers chipped away at Mike Mussina, scoring single tallies in four innings and evening the series by a score of 4-3.

Game 3 was a matchup of 40-year-old pitchers, and Kenny Rogers emerged the victor over Randy Johnson. This was Detroit's day for an early-game big inning: In the second inning, the Tigers sent eight batters to the plate and scored three runs. From then on, it was only a question of whether Rogers would hold up, and for the first time of many in the postseason, he did. He threw 7.2 innings of scoreless baseball, striking out eight and allowing only seven base runners. Joel Zumaya and Todd Jones closed out the shutout victory.

Facing elimination, the Yankees couldn't have liked the odds of a Jaret Wright-Jeremy Bonderman matchup. Just like Game 1, Game 4 went according to script, only this time in the Tigers' favor. Bonderman was nearly as good as Rogers, pitching into the ninth inning and allowing only two runs. The same couldn't be said for Wright and Cory Lidle, who put the Yankees in a 7-0 hole before the end of the fifth inning. Every Detroit batter except Curtis Granderson got a hit, and after the Tigers' three-run rally in the fifth, the game's outcome was never in doubt. In four games, Detroit eliminated one of the greatest offenses ever assembled and advanced to face the Oakland A's in the ALCS.

NLDS: St. Louis Cardinals vs. San Diego Padres

Cardinals: Despite its worst record (83-78) since 1999, St. Louis qualified for its fourth consecutive playoff appearance. Beset by injuries and a disappointing September that nearly lost them their postseason berth, the Cardinals looked like the 2005 Padres of this postseason: easy pickings for their first-round opponent. However, it was tough to write off a team featuring Albert Pujols and Chris Carpenter, arguably the best hitter and pitcher in the league, respectively. The Cardinals lost closer Jason Isringhausen to injury, so the biggest question mark appeared to be a patchwork bullpen built around rookie Adam Wainwright.

Padres: San Diego tied Los Angeles with 88 wins, but they earned themselves a better playoff seeding by winning the season series against the Dodgers. This appeared to be a huge edge, as it meant they would face the 83-win Cardinals instead of the 97-win Mets. Playing in the league's lowest-scoring ballpark, the Padres allowed the fewest runs per game but scored more than only two other teams. Their offense was of higher quality than that number suggests: their OPS on the road was 70 points higher than at home, and their runs per game away from PETCO Park put them ahead of the Cardinals in sixth place among NL teams.

The Series: Game 1 was a replay of the opener from the 2005 NLDS. Once again, Carpenter outpitched Padres ace Jake Peavy. Pujols picked up where he left off in the '05 postseason, breaking a scoreless tie in the fourth inning with a two-run home run. The Cardinals bullpen passed its first test: Wainwright and Tyler Johnson each pitched 1.1 scoreless innings and struck out a pair.

Both Game 2 starters began the season in the American League: San Diego's David Wells opened the year with the Red Sox, while Cardinals hurler Jeff Weaver was an Angel. Wells, known for his prowess in the postseason, was traded in August after the Sox fell out of the race, while Weaver was so bad in Los Angeles that he was placed on waivers. It was a surprise, then, that Weaver outdueled Wells for a Game 2 Cardinals victory. Both pitchers went five innings, but Wells gave up seven hits and two runs, while Weaver held the Padres scoreless. Again, the Cards bullpen was flawless: Four relievers combined to complete the shutout, and St. Louis was a game away from its second consecutive NLDS sweep of the Padres.

The Padres would make them wait to clinch, however. In Game 3, Chris Young delivered what may have been the best pitching performance of the series, striking out nine in 6.2 scoreless innings. Aside from a So Taguchi home run off of Scott Linebrink in the eighth, the Padres pitching couldn't have been better. The Cardinals bullpen was excellent, as well, keeping its team in the game for 4.2 innings, but the Padres' three-run fourth was enough to keep them alive.

For Game 4, Tony La Russa went with his ace, while Bruce Bochy held Jake Peavy back for a possible Game 5 and started Woody Williams instead. Carpenter struggled in the first inning, as he loaded the bases on two singles and a walk and then let in two runs on a walk and a fielder's choice. The Cardinals came back to tie the game in the bottom half on a two-run Ronnie Belliard single. Both Carpenter and Williams settled down until the sixth, when the Cards put the game out of reach. Juan Encarnacion broke the tie with an RBI triple, and Scott Spiezio, Carpenter, and David Eckstein tacked on RBIs against reliever Cla Meredith. Once again, the Cardinals' bullpen was superb, and St. Louis advanced to the NLCS for the third consecutive year.

NLDS: Los Angeles Dodgers vs. New York Mets

Dodgers: Thanks to a seven-game winning streak and 41-19 finish to the regular season, the NL Wild Card Dodgers were the popular upset pick against the 97-win NL East champion Mets. They gained more at the July 31 trading deadline than any other NL team: Greg Maddux helped solidify their starting rotation, while Wilson Betemit and Julio Lugo added to the already accomplished offensive attack. The injuries that bedeviled the Dodgers in 2005 didn't return in force; even J.D. Drew and Nomar Garciaparra stayed healthy for much of the season.

Mets: During the regular season, New York was the class of the National League. But without Pedro Martinez and midseason pickup Orlando Hernandez, their stature was lessened. With their starting pitching in question, the Mets resembled the Yankees: a bunch of No. 3/No. 4 starters supporting a world-class offense. The Mets featured MVP candidates Carlos Beltran and Jose Reyes along with sluggers David Wright and Carlos Delgado. It was no surprise that this Mets team was among the top three NL teams in runs scored; it's more unexpected that the Phillies and Braves both outscored them.

The Series: Many pundits liked the Dodgers' chances to win a Game 1 matchup between LA's Derek Lowe and New York's John Maine. With runners on first and second and none out when Los Angeles catcher Russell Martin blasted one off the right-field wall in the top of the second inning, the Dodgers should have been shoo-ins to score a run or at least avoid, say, the most unlikely double play baseball had seen in a couple of decades. Instead, in a single moment that defined the series, confused Los Angeles baserunners Jeff Kent and J.D. Drew were both thrown out at the plate trying to score almost at once ahead of Jose Valentin's relay from Shawn Green to Paul Lo Duca. Los Angeles still emerged from that dysfunctional inning with a 1-0 lead before staff ace Lowe allowed four runs over 5.1 innings to New York in his worst start since July. The Dodgers then rallied from a 4-1 deficit in the seventh inning to tie the game, but manager Grady Little chose the slumping Brad Penny to relieve, reinjecting the Mets with enough run-producing serum to generate a 6-5 New York win.

The Mets owned Game 2, riding Tom Glavine to a 4-1 victory over Hong-Chih Kuo, who couldn't get the offensive support he needed to become the first pitcher in modern baseball history to win a postseason game with only one regular-season victory to his credit. While the New York bullpen was plenty good enough to hold on for the win, the Betemit home run allowed by Aaron Heilman in the eighth inning was symptomatic of a larger problem. The Mets bullpen was one of the best in the league during the regular season but gave up runs in every game of the NLDS.

Game 3, however, fell one rally short of a classic. Back home in California, Los Angeles spotted New York and Steve Trachsel a 4-0 lead, rallied to go ahead, 5-4, against Darren Oliver in the fifth, but once again melted down in the bullpen, with the Mets nipping and tucking three runs in the sixth and two more in the eighth to take the series.

ALCS: Detroit Tigers vs. Oakland A's

Game 1: Since neither ALDS went to the maximum five games, both the Tigers and A's were able to bring their ALDS Game 1 starters back for the first game in the LCS. Nate Robertson pitched five scoreless innings and made that option look like a blessing; Barry Zito was shelled. Zito retired the first eight batters he faced, but a Brandon Inge home run in the third, followed by a four-hit explosion in the fourth, chased Zito and put the game out of the reach of Oakland's mediocre offense. The A's scattered eight hits, but scored only a single manufactured run off of Joel Zumaya in the eighth.

Game 2: Milton Bradley came up big for the A's, but his two home runs, four hits, and four RBIs weren't enough to even the series. Neither Justin Verlander nor Esteban Loaiza brought his best, but Verlander was able to keep his team in a game in which 13 runs scored, seven on the long ball. Detroit's big fourth inning, though, didn't depend on home runs: The Tigers put together four singles, a walk and a sacrifice fly to score four of their seven runs against Loaiza. While Oakland's offense woke up in its effort to catch up—in addition to Bradley's outburst, Eric Chavez homered and Mark Kotsay collected three hits—Frank Thomas's bat remained conspicuously silent. In five Game 2 at-bats, he struck out three times.

Game 3: The A's offense wasn't nearly so potent as the Yankees, and Kenny Rogers took advantage of that by beating Oakland even more handily than he disposed of New York in the ALDS. This time around, he threw 7.1 innings of shutout ball, allowing just five baserunners and striking out six. Rich Harden, making only his fourth appearance since June, pitched decently, limiting the Tigers to three runs despite issuing five free passes.

Those three runs, however, were too much: Rogers pitched the Tigers into a commanding 3-0 series lead.

Game 4: After three games in which Detroit outscored Oakland 16-6, Game 4 felt a little bit like a formality. That is, until the Tigers and A's found themselves in the first close game of the series. Both Jeremy Bonderman and Dan Haren held their opponents to three runs, and the score was knotted at three well into the bottom of the ninth. Ken Macha, managing his bullpen in an elimination game, went to closer Huston Street with two outs in the seventh. Street ended a threat in the seventh, retired the side in order in the eighth, and got two quick outs in the ninth. He didn't have much left in the tank after allowing singles to Craig Monroe and Placido Polanco, but Macha left him in to pitch to Magglio Ordonez. Ordonez sent the second pitch over the left-field fence and his team into the World Series.

NLCS: St. Louis Cardinals vs. New York Mets

Game 1: The Mets, who swept the Dodgers in their first round, chose their surviving ace, Tom Glavine, to start the opener. The Cardinals, having used Chris Carpenter to finish off the Padres, didn't have the same luxury and tabbed Jeff Weaver. The matchup appeared to favor the Mets, and New York indeed came out on top, but only after struggling for nearly six innings to make something happen against Weaver. The difference in the 2-0 game came in the sixth inning, when Carlos Beltran hit Weaver's 89th pitch over the right-field fence for all the scoring in the game. Both bullpens were excellent. Tyler Johnson, Brad Thompson, and Braden Looper combined to throw 2.1 scoreless innings for the Cards, while Guillermo Mota and Billy Wagner shut down St. Louis in the eighth and ninth.

Game 2: Runs may have been at a premium in Game 1, but neither team had trouble scoring in Game 2. In fact, at least one team scored in seven of the nine innings. John Maine and Carpenter were equally ineffective. Maine allowed four runs on two hits and five walks in just four innings, while Carpenter allowed five runs in five innings. After Mota gave up a two-run triple to Scott Spiezio in the seventh, the game was tied at 6. Amazingly, the tie-breaking moment came with Billy Wagner on the mound and So Taguchi at the plate, as Taguchi hit a solo home run to lead off the ninth. The Cardinals tacked on two more runs against Wagner, and the St. Louis bullpen kept the Mets' bats silent once again.

Game 3: In the next game, the Cards bullpen was hardly necessary. Jeff Suppan threw eight shutout innings and even hit a solo home run in the second on the way to a 5-0 St. Louis victory. Steve Trachsel removed himself from the game after giving up all five runs in the first two innings, and the only bright spot for the Mets was Darren Oliver's six-inning relief appearance, which saved the rest of the bullpen for another day.

Game 4: The various injuries to the Mets' pitching staff meant that they turned to Oliver Perez for a start, while the Cardinals looked to Anthony Reyes. Reyes gave up only two runs but didn't pitch past the fourth inning. Perez coughed up five runs in 5.2 innings but was supported by the better bullpen. Leading 5-3 on the strength of home runs from Carlos Beltran, David Wright and Carlos Delgado, the Mets turned their slim lead into an unreachable one against Josh Hancock and Tyler Johnson. Hancock faced five batters, allowing two singles, two walks, and a three-run ground-rule double to Delgado. The Mets bullpen didn't match the implosion, and New York evened the series with an 11-5 victory.

Game 5: In Glavine-Weaver, the rematch, Weaver was just as good as the first time—six innings, two runs—while Glavine was a fair bit worse. The Mets' starter didn't record an out in the fifth inning, and by that time he had given up three runs. Back on track, the Cards bullpen kept the Mets from coming back, and Chris Duncan added a St. Louis insurance run in the sixth to give the Cardinals a 4-2 victory.

Game 6: Facing elimination, the Mets came up with a 4-2 victory of their own. Both Maine and Carpenter pitched much better than their Game 2 outings, but Maine's 5.1 scoreless innings gave his team the edge. Carpenter gave up two runs, as did Braden Looper, who managed only two outs in the seventh. Taguchi again led a ninth-inning charge against Billy Wagner, but this time it wasn't enough; Wagner only allowed St. Louis to make up half of the four-run deficit.

Game 7: Against all odds, the deciding game turned into a Jeff Suppan-Oliver Perez pitcher's duel. Suppan allowed only one run in seven innings, while Perez permitted the same in his six innings of work. It took an astonishing play in the sixth inning from Endy Chavez, though, to save Perez's excellent outing. With one out and Edmonds on first, Rolen hit a fly ball that easily cleared the fence—but didn't exceed the reach of Endy's glove. Edmonds was doubled off to end the inning, and Chavez was prevailed upon for perhaps the first post-defensive-play curtain call in NLCS history.

Despite keeping the game knotted at 1, the Mets couldn't break through. The bullpens took over and preserved the tie through eight. Aaron Heilman, who had pitched a nearly perfect eighth, stayed in the game for the top of the ninth. After striking out Edmonds and allowing a single to Scott Rolen, Heilman gave up a two-run homer to Yadier Molina, a hero even unlikelier than Suppan. Adam Wainwright, attempting the save for St. Louis, almost matched Heilman for ineffectiveness. He loaded the bases with two outs on a pair of singles and a walk to Paul Lo Duca, but with a sold-out Shea Stadium crowd rooting against him, he struck out Carlos Beltran to seal the series victory.

World Series: Detroit Tigers vs. St. Louis Cardinals

Game 1: The Tigers had a week off between the end of their LCS and the beginning of the World Series; the Cardinals had a day. Jim Leyland was able to line up his starting rotation however he wanted; Tony La Russa had few choices outside of handing the ball to rookie Anthony Reyes. As it turned out, Reyes pitched into the ninth inning while Justin Verlander had his worst outing since August. The Cards took the opener 7-2 behind solid offensive performances from Albert Pujols, Jim Edmonds and Scott Rolen, their ailing trio of sluggers. In nine innings, the 83-win team from the weaker circuit took home-field advantage from the 95-win club representing the stronger league. Things quickly changed from "This Time It Counts" to "A Championship is in the Cards."

Game 2: Before 2006, Kenny Rogers was a postseason goat with a playoff ERA of nearly 9.00. In his first World Series start in a decade, Rogers threw eight more scoreless innings, evening the series at one apiece. He didn't do so without controversy, though. In the first inning, La Russa discussed a dark spot on Rogers's pitching hand with the umpires. Cardinals batters had complained that the ball was "acting a little funny," and whatever the blemish was, umpires made Rogers remove it. La Russa and his players stayed strangely mum about it after the game, refusing to point fingers. Regardless of what it was, whether Rogers knew about it (he claimed that he didn't) or whether some substance had helped the Tigers get this far, he continued to shut down the Cardinals with an apparently clean hand. Jeff Weaver allowed only three runs in his five innings, but with Rogers on the mound, the Tigers didn't need more.

Game 3: Chris Carpenter wasn't consistently great in the NLCS, but he pitched like a Cy Young Award winner in the World Series. Nate Robertson wasn't bad either, but Carpenter shut out the mighty Tiger offense for eight innings, allowing only three baserunners and striking out six. Only one Tiger got past first base, and Detroit's bullpen allowed the Cardinals plenty of insurance. In the seventh inning, two runs scored on a Joel Zumaya throwing error, and the Cardinals' fifth run scored in the ninth on a Zach Miner wild pitch. The Cards took a 2-1 series lead with their 5-0 victory.

Game 4: While the World Series up to this point had offered its share of great pitching performances, it had been lacking in the late-inning drama department. Game 4 changed that. Jeremy Bonderman and NLCS hero Jeff Suppan gave their teams solid starts, leaving the game to the bullpens with a 3-2 Detroit lead. Detroit fell victim to another pitcher's throwing error in the seventh to even up the game. David Eckstein scored from second when Fernando Rodney threw away a ground ball. Then, with two outs, when the inning should have been over, Preston Wilson singled home another run to move the Cardinals into the lead. The Tigers tied things up again in the top of the eighth on Ivan Rodriguez and Brandon Inge doubles, but Adam Wainwright struck out both Alexis Gomez and Curtis Granderson with Inge at second. Zumaya came in to preserve the tie in the bottom half but walked Yadier Molina to lead off the inning. Aaron Miles reached on a fielder's choice, then advanced to second on a wild third strike to Juan Encarnacion. Then, for the second time in the game, David Eckstein delivered an RBI double. Wainwright gave the Cardinals a 3-1 series edge with a perfect ninth.

Game 5: For the final game in St. Louis, Leyland gave the ball to Verlander, while La Russa skipped Reyes and started Weaver. Weaver capped his post-season of solid performances with his best yet, allowing a single earned run over eight innings. For the first time in the playoffs, Weaver struck out more than one per inning; he also walked only a single batter. Verlander also limited the Cards to one earned run, but St. Louis scored three on his watch, one of them on yet another pitcher's throwing error. A fourth-inning Sean Casey home run briefly gave the Tigers a 2-1 lead, but a pesky Cardinals rally—including Verlander's crucial misplay—immediately swung the lead back in the home team's favor. The Cards added another run in the seventh and Wainwright sweated his way through the ninth inning to clinch St. Louis' first World Series victory since 1982.

The Cardinals were the weakest regular-season team ever to win the World Series, and only the third team to win the championship after winning fewer than 90 games in a 162-game season (the 2000 Yankees won 87 and the 1987 Twins won 85). Yet, their starting rotation showed up when it needed to, their bullpen solidified just in time and the offense produced like the balanced attack it was built to be, not the one-man show it looked like in August and September. The Tigers may have literally thrown away three of their four losses, but consistently strong pitching gave the Cardinals a chance to capitalize on those mistakes in each of the last three games. The 2006 Cardinals are not a team you'll probably speak of in hushed tones decades from now, but for a couple of weeks in October, they outplayed three of the best teams in baseball.

2006 Commentary

Deadspin's Look Back at 2006

by Will Leitch

We can find ourselves, sometimes, so far deep inside the game of baseball that we forget that it's supposed to be *fun*. Fortunately, there's always enough off-the-field weirdness to remind us that no matter how seriously we take the great game, its participants and those who cover it will always make sure they remind us how silly they can truly be.

Here's a look at a season's worth of goofiness and malfeasance.

April

During the Colorado Rockies' first homestand, closer Brian Fuentes warms up in the bullpen, waiting for his "rocking" entrance music—Staind's "For You"—to blast over the loudspeaker, his cue to sprint toward the mound. As he readies his entrance, the public address system announces his name and begins playing … the Village People's "YMCA." "It was a downer," Fuentes says, echoing the sentiment of any Rockies fans who realized they root for a closer who legitimately likes Staind.

Roger Clemens, still "debating" whether or not he would "unretire," decides to pitch for the United States in the World Baseball Classic. He acknowledges that the event, while important to him, probably means more to the other countries involved, particularly the Asian countries. How does he know this? He has a hard time getting his dry cleaning done. According to Clemens' hopefully true story—because if it's not, Clemens could have some fascinating conversations with Chan Ho Park—when he asked if his suit could be ready in two days, he was rebuffed. He retold the story: "They said, 'You've got no chance,' they told me," Clemens said. "I said, 'I'm going to get it tomorrow, right?' And then she goes, 'No chance, we're going to the game.' So we couldn't get dry cleaning done out there, but I guess the neatest thing about them was there were about 50,000 of them at Anaheim Stadium, Korea and Japan." Clemens resists the urge to point out that Puerto Rico's success makes it extremely difficult for his house to be cleaned.

May

White Sox pitcher Freddy Garcia can only watch as news lets out that he sat out the WBC because of a positive test for marijuana. It can be understood, though, if he needs the demon weed to withstand a single episode of "Bonds On Bonds," the reality program starring Barry Bonds that manages to transform the single most fascinating athletic figure of our generation into Colby from "Survivor." The show barely lasts a month and a half, but it lives on in the hearts and minds of those who have a desperate desire to watch a grown man with a huge head dress like Paula Abdul and roll around on the couch with his bewildered children.

While visiting the San Diego Padres broadcast booth after a night out drinking with, of all people, Bill Murray, ESPN broadcaster Rick Sutcliffe, visibly intoxicated, slurs out a long discussion of the political progressiveness of actor George Clooney. Specifically, he talks about how Clooney is over in Israel, "tryin' to solve that thing." Sutcliffe does not elaborate on the "thing" Clooney was there to "solve," but ESPN solves the problem of Sutcliffe's public drunkenness by suspending him for a week. When he returns, his broadcast partner is, sadly, Gary Thorne, not Bill Murray or, for that matter, George Clooney.

Jose Canseco, the most bizarre soothsayer of his age, decides to follow up his riveting bestseller *Juiced* by signing up for the Los Angeles Men's Senior Baseball League. Not only will Canseco be the cleanup hitter, he also insists on pitching, throwing his vaunted knuckleball special, which, just by rote of habit, he aims squarely at the ass of the opposing batter. After one game, in which he hits a homer and gives up two runs, Canseco asks for a trade, which is granted.

June

It's not easy for a middle reliever to make headlines, so Cleveland Indians pitcher Scott Sauerbeck breaks the mold by being arrested in the middle of the night after a road game. What happened? While driving at 3 a.m. with a "female companion," Sauerbeck is spotted by police weaving drunkenly through traffic. To dodge them, he parks the car and, with his "companion," leaps into the backyard of a random house and hides in the bushes. When the home's owner realizes they have a middle reliever in their backyard, rather than someone with the respectable closer's mentality, they call the police and Sauerbeck is arrested.

The federal affidavit involving the use and distribution of human growth hormone by journeyman reliever Jason Grimsley is released to the public, with the juicy names blacked out. Players as celebrated as Albert Pujols and Jason Giambi (both later debunked) and Roger Clemens and Andy Pettitte (both denied) are floated into the public square, but no name is verified, other than former Baltimore Oriole David Segui, who admits to using HGH for treatment of a medical condition. Segui's confession is treated with little regard in the public square, as it is decided that he ranks above Matt Lawton but below Derrick Turnbow on the ever-dynamic Sliding Scale Of Steroid Outrage.

After being dropped from his spot in the rotation by Dodgers manager Grady Little, pitcher Odalis Perez, furious, announces that he will discontinue his "O's 45" program, in which he buys 45 tickets for inner-city school children to attend his starts. When he later is put back in the rotation, he says he will not reinstate the program. He explains in an oddly forthright fashion: "When you spend your own money you want to be recognized for that. I don't want to be a hero, but just pay more attention to what I'm doing. People don't want to give me the recognition for it."

Joe Mikulik, manager of the Colorado Rockies' Single-A affiliate, frustrated about an out call at second base, loses his mind at the beleaguered umpire and pulls out every trick in the disgruntled manager playbook. He tries the patented Dirt Kick, Base Toss, Bat Hurl, Backwards Hat Facial Confrontation and Squeezed Vein Howl before ultimately, and dramatically, strolling out of the "stadium" through the right field exit. In the future, the act of throwing their computers out the window and then heading to ground level to destroy them with a sledgehammer before burying them in a pile of cat feces will be known as "The Mikulik."

July

Responding to repeated criticism from *Chicago Sun-Times* "columnist" Jay Mariotti, White Sox manager Ozzie Guillen, otherwise known for his stoic restraint, unleashes a tirade at the (as usual, non-present) "journalist" and eventually refers to him as a "fag." The public uproar is immense, particularly among the media, but perhaps not in the way one would expect; many journalists, while deriding Guillen's choice of words, take the opportunity to deride Mariotti for refusing to attend the games he writes about. Mariotti, taking the high road, calls for Guillen to be suspended for his remarks in his next column. Guillen does the modern apology non-apology shuffle, saying he's sorry if was anyone was offended, excluding, presumably, Mariotti.

Before a start in Fenway Park, Phillies pitcher Brett Myers is arrested after several Boston residents call 9-1-1 and report that he was "punching his wife in the face." Myers pitches the next day and is booed lustily, though he is afforded more welcoming treatment in San Francisco later that week. In response to the story, elderly Phillies co-owner Bill Giles says the Phillies have a source that says Myers' wife made up the story, though he is unable to account for the throng of witnesses. As tends to happen, months later, reunited with her *tae kwon do* specialist husband, Myers' wife drops the charges.

ESPN baseball analyst Harold Reynolds is fired by the network for unspecified conduct detrimental to the network. They will ultimately never discuss the matter further, but several sources—and, eventually, Reynolds himself—confirm that he was fired for sexual harassment. Depending on whom you talk to, it was either a "pattern of behavior" (most sources) or a "misunderstanding" (Reynolds). He never returns to the network and is rumored to be joining TBS for baseball broadcasts next season. The instigating incident is rumored to be an "inappropriate hug" at a Boston Market in Bristol, a rumor Reynolds denies. With Reynolds gone and Peter Gammons recovering from an aneurysm, "Baseball Tonight" viewers are treated to countless debates about proper closer usage and the right way to throw at a batter from great minds John Kruk and Jeff Brantley.

August

In an effort to expand their reach among the Latino fan base, the Milwaukee Brewers introduce the chorizo to their famous sausage race. The chorizo, to much fanfare, participates in one race and loses. He is then retired for the rest of the season as Major League Baseball re-evaluates the sausage, which runs around the bases in a sombrero and sports a bushy mustache.

Cincinnati Reds utilityman Ryan Freel, a fan favorite for his hustle, versatility and skin pigment, tells *Dayton Daily News* reporter Hal McCoy that the key to his success is his imaginary friend "Farney." Freel says: "He's a little guy who lives in my head who talks to me and I talk to him. That little midget in my head said, 'That was a great catch, Ryan,' I said, 'Hey, Farney, I don't know if that was you who really caught that ball, but that was pretty good if it was.' Everybody thinks

I talk to myself, so I tell 'em I'm talking to Farney.'" Freel struggles the rest of the season as the Reds fade from the National League Central race, though Farney earns a decent living as the gremlin in Ken Griffey Jr.'s hamstring.

During a Boston Red Sox broadcast on the New England Sports Network, comedian and actor Denis Leary joins the booth and notices, with a start, that the Red Sox start a Jewish first baseman named Kevin Youkilis. Inspired by the recent arrest of reportedly anti-Semitic actor/director Mel Gibson for drunk driving in Malibu, CA, Leary goes on a full inning's rant against Gibson, cheering a diving play by Youkilis by screaming, "TAKE THAT MEL!!!!!" Youkilis is not Greek, by the way; he's actually from Cincinnati.

September

Distressing any Red Sox fans able to conjure up the intestinal fortitude to look, superstar designated hitter David Ortiz appears in a Dominican commercial for a product that cures erectile dysfunction. In the commercial, he implores potential customers to "get back in the game." Unlike former boner pitchman Rafael Palmeiro, he resists the urge to make it clear that he does not use the product he is being paid millions to endorse, which of course totally means he uses it.

During a late-season, meaningless contest between the Braves and the Nationals, a camera spies a woman in the top row of the upper deck performing an act on her boyfriend that has been known, in the past, to force people to face impeachment. Supposedly video of the incident exists, but has never been found. No truth so far to reports that the Nationals are considering working the incident into a promotion for next season, but if they do, attendance amongst members of Congress is expected to increase tenfold.

October

In the FOX booth with Thom Brenneman and future Cubs manager Lou Piniella, "analyst" Steve Lyons makes an inexplicable—and, frankly, entirely nonsensical—comment about Piniella speaking Spanish and stealing Lyons' wallet. All three broadcasters laugh at the comment, because it's in the contract of all FOX personalities that they are required to make Steve Lyons think he's funny. After the game, however, FOX suits decide the comment is racist and fire Lyons, who, for perfectly legitimate reasons (for once), is befuddled, confused and speechless.

During Game 2 of the World Series, Tigers pitcher Kenny Rogers, apparently too old to understand the intricacies of high definition television, takes the mound with a pound and a half of pine tar attached to his left palm. (It is so obvious that Tim McCarver notices it.) Cardinals manager Tony La Russa, perhaps because of his past marriage to Tigers manager Jim Leyland, decides not to protest the pine tar, though Rogers removes it between innings and goes on to shut out the Cardinals. The incident serves a crushing blow to Rogers' otherwise sterling, impeccable reputation as one of baseball's Good Guys and gives plenty of white guys in ties and pitstains the opportunity to write plenty about a World Series they hadn't much cared for heading in. As punishment, Rogers is ultimately dragged into the public square and tickled until he turns green, part of commissioner Bud Selig's controversial "Yellow means National League gets home-field advantage, Blue means American League" World Series initiative. The final verdict of green causes Selig to cancel the All-Star Game and just have a home run derby instead. *Back back back back back … GONE!* Man, chicks do dig the long ball.

The Best Ideas of 2006

by Ben Jacobs

Many of the moves that shape each baseball team every year are made in the offseason. From free agent signings to trades to promotions from the minor leagues, most teams receive at least a partial overhaul between the beginning of November and the end of January.

But while the building blocks for the season are put in place over the winter months, there's still plenty of room to adjust the final design as each team's general manager and manager combine to make hundreds, if not thousands, of decisions that impact their club's success or failure.

Below are five teams that made a decision, or group of decisions, after the beginning of Spring Training that turned out to greatly improve said team's fortune in 2006. No-brainer moves that merely required throwing a pile of cash at a problem, such as Houston re-signing Roger Clemens or the Yankees trading for Bobby Abreu, aren't included.

Boston Red Sox

The Red Sox entered the season with a lot of uncertainty at closer. After helping Boston win the World Series for the first time in 86 years in 2004, Keith Foulke was an absolute mess in 2005.

He struggled with injuries throughout the season, and when he was able to pitch, he posted a 5.91 ERA in 45⅔ innings. While the Red Sox hoped the offseason would allow him to heal enough that he could close, he clearly wasn't someone they could rely on.

When it wasn't Foulke, or converted starter Curt Schilling, closing games, it was Mike Timlin. He did an excellent job in 2005, with 13 saves and a 2.24 ERA in 80⅓ innings, but he was also going to be 40 years old by the start of the 2006 season, making him a risk to close as well.

The Red Sox had two rookies with potential: Jonathan Papelbon and Craig Hansen. Hansen was the team's first-round draft pick in 2005, and he was immediately tabbed as the closer of the future. The only question was whether he'd be ready for the majors in 2006.

Papelbon pitched 34 innings in the majors in 2005, splitting time as a starter and reliever, and it was clear that he'd have some sort of role in Boston in 2006.

The specifics, however, were unclear at the start of the season.

It looked as though the Red Sox would go with Foulke at closer until he proved he couldn't handle it and then switch to somebody else. But when they had a 2-1 lead to protect in the third game of the season, Terry Francona gave the ball to Papelbon in the ninth instead of Foulke, saying that Foulke wasn't ready yet and would get to close when he was.

Except Francona kept on giving the ball to Papelbon. Papelbon got the ball in the ninth as he started the season with 15⅓ scoreless innings, and he got the ball in the ninth as he successfully converted his first 20 save opportunities.

While Papelbon eventually got hurt and missed the final month, he still finished with 35 saves in 41 chances and a sickeningly good 0.92 ERA in 68⅓ innings. Without the decision to make him the closer right at the beginning of the season, Boston's season may have fallen apart much sooner than it did.

Cincinnati Reds

The Reds made two trades, one during Spring Training and the other in the first week of the season, that allowed them to remain in playoff contention until the final week of the season. They finished 80-82, good enough for third place in the NL Central, when most people probably expected them to lose 90 to 100 games and contend for the cellar.

First, the Reds bolstered their pitching staff by trading outfielder Wily Mo Pena to Boston for starting pitcher Bronson Arroyo. The next move looked relatively meaningless, as they sent a player to be named later (eventually minor leaguer Jeff Stevens) to Cleveland for Brandon Phillips, who had showed no ability to hit in the majors.

The 2005 Reds got a 5.38 ERA from their starting pitchers, as only one pitcher threw at least 200 innings (Aaron Harang at 211⅔) and only one had an ERA below 4.00 (Harang again at 3.83).

Arroyo came in this season and tossed 240⅔ innings with a 3.29 ERA. That contribution helped the Cincinnati rotation shave nearly a run off its ERA, down to 4.58 in 2006.

Phillips didn't do anything earth-shattering, but he did play 149 games and post a .751 OPS, hitting .276 with 17 home runs. That might not seem very good until you realize that without Phillips, the Cincinnati second baseman likely would have been Tony Womack. Womack, of course, managed just a .556 OPS in 2005 with the Yankees, and has a career OPS of .673.

Between the addition of Arroyo to stabilize the rotation and the upgrade at second base from Womack to Phillips, the Reds made early alterations that helped the team exceed expectations and contend for a playoff spot.

Detroit Tigers

Before this season, Justin Verlander and Joel Zumaya had combined for all of 55⅓ innings of experience above Double-A in their careers. Verlander went from Double-A to an 11⅓-inning stint in the majors last year, where he posted an ugly 7.15 ERA as a 22-year-old. Zumaya graduated to Triple-A late in 2005 and posted a 2.65 ERA in 44 innings as a 20-year-old.

It would have been perfectly understandable, and perhaps even sensible, for the Tigers to send both of them to Triple-A to start the season. Instead, Detroit opted to leave both on the major league roster, giving Verlander a spot in the rotation and putting Zumaya in the bullpen for the first time in his career.

It turned out to be a very fortuitous decision.

Verlander made 30 starts for the Tigers, going 17-9 with a 3.63 ERA in 186 innings. His peripheral numbers (124 strikeouts, 60 walks, 21 home runs allowed) weren't great, but he was able to get the job done more often than not.

Zumaya may have been even better pitching as the primary setup man for most of the season. He posted a 1.94 ERA in 83⅓ innings while striking out 97 batters and walking 42.

Their strong pitching in the first half of the season—Zumaya posted a 2.25 ERA in 40 innings and Verlander was 10-4 with a 3.13 ERA in 103⅔ innings in the season's first three months—helped the Tigers win 55 of their first 80 games and give themselves plenty of margin for error to make the playoffs.

Zumaya then got even better down the stretch, and Verlander did just enough to help the Tigers reach the playoffs for the first time since 1987, even if they did lose the division title on the final day of the season.

Detroit wound up winning the Wild Card by five games. If they had spent part of April and May with Verlander and/or Zumaya in the minor leagues, there's no telling how many games would have been moved from the left column in the standings to the right.

Los Angeles Angels of Anaheim

On May 27, with Bartolo Colon on the disabled list and Kevin Gregg not working out all that well as a spot starter, the Angels called up then-23-year-old Jered Weaver from Triple-A.

Weaver, who had posted a 2.05 ERA in eight starts at Triple-A, pitched seven scoreless innings in his major league debut to earn the win. He won his next three starts as well, going at least six innings and allowing no more than two runs each time.

After that, with Colon back from the disabled list, Weaver went back to Triple-A despite the fact that older brother Jeff (3-9, 6.15 ERA) seemed a much better candidate to lose his spot in the rotation.

It took just over two weeks for the Angels to reach the same conclusion. They recalled Jered Weaver from Triple-A on June 30, and they traded Jeff to the St. Louis Cardinals a week after that.

Jered made 15 more starts in the last three months of the season, and he finished with an 11-2 record, a 2.56 ERA and 105 strikeouts in 123 innings. Jered Weaver's permanent promotion to the major leagues wasn't the only factor in their turnaround, but the Angels were 35-44 at the end of June and then went 54-29 with him on the roster the rest of the way.

It's impossible to know what would have happened had the Angels started Jered Weaver in the major leagues as Detroit did with Verlander and Zumaya, but at least they salvaged a decent season by getting their best starting pitcher in their major league rotation at midseason.

San Diego Padres

A lot of people took the Padres to task last offseason when they traded Mark Loretta to the Red Sox for Doug Mirabelli. Loretta had finished in the top 10 in the NL in hitting two years in a row before injuries limited him in 2005, while Mirabelli was merely a backup catcher.

The move ended up not hurting the Padres, as Josh Barfield posted a .741 OPS (94 OPS+) while Loretta struggled to a .706 OPS (82 OPS+). More importantly, that trade set the Padres up to make a spectacular trade later in the season.

After trading Mirabelli to the Padres, the Red Sox didn't have anybody to serve as the personal catcher for Tim Wakefield. When Bard had trouble catching Wakefield's knuckleball, Boston panicked and went after the one player they knew could catch it: Mirabelli.

And what did San Diego get in return for giving back a player they never really needed to begin with? Just Bard and relief pitcher Cla Meredith. Since neither one is a household name, you probably wouldn't expect that this move would have such a big impact, but it may have been the difference between the Padres making and missing the playoffs.

After the trade from Boston to San Diego, Bard played in 93 games and racked up 231 at-bats. And after failing to post an OPS+ above 80 during any previous season in which he played more than seven games, Bard hit .338/.406/.537 for an outstanding 147 OPS+.

Meredith's pitching may have been even more important than Bard's hitting, however. The 23-year-old sidearmer threw 50.2 innings for the Padres after the trade, allowing just six runs for a 1.07 ERA. He only struck out 37 batters, but he also only allowed six walks and 30 hits for a 0.71 WHIP. Included in that amazing performance was a 34-inning scoreless streak that stretched from mid-July to mid-September.

The 2006 performance of Bard and Meredith alone would be enough to make this trade a great move for the Padres. But that doesn't even take into account the fact that Meredith will be under San Diego's control for another five seasons before free agency and Bard could remain a Padre for three more years.

All told, the Padres' decision to promote Barfield to be their starting second baseman and trade Loretta worked out better than they could possibly have dreamed.

Looking for Blunders

by Rob Neyer

Regarding the Minnesota Twins in 2006, you can pick your own low point. My choice is the 10th of June. On the 10th of June, the Twins lost to the Orioles, 9-7. Carlos Silva started for Minnesota, and his ERA ballooned to 7.73 (in 2005, it was 3.44). After that evening's games, the Twins were sitting in fourth place, 11.5 games behind the first-place Tigers and two games behind the third-place (and terribly disappointing) Cleveland Indians.

I knew, on the 10th of June, that I would be writing this article for this book, and on the 10th of June I'd have bet you the entire contents of my piggy bank—actually a giant plastic baseball, good for at least $120 at the moment—that my lead item, my No. 1 Blunder, when I sat down to write in late October, would be the Minnesota Twins' failure to trust their young players early in the season. At third base, the Twins had given far too many plate appearances to Tony Batista and Luis Rodriguez instead of Nick Punto. At shortstop, they'd given far too many plate appearances to Juan Castro instead of Jason Bartlett. At DH, they'd given far too many plate appearances to Rondell White instead of Jason Kubel (though I must admit that I expected White to play much better than he did).

Of course, nobody outside of Minnesota paid much attention to any of those guys. Not in June or any other month. The *guy* was Francisco Liriano. Widely considered the No. 1 pitching prospect in the game, Liriano spent September of 2005 with the big club and struck out 33 batters in 24 innings. If there was a single rookie pitcher who seemed to deserve a rotation slot entering the 2006 season, it was Liriano. But of course he didn't have it. Liriano pitched in the World Baseball Classic, and according to the Twins he simply wasn't ready to pitch as a starter when the real season opened. Liriano didn't join the rotation until May 19, which meant a few too many games were started by Scott Baker (5-8, 6.37 for the Twins in '06) and Kyle Lohse (2-5, 7.07).

When the Twins were 11.5 games out, I figured all this had killed their chances . . . though in fairness, when a team is that far out of contention you can't believe that *anything* would have made a real difference. Nobody . . . wait, let me be very clear about this . . . NOBODY could have guessed that the Twins, even with all the pieces finally in place, would go 69-32 after the 10th of June and win a division title. Nobody.

But of course that is exactly what the Twins did. What's more, Liriano managed only six innings after July 28 because of an elbow injury—and as you read this, he is recovering from Tommy John surgery—suggesting that maybe the Twins' caution in the spring was presciently appropriate. They might have been right about Liriano in April, and they did finish in first place. All of which is my long-winded way of saying, "Move along, folks; no (consequential) blunders to look at here."

The same might be said of the Nationals' trading Brad Wilkerson for Alfonso Soriano. I believed, at the time, that it was an awful deal for Washington. After all, even without accounting for the stadium switches—the Nats play in an extreme pitcher's park, the Rangers in an extreme hitter's park—reasonable projections showed Wilkerson doing just as well in 2006, as a hitter, as Soriano. In *Ron Shandler's Baseball Forecaster*, both players were projected to post .822 OPS's; in *Baseball Prospectus*, park-adjusted projections showed an .835 OPS for Wilkerson, .778 for Soriano. Speaking of BP, I don't mean to throw them under the bus—because after all, I agreed with them—but here's their closing line about Soriano: "He's about to become a massive disappointment."

It should be said that Soriano was not, in the end, a great player in 2006. A left fielder with a .351 on-base percentage and a so-so success rate when attempting to steal bases, Soriano certainly was one of the 25 best non-pitchers in the National League. He was not one of the ten best. But neither was a he a "massive disappointment" . . . or any other kind of disappointment.

Wilkerson, on the other hand . . . now *there* is a massive disappointment. He played in only 95 games, and when he played he was awful. Which isn't to say the trade was an unmitigated success for the Nationals. Even though they won their arbitration case with Soriano, they did have to pay him $10 million. They did finish in last place by an unhealthy margin, and they will lose Soriano to free agency with naught but a couple of 2007 draft picks in return. I still say trading for Soriano was a blunder . . . just not nearly the blunder I expected, and if the draft picks are useful it might even look *smart* in a few years.

So last spring I thought I'd have two mega-blunders to chronicle in this space, and I wound up with one non-blunder (Liriano, etc.) and one semi-blunder (Wilkerson-for-Soriano). And considering 1) that one of the criteria for a blunder is that it must have some significant impact, and 2) there was, in the end, little competition for spots in the World Series derby, it's not so easy to find "good" blunders in 2006. In the American League, the closest non-qualifiers were the White Sox (five games out in the Wild Card standings) and the Angels (four out in the West). There's no single thing that, if undone, would have pushed either team over the top. In the National League, the Phillies finished three games out of the Wild Card—actually, out of a tie for the Wild Card—while the Astros and Reds finished 1.5 and 3.5, respectively, behind the Cardinals in the Central.

I would like to focus on the Astros, as they wound up—after a late rush—so close to qualifying. And I would like to focus particularly on five hitters who sucked up—or if you prefer, sucked *during*—too many plate appearances...

2006 Results

Player	PA	OBP	SLG
Craig Biggio	607	.306	.422
Brad Ausmus	502	.308	.285
Preston Wilson	417	.309	.405
Jason Lane	345	.318	.392
Orl. Palmeiro	128	.294	.319

Obviously, none of these fine specimens hit much in 2006, and replacing just one of them with an *average* hitter might have pushed the Astros into, at the very least, a tie with the Cardinals. But in my book (literally) it's only a blunder if it wasn't a good move *before* it didn't work out. With that in mind, let's check *Baseball Prospectus*' projections for each of these guys...

2006 Projections

Player	PA	OBP	SLG
Craig Biggio	508	.321	.445
Brad Ausmus	287	.329	.330
Preston Wilson	401	.329	.473
Jason Lane	560	.340	.491
Orl. Palmeiro	98	.335	.389

More than anything else, the Astros were simply unlucky with these five. There's one thing I want to point out, though . . . While one cannot fault management for thinking Biggio and Ausmus would play better than they did, one can fault management for letting Biggio and Ausmus play as *often* as they did. BP assumed that Biggio would play five games per week; he played six. BP's method assumed that Ausmus would play three games per week; he played five. And if management erred, it was on the side of the veterans. If Biggio and Ausmus had played less and Chris Burke and Eric Bruntlett and Eric Munson had played more, the Astros might have won a couple of "extra" games.

The Phillies and the Reds? Not much there, really. One might quibble with trading Bobby Abreu, but 1) Abreu probably wouldn't have been worth three games, all by himself, and 2) this probably was the best thing for the franchise in the long term, and that counts, too. As for the Reds, I wasn't wild about Wayne Krivsky's various in-season moves to change (and theoretically improve) the pitching staff, but on balance I don't think he cost them a playoff spot, either.

Finally, there's October, and the seven teams that did not win the World Series Derby. Without belaboring things too much, I will point to a couple of things that seemed obviously wrong to me, at the time.

First, there was Joe Torre panicking like a first-time mother with a baby that won't stop crying. Following a rough June, Alex Rodriguez batted .300 with patience and power after the All-Star break; his best month of the season was September. In the Yankees' first Division Series game against the Tigers, Rodriguez batted sixth; he'd batted fourth and (occasionally) fifth all season long. In four at-bats that evening, he singled. In the Yankees' second game, he batted sixth again and went 0-for-4. They lost that one.

In the Yankees' third game, a left-hander pitching for the Tigers, Torre moved Rodriguez to his accustomed cleanup slot. He went 0-for-3. At which point Torre panicked. With the Yankees facing elimination in the fourth game, Torre dropped Rodriguez to a spot in the order he hadn't seen in more than a decade: eighth. Conveniently enough for today's little diatribe, Rodriguez went 0-for-3 and the Yankees lost.

I believed, at the time, that either Torre or Rodriguez would be gone by Opening Day in 2007. At this writing (early November), though, it looks like both will return. And considering the manager's easy manner and the third baseman's obvious talents, the likelihood is that this whole thing will be forgotten by May.

In the seventh game of the National League Championship Series, Mets manager Willie Randolph made two huge, second-guessable decisions about his pitchers. In the first, he chose Oliver Perez as his starting pitcher. It's not what I recommended. I recommended Aaron Heilman. But Perez, who posted a 6.55 ERA during the season, made Randolph look like a genius, giving up only one run in six innings. Chad Bradford followed with a perfect seventh. Heilman entered in the eighth, and retired all three Cardinals he wanted to retire (Albert Pujols drew an intentional walk). After eight innings—by the way, the game was in New York—the score was still 1-1, as it had been since the second.

And so another tough decision faced Randolph: Should he give Heilman another inning, or should he summon Billy Wagner?

In Heilman's favor: He's got good stuff; he pitched well during the season; excluding the four wide ones to Pujols, he'd thrown only fourteen pitches in the eighth; his 2006 included 15 two-inning relief stints.

In Wagner's favor: He's arguably the National League's best closer, and for many years I've been criticizing managers for losing close games without using their best reliever. In my book, I devoted a chapter to Joe Torre's non-use of Mariano Rivera in Game 5 of the 2003 World Series, which the Yankees lost in the 12th inning when Alex Gonzalez homered off Jeff Weaver.

The Mets lost, too. In the ninth, Heilman struck out Jim Edmonds. But Scott Rolen singled, and then Yadier Molina, who'd batted .216 with six home runs during the season, hit a two-run homer to put the Cardinals ahead. Heilman got the next two guys, Adam Wainwright escaped a scary jam in the bottom of the ninth, and the Cards were on their merry way to destiny.

So is Aaron Heilman the new Jeff Weaver, and Willie Randolph the new Joe Torre? Of course not, and not least because Weaver and Torre are still very much in the middle of things. Weaver was perhaps the *worst* pitcher in Torre's bullpen; Heilman was one of the best in Randolph's. And there's a big difference between the ninth inning and the twelfth inning. With the game quite possibly destined for multiple extra innings, Randolph wanted to get more than one inning from one of his best guys, and one can hardly blame him for that.

I'm not going to argue that Randolph made the *right* move, exactly. But I'm not willing to argue he made the wrong one, either. Which was the story of 2006, blunders-wise. There were certainly plenty of questionable decisions, as there are in every season. But if I were writing my book today, I suspect that double-aught-six would get a free pass. So here's hoping for some obvious and meaningful stupidity in '007...

2006: The Year of the Rookie

by Rich Lederer

Jim Morris (Dennis Quaid) may be *The Rookie* but the 2006 baseball season was The Year of the Rookie. Although Disney isn't expected to come a-calling, a movie about the Class of 2006 would feature numerous stars, including a select group of pitchers in the American League and a deep contingent of position players in the National League.

Among hitters with 250 or more plate appearances, major league rookies last year posted higher batting averages, on-base percentages and slugging averages than their counterparts in any of the previous five seasons.

Rookie Batters by Year

	AVG	OBP	SLG	OPS
2001	.272	.323	.417	.740
2002	.263	.330	.414	.743
2003	.268	.325	.414	.743
2004	.274	.334	.435	.769
2005	.264	.329	.410	.739
2006	.275	.339	.443	.782

Yes, the 2006 rookie crop out-hit the 2001 rookie class led by NL ROY Albert Pujols and AL ROY and MVP Ichiro Suzuki (as well as Adam Dunn, Alfonso Soriano, and Mike Young, among others). It also outproduced those in 2002 (Carl Crawford and Nick Johnson), 2003 (Miguel Cabrera, Travis Hafner and Mark Teixeira), 2004 (Jason Bay, Justin Morneau and David Wright), and 2005 (Garrett Atkins, Robinson Cano and Ryan Howard).

At the same time, among pitchers with at least 60 innings pitched, the 2006 rookies had the lowest WHIP and the highest K/9 and K/BB rates, plus the second-stingiest ERA, of the previous five campaigns.

Rookie Pitchers by Year

	ERA	WHIP	K/9	K/BB
2001	4.64	1.41	6.0	1.8
2002	4.42	1.43	6.4	1.7
2003	4.55	1.42	6.1	1.7
2004	4.34	1.40	6.7	1.9
2005	4.19	1.39	6.3	1.8
2006	4.21	1.35	7.0	2.0

Once again, the 2001-2005 rookie classes had their share of quality pitchers, including Roy Oswalt, C.C. Sabathia and Ben Sheets (2001); Josh Beckett, Aaron Harang, Jason Jennings, John Lackey, Brett Myers, Jake Peavy, Mark Prior and Carlos Zambrano (2002); Jeremy Bonderman, Rich Harden, Dan Haren, Brandon Lidge, Brandon Webb and Dontrelle Willis (2003); Erik Bedard (2004); and Felix Hernandez, Scott Kazmir, Huston Street and Chien-Ming Wang (2005).

Hitting and pitching. Quality and quantity. The Class of 2006 had 'em all.

Based on performance rather than long-term projection, we present:

The Hardball Times All-Rookie Teams

POS	First Team	Second Team
C	Kenji Johjima	Russell Martin
1B	Prince Fielder	Mike Jacobs
2B	Dan Uggla	Ian Kinsler
3B	Ryan Zimmerman	Willy Aybar
SS	Hanley Ramirez	Stephen Drew
OF	Josh Willingham	Luke Scott
OF	Nick Markakis	Melky Cabrera
OF	Chris Duncan	Andre Ethier
SP	Justin Verlander	Scott Olsen
SP	Francisco Liriano	Cole Hamels
SP	Jered Weaver	Anibal Sanchez
SP	Josh Johnson	Chuck James
SP	Matt Cain	Boof Bonser
CL	Jonathan Papelbon	Takashi Saito
SU	Joel Zumaya	Jonathan Broxton

We admittedly fudged a bit by going with three outfielders rather than a left fielder, center fielder and right fielder. Simply put, there was an abundance of corner outfielders and a dearth of center fielders among rookies in 2006. In fact, Brian Anderson (.225 AVG/.290 OBP/.359 SLG) of the Chicago White Sox was the lone rookie who patrolled center field on a regular basis. In the meantime, there were numerous left and right fielders to choose from, including the six listed above plus honorable mentions such as Milwaukee's Corey Hart (.283/.328/.468) and Arizona's Carlos Quentin (.253/.342/.530).

The Cream of the Crop

At the All-Star Break, Francisco Liriano, Jonathan Papelbon and Justin Verlander were not only candidates for American League Rookie of the Year but the Cy Young Award as well. Owing to a late start, Jered Weaver never quite joined either discussion, even though he ended up with a similar win-loss record and ERA to Liriano and rate stats superior to Verlander's.

It all seems so obvious now but who'da thunk it last spring? Hard to believe but not one of these four standout pitchers was guaranteed much of anything a year ago. Liriano, who started the season as a relief pitcher, didn't make his first start until May 19. Papelbon, on the other hand, went to Spring Training not knowing if he would wind up as a starter or reliever, and he became the league's best closer from the onset of the season.

Verlander, who was among several Detroit starters vying for the No. 5 spot in the rotation last March, became the first rookie pitcher in baseball history to win 10 games before the end of June. Weaver began the season in Triple-A Salt Lake, pitched a seven-inning shutout in his MLB debut on May 27, and went on to become the only pitcher in 25 years to earn victories in his first seven starts (hello Fernando Valenzuela) and the only AL pitcher since 1950 to win his first nine decisions (the last: Hall of Famer Whitey Ford).

Spearheaded by the foursome of Liriano, Papelbon, Verlander and Weaver, this class of first-year pitchers could be the best since 1984 when Rookies of the Year Dwight Gooden (17-9, 2.60) and Mark Langston (17-10, 3.40) were joined by Roger Clemens (9-4, 4.32), Orel Hershiser (11-8, 2.66), Ron Darling (12-9, 3.81) and Mark Gubicza (10-14, 4.05). Given the unpredictable nature of pitchers, this year's Fab Four could be caught or surpassed in due time by any number of their fellow rookies, including Chad Billingsley, Boof Bonser, Matt Cain, Cole Hamels, Rich Hill, Chuck James, Josh Johnson, Adam Loewen, John Maine, Scott Olsen, Anthony Reyes, Anibal Sanchez, James Shields and/or Jeremy Sowers.

Suffice it to say, the 2006 collection of pitchers is about as strong as they come. And the strength starts at the top with Liriano. Although the Twins refrained from using their prized rookie as a starter for the first seven weeks of the season, the 22-year-old Liriano was the favorite to win the league's Cy Young Award at the end of July when he was 12-2 with a 1.96 ERA. Unfortunately, the southpaw only made two more starts the rest of the way—a four-inning outing in August in which he surrendered a season-high 10 hits against the Detroit Tigers and a shortened two-inning effort vs. the Oakland A's in September. Pitching for the first time in more than a month, Liriano breezed through the first two innings, then felt a pop in his left elbow in the third inning. You might say it was the "Pop Heard 'Round Minnesota." He walked off the mound to a standing ovation and never pitched again, finishing with a 12-3 record, a 2.16 ERA, and an impressive array of peripheral stats (1.00 WHIP, .205 BAA, 10.71 K/9, and 4.50 K/BB) in 121 innings.

Liriano, who throws a 97-mph fastball along with a wicked slider and a "plus" changeup, is a rare breed—a strikeout artist who induces twice as many ground balls as fly balls. *If* healthy, Francisco and teammate Johan Santana, who won his second Cy Young Award this season, are undoubtedly the best 1-2 punch in the majors and one of the finest pairs of left-handed pitchers in the game's history.

However, as with all arm troubles, that is a big "if." Liriano underwent ligament replacement surgery a la Tommy John in early November and will miss the entire 2007 season. He is not the first pitcher to have such an operation after a sensational rookie campaign. Kerry Wood went 13-6 with a 3.40 ERA and 233 strikeouts in 166.2 innings (including 20 SO and 0 BB in a CG SHO a month before his 21st birthday) in 1998, had elbow surgery in March 1999 and did not return until May 2000. You can read more about pitchers who have undergone Tommy John surgery in David Gassko's article.

Like Liriano, Papelbon was shut down early due to a minor shoulder injury. Nevertheless, the Boston Red Sox closer saved 35 games in five months of action while posting a microscopic 0.92 ERA along with a 0.78 WHIP and a .167 BAA. Paps, who had already saved 10 games before he allowed his first run of the season in May, never had an ERA higher than 1.00 throughout the entire season. That is not a typo.

To put Papelbon's dominance in perspective, he recorded the highest ratio of strikeouts-to-earned runs of any pitcher with 50 or more innings since Dennis Eckersley in 1990. The 6-foot-4, 230-pound right-hander struck out 75 and allowed just seven earned runs (10.7 SO/ER) in 68.1 innings. What was the AL average SO/ER ratio, you ask? 1.41. General manager Theo Epstein recently announced that Papelbon will become a starting pitcher next season in a move designed to appease the youngster and protect his long-term health.

The Detroit Tigers featured two rookies with fastballs known to reach triple digits on the radar gun. Justin Verlander placed seventh in the AL in wins (17) and ERA (3.63). He benefited from strong run support, ranking second (behind Randy Johnson) among all major league starters with 6.77 runs per nine innings. The 23-year-old righthander threw 186 innings during the regular season, 56 more than in 2005 when he spent all but two games in the minors. Not surprisingly, he tired down the stretch (5.82 ERA, 1.79 WHIP, and 1.50 K/BB from August on) and was held out of the final six games of the season. Verlander returned in October and helped lead the Tigers to the ALCS title but lost two games in the World Series. All told, the fireballer tossed 208.2 innings, facing 876 batters and making 3,381 pitches.

The other half of the Tigers' 100-mph club was none other than Joel Zumaya, who just may be the hardest thrower to ever don a big-league uniform. According to John Dewan of Baseball Info Solutions, Zumaya threw 233 pitches of at least 100 mph, more than twice as many as the rest of MLB combined and greater than any other season total for the entire majors on record.

As a relief pitcher, Zumaya can come in and let it all out for an inning or two. He was a dominant middle reliever and setup man for Detroit, striking out 10.48 batters per nine innings while limiting opposing batters to .187/.287/.270. He blew away right-handed batters (.188 BAA) and left-handed batters (.183), no matter if he was at home (.191) or away (.182), or during the first half (.175) or second half (.199). Interestingly, Zumaya actually performed his best after he reached the 30-pitch count. Hitters—if you can call them that—were 4-for-37 with three walks and 18 strikeouts in such situations. The 21-year-old threw more than one inning in 30 of his 62 games and allowed just seven runs in 56.2 innings during those outings.

Weaver was 4-0 with a 1.37 ERA when he was inexplicably sent back down to Salt Lake to accommodate the return of Bartolo Colon from the disabled list in June. He made three starts in the minors (including a pair in which he struck out 25 batters while allowing just eight hits and one walk in 15 innings) before being recalled on June 30 to replace his brother Jeff who was designated for assignment that same day. Jered won his next three starts to run his record to 7-0 with a 1.15 ERA. He was involved in three straight no-decisions, then ripped off two more victories to go 9-0. Weaver went 2-2 the rest of the way to finish the year with an 11-2 record and a 2.56 ERA. The 2004 College Player of the Year allowed the second-fewest runs per nine innings (behind Liriano and ahead of Clemens) among pitchers with 100 or more innings pitched.

A School of New Fish Swims in Florida

Over in the National League, the Florida Marlins generally started rookies at first base, second base, shortstop and all three spots in the outfield. In addition, four of the team's top six starting pitchers in terms of innings pitched were also rookies. It wasn't unusual for the Marlins to have seven first-year players in the lineup at the same time. The youngsters not only played, but they fared quite well. For a team that many expected to lose 100 games, the Fish were still in contention for the Wild Card midway through September when the club was one game over .500.

Jeremy Hermida was the organization's top prospect in each of the past three years (as determined by *Baseball America*) and a preseason favorite to capture NL Rookie of the Year honors. In 2005, he became the second player in the history of the game to hit a grand slam in his first major league plate appearance, and he went on to slug four home runs in just 41 at-bats. Hermida's 2006 season, however, didn't go as planned. He spent five of the first seven weeks on the disabled list and missed most of September as well. While Florida's first-round draft pick in 2002 was a disappointment, the Marlins more than made up for his absence with the likes of fellow rookies Hanley Ramirez, Dan Uggla, Josh Willingham, Josh Johnson, Scott Olsen, Ricky Nolasco and Anibal Sanchez.

Ramirez and Sanchez were acquired in November 2005 in a blockbuster trade with the Boston Red Sox for Josh Beckett, Mike Lowell and Guillermo Mota. Although they had only appeared in a combined total of two major league games at that point, the 22-year-olds played a significant role in the rebuilding of the Marlins. Ramirez ranked in the top 10 in the NL in games (158), at-bats (633), runs (119), hits (185), doubles (46), triples (11), and stolen bases (51). He led all rookies in each of the above categories except for doubles, falling one shy of Ryan Zimmerman's 47. A five-tool player, Ramirez also slugged 17 home runs, including an NL rookie record six when leading off the first inning.

Sanchez was called up on June 25 and beat the New York Yankees in his first major league game. The righthander finished the season with a 10-3 record and a 2.83 ERA, not to mention a no-hitter vs. the Arizona Diamondbacks in September. He had the second-lowest ERA (2.27) in the majors (behind Clemens) after the

All-Star Break. Sanchez allowed just 6.25 hits per nine innings during this span, holding opponents to an unsustainably low batting average on balls in play (BABIP) of .212. Look for his rate stats to regress in 2007.

As good as Sanchez was last year, he may not have been Florida's best rookie pitcher. Most would give that nod to Johnson (12-7, 3.10), the Marlins' minor league pitcher of the year in 2005. A reliever at the beginning of the season, Johnson became the ace of the staff when he beat three former Cy Young Award winners (Pedro Martinez, John Smoltz and Roy Halladay) in a five-game stretch from May 26 to June 18. Only a strained right forearm prevented the 6-foot-7, 240-pound righthander from having a chance at becoming the first rookie to lead the league in ERA since Detroit's Mark Fidrych paced the AL in 1976. He missed three starts at the end of the season and fell five innings shy of the necessary 162 innings and 0.12 runs behind Roy Oswalt's NL-leading 2.98 ERA.

The Marlins pitcher with the most upside may, in fact, be Olsen. He had the highest K/9 (8.27) of them all, ranking sixth in the NL and ninth in the majors. Olsen, 22, is the same age as Johnson and Sanchez, but his strikeout proficiency and the fact that he throws from the left side may give him the long-term edge. He went 12-10 with a 4.04 ERA but was victimized by poor bullpen support in several starts. Olsen was among the league's best pitchers from late May through the end of season, fashioning an ERA of 3.31 over 141.1 innings.

Switching back to the offensive side of the Marlins, Uggla was named *The Sporting News* National League Rookie of the Year despite getting little, if any, preseason press. Uggla, buried in the Diamondbacks' minor league system, was selected by Florida in the Rule 5 draft in November 2005. The 26-year-old second baseman not only broke camp with his new team in April, he was in the starting lineup on Opening Day. Uggla never looked back, playing 154 games while making the National League All-Star team and setting a major league record for rookie second basemen with 27 home runs. He also scored 105 runs and knocked in 90 in a highly productive season for any rookie, much less a middle infielder.

Willingham (.277/.356/.496 with 26 HR in 502 AB) had a solid season as Florida's everyday left fielder. A former catcher, Willingham doesn't run particularly well and is no better than average defensively. However, the 27-year-old can flat-out hit. His overall numbers were held back in part by the tough hitting

environment at Dolphins Stadium in Florida (its park factor is 95, so it depresses runs by 5%). His away stats (.310/.389/.565) may provide a better gauge of his true offensive potential.

You know a franchise is loaded when someone with 58 extra-base hits (including 20 home runs) and 77 RBI rates as the seventh-best rookie on the team. After going yard 11 times in 100 at-bats in 2005, Mike Jacobs was traded by the New York Mets along with two others to the Florida Marlins for Carlos Delgado and cash. The minor-league-catcher-turned-major league first baseman hit .348 and slugged .627 in July and August but started and finished poorly, hitting .190 and slugging .365 in April and September. Going forward, the left-handed-hitting Jacobs looks like a good platoon partner at first base but not much more than that unless, of course, he can solve his woes vs. left-handed pitchers (.182/.234/.295).

Yes, They Are Considered Rookies, Too

Kenji Johjima and Takashi Saito became the latest imports from Japan to make a big splash in the States. The 30-year-old Johjima and the 36-year-old Saito were rookies despite playing 11 and 14 years, respectively, in the Japanese Leagues. Like it or not, there is no restriction on age or experience outside of the major leagues in order to qualify for the Rookie of the Year Award. The only requirements are as follows: a player must not have had 130 career at-bats, pitched 50 innings, or spent 45 days (excluding September and time on the DL) on an MLB roster.

The award has had its share of controversy since Hideo Nomo took home NL honors in 1995. If Johjima were to win the award this year, he would become the third Japanese-born player in the past seven years to capture the AL Rookie of the Year Award while playing for the Seattle Mariners. Kazuhiro Sasaki (2000) and outfielder Ichiro Suzuki (2001) were the previous winners. Johjima (.291/.332/.451 with 18 HR) set an AL record for hits in a season by a rookie catcher with 147 and had the second most RBI (76) by a rookie catcher ever.

Saito was released by the Whales/BayStars franchise at the end of the 2005 season and signed by the Dodgers as a free agent in February 2006. He succeeded in middle relief and gradually worked his way into the closer role after Eric Gagne was injured and Danys Baez failed to hold down the role. Saito was 6-2 with 24 saves and a 2.07 ERA. He struck out 107 batters while giving up only 48 hits in 76.1 innings.

The Future is Not What It Used to Be

Which rookies are the most likely to make a big impact over the next ten years? To answer that question, let's turn to Bill James. Age, as James first pointed out in his 1982 *Baseball Abstract*, is one of the most important indicators of a player's long-term success.

In all of my baseball research, I have discovered only one thing which could be described as an absolute rule. That rule is this: Any hitter who is destined to become a great ballplayer will reach the majors at an early age. I know of no clear-cut exception to this rule in the history of baseball.

Based on this tenet, the rookie position players that could well have the most upside include Ryan Zimmerman, who didn't turn 22 until the last week of the season; Melky Cabrera (22 last August); Prince Fielder (22 last May); Nick Markakis and Hanley Ramirez (both of whom turn 23 this offseason); and Stephen Drew and Russell Martin, two youngsters who won't celebrate their 24th birthdays until next spring.

Zimmerman tied Ramirez for the most Win Shares among all rookies with 25. The fourth pick overall in the 2005 draft, Zimmerman went from the University of Virginia to the big leagues in one summer and proceeded to hit .397 with 10 doubles in just 20 games. Zimmerman, known as much for his glove at third base as his bat, hit .287 with 47 doubles, 20 home runs, and 110 ribbies in 2006. He has catapulted himself into one of the brightest young stars in the game today.

Cabrera (.280/.360/.391) filled in admirably for the injured Hideki Matsui, yet heads into next season as a player who may be without a starting job unless the Yankees see fit to trade him this winter. The power-hitting Fielder (.271/.347/.483) cranked 35 doubles and 28 homers and should be a feared hitter for years to come. Markakis (.291/.351/.448) got off to a slow start but bounced back to hit .366 in June, July, and August, including 10 HR in the latter month and three in one game. Arizona's Drew (.316/.357/.517) and L.A.'s Martin (.282/.355/.436) are among a number of young Diamondbacks and Dodgers destined to become stars over the next decade.

In addition to age as a metric in determining a player's upside, James, in the 1988 Baseball Abstract, made the following observation:

The position that every player has to play a full season of AAA ball is, I think, intellectually indefensible. The vast majority of the greatest players in baseball history played fewer than 300 games of minor-league ball.

This rule of thumb also validates Zimmerman (67 MiL games), Drew (167), and Markakis (279) as youngsters with potentially high ceilings, while casting a certain level of skepticism over the likes of Mike Jacobs (821), Willy Aybar (706), Chris Duncan (685), Luke Scott (648), and Dan Uggla (568).

Scott, for his part, had a Willie McCovey-like rookie season. Scott batted .336 with 10 HR in 214 AB as compared to .354 and 13 HR in 192 AB for the Hall of Famer when he was unanimously named the 1959 NL ROY. The main difference between the two? McCovey was 21 that season, while Scott turned 28 last June. In other words, Big Mac's first year was a sign of things to come, whereas Scott's rookie season may turn out to be as good as it gets.

While on the subject of James and career value, it is also important to recognize the value of the Defensive Spectrum:

DH | 1B | LF | RF | 3B | CF | 2B | SS

All else being equal, players are more valuable if they play at the positions on the right side of the Defensive Spectrum since these positions are more difficult and require more athleticism than those on the left side.

As a player grows older, and in certain other cases, he tends to be shifted leftward along this spectrum. Sometimes he moves in dramatic leaps, like Ernie Banks, a shortstop one year and a first baseman the next, or Rod Carew, from second to first. Sometimes he crawls unevenly along the spectrum, like Pete Rose. Sometimes, like Willie Mays, the only movement in a player's career is within the area covered by one position; that is, the player moves gradually from being a center fielder who has outstanding range to being a center fielder with very little range. But always he moves leftward, never right. Can you name one aging first baseman who has been shifted to second base or shortstop to keep his bat in the lineup?

James concedes that certain young players whose position-specific skills are either undeveloped or under-utilized can move rightward but notes these shifts are always dangerous and often disastrous. He also points out the implications of the leftward drift in building a ballclub, including the need "to allow the talent at the left end of the spectrum to take care of itself, as it will, and to worry first about the right end."

The Best of the Rest

There were several players who just missed being named to The Hardball Times All-Rookie Teams not previously mentioned that deserve recognition, including catchers Eliezer Alfonzo (.266/.302/.465 with 12 HR in 87 games), Mike Napoli (.228/.360/.455 with 16 HR and the 92nd player to homer in his first at-bat in the big leagues), and Ronny Paulino (.310/.360/.394), who played in relative obscurity for the Pittsburgh Pirates. First basemen Ryan Garko (.292/.359/.470), Conor Jackson (.291/.368/.441 with 15 HR and 79 RBI), James Loney (.282/.342/.559), and Ryan Shealy (.277/.333/.450 with 37 RBI in 202 AB) showed signs of things to come. Second basemen Josh Barfield (.280./.318/.423 with 32 2B, 13 HR, and 21 SB) and Howie Kendrick (.285/.314/.416) displayed their talents, while 26-year-old Ryan Theriot (.328/.412/.522) gave Cubs fans something to cheer about in the final couple of months. Outfielders Shin-Soo Choo (.280/.360/.452),

Matt Kemp (seven HR in his first 15 games in the big leagues), and Delmon Young (.317/.336/.476) appear to be stars in the making. Young, in fact, is already on the short list of candidates most likely to garner AL ROY honors in 2007.

Or how about 33-year-old catcher Chris Coste (.328/.376/.505 in 65 G and 198 AB), who finally made it to the Show after spending more than 10 years in the minors, including four in the independent Northern League during the 1990s?

On the pitching side of the ledger, Cla Meredith (5-1, 1.07 ERA, 0.71 WHIP) and Pat Neshek (4-2, 2.19 ERA, 53 K and 6 BB in 37 IP) proved quite effective in relief with their unique deliveries. Adam Wainwright (2-1, 3.12 ERA) set up Jason Isringhausen until the St. Louis closer went down with a bad left hip in the middle of September. The tall righthander with the hammer curve wound up saving two games in the final week of the season and four more during the postseason when he threw 9.2 scoreless innings with 15 strikeouts. Wainwright may move into the Cardinals starting rotation next year.

This article wouldn't be complete without mentioning Jon Lester, the Boston Red Sox rookie southpaw who was diagnosed with anaplastic large cell lymphoma cancer in September. All of us at *The Hardball Times Annual* hope to see him back on the mound next spring, displaying the flashes of stardom that were evident last summer.

Anatomy of a Champion

by Bryan Tsao

Thanks to the salary cap and extreme revenue sharing, the NFL is the ultimate copycat league. Take a look around the league on Sundays, and you'll see a plethora of 3-4 defenses (thank you, Patriots) and spread formations (thank you, Colts). Major League Baseball is different. Tell the Devil Rays that they should sign Barry Zito and trade for Alex Rodriguez so that they can match the Yankees' success and they'll just laugh at you. That's why over the past few years, we've had World Series champions ranging from the youth-and-pitching Marlins in 2003 to the grizzled vets of the 2001 champion Arizona Diamondbacks.

So while many might deride the St. Louis Cardinals' triumph over the Detroit Tigers in the 2006 World Series, even a cursory glance at baseball's recent history will show that there are many ways to skin a cat in Major League Baseball, and every team needs to construct itself in a way that maximizes its organizational strengths—whether it's scouting, player development or negotiating trades—within their budget structure.

So how did the St. Louis Cardinals put together the reigning world champs? A close look at the main players on last year's roster shows that general manager Walt Jocketty tends to acquire players in three ways:

- Trading for players nearing free agency
- The draft
- Relatively cheap "value" free agents

In addition, the Cardinals, whether by chance or design, adopted an extreme "stars and scrubs" model of roster construction, with Albert Pujols, Scott Rolen and Chris Carpenter basically carrying their team this season. While this has more or less been the case during the Pujols era, as the Cardinals' middle-of-the-road payroll (11th on opening day last season) doesn't allow them to fill their roster with stars, the departure of strong supporting characters like Larry Walker or Reggie Sanders made the chasm even more extreme.

Taken together, the strategy of trading for players near free agency and concentrating money on top tier hitters has been an exceedingly successful formula, winning the Cardinals six division titles, two pennants and one World Series under Jocketty despite relatively middle-of-the-road payrolls. So while I'm not in a position to write a bestseller about him, the least I can do is devote a chapter of this year's Annual to the roster he put together.

Trader Jocketty

Scott Rolen and Jim Edmonds are certainly the poster boys of Jocketty's penchant for acquiring soon-to-be free agents and signing them to extensions. This strategy has allowed the Cardinals to stockpile talent in trade without giving up big time talent in return. It's not just Rolen and Edmonds though; Jocketty has used the same strategy to acquire other regulars on this year's

Key Cardinals Acquired Through Trades

Player	From	For	Years to FA	Notes
Scott Rolen	PHI	Placido Polanco, Mike Timlin, Bud Smith	1	Signed eight year, $90 million extension
Jim Edmonds	LAA	Adam Kennedy, Ken Bottenfield	1	Signed six year, $57 million extension
Jeff Weaver	LAA	Terry Evans, Cash	1	Went 3-2, 2.43 ERA in playoffs
Ronnie Belliard	CLE	Hector Luna	1	Started 14 games this postseason
Mark Mulder	OAK	Danny Haren, Kiko Calero, Daric Barton	1	Picked up 2006 $7.75 million club option
Jason Marquis	ATL	J.D. Drew, Eli Marrero	3	Also landed the Cardinals Ray King
Aaron Miles	COL	Ray King	4	Replaced by Belliard at the trade deadline
Adam Wainwright	ATL	J.D. Drew, Eli Marrero	6	Went 4-0 in save opportunities this October

playoff roster, from Ronnie Belliard to Jeff Weaver, for cents on the dollar.

Overall, Jocketty has acquired as much talent via trade as any other successful team in recent memory. As a group, these players contributed 48 Win Shares, good for 19% of the Cardinals total, with Weaver, Wainwright and Belliard primarily making their impact in the playoffs. Now, normally I wouldn't necessarily give full credit for trading for a player and then signing him to an extension, but given St. Louis's reputation as a player-friendly atmosphere and the circumstances surrounding the Rolen and Edmonds trades, I'm willing to give the team the benefit of the doubt in those cases.

It's also interesting to see one of Jocketty's two significant misses on this otherwise highly successful list of trades: Mark Mulder. Based on past form, it's clear that Jocketty saw Mulder as the next Rolen or Edmonds, but after pitching well all season and into the postseason in 2005, Mulder collapsed in 2006 with a 7.14 ERA in 17 starts. Still, the Cardinals were able to overcome Mulder's suckitude—his $7.75 million salary this season represented almost 9% of the team's payroll—thanks to the midseason acquisition of Jeff Weaver, who helped carry the team in the playoffs.

Build from within

There are some nice homegrown players on this team, but really, when we're talking about the Cardinals' current draft successes, the discussion begins and ends with Albert Pujols. Pujols is arguably the best player in baseball now, and continues the trend we've seen of Jocketty spending on internal options rather than free agents.

Looking at the table of draft acquisitions, it's actually quite amazing how successful the Cardinals have been in the later rounds of the draft. Also, the organization's ability to develop useful players in addition to Pujols certainly saved the Cardinals this season, with

Anthony Reyes and Chris Duncan playing key roles in the postseason.

Dumpster Diving

As alluded to before, the Cardinals have not been major players in the free agent market in recent years, preferring to take fliers on more value-priced players to complement their core. Given the research presented in "Net Win Shares Value" that shows that the cost of wins on the free agent market is roughly $4.4 million per win, that might not be a bad idea. Perhaps due to pitching coach Dave Duncan's guru reputation, Jocketty has been more inclined to take fliers on free agent pitchers rather than hitters. Let's take a look:

Cardinals' Free Agent Deals

Player	Deal
Jason Isringhausen	3 years/$25.75 million
Chris Carpenter	2 years/$13 million
Juan Encarnacion	3 years/$15 million
Braden Looper	3 years/$13.5 million
David Eckstein	3 years/$10.25 million
Jeff Suppan	3 years/$10 million
Preston Wilson	Minimum*
Josh Kinney	Minimum*

Both Wilson and Kinney joined the Cardinals midseason: Wilson after being released and Kinney from the minors. Thus, no salary data was available for them.

Just as Pujols was the star of the Cardinals' drafts, Chris Carpenter is unquestionably the main success here. Signed before the 2003 season coming off Tommy John surgery, the Cardinals basically paid Carpenter $300,000 not to throw a single pitch, but to focus on his rehab instead. After resigning him for the minimum again for 2004, Carpenter rewarded the Cardi-

Key Cardinals Acquired Through the Draft

Player	Draft round	Draft year	Notes
Albert Pujols	13	1999	Signed a seven year, $100 million extension after the 2004 season.
Anthony Reyes	15	2003	Went 2-0 with a 3.00 ERA in the playoffs
Chris Duncan	1	1999	Ninth on the team in Win Shares despite just 90 games
Yadier Molina	4	2000	Hit the series-winning home run in the NLCS
Tyler Johnson	34	2000	1.23 ERA in 7 1/3 postseason innings

nals with 182 innings of 3.46 ERA ball, which earned him his current two-year, $13 million extension.

While not all of Jocketty's signings have been as successful as Carpenter, it does epitomize the strategy of taking advantage of free talent and not handing out long contracts to pitchers. To put this in perspective, the Yankees paid nearly as much for Johnny Damon and Hideki Matsui—only the eighth- and ninth-highest paid players on their team—last season as the Cardinals paid for all of their free agents combined.

What really jumps out though is not only the relatively small annual values, but that none of the Cardinals' current free agent deals is for longer than three years, especially in the case of pitchers. Projecting player performance is hard enough—even the best scouts and analysts basically have an impossible time predicting how good a player will be next year—which is why teams often get burned signing long-term contracts (think Carl Pavano or Joe Mays).

By limiting the number of years he hands out, Jocketty has also managed to limit any mistakes he's made. Case in point: Jason Isringhausen. Even though he may be overpaid at more than $8 million per year, Izzy's contract comes off the books next season, reducing the amount of dead weight on the Cardinals payroll.

The other pattern that emerges here is the relatively drastic spending on free agent relievers. Jason Isringhausen, who didn't even pitch in the postseason after getting injured, is actually the highest paid pitcher on the staff, making more this season ($8.75 million) that Chris Carpenter has made in his entire Cardinals career to date ($7.6 million). Not to say that the bullpen is not important—in fact, the Cardinals bullpen was invaluable during its run to the World Series this season. However, that pen was anchored by Adam Wainwright, Tyler Johnson and Josh Kinney. So although Jocketty has managed to survive his case of edwadeitis to cobble together decent pitching staffs, it's safe to say that he's succeeding in spite of his penchant for free agent relievers and not because of it.

The Big Picture

So what's the big picture here? With an $89 million opening day payroll, 4th among last season's playoff teams, the Cardinals couldn't afford to match the Yankees or Mets star for star, dollar for dollar. So instead of relying on free agent spending sprees, the Cardinals have ridden one great draft pick (Pujols), some great trades (Rolen) and some savvy, value-oriented free agent spending (Carpenter) to a string of playoff appearances and a title. Even though I've spent the entire chapter so far writing about them, I really can't overstate how big a difference those three key decisions made for the Cardinals this past year. Here's a look at the 2006 playoff teams, and the percentage of Win Shares accrued by their top one and three players:

Percent of Win Shares from Top Players

Team	Top 1	Top 3
Cardinals	16	32
Mets	13	34
Yankees	11	28
Twins	11	29
Padres	11	27
Dodgers	10	25
Athletics	8	24

Only the Mets' trio of Carlos Beltran, David Wright and Jose Reyes topped Pujols, Rolen and Carpenter, while Pujols played the largest role in his team's success of all the players on playoff teams last season. Fittingly, Rolen, Pujols and Carpenter also represent the organization's greatest strengths: strong trading (both in targeting players and negotiating the best deal), good drafting and savvy spending.

There are three main ways to acquire talent in Major League Baseball: the draft, free agency and trades. Different teams focus on different modes of player acquisition, based on their relative strengths: the Yankees sign free agents, the Twins draft well and the A's have made a lot of great trades over the years. The beauty of baseball is that each of these teams is able to be successful on its own terms. This past season, the Cardinals' magic formula was a mix of deft trades, a great draft pick and conscientious free agent spending. Just don't expect to see 29 other teams trying to steal that formula next year—after all, this ain't the NFL.

Prospecting for Ballplayers

by Chris Constancio

The value of developing young talent was never more obvious than during the 2006 season. The Marlins won 78 games with a miniscule payroll by major league standards due to the success of rookies like Hanley Ramirez, Dan Uggla, Anibal Sanchez, Josh Johnson, and Scott Olsen. The Detroit Tigers relied heavily on rookies Justin Verlander and Joel Zumaya during their playoff run. Other talented young ballplayers like Ryan Zimmerman, Russell Martin, Francisco Liriano, Jon Papelbon and Jered Weaver made important contributions to their teams.

The following list is designed to identify the 30 players with the greatest chance of making an impact at the major league level by age 25. Each player's ranking was generated by comparing his recent performance data with similar minor leaguers' performances from the past 10 years. Hitters are compared using league- and park-adjusted contact rates, walk rates, and isolated power. Pitchers are compared using league- and park-adjusted strikeout rates, walk rates, and ground ball/fly ball rates. In addition to these performance measures, other informative characteristics such as player handedness, height, weight, defensive position and even draft position are considered. Using a pool of similar players from the past, I project each target player's future by looking at the similar players' status as of age 25, when most players are entering the prime of their careers.

The resulting estimate suggests each player's chances of becoming an active major leaguer, a regular player, or a star at the age of 25. The *active* estimate represents the probability that the player will be at least a part-time player in the major leagues. The *regular* estimate represents the probability that a hitter will start in at least 120 games and a starting pitcher will pitch at least 100 innings. The *star* estimate represents the probability that a hitter's offensive production will be among the top third of all regular players at their position. For pitchers, the *star* estimate represents the probability that they will be among the top third in run prevention relative to other starting pitchers.

Keep in mind that these probabilities work best at the group level. If you see a group of players with about a 33% chance of becoming "stars" by age 25, I am not suggesting all of those players will probably fail to become stars. Instead, you could look at the group and imagine that three out of nine (33%) of those players will go on to become stars by age 25.

Finally, the following list only includes young players who have not yet reached 130 plate appearances or 50 innings pitched in the major leagues. Without further ado, allow me to introduce the top 30 baseball prospects entering the 2007 season:

1. Chris Young

OF | Arizona Diamondbacks | 23
Age 25 Probabilities:

Active: 96%	Regular: 78%	Star: 46%

Young is a spectacular center fielder who is strong enough to hit 20 to 30 home runs in a major league season. The most pleasant development of his 2006 season was an improved contact rate. Young recorded well over 100 strikeouts in each of his two previous minor league seasons, but he only struck out 71 times in Tucson, or about 16% of his plate appearances. Young already walks once every 10 plate appearances, and if he can maintain his ability to make contact, Young will complement his power with above-average on-base skills. He will be Arizona's starting center fielder in 2007 and is a strong contender for Rookie of the Year honors.

2. Alex Gordon

3B | Kansas City Royals | 23
Age 25 Probabilities:

Active: 97%	Regular: 77%	Star: 44%

The second overall pick of the 2005 draft may be more important to the Royals' future than anyone. Alex Gordon is a complete ballplayer. He launched 29 home runs for the Wichita Wranglers in 2006, but he also worked hard on his defense, reached base in 43% of his plate appearances, and stole 22 bases in 25 attempts. Gordon is good enough to hit in the middle of the Kansas City lineup right now, but the Royals will probably send him to the International League in April while they figure out what to do with their logjam at third base.

3. Troy Tulowitzki

SS | Colorado Rockies | 22

Age 25 Probabilities:

Active: 91%	Regular: 75%	Star: 45%

The Rockies were pleasantly surprised when six other teams passed on Tulowitzki in the first round of the 2005 draft. The Long Beach State University alum now has a chance to be the Rockies' starting shortstop in 2007. Although Tulowitzki is a big-bodied shortstop who projects to hit for power, he only managed 13 home runs in the Texas League last season. The right-handed hitter also hit over twice as many line drives to right field than left field, so he has some work to do before becoming a major power threat. The Rockies wanted him to work on his plate discipline in 2006, and he responded by taking more pitches and improving his walk rate and contact rate. He looks to be at least an average big-league shortstop in the near future and could be a special player if he continues to develop at the plate over the next few years.

4. Elijah Dukes

OF | Tampa Bay Devil Rays | 22

Age 25 Probabilities:

Active: 90%	Regular: 72%	Star: 46%

There is probably no player on this list who is more of a risk than Elijah Dukes. Dukes spent a lot of time off the field last year due to arguments with umpires, a coach, and a teammate. He also briefly considered quitting baseball during a season-ending suspension in August. The Devil Rays continue to support Dukes, however, and he is voluntarily attending anger management classes in the offseason. His baseball skills are outstanding, and his production on the field continues to improve even as he faces better competition. In each of the past three seasons, Dukes has significantly improved his contact rate while maintaining above-average walk rates and power. At only 22, he is already capable of .290/.350/.450 production in the big leagues. If not for serious questions about his makeup, Dukes would be baseball's top prospect right now. The reality is that Dukes needs to make some non-trivial improvements in how he handles himself on and off the field just to get a chance with a big-league team.

5. Daric Barton

1B | Oakland Athletics | 21

Age 25 Probabilities:

Active: 94%	Regular: 76%	Star: 37%

An elbow injury sidelined Barton for much of the 2006 season and delayed his inevitable promotion to Oakland. Barton is slow and does not hit a lot of home runs, but his patience at the plate is as good as it gets. He has drawn more walks than strikeouts at every level during the past three seasons and his .389 OBP with Sacramento last year was actually the lowest of his career. His ability to get on base should take him far, but it's still too soon to write off his power potential.

6. Philip Hughes

RHP | New York Yankees | 20

Age 25 Probabilities:

Active: 88%	Regular: 75%	Star: 44%

Hughes demonstrated outstanding control while striking out more than a batter per inning against older hitters last year. It's hard not to get excited about Hughes's future, but it's important to remember that he is very young and pitching is a dangerous pastime. His dominating 2006 performance most closely resembles former Orioles prospect Matt Riley's 1999 season as a teenager in the Eastern League. Since then, Riley has contributed fewer than 100 innings in the big leagues while recovering from three serious elbow injuries. Hughes' ability to stay healthy is his only major obstacle to fulfilling his potential as a front-of-the-rotation pitcher for the Yankees.

7. Homer Bailey

RHP | Cincinnati Reds | 20

Age 25 Probabilities:

Active: 82%	Regular: 72%	Star: 45%

Bailey's lively fastball and breaking ball are outstanding, and his upside is as high as any minor league pitcher in the game today. I do worry about his occasional lapses in control. In the final month of the 2006 regular season, Bailey walked 20 batters in 31 innings before struggling with walks and wild pitches in his only playoff start.

8. Billy Butler

OF | Kansas City Royals | 20
Age 25 Probabilities:

Active: 78%	Regular: 70%	Star: 45%

Butler is an excellent contact hitter who can drive the ball to all parts of the field. He hit .331 with nearly 50 extra-base hits for the Double-A Wichita Wranglers last season. Butler has a strong arm in the outfield, but his defense is a work in progress. The Royals will keep him in right field for as long as possible, but he can hit enough to be a designated hitter. The organization will find a way for him to join Alex Gordon in the middle of their major league lineup before 2008.

9. James Loney

1B | Los Angeles Dodgers | 22
Age 25 Probabilities:

Active: 85%	Regular: 75%	Star: 31%

Loney doesn't hit for much power, but his 26% line drive rate in the Pacific Coast League suggests he will hit enough to generate Sean Casey-like production in the Dodgers lineup. He lifted the ball to center field as often as anyone in the minor leagues last year, and he might start hitting more home runs if he begins to pull the ball more often in game situations. Loney is athletic enough to make occasional starts in left field, but he is an above-average fielder at first base.

10. Yovani Gallardo

RHP | Milwaukee Brewers | 21
Age 25 Probabilities:

Active: 91%	Regular: 77%	Star: 27%

Gallardo led the minor leagues with 188 strikeouts in 2006. He doesn't have the overwhelming stuff like other pitchers on this list, but his exceptional poise on the mound and command of three above-average pitches have taken him far. Gallardo seemed to get better as the 2006 season progressed; he actually put up more impressive numbers after a promotion to the Double-A Southern League. He was at his best during the playoffs, when he struck out 17 batters and only allowed one walk in 12 innings over two starts.

11. Delmon Young

OF | Tampa Bay Devil Rays | 21
Age 25 Probabilities:

Active: 84%	Regular: 68%	Star: 28%

Delmon Young has been a consensus top prospect for a long time now. If we evaluate him solely on his most recent performances, however, he looks like an incomplete baseball player. He did not show much power at Durham and his patience at the plate remains abysmal. Young also raised questions about his makeup when he tossed a bat at an umpire after a called third strike early in the 2006 season. I think he will be a star in the long run, but Young might need more time than most people realize before he reaches such lofty expectations. Look for Young to hit .280 and collect 15 to 20 stolen bases, 15 to 20 home runs, and 15 to 20 walks for Tampa Bay this season.

12. Cameron Maybin

OF | Detroit Tigers | 20
Age 25 Probabilities:

Active: 81%	Regular: 78%	Star: 24%

Cameron Maybin hit .304 and was 27-for-34 in stolen base attempts during his first full season as a professional, but those nice-looking numbers obscure some problems in the young outfielder's game. Maybin experienced a lot of success by slapping 40% of his batted balls to the left side of the infield, but he won't be successful trying to outrun more polished infielders in the upper minor leagues. His high strikeout rate is also a cause for concern, but it isn't an insurmountable obstacle. Carlos Beltran and Elijah Dukes are a couple of recent examples of athletic center fielders who developed into well-rounded hitters after struggling to make contact as a teenager. Maybin will probably develop into a useful big league outfielder in the long run, but I don't expect him to repeat last year's level of performance as he faces more advanced competition in 2007.

13. Humberto Sanchez

RHP | New York Yankees | 23
Age 25 Probabilities:

Active: 60%	Regular: 54%	Star: 41%

Sanchez was averaging at least one strikeout per inning when facing both Double-A and Triple-A hitters in 2006 until elbow soreness eventually landed him on the disabled list. Sanchez's elbow problem won't require surgery, and he will return to the mound in Spring Training. The burly righthander was traded to the Yankees as this book was going to print.

14. Brandon Wood

SS | Los Angeles Angels of Anaheim | 22
Age 25 Probabilities:

Active: 73%	Regular: 59%	Star: 38%

Wood followed up his breakout 2005 season with over 70 extra-base hits in just 453 at-bats with the Arkansas Travelers of the Southern League last year. His error-prone defense at shortstop and high strike-out rate at the plate are reasons for concern, however. The most recent Angels infielder to swat 20 home runs while striking out in about one in every four plate appearances in Arkansas was Dallas McPherson. Like McPherson, Wood may disappoint Angels fans if he doesn't learn to make contact more consistently against advanced pitching.

15. Reid Brignac

SS | Tampa Bay Devil Rays | 21
Age 25 Probabilities:

Active: 74%	Regular: 69%	Star: 28%

The 21-year-old shortstop posted a .540 slugging percentage across the California League and Southern League last year. Brignac has impressive pull power, and if he can stick at shortstop it's hard to imagine he won't be in the big leagues in a couple of years. My only concern is that he won't get on base often enough to be a real asset at the plate. Brignac doesn't walk much and his aggressive approach at the plate sometimes leads him to chase too many pitches out of the zone.

16. Evan Longoria

3B | Tampa Bay Devil Rays | 21
Age 25 Probabilities:

Active: 76%	Regular: 70%	Star: 25%

The first position player selected in the 2006 draft made a huge impression when he belted 18 home runs and drove in 58 runs in just 62 games across three levels of the minor leagues. His hot hitting continued during the postseason, where he hit a two-run walk-off homer to send the Montgomery Biscuits into the Southern League Championship Series. Longoria will probably return to Double-A Montgomery in 2007, but he could be promoted aggressively and eventually take over third

base for the Devil Rays if B.J. Upton struggles in that role.

17. Colby Rasmus

OF | St. Louis Cardinals | 20
Age 25 Probabilities:

Active: 70%	Regular: 58%	Star: 28%

Rasmus is the lucky guy who will get to fill Jim Edmonds' shoes in center field at Busch Stadium in a few years. The lanky young left-handed hitter's combination of above-average contact skills and power is rare among teenagers, and I expect him to move quickly through the Cardinals' farm system.

18. Andrew McCutchen

OF | Pittsburgh Pirates | 20
Age 25 Probabilities:

Active: 72%	Regular: 60%	Star: 25%

The 5' 11" McCutchen pleasantly surprised the Pirates with 17 home runs in his first full season of professional baseball. McCutchen already looked like a good candidate to lead off for the Pirates in a few years due to his above-average speed and on-base skills, but he could evolve into something more if he continues to develop his power at the plate.

19. Ubaldo Jimenez

RHP | Colorado Rockies | 23
Age 25 Probabilities:

Active: 80%	Regular: 69%	Star: 24%

Jimenez's arsenal includes an outstanding 98-mph fastball and above-average offspeed stuff. He has also walked nearly five batters per nine innings over the past two season, so his control remains a major obstacle to sustained success in the big leagues. Jimenez has remained a starting pitcher in the Rockies' system, but he may be better suited for a bullpen role.

20. Adam Jones

OF | Seattle Mariners | 21
Age 25 Probabilities:

Active: 73%	Regular: 70%	Star: 25%

Jones hit 16 home runs in the Pacific Coast League and earned a promotion to Seattle while making the transition from shortstop to center field in 2006. He is not a strong contact hitter, and he looked overmatched while striking out 22 times in his first 72 major league at-bats. He could use some more time refining his approach at the plate in the minor leagues before taking over center field in Seattle.

21. Justin Upton

OF | Arizona Diamondbacks | 19

Age 25 Probabilities:

Active: 82%	Regular: 72%	Star: 19%

Justin Upton's first full season of professional baseball was somewhat disappointing and reminiscent of Brandon Phillips, his top comparison player in my database of minor league performances. Like Phillips, it might take some time before Upton's much-talked-about tools translate to reasonable performance in the upper minor leagues and major leagues. There are very few examples of star major league outfielders who made the kind of debut Upton did in the Midwest League, but he is still very young and has plenty of time to prove me wrong.

22. Fernando Martinez

OF | New York Mets | 19

Age 25 Probabilities:

Active: 73%	Regular: 57%	Star: 24%

Signed as a 17-year-old out of the Dominican Republic, Fernando Martinez excelled against older and more experienced competition during his first full season in the Mets organization. He hit .333/.389/.505 for Low Single-A Hagerstown in the first half of the season and earned a promotion to the Florida State League in August. Although Martinez struggled to reach base after the promotion, he showed surprising power (five home runs in 32 games) for such a young player. Martinez was slowed by various injuries and made up for lost time by participating as the youngest player in the Arizona Fall League in October. He will return to the Florida State league in 2007 and could appear in New York's outfield as soon as 2008.

23. Jose Tabata

OF | New York Yankees | 18

Age 25 Probabilities:

Active: 72%	Regular: 53%	Star: 24%

The Yankees' future right fielder hit .298 with five home runs as a teenager in the South Atlantic League last year. His power numbers were a bit below expectations, but he is very young and his mature approach at the plate was evident in his above-average walk rate and league-leading proportion of line drives hit to the right-center gap. He profiles as an average right fielder

defensively and has enough speed to steal 15-20 bases per season.

24. Jason Hirsh

RHP | Houston Astros | 25

Age 25 Probabilities:

Active: 76%	Regular: 52%	Star: 24%

The 6-foot-8-inch, 250-pound hurler went 13-2 with a 2.10 ERA for Round Rock of the Pacific Coast League before earning a promotion to Houston. Hirsh is an extreme fly ball pitcher, so Minute Maid Park is probably not the best fit for him. He surrendered three home runs in one inning during his first start in Houston and the longball was a problem for him during the remainder of the season. His strikeout and walk rates are strong, however, and he has a good chance to be at least an average pitcher in the back of Houston's 2007 rotation.

25. Mark Reynolds

2B | Arizona Diamondbacks | 23

Age 25 Probabilities:

Active: 75%	Regular: 50%	Star: 23%

A 16th-round pick in 2004, Mark Reynolds had a breakout year while playing second base, third base, and left field in the Diamondbacks organization and for Team USA. Reynolds hit .318 with 31 home runs across two levels of play, and while much of his damage was done at hitter-friendly Lancaster, his .297/.373/.551 numbers on the road in the California League don't look bad at all. Reynolds' batting average of balls in play was unusually high last year. That suggests he won't repeat his .300 batting average in the near future, but his power and ability to handle multiple positions on the field will take him to the big leagues.

26. Jarrod Saltalamacchia

C | Atlanta Braves | 22

Age 25 Probabilities:

Active: 80%	Regular: 73%	Star: 14%

He was one of baseball's most popular prospects after his .314/.394/.519 effort at Myrtle Beach one year ago. Saltalamacchia followed up that impressive performance by struggling to hit .200 during the early part of the 2006 season with Mississippi. He was still hitting the ball hard and demonstrating his usual patience at the plate, but the results were not there. After taking some time off for a hand injury in July, Saltalamacchia smacked five home runs and posted an on-base percentage of .475 in his final month with Mississippi. Saltalamacchia also made progress behind the plate, particularly in throwing out would-be base stealers. His performance was clearly one of the great disappointments of the 2006 season, but I think evidence suggests it's too soon to write him off, and I expect a big rebound performance from him in 2007.

27. Carlos Gonzalez

OF | Arizona Diamondbacks | 21
Age 25 Probabilities:

Active: 56%	Regular: 49%	Star: 25%

Gonzalez recovered from a slow start to the 2006 season and managed a .300 batting average and 60 extra-base hits in the California League. The five-tool outfielder has an exceptional throwing arm, but he is also error-prone on the field. The Diamondbacks do not have a shortage of outfield prospects, so they can afford to be patient with Gonzalez.

28. Ian Stewart

3B | Colorado Rockies | 22
Age 25 Probabilities:

Active: 72%	Regular: 50%	Star: 19%

Stewart was the Rockies' top prospect two years ago, but since then he has watched teammates like Chris Iannetta and Troy Tulowitzki pass him on the way to Colorado. Stewart has been plagued by inconsistent production at the plate, and wrist injuries have probably sapped some power from his bat. Garret Atkins' emergence has the Rockies strongly considering moving Stewart to the outfield in 2007. If that happens, Stewart will need another year in the minor leagues to learn his new position and develop some consistency at the plate before contributing to the parent club.

29. Dustin Pedroia

SS | Boston Red Sox | 23
Age 25 Probabilities:

Active: 79%	Regular: 58%	Star: 15%

The above estimates are consistent with common sentiments about Dustin Pedroia; he is very close to being a useful major league infielder, but his upside is very limited. Pedroia is smaller than a typical big leaguer and probably won't ever hit for much power, but he is patient at the plate and was among the minor leagues' best contact hitters in 2006. The scrappy infielder only hit .191 during his cup of coffee with the Red Sox in 2006, but his track record in the minor leagues and the fact that he only struck out seven times in nearly 100 plate appearances with Boston suggests he will be a perennial threat to hit .300 in the big leagues. Pedroia split time between shortstop and second base in 2006, and the Red Sox don't have an incumbent at either position in 2007.

30. Jay Bruce

OF | Cincinnati Reds | 20
Age 25 Probabilities:

Active: 68%	Regular: 49%	Star: 20%

Bruce did a little bit of everything with the Dayton Dragons of the Midwest League last year. He hit .291, belted 63 extra-base hits including 16 home runs, and stole 19 bases. A reasonable case can be made that Bruce should be ranked ahead of his outfield peers from the Midwest League, including Upton, Rasmus, and Maybin. Bruce might be the best all-around hitter among that group right now, but he has already made the move to right field, and his position-relative value is not as high as it would be if he were sticking in center field like those other three outfielders. Sarasota is not a bad place to hit compared to most other Florida State League parks, so Bruce should continue to put up impressive numbers when he faces Advanced Single-A competition in 2007.

The World Baseball Classic

by Jeff Sackmann

2006 was perhaps the first time in the history of the game that more exciting baseball was played in March than in April. After years of planning, we were finally able to witness the inaugural World Baseball Classic, which brought together many of the greatest players in the world to compete for national pride. Before the event began, it was an unknown quantity, perhaps most interesting to those who would've created Strat-O-Matic versions of the tournament had it not been presented in reality.

How quickly things change. By the time Japan defeated Cuba in the final game on March 20, the WBC seemed like an established part of the baseball landscape. It was far from perfect, and we can expect to see plenty of tweaks to the framework before the next event in 2009, but the first go-round succeeded beyond (dare I say it?) even Bud Selig's wildest dreams.

The Format

When planning an event that figures to include a hefty number of major leaguers from the United States, Japan and Korea, one of the foremost concerns is scheduling. Rather than tacking on the WBC to the end of the major league season in November, it was planned for the middle weeks of March. Playing the games three weeks before the beginning of the Major League Baseball regular season wasn't ideal. Some participants clearly weren't at 100 percent for the first round of games, and many weren't able to rejoin their teams until less than two weeks before opening day. The schedule of the event effectively minimized many of these problems: for non-Asian teams, the event could take no longer than two weeks to complete, and no team played more than eight games.

The first WBC included teams from 16 countries, from the mighty United States and Japan to overmatched China and South Africa. The tournament began with pool play, dividing those sixteen teams into four groups as follows:

Pool A: China, Chinese Taipei (Taiwan), Japan, Korea

Pool B: Canada, Mexico, South Africa, United States

Pool C: Cuba, Netherlands, Panama, Puerto Rico

Pool D: Australia, Dominican Republic, Italy, Venezuela

Each team began the tournament by playing a three-game round robin against the other members of its pool. The top two teams from each quartet advanced to another pool of four to play another round robin. The winners from Pools A and B matched up, as did those from Pools C and D. The two best clubs from each second-round pool played a semifinal match against each other, the winners of which advanced to a one-game final.

Pool A

Teams

In last year's Annual, Craig Burley and Thomas Ayers wrote, "As the host for the first round in Pool A, Japan is a clear favorite to go 3-0 and cruise into the second round." Especially since Pool A games were held in the Tokyo Dome, Team Japan indeed appeared to have a huge advantage. Japan has a tradition of professional baseball that far outstrips those of their Pool competitors—the presence of manager and home run king Sadaharu Oh was a constant reminder of that—and many of their players are considered to be among the best in the world.

While Ichiro Suzuki headlined Team Japan, many Japanese stars from MLB didn't participate. Kenji Johjima, Tadahito Iguchi and Hideki Matsui all opted to spend March in major league spring training. In fact, the only other MLB player on Japan's roster was reliever Akinori Otsuka. That did little to lessen the star power of the team, though. Daisuke Matsuzaka and Toshiya Sugiuchi, both under 26 years of age, are perhaps the best Japanese pitchers playing anywhere in the world, and Japan's first baseman, Nobuhika Matsunaka, is only two years removed from a triple crown. Japan's National Professional Baseball (NPB) may not be as strong as the American major leagues, but the NPB all-star squad promised to be a powerful one.

Korea's roster, while it contained more players with MLB experience, didn't compare favorably to Japan's. The pitching staff appeared to be a strength—Jung

Bong, Byung-Hyun Kim, Sun Woo Kim, Dae Sung Koo, Chan Ho Park and Jae Seo all have an American pedigree—but the same couldn't be said of the offense. Korea did feature two strong first basemen in Hee Seop Choi and Seung Yeop Lee, a slugging star of the NPB's Chiba Lotte Marines, but the remainder of the lineup paled in comparison.

Whatever the difference between Japan and Korea, though, the gap between Korea and rest of its pool competition was greater. Taiwan's roster included a few players with professional experience in the NPB and in the American minor leagues, but their chances of advancing out of the first round were dealt a huge blow when Yankees pitcher Chien-Ming Wang opted to skip the event. Mainland China's team was weaker still. Aside from other international competitions, no players on China's roster had played outside of their own national league.

Results

The first five games of pool play went exactly according to plan. Korea beat Taiwan in a low-scoring game that seemed to clinch Korea's place in the next round. China lost three blowouts—18-2 against Japan, 10-1 against Korea, and 12-3 against Taiwan—and Japan handily disposed of Taiwan.

The final game was almost a formality, as Japan and Korea had both clinched their berths in Round 2. However, with national pride on the line in the Tokyo Dome, the two teams treated it like the most important contest in the pool. As expected, it was a low-scoring game. Through seven innings, Japan led 2-1. In the top of the eighth, though, DH Seung Yeop Lee smacked a two-run home run off of Hirotoshi Ishii to move Korea into the lead. Dae Sung Koo and Chan Ho Park each pitched a scoreless inning, and Korea emerged from Pool A the only undefeated team.

Pool B

Teams

If Pool A looked like an obvious win for Team Japan, Pool B appeared to be even more of a lock for Team USA. After years of sending minor leaguers and college players to international competition, the United States finally assembled a dream team to take on the world. Virtually every member of the team was an All-Star, and the infield was particularly historic. Each game, manager Buck Martinez had a choice between Mark Teixeira and Derrek Lee at first base, Derek Jeter and Michael Young at shortstop and Alex Rodriguez and Chipper Jones at third.

Making those decisions may have been easier than arranging his bullpen. In the late innings, Martinez could choose from closers Chad Cordero, Brian Fuentes, Todd Jones, Brad Lidge, Joe Nathan and Huston Street. Team USA may be the only team ever assembled in which a starting pitching trio of Roger Clemens, Jake Peavy and Dontrelle Willis wouldn't appear to be the club's top asset.

Making things even easier for Team USA, Pool B didn't seem to offer much in the way of competition. Mexico, at least, had a slew of MLB players, including Esteban Loaiza and Rodrigo Lopez on the pitching staff and a strong infield that included Jorge Cantu, Vinny Castilla, Erubiel Durazo and Adrian Gonzalez.

Team Canada also had something to offer. While the Canadians were hurt by the non-participation of a couple of great players (Rich Harden and Larry Walker), they could nonetheless put a respectable team on the field. Jason Bay and Justin Morneau highlighted the offense, surrounded by MLB players Corey Koskie, Pete Orr, Matt Stairs and Adam Stern. Their pitching options, though, were weak: Erik Bedard, Adam Loewen and Jeff Francis offered stuff but not experience; relievers like Mike Meyers, Paul Quantrill, and Chris Reitsma contributed the opposite. From Team Canada's pitching staff, only Rheal Cormier would've had a chance of cracking Team USA's provisional roster.

The pools were arranged, apparently, so that every group would have a whipping boy. In Pool A, that was China; in Pool B, the honor went to South Africa. Barry Armitage, the ace of South Africa's pitching staff and an uninspiring right-handed reliever in the Kansas City Royals minor-league system, was one of the few players on the roster with any pro experience.

Results

The first day of play quickly adjusted expectations. While Peavy and six relievers combined to shut out Team Mexico, the U.S. offense only managed two runs. The shock of the day, however, was the near-upset of Canada by South Africa. Going into the top of the ninth inning, South Africa led 8-7, but Canada tied the game on an Adam Stern RBI double and tacked on three more runs for the win.

That surprise was nothing compared to what would quickly follow. In the first pool game on March 8, Canada upset Team USA. Led by a four-hit outing from Stern, including an inside-the-park home run, Canada scored five runs off of Willis and tacked on another two against Al Leiter. The United States made a mighty comeback as Jason Varitek's grand slam highlighted a six-run fifth, but adequate relief pitching and a sensational, game-saving catch by Stern in the eighth gave Canada the victory. Due to the somewhat arcane WBC tiebreak rules, Team USA's fate was partially out of its own hands. Even if the U.S. beat South Africa, it wouldn't advance if Mexico won its game against Canada without scoring more than two runs.

A day later, Mexico eliminated all of those what-ifs, scoring four runs in the first inning of a 9-1 win to clinch a spot in the second round. The U.S. joined the party the next day with a 17-0 win over South Africa.

Pool C

Teams

Pool C was perhaps the most even of the four initial groupings. It was also the most difficult to predict. For the duration of the tournament, Cuba was the wild card, an unknown quantity among the other star-studded rosters. Cuba has dominated international competition in recent years, and there's no doubt that several of their players, especially infielder Yulieski Gourriel, could make an impact in the United States. However, they had never played teams as strong as those representing the U.S., the Dominican Republic and Venezuela.

Of the known quantities in Pool C, Puerto Rico was the clear favorite. While the starting pitching was weak behind Javier Vazquez, the offense featured Ivan Rodriguez, Javy Lopez, Carlos Beltran, Jose Cruz Jr. and Bernie Williams, with Carlos Delgado available to pinch-hit. The bullpen also appeared credible, with Fernando Cabrera, Kiko Calero, Pedro Feliciano and J.C. Romero ready for late-inning duty.

Panama's roster was a sort of low-rent version of Canada's. It featured slugger Carlos Lee, infielder Olmedo Saenz and a few decent pitchers (Bruce Chen, Manuel Corpas and Davis Romero), but very little behind that. Because Curacao is part of the Dutch Antilles, Andruw Jones (and fellow MLBer Randall Simon) could play for The Netherlands, but there aren't enough stars hailing from the Dutch Antilles to make the team competitive.

Results

Pool C provided plenty of drama, mostly involving Panama. In the first game, Puerto Rico edged Panama

2-1. Panama starter Luis Picota was the equal of Javier Vazquez, and Braves farmhand Manuel Acosta was stuck with the loss despite giving up just one run and two hits in three innings. Panama gave Cuba an even bigger scare. Tied 4-4 going into the eighth inning, both teams scored two more in the ninth. Finally, Cuba's Yoandry Garlobo delivered a pinch-hit single in the 11th to give Cuba the victory.

In its final game, Panama again surprised viewers around the world, but this time it didn't make the fans at home proud. The Netherlands' Shairon Martis, a Single-A pitcher in the San Francisco Giants system who has since been traded to the Nationals, no-hit Team Panama over seven innings before the mercy rule came into play. Amazingly, he did so despite the WBC's strict Round 1 pitch limits. No hurler was permitted to throw more than 65 pitches in the opening round (except to finish a plate appearance); Martis retired 21 batters using exactly that many.

By the time Martis threw his first pitch, Cuba and Puerto Rico were already guaranteed spots in the Round 2. The next day, those two teams played their final game and PR mercy-ruled Cuba. By this time, only a little more than a week into the tournament, it was clear that the WBC was here to stay. Bernie Williams, a key part of PR's victory, spoke for many players when he said, "Most definitely this home run that I hit was very important—it was a milestone in my career. I felt that I was playing the World Series in the month of March."

Pool D

Teams

Pool D's 300-pound gorilla was the Dominican Republic. In their opening game against Venezuela, the Dominicans started Alfonso Soriano, Miguel Tejada, Albert Pujols, David Ortiz, Moises Alou, Adrian Beltre and Juan Encarnacion in the top seven spots in the lineup. It's amazing, then, to consider that much of the pre-WBC news surrounding the DR roster had more to do with who didn't end up on the team. Alex Rodriguez apparently considered playing for the DR, as did Manny Ramirez. Vladimir Guerrero was on the roster but didn't play due to personal issues. Pedro Martinez may have played if not for injury. Team DR's pitching was not nearly as strong as its incredible offense, but it appeared that few teams could survive the bludgeoning that would surely face them.

If any team had a chance of stopping them, it appeared to be Venezuela. The offense couldn't compare with DR's (despite including Bobby Abreu, Magglio Ordonez, Miguel Cabrera, Carlos Guillen and Victor Martinez), but starters Johan Santana, Carlos Zambrano, Freddy Garcia and Kelvim Escobar and relievers Francisco Rodriguez and Rafael Betancourt anchored what looked like the best pitching staff in the tournament.

Against that kind of competition, Italy and Australia didn't stand a chance. Italy's roster included some talented second-generation players, including Mike Piazza, Frank Catalanotto, Jason Grilli and Mike Gallo. Team Australia also featured some familiar players, among them Damian Moss, Trent Durrington, Justin Huber and former Milwaukee Brewers catcher Dave Nilsson.

Results

The talent levels in Pool D were so lopsided in favor of Venezuela and the Dominican that only two games appeared to be close ones, both of which took place on the first day. DR beat Venezuela 11-5 behind a strong start from Bartolo Colon and two David Ortiz home runs. The other unpredictable game, between Italy and Australia, was a rout for the Italians. Jason Grilli allowed only one hit in 4.2 innings, and Riccardo De Santis followed by retiring seven straight. DR and Venezuela both swept Italy and Australia to predictably reach the second round.

Round 2

Pool 1

Like many of the first-round pools, Pool 1 had a pair of early favorites. Despite their surprising losses in Round 1, Japan and the U.S. still looked too good on paper to be discounted. Korea—the only undefeated team in Pool 1—was a wild card, but Mexico simply appeared to be too weak to seriously threaten the bigger guns.

The first day of play, March 12, pitted the USA against Japan and Korea against Mexico.

Team USA won its first game, 4-3 over Japan, on what would be the most controversial call of the Classic. With the game tied 3-3 in the eighth inning, Japan loaded the bases against Joe Nathan with one out. Akinori Iwamura flied out to left field and Tsuyoshi Nishioka tagged up at third base and appeared to beat the throw for the go-ahead run. The U.S. appealed and second base umpire Brian Knight indicated that Nishioka was safe.

However, the umpires gathered to review the situation and ultimately decided that home plate umpire Bob Davidson should have made the call. Davidson claimed he was in position to make the call and clearly saw that Nishioka left early. Sadaharu Oh argued the overrule to no avail, and instead of taking the lead, Japan lost its momentum and, an inning later, the game.

Later that day, Korea and Mexico played another low-scoring game. Aided by a strong start from Jae Seo, Korea remained undefeated in the tournament. Mexico's offense managed only five hits, and Korea won on the strength of a Seung Yeop Lee two-run homer.

The following day, the U.S. took on Korea with the opportunity for either team to go 2-0 and very nearly clinch a spot in the semifinals. En route to a 7-3 loss, Dontrelle Willis gave up three runs in three innings, helping Korea by issuing four walks in that span. Dan Wheeler couldn't stop the bleeding, letting in three more runs in the fourth. Korea's starter, Min Han Son, was the exact opposite, allowing only four baserunners (including a solo home run to Ken Griffey) in his three innings of work. The U.S. mounted a comeback against Tae Hyon Chong in the ninth but only shrunk the gap from six runs to four.

Japan's win over Mexico on the third day of Pool 1 play was the only game in Pool 1 without any particular drama, but it was the first chance for stateside fans to watch Japanese pitching sensation Daisuke Matsuzaka. Matsuzaka didn't disappoint: He threw five shutout innings, allowing only one hit and leading Japan to an easy 6-1 victory.

Next, Japan took on Korea. A low-scoring Japan victory would have made both Asian teams 2-1 and eliminated the U.S. Thus, manager Buck Martinez and his squad found themselves rooting for the team that had beaten them only two days before. Korea turned to Chan Ho Park, who had served as closer in the first five games, while Japan gave the ball to Shunsuke Watanabe. Both were outstanding. Park struck out three, allowing three hits, no walks, and no runs in five innings, while Watanabe allowed only a hit and two walks in his six frames. It wasn't until the eighth inning that Korea broke the scoreless tie. Center fielder Jong Beom Lee drove in two runs with a double, and once again the Korean bullpen was good enough to hold the lead. Korea kept its perfect record, Japan fell to 1-2 and the U.S. had the opportunity to advance to the semifinals with a victory over Mexico.

The U.S. wasn't up to the task, however, as Oliver Perez and the Mexico bullpen outpitched Roger Clemens and company for a 2-1 victory. With Mexico, the U.S. and Japan all 1-2, the second berth in the semifinals was decided by each team's runs allowed. Mexico allowed eight, the U.S. 16 and Japan seven, so Japan advanced to face Korea for a third time in the semifinals.

Pool 2

The second Round 2 group didn't have the pitching and defense that made for such gripping baseball in Pool 1, but the competition was just as fierce and every game mattered. Pool 2 opened with Cuba playing Venezuela: the masters of international competition against some of the best MLB players in the tournament. Johan Santana allowed one run and two hits in five innings, but the Cuban squad took a commanding lead as soon as it saw a different arm. Giovanni Carrara coughed up five runs and retired only two batters, thanks in large part to a missed double play by Omar Vizquel, and Cuba jumped to 1-0 in the pool behind the strong pitching of Yadel Marti and Pedro Lazo.

Later that day, more MLB sluggers found their bats silent. Puerto Rican pitchers Javier Vazquez, Jose Santiago, Kiko Calero and J.C. Romero held the imposing Dominican offense to just one run, an Adrian Beltre home run. Suddenly, the favored Dominican Republic team found itself facing a couple of games it almost certainly had to win.

All four teams played again the following day. In the afternoon game, some fans chanted "Down with Fidel," while Team DR merely defeated the Cubans on the field. The Dominican bats awoke as David Ortiz homered and Placido Polanco and Ronny Paulino enjoyed multi-hit games in a 7-3 win over Cuba.

Venezuela also improved to 1-1 as Carlos Zambrano pitched much better than he did in the first round, joining several relievers to shut out Puerto Rico. Venezuela received offense contributions from sources both likely and unlikely. Victor Martinez sealed his team's victory in the eighth with a grand slam, but the go-ahead runs came on a two-run shot from Endy Chavez. It was Puerto Rico's first loss in the tournament, and it meant that the winners of the final two games—Cuba vs. PR and Venezuela vs. DR—would advance to the semifinals.

The Dominican Republic claimed the first spot with a 2-1 win over Venezuela. Daniel Cabrera, who couldn't even hold on to a rotation spot for the Baltimore Orioles during the 2005 regular season, threw four no-hit innings, striking out seven and allowing only a walk.

Francisco Liriano gave up a run in the sixth, but Miguel Batista and Duaner Sanchez combined for 2.2 hitless innings to finish off the game.

Cuba joined the Dominican Republic by beating Puerto Rico 4-3. The Cubans took a 4-1 lead in the fourth and held on after Puerto Rico scored twice in the seventh off Adiel Palma. The key play came when Ivan Rodriguez tried to score from first after Cuban center fielder Carlos Tabares bobbled a Carlos Beltran single and Yuliesky Gourriel nailed Rodriguez at the plate to end the seventh.

Semifinals

If there is one problem with the elimination method in the World Baseball Classic, it was well illustrated by Korea's departure from the tournament. Korea beat Japan twice in the first two rounds, but that meant nothing after Japan's 6-0 semifinal victory. Koji Uehara shut out the Koreans for seven innings, striking out eight and allowing just three baserunners. Jae Seo was nearly as good through five innings, and the scoreless tie held into the seventh. But Byung-Hyun Kim relieved Byung Doo Jun after a Nobuhiko Matsunaka double, and he yielded a two-run homer to pinch-hitter Kosuke Fukudome that opened the floodgates and sent Japan to the final

Like Korea, the Dominican Republic was punchless in its semifinal matchup, falling 3-1 as Cuban pitchers Yadel Marti and Pedro Lazo combined to allow just one unearned run. Bartolo Colon did his part to shut the Cubans down, but Odalis Perez, Salomon Torres and Julian Tavarez allowed three runs in the seventh.

Final

After a tournament full of pitchers' duels, the WBC final was the exact opposite. Because of the Classic's rules regarding pitcher usage, both Yadel Marti and Pedro Lazo were ineligible to pitch in the final. The same was true of Koji Uehara, who so handily defeated Korea. Both teams, though, were able to start their first-line offenses, and it was that part of the game that dominated the final matchup. Cuba outhit Japan 11-10, but Japan took the game 10-6.

Japan attacked early, scoring four runs in the first inning. Cuba's Ormani Romero left the game after allowing three of the first four batters to reach base, giving way to Vicyohandri Odelin. Odelin also failed to finish the first, allowing another walk and a hit before leaving. Despite using eight pitchers, Cuba stayed close.

Cuba fought back with an Eduardo Paret solo home run off of Matsuzaka in the first and two runs against Shunsuke Watanabe in the seventh. By the time Japan came to the plate in the top of the ninth, Cuba had cut the lead to 6-5. Adiel Palma, who had already thrown 3.2 innings of scoreless relief, stayed in the game and allowed Japan to break things open with four ninth-inning runs. Akinori Otsuka allowed a run in the ninth but closed out the game—and the tournament—for a save.

Reactions

Fan response to the WBC was overwhelmingly positive, and not just in the countries that advanced deep into the tournament. The final game, played at PETCO Park in San Diego, drew a sold-out crowd, and total attendance for the games topped 73,000. However briefly, names like Shairon Martis, Seung Yeop Lee, Adam Stern, Koji Uehara and Pedro Lazo were familiar ones, while Albert Pujols and Alex Rodriguez were hardly factors.

The new and sometimes arcane rules weren't as generally accepted. The restrictive pitch counts may be a good way to soothe the worried minds of MLB owners but are perhaps not appropriate for teams such as Cuba, for whom the WBC is a central goal, not merely a diversion in March. The tiebreaker system, while necessary in a short, round-robin format, created an incentive system that technically could have rewarded Team Mexico for refusing to score a run against the U.S. And when Japan takes a 4-3 record into the final while Korea goes home after a 6-1 showing, there may be room for improvement.

The response from the players, however, was sufficiently encouraging to overcome any nitpicking about the rules. Bernie Williams called a WBC home run the most important he ever hit. Ichiro Suzuki claimed that, during the Classic final, he didn't care if he got hurt and missed the regular season, so long as Japan won the tournament. The stars who made up Team USA appeared to be genuinely ashamed to make their early exit. This was no exhibition, even to the players who were most likely to view it as one. If the player reaction in 2006 was any indication, the biggest stars from all over the world will be fighting for roster spots to represent their countries in 2009.

The Business of Baseball Report

by Brian Borawski

In several ways, 2006 was a historic year for the business of baseball. Major League Baseball finally sold the Montreal Expos, finishing what they started when they purchased them in 2002. Even more importantly, a new Collective Bargaining Agreement was negotiated nearly two months before the actual deadline took place. Games were played, and outside of a few teams who had to contend with ownership changes or stadium issues, there were very few distractions. The focus was mostly on the field, which is where it should be. That doesn't mean there wasn't any drama or political intrigue, but as you'll see, much was actually accomplished in the business of baseball.

MLB Sells the Washington Nationals

On February 12, 2002, MLB purchased the Montreal Expos. What started out as a temporary solution to prop up an ailing franchise turned into more than four years of broken promises and political mishaps. This year, things finally came to a head and the league sold the Washington Nationals. Like most things, the road to the sale was much more newsworthy than the sale itself.

At the end of 2004, just days before MLB's deadline for a stadium bill, the Washington, D.C. city council finally passed a stadium bill that would allow for the construction of a new stadium along the Anacostia River waterfront. With the stadium "problem" out of the way, the league began soliciting bids for the team, but once again, a road block developed. Comcast Sportsnet filed a lawsuit against the Baltimore Orioles, majority owner of the Mid-Atlantic Sports Network (MASN), over broadcasting rights to Orioles games. Comcast felt shut out of an exclusive negotiating process for Orioles games and sued the team for breach of contract. MASN not only had broadcast rights to Nationals games, but it was partially owned by MLB, which hoped to package its share of MASN (currently a 10% ownership stake, which increases to 33% over the next 28 years) into the sale of the Washington Nationals. With this lawsuit pending, the league once again held off on selling the team.

In late July 2005, a Montgomery County Circuit Court Judge dismissed Comcast's case, opening the door for the sale of the Nationals until things hit yet another snag. MLB didn't want to sell the team until there was an agreed-upon lease between the Nationals and Washington, D.C. Negotiations went into November; at issue was whether the league would guarantee the $6 million in finance costs as a rent payment, regardless of whether the team were to play in the prospective stadium or not. Then in early December, the city began asking for $20 million to help build the stadium. MLB finally agreed to a tentative lease that included $24 million in rent guarantees in the event of a terrorist event or a players' strike and $20 million to cover cost overruns on the stadium. Now all that had to happen was for the Washington, D.C. city council to vote on the matter.

Then the proverbial "stuff" hit the fan. In mid-December, Washington, D.C. mayor Anthony Williams asked the city council to delay the vote on the stadium lease, citing a need to make changes to it. The unofficial reason: there weren't enough votes to push the lease through the city council. Unlike at the end of 2004, there was no happy ending here. Negotiations continued, but a December 31, 2005 deadline to iron out the lease came and went with no resolution.

Shortly after the start of 2006, MLB filed a claim with the American Arbitration Association; a 15-day mediation process began in the middle of January with former Detroit mayor Dennis Archer as mediator. The city council was now looking for a $535 million spending cap on the new stadium, along with more community benefits from the league.

In late January, the two sides finally came to an agreement, which required that the city use traditional tax-exempt financing and that it split the proceeds with MLB on any land sold around the area of the ballpark that would be used for future developments. Under the agreement, MLB has to lease RFK Stadium in 2008 if the new ballpark isn't ready. MLB is also required to build a youth baseball facility and increase the number of tickets given to disadvantaged children. All that was needed was a positive vote from the city council.

The city council met on February 7, and both MLB and the mayor hoped for the best. But it wasn't to be. In a much shorter meeting than expected, the stadium lease was voted down by a vote of 8-5. Then, in a closed-door meeting, all of the respective parties ironed out their differences. The meeting reconvened later that night, and very early on February 8, the city council finally approved a lease, albeit one that deviated quite a bit from the original agreement made way back in 2004. The major difference was a $611 million spending cap for the new stadium.

On March 5, MLB finally relented, and later that week, the city council approved the construction contract for the new stadium. All that was needed now was a new owner.

In late April, rumors surfaced that the league had made it a two-team race for the Nationals led by Theodore Lerner, a local real estate developer. In early May, those rumors proved true when MLB announced the $450 million sale to the Lerner Group. The groundbreaking for the new stadium was held the next day.

You'd think this would be the end of the drama, but unfortunately it's not. The city's plan to develop the surrounding area with two multi-use towers fell through. The towers would have contained everything from parking to condominiums to retail, but the team was never on board because of doubts that it would be finished by the 2008 deadline. At press time, Mayor Williams was trying to get the spending cap increased by $75 million to pay for parking for the new stadium and to possibly keep the multi-use tower idea alive. The drama will never end, but it looks like the Nationals are going to be in the nation's capital to stay with the Lerner group as owners.

The 2006 Florida Marlins

The only person who had been seeking public funding for a new stadium longer than Florida Marlins owner Jeffrey Loria was Minnesota Twins owner Carl Pohlad. And when the Florida state government once again balked at providing the Marlins with funding, Loria decided to throw up his hands and sell the farm. Carlos Delgado, Paul Lo Duca, Josh Beckett and Mike Lowell were all traded away and A.J. Burnett signed with the Toronto Blue Jays as a free agent. Even manager Jack McKeon was replaced with rookie manager Joe Girardi to go along with all of the rookies that would be starting for this team. By the end of the season, 33 rookies would go through the Marlins roster. The team started the season with a team payroll just under $15 million, which was less than one-third the payroll of the 1997 World Series Champion Marlins. Even the 1993 inaugural Marlins had an Opening Day payroll of just over $18 million.

Through mid-May, the team definitely struggled. On May 21, the Marlins were an unimpressive 11-31 after a seven-game losing streak. After that though, something happened—the Marlins started winning. By June 20, after winning nine straight, the team stood just seven games below .500, and on September 4, in the middle of a crazy National League Wild Card race, the Marlins passed the .500 mark at 69-68. They became the first team to ever reach a winning record after starting a season 20 games under .500. The Marlins missed making the playoffs, but they were in it until the final weeks of the season.

This didn't help them at the ticket office though. The Marlins finished dead last in attendance with fewer than 15,000 fans on average at home games. And then a rift between Girardi and Loria came to a head in August when the two got into a shouting match. At season's end, Loria fired Girardi and replaced him with Atlanta Braves third base coach Fredi Gonzalez.

While all this was going on, Loria was doing his best to get that funding for a new stadium. He received permission to relocate the team, and it looked like San Antonio, TX might be a potential option. The hope was that an extension of a car rental tax and a hotel tax would allow San Antonio to give the Marlins a nice new stadium. A May 15, 2006 deadline for the team to decide on San Antonio came and went. Once again, a major league owner was using another city as leverage in an attempt to get what he wanted.

Now it looks like the Marlins have found prospective locations in downtown Miami and Hialeah. To date though, not much has been done because of a lack of public financing.

A Team Sold and a Team Kept

There were just as many rumors of team sales in 2006 as there were actual sales. One other team was sold in 2006: the Cincinnati Reds. In November 2005, Cincinnati Reds owner Carl Lidner agreed to sell a controlling interest in his club to local businessman Robert Castellini. In January, the owners approved the sale, and Castellini didn't waste much time in firing general manager Dan O'Brien. The Reds then hired Wayne Krivsky, the assistant general manager for the Twins.

Just as interesting are the sales that didn't happen. Pittsburgh Pirates owner Kevin McClatchy played coy in the second half and wouldn't commit to selling his controlling interest in the team during the offseason. There was even a rumor that Dallas Mavericks owner Mark Cuban was interested in purchasing the team. And in June 2006, a lot was made about a meeting between former New York mayor Rudy Giuliani and Chicago Cubs Hall of Famer Ernie Banks a couple of weeks after Banks approached the owner of the Chicago Cubs, The Tribune Company, about purchasing the team. Nothing, however, came out of these rumors.

The Braves were also put up for sale during 2006. Atlanta Falcons owner Arthur Blank was the first suitor. He received permission to negotiate the purchase with

Time Warner in January, and things went well until it became clear that Time Warner wouldn't budge from its $400 million price. By late February, Blank had walked away from the negotiating table, at least temporarily.

In April, Blank got some very solid competition. Liberty Media, a Colorado-based media conglomerate, became a legitimate rival to Blank for the simple reason that Liberty held $3 billion worth of Time Warner stock. By taking advantage of a tax loophole, Time Warner would be able to unload the Braves and a boat load of cash for a large chunk of that Time Warner stock and neither side would have to pay any taxes on the transaction.

When it appeared that the out-of-state mega-corporation would be buying the Braves, local businessman Ron Terwilliger made one last pitch to Time Warner to sell the team to an Atlanta native. But Time Warner decided to go the tax-free route and since then has been negotiating exclusively with Liberty Media. These transactions are never easy though, and a nice chunk of those tax savings are being eaten up by legal and accounting fees because the sale has yet to close. It'll be interesting to see how Time Warner approaches the off-season as a lame-duck owner.

The Los Angeles Angels of Anaheim, Chapter Two

In November 2004, the Anaheim Angels received permission from MLB to change the team name; prior to the 2005 season, they became the Los Angeles Angels of Anaheim. Team owners wanted to profit from being associated with the second-largest media market in the country. Anaheim, however, didn't take this lightly; the city filed a breach of contract lawsuit, stating that the spirit of the stadium lease required that Anaheim be the primary city. The city tried to get restraining orders from two different courts to block the name change, to no avail. For several months, the two sides unsuccessfully tried to resolve their differences.

Mediation continued without resolution, and in December 2005, Angels owner Arte Moreno took things to the press. He said the city of Anaheim was effectively trying to run him out of town and if he ultimately won the legal battle and the city decided to appeal the decision, he might be forced to relocate the team. A short time later, the city announced that as long as the Angels kept "Los Angeles" in the team name, Anaheim would not renovate or replace the Angels' current stadium and would expect the team to opt out of the stadium lease in 2016.

On January 9, the jury trial began in Orange County Superior Court. Judge Peter Polos gave the city an early

victory when he ruled that it could argue the team broke the spirit of the lease, if not the exact wording of the agreement. The city then called on former Angels president Tony Tavares to determine why the wording in the lease, which states the team must "include the name of Anaheim therein," was added at the time of the agreement.

Moreno was pulling out every stop he could. Sparing no expense, he hired Jo-Ellan Dimitrius as jury consultant. Dimitrius became nationally renowned after she had advised the O.J. Simpson defense team. On January 13, with a jury of five men and seven women, the lawyers for both sides gave their opening statements.

In late January, Moreno took the stand, and after cracking a few jokes, he did admit that the team had violated one provision of the lease. The team didn't include "of Anaheim" on any of the team's ballpark signs and instead just stated "Angel Stadium." An expert witness was also called to the stand that week to determine the amount of money that the city could potentially lose because of the name change. The witness contended that the city could lose as much as $191 million by 2016 and $373 million by 2029. The city never asked for a specific amount in damages; Anaheim city officials hoped these figures would be what the jury used to determine damages in the event of a favorable ruling.

The city of Anaheim scored some points near the end, when Angels president Dennis Kuhl testified that the language of the lease is vague, which lends credence to the city's argument that the team violated the lease's spirit. But the city's final witness, Anaheim mayor Curt Pringle, also conceded that Anaheim is in the center of the Los Angeles media market, in a way validating the two-pronged name.

With things now in the Angels' court, they called a former business strategist involved in the initial lease negotiations that claimed Disney never intended for "Anaheim" to be a requirement in the team's name. The team also called on their own expert witnesses who claimed that the city will lose virtually nothing because of the name change.

The jury didn't waste much time in deciding in favor of the Angels. In a double bagel, the jury decided that the team could retain the current Los Angeles Angels of Anaheim name and gave no monetary compensation to the city of Anaheim. There was also speculation that the city could be on the hook for the $7 million legal tab that the Angels ran up while defending themselves in the lawsuit. The city made one last stab by asking Judge Polos to force the Angels to change their name back, but in early March, he once again denied their request.

In late May 2006, Anaheim's city council voted to appeal the decision. While this seemed like a lost cause, there was speculation that it was an attempt to get the Angels to back off from their push to get the $7 million in legal costs reimbursed from the city. It looks like there won't be a conclusion until the city of Anaheim exhausts all of its legal options.

Stadium Developments

Twins owner Carl Pohlad had waited a long time for public funding for a new stadium. In the past, he threatened to relocate the team and even worked to get the team contracted right out of the league. Despite the threats, year after year the people of Minnesota failed to give him what he wanted. He appeared close in 2005 when Hennepin County stepped up and was about to fund a new stadium with a sales tax increase, but the measure fell off the docket when the state ran into a budget crisis. In late 2005, even Minnesota governor Tim Pawlenty admitted that the team might relocate if the state didn't pass a stadium bill, and he pledged to help with the process.

In January 2006, the Twins scored a victory in Hennepin County District Court when Judge Charles Porter, Jr. ruled that the Twins had no legal obligation to play in the Metrodome beyond the 2006 season. The last lease signed between the Twins and the Metropolitan Sports Facility Commission expired at the end of 2003, but the two parties continued to do business despite the lack of a long-term lease. The commission argued that the team had been conducting itself just as if it were a long-term tenant, but the judge saw otherwise.

In late February, things began heating up. The same stadium plan as the previous year, which involved a 0.15 percent sales tax increase in Hennepin County, appeared to have the votes necessary to pass both houses of the state legislature. The state vote was required in order to bypass the public, who in the past hadn't been very sympathetic to a tax increase for a baseball stadium. It passed the Minnesota House of Representatives, but the Senate Tax Committee voted to allow county residents a chance to decide their own fate.

In early May, the Minnesota Senate approved a different stadium bill with a multi-county sales tax increase that allowed for a public referendum. The bill didn't have the support of Pawlenty, who could veto it if passed.

Things finally came to head on May 20. With the legislative session set to end, the Senate passed the House version of the stadium bill by a razor-thin margin (34-32), and just like that, Pohlad had his new stadium.

The final price tag for the open-air stadium is estimated at $522, most of which will be paid for by the sales tax increase to Hennepin County residents.

Both New York teams were also able to get their new stadiums approved. The Yankees faced some resistance at first because of their plans to demolish a nearby park. In the end, the Yankees got the necessary approvals. And the New York Mets plan to build a stadium similar to Ebbets Field, the former home of the Brooklyn Dodgers. Both stadiums are expected to open for the 2009 season.

The St. Louis Cardinals opened their new stadium in 2006 and proceeded to sell out all 81 home games. The team rewarded their fans by winning 49 games at home; only the Mets topped that number in the National League with 50. Home attendance was 3,379,535; the second-best draw in the franchise's record.

Fantasy Baseball Goes to Court

In January 2005, Major League Baseball Advanced Media (MLBAM), the leagues' Internet arm, came to an agreement with the Major League Baseball Players Association (MLBPA) on a five-year deal providing MLBAM the exclusive rights to use MLB player group rights for the development and creation of online games. This, of course, includes fantasy baseball statistics, so only licensed companies can use fantasy baseball statistics in conjunction with player names. The number of licenses was shaved from 20 to seven, and while high profile companies like ESPN, CBS Sportsline and Yahoo were all given licenses, even more companies were locked out.

CDM Sports, which is owned by CBC Marketing and ran online fantasy baseball leagues, decided to not renew their license when it expired at the end of 2004. Instead, the company sued MLBAM, saying that the statistics are part of the public domain and continued to operate fantasy baseball without a license in 2005 and 2006.

In August 2006, United States District Court Judge Mary Ann Medler upheld CBC's argument and ruled that MLBAM could not force businesses to pay for baseball statistics. She claimed that CBC hadn't violated the player's claimed right of publicity and that MLBAM could not stop CBC from offering fantasy baseball leagues using MLB statistics.

In September 2006, both MLBAM and the MLBPA appealed the decision. This battle is hardly over, but the league has been dealt a blow. For the time being, sites like CDM Sports can sell fantasy baseball games for profit without paying a dime to MLBAM. Fair or not, we'll have to wait and see how the appeal goes until this issue is resolved.

A Historic Collective Bargaining Agreement

The collective bargaining agreement (CBA) that was in place at the beginning of the 2006 season between the MLBPA and MLB was set to expire on Dec. 19, 2006. The CBA was historic because it was the first agreement that didn't result in a work stoppage. This time around, it seems everyone is cashing in big time in what appears to be a baseball boon. Paid attendance (tickets sold) continues to set records, both league-wide and amongst individual teams, and MLBAM continues to be a cash cow for the league. Conditions were ripe for a fruitful negotiation.

The only sore spot appeared to be performance-enhancing drugs. In 2006, the MLBPA opened up the CBA and added a Joint Drug Agreement (JDA) to add stiffer penalties for those who test positive for performance-enhancing drugs. Even amphetamines came under fire this time around.

As the season progressed, rumors began to circulate that the sides were busy negotiating a new agreement, but little was said. In the past, both sides used the press to get their message across; but this time around, MLB commissioner Bud Selig issued a gag order. By the end of the regular season, the only item that had leaked was that there might be an end to compensation for teams that lose players to free agency.

Then, in the middle of the playoffs, something strange happened. Rumors started swirling that the league and player's union were actually close to an agreement and that something might be announced during the World Series. The reason this was so strange was that it was completely unprecedented. The previous time that a work stoppage didn't occur because of CBA negotiations, things went right down to the final hour. So to have a new CBA in place nearly two months before the current one was set to expire was absolutely ground breaking.

On Tuesday, Oct. 24, 2006, prior to Game 3 of the World Series between the St. Louis Cardinals and the Detroit Tigers, Selig announced that a new CBA had been agreed upon. The actual CBA was not yet available but as I was finishing this story, details surrounding the new CBA were coming to light. The new agreement is a five-year deal, making it the longest ever.

Revenue sharing remained largely intact and one rate will apply for all clubs. In the past, lower revenue-making clubs were forced to pay a higher percentage (48 percent) than higher revenue-making clubs (40 percent). Now all clubs will pay the same percentage (31 percent). The luxury tax also remained largely unchanged with the exception of the

salary thresholds. In 2006, teams with a payroll over $136.5 million were subject to the luxury tax. This number will go up to $148 million in 2007 and by 2011, it will increase to $178 million. The minimum salary was increased from $327,000 in 2006 to $380,000 in 2007 and will go up to $400,000 in 2009, with cost of living adjustments increasing the minimum payroll after that through 2011.

There were also changes to when a team has to sign a player from that year's amateur draft. Now players that were drafted must be signed by Aug. 15 of that year. There were also some changes to the key dates surrounding free agency, and the JDA was folded into the CBA.

Again, until the actual agreement is made available, it's hard to speculate as to exactly what all of the details are. Regardless, five years of labor peace in baseball is definitely a good thing, so baseball fans have little chance of seeing a repeat of the 1994 strike in the foreseeable future.

MLB Sets Attendance Record for Third Straight Season

Total attendance for Major League Baseball games in the 2006 season reached a record total of 76,043,902. This was 1.5% better then last year's record of 74,926,174, and it was even sweeter because there were no extraordinary circumstances. The 2005 record had been largely due to the increase in attendance because of the move of the Montreal Expos to Washington, D.C.

A record eight teams crossed the 3 million mark, and all but six stadiums topped two million. The New York Yankees set a new American League and franchise standard by drawing 4,248,067 fans. The Yankees also became the second team to top 4 million fans in two separate seasons, and they set a record for combined home and road attendance with 7,328,332.

Several other teams set new records as well. The Los Angeles Dodgers drew 3,758,545 fans, breaking a record set way back in 1982. The White Sox edged their previous mark by fewer than 25,000 fans when they drew 2,957,414 fans. The Boston Red Sox drew a record 2,930,588; they became what is believed to be the only team to set its franchise attendance record for seven straight years. The Los Angeles Angels of Anaheim drew a record 3,406,790, the Tigers set a Comerica Park record when they drew 2,595,937 and the St. Louis Cardinals sold out every game at their new ballpark and drew 3,407,104 fans.

The love for the game extended beyond MLB. Minor League Baseball set a third consecutive attendance record by drawing 41,710,357. Even the Independent Leagues set a record with 7,554,512 fans this year.

As Clear as Mud: Drug Testing's Impact on the Stats of 2006

by Steve Treder

In 2006, for the first time in history, Major League Baseball implemented a Performance Enhancing Drug (PED) policy with genuine teeth. The sport instituted serious testing for and sanctions against not only steroids, which have almost certainly been employed by many players in recent years, but also amphetamines, which in various forms have been baseball's open secret for decades (the "greenies" pervasive in Jim Bouton's *Ball Four* way back in 1969).

While one might imagine that this new get-tough drug ban was motivated by concern for players' health, to do so would be naïve. The plain truth is that the groundswell of media and public outcry (and congressional grandstanding—er, pressure) that drove MLB to enact the new policy and the Major League Baseball Players Association to accept it (after years of apathy and foot-dragging by both parties) wasn't prompted by fear that the use of PEDs put pro ballplayers' long-term wellness in jeopardy. Instead, what stimulated the agitation was fear that the use of PEDs put familiar benchmarks in the sport's *record book* in jeopardy.

Beginning with the power-hitting exploits of Mark McGwire and Sammy Sosa in the late 1990s, and coming to a head with the slugging barrage exhibited by Barry Bonds from 2001 through 2004, while punctuated with eyebrow-raising long-ball prowess suddenly discovered by the likes of Brady Anderson, Bret Boone, and Luis Gonzalez, the galvanizing issue was home runs, not hormones. When late-career home run hero Rafael Palmeiro was outed as a steroid user in 2005 and Big Bad BALCO Barry approached the hallowed career home run marks of Babe Ruth and Hank Aaron, the tipping point was reached: MLB and the MLBPA *had* to do something to curb the use of PEDs. No more excuses, empty talk, and half-measures would be tolerated; this was a crisis.

Proponents of the new policy, as well as opponents, and those who couldn't care less about the issue, can all agree on one point: the new policy is authentically powerful. (Whether it's authentically effective is, as we'll see, a separate question.) The testing regime and the penalties for violation comprise the most significant effort the sport has ever taken to eradicate PEDs—

indeed, baseball's *first* serious effort to eradicate PEDs. Whatever one's view of the effort's appropriateness, its establishment provides the first opportunity to meaningfully assess just what the impact of the presumably widespread usage of PEDs has been on the nature of the game on the field.

Or does it?

The "C" Word

Here's where complexity raises its head—its ever-present, ever-dreaded, ever-ugly head.

In the first place, understand that long ago, long before PEDs were anything but a gleam in some imaginative biochemist's eye—*really* long ago, like in the late 1800s and early 1900s—run-scoring rates, and production of such events as home runs, extra-base hits, and so on, fluctuated all over the place from year to year and from era to era. Such fluctuations have continued ever since.

Given that, there are obviously factors other than PEDs—ballparks, the strike zone, pitchers' mounds, player techniques, team tactics, the resiliency of the ball itself, and so on—that have abundant influence on the rate of hitting and scoring in baseball games. We may not be able to identify all of these factors or isolate their precise impacts, but the influence nonetheless significantly applies. And whatever influence these various factors exert on the nature of play, they certainly continued to do the same in 2006. Given *that*, whatever the impact drug testing had on the baseball outcomes we witnessed in 2006 has to be understood as operating within the context of the other factors, timeless and universal, that haven't disappeared.

And given even *that*: PEDs themselves are anything but simple, and their influence over baseball outcomes is anything but obvious. Questions as to exactly who has been using what PED, and when, and exactly what impact which PED has had on the performance of which player—let alone such further questions as whether, say, steroids in particular have generally been used more by hitters than by pitchers—are equally wide open.

And on top of all *that* remains yet another crucially relevant unknown: Just how effective is the new testing program at eliminating or reducing PED usage? The experience of other sports demonstrates that many athletes continue to use PEDs despite testing regimes. We know this simply because so many continue to get caught: The persistence of athletes getting caught stands as strong circumstantial evidence for the likelihood of others (no one knows how many) not getting caught. No net captures every fish; even hawkish anti-doping warriors generally accede to the imperfection of even the most sophisticated testing protocols, for a variety of reasons not limited to dosage cycling patterns, masking agents, and of course the near-inevitability of untested-for PED compounds.

But with all of this messiness acknowledged, it was still a simplistic focus on a single narrow issue of the perceived influence of PEDs on the nature of play—specifically, on the capacity of sluggers to hit home runs—that drove the PEDs-in-baseball scandal, and led to the imposition of the drug testing regime of 2006. If not for the widespread suspicion (frequently expressed as beyond-any-doubt conviction) that PEDs (steroids in particular) were having a dramatic effect on home run totals, it's a virtual certainty that no such serious drug testing policy would now be in place.

Thus one is compelled to examine the issue of just what kind of an impact the adoption of the policy actually made in 2006 in terms of on-field outcomes. The potential influence of any number of factors other than PEDs is all well and good, but they're all inherently foggy. In contrast, one crystal-clear fact is that the new, tough drug policy took effect in 2006. If indeed PEDs *have* had a profound effect on increasing the home run production of many prominent sluggers, and if indeed the tough new policy *has* had a significant effect on reducing or eliminating the usage of those PEDs, then it would stand to unassailable reason that the policy would have the effect of reducing home run output.

The Big Flies of 2006

So, the first obvious question that arises in examining the results of the 2006 season is: What about home runs? Let's look at a graph of the number of home runs hit per game from 1996 through 2006 to see what it can tell us. Was home run production reduced in 2006?

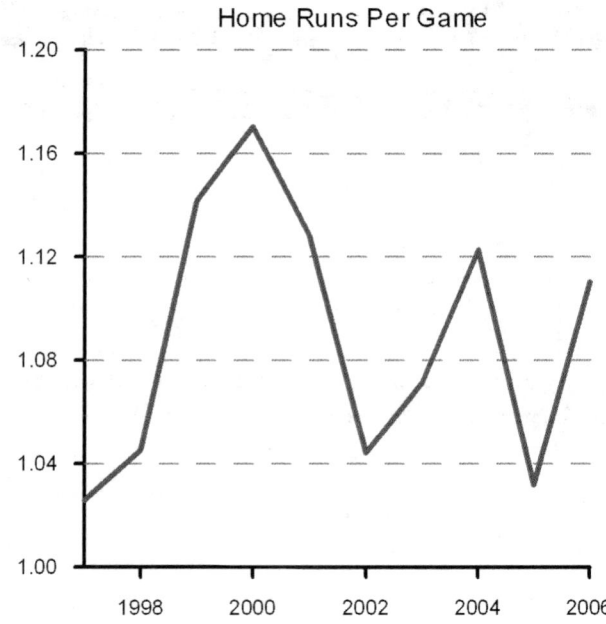

Home Runs Per Game

In a word: no.

MLB-wide home run production was not reduced in 2006; in fact, it increased by a factor of about 8% over 2005. Home runs were hit in '06 at a rate nearly equal to that seen in '04 (the season before MLB introduced the semi-serious PED-testing protocol that was strengthened in '06) and greater than the rate produced in 2002 or 2003 (seasons effectively without any PED sanctions whatsoever).

The increase from 2005 to 2006 was pretty sharp within this 10-season perspective, but not quite as distinct as the increase from 1998 to 1999. So, is such a year-to-year change in home run rate as we witnessed in either '05 to '06 or '98 to '99 unusual? Here's a look at what the fluctuation in home run production has been over the past quarter-century:

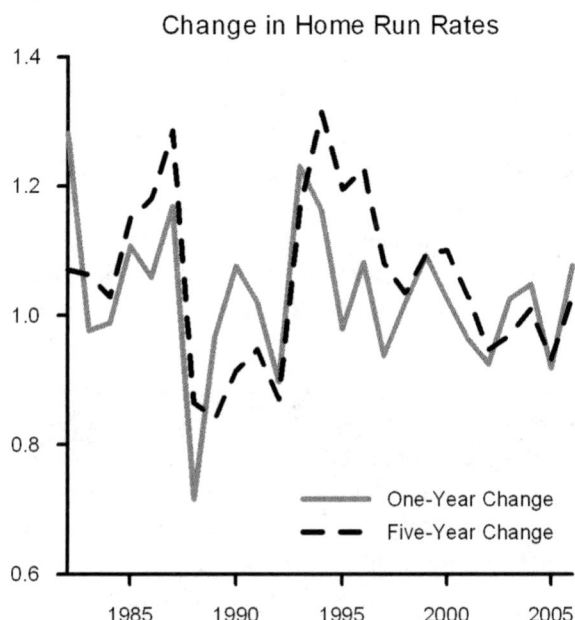

Change in Home Run Rates

One-Year Change
Five-Year Change

The uptick from 2005 to 2006 was noticeable on a multi-decade scale, but hardly dramatically so. The 2006 increase, both in terms of its change from the previous single season as well as its change from the average of the previous five seasons, was well within the range of those routinely witnessed over the past 25 years. It wasn't nearly as startling as the jumps that occurred in 1982, 1987, 1993, and 1994, nor was the upward movement of 2006 nearly as significant as the drops that took place in 1988 and 1992.

In short, the 2006 increase in home run production wasn't anything different than the sort of year-to-year fluctuation in home run production that typically occurs.

Hmmm ...

So what's up with that? Baseball finally responds to widespread concerns about steroid-fraudulent home runs and invokes its first serious stamp-out-steroids program, but home run production goes up moderately. (And it does so, by the way, despite the fact that the sport's erstwhile most home-run-friendly haven, Coors Field in mile-high Denver, was humidor-tamed in 2006 to play more near-neutral than ever before.) Alas, it seems the concerns I expressed earlier that this impact-of-PEDs issue isn't entirely simple might, frustratingly, might be justified.

To explore it more deeply, let's examine not just tater rates, but more of the elements that comprise batting production. Let's look at extra-base hits alongside singles, and while we're at it let's include walks and strikeouts. And what the heck, if we're going to do that, let's also include the entity that all these elements combine to produce: runs themselves. Let's see just what kind of a season 2006 was, compared to those of the past 25 years.

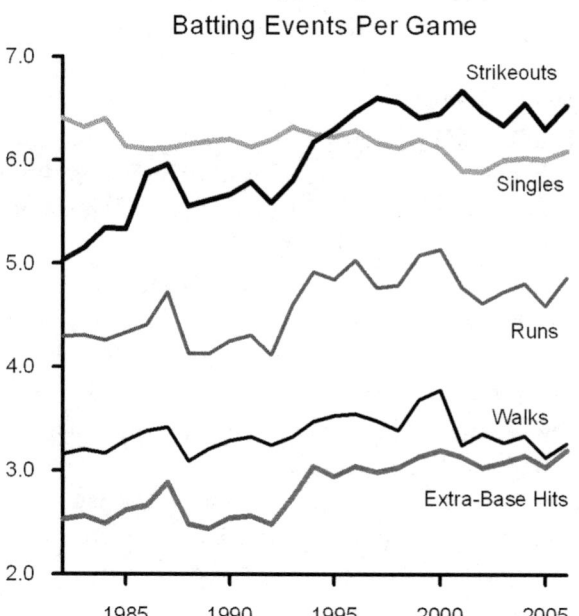

Batting Events Per Game

Viewed in this fuller context, it becomes clear that 2006 wasn't a particularly extraordinary year for offensive production of any sort. The rate of everything was up from 2005—singles as well as extra-base hits, walks as well as strikeouts, and runs were up as well—but nothing spiked dramatically, and every element was in the range of where it's been for the past decade. It was a good hitters' year, but not the best in the modern hitter-friendly era, and not a season in which the production of any result stands out as atypical. If someone unfamiliar with baseball was asked to take a look at this chart and identify which season it was in which the sport introduced a significant new PED-regulation policy, he or she would likely not conclude 2006.

The Powder River Leaderboard

But perhaps I'm looking in the wrong place. Maybe the impact of PEDs doesn't manifest itself in league-wide aggregate rates so much as it's revealed in the performances of a few individuals: the outliers, the most prolific sluggers. What sort of a year was 2006 for those guys?

A banner year, actually:

- Ryan Howard, in his first full big-league season, blasted 58 home runs, the 10th-highest total in major league history.

- David Ortiz detonated a career-high 54 bombs, making it the first time since 2002 that two players exceeded 50 homers.

- The league-leading marks in slugging percentage were up from 2005 in both leagues, as NL leader Albert Pujols and AL leader Travis Hafner each achieved career highs in home runs and RBIs as well.

- Each league leader in extra-base hits, the AL's Grady Sizemore and the NL's Alfonso Soriano, also reached personal bests in homers.

- Other bruisers establishing career highs in home runs (all with at least 35 dingers) included Lance Berkman, Jermaine Dye, Carlos Beltran, Aramis Ramirez, Carlos Lee, Bill Hall, Jason Bay, and Nick Swisher.

- *All* of the above recorded personal bests in slugging percentage with the exception of Ramirez (whose mark was .017 behind his career high). Others who achieved career highs in slugging, all with figures above .550, were Matt Holliday, Miguel Cabrera, Adam LaRoche, Justin Morneau, and Garrett Atkins.

- 34-year-old Manny Ramirez and 35-year-old Jim Thome each produced his highest slugging percentage since 2002. 38-year-old Frank Thomas produced the third-highest home run total in history by a player of his age.

Two of the sport's veteran sluggers whose names have been most notoriously associated with the steroid scandal enjoyed strong comeback performances in 2006. Jason Giambi, at age 35, despite being hampered by a chronic wrist injury that required immediate surgery at season's end, produced:

- his most home runs since 2003
- his highest slugging percentage since 2002
- his highest isolated power since 2001

Barry Bonds, coming off of dual knee surgeries complicated by infection that had limited him to 14 games in 2005, and despite being hampered by a chronic elbow injury that required immediate surgery at season's end, produced a season that ranks among the historical seasons of 41-year-olds:

- ninth in doubles
- sixth in runs
- fifth in total bases
- fourth in RBIs
- third in times on base, extra-base hits, and runs created
- second in home runs, home runs per at-bat, slugging, OPS, and OPS+
- first in on-base percentage, walks, intentional walks, and hit by pitch

That's quite a year for the long-ball elite. Nearly all of these power plants are very big and very muscular, well over 200 pounds and obviously intimately familiar with the weight machine. In the absence of the 2006 drug-testing policy, would such a litany of power-hitting attainments, especially including the remarkable performances of Giambi and Bonds, be blithely accepted as drug-free? Under the actual circumstances, should they be?

The issue, of course, is that assuming the sport's drug-testing program has ensured that all these 2006 slugging exploits, both aggregate and individual, were achieved without the assistance of PEDs, then it calls into serious question the validity of the widespread suspicion that many comparable achievements in recent seasons were meaningfully impacted by PEDs. And if the abundance of such 2006 slugging achievements causes us to remain suspicious about whether the usage of PEDs has been substantially reduced, then it calls

into question the efficacy of the drug-testing program itself.

In short, the evidence produced by the statistically-measured performance of players on the field leads to no conclusion at all regarding the degree to which PEDs have been employed by baseball players prior to 2006, the degree to which they continue to be employed despite testing, and the degree to which that employment has influenced and continues to influence players' results.

Well, Where's the Fun in That?

Not that the absence of even mildly compelling factual evidence has hindered sportswriters, broadcasters, players, pundits, politicians, and most especially those ever-eloquent callers to sports talk radio shows from making bold, confident assertions in this regard (and all others), nor is there any reason to suspect any of that will change. *C'est la vie*; it's just baseball, after all. Part of the fun is for all of us to fool ourselves into thinking we know and understand a lot more about the sport and its contestants than we actually do.

So in that cheeky spirit, herewith some utterly unprovable theorizing:

- The use of amphetamines in baseball has been ubiquitous for half a century.
- The impact of amphetamines on player performance is probably minor, especially long-term, and may indeed be deleterious, especially if dependence develops.
- The 2006 drug testing policy may have had a meaningful effect on curbing amphetamine use, as these compounds are fairly easily tested, and many players may see the risk of detection outweighing the benefit of use.
- In any case, given their likely minor performance-enhancing effect, the impact of amphetamine testing on the nature of play isn't and won't be large.
- Steroids and related compounds haven't been as widely used as amphetamines, but they still have been extensively employed by players at all levels of the sport for at least the past 15-20 years.
- The media's focus on a few prominent sluggers (Bonds, McGwire, Sosa et al) has missed the point that usage has probably been more prevalent among scrubs struggling to gain and hold roster spots than among established stars.

- Media have also largely ignored the issue that usage has quite possibly been at least as widespread among pitchers as among position players.

- Unlike amphetamines, the impact of steroids and related compounds on player performance is likely substantially positive, especially if employed as part of a robust, comprehensive training and conditioning regimen—and that regimen itself almost certainly has more positive impact than anything else.

- Also unlike amphetamines, the huge diversity of steroid and related compounds creates a great challenge for drug testers and provides a great opportunity for drug developers.

- Therefore, the degree to which the 2006 testing program has reduced steroid and related compound usage is probably less than that of amphetamines, as players see a lower risk of detection and a higher benefit to usage.

- Therefore, the degree to which the 2006 testing program has impacted the nature of play probably isn't and won't be large.

- Perhaps already, and certainly in the years ahead, development of ever-more sophisticated performance-enhancing compounds and techniques, including gene doping and possibly nanotechnology, render the tester's challenge more daunting still.

- So long as the economic, social and psychic rewards for excellent performance in baseball remain as enormous as they are, for both individuals and teams, the reality of doping in some form will abide.

What About the 2006 Stats, Then?

So the impact of drugs and drug testing on the '06 stat sheet was effectively undetectable, and the notion that with the imposition of testing we'd rid ourselves of record-stalking slugging stats was foolish. What, then, can be said about the level of 2006 hitting and scoring, and what kind of an offensive game can fans expect in the years ahead?

To help answer that, let's take another look at that total-offense graphic, only this time let's get a tighter focus and consider the 15-year perspective at the top of the next column.

As stated before, you can see that 2006 doesn't stand out as an unusual individual season in any regard. But the general uptick '06 demonstrated, back to or slightly above the rates displayed in 2004 might be significant,

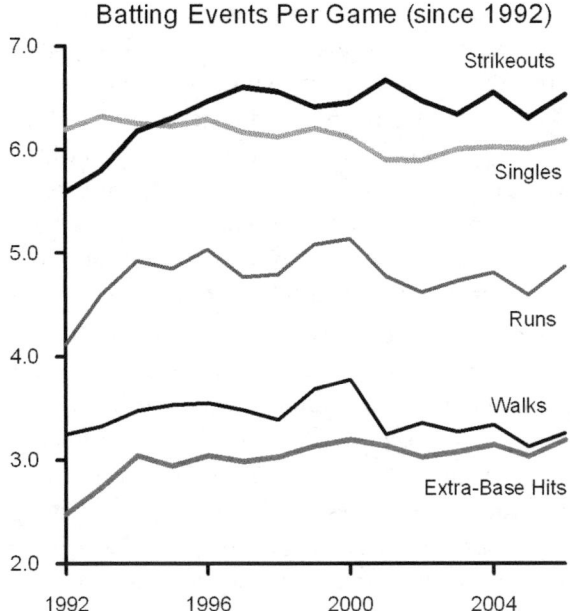

Batting Events Per Game (since 1992)

given that '04 was itself something of an uptick season as well.

We see that the general trend for several years before 1997 had been one of increasing rates in most all of these events (including, interestingly, strikeouts). A fairly dramatic dropoff (in everything except strikeouts) occurred in 2001 as a result of MLB's reinforcement of the rule book strike zone, including the imposition of the QuesTec system; following 2000, offense stabilized at a lower level, but not as low as it had been prior to 1993. And the '04 and '06 upturns in combination might be seen as a continuance of the longer-term trend toward increased offense that spans the entire era.

Assuming this is so, what stimulates this trend, if not PED usage *per se*? The benefit of weight training for hitters, whether steroid-aided or not, is clearly a contributor. Moreover, the balance of new ballparks coming on line (and reconfigurations of existing parks) has continued the pattern begun in the early 1990s of an ever-more hitter-friendly overall environment. The ball itself may have gotten more lively in 1993-94 (though not officially and perhaps not intentionally), and in any case it shows no sign of getting any less so. Batters crowd the plate with greater confidence as the brushback pitch has effectively been removed from the game. And probably most importantly, teams increasingly demonstrate a proclivity toward roster and lineup choices erring on the side of offense, such as developing and deploying bigger, stronger, non-strikeout-avoidant power-oriented athletes with limited defensive range, often even at the traditionally defense-first positions of shortstop, second base and center field.

"Chicks dig the long ball," went the advertising campaign slogan from several years ago. There's a lot of truth to that, and not only with regard to the fairer sex. Fans of both genders and all ages appear to love the high-octane power-centric mode of play with which they've been presented for the past decade-plus: major league-wide per-game attendance in 2006 was the very highest of all time, finally eclipsing the mark set in the infamously strike-shortened season of 1994.

Baseball's hottest-selling product has been and remains the home run. Owners understand this, and players do too; the power game is where the big money is, for investors and contracted labor alike. Thus there's no reason to anticipate the sport's powers-that-be instituting structural changes, or its athletes modifying training programs and batting approaches, that significantly arrest the long-term tendency toward muscular, strikeout-saturated, long ball-laden results—the very results that have generated such angst among those concerned with the sanctity of the record book.

Drug testing notwithstanding, in 2006 we witnessed just one more in a long line of fence-busting seasons.

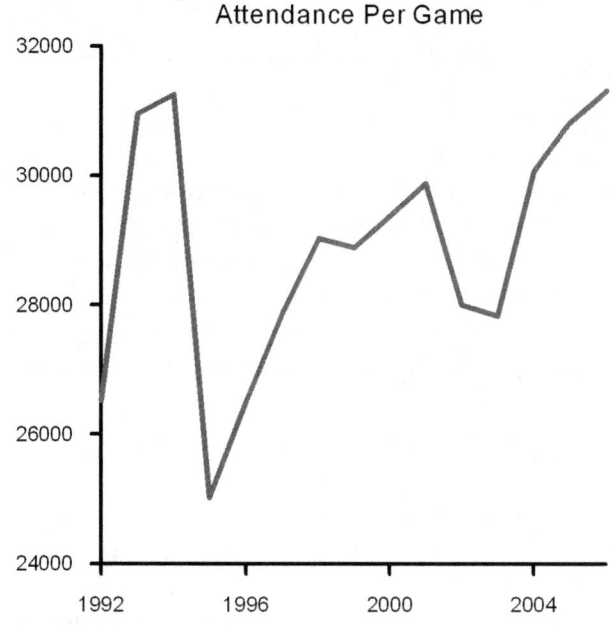

Attendance Per Game

Basic economic logic dictates that we should expect this dynamic to continue, with established power standards rendered ever-more obsolete in the seasons to come.

The Illusion of Competitive Balance

by Vince Gennaro

Following the work stoppage of 1994, Major League Baseball revamped the postseason structure by adding the Wild Card and doubling the number of teams. Extra postseason spots would keep more teams in contention longer and produce a variety of champions. Yet in 2000, after the Yankees won their fourth World Series title in five years, the commissioner's Blue Ribbon Panel issued a report citing growing economic disparities between the "haves" and the "have nots" that made it nearly impossible for the latter to compete. Competitive balance became the new catchphrase.

Coupled with the recent success of many Wild Card qualifiers, MLB's changes helped create the perception that everyone has a chance. Those who say competitive balance is alive and well tend to cite the winners and losers from year to year, counting the number of different teams that have reached the World Series—more diverse than any sports championship series. Others offer as evidence the number of small-market teams reaching the postseason in recent years, notably Oakland, Minnesota and Florida.

This all-too-common approach of judging competitive balance based on the actual results of who reaches the postseason is "contaminated" and obscures the real issue: the fundamental design of MLB's economic system, which forms the foundation for on-field competition. If a team reaches the postseason due to superior management, or a miniscule payroll, or through player performance that was beyond all expectations, the team's achievement may tell us little about competitive balance.

From time to time an owner of one of the "have-nots" is willing to spend lavishly to field a winning team, only to learn that his exorbitant spending is not rewarded by the fans, as they stay away from the ballpark in droves. If the franchise hemorrhages cash from an unsustainable payroll but wins on the field, is competitive balance alive and well? Even a winning team that repeatedly loses money will ultimately need to balance the checking account. It may be more productive to analyze competitive balance by focusing on baseball's economic structure, not on whether personal heroics or irrational spending can overcome design defects in baseball's economic model.

In order to frame the analysis, we need a definition of competitive balance. I define competitive balance simply as *an economic framework for MLB that provides motivation for all teams to compete for a berth in the postseason.* In other words, it's a framework that does not penalize teams in their quests for the postseason. The postseason seems to be the right aspiration for two reasons—it is the dream of every team owner and fan, and it is accompanied by a bounty that can improve a team's financial situation for several years. During the inevitable mad scramble for playoff tickets, fans disappointed with the availability or pricing of playoff seats vow to avoid the chaos in the future by buying season tickets for the following year with options for future playoff seats. Even if the team does not return to the playoffs, it takes several years of attrition for the new season ticket holders to vanish, creating a "bonus" revenue stream for the team in the meantime. Winning also promotes greater fan interest and helps to build an emotional bond with fans, leading to higher future attendance and revenues.

An analysis of competitive balance begins with a look at a team's local revenues—a core driver of MLB's business model. In contrast to the NFL, which evenly distributes about 80% of all revenues, the largest portion of which is from national television contracts, only about 25% of MLB revenues are shared among all teams. A baseball team's financial fate lies largely in its ability to cultivate the local market through various revenue streams—attendance, broadcast, luxury suites, concessions and local merchandise sales—that are "owned" by each individual team.

In an effort to take chance, management quality and unsustainable spending levels out of the equation, I analyzed the historical relationship between a team's revenues and its on-field performance. By using statistical analysis to quantify this relationship, I can compare the revenue a team can expect for 70-win and 90-win seasons. By gauging the local revenues at each win total, I can drill to the core of the competitive balance question by estimating the "affordable payroll" for each team as it chases the postseason.

The analysis divides a team's revenues into two components: baseline revenues, the amount of local revenue a team can expect to generate in a non-competitive season; and marginal revenue from winning, the amount of incremental revenue a team would generate as it pursues a playoff spot. Using a hypothetical 70-win season as the threshold, I statistically estimated the baseline revenues of each team, which is based on the loyalty of a team's fans and the size and popularity of baseball in the local market. I defined the marginal revenue from winning as the incremental revenue attributable to a 95-win season, which would likely qualify a team for the postseason (or at least place it in serious contention) and represent the financial payoff from producing a winning team. By statistically analyzing the historical relationship between a team's on-field performance and revenues, I have developed a series of "win-curves" for all 30 teams. (More about the "win-curve" and related topics can be found in my book, *Diamond Dollars: The Economics of Winning in Baseball*, from Maple Street Press.)

While team revenues are also affected by the strength of a team's marketing efforts, whether or not it has marquee players with gate appeal, and ticket pricing, the win-curves isolate the impact of winning by estimating local fans' response—in the form of attendance, broadcast, and other revenues—to changes in team wins. As part of the win-curve analysis, I include the financial windfall from a postseason appearance. The net result is an estimate of the revenue each team can expect to earn at each win level. Here is an example of the Los Angeles Angels' win-curve:

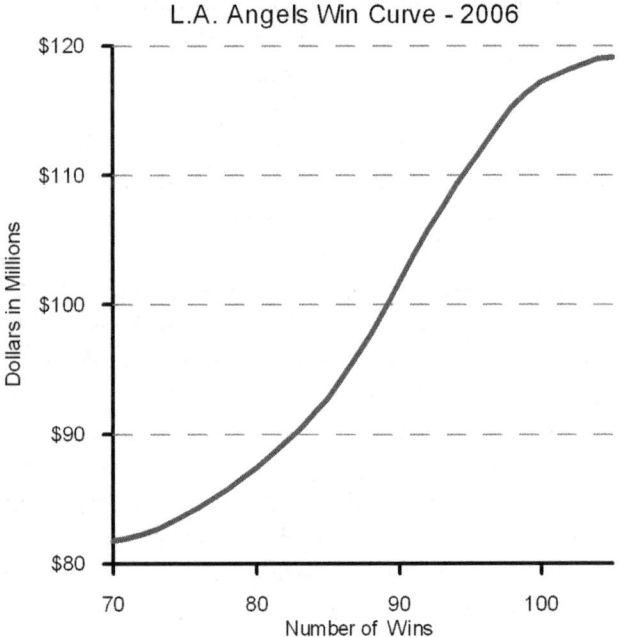

way to get a sense of which teams are the "haves" and which are the "have-nots" is to categorize them in a 3x3 grid—high, medium and low, on two dimensions, baseline revenue and marginal revenue. In the Revenue Opportunity Index on the next page, teams in the top row, the high marginal revenue teams, experience the highest dollar payoff from producing a winner, while teams in the right-hand column, the highest baseline revenue teams, have the highest revenue base when all teams are "non-competitive." Teams with both the "high/high box (the top right), have a decided advantage over teams in the "low/low box" (the bottom left).

To show the dollar implications of the teams in the two extreme boxes (top right and bottom left), I compared estimates of the teams' local revenue at the 95-win mark. Even after incorporating revenue-sharing distributions (based on the 2002 Collective Bargaining Agreement), intended to level the playing field, the average of the six highest local revenue teams is $227 million, while the average of the nine teams with the lowest estimated local revenue at 95-wins is $96 million. Four teams (the Yankees, Cubs, Red Sox, and Dodgers) would generate revenues greater than $200 million, while seven teams would be below $100 million. The following table shows the Yankees, Cubs, Dodgers, Red Sox, Giants and Mariners as the high-revenue teams, while the Twins, Royals, Devil Rays, A's, Reds, Pirates, Brewers, Tigers and Marlins are the lowest revenue teams, under our hypothetical 95-win scenario.

Estimated Local Revenue for 95-win Season

"Haves"		"Have-nots"	
NYA	$300	DET	$111
CHA	$248	MIL	$102
BOS	$240	TB	$99
LAN	$206	FLA	$99
SEA	$193	PIT	$96
SFG	$180	CIN	$91
		OAK	$90
		KC	$90
		MIN	$83

Annual Local Revenue Estimated in Millions of Dollars

This snapshot of team revenues, from two different angles—marginal revenue from winning and baseline revenue—is a first step in calibrating a team's ability to spend payroll dollars to build a competitive team. One

The disparity in local revenues for these two groups of teams averages $131 million in annual local revenue, while the spread between just the Yankees and the low-revenue teams is about $200 million. While this analysis focuses on the revenue side, including estimates of the non-payroll operating costs may narrow the gap some-

Revenue Opportunity Index

Marginal Revenue	Low	Medium	High
High		CHA CLE HOU STL	NYY SFG BOS SEA NYM CHN
Medium	COL	LAA ARI ATL TOR WAS	BAL PHI LAN TEX
Low	CIN DET OAK FLA KC PIT MIL MIN TB	SDP	

Baseline Revenue

what. According to data released by the commissioner's office in 2001 (which I inflated to 2006 dollars), non-payroll costs can vary across teams by as much as $60 million annually from the highest to the lowest. Even if our highest-revenue teams were saddled with the highest non-payroll costs and the lowest-revenue teams had the lowest non-payroll costs, *it would leave us with an "affordable payroll" average gap of $71 million—$131 million revenue gap, less the $60 million cost gap.*

Defenders of MLB's competitive balance will no doubt argue that a higher affordable payroll does not guarantee success. While any number of factors can breach the relationship between payroll and wins, including luck, injuries or unexpected performance by key players, a higher payroll does raise the probability of success. By analyzing the win contribution of players relative to their salary, we can determine the cost of a "marginal win." In "Net Win Shares Value," Dave Studenmund finds that the going rate in the free agent market for a marginal win is in the $3.5 to $4 million range. If teams with the highest affordable payroll—the teams in the top right box on our grid—were to deploy their $65 million payroll advantage with average efficiency in the free agent market, they could theoretically buy 16 to 18 more wins than the teams in the lower left corner of our grid. So while chance, under- or over-performing players, an unsustainable spending level by a team's owner, or even superior talent evaluation and management, can cause a team to play better than its payroll, the economic framework that forms the foundation for fair competition is arguably broken.

MLB's current economic system, which allows 20% of the teams (top right box) the resources to outspend 30% of the teams (lower left box) by $65 million-plus in annual payroll is hardly a level playing field. The disparity in "affordable payroll" between the "haves" and the "have-nots" is evidence that competitive balance does not exist today, as it strips the economic motivation for nearly one-third of the teams to compete for the postseason. The Kansas City Royals and their eight colleagues in the lower left box of the grid would need to lose $50 million annually to match the affordable payroll of the Cubs, Red Sox, and Dodgers, which might still leave them an additional $50 million short of the Yankees' affordable payroll. The $50 million loss by the have-nots assumes they succeed in reaching the postseason. The losses would be greater if they spent the payroll dollars to match the big boys, but fell short in the win column.

If the revenue sharing and luxury tax provisions in the 2002 Collective Bargaining Agreement were insufficient to level the playing field, is there a potential solution to the competitive balance problem? For starters we could alter the provision that taxes teams' actual revenues, in favor of a method that taxes teams on structural factors that reflect the *strength of their revenue opportunity*. Under the 2002 CBA revenue sharing formula, if the large-market Dodgers performed poorly for several years and their fan base eroded and revenues plummeted, they could *receive* payments under the 2002 provision, based on their lower revenue level. In my alternative system, teams would be classified based on their revenue opportunity and assessed an annual fixed fee, with the cash from the haves, redistributed to the have-nots.

Another useful modification to the way in which revenue sharing has been implemented historically is to add a kicker for the have-nots based on their win-loss record. For example, if the Kansas City Royals are pegged to receive $40 million annually from the revenue sharing pool, they could be given an additional $10 million if they achieved a .500 winning percentage or an additional $20 million if they won 90 games. By adding a kicker for on-field performance, we effectively raise the marginal revenue from winning, which is precisely the deficiency from which the teams in the lower left corner of the grid suffer. Any revenue-sharing system which narrows the marginal-revenue-from-wins gap from the "haves" to the "have-nots" will help promote competitive balance.

How badly does MLB want true competitive balance? Conventional wisdom says that in the absence of competitive balance, fans of disadvantaged, under-performing teams will eventually lose interest. The lack of fan interest will cut into revenues through lower attendance, higher sensitivity to ticket prices and lower broadcast ratings. It will ultimately threaten the very existence of those franchises. If a team has virtually no realistic chance of competing for a postseason berth, then the regular season games become an exhibition rather than a competitive contest. Fans of an exhibition would likely be less loyal and therefore less willing to forego alternative events to attend or watch broadcasts of the team's games or bear ticket price increases.

On the other hand, if MLB had true competitive balance and teams in large media markets (e.g., the Yankees, Mets, Dodgers, Cubs, etc.) did not have a better-than-fair chance to reach the postseason, how might national broadcast contracts be affected? The viewing audience for the postseason, and ultimately the networks' ability to command advertising dollars, is closely related to the size of the market of the play-off teams. A World Series between Kansas City and Pittsburgh, would likely draw far fewer viewers than a Yankees-Dodgers matchup or a Mets-Cubs pairing. (Excluding the magical journey of the 2004 Red Sox, there is a .93 correlation between the national television ratings for the World Series and the size of the markets of the participating teams, from 2001-2005.) Is MLB's total revenue base higher if larger market teams have a built in advantage to reach the postseason, and are the Royals and Pirates better off collecting their share of a larger national broadcast deal, rather than having a level playing field? By virtue of the approach MLB has taken, maybe we can conclude that the illusion of competitive balance is better than the real thing.

GM in a Box: John Schuerholz

by Mac Thomason

In last year's Annual, Brian Gunn reviewed Walt Jocketty's record as General Manager of the St. Louis Cardinals. Using a format similar to Bill James's old "Manager in a Box," Brian sought not to judge Jocketty, but to describe his tendencies, preferences, likes and dislikes.

Brian's article was very well-received, and we're pleased that Mac Thomason agreed to approach Braves General Manager John Schuerholz in the same manner for this year's Annual.

Record and Background

Age: 65

Previous Organizations:

1967-68: Orioles, administrative assistant to Farm Director Lou Gorman. The general manager was Harry Dalton.

1969-90: Royals, various roles in the minor league operations (under Gorman and general manager Cedric Tallis), rising to farm director (1976 under Gorman and general manager Joe Burke) and director of scouting (1977-80); assistant general manager (1981); general manager (1982-1990).

Years of service with current organization: 16 (longest in majors)

Cumulative record: 2,185-1,633, .572 winning percentage (Braves: 1,431-931, .606)

Did he play professional baseball, and if so, what type of player was he? Schuerholz never played professional ball; he was an infielder at Towson State, but he says that scouts thought that he was too small to play professionally.

Personnel and Philosophy

Any notable changes from the previous regime?

Well, they started winning every year instead of finishing last every year. In terms of *philosophy*, Schuerholz brought two major changes to the Braves:

Firstly, he brought a focus on defense. He signed three free agent position players before his first season with the team. They were all players whose value was largely (Terry Pendleton, Sid Bream) or entirely (Rafael Belliard) in defense. At the beginning of the season, he added a fourth glove man, Otis Nixon, via trade. Even

before them, he hired Ed Mangan as the head groundskeeper at Fulton County Stadium in an effort to keep the field there (then a multi-purpose stadium used for football and concerts) in better shape to help infielders. The Braves had been a poor defensive team for years; Schuerholz put an end to that, which played a huge role in the 1991 turnaround.

Secondly, he brought a new sense of professionalism into a lackadaisical and largely incompetent organization. Some of that was reflected in corporate-type things—always wearing ties and the like—but the Braves, very rapidly, took on the identity of their general manager.

What characterizes his relationship with ownership? What types of people does he hire to work under him? Is he more collaborative or authoritative?

A relationship with a corporate entity like Time-Warner is hard to establish. It seems that his closest relationship with a superior in the Braves organization was with Stan Kasten (Schuerholz was never an intimate of Ted Turner) and that he is not as close with any of the current people in charge, but that may just be perception. He was close with Ewing Kauffman in Kansas City.

Schuerholz is intensely collaborative, surrounding himself with skilled people, a trait that probably carries over from his very early days in the Orioles' front office (which had a ridiculous number of longtime baseball executives—Frank Cashen, Harry Dalton, Frank Lane, and Lou Gorman were among Schuerholz's superiors). He's had young people who've risen through the ranks, but has also hired some veteran baseball people who were out of jobs.

What kinds of managers does he hire? How closely does he work with them?

Schuerholz has never hired a manager with the Braves; he inherited Bobby Cox (also his predecessor as general manager) and the two have a close working relationship.

With the Royals, he inherited Dick Howser and would likely have stuck with him as well if not for Howser's brain tumor and death. He had a difficult time replacing Howser, going through Mike Ferraro and Billy Gardner before settling on John Wathan. Unlike the other managers, Wathan was a fairly young guy who had only recently retired as a player.

Player Development

How does he approach the amateur draft? Does he prefer major league-ready players or "projects?" Tools or performance? High schools or college? Pitchers or hitters?

From 1992 (his second draft with the team) to 2004, the Braves selected a high school player with their first pick *every year*. What's noticeable about these picks of high schoolers is that they never panned out. From 1992 to 2000, none of the Braves' first picks had a successful major league career. That seems to be changing; 2000 first rounder Adam Wainwright, traded to the Cardinals, should have some sort of a career, even if he comes short of stardom (Note: this was written before his postseason success). Their first pick in 2001, Macay McBride, should at least have a long career as a lefty specialist, and Jeff Francoeur, their first pick the next year, has a chance at stardom if he can achieve some semblance of plate discipline. Some of this change may have to do with the rise of Dayton Moore, now in Schuerholz's old job as Royals GM, as the head of player development in the Braves' organization.

In 2005, Joey Devine became the first college player picked first by the Braves since Mike Kelly in 1991, and he was in the big league bullpen by the end of the season.

The Braves have favored pitchers rather than hitters, and high school pitchers are a risky commodity. Another notable point is that they like to draft regionally and even locally. Nine of 11 first picks from 1992 to 2002 were Southerners (including Texans); three were from Georgia. Of the massive 2005 rookie class, six players (Francoeur, McBride, Brian McCann, Kyle Davies, Blaine Boyer and Chuck James) were high draft picks from the Atlanta area. There may be some carryover from the Royals, who also liked local talent.

Under Schuerholz, the Braves have been more successful with Latin American talent; he's chosen to focus there while mostly staying out of Asia. Javy Lopez, Andruw Jones, Rafael Furcal and Andy Marte are some of the results of the Braves' Latin American scouting. They've stayed away from the high-profile Cuban refugees, but signed a lot of younger Cuban players. The Braves have also been active in Australia, although they have relatively little to show for it so far except for one good year from Damian Moss.

Does he tend to rush guys to the majors or let them marinate?

Some of both. Some notable "rushed" players include Andruw Jones, Furcal, Francoeur and Devine. Jones started the 1996 season in Single-A ball and finished it in the World Series. Furcal won the shortstop job in Spring Training of 2000 with only a few weeks of experience above Single-A ball. Francoeur was promoted from Double-A even though he was far from a finished product and has had to do a lot of on-the-job training in the bigs. As for Devine, see above.

However, sometimes Schuerholz has left a player in Triple-A maybe a bit longer than he should have—Marcus Giles comes to mind. Generally, the players who have been rushed have been great athletes who supposedly could survive as unfinished products, while the players who have marinated in Richmond have been less toolsy. What he *won't* do is push a player into the big leagues only to sit on the bench (except for September callups or as a short-term stopgap); there is a stated desire for the young players to play. If a young player is kept on the major league bench (or a young starter in the bullpen) before he's out of options, that's a sign that the Braves don't see him as a regular (or a starter).

Roster Construction

Are there any types of players of whom he's especially fond? Does he like proven players or youngsters? Offensive players or glovemen? Power pitchers or finesse guys?

One type of player that's noticeable as a Schuerholz staple isn't actually a type of baseball player exactly—he loves football players. Three players of the 1980s and 1990s had significant careers in both the major leagues and NFL: Bo Jackson, Deion Sanders and Brian Jordan. All played for Schuerholz, who drafted Jackson with the Royals, signed Sanders off the scrap heap as a utility outfielder in 1991 during the pennant chase, and signed Jordan to a big free agent contract in 1999. Francoeur was a first-round pick he signed away from a football scholarship, George Lombard was a second-round pick he signed away from another scholarship, and Chad Hutchinson was a first-round pick he *couldn't* sign away from football. The Braves also spent low-round draft picks on Terrell Buckley (who actually played in the minors for a time) and Mark Brunell, several failed high draft picks who eventually went back to football, and others less famous than Buckley and Brunell who stayed with football.

As you'd expect from the football obsession, Schuerholz likes speed, a trait going back to the Kansas City days when they at times had three centerfield types on the field at once. The Braves drafted *a lot* of guys who could run in the '90s; the best of them turned out to be Lombard, who wasn't actually any good. However, this pattern hasn't been particularly evident with major league acquisitions (through trade and free agency), many of whom have been downright slow.

What the major league acquisitions tended to have in common is defensive skill. As mentioned above, he acquired four glove men within a few months of taking the job. For that matter, of his four most prominent free agent acquisitions, three (Pendleton, Greg Maddux, and Andres Galarraga) were Gold Glove winners, and the fourth (Jordan) maybe should have been one. To that you can add lesser lights acquired as free agents such as Walt Weiss, Belliard, and Bream.

The Braves offense tends to be more based on power than on anything else, while the pitching staff has been based upon minimizing the other team's power. It's hard to say what's due to Schuerholz and what's due to Cox (or Leo Mazzone, the pitching coach every year of that partnership until 2006), but the Braves, while rarely leading the league, usually were among the league leaders in homers, and they always allowed relatively few homers. (As part of a general pitching collapse this past season, the Braves allowed the sixth-most homers in the National League, suggesting it was largely Mazzone.) You can win a lot of games like that, especially if you have a good defense behind the pitchers, who mostly follow a put-it-in-play philosophy.

Schuerholz prefers to promote players from within, but if he doesn't have a quality player to fill a hole in the farm system, he prefers to acquire veterans, even if those veterans aren't really that much better than the internal solution. Basically, if a young player has star ability he'll get every chance, but Schuerholz would prefer an established mediocrity to risking a young player who *might* be good but *might* be a disaster. In recent years, he's been a little more willing to plug in a youngster, but that may be more because of lack of finances than choice.

Does he tend to allocate resources primarily on impact players or role players? How does he flesh out his bullpen and his bench? Does he often work the waiver wire or sign minor league free agents or make Rule 5 picks?

A relative few players—mostly All-Star-level players like the Joneses, Smoltz, Hudson and Hampton—have eaten up most of the Braves' payroll in recent years. It's particularly extreme right now, because the team is playing so many first- and second-year players who make little more than the minimum. When Schuerholz was allowed to spend more money, he was willing to spend relatively large amounts on players who weren't a whole lot better than free alternatives, but he's cut out most of those players. This has hurt the bullpen but probably helped the bench, because instead of mediocre veterans, talented youngsters are filling the end of the roster.

As I'll cover in a minute, Schuerholz hasn't signed many big-ticket free agents, but he has had a lot of success with fringe free agents and trade throw-ins. The Braves have gotten big years from players no one else wanted, like Chris Hammond and John Burkett.

When will he release players? On whom has he given up? To whom has he given a shot? Does he cut bait early or late?

He's usually reluctant to just give up on a player signed to a major league contract, but if a young player is available and makes himself impossible to ignore, sometimes Schuerholz will jettison a veteran to make room. A couple of examples: Ozzie Guillen was cut late in Spring Training when Rafael Furcal burst on the scene. In 2005, Raul Mondesi was so bad that there was no choice but to get rid of him and bring up Kelly Johnson.

Defining "giving up on" can be hard. Was Ryan Klesko "given up on" or just traded in what turned out to be a bad deal? Bret Boone, also dealt in that deal, pretty clearly was given up on. Schuerholz and Cox eventually got sick of dealing with Deion Sanders and traded him. Schuerholz made no real effort to retain Kenny Lofton as a free agent, and he traded Jermaine Dye after his rookie season. He's hung with a lot of guys (Mark Wohlers comes to mind) long after everyone else had given up. Some prospects (e.g. Mike Kelly) have hung on long past their sell-by date, but he's managed to get some good work out of some (e.g. Wilson Betemit) who seemed busts.

A lot of fringe veterans have gotten last shots with the Braves, some of them with remarkable success (see Hammond and Burkett above.) The Braves have had lots of success with pitchers nobody thought were major league material, such as Rudy Seanez (out of the majors for two years before being signed before the 1998 season—the Braves got three good years out of him and he's still pitching), Kerry Ligtenberg (acquired from a Northern League team for equipment), Greg

McMichael, and Ken Ray. Relatively few position players have surprised, and a lot of this success may be due to Leo Mazzone and/or the Braves' minor league development system.

Is he active or passive? An optimist or a problem solver? Does he tend to want to win now or wait out the success cycle?

There hasn't been any "success cycle" in Atlanta, of course; it's just been success, until the 2006 season. He'll trade a prospect to get a veteran, and he's generally done a magnificent job of doing so; few prospects have come back to bite him later, and most of those have happened only years after the trade. He is a more aggressive trader when he can afford to take on salary, but he'll usually add a player late in the year. Overall, it's a sort of "aggressive patience"—he'll wait for someone who is likely to come around, but if the incumbent isn't likely to get any better, he'll make the move. He's been accused of trying too hard to keep the winning streak going, giving up prospects for short-term gains.

Does he favor players acquired via trade, development or free agency?

The bias is to development; most of the Braves' (and the Royals') best players have been native sons. The current team is mostly homegrown talent—old stars (Smoltz, the Joneses and Giles) mixed with a lot of young players. Edgar Renteria was the only regular on the 2006 team not developed by the Braves, though more pitchers are from outside.

When it comes to acquiring veterans, the preference has been to make trades. Some of the better players he's traded for include Fred McGriff, Denny Neagle, Marquis Grissom, Kenny Lofton, Gary Sheffield, J.D. Drew, Johnny Estrada, Tim Hudson and Renteria.

However, his periodic forays into the free agency market have been remarkably successful. He's only signed four top-tier free agents in Atlanta (none in the last five years), but all were big wins. Greg Maddux ranks among the most valuable free agent signings of all time, winning three Cy Young Awards in his time in Atlanta and ranking as the best National League pitcher of the 1990s. Terry Pendleton won the MVP in his first year in Atlanta and was actually better his second year. Andres Galarraga missed the second year of his three-year contract, but in the other two seasons he made the All-Star team. Brian Jordan made one All-Star team in three solid years and then was traded for Sheffield.

One group of players to throw in here is, well, throw-ins. The last player in the deal that brought Bret Boone to Atlanta was Mike Remlinger; Remlinger was by far the most valuable player in the deal to the team acquiring him, giving the Braves four years of top-notch middle relief. (He is probably the best reliever the franchise has had in the Schuerholz regime.)

He's had other successes that were less spectacular but still notable. Though the Braves never got much out of him, they got Joe Borowski when Schuerholz salary-dumped Kent Mercker in 1995. When they gave up on Greg McMichael (pretty much a salary dump as he was entering arbitration) in 1996, he got Paul Byrd in exchange. The Braves generally know what they're doing when it comes to picking guys out of other teams' systems, even if they don't always know themselves how to make use of the talent they receive.

Trades and Free Agents

Is he an active trader? Does he tend to move talent or horde it? To whom does he trade and when?

He's a fairly active trader who makes a major trade or two a year and a blockbuster (McGriff, Neagle, Sheffield, Hampton, Hudson) every few years. Schuerholz's tendency is to fill holes via trade, rather than free agency; since the bullpen is where you're most likely to have a hole (especially with today's seven-man bullpens), he ends up trading a lot of prospects for a lot of relievers. A typical trade would be two pitching prospects for one established setup man who's fallen into the closer role. In 2004-05 he made three trades of just this type, for Chris Reitsma, Dan Kolb and Kyle Farnsworth. Normally this doesn't hurt, because most of the pitching prospects flame out as pitching prospects do, but then a Zach Miner (traded for Farnsworth) goes 7-6 with the Tigers when you're down to using Lance Cormier and Kevin Barry to patch rotation holes, and you don't feel so hot.

But consider the five blockbuster additions I listed above. The three players traded for McGriff (Mel Nieves, Donnie Elliot and Vince Moore) were all legitimate prospects, and Nieves was an A or B+ prospect; none of them panned out. The only really good player Schuerholz traded to get those five players is Jason Schmidt, and he didn't break through until he joined the Giants, five years after the deal. He's lost a few good players in trades, but not many compared to the number of good players he's added.

He's made a few trades of veteran players, but usually for salary reasons. Grissom and Justice were traded for Kenny Lofton because Schuerholz needed to conserve to pay for extensions of Maddux and Glavine. Kevin Millwood was traded because the Braves were over their imposed payroll limit.

As I mentioned above, in recent seasons, a few people think that Schuerholz was trying a little *too* hard to keep the division streak going, trading off core prospects for more marginal improvements, or (most notably) giving up six seasons of Adam Wainwright as part of the deal for one season of J. D. Drew. Schuerholz thought he could re-sign Drew at a discount but failed to take Scott Boras into account. Drew had a great season in Atlanta and made himself a lot of money, but they sure could use Wainwright now.

Unlike minor leaguers, he's been known to horde major league talent for depth rather than deal it at a loss. He could have dealt John Thomson, who was pushed out of the rotation, for needed relief help or a right-handed bat this spring, but he held onto Thomson; after a few good starts he turned ineffective and then got hurt. There are a number of examples of this, of players held onto just long enough to lose most of their value.

Will he make deals with other teams during the season? How does he usually approach the trading deadline?

He'll usually make one or two deals in July or August, most often for relief help. McGriff is basically the only major hitter added during the season under Schuerholz; since it was one of the greatest in-season deals ever made, it doesn't need any help. Neagle (who came in as a waiver deal) is the most prominent starting pitcher he's added, though there have been one or two others. Generally, though, it's been for relievers. Beginning in 1991 (when Alejandro Pena came over and put the bullpen on his back for the last two months of the season) and continuing to 2006 (with the additions of Bob Wickman and Danys Baez) Schuerholz usually adds one or two relievers a year. This may just be because the bullpen is usually in flux. Sometimes he'll also add a veteran outfielder as a bench bat, less often now than in the 1990s.

Are there any teams or general managers with whom he trades frequently?

Not really. He's made more trades with the Reds (under, I believe, three different general managers) than with anyone else. Schuerholz is more willing than most general managers to trade within his division and has made trades (involving major leaguers) with all four NL East teams since the advent of three-division play. The trade of Millwood to the Phillies was controversial, to say the least.

Under what circumstances will he sign free agents?

Today, only if they're cheap. When he had a big payroll to work with, he made sporadic splashes in the free agent market but even then preferred to trade for players.

He signed a lot of free agents in 1991, but then he had a lot of holes and was trying to make over the team in his own image. Since then, free agents have not necessarily been to fill a hole. The Braves didn't really *need* Maddux in 1993, what with an established rotation of Glavine-Smoltz-Avery-Leibrandt, but they could use the upgrade, and then sent Leibrandt packing for a prospect. His signings of Galarraga and Jordan were basically to fill holes on a team that was thin at the left end of the defensive spectrum and at a time when he was looking for right-handed power.

The only player on the 2006 roster acquired as a major league free agent was John Thomson, who was signed in 2004 to a two-year deal with an option. The only major league free agent acquired since Thomson was Raul Mondesi in 2005, and he was cut in the middle of that season.

Contracts

Does he prefer long-term deals or short? Does he backload his contracts very often? Does he lock up players early in their careers or is he more likely to practice brinksmanship? Does he like to avoid arbitration?

Short-term, for the most part. The Braves lost Tom Glavine basically because they wouldn't add a year to his deal. But other than Glavine, keystone players (Smoltz, Chipper Jones, Andruw Jones, even Glavine when he was younger) have often been signed to deals taking them five or more years out. The Braves have also extended some of these players as part of renegotiations to save money in the present; Chipper's deal in particular has been edited more than once.

While Schuerholz has had backloaded contracts in recent years (Tim Hudson in particular, but also a few other players), I don't believe he actually prefers this; he's done it out of necessity. The imposed cap has forced him to look ahead in a way he probably would not like to. During the 1990s, players were signed to contracts that slowly built up.

Schuerholz doesn't generally practice the John Hart policy of locking up players' arbitration years. He does try to avoid arbitration via a settlement, but his typical signing would be to take a player with a year or two of arbitration left and *then* sign him for four or five years, a la David Justice or the Joneses.

Anything unique about his negotiating tactics? Is he vocal? Does he prefer to work behind the scense or through the media?

In recent seasons, Schuerholz has tended to be more vocal. Perhaps this is because he's more the face of the franchise since Stan Kasten's departure, maybe it's just cranky old man syndrome, but it seems like not a free agency period goes by without either Schuerholz complaining about a player or a player complaining about him. The free agency departures of Tom Glavine, J.D. Drew, and Kyle Farnsworth all involved either one side or the other complaining about lack of communication or even out-and-out lying. Early in the 2006 season, Glavine, long since departed to the Mets, complained about Schuerholz's depiction of his departure in *Built To Win*. It may be significant that Glavine was a longtime Brave and Drew and Farnsworth are Georgians; Schuerholz felt that he could sign all three for a discount and could not.

This isn't a tactic, but he doesn't like to negotiate during the season—though he made an exception for Maddux and Glavine when their first extensions with the team came up.

Bonus

What is his strongest point as a GM?

Professionalism. The Braves of the 1980s were a mockable organization; people openly questioned why Schuerholz would leave Kansas City for Atlanta, of all places. The Braves succeeded the Royals as baseball's most stable and corporate of franchises at just that time. Schuerholz didn't establish that in Kansas City, but he brought it to Atlanta just as it was fading. I personally think that things such as requiring jacket and tie while traveling are silly, but Schuerholz believes in it and it's all part of the style he employs.

The Braves have a reputation in baseball for being cold, even robotic, in their professionalism. In some ways that's not fair, but in a lot of ways it is, and that's the way Schuerholz likes it. Is Bobby Cox the reason that the Braves underachieved in postseason, or is John Schuerholz? Is it a manager who can't adjust to a different style of play, or a team full of even-keel types who couldn't turn on the emotions to reach higher when the stakes rose? The Braves won 14 division titles in a row by taking one game at a time and realizing that most of those games are equally important, and that the season is a marathon, not a sprint. The postseason is a sprint. Maybe Schuerholz's shit doesn't work in postseason any more than Billy Beane's does.

At any event, Schuerholz's professional style has been wildly successful. It's when he gets personal—as in the recent free agency sniping – that he has problems.

What would he be doing if he weren't in baseball?

He was a schoolteacher before he talked his way into the Orioles' front office. I'm guessing that after a few years he would have gone into administration and would now be wrapping up his 20th and final year as a principal of a high school in Maryland and getting ready for a well-earned retirement.

A primary source for this article was Built To Win, by Schuerholz with Larry Guest, published by Warner Books.

History

The Most Valuable Pitchers of All Time

by David Gassko

I've always been a fan of pitching. My favorite player growing up was Pedro Martinez, and he still is. When I bought *The New Bill James Historical Abstract* (sorry, wasn't alive for the original), the first section I turned to was his pitcher ratings. My first foray into sabermetrics was an embarrassingly sad formula for evaluating pitchers. It's hidden somewhere deep in the archives of the interweb, and I pray no one ever sees it. Since then, I've worked hard on coming up with a system that works.

I am about to present a system for rating pitchers that, in my opinion, does indeed work. More importantly, I think it is highly logical, and if you buy into the logic of the system, then you have no choice but to buy into the results. You're probably going to disagree with many of the numbers and ratings I provide here, and it's understandable why. But intuitively, the math makes sense, and I think that if you really think about it hard, so do the ratings. And if you love Bert Blyleven, then this article is for you.

The Method

So how do I determine the value of a pitcher? Let's start by asking a simpler question: What can a pitcher do to contribute to a win or a loss? The answer is simple: prevent runs. The fewer runs a pitcher allows, the better his team's chances of winning; that's simple enough. So let's start with that.

But there are plenty of factors that can affect the number of runs a pitcher allows like park, defense and the quality of competition; we have to adjust for those factors as well to come up with a proper pitcher valuation. Adjusting for park effects is simple enough, so I'll focus on how I do the latter two.

Defense. We can get a good measure of a team's fielders by calculating its Defensive Efficiency, the percentage of balls in play that the defense converts into outs. This is not a new discovery; Bill James wrote about it almost 30 years ago. What is a newer discovery is the controversial Defense Independent Pitching Statistics (DIPS) theory, postulated by Voros McCracken, which states that pitchers have little if any control over the results of their balls in play. Essentially, the batting average on balls put into play against

a pitcher, according to DIPS, is purely a combination of luck and fielding—it has nothing to do with the pitcher.

I've decided to go with a much weaker version of that theory. I credit a pitcher for his batting average on balls in play, but I remove the difference between the batting average on balls in play allowed by the team's fielders and the league average. Essentially, this allows me to control for the quality of the team's defense, while leaving the luck component in there. I don't know if it is a perfect solution, but I'm not the first to think of it, and to me, at least, it makes sense.

Quality of competition. This one is a little bit tougher. First, let's be clear on what I mean by quality of competition. I do not mean the quality of batters a pitcher has faced, as opposed to the league average or anything like that, though this is what is normally meant when people talk about the quality of competition. I am talking about the quality of the league that determines the pitcher's statistics.

Let's say a pitcher has a 4.00 ERA. What does that number mean? Nothing, really, without context. If he has a 4.00 ERA in 2006, well then he's pretty damn good. If he has a 4.00 ERA in 1968, that's terrible! A player's quality is directly tied to the baseline with which is he is being compared.

The baseline in 1968 was different from the one in 2006 in a couple of ways. First of all, teams scored runs at a much lower pace in '68, making a 4.00 ERA much less valuable than in '06.

Secondly (and more to the point), the pool of talent from which Major League Baseball drew its players was markedly smaller 40 years ago. The U.S. population was smaller in general, and we didn't have the influx of Latin American players we have today, let alone players from Asia. And if you compare today's pitchers to those who pitched in the era before integration, you're talking about an even larger difference in available talent.

Simply put, a pitcher who won 60 percent of his games in 1968 would not win 60 percent of his games in 2006, because he would be matched up against better pitchers. In 2006, we have huge baseball academies all over Latin America, Asian players coming to the major leagues, and even better scouting in the United

States. If I'm going to be fair to pitchers who pitch in the modern era, well, I have to adjust for that.

How do I adjust? That's where the issue gets mucky. There are a few different systems out there that try to generate such adjustments, but because I like doing things my own way, I've devised my own. I don't claim that it's the best, but I'm not sure that it isn't either.

My era adjustments are entirely dependent on two things: the population from which major league baseball players are drawn and the number of regular starters in the league. I won't bore you with the math, but a simple explanation is in order. First, I calculate the difference in runs allowed between the theoretical best pitcher in a league in a given year and a replacement-level pitcher, based on the number of "regular" pitchers in the league. I then calculate the same theoretical difference between a replacement-level pitcher and the average person in the population from which MLB is drawing. We count a country's population as part of the MLB population once at least three pitchers from that country have pitched in the majors in the same season. (I also subtract the black population from the U.S. population prior to integration.) The population is cut in half because women don't play professional baseball.

Essentially, my assumption is that the average person in a population has equivalent baseball talent across the years. The further away a replacement-level player is from that "average person" in the population, the higher the quality of major league competition. To find the adjustment for each era, we calculate this difference in runs and add it to a replacement player's run average. From 1901 to 2005, this produces the following graph:

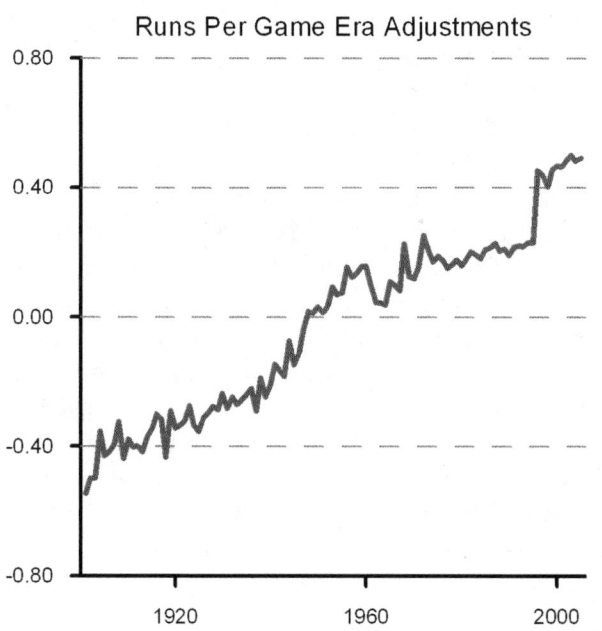

Runs Per Game Era Adjustments

As you can see, the quality of play has increased steadily over the past 100-plus years. The numbers prior to 1901 are wacky because the leagues were small and weren't really drawing players from across the country. The scouting system was poor and many baseball players were not really worthy of being professionals. So I have fitted a trend line to this data and extended it back to 1871. The numbers given by that trend line are what I use for the era adjustments; they also smooth out small changes in the data that don't really represent anything.

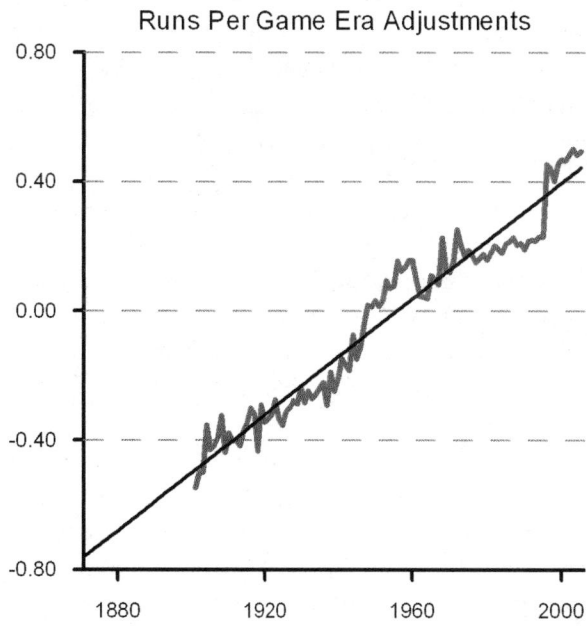

Runs Per Game Era Adjustments

Park. This one is pretty obvious. I adjust each pitcher's run average for park. This does somewhat double count the adjustment for defensive efficiency (because some parks cause more or fewer hits on balls in play), but the effect is not great.

Finally, I take the pitcher's adjusted runs allowed average and compute his expected winning percentage in a season given an average offense for that league and year, using a variation of Bill James' Pythagorean record, known as Pythagenpat. His expected winning percentage is then multiplied by innings and divided by nine to calculate Pitching Wins. Pitching Losses are equivalent to one minus the pitcher's expected winning percentage, multiplied by innings pitched and divided by nine.

Finally, Pitching Wins above Replacement (pWAR) are calculated by comparing the pitcher to an era-dependent replacement-level winning percentage. The historical average replacement level is .410, which is one standard deviation below an average pitcher. But the replacement level gets lower and lower as time goes on (from about .470

to .365), which is how I incorporate the era adjustment into my system.

Career Rankings

On the next page there is a list of the top 100 pitchers in the history of the game based on Pitching Wins above Replacement prior to the 2006 season. I want to make it clear that this is not a list of the 100 greatest pitchers of all time, or the 100 best, or the 100 handsomest; it is simply a list of the 100 pitchers who provided the most value over their careers. Longevity is rewarded heavily in these rankings, because no matter how good you are over half a decade, a pitcher half as good will have as much or more value over his career. It's easiest to think about this in monetary terms: Sandy Koufax was great, but for about four years. How much would you have paid him for his performance between 1963 and 1966 (in modern cash, of course)? $20 million a year? $25 million? A decent pitcher these days will get $8 million a year; it would take him 12-and-a-half seasons to match Koufax's total value. Few can pitch effectively for that long, but those who do rank high on my list. It doesn't make them better than Koufax ever was.

I'd like to review each group of 10, explaining why a player ranks where he does and providing a little commentary whenever it strikes my fancy. I hope that the following list provides a step forward in objectively valuing pitchers in a historical context and re-ignites at least a few arguments about the greatest pitchers of all time. They might be futile, but I still find them enjoyable…

The Most Valuable Pitchers: 1-10

Rank	First	Last	pWAR
1	Roger	Clemens	153
2	Walter	Johnson	140
3	Cy	Young	138
4	Greg	Maddux	123
5	Pete	Alexander	117
6	Tom	Seaver	116
7	Bert	Blyleven	113
8	Randy	Johnson	110
9	Steve	Carlton	107
10	Lefty	Grove	106

Clemens, Maddux, Blyleven and Randy Johnson? Is that era adjustment too great? Not at all.

It's key to understand that a pitcher's record is really just his performance compared to the performance of all other pitchers in the league. Per inning, Lefty Grove has a slightly better park-adjusted ERA versus his league than Johnson, and he pitched about 400 more innings (not including 2006). But, when we say that Grove was better than Johnson on a per-inning basis, we're comparing Grove to his contemporaries. So if the average pitcher is worse in Grove's time, Grove will look better.

Now think about it: Johnson and Clemens compete against Pedro Martinez (18th all-time), Johan Santana, Dontrelle Willis—guys who would not have pitched in Grove's time. If Johnson and Clemens didn't have to compete against foreign-born or black pitchers, just think of how much better they'd be.

Replacement level varies by year, based on the quality of the competition. The more players competing, and the fewer spots they're competing for, the better a replacement-level player will be. If we were to exclude foreign-born or black players from the major leagues, they would be replaced by a bunch of Triple-A pitchers and long relievers. But then, if a pitcher got injured, his replacement would be much worse, because the guys who were the best Triple-A pitchers and long relievers would now be major league regulars. I adjust for this by adjusting run average. How accurate are the adjustments?

Without adjusting for era, foreign-born pitchers in 2005 were 130 Pitching Wins above Replacement. That's 130 wins that American pitchers are not going to get, since the number of wins in the league is limited to 2,430. That's a difference of .054 wins per game; my era adjustments say that the quality of competition today is .056 wins per game better than it was in 1930, when Grove was in his prime. Factor in the performance of black pitchers in 2005, and if anything, I'm not adjusting enough!

And why shouldn't Clemens rank ahead of Walter Johnson and Cy Young? Young's career was over in 1911, Johnson's in 1927. Have there really been no pitchers more valuable than those two in the 80 years since? I find that hard to believe. What is more astonishing is that we're seeing so many great pitchers at the tail ends of their careers right now. Clemens, Maddux, Johnson, Martinez, and Tom Glavine all fall into the top 20 of the all-time rankings. Is that excessive? Not at all, if you ask me. Even before the 2006 season, four of these pitchers fell into the top 40 all-time in wins, which is extremely impressive given

The Hardball Times Baseball Annual 2007

Rank	First	Last	Debut	pW	pL	pWAR	Rank	First	Last	Debut	pW	pL	pWAR
1	Roger	Clemens	1984	348	175	153	51	Billy	Pierce	1945	211	157	63
2	Walter	Johnson	1907	425	232	140	52	David	Wells	1987	195	161	62
3	Cy	Young	1890	504	313	138	53	Tim	Keefe	1880	320	241	62
4	Greg	Maddux	1986	306	184	123	54	Dazzy	Vance	1915	201	128	61
5	Pete	Alexander	1911	366	211	117	55	Ted	Lyons	1923	256	207	61
6	Tom	Seaver	1967	322	210	116	56	Orel	Hershiser	1983	192	156	61
7	Bert	Blyleven	1970	326	227	113	57	Early	Wynn	1939	266	241	61
8	Randy	Johnson	1988	258	141	110	58	Red	Faber	1914	255	199	60
9	Steve	Carlton	1965	332	248	107	59	Eppa	Rixey	1912	274	225	60
10	Lefty	Grove	1925	291	147	106	60	Mickey	Lolich	1963	218	187	59
11	Phil	Niekro	1964	336	265	103	61	Frank	Viola	1982	179	137	59
12	Gaylord	Perry	1962	331	263	100	62	Larry	Jackson	1955	203	159	59
13	Fergie	Jenkins	1965	292	208	97	63	Dennis	Martinez	1976	227	218	58
14	Warren	Spahn	1942	331	252	96	64	Sandy	Koufax	1955	161	98	58
15	Christy	Mathewson	1900	330	201	96	65	Dwight	Gooden	1984	175	136	58
16	Bob	Gibson	1959	263	169	93	66	Bob	Friend	1951	218	183	58
17	Nolan	Ryan	1966	321	277	91	67	Ed	Walsh	1904	202	128	57
18	Pedro	Martinez	1992	194	85	91	68	Jimmy	Key	1984	165	123	56
19	Tom	Glavine	1987	252	187	89	69	Kenny	Rogers	1989	174	144	56
20	Kid	Nichols	1890	341	221	88	70	Steve	Rogers	1973	177	138	56
21	Robin	Roberts	1948	295	226	85	71	Jamie	Moyer	1986	185	164	55
22	Curt	Schilling	1988	203	120	83	72	Mark	Langston	1984	179	150	55
23	Don	Sutton	1966	309	278	82	73	Tommy	Bridges	1930	186	128	55
24	Jim	Palmer	1965	251	188	80	74	Milt	Pappas	1957	194	160	54
25	Mike	Mussina	1991	203	132	79	75	Wilbur	Wood	1961	171	128	54
26	Dennis	Eckersley	1975	218	147	78	76	Bobo	Newsom	1929	227	190	54
27	Rick	Reuschel	1972	230	165	78	77	Hoyt	Wilhelm	1952	154	97	54
28	Kevin	Brown	1986	212	150	77	78	Ron	Guidry	1975	156	110	54
29	Tommy	John	1963	279	245	76	79	Jack	Morris	1977	215	210	53
30	Luis	Tiant	1964	227	161	76	80	Red	Ruffing	1924	256	227	53
31	Eddie	Plank	1901	295	204	75	81	Jack	Quinn	1909	240	195	53
32	Jim	Bunning	1955	240	177	75	82	Vida	Blue	1969	196	175	53
33	John	Smoltz	1988	195	130	74	83	Vic	Willis	1898	250	194	53
34	Carl	Hubbell	1928	237	162	70	84	Eddie	Cicotte	1905	208	150	52
35	Bob	Feller	1936	243	182	68	85	Joe	McGinnity	1899	222	160	52
36	Bret	Saberhagen	1984	175	110	68	86	Al	Spalding	1871	203	118	52
37	David	Cone	1986	188	134	67	87	Rube	Waddell	1897	198	131	52
38	Hal	Newhouser	1939	203	129	67	88	Charlie	Hough	1970	213	210	52
39	Frank	Tanana	1973	245	221	67	89	Dizzy	Trout	1939	176	127	52
40	Jim	Kaat	1959	264	240	66	90	Danny	Darwin	1978	178	157	52
41	Jerry	Koosman	1967	232	195	66	91	Dutch	Leonard	1933	199	158	52
42	Don	Drysdale	1956	218	164	66	92	Mordecai	Brown	1903	207	146	51
43	Chuck	Finley	1986	199	156	66	93	Charley	Radbourn	1880	282	221	51
44	Whitey	Ford	1950	207	146	66	94	Brad	Radke	1995	144	110	50
45	Juan	Marichal	1960	219	171	65	95	John	Candelaria	1975	158	123	50
46	Stan	Coveleski	1912	211	131	64	96	Bob	Welch	1978	181	163	50
47	John	Clarkson	1882	294	210	64	97	Jim	Perry	1959	194	171	50
48	Dave	Stieb	1979	186	136	64	98	Virgil	Trucks	1941	171	127	50
49	Pud	Galvin	1875	371	296	63	99	Babe	Adams	1906	194	138	50
50	Kevin	Appier	1989	170	118	63	100	Waite	Hoyt	1918	227	191	49

the decreased number of innings pitchers throw today and the improving quality of competition. Martinez does not yet rank that high in wins, but he has been by far the greatest starting pitcher on a per-inning basis in the history of the game. Grove's ranking might seem a little low, but he's 10th all-time in pitching Win Shares, so I think it's actually just right.

Of course, I can't move on without mentioning Bert Blyleven's rank. I've done these rankings a dozen different times, with the math changing somewhat every time. I've done them with no era adjustment, with severe adjustments, adjusting for defense, without adjusting for defense, and so on and so forth. And there has been no list on which Blyleven has fallen out of the top 20 or even, I think, the top 15. It has become clear to me that Blyleven is not only a Hall of Famer but one of the greatest pitchers of all time. Even if we look at pitching wins above average instead of above replacement to give more weight to great performance and less to longevity, Blyleven still ranks near the top. If there's one thing I've learned from this project it is that even those arguing for his inclusion in the Hall of Fame have greatly underestimated Blyleven as a pitcher.

Sidebar: Where They Came From

Here is the list of countries whose populations count as part of the MLB population, and the year in which they are first included:

Country	Year
USA	1871
Canada	1883
Cuba	1920
Puerto Rico	1955
Dominican Republic	1960
Mexico	1968
Venezuela	1980
Nicaragua	1982
Australia	1996
Japan	1996
Panama	1997
South Korea	1999

The Most Valuable Pitchers: 11-20

Rank	First	Last	pWAR
11	Phil	NIekro	103
12	Gaylord	Perry	100
13	Fergie	Jenkins	97
14	Warren	Spahn	96
15	Christy	Mathewson	96
16	Bob	Gibson	93
17	Nolan	Ryan	91
18	Pedro	Martinez	91
19	Tom	Glavine	89
20	Kid	Nichols	88

Ryan has become somewhat underrated by particular stat-conscious fans. Sure, he holds the all-time record in walks, but that only puts a damper on his strikeout record; it does not negate it. Ryan's walks and strikeouts were worth -.56 runs per game; that's around a third of a run better than the average pitcher in Ryan's day in what I like to call umpire-related events. Of course, if Ryan is somewhat underrated by saber-types, he's more overrated by the people who want to suggest he is the greatest pitcher of all time. (Yes, they exist.) He never even won a Cy Young award!

The Most Valuable Pitchers: 21-30

Rank	First	Last	pWAR
21	Robin	Roberts	85
22	Curt	Schilling	83
23	Don	Sutton	82
24	Jim	Palmer	80
25	Mike	Mussina	79
26	Dennis	Eckersley	78
27	Rick	Reuschel	78
28	Kevin	Brown	77
29	Tommy	John	76
30	Luis	Tiant	76

First on Reuschel. Bill James in the *New Historical Abstract* ranks him 81st among all pitchers. Other lists have him about as low or nowhere at all. So what gives? Of the 10 most similar players to Reuschel, two are Hall of Famers and the rest of the list is populated by pretty good players in their own right. Between 1973 and

1980 Reuschel pitched 230 innings in each year, and he was pretty good doing it too. He finished third in Cy Young voting in 1977 and again in 1987. He was an All-Star three times.

Reuschel's record is obscured by a few facts. He played on some pretty bad teams—he did not get to the postseason until after his eight-year peak. He only had two seasons in which he was great; in one, he played for a team that lost 104 games and scored 568 runs all season, and in the other he played in a park that inflated his ERA by almost half a run. And though his peak came in the mid-to-late 70s, Reuschel had another good five-year run in the late 1980s.

Sidebar: Who had the best fielders?

Which pitchers have been helped most by their defense? Which have been hurt the most? Negative means a good defense, positive means a poor one:

Rank	Pitcher	Fielding Runs vs. Average
1.	Kid Nichols	-261.13
2.	Tim Keefe	-208.96
3.	Charley Radbourn	-208.00
4.	Al Spalding	-193.93
5.	George Bradley	-168.11
6.	Mickey Welch	-157.56
7.	John Clarkson	-156.18
8.	Jim Palmer	-155.97
9.	Will White	-155.78
10.	Silver King	-152.87

Rank	Pitcher	Fielding Runs vs. Average
1.	Bill Stearns	159.51
2.	Pud Galvin	146.99
3.	Win Mercer	140.02
4.	Stump Wiedman	135.91
5.	John Coleman	133.25
6.	Kid Carsey	123.85
7.	Case Patten	119.43
8.	Jim Whitney	113.56
9.	Ned Garver	102.59
10.	Claude Passeau	97.78

Reuschel was never *perceived* to be a great pitcher, and he wasn't so consistent as to get noticed for that either. But for two decades, Reuschel ate innings and pitched well; in a set of rankings like these, that's going to get rewarded.

Brown and Mussina I'll tackle together. They have both pitched almost 1,000 more innings than Sandy Koufax, with almost the same effectiveness. Koufax is regularly rated in the top 10 and never outside the top 20 among the greatest pitchers that ever lived. So why shouldn't these two rank only somewhat further down? The answer, of course, is that Koufax had one of the greatest peaks in the history of the game. And while I won't argue with that fact, I would argue that it wasn't *that* much better than those of Mussina or Brown.

Between 1962 and 1966, Koufax collected 44.8 pWAR. That's damn good, but between 1996 and 2000, Kevin Brown collected 42.7 pWAR. And from 1997 to 2001, Mussina collected 32.4 pWAR. So Mussina's peak doesn't quite match up, but Brown's clearly does. I write this because I think most people, at this point, would rank the Moose ahead of Brown, or at least not far behind him. Mussina, who will be just 38 next season, is 61 wins away from 300 and has posted double digits in wins in every season since 1992. In terms of career value, I'm not sure that you could make a very good argument for any pitcher ranked below these two as being clearly better, no matter what metric you use.

The Most Valuable Pitchers: 31-40

Rank	First	Last	pWAR
31	Eddie	Plank	75
32	Jim	Bunning	75
33	John	Smoltz	74
34	Carl	Hubbell	70
35	Bob	Feller	68
36	Bret	Saberhagen	68
37	David	Cone	67
38	Hal	Newhouser	67
39	Frank	Tanana	67
40	Jim	Kaat	66

I"m not sure you can convince me that Feller was a significantly better pitcher than Newhouser, once you remove the myth surrounding Feller's fastball and his general dominance. It is true that Newhouser's best years came during the war, but it's not his fault that the Axis powers decided to engage the United States in a war in the midst of his prime. While the major leagues certainly were worse in the early 40's than immediately prior, the extent of the worsening quality of competition is greatly exaggerated; it was only slightly worse. Newhouser won the MVP in 1944 and 1945; he was second in 1946, and actually performed better than he did in '44.

Newhouser had a very concentrated peak between 1944 and 1949, but he was 51 Pitching Wins over Replacement in that six-year period. Feller also had a relatively concentrated peak between 1939 and 1947 (six years because of the war), and he was 44 Pitching Wins better than Replacement in that time. Newhouser's best season was better than Feller's best, his second-best season was better than Feller's second-best, his third-best season was better than Feller's third-best. If you want to talk about peak, Newhouser clearly wins out, and they're just about tied with it comes to career value.

Hal Newhouser is an extremely underrated pitcher, and Feller overrated; once you remove the myth, it's impossible to say that one was definitely better than the other.

The Most Valuable Pitchers: 41-50

Rank	First	Last	pWAR
41	Jerry	Koosman	66
42	Don	Drysdale	66
43	Chuck	Finley	66
44	Whitey	Ford	66
45	Juan	Marichal	65
46	Stan	Coveleski	64
47	John	Clarkson	64
48	Dave	Stieb	64
49	Pud	Galvin	63
50	Kevin	Appier	63

Chuck Finley? I must be nuts.

Between 1990 and 1996, Finley played for a team that averaged just under 87 losses a year, and only four other pitchers—Greg Maddux, Tom Glavine, Jack McDowell, and John Smoltz—won more games than he did (99). Note the conspicuous absence of the greatest pitcher of all time from that list.

Finley was a five-time All-Star, but he never really had that one big season. His best year came in 1990, when he was the second-best pitcher in the major leagues but still more than two full wins above replacement worse

than Roger Clemens. In 1993, Finley pitched 251.1 innings with a 3.15 ERA, but there were still five pitchers in the American League who were better. Finley was the fifth-best pitcher in the league in 1998, when he pitched 223.1 innings with a 3.39 ERA. But in those three seasons, Finley combined for just 45 wins and 32 losses. It's hard to see any kind of greatness in a pitcher who averages 15 wins and 11 losses in the best years of his career.

But these are career rankings, and the fact is, Finley had a heck of a career. He won 200 games, tossed 3,200 innings and maintained an ERA that was 15 percent better than average. He was one of the best and most consistent pitchers in baseball for a decade.

One more way to look at it: Between 1989 and 2000, there are only six pitchers better than Finley, four of whom either already have 300 wins or will. There are 23 300-game winners in baseball history; 25 if we include Randy Johnson and Tom Glavine, who are almost certain to get there. So for every 12-year "era," there are about two guys who will win 300 games. In Finley's dominant period, there were four. So to be fair to him, let's get rid of two of them. That makes Finley the third-best pitcher of a 12-year era. Not including 2006, we've seen 135 years of professional baseball, or a little more than 11 such eras. So shouldn't Finley be around the top 35 pitchers in history?

The Most Valuable Pitchers: 51-60

Rank	First	Last	pWAR
51	Billy	Pierce	63
52	David	Wells	62
53	Tim	Keefe	62
54	Dazzy	Vance	61
55	Ted	Lyons	61
56	Orel	Hershiser	61
57	Early	Wynn	61
58	Red	Faber	60
59	Eppa	Rixey	60
60	Mickey	Lolich	59

Do you think it would be easier to convince a group of baseball fans that Barry Bonds is the greatest hitter of all time, or that David Wells is one of the sixty most valuable pitchers? Or would it be more productive to try to convince them that you are the son of a wealthy Nigerian banker?

The Most Valuable Pitchers: 61-70

Rank	First	Last	pWAR
61	Frank	Viola	59
62	Larry	Jackson	59
63	Dennis	Martinez	58
64	Sandy	Koufax	58
65	Dwight	Gooden	58
66	Bob	Friend	58
67	Ed	Walsh	57
68	Jimmy	Key	56
69	Kenny	Rogers	56
70	Steve	Rogers	56

The Most Valuable Pitchers: 71-80

Rank	First	Last	pWAR
71	Jamie	Moyer	55
72	Mark	Langston	55
73	Tommy	Bridges	55
74	Milt	Pappas	54
75	Wilbur	Wood	54
76	Bobo	Newsom	54
77	Hoyt	Wilhelm	54
78	Ron	Guidry	54
79	Jack	Morris	53
80	Red	Ruffing	53

Three surprises here: Viola, Key and Martinez. Let's take those in order.

For a decade, between 1983 and 1992, no one started as many games as Viola, and only one pitcher (Jack Morris) pitched more innings or accumulated more wins. He was a bulldog, and I'm surprised he doesn't rate higher on other lists; he didn't have that huge peak, but his value is all concentrated in a 10-year period.

Key is a lot like Viola: very good decade of performance (1985-1994) and not much else. It should be no surprise that the two have ended up in the same group.

Dennis Martinez reaps the benefits of a 23-year career. He was barely above average, but he retired just an out away from 4,000 career innings.

Oh, and you thought I was going to ignore Koufax. Look, his ranking is solely the result of the baseline I chose to use. If you look at Win Shares, which have an effective baseline around .300, Koufax ranks even lower. If you were to calculate Pitching Wins above average, or use Total Player Rating, he would rank a bit higher (36th, using Pitching Wins) because he'd be compared to a higher baseline. I choose to compare all players to a .410 baseline, because in my opinion that best defines value. Replacement-level play can be obtained for free; anything above that will cost you.

But instituting a replacement baseline means that pitchers will benefit from long careers, and the lower the baseline, the more benefit. I think .410 is as fair a baseline as any. My point is that in terms of career value, Koufax is only the 64th-most valuable pitcher in the history of the game. In terms of greatness, he obviously would rank much higher.

Wilhelm would probably rank right around where Bill James has him if I were to adjust for leverage. So he's 40 or 50 spots too low.

Pappas is the type of guy who really benefits from focusing solely on career value. Excluding his cup of coffee in 1957, Pappas pitched for 16 seasons, making more than 20 starts each year. He was a quality pitcher, with a career 209-164 record and 3,000 innings pitched. Pappas had four years when he could have been the ace of a good pitching staff and five more when he could have headed a not-so-good staff. He was never great, but he was consistently good, and while that doesn't make for a storied career or a title as one of the greats, it does make for a valuable pitcher—valuable enough to make this list.

The Most Valuable Pitchers: 81-90

Rank	First	Last	pWAR
81	Jack	Quinn	53
82	Vida	Blue	53
83	Vic	Willis	53
84	Eddie	Cicotte	52
85	Joe	McGinnity	52
86	Al	Spalding	52
87	Rube	Waddell	52
88	Charlie	Hough	52
89	Dizzy	Trout	52
90	Danny	Darwin	52

Hough, if anything, is ranked too low. From 1982 to 1993 he was a very effective starter—very good through the 80s and still an innings eater after. He was also, in those years, in his mid-to-late 30s and early-to-mid-40s.

Sidebar: The Greatest Pitching Seasons Ever

Which seasons were the greatest of all time? First of all, here's a list of the greatest seasons before 1900:

Rank	First	Last	Year	pWAR
1	Pud	Galvin	1884	18.90
2	Charley	Radbourn	1884	15.31
3	Charlie	Buffinton	1884	14.28
4	John	Clarkson	1889	14.01
5	Tim	Keefe	1883	13.98
6	Guy	Hecker	1884	13.66
7	Silver	King	1888	13.15
8	Al	Spalding	1875	12.73
9	Tommy	Bond	1879	12.51
10	Jim	Devlin	1877	12.23

Everyone knows about Radbourn's amazing 1884, so how is it that he wasn't even the best pitcher in the league that year? In 1884, Radbourn set the major league record for wins, pitching 678.2 innings (just 1.1 back of the record) while putting up an ERA less than half of the league average. So how does Galvin end up at the top?

Well, first of all, Galvin was no slouch himself. He threw about 40 fewer innings that season, with an ERA almost 60 percent better than average. But what struck me in my analysis is that Radbourn was playing in front of a great defense. In a league where the average team allowed 28.8 percent of all balls in play to fall in for hits, the Providence Grays allowed hits on just 25.1 percent of balls in play. That number is about

the same if you include Radbourn in the analysis or if you don't.

How big a difference does that make? I estimate that if Radbourn had been pitching in front of Galvin's defense, he would have pitched 49 fewer innings and allowed 70 more runs than he did. Our new comparison would look something like this:

Pitcher	Innings	Run Average
Galvin	636.1	3.59
Radbourn	629.2	4.09

And that's why Galvin rates better.

Here's the list of greatest pitching years since the 20th Century began:

Rank	First	Last	Year	pWAR
1	Steve	Carlton	1972	13.90
2	Walter	Johnson	1913	13.76
3	Roger	Clemens	1997	12.66
4	Pete	Alexander	1920	12.66
5	Christy	Mathewson	1908	12.66
6	Walter	Johnson	1912	12.51
7	Bob	Gibson	1968	12.48
8	Dwight	Gooden	1985	12.33
9	Wilbur	Wood	1971	12.12
10	Pedro	Martinez	2000	11.70

If Hough had been given a chance to start at the beginning of his career, he almost certainly would have won 300 games, and maybe many more. Here are the pitchers with the most innings pitched after turning 34:

First	Last	IP
Phil	Niekro	3735.1
Cy	Young	3313.0
Charlie	Hough	2858.1
Warren	Spahn	2810.2
Gaylord	Perry	2713.0

Darwin is an interesting guy because he finished his career with a 171-182 record. How can a guy with a losing record have more value than all but 77 pitchers in the history of the game? Well, if you don't like the Pitching Wins and Losses system, you'll probably blame the construction, but I wouldn't. Simply put, Darwin had some awful, awful luck in his career.

In 1983, his ERA was 16 percent better than the league average, and he finished 8-13. In 1984, his ERA was 5% better than average; he finished 8-12. In 1985, 9 percent better than average; 8-18. In 1986, he was 31 percent better than average, and he finished 11-10. In 1987, he was 9 percent better than average with a 9-10 record. He did allow a lot of unearned runs, but still, in those five years, I estimate that Darwin should have gone 59-53. His actual record was 44-63. In 1993, I estimate Darwin should have gone 17-9, and he went 15-11. In 1996, Darwin went 10-11, when he should have won 10 and lost 8. Overall, I estimate that Darwin should have had a career record of 178-157 instead of 171-182, which certainly would have led to different perceptions of him.

The Most Valuable Pitchers: 91-100

Rank	First	Last	pWAR
91	Dutch	Leonard	52
92	Mordecai	Brown	51
93	Charley	Radbourn	51
94	Brad	Radke	50
95	John	Candelaria	50
96	Bob	Welch	50
97	Jim	Perry	50
98	Virgil	Trucks	50
99	Babe	Adams	50
100	Waite	Hoyt	49

It might look like Mordecai Brown and Radbourn both rank way too low, but I don't think so. Both benefited from great defenses in their careers, and both pitched in a completely different era, where their numbers were not quite so outstanding as they look today. Brown didn't pitch that many innings, and for that matter, neither did Radbourn, given that he tossed almost 700 in one season. In terms of ERA, Radbourn was 20 percent better than the league average for his career. He also benefited from a great defense to the tune of almost a third of a run per game. Take that away, and his advantage over average is just under 8 percent. Isn't it reasonable, then, that an era adjustment for a guy who played more than a century ago would take him down to just barely above average?

Brad Radke is going to retire after this season because his shoulder resembles a pile of Enron documents. I've always been a Radke fan, not for his toughness, but because he managed to win and remain loyal to a team that averaged 93 losses a year for the best years of his career. The Twins' role as national laughingstock has since been assumed by the Kansas City Royals—I wonder what it is about the American League Central?

In 1997, Radke managed to win 20 games for a team that lost 94, which is about as impressive as it sounds. Here are the biggest difference between a pitcher's winning percentage and that of his team on a team that won 42% of its games or less (minimum 30 decisions):

First	Last	Year	Diff
Steve	Carlton	1972	0.352
Ned	Garver	1951	0.287
Brad	Radke	1997	0.247
Walter	Johnson	1911	0.242
Red	Faber	1921	0.222

Some Thoughts

The first player that Bill James and I rate vastly differently is Bert Blyleven; I have him sixth, while James has him 39th. If James had just ordered pitchers in terms of career Win Shares (which is similar to what I do), Blyleven would have been 16th; he would have been 11th if you remove all 19th century pitchers but Cy Young from the discussion. You'll generally find that the same is true for most of the other pitchers who are ranked significantly differently here than they are by James.

There are certainly more pitchers on this list whose careers began during or after the 1960s than in any decade before, even if you remove black and foreign-born pitchers. I don't think this is necessarily wrong. First of all, it's not just that we're including more pitchers from other countries; Major League Baseball also has a much greater scouting system in place today than ever before. There are plenty of legends about players being "discovered" by scouts in the early 20th century and of course the 19th as well. Today, there is a streamlined feeder system that means practically no player will slip through the cracks, and of course, players learn to pitch in Little League rather than in the minor leagues.

In addition, since this list relies on career value, I would suggest that modern medical advances in diagnosis and treatment, as well as modern knowledge of the effects of pitch counts, has extended the careers of dozens of pitchers who would have been toast after

less than a decade back in the day. When it comes to seasonal value, they may not be as effective, but it is actually *easier* to throw 3,000 or so innings nowadays than in the past. Mordecai Brown, who once threw 342 innings in a season, has fewer career innings than Chuck Finley.

Everything presented here is simply what the numbers tell me. They are not my personal opinions, nor should they be gospel for anyone else. They are only meant to provide actual numerical evidence to be used in any way you see fit. Now let the arguments begin.

I owe much gratitude to Bill James, Nate Silver, and Tom Tango for inspiring this analysis, as well as Joe Dimino, Vinay Kumar, Dave Studenmund, Steve Treder, and John Walsh for helping me develop Pitching Wins and Losses.

Looking Back: The Federal League

by John Brattain

Major League Baseball Players Association executive director Don Fehr once commented: "You go through *The Sporting News* for the last 100 years, and you will find two things are always true. You never have enough pitching, and nobody ever made money."

And so it goes.

George Bernard Shaw once opined that the only thing man learns from history is that man never learns from history. The Federal League had a relatively short cameo on the baseball stage, but its storylines would be as familiar today as they were then. While the theme is familiar, its impact was so deep that its impression is still felt on the game we so love.

It was a period of baseball when players were jumping from team to team, chasing the highest bids for their services without any concern for the fans or team loyalty. Owners were howling over player salaries and dumping salary. Baseball talked about salary caps and restricting player movement, and ultimately both sides were so busy scrapping over every last nickel that the poor fans of the game wondered if anybody really cared about them.

The more things change...

A little background is in order:

Before the dawn of the 20th century, many professional leagues claiming major league status came and went: the American Association, the National Association, the Union Association and the Players' League.

Finally, come 1901, a league did succeed in rising up against the incumbent National League. Originally named the Western League, it moved into major markets, announced that it too was "big league" and changed its name to "The American League"—the same one that we enjoy today.

Things didn't end there, however. With a wide-open marketplace where free enterprise, capitalism and the entrepreneurial spirit reigned supreme, more men of vision made plans for "major leagues." The vast majority of plans were stillborn, but in 1913 a plan finally got beyond the drawing board and saw the light of day.

What made this league different from the other failed attempts? As Deep Throat said so well over a half century later: "Follow the money." By the standards of upstart leagues, this new enterprise had substantial startup capital, enough even to capture the attention of major stars—not to mention the magnates—of the senior and junior circuits. It was the Federal League.

John Power, who had been a member of a previous attempt to form a "major league" (the Colombian League, which never played a game), was elected president of the enterprise. Setting the tone as a renegade league, the Federal League planned to be no part of the National Association and its regulation over the NL and AL. Preferring independence, it stated that it would develop its own players and wouldn't engage in the expensive player raids that ultimately doomed earlier challengers.

The Federal League hoped to imp the incumbents by launching an eight-team league in 1913, yet it was forced by time constraints to open with franchises in six cities: Chicago, Pittsburgh, Cleveland, St. Louis, Indianapolis and Cincinnati. This would put the Federal League into competition with five major league markets and one minor league market. It also increased the number of major league franchises to three in both Chicago (White Sox and Cubs) and St. Louis (Cardinals and Browns). The Cincinnati market immediately proved too small to support two teams and the club quickly relocated to Covington, Kentucky—a dubious decision at best. They took wing again before the inaugural season concluded and decided to compete with the American Association's Blues in Kansas City.

The Federal League vowed not to interfere with the National Association's (from this point on, the term 'National Association (NA)' will be understood to stand for the National and American Leagues) player contracts and would sign only "free agents."

The trouble, however, came in the interpretation of what constituted a free agent. The National Association had Rule 10 A—better known as "the reserve clause":

On or before January 15 ... the Club may tender to the Player a contract for the term of that year by mailing the same to the Player. If prior to the March 1 next succeeding said January 15, the Player and the Club have not agreed upon the terms of such contract, then on or before 10 days after said March 1, the Club shall have the right ... to renew this contract for the period of one year.

The question, which wouldn't be finally settled until arbitrator Peter Seitz decided Messersmith-McNally, was whether a player who had played out his option was still "under obligation" to the club holding his contract, or was free to negotiate with other teams. The question was put to the test when three players considered "under obligation" by organized baseball signed with the Pittsburgh Federal League franchise.

Invariably, organized baseball did as organized baseball does—it reacted badly and made an awkward situation worse by raiding FL (Federal League) rosters. The Chicago Cubs were the most aggressive, offering contracts to a number of the Chicago Whales (or Chifeds, as they were also known) players.

Bear in mind that this action predated baseball's antitrust exemption. Of course, that didn't stop the National Association from acting like monopolists. When the NA pressured Western Telegraph to not put FL scores on its service, the Feds dispatched one E. E. Gates to appear before the Interstate Commerce Commission to argue their case.

Gates contended that the FL had offered to pay for the service yet was refused because of the National Association's influence. He later met with a U.S. government representative and requested a resolution to Congress to investigate whether the NA had violated antitrust laws. Gates made the case that baseball had been bestowed certain privileges not available to other businesses and claimed that the NA was trying to monopolize the baseball marketplace, which of course is quite illegal without an antitrust exemption. If the NA was found to have violated antitrust laws they would be liable to treble damages. (More on that later.)

Meanwhile, on August 2 of that year, things started to get really interesting. Powers was kicked out as league president and Chicagoan James Gilmore was elected. He quickly brought significant new capital into the FL by enlisting the support of wealthy restaurateur Charles Weeghman for the Chicago franchise and oil magnates Harry Sinclair and Phil Ball for the Newark and St. Louis franchises, respectively. During these maneuverings, the Indianapolis entry won the inaugural Federal League pennant.

The FL learned what other rival leagues had come to grips with: A pennant was nice, but the money was in the postseason. Of course, knowing this was one thing, trying to come up with a workable postseason format that satisfies all parties (something baseball is still trying to achieve) is quite another.

In the early and late 1960s, late 1970s and twice in the 1990s, major league baseball claimed to be losing money as an industry and so expanded teams to raise capital. This was hardly a new phenomenon; the FL did the same thing in 1914; claiming losses and deciding to add clubs.

A team was added in Brooklyn and awarded to the Ward brothers, wealthy bakery magnates who evidently had a lot of dough (sorry). The Wards felt a major league team would be a dandy promotional vehicle for their other business interest and promptly christened the team "The Tip Tops" in honor of their line of breads.

Shockingly, the New York media was aghast at this commercial prostituting of the game and raised such a mighty stink that the brothers Ward renamed their franchise the Brookfeds.

The Federals added two other franchises in direct competition to International League teams in Buffalo and Baltimore. This devastated those minor league teams, since baseball fans in these cities considered the FL to be "big league." The immediate impact was the relocation of the Baltimore franchise to Richmond, Va., and the FL nearly destroyed the International League.

To bring the league to the ideal number of eight franchises, the FL dropped the Cleveland entry. With this alignment in place, the FL finally stepped up and proclaimed itself a major league in 1914 with eight franchises challenging organized baseball in four major league cities and four minor league cities. The league also led all three circuits in innovations. The FL recognized that they would either hang together or hang separately, and organized itself as a single corporation with stock divided among ownership. There were also incentives for the players.

In order to maintain a hold on their players, the Feds introduced a profit-sharing program where a certain percentage of the profits generated by the league would be set aside to be divvied up among the players at the conclusion of each season. Further, after ten years of FL service, a player could be given his unconditional release, making him a free agent. Of course, this generosity didn't come without a price. With salaries escalating, the FL brought in a team salary cap.

Major league baseball—or at least the Federal League version of it—now had free agency, a salary cap and revenue sharing (or stock sharing) among the clubs.

Feeling on solid ground and annoyed by the preemptive player-raiding strike from the NA, the FL felt it was time to return the favor and snag of few of the NA's gate attractions. This served to put the two leagues under pressure, as well as adding legitimacy to the FL's "major league status." The biggest prize from that initial foray was Joe Tinker of the immortal Cubs infield trio of Tinker-to-Evers-to-Chance. Another member of the trio, Frank Chance, had just been sold from the Cincinnati Reds to the Brooklyn Superbas.

Chance mulled two offers: The Superbas offered $7,500, the Chicago Whales $12,000 plus stock in the franchise and the position of manager. He followed the money. Other notable players induced to jump the NA ship for managerial posts in the new league were George Stovall (Kansas City) and Mordecai "Three Finger" Brown, who would pilot the St. Louis Terriers.

The Federal League was a godsend to the players in all three leagues. For the first time since the advent of the AL, major league players had a degree of leverage when negotiating contracts. This sent shock waves throughout baseball.

It was the Federal League that prompted the venerable Connie Mack to dismantle his first great dynasty and invent the team-wide salary dump. He sold Hall-of-Fame bound second sacker Eddie Collins to penurious Charles Comiskey. He requested waivers on Hall-of-Fame hurlers Chief Bender and Eddie Plank to try and get something for his stars. However, both of them signed with the Feds. Mack sold Hall-of-Fame hot cornerman Frank "Home Run" Baker to the Yankees (starting yet another tradition) and effectively consigned the A's to baseball purgatory for over a decade and a half—heroes to zeroes, courtesy of the Feds.

The uniform player contract was called into question because the contract basically stipulated that a player was the property of the franchise for life, yet the team could release a player on 10 days notice. This went to court in the case of Chief Johnson, a pitcher of no particular renown and the 1910's version of Andy Messersmith. As Messersmith would decades later, Johnson won out.

This prompted star first baseman Hal Chase, who could smell money as well as any owner, to give his club ten days notice and jump to the Feds. The court ruled in his favor, saying that his contract lacked mutuality (the Supreme Court would be unable to see this years later in Flood vs. Kuhn).

The organized baseball magnates—never ones to take defeat (or being forced to not treat players as chattel) lying down—struck back. The National Association rules were amended to specify a three-year suspension for reserve rule jumpers (defined as players who played out their option year and left) and five-year suspensions for contract breakers. The May 4, 1914 *Boston Herald* reported that American League boss Ban Johnson, in an attempt to tighten the screws on those who exercised the same rights enjoyed by ordinary citizens (the right to change employers when a work contract expired), stated:

No player of the Federal League can ever play in the American League ... a man may be reinstated by the National Commission, but can never hope to get into the American League. The National and other leagues may accept him, but as for the American League, never.

The Herald of June 21 of that same year reported that the NA was considering a squeeze play—launching a third major league of its own within the National Association to combat the Feds. The discussions went so far as to consider how to handle the World Series with three participants, perhaps holding a World Series round-robin tournament.

Despite these shenanigans, the Feds pressed on with their second campaign leading to an Indianapolis repeat. Players were beginning to develop reputations and fan recognition. Benny Kauff of the pennant-winning Hoofeds (Hoosiers + Federals) was dubbed "The Ty Cobb of the Federal League" and won the batting title with a sparkling .370 average (and 166 OPS+).

Other notable achievers included Yankees defector (and Canadian) Russ Ford, who enjoyed a superlative season on the mound, going 21-6 with a minuscule ERA of 1.82 (181 ERA+). Sadly, this was the last hurrah for a once-promising hurler. In his first two seasons with the Yankees, he posted won-loss marks of 26-6 and 22-11, yet in 1915 he went 5-9 (4.52 ERA, 69 ERA+) in his second campaign with the Buffeds.

Claude Hendrix of the Whales led all hurlers with a stunning 29-10 ledger to go along with a minute earned run mark of 1.69 (174 ERA+). He logged 362 frames while averaging less than two walks per game. Gene Packard, the only FL moundsman to have a pair of 20-win seasons, finished 20-14 despite an earned run mark of almost 3.00 (106 ERA+). Like Hendrix, Packard logged 300-plus innings.

Although Kauff was the headliner with the lumber, other batters gave notice as well. Ennis "Rebel" Oakes, a player of no import in organized baseball, batted .312 (121 OPS+) for Pittsburgh and drove in 75 runs. Edward Zwilling, whose claim to fame is currently being the last entry in the "Baseball Encyclopedia," was unique in that he played out his four-year baseball career with all three major league teams in Chicago. While in NA he was a nobody, with the Whales he was a star slugger. In the midst of the dead-ball era he slugged a mighty .485 (146 OPS+) in 1914. He batted .313 while smacking 38 doubles, ripping eight triples, blasting a league-leading 16 home runs and driving in 95 runs. He followed that with a 143 OPS+ in 1915. He wasn't a hulking slugger in anybody's book, being about the size of Phil Rizzuto.

If there's one thing that'll catch a baseball magnate's attention, it's losing money. At the conclusion of the 1914 baseball season, the three leagues quietly entered into negotiations in an attempt to end this costly war. Although new money had come into the FL when Sinclair, Weeghman, Ball and the Ward brothers acquired franchises, the Feds were losing money. The National Association was in the red too, but its financial losses were not as great.

And if there's one thing that'll catch a baseball player's attention, it's the possibility of making more money elsewhere. Thus, the question of whether to jump or not was splintering clubhouses.

Despite the National and American Leagues' frustration at losing marquee names to the Feds, the talks between the three leagues reached an impasse, as the Federal League's insistence on being recognized as a major league was a deal-breaker to the monopoly-minded National and American Leagues.

So on with the war.

Finally, on January 5, the FL filed an antitrust suit against organized baseball. FL president James Gilmore contended that the de facto monopoly status enjoyed by the National Association resulted in such "illegal acts" as farming out players—thereby allowing AL/NL clubs to maintain control of players both in the minors and the majors and preventing them from joining the Feds—and was a restraint of free trade.

Organized baseball wet their collective britches after learning that the case landed in the court of a notorious "trust buster" who had recently ruled that Standard Oil had been guilty of anti-trust violations (later overturned). The judge's name?

Kenesaw Mountain Landis.

Just when the National Association thought things couldn't get any worse, "The Big Train" jumped the tracks when Walter Johnson rejected Washington Senators owner Clark Griffith's contract offer in favor of signing with the Chicago Whales.

Like many baseball contract negotiations, Johnson wasn't looking to leave the Nats but rather to use the Federals as a stalking horse to boost Griffith's offer. Johnson had asked for either a one-year deal for $15,000, a three-year deal for $36,000 or a five-year offer of $50,000. When Griffith curtly told Johnson that he didn't want to "purchase the whole state of Kansas," (Johnson's home state) Johnson opted to play in the Windy City for Joe Tinker, earning $40,000 over two years.

Griffith traveled to Kansas City to visit eyeball-to-eyeball with Johnson and appeal to his star's better nature. Griffith reminded him that he had always acted in good faith toward his storied hurler and felt his actions should be reciprocated.

Johnson agreed but felt that it would hurt the Whales if he were to jump back. Griffith pointed out that he would hurt Washington, and by extension his many fans, if he stayed in Chicago. In effect, Griffith said that Johnson had created a situation where his defection would ultimately hurt either Washington or Chicago and he'd have to choose whether to hurt the people who had cheered him for years or a city that wouldn't hold him in such high regard.

Swayed, Johnson returned his signing bonus to Weeghman's club and returned to the Senators while receiving a healthy raise for his troubles, which was all he really wanted in the first place. Ultimately, "The Big Train" never pulled up to the Chicago Federal League station. In an interview with the *Washington Post* (Sunday, May 14, 1915) he candidly admitted:

> ... *I deserve the blame for what I have done, and I admit in the light of experience, that I did not act wisely, I make no excuses and ask no consideration. I am willing to accept whatever blame is due me.*

Of course this was one of the few conflicts with an amicable resolution.

Now things were about to get ridiculous, as pompous self-importance started to rule the day.

Organized baseball decided to renew hostilities with the FL by signing away from Brooklyn "The Ty Cobb of the Federal League"—Benny Kauff (he had been 'transferred' there from Indianapolis).

However, this wasn't a player raid—he was actually bought from the Brookfeds, a transaction that started a major firestorm.

The first problem was that Kauff was signed by the New York Giants, but Giants manager John McGraw wanted nothing to do with him.

The second problem was that Kauff was considered the property of the Boston Braves, although he was a Yankee prior to going to the Federal League, and the Braves claimed that he was blacklisted because he had jumped his contract there.

Kauff, in a bridge-burning move, stated that "he was through with the Federal League" and applied to the National Association for re-instatement stating: "If I can't play with the Giants, I'll quit the game for good."

The third problem was that the National Association refused his reinstatement.

Kauff was forced to eat his words (and no doubt some more Tip Top bread) and return to the Brookfeds.

Despite all the off-field fireworks, the Federal League enjoyed one of its finest pennant races (not difficult when you consider that they only had three), going down to the final few games of the season, when Chicago split a doubleheader with Pittsburgh to finish ahead of St. Louis by percentage points. Chicago finished 86-66, with St. Louis at 87-67 and Pittsburgh at 86-67, marking the first time that the team with the most wins didn't win the pennant. The other time, of course, was the players' strike year of 1981 when the Cincinnati Reds won a division-high 66 games and did not qualify for the postseason under the split-season format.

Benny Kauff won his second straight batting title, hitting .342 (182 OPS+), and enjoyed a monster season, leading the loop in OBP, SLG and stolen bases.

At the conclusion of the 1915 campaign, several developments brought peace to the game. Just as the appearance of one man gave the Federal League new life, it was the exit of one man that caused the FL to shuffle off its mortal coil. Robert Ward—wealthy owner of the Brooklyn Tip Tops—died in the fall of 1915; much of the fight, spunk and vision died with him.

Like Walter O'Malley, he was the center of consensus within the league and its chief power broker.

Despite a thrilling pennant race in the waning days of 1915, attendance was poor. While rumors of the U.S. entering into World War I also negatively affected organized baseball, it was in better shape to handle the stormy days still ahead. Even slashing ticket prices in several FL cities couldn't reverse the trend.

Federal League president Jim Gilmore saw the writing on the wall, but was loath to just throw in the towel and abandon his investors. The league had lost a lot of money and Gilmore (as well as the other team magnates) didn't want to walk away empty-handed. Gilmore, who had the guts of a gambler (not to mention a bang-on assessment of who he was dealing with), orchestrated and executed a plan that eventually resulted in an extremely generous settlement from the National Association.

Gilmore and Harry Sinclair had planned to place a franchise in New York, but with the league on the verge of financial collapse, the move wasn't viable. Of course, the NA didn't know that, and the Feds figured that appearing to go ahead with a New York Federal League franchise would be an excellent bargaining chip.

They also had a perfect cover story, in the guise of a property at the corner of 145th St. and Lenox Ave. that the FL had purchased for the magnificent sum of $1.25

million. At the time it was bought, Gilmore figured that he could build a stadium in a matter of months for about $475,000, and he had a blueprint made which called for a stadium that could ultimately hold 55,000 patrons.

Not coincidentally, the New York Yankees were also looking to build a stadium, having been informed by the Giants that they wished to occupy the Polo Grounds alone. This panicked the National League, which now wanted to negotiate with the Feds. When rumors were spread among the leagues that Sinclair and Gilmore didn't have the money to pull it off, Sinclair put on his best poker face and dropped the gauntlet:

> *I'll meet you people (the A.L and N.L. magnates) on the waterfront and we'll toss dollar for dollar into the Hudson River. Then we'll see who runs out of money first.*

At this, the AL also folded and negotiations began in earnest. Someday, Marvin Miller would also discover that the mighty Lords of Baseball were often more bark than bite.

The Federal League received an excellent settlement from organized baseball, as the AL and NL, in effect, bought out the Feds. Some of the terms of the agreement included:

- Allowing Charles Weeghman to buy the National League Cubs, which he did. This is how the Cubs ended up in Wrigley Field. Wrigley was initially constructed for the Whales, with the Cubs occupying South Side Park at the time.

- Phil Ball, owner of the St. Louis Terriers, was permitted to buy the AL St. Louis Browns.

- Weeghman and Ball then merged their two clubs, taking the best from the NA and Federal League clubs. Although syndicate ownership was supposedly illegal within the National Association, this wouldn't be the last time organized baseball would break its own rules to make a problem go away.

- The Ward estate was awarded $400,000.

- The Pittsburgh franchise was given $50,000 and the right to make bids on major league franchises that would become available.

Sinclair probably received the best settlement when he was paid $100,000 and given the rights to all the players from the Newark, Kansas City and Buffalo teams. He was also given the rights to Lee Magee, Benny Kauff and George Anderson, which he sold to National Association teams.

Another provision of the agreement was that all the Federal League players were to be granted amnesty and have the remaining parts of their Federal League contracts paid in full. And the Feds asked Landis to dismiss the antitrust case.

However, not everyone was thrilled with the settlement. The International League refused to be part of the settlement due to the damage the Feds had brought to their league, and the Federal League teams that weren't located in major league cities received little-to-no compensation.

The Baltimore Terrapins, in particular, rejected an offer of $50,000 and filed their own antitrust lawsuit charging that the NA conspired to destroy the Feds. A similar scenario unfolded in Buffalo. The saga of the Federal League ended, but its participants did not all go quietly into that good night.

Epilogue

The Federal League is now 90 years in the past. However, it's more than a mere historical curiosity. Baseball's unique antitrust exemption sprang directly from the suit that was launched by the Baltimore Terrapins against organized baseball. The suit that was presented before the court of Kenesaw Mountain Landis between 1914 and 1915 was never decided. The Federal League dropped the suit as part of the "peace agreement." Landis deliberately delayed ruling on the matter anyway. Landis was a baseball fan himself and, in the trial transcripts, he said to the Federal League attorneys:

"Do you realize that a decision in this case may tear down the very foundations of this game so loved by thousands?"

The great trust buster lost his nerve—not the first time the courts were overcome by the glare of the National Pastime.

When the owners saw a man who was willing to suppress his own principles and look the other way when the law was being broken to benefit private enterprise, they knew they had found their first commissioner.

Of course, history shows us they got a lot more than they bargained for.

As to the player raids, in retrospect, it was much ado about nothing.

Like today, many of the marquee names that jumped were at the end of their careers but had a great year or two left in the tank. A modern equivalent would be the recent New York Yankees, who routinely pick up big names whose best days are past: Randy Johnson, Kevin Brown, Jose Canseco, Gary Sheffield, Robin Ventura, etc.

Their only real value was as gate attractions, since they had name recognition. Philadelphia A's and Hall-of-Fame pitcher Eddie Plank enjoyed his final quality season with the Feds, when he went 21-11. Chief Bender's first campaign with the Feds went 4-16. Mordecai "Three Finger" Brown went 31-19 in his two years with the Feds, but he too was at the end of the line.

Benny Kauff ultimately signed with the Giants and enjoyed a handful of solid, though unspectacular, seasons before being banished from the game. (He was charged with auto theft, acquitted by the court and was banished anyway because Landis figured that he was probably guilty.)

Craig Burley's excellent history of the Benny Kauff affair can be found at the Hardball Times web site (http://www.hardballtimes.com/main/article/free-benny-kauff-part-one/).

Federal League slugger Dutch Zwilling played in only 35 games with the Cubs following a superlative Federal League career, batting an anemic .113.

For the most part, the Federal League stars failed to make any real contribution back in MLB, but there were exceptions. Jack Tobin, who began his major league career with the Federals, went on to play through 1927 and accumulated a lifetime batting mark of .309 (109 OPS+). Tobin topped 200 hits in four consecutive seasons (1920-1923), garnering 236 hits in 1921. If you never heard of him, it is probably because he spent a large part of his career with the St. Louis Browns.

The real jewel of the Feds was unquestionably Edd Roush. He, like Tobin, debuted in the Federal League. However, unlike Tobin, you will find Roush's visage gracing the Hall of Fame.

People don't change, which is why history repeats itself so often. Despite the money, the greed and the short-sighted ineptitude of those in charge, the saga of the Federal League shows the enduring nature of baseball because all of that is balanced by our enduring love for the game.

The Best Outfield Arms of Our Time

by John Walsh

There is something about the strong-armed outfielder that has always captured the imaginations of baseball fans. It's not hard to see why. For one thing, gunning down an opposing runner from the outfield is a spectacular play, one that might turn an extra-base hit into an out or a run scored into a double play. A strong outfield throw is often the turning point in a close game.

And it's, well, *impressive* when a cannon-armed fielder cuts loose with a laser beam that comes in knee-high, just in time for the tag to be applied. The rifle arm is something that even the casual fan can observe and appreciate. We don't need stats to tell us who has a strong arm and who doesn't—we can tell the difference between Vlad Guerrero and Johnny Damon. In fact, most of us have a good idea of the best outfield arms in baseball today. Ichiro, Guerrero and Andruw Jones are three that often come up in these discussions. Some older fans will remember great arms from the past: Roberto Clemente and Al Kaline and (going back further) Carl Furillo.

But maybe the statistics can tell us something after all. We all agree Clemente was great. But how great was he? And how many runs is that strong arm worth to a team? Ichiro and Vlad have cannons, but is one of them better than the other? Can we measure that and if so, how?

Outfield assists are one measure of throwing ability—strong-armed outfielders will tend to throw out more runners than weak-armed ones. However, assists only tell a part of the story. Controlling the running game by discouraging runners from taking an extra base is probably just as important as throwing out the occasional runner. And traditional fielding statistics cannot tell us who is good at holding runners and who is not.

The solution to this problem is to make use of the wonderful play-by-play data published by the folks at Retrosheet. Retrosheet has published this data for virtually all major league games played from 1957 through 2005 (the 1999 season is not yet available). The data allow us to measure precisely how many times an outfielder prevented a runner from taking an extra base and how many times he failed to do so. This level of detail in the data will give an accurate picture of which outfielders in the Retrosheet era had the best arms.

Evaluating Outfield Arms

I've isolated five different outfield plays (henceforth referred to as "situations") that make up a good portion of an outfielder's throwing duties:

1. S-1B: A single is hit to the OF with a runner on 1B and 2B unoccupied.
2. S-2B: A single is hit to the OF with a runner on 2B.
3. D-1B: A double is hit to the OF with a runner on 1B.
4. F-3B: An OF fly is caught with a runner on 3B, fewer than 2 outs.
5. F-2B: An OF fly is caught with a runner on 2B and 3B unoccupied, fewer than two outs.

For each play that falls into one of these categories, I classify the play into one of three possible outcomes:

1. Kill: an assist was recorded by the outfielder.
2. Hold: the runner did not take the extra base.
3. Advance: the runner took the extra base.

If the outfielder records an assist on the play, on any runner (including the batter), he gets a kill. If there is no kill, then I look at the "key" runner. If he takes the extra base, that is an "advance" charged to the fielder. Otherwise, the outcome is considered a "hold."

Outfielders are evaluated by considering how they did compared to an average outfielder, given the same opportunities. I determine average performance based on the situation, the outfield position, the number of outs and the year. For example, in the year 2000, with fewer than two outs, a runner on first base and a single to right field (situation S-1B), the runner will hold second 56% of the time, he'll make it to third 42% of the time and he'll be thrown out 2% of the time.

If the ball is hit to left field, the throw is much shorter and the runner is less inclined to try to take third; in fact, he only attempts it 15% of the time. If there are two outs, runners will advance more easily because they can run on contact, without worrying if the ball will be caught on a fly.

A runner's tendency to try for the extra base also depends on when he played. Baserunners have gotten more conservative over the period of 1957-2005. This makes sense, given the general increase in offense over that period; better not to get thrown out when the next guy up has a good chance to hit a home run. Going back to our runner going from first to third on a single to right: in 1960 he tried for the extra base 59% of the time and was thrown out 4% (compared to 44% and 2%, mentioned above).

A Pretty Good Arm

By way of example, let's look at some numbers for a right fielder. How about Paul O'Neill? I remember O'Neill as an agressive outfielder with a strong arm, but what do the numbers say? Here's a table summarizing his performance:

Paul O'Neill's Arm

Situation	Opps	H	K	Hexp	Kexp
S-1B	555	302	13	285.3	11.9
S-2B	390	129	34	113.5	31.3
D-1B	204	132	8	125.1	9.3
F-3B	173	45	8	38.4	8.9
F-2B	240	136	3	135.4	5.8
Overall	1562	744	66	697.7	67.2

The first five rows of the table show the five situations, followed by the grand total. Looking at the first row, we see that O'Neill fielded a single with a runner on first 555 times. He "held" the runner at second base 302 times (column labeled "H"), while an average outfielder would have held around 285 runners ("Hexp"); so O'Neill was definitely better than average in holding the runner in this situation. He also threw out the runner 13 times (column labeled "K"), about once more than the expected number (column "Kexp").

Overall, summing up the five situations, we see that O'Neill held more runners than the average fielder and threw out (virtually) the same number. I will call the ratio of runners held to the average "Hold+", while "Kill+" will be the number of runners eliminated divided by the expectation. O'Neill achieved Hold+ and Kill+ values of 107 and 98.

The Value of a Strong Arm

I'd like to assign a run value to an outfielder based on his throwing performance, using the Run Expectancy matrix. This matrix tells you, given a combination of outs and runners on base, how many runs a team will score in the rest of the inning. These run values are averages: they assume average hitters coming to the plate, an average pitcher, average defenders, etc. By considering the run value before and after any given play, you can assign an average run value to the play itself.

I have calculated average run values for the different outcomes (Kill, Hold, Advance) for the five situations. I also split the data up according to the number of outs: fewer than two outs or two outs. I have purposely not taken into account the variation in run scoring over the last 50 years. All run values will be expressed in "year 2002 runs," so we can compare outfielders across the years. This is akin to how economic data is sometimes presented; incomes or prices are sometimes presented in terms of "1990 dollars" to remove the effects of inflation. Same thing here: I'm removing the effects of run inflation.

Ok, enough technical stuff; let's get to the players. I've found it convenient to divide the whole period into three eras, each of which is discussed below.

The Clemente Era

Any discussion of great outfield arms invariably includes the name Roberto Clemente. Many consider his arm to be the best ever, simply a thing of wonder. Bill James wrote about Clemente in the Historical Baseball Abstract:

> For younger fans, you just can't believe what it was like [watching Clemente play]; I hope we see another one like it, or you'll never believe that it was possible. His throws combined strength, accuracy, and speed of release in whatever proportions were necessary to get the job done....I saw him grab a double in the gap and fire it to second base to make it an oops/single, when the entire transaction was so lightning fast that even having seen him do it four or five times, you still couldn't believe it was possible.

James' description of Clemente reminds us that controlling the running game is not simply a matter of having a strong arm. Getting to the ball quickly, getting the throw off quickly, accuracy and hitting the cutoff/relay man are all essential aspects of good "throwing." Clemente was great at all aspects of throwing.

Of course, Clemente's was not the only rifle arm in the Clemente Era (which includes players born before 1950); we also had Al Kaline and Hank Aaron in right field, Willie Mays in center and Carl Yastrzemski in left. Let's see how these and others fare in our analysis. Here is a list of the top 10 right fielders from the Clemente Era:

Right Field -- Clemente Era

	Opps	Kill+	Hold+	Runs	Runs/162
Clemente, Roberto	1998	135	118	67.1	5.4
Callison, Johnny	1648	132	107	43.3	4.3
Staub, Rusty	1558	124	103	28.9	3.0
Kaline, Al	1473	89	115	26.5	2.9
Aaron, Hank	1645	117	104	24.9	2.4
Kirkland, Willie	740	148	110	21.1	4.6
Brown, Ollie	798	113	115	19.5	4.0
Johnstone, Jay	529	139	106	12.8	4.0
Colavito, Rocky	1045	93	110	12.6	1.9
Rose, Pete	619	108	110	11.5	3.0

A word of explanation: "Runs" means runs prevented above average. "Runs/162" is the number of runs saved per 162 opportunities. It turns out that there is about one opportunity per game played, so this just corresponds to runs saved per season. Players are ranked by Runs. To make this list, a player had to have a minimum of 500 opportunities.

Not surprisingly, Clemente tops the list. His total of 67.1 runs saved is tops in this group, but it's also the most (virtually tied with Yaz, as we'll see) for any outfielder in the full Retrosheet period. This is one case where the numbers really agree with what our eyes have been telling us. I'm glad to see that, because any metric that doesn't rate Clemente's arm highly is a flawed metric.

Johnny Callison was the All-Star right fielder for the Phillies in the 1960s. He was a good hitter, twice knocking in 100 runs and finishing second in the MVP vote in 1964. Callison passed away this past October, and just about everybody who reminisced about him mentioned the cannon arm. Teammate Dick Allen said: "He was a terrific player with a great arm from right field." Tim McCarver: "Cannon for an arm. Compact power. Just a superb ballplayer."

I thought Kaline would rank higher, to be honest, and was surprised to see that his Kill+ was less than average. Still, his Hold+ of 115 is excellent; it's clear that runners respected his arm. One thing to keep in mind: the players with long careers will experience a decline phase in their later years, which will tend to depress their rate stats (Hold+, Kill+ and Runs/162). I'm sure this affected the numbers of Kaline and

Aaron, as they struggled with age and injury in their final years. Clemente's excellent rate stats are even more impressive considering the length of his career, although it was cut short at age 37 by his accidental death in 1972.

The top center fielders from this era stack up like this:

Center Field -- Clemente Era

	Opps	Kill+	Hold+	Runs	Runs/162
Blair, Paul	1414	129	109	31.0	3.6
Mays, Willie	2337	97	110	28.8	2.0
Geronimo, Cesar	1010	106	112	18.6	3.0
Pinson, Vada	1818	101	105	15.4	1.4
Unser, Del	1236	128	103	15.1	1.9
Smith, Reggie	864	112	109	12.5	2.3
Davis, Willie	2284	110	102	12.1	0.9
Tuttle, Bill	674	136	104	9.1	2.2
Piersall, Jim	930	97	107	8.8	1.5
May, Dave	524	125	104	7.5	2.3

Paul Blair was the premier American League center fielder in this period, winning eight Gold Gloves between 1967 and 1975. He had excellent range and a great arm. Willie Mays's totals are hurt by the fact that his first five years in the majors are not covered by Retrosheet. Cesar Geronimo was the center fielder for Cincinnati's Big Red Machine. An excellent defender, Geronimo won four Gold Gloves with the Reds. His defensive arsenal included an excellent arm, for which he was justly renowned.

There are not very many left fielders known for their throwing arms. Of a team's two corner outfielders, the one with the better arm will generally be found in right field. Still, a left fielder has as many throwing opportunities as a center or right fielder. These are the top left fielders in the Clemente Era:

Left Field -- Clemente Era

	Opps	Kill+	Hold+	Runs	Runs/162
Yastrzemski, Carl	1974	128	111	67.3	5.5
Stargell, Willie	1069	145	101	19.7	3.0
Colavito, Rocky	532	125	110	18.3	5.6
Rose, Pete	677	116	108	13.9	3.3
Moon, Wally	533	107	107	10.2	3.1
Rudi, Joe	1057	74	107	9.2	1.4
Skinner, Bob	771	143	100	7.9	1.7
Reichardt, Rick	705	115	104	7.8	1.8
Oglivie, Ben	1159	118	100	7.1	1.0
Hisle, Larry	590	109	103	6.5	1.8

Yaz was well known for his good arm and the numbers bear that out. Keep Yaz in mind, because we'll be looking at other Boston left fielders in a bit. Fenway may be having an effect here. Colavito and Stargell were also reputed to have powerful arms. I never thought of Rose as having an exceptional arm, but this analysis suggests that he did. As we saw above, Rose was also very good in throwing from right field.

The Jesse Barfield Era

Jesse Barfield, right fielder of the Toronto Blue Jays in the 1980s, is widely considered to have had the best throwing arm of his time, so I named this era after him. This era (birth year between 1950 and 1965) doesn't have the number of heroic figures of the Clemente Era: I count something like a dozen Hall of Fame outfielders in the Clemente Era and only five in this era (including Barry Bonds and Rickey Henderson). Still, there were some really excellent outfield arms playing in this period. Let's look first at the cannons in right field:

Right Field -- Barfield Era

	Opps	Kill+	Hold+	Runs	Runs/162
Barfield, Jesse	1145	172	118	58.8	8.3
Valentine, Ellis	768	143	119	38.6	8.2
Evans, Dwight	1937	106	111	30.8	2.6
Winfield, Dave	1690	95	110	17.7	1.7
Wilson, Glenn	743	135	113	17.5	3.8
Snyder, Cory	773	140	108	17.5	3.6
Clark, Jack	1006	118	109	16.6	2.7
O'Neill, Paul	1562	98	107	15.6	1.6
Parker, Dave	1587	107	107	14.3	1.5
Cowens, Al	1182	95	107	9.8	1.4

Bill James called Jesse Barfield the best outfielder of the 1980s "by far." He also named Ellis Valentine, right fielder for the Expos in the late 1970s, the best outfielder of that decade. Pretty smart guy, Bill James. Note that Barfield and Valentine both have Runs/162 values that are higher than anything we saw in the Clemente Era. They both had relatively short careers and missed the worst part of their defensive decline phase. Valentine, who seemed to be on a Hall of Fame track at the age of 25, was out of the game by age 30. Barfield

played in 12 seasons, mostly with the Jays, and was a fine defender and solid hitter. He fell off very quickly though, and at age 32 he retired from baseball. Valentine and Barfield were so dominating at controlling the running game that they rank high on the all-time list of runs saved for right fielders, despite their short careers. Impressive.

I should mention here that there is a hole in the data for the Barfield Era. For 1984 and 1985 the Retrosheet play-by-play data do not contain enough detailed information to perform this analysis. So I have to exclude these years. This probably hurts Jesse Barfield more than many others, since he was at his peak in this period and, in fact, threw out 33 baserunners in 1984-1985 (best among major league right fielders).

The top center fielders:

Center Field -- Barfield Era

	Opps	Kill+	Hold+	Runs	Runs/162
Van Slyke, Andy	1113	159	117	44.2	6.4
Dawson, Andre	1123	126	116	35.5	5.1
Moreno, Omar	1215	105	109	18.6	2.5
Murphy, Dwayne	998	119	109	18.3	3.0
Henderson, Dave	930	127	110	17.4	3.0
Cedeno, Cesar	1548	101	109	17.4	1.9
Puckett, Kirby	1194	138	102	13.9	1.9
Murphy, Dale	812	95	114	10.9	2.2
McGee, Willie	1071	130	102	9.1	1.4
Shelby, John	510	132	110	8.2	2.6

Andy Van Slyke's throwing arm was well-respected in his time, and we see now just how fabulous it truly was. Van Slyke was a right fielder with the St. Louis Cardinals early in his career, but he moved to center when traded to Pittsburgh in 1987 (forcing Barry Bonds to left field). Dawson, the two Murphys, Puckett—heck just about all of these guys were known to have good throwing arms. Dawson actually spent the second half of his career in right field, where his numbers were only average. This probably has more to do with age than the position change though. Dale Murphy did not throw out a large number of runners, but he commanded respect, with an admirable Hold+ of 114.

Kirby Puckett is another player who suffers from the missing data from 1984-1985: he led all major league outfielders with 35 assists in that period.

eft fielders in the Barfield Era are:

...eld -- Barfield Era

s	Kill+	Hold+	Runs	Runs/162
9	111	106	33.2	2.2
5	122	110	22.5	4.9
6	121	102	15.8	1.8
7	140	103	15.2	3.1
2	140	99	14.3	2.2
4	141	101	11.9	3.2
0	102	104	10.6	1.9
2	153	99	9.3	3.0
1	119	102	7.0	1.6
7	123	100	6.2	0.6

...to admit that I found this list a bit ...eman did not seem to me to have ... arm, and his Hold+ of only 99 ...ng base runners were of the same ...ctually threw out 40% more base ...erage left fielder. However, as Bill ... Clemente pointed out, throwing is not only about arm strength. Coleman had great speed and was effective at getting to the ball and getting rid of it quickly. The same argument can be made on Bonds's behalf—he was very effective at controlling the running game despite lacking a strong throwing arm.

The Vlad Guerrero Era

We are now in the Vlad Guerrero Era, which includes players born since 1965. Most of us are more familiar with the cannon-arms from today's game: Vlad, Ichiro, Bradley and Higginson. Higginson? Wait, he was a left fielder, so I'll stick to the program and show the top right fielders first:

Right Field -- Guerrero Era

	Opps	Kill+	Hold+	Runs	Runs/162
Walker, Larry	1670	135	112	51.3	4.9
Mondesi, Raul	1326	117	120	44.8	5.5
Abreu, Bobby	1092	115	109	26.6	4.0
Guerrero, Vladimir	1154	122	112	25.3	3.6
Merced, Orlando	619	145	116	22.6	5.9
Whiten, Mark	684	127	116	20.4	4.9
Suzuki, Ichiro	906	115	111	18.5	3.3
Sanders, Reggie	1009	129	103	16.3	2.6
Hidalgo, Richard	552	115	114	13.5	4.0
Jordan, Brian	829	113	101	9.5	1.9

Now this is a list of strong outfield arms. Orlando Merced only played a few years as a regular before assuming more of a fourth outfielder role. His best attributes were his good batting eye and very effective arm. Bobby Abreu gets mixed reviews for his defense, and I haven't heard him touted as having a great arm very much, but this analysis suggests he has a good one. The other eight players on this list are all considered to have very strong arms.

The list of top center field arms also contains some expected names:

Center Field -- Guerrero Era

	Opps	Kill+	Hold+	Runs	Runs/162
Edmonds, Jim	1503	158	111	41.1	4.5
Griffey Jr., Ken	2142	130	111	40.4	3.1
Jones, Andruw	1259	126	114	36.5	4.7
Lofton, Kenny	1762	127	107	31.1	2.8
Hunter, Brian	776	178	101	19.8	4.1
Bradley, Milton	514	162	108	15.3	4.9
Kotsay, Mark	797	151	102	12.7	2.6
Glanville, Doug	714	112	107	11.6	2.6
Curtis, Chad	835	111	105	11.5	2.2
Finley, Steve	2068	109	104	11.4	0.9

Edmonds, Griffey, Jones, Bradley, Kotsay: all of these guys are considered strong throwers. Kenny Lofton doesn't seem to possess a strong arm nowadays, but over his career he was apparently effective in controlling the running game. Milton Bradley moved to right field in 2006, and it will be very interesting to see how he did there, once the data for 2006 is available.

And finally, we come to the left fielders:

Left Field -- Guerrero Era

	Opps	Kill+	Hold+	Runs	Runs/162
Higginson, Bobby	846	171	105	26.6	5.1
Gilkey, Bernard	954	172	103	24.1	4.0
Burrell, Pat	817	123	108	15.8	3.2
Ramirez, Manny	632	115	101	6.8	1.7
Dunn, Adam	583	108	103	6.7	1.9
Jenkins, Geoff	691	151	100	6.5	1.5
Conine, Jeff	761	122	102	6.0	1.3
Alou, Moises	1018	106	100	4.7	0.7
Anderson, Garret	1103	97	103	3.5	0.5
Giles, Brian	663	107	98	2	0.5

What can I say? I wouldn't have named any of these guys, except for Geoff Jenkins, as strong-armed outfielders. Bobby Higginson? I must confess, I remember the Tiger outfielder (1995-2005) as a guy who had a couple of good years, was signed to a long-term over-valued contract and was crappy thereafter. But it turns out that he had a great arm. He led all left fielders by a wide margin in assists per game in the period 1996-2005. Bernard Gilkey, another offensive one-hit wonder (his great year offensively was 1996), had a fabulous arm; he was second in assists among all outfielders during the 1990s and, on a per-game basis, he threw out more runners than any outfielder.

In fact, many left fielders have good arms, but you never would know it, because nobody talks about guns in left field.

The presence of Manny Ramirez on this list may or may not surprise you. Ramirez, of course, played right field before coming to Boston, so you might expect an ex-right fielder to be good in left field (his throwing numbers in right were about average).

But, when you see Manny throw, he just doesn't look very imposing. He doesn't have a powerful arm and he doesn't have good speed to allow him to get to balls particularly quickly. The best that can be said is that he gets rid of the ball in a hurry once he's gotten hold of it. It makes you wonder if Fenway Park is helping him. After all, we've already seen two other Boston left fielders, Yaz and Rice, among the best throwing left fielders of their time.

I have not studied the question in detail, but it's logical to think that Fenway Park, with its short, high fence in left, could make throwing easier for Red Sox left fielders. Left fielders are forced to play shallow at Fenway, making for a shorter throw back to the infield.

Also, the Green Monster can make base running hazardous—it's not that difficult to catch a ball off the wall and get it back into second base in time to turn a double into an "oops/single," as Bill James put it.

This is an area for further research—doing the analysis for home and away games would be the logical first step. For what it's worth, Mike Greenwell and Troy O'Leary, the two regular Boston left fielders between the Rice and Ramirez years, do not have particularly good throwing numbers; Greenwell was about average, while O'Leary was below average.

Hall of Famers

Here are the results for Hall of Famers who had significant playing time in the Retrosheet era. I've included a few players who are not eligible for the Hall but would otherwise go in based on their career statistics: Rose, Bonds, Sosa and Griffey Jr.

HoF Right Fielders

	Opps	Kill+	Hold+	Runs	Runs/162
Clemente, Roberto	1998	135	118	67.1	5.4
Kaline, Al	1473	89	115	26.5	2.9
Aaron, Hank	1645	117	104	24.9	2.4
Winfield, Dave	1690	95	110	17.7	1.7
Rose, Pete	619	108	110	11.5	3.0
Sosa, Sammy	1911	102	99	6.2	0.5
Jackson, Reggie	1644	100	100	0.3	0.0
Robinson, Frank	1062	78	95	-15.5	-2.3

HoF Center Fielders

	Opps	Kill+	Hold+	Runs	Runs/162
Griffey Jr., Ken	2142	130	111	40.4	3.1
Mays, Willie	2337	97	110	28.8	2.0
Puckett, Kirby	1194	138	102	13.9	1.9
Mantle, Mickey	1094	64	100	-6.9	-1.1
Yount, Robin	1152	99	89	-14.0	-1.9
Ashburn, Richie	783	67	89	-19.3	-4.0

HoF Left Fielders

	Opps	Kill+	Hold+	Runs	Runs/162
Yastrzemski, Carl	1974	128	111	67.3	5.5
Bonds, Barry	2419	111	106	33.2	2.2
Stargell, Willie	1069	145	101	19.7	3.0
Rose, Pete	677	116	108	13.9	3.3
Robinson, Frank	562	124	99	-0.7	-0.2
Williams, Billy	1714	118	98	-1.1	-0.1
Henderson, Rickey	2349	74	101	-10.7	-0.7
Brock, Lou	2148	76	97	-30.6	-2.3

I suppose Lou Brock had the worst outfield arm of any Hall of Famer. Richie Ashburn doesn't count, since the first 10 years of his career are not covered by Retrosheet. Ashburn is reputed to have had a strong throwing arm. Mantle also loses the best part of his career and likely was a better thrower than indicated by the numbers you see here.

The Worst Outfield Arms

Here, without comment, are the outfielders that fared worst with this analysis.

Worst Right Field Arms

	Opps	Kill+	Hold+	Runs	Runs/162
Singleton, Ken	1114	70	89	-29.2	-4.2
Burnitz, Jeromy	1162	85	93	-21.7	-3.0
Washington, Claudell	931	91	86	-20.3	-3.6
Burroughs, Jeff	862	87	85	-18.6	-3.5
Eisenreich, Jim	554	62	90	-17.1	-5.0

Worst Center Field Arms

	Opps	Kill+	Hold+	Runs	Runs/162
Williams, Bernie	1911	55	92	-44.3	-3.7
Pierre, Juan	871	50	88	-29.3	-5.4
Damon, Johnny	1190	68	91	-22.5	-3.1
McRae, Brian	1243	64	96	-21.6	-2.8
Bumbry, Al	806	87	85	-20.6	-4.1

Worst Left Field Arms

	Opps	Kill+	Hold+	Runs	Runs/162
Howard, Frank	874	76	86	-33.4	-6.2
Brock, Lou	2148	76	97	-30.6	-2.3
White, Roy	1687	74	95	-30.5	-2.9
Baylor, Don	678	52	88	-25.7	-6.2
Gant, Ron	995	84	96	-16.9	-2.8

Final Thoughts

The wealth of detailed play-by-play information made available in recent years makes it possible to get a good, quantitative handle on which outfielders were successful in controlling the running game. By considering the outcomes of key throwing situations for each fielder, I can determine how many runs he saves (or costs) his team. The analysis is by no means perfect—the five situations considered are not 100% exhaustive. Part of outfield throwing is not captured in this analysis, although I believe it's a relatively small part.

By and large, the results of this analysis agree with our notions of who throws well and who doesn't. The study, though, has unearthed a few unexpected (at least to me) names, especially among left fielders, who don't get much attention for their throwing ability.

This study gives us some idea of how much a strong outfield arm is worth, although the numbers need to be interpreted with some caution. First, as I've already mentioned, not all throwing is covered by the five situations, so the runs saved figures can be regarded as a lower limit, in some sense. Clemente probably saved more than 67 runs over his career, because we haven't taken into account the full body of his throwing work. The second point is that the Runs/162 numbers shown above are career stats; values for a single season will tend to fluctuate more and the difference between the best and worst arms in a given year will be larger than what one might deduce from the numbers given above.

For example, from the tables above, it appears that generally the best arms are three to five runs above average and the worst are perhaps three to five below average, for a difference of about six to 10 runs. However, if you look at seasonal numbers, the differences are larger. In 1986, for example, the difference in Runs/162 between Dwight Evans (7.8 Runs/162) and Kirk Gibson (-7.0) was about 15 runs. In 1964, the difference between the best throwing left fielder (Yastrzemski) and the worst one (Tito Francona) was 19 runs (in terms of Runs/162). These numbers are better indicators of the value of a good outfield arm over the course of a single season.

Sources

This study builds on an analysis that I performed in 2006, the results of which were written up as two articles on the Hardball Times Website:

http://www.hardballtimes.com/main/article/cannons-and-popguns-rating-outfield-arms/

http://www.hardballtimes.com/main/article/more-guns-in-the-outfield-center-and-left-field/

Bill James' *Historical Baseball Abstract* is by now a classic of baseball writing. The quote on Clemente is taken from the original (1985) version.

Retrosheet (www.retrosheet.org) is a non-profit organization run by people who love baseball.

Tommy John Surgery

by David Gassko

It was mid-July in 1974 and Los Angeles pitcher Tommy John was having a great season. He was 13-3 with a 2.50 ERA and his Dodgers were in first place with a 61-31 record, 5½ games up on the Cincinnati Reds. He had a start against the Montreal Expos, and it was that day, July 17, that everything went wrong. He pitched two innings, allowed two runs, and came out of the game with a sore elbow. He knew what it meant—his career was over. It had happened to countless pitchers before him, including Sandy Koufax. They would call it "dead arm" and call it a career.

He went to team doctor Frank Jobe and said, "I don't want to be done. Can't you make something up?" Two months later, Jobe did and John went under the knife. Jobe gave John a 1-in-100 shot of making it back to the major leagues. A year later, John was back; he played 14 more seasons. The surgery would come to be known as "Tommy John surgery," and it would save hundreds of pitchers' careers.

How does it work?

So what did Jobe do to save John's career? What procedure did he make up in that operating room? Well, it took Jobe four hours to repair John's elbow, though the procedure takes just over an hour these days. The surgery is not really any different, though—essentially, doctors take a useless tendon from the pitcher's forearm or hamstring and loop it through his elbow in a figure-eight shape.

The ulnar collateral ligament (UCL) is located in the elbow, and every time a pitcher throws a baseball, he places extreme stress on the UCL, which stabilizes the elbow during the pitching motion. Pitchers often have damaged UCLs, and sometimes the ligament will just give out. An injury to the UCL can be difficult to spot, but it saps a pitcher's velocity and throwing ability. Not all Tommy John surgery patients have torn UCLs—if the ligament is damaged enough, it may be better to operate on it than to attempt rehab. As the ligament stretches, the pitcher is going to lose effectiveness, even if the UCL is not completely torn.

To replace the UCL, a doctor will harvest a tendon from the pitcher's forearm—the tendon serves no real use; in fact 12-15 percent of us don't even have it—or hamstring, if the forearm tendon is not present or for some other reason is unusable. The tendon is then looped into the elbow through the humerus and ulna bones using a figure-eight pattern that is supposed to make it maximally strong and resistant.

This part is easy. What comes next is not. The tendon must be converted to a ligament, learn to function as a ligament, and start carrying blood. It's a long, arduous process that doesn't just involve rehabbing the elbow, but the whole arm. Seattle prospect Matt Hrynio said that his forearm "shriveled from the surgery." According to Dr. Tim Kremchek, who does 120 Tommy John surgeries a year, the "difference maker is the rehab people, not the surgeon."

The first week after surgery, the pitcher has to wear a hard brace; the next, he wears a sling, and after that he can slowly return to his full range of motion, which takes about a month. At four months, he can begin a soft-tossing program, and six months after surgery, the pitcher can finally throw from 60 feet. It takes almost a year before he is allowed to go full speed again, though often the pitcher feels like he can pitch seven or eight months in. The new ligament, however, is not yet ready to withstand the force of a major league fastball.

The recovery is long and it can be embarrassing. When Randy Wolf first played soft-toss after having the surgery, about a third of his throws bounced off the ground. It took months to get from there to the mound. In the week after surgery, the only exercise a pitcher is allowed to do is to squeeze a soft ball or putty. Forget about carrying groceries or doing other simple tasks.

Even as the pitcher's range of motion increases, and his elbow strengthens, it is imperative that he take his time coming back from the surgery. The ligament has to mature and then be strengthened, and that takes time, regardless of the pitcher's personal healing abilities. Rushing a comeback can not only hurt the elbow,

> **Which pitchers have come back strongest from Tommy John surgery?**
>
> 1. Odalis Perez (2000), -.1.97
> 2. Ryan Dempster (2004), -1.74
> 3. Chris Carpenter (2003), -1.73
> 4. Steve Karsay (1995), -1.71
> 5. Jason Isringhausen (1998), -1.39
>
> (Measured by improvement in ERA post-surgery)

it can also hurt the pitcher's shoulder, because he will try to compensate for his elbow's weakness by changing his mechanics. In fact, Dr. Craig Morgan, a Tommy John surgery specialist, has concluded that pitchers who have UCL damage tend to drop their elbow below their shoulder during their release, placing extra stress on their arms. Players with elbow problems tend to have shoulder problems as well.

Tommy John injuries are therefore correlated with poor mechanics in general. Morgan believes that Tommy John surgery could be done away with completely if clubs did more to correct pitcher mechanics. Jobe says that fatigue and overuse lead to a breakdown in mechanics which in turn can cause injury problems—a statement echoed by a multitude of pitchers. For that reason, he supports the five-man rotation.

But a torn UCL is still something of a freak injury. Throwing overhand is a highly unnatural motion, so every time a pitcher rears back to throw, he risks popping that ligament. (Jobe theorizes that sidearm pitchers should be less susceptible to injury.) Good mechanics and avoiding overuse can do a great deal to steer clear of elbow problems, but there's no way to totally prevent them.

Who has had it done?

The second pitcher, after Tommy John, to have a successful surgery and rehab was Tom Candiotti in 1982, although according to him, Jobe had done the surgery on eight pitchers by that point, and none but John had come back.

The surgery has since exploded in popularity, with many hundred Tommy John cases each year. Most estimates say that about 10% of all current major league pitchers have had the procedure, or about 70 hurlers total. I was able to compile a list of 182 past and current pitchers who have had Tommy John surgery. Only about 20% of Dr. James Andrews's UCL patients these days are major leaguers. The majority of his patients are college or high school players. San Diego pitcher Dewon Brazelton had surgery when he was just 16, and five years later the Tampa Bay Devil Rays made him the third overall pick in the 2001 amateur draft.

David Wells and Mariano Rivera both had the procedure done as minor leaguers, and Chris Carpenter has had three straight great seasons since he had Tommy

John surgery. Jose Rijo owns the greatest comeback from Tommy John surgery: he missed six years, garnered a vote for the Hall of Fame, and had multiple procedures before coming back in 2001. Rijo is the only player to ever play in a major league game after receiving a vote for the Hall of Fame, and he managed to pitch effectively after his grueling comeback.

Then, of course, there's the most famous non-patient of all-time: Sandy Koufax. Following a spectacular 1966 season, in which he won the Cy Young and finished second in MVP voting, Koufax retired with "dead arm." Many believe that his elbow problems were due to a damaged UCL; had Tommy John surgery come into existence 10 ten years earlier, Koufax's career might have been saved (and maybe they would be calling it "Sandy Koufax surgery" instead). Who knows what could have been? Another famous suspected UCL case is Smoky Joe Wood. In 1912, Wood pitched 344 innings with a 1.91 ERA and 35 complete games. Wood was never the same after the season, and many believe that he might have had a damaged UCL as well. Eventually, Wood was converted to an outfielder so that he could extend his career.

With John still eligible for the Hall of Fame, and Rivera almost certain to make it to Cooperstown once he retires, Tommy John surgery has not just been a career-lengthening procedure; it has given us greats that would have otherwise had to retire.

What is the effect of Tommy John surgery?

So we can see that some, like Rivera or Wells, have benefited greatly from the procedure—they wouldn't have had a career without it. Others, like Jeff Zimmerman and Denny Neagle, have seen their careers ruined following the surgery. So how does Tommy John surgery affect the average pitcher?

Some pitchers swear that Tommy John surgery improved their fastball velocity. Chad Fox says that each of his two surgeries added a couple of miles per hour to his four-seamer. Kerry Wood has said the same. So has Billy Koch. Jobe insists that Tommy John surgery can't make you any better than you have been, but that pitchers may throw better than they have in years because even before the UCL pops, a pitcher's elbow might have been in bad shape for some time. All pitchers have some structural damage—it's the extent

> ### Which pitchers' careers have been extended the most by Tommy John surgery?
>
> 1. David Wells (1985), 3206.33
> 2. Tom Candiotti (1982), 2725.00
> 3. Tommy John (1975), 2544.67
> 4. Cory Lidle (1998), 1070.33
> 5. Matt Morris (1999), 1046.67
>
> (Measured by number of innings pitched, post-surgery)

that determines just how much they're going to be hurt. Essentially, Tommy John surgery takes a pitcher back to square one—his elbow is as sound as it was before he ever picked up a baseball.

Of course, on the other hand, the surgery has other effects as well. It forces pitchers to adapt their repertoires—Wood had to drop his nasty curveball for a slurve that puts less stress on his arm, but moves less well. Many pitchers simply can't make the recovery, or if they do, they don't come back the same. Can it be that Tommy John surgery hurts pitchers then?

Luckily, this question can be examined by looking at my database. Of the 182 pitchers who have had Tommy John surgery that I could identify, 74 pitched in the major

Rehabilitation program following Tommy John surgery:

0-7 days: Splint is worn; squeeze soft ball.

1-4 weeks: Discontinue splint; sling worn for one more week; gradually achieve full range of motion.

1-2 months: Full range of motion at elbow, wrist, forearm, shoulder; lightweights for forearm exercises.

2-3 months: Continue lower body conditioning program; continue exercises for upper extremities, including rotator cuff.

3-4 months: Easy tossing (no wind-up), 25-30 throws building up to 70.

4-5 months: Continue throwing program with easy wind-up, 20-50 feet, 10-40 throws.

5-6 months: Throwing program extends to 60 feet at half-speed.

6-7 months: Gradually increase distance to 150 feet.

7-8 months: Progress to a mound at half- to three-quarters speed, using proper body mechanics (stay on top of ball, keep elbow up, throw over the top, follow through with arm and trunk).

9-10 months: Simulate game situations.

10-12 months: Begin normal routine and make appropriate rehab starts.

(Originally provided by Dr. Craig Morgan to the *Courier Post Online*)

leagues both before and after the procedure (excluding 2006). By weighting each pitcher's totals by the lesser number of innings pitched in either half of his career (that is, if a pitcher throws fewer innings before the surgery than he does after, I weight the changes in his statistics by the number of innings he threw before having the procedure, and vice-versa), I found that the average pitcher's ERA increased by .18 runs post-surgery. This is actually an improvement over average, because the average age at surgery is 26, and most pitchers get worse after 26 to a greater degree than just .18 runs. In total, we have over 13,000 "weighted innings" in our sample.

Unfortunately, Tommy John did a little too well both before and after his surgery—his numbers represent over 16 percent of the total sample. That's a bit too much for my taste, so I'll remove him. We still have 11,000 "weighted innings," which should be plenty. Now I see an increase of just eight-hundredths of a run post-surgery, no change in strikeout rate, a decrease of .28 walks per game, and an extra .09 home runs per nine. The home run and walk numbers are consistent with normal aging patterns, but the strikeouts are not.

Looks like Fox and Wood and Koch are right: For whatever reason, Tommy John surgery actually helps pitchers, if only a little.

What's next?

The Tommy John procedure is pretty much perfected by now, and if the pitcher does his part in rehab, his chances of coming back are very good. Jobe speculates that the future is in stem cell research, and that some day, surgeons may be able to regenerate the elbow ligament, instead of having to replace it. Until then, pitchers will have to go through the one-hour surgery and the one-year rehab to make it back as good as new.

It would be interesting to see how pitchers are affected by other types of surgery—my guess is that the results would not be nearly as favorable. Tommy John surgery is indeed a medical miracle; it doesn't just repair the pitcher, it makes him good as new.

And, according to my database, Tommy John surgery has given us around 40,000 innings from pitchers whose careers would have otherwise been done. That's a hell of a shot Jobe fired 30 years ago, what with his 1-in-100 odds.

Analysis

WPA in the USA

by Dave Studenmund

On July 14, the Braves and Padres played a roller coaster of a game. The Braves took a 4-0 lead in the first on home runs by Chipper and Andruw Jones, but the Padres came back to tie it in the third, 5-5, on a double by Mike Piazza and a home run by Adrian Gonzalez. Atlanta scratched back to take the lead again, 8-5 in the fifth, but the Padres scored three in the sixth and one more in the seventh to take their own lead, 9-8.

The Braves were not going to relinquish the game easily, however, and they scored three runs off Trevor Hoffman in the top of the ninth for an 11-9 lead. Not so fast, said the Padres, who scored two of their own in the bottom of the ninth on consecutive hits by the Joshes (Barfield and Bard) that sent the game into extra innings.

In the 10th, Adam LaRoche homered to put Atlanta up by one, but the Padres once again refused to yield, scoring one more in the bottom of the inning. Finally, the Braves scored three runs in the top of the 11th to put the game away, 15-12, and everyone went home exhausted.

There were so many lead changes and comebacks that day in San Diego that this game deserves to be called the ultimate roller coaster of 2006, based on a little statistic called Win Probability Added (WPA).

WPA is a relatively simple idea, though the math is kind of complex. I'll try to explain WPA with an example. We can calculate, based on the number of times an average team scores per inning, that an average team with a one-run lead in the top of the ninth has an 83% chance of winning. And, if we look up that situation in actual baseball games over the past 25 years (no one out, no one on, top of the ninth, one-run lead), we find that the leading team has actually won the game about 85% of the time. The numbers don't match exactly, because teams use their best relievers with one-run leads (increasing their probability a bit), but the results are pretty close.

Apply that math to every situation in a game, and you have an average team's win probability for every situation in every inning. For instance, when the Braves took a four-run lead over the Padres in the very first inning, their win probability was about 80%. When the Padres took a 9-8 lead in the bottom of the seventh, their win probability was 74%. Two-run lead for Atlanta in the ninth? 90%. Padres come back to tie in the bottom of the ninth? 50%.

And on and on. Each change in win probability is the Win Probability Added of that play. So once you add up all of the WPA swings in that July 14 game, you get a total of 793% or .69 WPA points of change per

The Roller Coasters of 2006: Games with Most Changes in WPA

Date	Winner	Score	Loser	Score	Innings	Tot WPA	Avg/Inning
7/14/2006	ATL	15	SD	12	11	7.63	0.69
9/18/2006	LAN	11	SD	10	10	6.84	0.68
9/27/2006	PHI	8	WAS	7	14	9.15	0.65
9/6/2006	WAS	7	STL	6	9	5.83	0.64
5/19/2006	ARI	10	ATL	9	9	5.80	0.64
5/14/2006	BAL	8	KC	7	9	5.72	0.63
8/30/2006	PIT	10	CHN	9	11	6.99	0.63
8/4/2006	HOU	8	ARI	7	9	5.68	0.63
4/16/2006	STL	8	CIN	7	9	5.62	0.62
6/26/2006	BOS	8	PHI	7	12	7.43	0.62

inning, more than twice the major league average of .30. That's a lot of action for one little ballgame.

Actually, Padres fans chewed quite a few fingernails last season, because their team was also involved in the second-wildest game of the year. Remember when the Dodgers hit four straight home runs in the bottom of the ninth (September 18 in Los Angeles) to tie the game and eventually won in the 10th on a Nomar Garciaparra home run? There were .68 WPA points exchanged per inning in that game, just .01 less than the Atlanta game. Given its record-setting home run heroics and pennant implications, I have no problem calling the September 18 game 2006's "game of the year."

On the previous page, you see a list of the 10 wildest games of the year, measured by total changes in WPA (per inning) during the game.

That September 27 game in Washington was a wild one. Philadelphia, hoping to make the postseason, walked Washington's Ryan Zimmerman with the bases loaded in the bottom of the ninth to tie it. Both teams scored in the 10th, but Philadelphia took a two-run lead in the 14th. It was good that Philly scored two, because Washington managed to load the bases with no one out in the bottom of the inning. After a sacrifice fly and a double play, however, the game belonged to the Phillies.

The most boring game of the year was Detroit's 15-4 victory over Kansas City on September 23. Detroit took a 10-0 lead in the first inning and led 15-0 after four; for all intents and purposes, the game was decided before the Royals even came to bat. There were only .07 WPA change points per inning that day in K.C.

Less than two weeks earlier, the Phillies' Tom Gordon had made the biggest WPA pitching play of the year. The Phillies were leading Houston 4-3 in the bottom of the ninth (79% win probability), but Gordon allowed a couple of hits, his fielders botched a couple of plays and the Astros had the bases loaded with one out. The Phillies' win probability had dropped to 46%. But Gordon got Humberto Quintero to ground into a double play, winning the game for the Phils and adding .54 win probability points in one play. (Once a team wins a game, its win probability is 100%, natch.)

There were two other similar plays last year. Baltimore's Chris Ray got Garrett Anderson to ground into a double play on May 28, and the Reds' David Weathers "got" Johnny Estrada to line into a double play on May 7. Both plays occurred with the bases loaded and one out in the bottom of the ninth and the visiting team winning by a run.

Given the pennant implications of Gordon's September save, we'll give him credit for the biggest "pitching" outcome of the year. Indeed, most of the biggest WPA defensive plays of the year involved double plays, which makes sense. Two outs have a bigger impact than one.

But a pitcher shouldn't get 100% of the credit for a double play, right? After all, his fielders helped. So let's ask a more specific question for pitchers: what was the biggest strikeout of the year?

It occurred on September 29, when the Twins were still trying to catch the Tigers for first place in the American League Central. They entered the bottom of the ninth losing to the White Sox 4-1, but scored two runs and had the bases loaded with two out and Phil Nevin at the plate and Bobby Jenks on the mound for the Sox. Jenks had pitched the entire ninth and let the Twins get back into the game. But with the bases loaded, Jenks struck out Phil Nevin on three pitches for a WPA gain of .28. The Twins had to wait a few more days to take over first place.

Okay, now let's turn the tables and uncover the biggest offensive play of the season. Which single swing of the bat did the most to win a game?

It turns out that there were two. On July 30, the A's were down by two runs when Milton Bradley came to bat with runners on first and second and two outs in the bottom of the ninth. Toronto had scored three runs in the top of the inning, and the A's winning probability at that point was just 10%, even though Mark Kotsay had just fouled seven straight pitches off of relief ace B.J. Ryan to earn a walk and get Bradley to the plate.

Bradley responded by smoking a home run to center field and giving the A's a 6-5 victory. That single hit changed Oakland's win probability from 10% to 100%; Bradley added .90 WPA points with one swing of the bat.

One other batter matched Bradley's WPA output. That was Boston's David Ortiz, who hit a home run in a very similar situation on June 11 against Akinori Otsuka and the Texas Rangers. Bradley's and Ortiz's home runs had bigger game impacts than any other hits all season.

Hopefully, these examples give you a feel for win probability and how it works. To recap, the specific probability of a situation is its Win Probability, and the phrase Win Probability Added describes the change in win probability from play to play. If you assign Win Probability Added to the players involved in each play, you have a fascinating way to judge which players did the most to help their teams win.

You probably noticed that Win Probability is a "real time" statistic. A home run in the ninth inning of a tie game has a much bigger WPA impact than a home run in the first inning of a tie game, because a team is much more likely to win the game when it goes ahead in the ninth.

That may strike you as unfair, but that's what WPA is. It reflects the tension and dynamic of game situations as they occur. That's why I like to use it to find the most thrilling and significant games and plays. And when used properly, it can also tell you a lot about individual players.

The Bullpen

For instance, WPA is a truly unique way to measure the impact of major league bullpens. WPA measures the impact of bullpens (and bullpen deployment) better than any other single statistic because it captures both performance and situation. The top five WPA bullpens in the majors last year were…

Top WPA Bullpens

Team	WPA	LI
Twins	11.2	0.85
Mets	11.1	1.06
A's	8.9	1.16
Angels	8.5	1.02
Padres	7.9	1.16

There's no doubt that the Twins' and Mets' bullpens were the best last year. They had the two lowest ERAs (2.91 and 3.25, respectively) among all major league bullpens, and they both accounted for about 11 WPA points. Since one win equals .50 WPA points (each team starts a game with a 50% chance of winning, so the winning team gains .50 WPA points during the game), this means that these two bullpens

each contributed 22 wins above .500 to their team's record.

The Mets and Twins both finished about 40 wins above .500, so their bullpens were responsible for roughly half of their above-average performance.

I didn't list it here, but the Texas bullpen was sixth in the majors in bullpen ERA (3.74), yet 19th in bullpen WPA (0.90). To understand why, let's kick around another WPA angle, perhaps the best angle of all.

The right-hand column in the previous table includes a statistic called Leverage Index (LI), an invention of baseball analyst Tom M. Tango, who is the leading champion of WPA today. Tom developed LI as a way of measuring the relative criticality of a play. The greater the potential impact of a plate appearance on win probability, the higher the Leverage Index.

For instance, when Bobby Jenks struck out Phil Nevin with the bases loaded, the Leverage Index was 11—the situation was 11 times more critical than the average situation. That's just about as high as LI gets. An average LI is one; most relief aces have an average LI around 2.0.

So why did Texas rank so low in bullpen WPA? Because they pitched best when it mattered least. I've put all Texas bullpen situations into the following Leverage Index groups, so you can see how their performance worsened as situations became more important:

Texas Bullpen

LI	WPA
0.0 - 0.5	0.90
0.5 - 1.0	0.03
1.0 - 1.5	0.90
1.5 - 2.0	-1.26
2.0 - 2.5	-0.43
2.5 - 3.0	1.72
>3	-1.69

When the Leverage Index was under 1.50, the Texas bullpen was fine. But in three of the four groupings above 1.50, the bullpen's WPA was negative. Overall, their stats looked good, but WPA captured how well (or poorly) they pitched to the situation. In this case, WPA tells the real story.

Let's look at the individual members of one of last year's best bullpens, the San Diego Padres', led by the all-time leader in career saves, Trevor Hoffman.

The San Diego Bullpen

Name	WPA	LI	Save Ops
Hoffman T.	4.05	2.08	51
Meredith C.	3.11	1.40	2
Linebrink S.	2.52	1.90	11
Embree A.	0.77	1.15	0
Adkins J.	0.37	0.96	0
Sweeney B.	0.13	0.45	3
Brocail D.	0.01	0.74	0
Cassidy S.	-0.95	0.92	2

Hoffman led the Padres in bullpen WPA, and he also compiled the highest Leverage Index. But he wasn't the only outstanding reliever in the pack.

If you were to look only at each pitcher's save opportunities, you'd think that Hoffman made many more critical appearances than any other San Diego reliever. But Scott Linebrink's LI was only slightly lower than Hoffman's. In fact, Linebrink's LI was higher than that of several closers on other teams. He also performed extremely well, with a WPA of 2.52

Linebrink and the remarkable Cla Meredith were among the top 16 relievers in all of baseball last year, along with Hoffman. The top ten relievers in 2006 WPA were:

Top Ten Major League Relievers

Name	Team	WPA	LI
Rodriguez F.	LAA	5.39	2.12
Papelbon J.	BOS	5.24	2.02
Nathan J.	MIN	5.19	1.62
Ryan B.	TOR	4.75	1.89
Putz J.	SEA	4.34	1.71
Saito T.	LAN	4.09	1.50
Hoffman T.	SD	4.05	2.08
Wagner B.	NYN	3.85	1.88
Zumaya J.	DET	3.70	1.60
Rivera M.	NYA	3.39	1.83

Hopefully, you can see that a glance at the saves leaderboard won't necessarily tell you who the best relievers were last year. WPA will. Want to see a list of the worst relievers? Here you go:

Ten Worst Major League Relievers

Name	Team	WPA	LI
Dempster R.	CHN	-3.13	1.77
Turnbow D.	MIL	-2.91	1.78
Burgos A.	KC	-2.13	1.68
Sisco A.	KC	-1.95	0.90
Carmona F.	CLE	-1.82	1.53
Messenger R.	FLA	-1.68	0.84
Seanez R.	BOS	-1.50	0.54
Herges M.	FLA	-1.48	0.95
Williams T.	BAL	-1.48	1.28
Wickman B.	CLE	-1.48	1.98

Dempster, Turnbow and Burgos had truly bad years, though they continued to pitch in high-leverage situations for much of the year. By the way, Bob Wickman's record includes only his time with Cleveland. He logged a WPA of 0.79 with Atlanta.

As you can see from these lists, relievers face different levels of intensity. The Angels' Francisco Rodriguez, for instance, had an LI almost 0.50 higher than Joe Nathan's. This is a result of both managerial usage and team opportunity.

Managers choose when to bring relievers into games. Hopefully, they use their best relievers in the most important situations, though that doesn't happen as often as you might think. LI is a good tool for judging when to bring in your best relievers.

The Twins played only 60 close games last year (games with a margin of only one or two runs), the fewest in the majors. So their bullpen LI was also the lowest in the majors, 0.85. This makes their bullpen WPA total even more impressive, because it's harder to rack up a lot of WPA in low-leverage situations.

If you'd like to adjust each pitcher's WPA to even out the opportunities he was handed, simply divide WPA by LI. That essentially gives you a "normalized" WPA. Here's the list of top relievers ranked by normalized bullpen WPA:

Top Ten "Normalized" WPA Relievers

Name	Team	WPA	LI	WPA/LI
Nathan J.	MIN	5.19	1.62	3.20
Saito T.	LAN	4.09	1.50	2.73
Carrasco H.	LAA	1.42	0.54	2.61
Papelbon J.	BOS	5.24	2.02	2.60
Rodriguez F.	LAA	5.39	2.12	2.55
Putz J.	SEA	4.34	1.71	2.54
Ryan B.	TOR	4.75	1.89	2.51
Zumaya J.	DET	3.70	1.60	2.31
Rincon J.	MIN	2.42	1.08	2.24
Meredith C.	SD	3.11	1.40	2.23

Joe Nathan rocked last year, and so did the Angels' Hector Carrasco. The guy had a great year, but fans might have overlooked him because he didn't pitch in many key situations.

Starting Pitching

Virtually all starting pitchers have a Leverage Index between 0.85 and 1.15, and their WPA generally reflects their overall performance. There are some exceptions, however. For instance, here's a list of the top 10 major league starters, ranked by WPA. I've also tossed in their Runs Saved Above Average (RSAA), a comparison of their total runs allowed compared to the major league average. Positive numbers are good:

Top Ten WPA Starters

Name	Team	WPA	LI	RSAA
Oswalt R.	HOU	4.43	1.00	42
Santana J.	MIN	4.18	0.97	49
Webb B.	ARI	3.69	0.96	34
Carpenter C.	STL	3.38	1.02	37
Smoltz J.	ATL	3.28	1.04	31
Sanchez A.	FLA	3.21	1.15	22
Halladay R.	TOR	3.20	0.97	38
Young C.	SD	3.14	0.98	24
Arroyo B.	CIN	3.01	0.91	31
Robertson N.	DET	3.00	1.04	16

The first name that jumps out at me is Florida's Anibal Sanchez, who had the sixth-highest WPA total among all major league starters, although his RSAA figure was tied for 24th. The reason for Sanchez's ranking lies in his Leverage Index which, at 1.15, was at the upper end of the starting pitcher spectrum. He faced relatively more critical situations than most starters, and he evidently pitched well in them.

A couple of other pitchers who rank surprisingly high, such as San Diego's Chris Young and Detroit's Nate Robertson, pitched very well in high-leverage situations. For instance, batters hit only .199 against Robertson with runners in scoring position. Or, using the language of WPA, his WPA total was 0.50 when LI was below one, but 2.50 when it was over one. He was the opposite of the Texas bullpen.

I should mention that the WPA statistics used here don't attribute any WPA to fielders, though future versions of WPA might.

One last point: you probably noticed that WPA totals tend to be lower for starters than relievers. This is primarily a matter of opportunity; relievers get to pitch in late innings when their performance has more impact. Once again, there is a simple way to adjust this: divide WPA by LI to derive a list of the pitchers who contributed the most to their teams' wins, regardless of opportunity:

Top Ten "Normalized" WPA Pitchers

Name	Team	WPA	LI	WPA/LI
Oswalt R.	HOU	4.43	1.00	4.44
Santana J.	MIN	4.18	0.97	4.30
Webb B.	ARI	3.69	0.96	3.84
Carpenter C.	STL	3.38	1.02	3.32
Arroyo B.	CIN	3.01	0.91	3.31
Halladay R.	TOR	3.20	0.97	3.30
Nathan J.	MIN	5.19	1.62	3.20
Young C.	SD	3.14	0.98	3.20
Smoltz J.	ATL	3.28	1.04	3.16
Liriano F.	MIN	2.91	0.93	3.12

On this list, there's only one reliever among the top 10 pitchers in the majors: Minnesota's Joe Nathan.

Batters

Here are the top 10 batters, ranked by WPA:

Top Ten Major League Batters

Name	WPA	LI
Pujols A.	9.24	1.03
Howard R.	8.20	1.06
Ortiz D.	8.04	0.99
Jeter D.	5.98	1.00
Berkman L.	5.37	1.04
Dye J.	5.14	0.98
Beltran C.	4.93	0.96
Bonds B.	4.74	1.01
Abreu B.	4.71	1.01
Morneau J.	4.46	1.04

Like starting pitchers, the typical batter's LI will be between 0.85 and 1.15. Batters don't have a lot of control over when they come to bat (except for pinch hitters), and their LI will usually average around 1.0, unless their team plays a lot of close games.

I didn't separate batters into teams, because Bobby Abreu ranks among the top 10 batters in the majors when you combine his WPA totals with the Phillies and Yankees. Thought you'd like to see that.

Even so, Albert Pujols, Ryan Howard and David Ortiz were the three most valuable batters by a wide margin last year, according to WPA. Over the past five years (2002 through 2006), only Barry Bonds has had a higher WPA count than Pujols' 2006 figure. Bonds surpassed it twice, in 2002 (9.83) and 2004 (a phenomenal 12.64). Despite his relatively low profile in 2006, Bonds still managed to finish eighth in the majors.

Clutchiness

If you put a bunch of baseball analysts in a room and ask them about clutch hitting, you're just asking for trouble. I guess if you were to push really hard, you might get a consensus that clutch hitting happens, but it can only be identified in retrospect. In other words, it's very hard to say which batters are "clutch hitters," but sometimes batters do have seasons in which they perform very well in the clutch.

But that would be the easy part. If you're really a troublemaker, you could sequester them in a room (like a jury) and ask them to define a clutch situation. They might never leave. If they were to somehow agree, you could send them back with another question: if a player usually hits .200 but bats .300 in the clutch, is he a better clutch hitter than a batter who bats .320 in all situations?

Be sure to order pizza.

The concept of clutch hitting is so elusive that blogger Dan Smith borrowed a page from the *Colbert Report* and dubbed it "clutchiness"—something that may exist but defies description for anyone but the describer, who absolutely knows it when he sees it. Clutchiness is baseball's equivalent of Colbert's truthiness.

I'll step into this quagmire and suggest that WPA and LI don't exactly define clutchiness but they come pretty close.

WPA is a real-time statistic, and isn't clutch hitting a real-time phenomenon? Wouldn't you say that a single with a man on third in the ninth inning and the score tied and the crowd standing and yelling is more "clutch" than that exact same hit in the top of the first? Well, maybe you wouldn't. But some people would, and that difference is exactly what WPA measures.

Leverage Index is a useful measure of the clutchiness of a situation. Milton Bradley's home run and Bobby Jenks' strikeout were both clutch performances because they occurred in clutch situations, as measured by LI.

If you're not totally on board with me, try one other mind game. Watch your favorite team play a close ballgame and track the game using the Baseball Graphs WPA spreadsheet. Pay particular attention to two things: your anxiety level during the game and the LI of each situation. My guess is that the two will match closely from play to play. If you believe that clutch hitting occurs when emotions are taut and the game hangs in the balance, then you've discovered a clutchiness monitor. You've defined the thing that can't be defined.

Maybe you're with me; maybe you're not. At least we're not sequestered in a motel room together. But here is something that is fairly straightforward: a list of batters who appeared in at least 10 plays with a Leverage Index of 3.0 or more. I would call these "clutch plays," because they had at least three times more impact on a game outcome than an average play.

By this measure, there were 6,250 clutch plays in 2006, and here is the list of the 10 batters who performed best in those plays. I've included their total WPA, average Leverage Index, the number of plays and the average

WPA per 10 plays (which is how I ranked the results). The names near the top probably won't surprise you, but the name at the very top just might:

The Clutchiest Hitters of 2006

Name	WPA	LI	Plays	Avg WPA
Kielty B.	1.68	3.8	10	1.68
Ortiz D.	3.47	4.0	24	1.44
Pujols A.	4.18	4.0	29	1.44
Griffey Jr. K.	2.58	4.6	19	1.36
Palmeiro O.	1.46	3.7	12	1.22
Durham R.	2.36	4.2	20	1.18
Monroe C.	2.33	4.3	20	1.16
Bradley M.	1.14	3.7	11	1.03
Catalanotto F.	1.02	4.4	10	1.02
Garciaparra N.	2.11	4.2	24	0.88

Least Clutchy Hitters of 2006

Name	WPA	LI	Plays	Avg WPA
Cedeno R.	-1.35	4.3	15	-0.90
Clark T.	-0.99	4.4	11	-0.90
Martinez V.	-1.54	4.1	18	-0.86
Rivera J.	-1.06	4.1	13	-0.82
Matsui K.	-1.23	4.0	16	-0.77
Blum G.	-0.97	4.2	13	-0.75
Hart C.	-0.74	3.9	10	-0.74
Sullivan C.	-1.03	4.7	14	-0.74
Hall T.	-0.94	4.1	13	-0.72
Teixeira M.	-1.36	4.0	19	-0.72

In 10 high-leverage plate appearances, Oakland's Bobby Kielty walked, singled three times, doubled twice and homered. He even sacrificed twice. Only once did Kielty make an out he wasn't trying to make. Yes, Bobby Kielty wins our Clutchinessest Player of the Year award.

I'm sure you're dying to know about chokiness, too. The worst clutch hitters of 2006 were...

Boy, Mark Teixeira really did have a disappointing year, didn't he? Although he had a fine second half, he had no power in the first half of the year (just nine home runs before the All-Star Break). And now it turns out he wasn't clutchy, either. In 18 plate appearances with an LI over 3.0, he hit just two singles, one double and drew one walk.

Small sample size? Of course. WPA is a snapshot of what happened in 2006, not an in-depth portrait for the ages. But what a snapshot.

Special Thanks to...

You and I might never have heard of WPA were it not for the efforts of Tom M. Tango. Tom's insight, effort and generosity are unparalleled. Close behind Tom in the generosity department is David Appelman, who runs FanGraphs (www.fangraphs.com). Fangraphs has WPA and Leverage Index stats for the last five years, and David supplied all the WPA stats used in the THT Annual. We can't thank either of these two guys enough.

Win Probability Added was first published (under a different name) by Harlan and Eldon Mills in 1970. Researchers who have moved WPA forward include George Lindsey, Jay Bennett, Doug Drinen and Keith Woolner. I think it was Newton who said something about standing on the shoulders of giants.

If you'd like to read more about WPA (and who wouldn't?), I'd suggest this THT articlee:

http://www.hardballtimes.com/main/article/the-one-about-win-probability

For more about Leverage Index, Tom Tango wrote an excellent overview in a series of articles at The Hardball Times:

http://www.hardballtimes.com/main/article/crucial-situations/

http://www.hardballtimes.com/main/article/crucial-situations-part-2/

http://www.hardballtimes.com/main/article/crucial-situations-part-three

Regarding the title of this piece, I know that major league baseball is played in Canada. I just couldn't resist the John Mellencamp reference.

Team Defense

by John Dewan

The New York Yankees had the best record in baseball in 2006, tying their cross-town rival New York Mets with 97 victories. Nevertheless, they had the second-worst defensive team in the American League, based on the plus/minus system developed last year at Baseball Info Solutions (BIS) and published in *The Fielding Bible*. But you know what? That's a good thing for the Yankees. In 2005 they were the worst team in all of baseball, with a plus/minus score of -167 (zero is average). Their score of -55 in 2006 was a significant improvement.

It was addition by subtraction, and their biggest subtraction was Bernie Williams. Williams was the regular center fielder in 2005, and he posted a -39 plus/minus figure, the worst score among all major league center fielders that year. In 2006, the Bronx Bombers signed a key leadoff man in Johnny Damon. The top of the order was solidified, but the defensive improvement in center field was just as important.

Damon is no Andruw Jones, but his near-average plus/minus figure of -2 in 2006 was a vast improvement over Williams.

The best defensive outfield plus/minus score was posted by the Atlanta Braves for the second year in a row. They scored a +63 in 2006 after their +61 in 2005. For 2006 they had regulars Andruw Jones at +30 in center, Ryan Langerhans at +15 in left field, and Jeff Francouer with a +2 in right. But when you add outfielder throwing performance into the mix, I have to give the title of Best Outfield Defense for 2006 to the Toronto Blue Jays.

The Jays outfield with their regular trio of Vernon Wells (+15 in CF), Alexis Rios (+20 in RF), and Reed Johnson (+12 in LF) scored at +52, a bit less than Atlanta. However, they ranked first in the majors in intimidation factor by allowing just 43.9% of runners to attempt an extra base on a single or a double, and they had 24 base runner kills as a unit. By comparison, Atlanta had 51.7%

Team Totals and Rankings - 2006

Team	PLUS/MINUS					GROUND DP				BUNTS				THROWING				
	Middle Infield	Corner Infield	Outfield	Total	Rank	GDP Opps	GDP	Pct	Rank	Opps	Score	Grade	Rank	Opps To Advance	Extra Bases	Kills	Pct	Rank
San Diego Padres	+31	+13	+47	+91	1	318	121	.381	22	53	.586	B	8	384	211	8	.549	28
Toronto Blue Jays	+1	+15	+52	+68	2	307	128	.417	13	39	.487	C	26	410	180	24	.439	1
Seattle Mariners	+8	+33	+27	+68	2	297	129	.434	9	37	.565	B-	13	486	229	20	.471	4
St Louis Cardinals	+10	+30	+19	+59	4	380	154	.405	18	51	.528	C+	21	446	235	4	.527	24
Chicago Cubs	+8	-3	+44	+49	5	283	96	.339	28	62	.555	B-	16	415	207	8	.499	11
San Francisco Giants	-5	+34	+13	+42	6	317	110	.347	27	61	.663	A	1	428	241	16	.563	30
Houston Astros	+43	+4	-8	+39	7	330	145	.439	7	60	.544	B-	19	397	209	16	.526	23
Milwaukee Brewers	+18	-1	+19	+36	8	315	113	.359	25	86	.585	B	9	426	235	12	.552	29
New York Mets	+44	-14	+1	+31	9	315	104	.330	29	49	.558	B-	15	412	221	26	.536	25
Detroit Tigers	+15	+31	-20	+26	10	301	139	.462	3	27	.620	B+	4	411	193	18	.470	3
Kansas City Royals	-5	+28	-3	+20	11	356	160	.449	6	36	.401	D	30	534	276	19	.517	16
Atlanta Braves	-15	-33	+63	+15	12	355	132	.372	24	58	.574	B	11	476	246	18	.517	15
Arizona Diamondbacks	+25	-14	+1	+12	13	345	142	.412	15	46	.490	C	25	434	236	8	.544	27
Minnesota Twins	+7	+5	-1	+11	14	295	111	.376	23	34	.603	B+	6	422	204	18	.483	7
Baltimore Orioles	+1	-8	+16	+9	15	312	127	.407	17	46	.416	D+	28	486	231	20	.475	6
Los Angeles Dodgers	-10	+2	+12	+4	16	374	155	.414	14	42	.583	B	10	466	233	14	.500	12
Texas Rangers	-17	+2	+4	-11	17	360	147	.408	16	30	.613	B+	5	517	244	28	.472	5
Tampa Bay Devil Rays	-19	-20	+22	-17	18	323	129	.399	20	36	.503	C+	24	521	274	24	.526	21
Cleveland Indians	-31	-22	+32	-21	19	329	144	.438	8	40	.559	B-	14	503	254	14	.505	13
Colorado Rockies	+30	-11	-42	-23	20	363	165	.455	4	43	.551	B-	17	490	257	22	.524	20
Florida Marlins	-4	-27	+2	-29	21	367	148	.403	19	53	.571	B	12	467	231	13	.495	10
Philadelphia Phillies	+32	-17	-48	-33	22	319	134	.420	11	56	.513	C+	23	437	229	21	.524	18
Oakland Athletics	-22	+9	-23	-36	23	320	151	.472	2	33	.515	C+	22	474	220	15	.464	2
Washington Nationals	-46	-6	+13	-39	24	324	88	.272	30	69	.635	A-	3	512	276	26	.539	26
Los Angeles Angels	-16	+4	-39	-51	25	297	129	.434	9	44	.486	C	27	411	201	26	.489	8
Chicago White Sox	-12	+2	-43	-53	26	281	127	.452	5	39	.529	C+	20	455	236	8	.519	17
New York Yankees	-19	-21	-15	-55	27	302	126	.417	12	25	.410	D	29	492	258	17	.524	19
Cincinnati Reds	-15	-8	-38	-61	28	317	111	.350	26	47	.551	B-	18	472	233	27	.494	9
Boston Red Sox	-20	+17	-69	-72	29	307	149	.485	1	32	.588	B	7	454	239	15	.526	22
Pittsburgh Pirates	-18	-24	-35	-77	30	381	145	.381	21	80	.639	A-	2	509	259	12	.509	14

of runners attempt an extra base (a middle-of-the-pack ranking at 15th) and killed 18 of them.

The title of Best Infield Defense is a battle between the Detroit Tigers, the San Diego Padres, and Adam Everett. The Tigers infield scored a +46 while the Padres tallied +44 from the four infield positions. Shortstop Adam Everett was at +43 all by himself for the Houston Astros. Everett needed a little help from his fellow Astro infielder friends to push them past Detroit, and he got it with a +4 for a team total of +47. That is the highest plus/minus infield team total in baseball.

The Tigers, however, ranked third in baseball in turning double plays and fourth in bunt defense, while the Astros ranked seventh and 19th, respectively. Therefore, the title of Best Infield Defense for 2006 goes to the Detroit Tigers. The regulars and their individual scores are: Brandon Inge (+27 at 3B), Carlos Guillen (-1 at SS), Placido Polanco (+4 at 2B) and Chris Shelton/Sean Casey (a combined +4 at 1B). Utility infielder Omar Infante scored a +7 playing a backup role primarily at second base.

Description of the Team Totals and Rankings

The team totals and rankings are broken into four groups: Plus/Minus, Ground DP, Bunts and Throwing. In the columns under the heading Plus/Minus we've broken down the data further into three groupings: Middle Infield (second base and shortstop), Corner Infield (first and third base), and Outfield (left, center and right). The next three main column headings each are associated with one of those same position groupings. Ground DP tells you how often the team turned double plays given their opportunities (ground ball with a man on first and fewer than two outs) and primarily applies to the middle infielders, though all GDPs are included in these team totals. Bunts apply primarily to the corner infielders, though all bunts are included in the team totals regardless of who fielded them. You'll see letter grades based on the traditional system in schools of A through F, so you can get an idea of how well a team performed on bunts. The entire bunt grading system is described in *The Fielding Bible*. Throwing applies to outfielders only.

The Plus/Minus System

My book, *The Fielding Bible*, goes into great length (ad nauseum to some) describing the new fielding system we developed at Baseball Info Solutions, the Plus/Minus System. Video Scouts at BIS review video of every play of every major league game and record detailed information on each play, such as the location of each batted ball, the speed, the type of hit, etc. Using this in-depth data, we're able to figure out how each player compares to his peers at his position. How often does Derek Jeter field that softly batted ball located 20 feet to the right of the normal shortstop position compared to all other major league shortstops?

A player gets credit (a "plus" number) if he makes a play that at least one other player at his position missed during the season, and he loses credit (a "minus" number) if he misses a play that at least one player made. The amount of the credit is directly related to how often players make the play. Each play is reviewed individually and scored. Sum up all the positives and negatives for each player at each position and you get his total plus/minus for the season. A total plus/minus score near zero means the player is average. A score above zero is above average, and a negative score is below average. Adam Everett turned in the highest score we've had in four years of using the system with his +43 at shortstop in 2006. That means he made 43 more plays than the average MLB shortstop would make.

There were several enhancements made to the system since the publication of *The Fielding Bible* in February 2006. Here's a summary:

- The system for outfielders was modified to count all batted balls hit within about five feet as the same location. This generally resulted in more extreme (higher and lower) plus/minus figures for outfielders. All years were restated.

- Also for outfielders: we added a new category called a "fliner." Prior to last year, we categorized balls hit in the air as a fly ball or a liner. But, as baseball fans know, there are a lot of balls hit in the air that are in between. We call them fliners, and using this new category we are able to get better precision. This was implemented for 2006.

- For balls hit in the air in the infield (pop-ups and line drives), all batted balls within about three feet count as the same location. Again, all years were restated for the "air" component of infielders' plus/minus.

- We reviewed several other possible enhancements, such as using multi-year data as a basis to calculate an individual year. Other than the three mentioned above, none provided any improvement in the system and were discarded.

The *Bill James Handbook 2007* has the final plus/minus leader boards for the 2006 season, plus the first-ever Fielding Bible Awards.

Net Win Shares Value 2006

by Dave Studenmund

Major League Baseball teams were caught in a salary squeeze this year, and it's not likely to get better anytime soon. As a result, the amount they pay per victory is continuing to rise.

Blame the rookies. In fact, blame the last two rookie crops. In 2005, there were 2,473 Win Shares (or 824 wins; see the Glossary for more about Win Shares) contributed by players not yet ready for arbitration. In other words, players who were only making the minimum salary (or a bit more) contributed about 34% of all wins.

In 2006, thanks to an outstanding rookie crop, that figure rose to 2,669 Win Shares (37%). You'd think that would be good news for owners' budgets, right? Players who make only the minimum contributing more to the team?

The problem is that free agent spending continued to rise, up from $1.5 billion (yes, billion) in 2005 to $1.6 billion in 2006—yet free agents contributed nearly 300 fewer Win Shares than in 2005 (down from 3,163 to 2,879). Teams paid more money for less productivity from free agents.

The overall result is that the price of a Win Share Above a Bench player (or WSAB) for all players rose from $750,000 in 2005 to $830,000 (an 11% increase). I'm pretty sure this is a bigger increase than the commissioner's office would like.

Let's back up. Major league teams paid $2.3 billion in player salaries last year, or about $2.6 million per player. Put another way, there were 2,430 wins last year, so teams paid a little less than $1 million per win.

This approach is too simplistic, however, because most teams could probably win 50 or more games by paying and playing players who make only the minimum salary ($327,000). Do the math and you'll see that those 50 wins would only cost a team about $163,000 per win in player salary.

It's the wins above 50 that cost a lot of money, and that is where Win Shares can lend a hand. Win Shares were developed by Bill James to allocate each team's wins to its players. Win Shares uses a lot of basic baseball stats—batting, stealing bases, hitting in the clutch, pitching ERA, saves, fielding stats—to quantify how much each player contributed to his team's win total. As an example, it says that Player X contributed five wins to his team, and then multiplies that by three (basically to make the number meatier). The final result is that Player X contributed 15 Win Shares.

So if you calculate the number of Win Shares a player contributed above what a typical "minimum salary" (or "bench") player would contribute, and you compare that to the salary he was paid over the minimum, you can figure out just how much those extra wins he contributed cost.

Are you with me? I hope so, because the results may surprise you. Here are a couple of findings I get from applying that logic to specific classes of player salaries:

- Teams paid players eligible for arbitration $470 million above the minimum for 597 WSAB last year, for an average of $788,000 per WSAB, or $2.4 million per win.

- Teams paid free agents nearly $1.6 billion above the minimum for 1,077 WSAB last year, for $1.5M per WSAB, or an astounding $4.4 million per win.

In other words, **the price of a win rose from $163,000 (for the first 50) to $2,400,000 (for additional wins from arbitration-eligible players) to $4,400,000 (for additional wins from free agents).**

If you assume Player X, who contributed five wins to the team, contributed two wins above a bench player and was paid an average salary for his class, he would have made…

- $327,000 if he was a first- or second-year player
- $4,800,000 if he was in his third to sixth year
- $8,800,000 if he was a free agent

That is salary inflation, and it also how small-market teams manage their payrolls and still win. Player X's Win Share totals, by the way, are about the same as an average major league ballplayer's.

Maybe you're someone who believes major league players are paid way too much. As the son of two teachers, I'm not going to disagree with you.

But the business of baseball is doing very well. According to *Forbes* magazine, the value of major league franchises has risen 15% each of the last two years. Attendance reached an all-time high this year, and Major League Baseball Advanced Media (MLBAM), the operator of MLB's Internet site, is a powerful new source of revenue.

Owners are flush with money, they want to win (because winning is good for business) and players are delighted to sign for as much as they can get. There's nothing really "wrong" with this scenario. It's Adam Smith's free market at work.

So instead of complaining about Alex Rodriguez's $26 million salary, let's accept baseball's salaries for what they are and ask whether or not Rodriguez's contract was a good deal in the context of what ballplayers were actually paid last year.

The system I've developed to answer that question is called Net Win Shares Value.

I'll put a detailed explanation of Net Win Shares Value at the end of the article, but suffice it to say that the system evaluates each player and his contract based on his classification (not eligible for arbitration, arbitration-eligible and free agent) and his production (as measured by Win Shares).

Net Win Shares Value is essentially the amount by which a player exceeded the average value of his classification. For instance, here's a list of the 10 best values of 2006:

Best 2006 Net Win Shares Value

Name	Tm	Cl	Salary	Net WS Value
Cabrera, Miguel	FLA	NA	$472,000	$17,121,203
Mauer, Joe	MIN	NA	$400,000	$16,334,200
Wright, David	NYN	NA	$374,000	$15,695,111
Howard, Ryan	PHI	NA	$355,000	$14,641,724
Beltran, Carlos	NYN	FA	$13,571,429	$14,495,338
Reyes, Jose	NYN	NA	$401,500	$13,343,969
Ortiz, David	BOS	FA	$6,900,000	$12,865,289
Morneau, Justin	MIN	NA	$385,000	$12,348,351
Hafner, Travis	CLE	A	$2,500,000	$12,012,263
Thomas, Frank	OAK	FA	$500,000	$11,838,943

Naturally, if you want to find the players who provided the best value, look for superstars not yet eligible for arbitration. Exhibit Number One is the Marlins' Miguel Cabrera, who had an MVP-type of year with 33 Win Shares, yet was paid only $472,000.

According to Net Win Shares Value, Cabrera's extra production was worth over $17 million, based on what the average major leaguer was paid. As long as he stays healthy, Cabrera will have his day in arbitration court, but the Marlins got their money's worth this year.

A few free agents made the top-10 list too. You actually might be a bit surprised to see that Carlos Beltran, he of the mega contract for mega years, was the best free agent value last year. But Beltran also had an MVP-type year, with 41 home runs, 116 RBIs, 127 runs scored, outstanding defense in centerfield, great base running and 38 Win Shares (27 WSAB). In 2006, at least, he was worth a lot more than what that contract paid him.

Indeed, the Mets had three of the six best contract values on their roster. We'll get to team rankings in a couple of minutes.

Before we do, let's look at the...

Worst 2006 Net Win Shares Values

Player	Tm	Cl	Salary	Net WS Value
Pineiro, Joel	SEA	A	$6,300,000	($10,015,092)
Mulder, Mark	STL	A	$7,750,000	($9,907,041)
Gagne, Eric	LAN	A	$10,000,000	($9,901,801)
Berroa, Angel	KC	A	$2,000,000	($8,570,974)
Perez, Odalis	LAN/ KC	FA	$8,750,000	($8,447,174)
Colon, Bartolo	LAA	FA	$14,000,000	($8,309,574)
Ortiz, Russ	ARI	FA	$7,800,000	($8,219,259)
Chen, Bruce	BAL	A	$3,800,000	($8,000,963)
Hillenbrand, Shea	TOR/ SF	A	$5,800,000	($7,662,720)
Alfonzo, Edgardo	LAA	FA	$8,000,000	($7,618,708)

People tend to complain about the big bucks paid to Beltran and A-Rod, but they forget about the impact that an injury to someone like Bartolo Colon, at $14 million, makes. Or the impact that a terrible year by Joel Pineiro (6.36 ERA, -5 WSAB) can have on the value of his contract.

In fact, seven of the 10 worst values last year were pitchers, emphasizing that pitching is risky business. And check out the terrible year that Angel Berroa had. Batting .234/.259/.333 and playing a subpar shortstop, Berroa was eight Win Shares **worse** than a bench player. His negative $8.5 million in Net Win Shares Value is the amount the Royals would have had to pay other players, on average, to compensate for Berroa's lack of production.

You can find the Net Win Shares Value of every major leaguer in our appendix. In this article, I thought I'd pursue a few interesting angles regarding this year's contracts.

First of all, I looked at each free agent contract based on the year it was signed. Just like last year, the most valuable free agent class was the most recent one, but the class of 2001 added a twist by producing the most value per WSAB.

Net Win Shares Value by Year of Contract

Year	WSAB	Net WS Value	Val/WSAB
1999	1	($5,790,025)	($4,067,909)
2000	65	($457,669)	($7,005)
2001	81	$6,919,803	$85,024
2002	85	($14,530,361)	($170,366)
2003	184	($7,934,558)	($43,018)
2004	319	($562,511)	($1,762)
2005	340	$22,355,321	$65,820

It makes sense that the most recent free agent year would be the most valuable, because it's easier to predict player performance one year out instead of three or four years out. Also, players often sign for significantly less salary in the first year of a contract.

Taking a closer look at free agent deals signed last winter...

Best 2005 Free Agent Net Win Shares Values

Name	Salary	Net WS Value
Ortiz, David	$6,900,000	$12,865,289
Thomas, Frank	$500,000	$11,838,943
Carpenter, Chris	$5,000,000	$9,561,070
Hernandez, Ramon	$4,000,000	$8,079,482
Ryan, B.J.	$4,000,000	$7,194,000

B.J. Ryan will make $12 million in a couple of years. Frank Thomas will make a whole lot more next year, as he signed a one-year deal with Oakland and enters the free agent market again this offseason.

In the *The Hardball Times Annual 2006*, the 2001 free agent class had the lowest value of all free agent classes. This year, they have the most value per WSAB. Part of the improvement came about because several contracts expired (Sosa, Boone, etc.) and part of the improvement came from a technicality. (I didn't include players who didn't play, so Jeff Bagwell was left out of the equation.)

But Barry Bonds's return to health certainly helped, as did improvements by Jorge Posada, Jason Schmidt and Jason Kendall.

That 1999 deal is Ken Griffey Jr. Yes, Junior hit 27 home runs last year, but he also posted a OBP of .316 and played terrible defense. From a production standpoint, he wasn't worth his $12.5 million salary.

Net Win Shares Value treats all arbitration-eligible players the same, but they're not paid the same way. In fact, the Collective Bargaining Agreement explicitly calls for player salaries to rise as they gain experience between their third and sixth years.

You can see the impact of the arbitration process in this table. Six-year players were paid about 75% of the value free agents were paid. This is why you'll sometimes see teams non-tender players entering their last years of arbitration.

Major League Service

Years	WSAB	Sal/WSAB
2-3	77	$247,325
3-4	219	$525,080
4-5	125	$1,071,087
5-6	175	$1,153,116

Which position generated the most contractual value? In 2006, that position was catcher, where players such as Joe Mauer, Brian McCann, Russell Martin, Dave Ross and Ronny Paulino had very good years at (or close to) the minimum salary.

Net Win Shares Value by Position

POS	WSAB	Net WS Value	Val/WSAB
DH	80	$12,409,655	$154,929
C	167	$62,160,589	$371,487
1B	225	$81,331,469	$362,008
2B	109	$32,981,932	$303,728
SS	125	$31,759,688	$254,837
3B	212	$72,780,499	$343,548
OF	544	$137,756,935	$253,007
SP	674	$115,973,461	$172,078
RP	326	$100,803,904	$309,461

Starting pitchers are definitely overpaid according to Net Win Shares Value. Win Shares has been criticized by many for underrating starting pitchers, but I've taken steps to appropriately value them in the WSAB process (see the end of the article for details). Was it enough of an adjustment? Not according to major league teams, who paid more for production from starting pitchers than any other position. (Except for designated hitter, where Carl Everett, Rondell White, Mike Sweeney, Dmitri Young and others had bad years. The designated hitter position appears to be the home of over-the-hill, injured and overpaid players.)

Team Payrolls

Teams follow different strategies to success. Big-market franchises sign free agents, small-market teams develop their farm systems and middle-market teams try a combination of the two.

Up to now, the best method for evaluating the effectiveness of team payrolls has been the late Doug Pappas's Marginal Payroll/Marginal Wins method. While Pappas' method is excellent, it doesn't account for differences in strategy. Teams that play the free agent market are obviously going to pay more for talent; successful teams that emphasize player development are obviously going to pay less.

Net Win Shares Value, when accumulated at the team level, does account for differences in strategy. For instance, the Marlins were obviously very good at payroll management last year, finishing at almost .500 with a $15 million payroll. But Net Win Shares Value says that the Twins were actually more successful in managing their payroll, due to the fine performances turned in by many of their arbitration-eligible players (Cuddyer, Santana and Nathan).

The least Net Win Shares Value award goes to the Cubs, who were wracked by injuries and terrible production from some players. We don't have to talk about that anymore, do we? You will find a table of every team's total Net Win Shares Value on the next page.

Looking at classifications, the Marlins captured the most Net Win Shares Value from their youngest players. In fact, 187 of Florida's 234 Win Shares were contributed by players in their first or second year.

Incredibly, the Marlins' cross-state rivals, the Tampa Bay Devil Rays, realized no Net Win Shares Value from their non-arbitration players. That's almost impossible, but the production of Tampa Bay's first- and second-year players was horrendous: -0.8 WSAB overall.

The team with the most valuable group of arbitration-eligible players was Arizona, who received nearly $27 million in Net Win Shares Value from players like Brandon Webb and Orlando Hudson. The team that got the least from arbitration-eligible players was Milwaukee, due to injuries to Ben Sheets and Tomo Ohka, and subpar years from players like Brady Clark.

Finally, the White Sox received more Net Win Shares Value from their free agents ($23 million) than any other team, particularly due to Jim Thome's and Jermaine Dye's great years. The team with the least free agent Net Win Shares Value was the New York Yankees (of course), at negative $21 million. Randy Johnson and Gary Sheffield deserve some of the blame, but there's plenty to go around.

For instance, Alex Rodriguez, who was paid $4 million more than any other player, contributed negative $4.3 million in Net Win Shares Value (the 56th-worst total). I figured you might be curious about that.

As I mentioned before, Net Win Shares Value is listed for most players in our statistical appendix.

Net Win Shares Value by Team and Classification (in thousands)

Team	NA	A	FA	Grand Total
MIN	$48,705	$16,175	($3,036)	$61,844
FLA	$52,382	$8,869	($1,819)	$59,432
OAK	$34,103	$6,687	$12,064	$52,854
DET	$37,270	$9,697	$5,572	$52,539
NYN	$40,043	($8,680)	$20,561	$51,924
SD	$33,709	$11,778	$764	$46,252
TOR	$15,580	$1,254	$18,500	$35,335
COL	$26,543	$6,181	$922	$33,646
LAN	$22,359	($15,689)	$20,943	$27,613
LAA	$23,106	$18,606	($14,630)	$27,083
CIN	$7,495	$19,476	$95	$27,065
PHI	$38,323	($982)	($11,146)	$26,195
CLE	$25,858	$8,469	($9,544)	$24,782
ARI	$11,080	$26,725	($13,142)	$24,662
ATL	$23,230	($6,905)	$5,766	$22,090
CHA	$5,680	($9,424)	$23,157	$19,413
MIL	$21,834	($17,635)	$13,197	$17,396
STL	$12,365	($11,581)	$14,384	$15,168
TEX	$12,295	$29	$2,450	$14,774
PIT	$38,033	($17,371)	($9,564)	$11,097
WAS	$19,157	$3,797	($13,104)	$9,849
SF	$9,088	($7,752)	$8,386	$9,722
SEA	$12,000	($7,941)	$4,977	$9,036
HOU	$13,223	$37	($7,745)	$5,514
BOS	$15,629	($3,786)	($9,165)	$2,678
TB	($935)	$10,858	($9,406)	$516
BAL	$3,725	($11,770)	$1,837	($6,208)
KC	$16,473	($11,208)	($12,839)	($7,573)
NYA	$22,250	($10,619)	($20,890)	($9,259)
CHN	$982	($7,293)	($17,542)	($23,853)

ADDENDUM

There are two basic steps to calculating Net Win Shares Value: first you calculate the anticipated performance of a player based on how much he was paid, and his classification (free agent, arbitration-eligible or not eligible). You then compare his actual performance to his anticipated performance and multiply the difference by the average amount paid per WSAB across all players.

To show how important it is to differentiate among classifications, let me list how much major league teams paid for each WSAB for each class of player:

Not arbitration eligible:	$17,907
Arbitration eligible:	$788,155
Free agent:	$1,452,474
Average:	$832,195

Here's an example of how it works: at the beginning of the season, David Ortiz signed a new five-year contract with the Red Sox that called for him to make $6.5 million this year; he also received a signing bonus of $2 million. By spreading the bonus over the five years of the contract, I come up with a 2006 salary of $6.9 million this year.

With seven years of major league service before the year began, Ortiz qualified as a free agent, even though he didn't put his services on the free agent market. The notion is that the Red Sox certainly negotiated with his agent as though he were a free agent.

Free agents received $1.45 million for every WSAB they produced last year. So, at a salary of $6.9 million, Ortiz's "anticipated" WSAB output was 4.5. He blew that away, of course, by compiling 29 Win Shares and 20 WSAB. That was 15.5 WSAB more than "anticipated."

Across all classifications, players received $832,195 for each WSAB last year. So we multiply Ortiz's WSAB above anticipated (15.5) times the average value of a WSAB to obtain his Net Win Shares Value. That figure ($12.9M) is how much value he delivered to the Sox beyond the expected value of his contract.

We use the "all market" figure for our final step because this puts all player contributions in the same context. In other words, expectations are set by the "market" in which the player signed, and incremental value is set by the average across all markets.

The process is different for players in their first or second year (and not yet eligible for arbitration). For these players, we multiply their WSAB by the overall average value of a WSAB, and then subtract any salary they are paid above the minimum.

This process has changed slightly from last year's. For one thing, we define bench players at 70% of expected Win Shares for all players except starting pitchers, for whom we use 50%. Last year, we had used 60% for starting pitchers.

Also, I put an artificial floor on negative values last year so that no player would have less value than the money spent on his salary. I eliminated that floor this year.

The key to this system is properly classifying players as free agents, arbitration-eligible and not eligible for arbitration. This is much trickier than it seems. For instance, there are many players who have not yet played six years in the majors (and so aren't eligible to file for free agency) who were free agents because they were released by their teams. I did my best to identify all players who were in this situation when they signed their contracts.

There is one caveat I should mention. This analysis included only players who actually played in 2006. There were a number of players who were paid good money but didn't make it onto the field last year. Here is a list of all non-playing major leaguers who received at least $1 million salary in 2006:

Player	Salary
Bagwell, Jeff	$17,000,000
Hampton, Mike	$16,000,000
Pavano, Carl	$8,000,000
Guzman, Cristian	$4,200,000
Wilson, Paul	$3,750,000
Lawrence, Brian	$3,600,000
Alvarez, Wilson	$2,000,000
Reed, Steve	$1,250,000
Ginter, Keith	$1,250,000
Spivey, Junior	$1,200,000

Which Way Did It Go?

by Greg Rybarczyk

Hit Tracker is a method and tool for detailed trajectory analysis of flying baseballs. It can provide interesting details about the flight of the ball, such as how fast it came off the bat, what direction it went and how far it went. It combines an aerodynamic model with observation data from home run events to recreate the precise trajectory the ball followed in flight, including the initial velocity of the ball as it left the bat, as described by three parameters: the speed off the bat, (SOB), the horizontal launch angle (HLA), and the vertical launch angle (VLA). Hit Tracker also calculates the impact of altitude, wind and temperature on the flight of the ball. More than 50,000 unique visitors to the Hit Tracker website, www.hittrackeronline.com, have viewed data on major league home runs since the beginning of the 2006 season.

On a deeper level, Hit Tracker can isolate the striking of the home run ball, which is a product of the combined actions of the hitter and the pitcher, from the flight of that ball through the air, which depends only on the atmospheric conditions at the moment the ball is put in play. This information can be used to answer some very challenging and important questions about player performance, particularly when a player changes teams and home ballparks. This article will explore several of these questions, using real data from the 2006 season.

Home run demographics in 2006

There were 5,386 home runs hit in 2,429 major league games during the regular season last year, or about 2.22 home runs per game. This is the fifth-largest season total in MLB history. 505 different hitters went deep, ranging from league leaders Ryan Howard (58) and David Ortiz (54) to the 75 players who each hit exactly one home run. They hit these homers off of 587 different pitchers, including Minnesota starter Carlos Silva, who surrendered a league-leading 38 long balls, and Kansas City's Ambiorix Burgos, who allowed a league-high 16 homers in relief, including 12 in the ninth inning.

Of the 5,386 homers hit, only 14 were of the inside-the-park variety, or just one of every 385. Slightly less uncommon were home runs by pitchers: a total of 32 home runs were hit by 21 different pitchers in 2006: 29 by NL pitchers and just three by AL pitchers (one each by NL veterans Josh Beckett and Kris Benson and one by career AL pitcher Jon Garland). Carlos Zambrano led the way among pitchers with six homers for the Cubs, with Atlanta's (later St. Louis') Jorge Sosa and Florida's Dontrelle Willis chipping in three home runs each.

The Chicago White Sox led all teams with 236 homers, one of seven teams to top the 200 mark. The Kansas City Royals trailed the field with just 124 homers. The Baltimore Orioles allowed the most homers, 216, while the San Francisco Giants and the Los Angeles Dodgers were the stingiest, each allowing only 152 home runs.

U.S. Cellular Field in Chicago saw the most home runs hit, 247, followed closely by Great American Ball Park in Cincinnati. The toughest park in which to hit a home run was AT&T Park in San Francisco, where only 129 balls left the yard.

How far they went: home run distances

The longest home run of the season, which carried 496 feet, was Matt Holliday's September 19 blast onto the concourse in left-center field at Coors Field. Philadelphia's Ryan Howard cranked a 491-foot shot into Ashburn's Alley at Citizens Bank Park on April 23 for the second longest of the season, while Yankee Alex Rodriguez launched a 488-foot home run on June 15 at Yankee Stadium for the third longest of the year.

At the other end of the distance spectrum, there's no more popular place for a cheap-shot home run than the Crawford Boxes in left field at Minute Maid Park, which gathered some of the shortest and softest home runs in the major leagues in 2006. Jason Lane lofted a 328-foot pop-fly homer there on April 17, and on June 21, Lance Berkman drove his 200th career home run a spare 331 feet into the first row of the boxes just off the left field line.

Left field at Minute Maid Park sees more homers, but no outfield seats are closer to home plate than those just past the Pesky Pole in right field at Fenway Park. There on September 9, Kansas City's Jeff Keppinger hit the season's shortest fence-clearing homer, which measured all of 311 feet.

While the long home runs earn our admiration, and the short ones inspire either disgust or glee (depending on one's team affiliation), most fall somewhere in between. In 2006, the average home run traveled 397.2 feet.

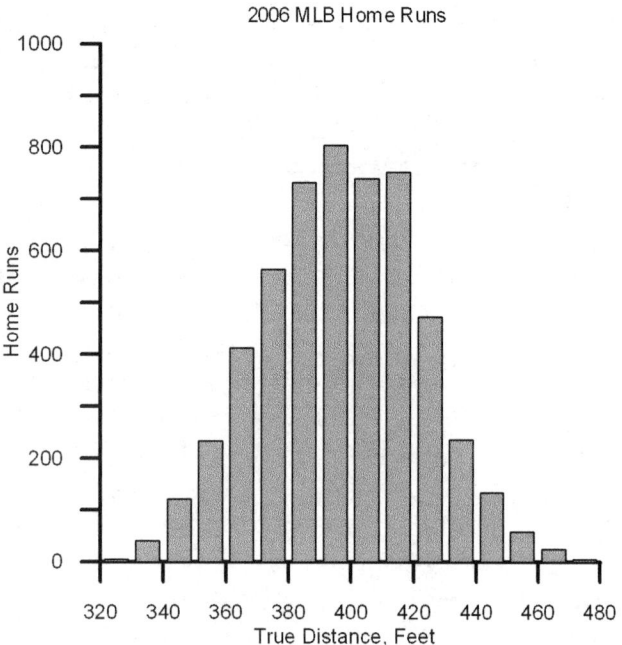

2006 MLB Home Runs

Atmospheric factors

Various ballparks around the major leagues have established their own reputations as either a pitcher's park or a hitter's park. Oakland's McAfee Coliseum is known as a pitcher's park, while Wrigley Field and Turner Field are known as hitter's parks. Often fans assume this is because of the fence distances and heights, but this is only part of the story; another major component is the prevailing atmospheric conditions at the parks during games. Let's consider the three most important factors: altitude, air temperature and wind direction and speed.

The altitude of the ballpark influences the density of the air, with higher altitude stadiums offering less air resistance and longer home runs for the same "launch" parameters. If a ball flies 400 feet when struck in "standard" conditions (which for Hit Tracker are defined as 70 degrees, sea level and no wind), that same ball will fly about 404 feet at Detroit's Comerica Park (altitude 600 feet), 408 feet at Chase Field in Phoenix (altitude 1,086 feet) and 438 feet at Coors Field in Denver (altitude 5,190 feet).

The air temperature also strongly influences the density of the air; warm air is less dense than cool air. Every ten degrees adds about four feet of distance to a

batted ball, so the difference between 40-degree weather and 90-degree weather is 20 feet—enough to make quite a dent in home run rates.

In most cases, the strongest atmospheric factor affecting the flight of the ball is the wind. A tail wind can add a lot of distance to a hard-hit fly ball, while a head wind can knock down a would-be home run and turn it into an out. The impact of wind on the distance of a standard 400 foot homer to center is shown in the plot below.

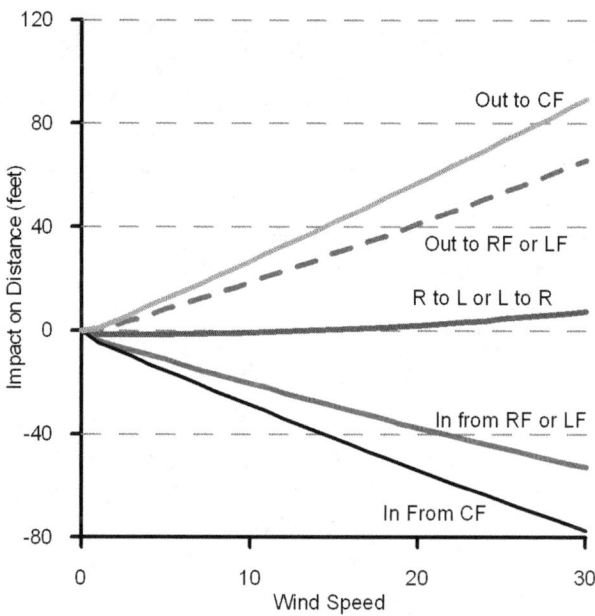

One other factor, humidity, is a weaker influence on the flight of a baseball. Humid air is less dense than dry air because water vapor (molecular weight 18) displaces other air molecules, chiefly nitrogen (molecular weight 28) and oxygen (molecular weight 32), and thus offers less resistance; humidity is such a minor factor, however, that it can typically be disregarded with minimal effect.

Changing Teams: Josh Beckett

Obviously atmospheric conditions can have a significant impact on the flight of a baseball, but how much impact can it have on a player's success?

In 2005, Josh Beckett pitched for the Florida Marlins with great success, recording an ERA of 3.37 with only 14 home runs allowed in 178.2 innings. After the 2005 season, Beckett was traded to the Boston Red Sox and proceeded to have a disappointing 2006 season, allowing 36 home runs and posting an ERA of 5.01. Why did this happen? Can any of this difference be attributed to the different atmospheric conditions in which Beckett pitched?

First, a comparison of Beckett's home ballparks: the Marlins' ballpark, Dolphins Stadium, is unquestionably a pitcher's park, an effect that is often attributed to its spacious dimensions, but which also derives from the direction and strength of the wind that blows during games there. The average wind conditions during the 81 games played at Dolphins Stadium in 2006 were a very consistent 10 mph, blowing from a very consistent direction: straight in from center field. Hit Tracker tells us that for a "typical" 400-foot home run, this wind will knock 29 feet of distance off a ball hit to center and 21 feet off a ball hit to right or left field, as compared to a windless day. Home run statistics reflect this, as Dolphins Stadium posted a 0.842 park factor for home runs over the past six years.

Over the same period, Fenway Park posted a park factor for home runs of 0.936, which means that home runs should be about 11% more common there than in Dolphins Stadium. However, upon moving north, Beckett's home run rate in his home park jumped by 100%, from one every 18.2 innings in Miami to one every 9.1 innings in Boston. Is this a simple matter of small sample size, or is it something that could have been predicted?

Using Hit Tracker to evaluate each of the 12 home runs Beckett allowed at Fenway Park in 2006, we will then see what the outcome for each would have been in Dolphins Stadium. This is done by first analyzing each home run where it actually occurred (Fenway), and determining the values of the three parameters that completely describe a batted ball as it leaves the bat: SOB, VLA and HLA. Next, Hit Tracker places those parameters into Dolphins Stadium's average atmospheric conditions (84 degrees, 10 mph wind in from center field), and we see where the ball would have landed in relation to the fences at Dolphins Stadium. The results are striking.

Of the 12 home runs Beckett allowed at Fenway Park in 2006, only six would have been home runs on a typical day at Dolphins Stadium. Of the six that would not have left the yard, five would have been caught for outs, and the sixth would have landed foul in the stands. This would seem to account for the rise in Beckett's home runs allowed at Fenway Park, but the trouble with this analysis is that it is not appropriate to only analyze home runs, which is in effect "cherry-picking" the data.

While it's not necessary to analyze every batted ball, it is important to examine ones that had a chance to turn out differently. A ground ball up the middle will turn out the same almost anywhere, so it can safely be left alone. Most short line drives can be excluded as well, since the positioning of the outfielders will not change

the outcomes of most of these hits (with the possible exception of a small percentage of line drives to left field at Fenway, which may be caught due to the left fielder playing shallow there). However, any fly balls hit "near" or over the outfield walls are likely to fly quite differently in the two parks and must be looked at closely.

In 17 starts at Fenway Park in 2006, Josh Beckett allowed 40 balls to be struck "near" or over the outfield walls. The breakdown of outcomes for these 40 balls was 18 flyouts, one single, nine doubles and 12 home runs.

Placing those same 40 hits (as described by SOB, VLA and HLA) in Dolphins Stadium under average 2006 conditions of 84 degrees and 10 mph wind in from center field, we get these results:

Fenway Park	Dolphins Stadium
18 Flyouts	16 Flyouts
	2 Home Runs
1 Single	1 Flyout
9 doubles	3 doubles
	6 Flyouts
12 home runs	6 home runs
	5 Flyouts
	1 foul ball

The net effect is -6 doubles, -4 home runs and +9 outs.

Certainly changes like these would affect Beckett's overall performance, but exactly how? To determine this, I looked at each changed outcome individually to see how it affected the game in which it took place. Using game logs and the revised outcomes for Dolphins Stadium, I can identify the impact of each change and tally the results. For example, on September 3, Toronto's Kevin Barker hit a solo home run to lead off the fourth inning against Beckett, who then retired the next three hitters in order. If the home run were instead a flyout (as would have been the case in Dolphins Stadium), then this would have changed a one-run inning to a zero-run inning and removed one earned run from Beckett's stats. This is obviously a simple case; for other more complicated innings, I simply make my best guess as to how the inning might have turned out and add up the results.

Overall, my best estimate is that Beckett would have allowed 17 fewer runs if he'd played his home games in Dolphins Stadium. This would have lowered his home ERA from 4.84 to 3.45 and his overall ERA from 5.01 to 4.27. This comes to a difference of 0.74 runs on Beckett's ERA due to the different atmospheric conditions and park configuration. Add this to the 0.49 runs that Baseball Mogul suggests typically come with a switch to the American League and you have an increase of 1.23 runs in Beckett's ERA. That goes a long way towards accounting for the actual 1.55 increase, from 3.46 (his career average through 2005) to 5.01.

Bad Luck: Glendon Rusch

Hit Tracker analysis can be projected forward as well, by taking a pitcher's 2006 batted balls and "placing" them in any major league ballpark's average atmospheric conditions, or typical conditions for a particular time in the season for those parks whose atmospherics are not as monotonously consistent as those in Miami or San Diego. To illustrate this point, we will examine one pitcher who suffered from extraordinary bad luck on the playing field in 2006, Glendon Rusch.

Glendon Rusch got off to a bad start in April, starting five games for the Cubs and losing four, posting an 8.46 ERA and allowing 11 home runs in only 22.1 innings. In May he was sent to the pen, and made only 4 starts and 16 relief appearances the rest of the season, posting a 7.46 ERA overall and allowing 21 home runs in just 66 1/3 innings before a blood clot in his lung ended his season on Sept. 12.

At a glance, Rusch might seem to be just another pitcher who had a bad year; however, Hit Tracker analysis tells a different story. Closer analysis shows that of Rusch's 21 home runs allowed, 20 were struck with a tail wind. This is a highly unusual occurrence; typically only about half of all homers get any help from the wind. Furthermore, the impact was quite substantial: Rusch's 21 homers each received an average of 27 feet of extra distance from the wind, enough to push almost any warning track fly into the stands. Then, on top of the wind impact, there was altitude: all 21 homers occurred at either Wrigley Field or another stadium with an altitude of at least 535 feet above sea level, providing another three-to-five feet of distance per homer.

Rusch was extremely unlucky to pitch on so many days in 2006 when the atmospheric conditions were so favorable for hitters. It is worth considering how those 21 home run balls that sank Rusch's season might have turned out had they been hit in conditions more favorable to pitchers. Ordinary statistics cannot answer this question, but Hit Tracker can. As it turns out, the answer *is* blowing in the wind!

Earlier in his career, Rusch pitched for the Mets and had a pretty good season in 2000 when he played his home games at Shea Stadium, tallying a WHIP of 1.26 in 190.2 IP, with a BB/K ratio of 44/157. What if the 21 home runs he surrendered in 2006 had been struck in the average conditions that prevailed in Shea Stadium during the 2006 season? Would his performance have been any different?

In 81 home games at Shea in 2006, the average game temperature was 72 degrees, the average wind was 11 mph in from left field, and the field sits at an altitude of about 10 feet above sea level. Using those atmospheric conditions, I found that if those 21 home run balls had been hit in Shea Stadium, Rusch's season would not only have been better, but spectacularly better.

Of the 21 home run balls Rusch surrendered in 2006, only **two** would have left Shea Stadium under average atmospheric conditions there: a Craig Wilson homer on April 16 at PNC Park and a bomb by Prince Fielder at Wrigley Field on April 29 that would have left any ballpark by a comfortable margin. One other ball would have hit the left-center field fence for a probable double, but the other 18 balls would have been harmless: 17 flyouts and one foul ball.

Of course, any pitcher's results will look better with an 11 mph wind blowing in from their "power field," so let's consider a modified scenario: instead of a highly favorable 11 mph wind blowing in from left field, I analyzed the 21 home runs balls at Shea with no wind. Analysis shows that that the change would be less dramatic, but Rusch's pitching line would still have been hugely improved: nine home runs, one double, nine flyouts and one foul ball out of 21 total balls hit.

Since the winds at Shea vary greatly from one game to the next, some days blowing in and other days out or across, this latter set of outcomes is probably closer to what would have happened than the former set.

In any event, Rusch would have had much more success had he simply pitched on days with more favorable weather. If he had been just fortunate enough to pitch in the average weather a Mets pitcher enjoys, his season would have turned out dramatically better. Assuming his recovery goes well, Glendon Rusch deserves another shot at the Cubs rotation in 2007, preferably on a cold day with the wind blowing in!

Inside the fence

Hit Tracker analysis has focused on home runs during its inaugural season, but it can also be performed on balls hit in the air that do not leave the park. For example, the Reds' Felipe Lopez' hit a 419-foot inside-the-park homer at Chase Field on May 6 against the Diamondbacks, which was the longest homer of the year to stay inside the fences.

Interestingly, the two longest hits of the season to NOT result in a homer were both singles: Barry Bonds' single on June 14, also against the Diamondbacks at Chase Field, and David Ortiz' single on June 15 at the Metrodome against the Twins. Bonds's blast struck a few feet from the top of the 25-foot-high center field wall at Chase, and if uninterrupted would have carried some 429 feet; Bonds's balky knees and a quick throw to the infield by Eric Byrnes prevented Bonds from making it past first. Ortiz's rocket struck a speaker suspended from the Metrodome roof in right-center field and rebounded into shallow center field, holding the Red Sox slugger to a single on what should have been a home run in the 430-440 foot range.

At least Bonds and Ortiz got credit for a hit for their trouble; Eric Munson probably feels worse than they do about the result of his 428 foot flyball in Houston's Minute Maid Park on July 7. Munson was robbed of extra bases by St. Louis' Jim Edmonds, who made one of his trademark over-the-shoulder catches halfway up Tal's Hill in the deepest center field in the major leagues. Munson picked the wrong aiming point for his hit: center field at Minute Maid is so far away that only one home run cleared the fence beyond Tal's Hill in 2006: Jacque Jones' 445 foot shot off Houston's Roger Clemens on August 15.

Sometimes something on the field gets in the way of a well-struck ball. On August 29, Vladimir Guerrero hit a line drive off of pitcher Rafael Soriano's head during an Angels-Mariners game. Hit Tracker tells us that the ball left Guerrero's bat at about 116 mph and had slowed only to about 107 mph by the time it hit Soriano's head. This is significantly faster than any pitch that ever hit a major league hitter, including the one that killed Ray Chapman 86 years earlier. Soriano is lucky to be alive.

What's Tougher?

There are a number of ballpark locations throughout the majors that are known to be (or believed to be) difficult to reach with a batted ball, so when a hitter knocks one there, players, fans and broadcasters alike take notice. Let's examine a few of those unusual landing spots through the lens of Hit Tracker.

Lansdowne Street, Boston (i.e. over Fenway Park's Green Monster): A home run ball that leaves the ballpark and disappears into the night is obviously a dramatic occurrence, but in this case, it's not very uncommon, or difficult for a major league hitter. In 2006, 29 home runs either cleared the Monster Seats at Fenway entirely or would have if they had not struck a sign or light tower. Difficulty Rating: **Moderate**.

Upper Deck at RFK Stadium, Washington: A blast to the cheap seats at the Nationals' home park generally draws a lot of oohs and aahs, but this feat is also a bit oversold. During the 2006 regular season, 24 home runs either reached the upper deck or struck the foul poles above that level, and one of those was a 368-foot homer straight down the right field line by Scott Spiezio. Difficulty Rating: **Moderate**.

Black Seats at Yankee Stadium: Here we have a feat that does a much better job of sorting out the sluggers from the rank-and-file major leaguers. To reach the closest corner of the black seats in deep center field at the Stadium, a ball needs to carry at least 420 feet. In 2006, only six home runs found the black seats, including three by New York's Alex Rodriguez. Difficulty Rating: **High**.

Catwalks at Tropicana Field: This is a very challenging target, but to hit a catwalk is not so much a feat of strength as it is a lucky shot. Only three batted balls at Tropicana in 2006 hit either of the two lowest catwalks for home runs; interestingly, two were hit by Jonny Gomes off two of the best AL pitchers: Curt Schilling and Roy Halladay. Difficulty Rating: **Very High**.

Splash Hits at AT&T Park: McCovey Cove is not too far from home plate if a ball goes straight down the right field line, but the water angles away sharply as you move towards center field. Only three home runs were hit into the water in 2006, one by perennial threat Barry Bonds and two by New York Mets Cliff Floyd and Carlos Delgado on consecutive days in April. Difficulty Rating: **Very High**.

Center Field at Comerica Park: The designers of Comerica Park obviously wanted to make the playing field "roomy," but they quite clearly went overboard in center field. The fence there is 420 feet from home plate at its closest and nearly 430 feet at the corners where it meets the right- and left-field fences. During the 2006 season, not one home run was hit over this fence. Though a difficult task, clearing this fence is far from impossible: one of every 35 major league plate appearances results in a home run, and one in

52 home runs in 2006 was hit to center field deep enough to clear this fence, so one could expect a ball to clear this fence once every 1,800 plate appearances, or about three times per season. The fact that no one did it in 2006 reflects well on the Detroit pitching staff (and perhaps poorly on the Tigers' hitters!). Difficulty Rating: **Extreme**.

Allegheny River, Pittsburgh (right field, PNC Park): No home runs landed in the river during the regular season, although five baseballs reached the river on the fly during the 2006 Home Run Derby, including Lance Berkman's first round bomb that traveled 473 feet, the longest homer of the event. To reach even the closest point, a hitter would need to blast the ball about 440 feet, making this one of the most challenging targets in baseball. Difficulty Rating: **Maximum**.

Coors Field: Whither the Humidor?

In 2002, the Colorado Rockies installed a humidor with the permission of MLB, to try to cut down on how far the baseball was flying at Coors Field. The theory was that the dry climate was drying out and shrinking the baseballs, which makes them travel farther than a baseball under more "normal" conditions. Since putting the humidor in operation, home run totals at Coors have dropped, but there are other potential causes for that, so it is not clear what impact the humidor has truly had. Hit Tracker analysis can be used to factor out the atmospheric impact of temperature, wind and altitude to see if balls are coming off the bats of major league hitters as fast in Coors Field as they do everywhere else.

The best way to evaluate the liveliness of the baseball at Coors Field is to use SOB. The average home run SOB for all of MLB in 2006 was 107.6 mph, while in Coors Field this average was 106.1 mph. This suggests there may be something to the idea that the humidor is making the baseballs less lively, but it's also possible that the dimensions of Coors Field and the altitude may allow more "cheap" homers to clear the fence, which could skew the data Therefore, I evaluated only the top 25% longest home runs at Coors Field and elsewhere in this study; these homers, with standard distances of at least 400 feet, would be home runs in every park in virtually every direction, and so provide a better basis for comparison.

The major league average SOB for the top 25% of homers is 113.9 mph, while the corresponding average for Coors Field is 112.1 mph, which ranks 29th in the league. This is a real, significant effect: the hardest-hit home run balls at Coors Field are among the weakest in MLB.

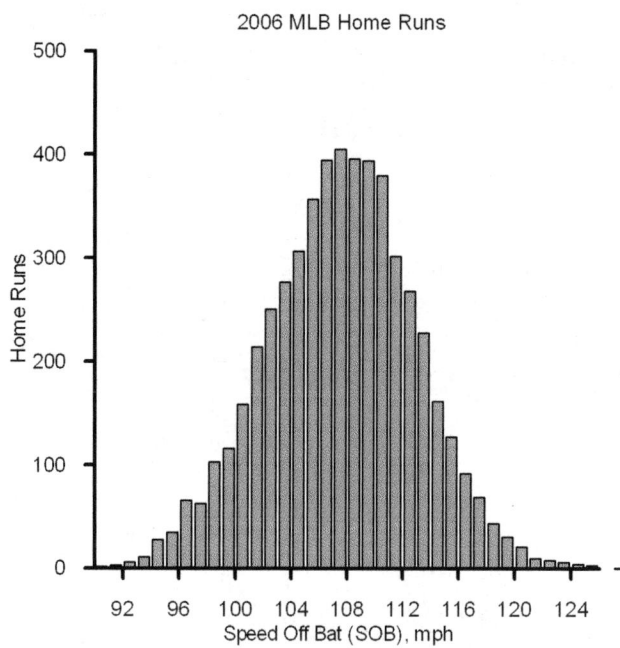

2006 MLB Home Runs

Let's split the data and look at pitchers' and hitters' performances at Coors Field and at all other sites:

Speed Off Bat (top 25% of HR's)		
	Coors Field	Other sites
Non-Rockies hitters	110.9 mph	114.0 mph
Rockies hitters	112.9 mph	112.7 mph
Non-Rockies pitchers	112.9 mph	114.0 mph
Rockies pitchers	110.9 mph	113.4 mph

The performance of the rest of MLB at and away from Coors Field supports the theory that the humidor is slowing down balls off the bat, with a huge difference of more than 3 mph. The Rockies hitters, however, do not seem to be affected in the same way—their data are about the same no matter where they hit. The reasons for this are not clear, but one possibility would place the responsibility not with the Rockies hitters but with the visiting pitchers, who, to put it another way, allow harder-hit home runs at Coors than do Rockies pitchers. Perhaps the non-humidor-related differences in pitching at Coors Field (difficulty in gripping the ball, less break on curveballs, etc.) weigh more on visiting pitchers than they do on Colorado's staff, who are more familiar with such factors.

In any event, the data are suggestive, but not conclusive. The humidor *might* be significantly changing the way balls come off the bat at Coors compared to the other 29 ballparks, but further study in the future is needed to make a final determination on this.

Alex Rodriguez and Ryan Howard: a study in opposites (fields)

During the 2006 season, Alex Rodriguez led all major league hitters who hit at least 20 home runs in average standard distance, logging an average of 416.1 feet per homer, compared to the league average of 390.3 feet. A-Rod led the next closest hitter, Tampa Bay's Jonny Gomes, by almost eight feet, an enormous margin. Clearly A-Rod has the raw power to hit a home run anywhere, in any direction, but in 2006 he didn't seem to use it.

A scatter plot of the landing points of A-Rod's homers shows that he doesn't hit very many home runs to the opposite field. I divided the 90-degree sector of the playing field into five equal sectors of 18 degrees each

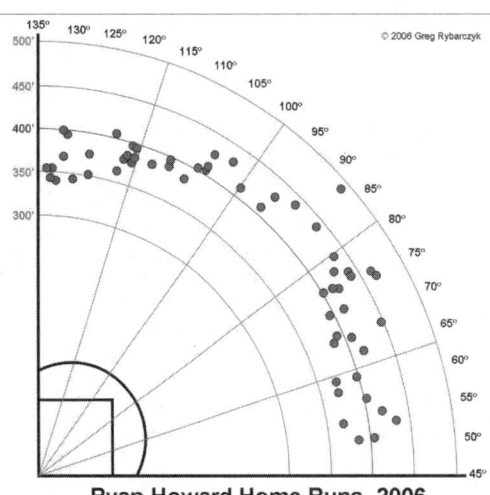

Ryan Howard Home Runs, 2006

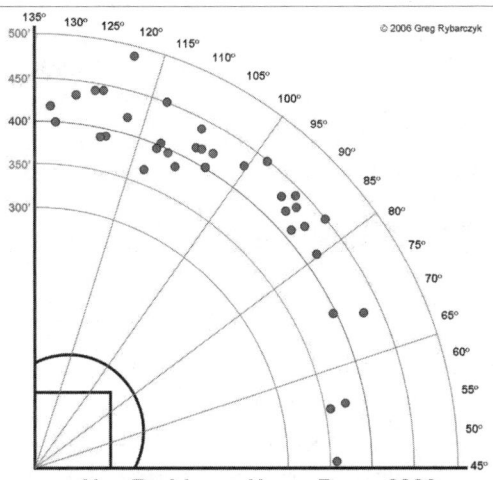

Alex Rodriguez Home Runs, 2006

and call them right, right-center, center, left-center and left field; this showed that A-Rod hit nine home runs to left field, 12 to left-center, nine to center, two to right-center and three to right field. Considering that he has the power to hit the ball out of the park in any direction and he plays half his games in a stadium whose right field fence is among the closest in baseball, Rodriguez should hit a lot of opposite-field homers. But the data clearly show that in 2006, he didn't.

There is no need to speculate about how many home runs A-Rod might hit if he used his power to all fields. All we need to do is look at Ryan Howard, the 2006 home run champion.

Howard's home run scatter plot strongly resembles A-Rod's on the "pull" side: nine to right, 16 to right-center and six to center field. But there the resemblance ends; Howard also stroked nine homers to right-center field and an amazing 18 home runs to left field. Early in 2006, many opposing pitchers tried to stay away from Howard's awesome power by pitching him outside, only to watch

him slap the ball 370 feet into the left field seats at cozy Citizens Bank Park. Later in the year, burned by that approach, pitchers tried to come back inside more often, and Howard proceeded to hammer several long home runs to center and right-center field. In 2006, the only effective strategy for averting Howard's home run trot was keeping his bat and the baseball apart, either by walking him (108 times) or striking him out (181 times).

Craig Biggio, living large at Minute Maid Park

Craig Biggio is perfectly adapted to hitting home runs at Minute Maid Park. It's as if his ancestors evolved there, only procreating after hitting a baseball into the Crawford boxes in left field. Biggio's consistency would make a champion dart thrower envious. His 21 home runs all landed within 23 degrees of the left-field line, and all traveled between 342 and 402 feet.

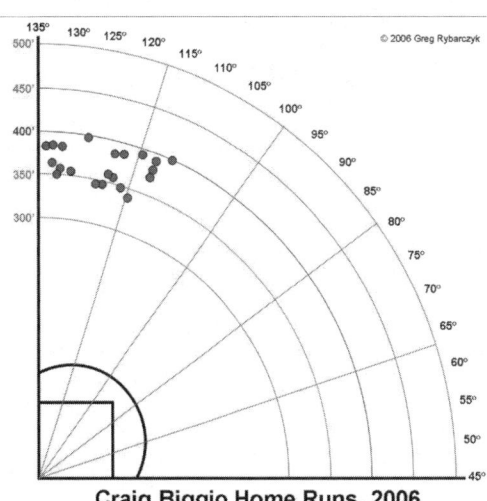

Craig Biggio Home Runs, 2006

Biggio, like most other Houston players, showed little inclination to try to hit a home run to center field at Minute Maid, which is as vast as left field is claustrophobic. As for right field, why bother when pitchers are still apparently willing to pitch him inside? So his homers are clementines to teammate Lance Berkman's oranges; they each still earn a leisurely trot around the bases and further cement Biggio's Hall of Fame career.

Injury Detection with Hit Tracker

Throughout the 2006 season, St. Louis' Jim Edmonds suffered from a number of injuries, but he nevertheless managed to play through the pain and appear in 110 games for the Cardinals. With Hit Tracker's ability to determine the speed that the balls are coming off a hitter's bat, is it possible to observe any trends in SOB and compare them to a player's health status?

Jim Edmonds' 2006 home runs are shown on the chart, which shows when they occurred and how hard they were hit.

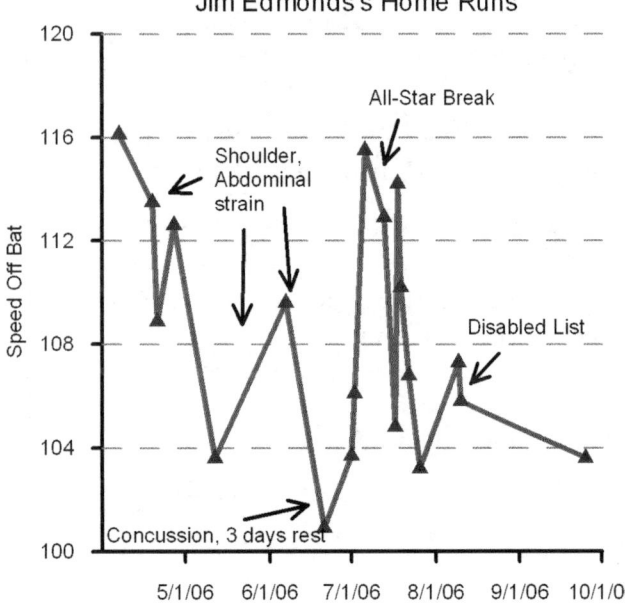

Jim Edmonds's Home Runs

The SOB for Edmonds' home runs started out high but steadily decreased over the first two months of the season, during which time Edmonds suffered from a sore shoulder and an abdominal strain. On June 21 he hit his slowest homer of the year (100.9 mph) and suffered a concussion later in the same game. After three days out of the lineup, he hit three more homers in six days, the last of which came off the bat at a robust 115.5 mph. After the All-Star Break, Edmonds steadily wore down again, according to observers' eyes and his SOB data, until he was diagnosed with post-concussive syndrome on Aug. 17 and went on the disabled list.

Throughout the year, the SOB data for Edmonds' home runs closely mirrored his actual health status. While Edmonds' injury status was no secret, it may prove possible to use SOB data to detect undisclosed injuries in MLB players, which would be valuable information. The SOB effect would likely be even more evident when SOB data for all hits, not just home runs, is available and analyzed.

What's next for Hit Tracker?

Hit Tracker's trajectory analysis has opened up a number of promising avenues of statistical exploration. The most promising is the use of Hit Tracker analysis on all batted balls, instead of only home runs. This would allow the creation of a three-dimensional distribution for each hitter, completely independent of atmospheric conditions, that would describe their "spray pattern" of hits in terms of SOB, HLA and VLA. This distribution would represent a description of a player's hitting performance at its most fundamental level and would also be useful for defensive positioning. These data could be analyzed season to season for trends, and data for minor leaguers could be collected and compared to their later major league performance, for the purpose of identifying predictive metrics.

Developing Power

by Chris Constancio

Which young baseball prospects are most likely to develop substantial power in the major leagues? I'll look at the relationship between young players' power development and their physical characteristics, their position on the field, other performance indicators, and their pedigree. The resulting analysis will give a clearer picture of what really matters in forecasting young hitters' power development.

Baseball researchers have long been interested in finding adequate ways to assess individual change over time. This is most apparent in the various approaches used to forecast player performances. Dan Szymborski's ZiPS and Tom Tango's Marcel projection system are good examples of techniques that effectively make use of general aging patterns. A major weakness of these systems is that they rely on average developmental trends to forecast the growth of complicated individuals with a wide range of traits that might affect their rate of growth. Other approaches to player projections, including Baseball Prospectus's PECOTA and FirstInning.com's FIPro, attempt to model individual players' development by looking at similar players' histories. While this is one way to account for individual variance in development, the systems do not result in any general rules we can use to better understand baseball players' development, and the results are limited by the small number of relevant comparison players that are available.

In this article, I will utilize multilevel modeling to analyze growth trajectories of hitters' power from age 21 to 26. This analytical approach, sometimes called growth curve modeling, reveals the structure and predictors of change over time. There are some important technical advantages to this technique, such as the ability to handle messy data with missing data points. Growth curve modeling is particularly useful because we don't need to assume that individuals develop similarly over time. We already know that players generally improve from age 21 to 25, but now we can see which individual characteristics explain various developmental paths.

Slugging percentage, or the "S" in OPS, is a well-known measure of a hitter's power, but it is not an appropriate focus for this study because it gives weight to singles. In lieu of slugging percentage, I will use an equally simple statistic often referred to as isolated power (ISOP) as the dependent variable in this study. ISOP can be calculated by subtracting batting average from slugging percentage. Travis Hafner and David Ortiz led the major leagues with ISOPs of .350 and .349 last year, while light-hitting Jason Kendall and David Eckstein had the lowest ISOP among qualifying major leaguers with figures of .047 and .052 respectively. All of the ISOP numbers in this study have been league- and park-adjusted so that we can study hitters in a range of contexts. Only hitters who were competing at the Single-A level or better before age 22 were included. This restriction won't exclude many noteworthy baseball prospects, but it is important to note that the conclusions in this article don't necessarily generalize to all professional baseball players.

Striking Out, Walking and Stealing Bases

The most obvious direction to take in this kind of study is to look at the relationship between isolated power and other performance measures such as strikeouts, walks and stolen bases.

It shouldn't surprise anyone reading this chapter that strikeouts and walks are both positively associated with isolated power. Major league sluggers tend to strike out and walk more often than other hitters, and this holds true among the younger professional baseball players. The relationship between isolated power and strikeout rates might be due to selection bias. That is, organizations are probably willing to tolerate guys who swing and miss a lot if they are at least hitting the ball hard when they make contact. The relationship between walks and isolated power might have something to do with the effect of patience on pitch selection, but it might also be the result of young pitchers avoiding the strike zones versus middle-of-the-order bats.

Although both of these performance traits are positively associated with hitters' isolated power at age 21, they have no effect on hitters' growth rates. Good contact hitters don't improve their isolated power at a better rate than hitters who strike out a lot. Free swingers who rarely walk don't improve their isolated power at a rate any different from patient hitters with above-average walk rates.

Finally, stolen base rates do not affect players' growth rates when controlling for all other variables in this study. This was surprising to me because I assumed hitters with speed would typically hit at the top or bottom of lineups and have more incentive to simply make contact and use their speed to get on base rather than try and drive the ball over the fences like bigger and slower baseball players. I might find something like this if I used another measure to assess player speed rather than stolen base rates. The current study, however, suggests that neither stolen bases, strikeouts, nor walks predict any change in players' rates of power development between the ages of 21 and 25.

Physical Characteristics

It's difficult to imagine a scrappy 165-pound infielder hitting in the middle of a big-league lineup, but prospect watchers tend to imagine great things for big young hitters. As we will soon discover, the numbers suggest size is in fact an important consideration in how a player's power develops.

My analysis of player size on power development focuses on players' weight rather than height. Height and weight should not co-exist in the model due to their collinearity, and as it turns out weight has much more explanatory power than height anyway. This result is consistent with David Gassko's findings in his "Does Size Matter?" series on The Hardball Times website. The average weight of players in my sample was about 195 pounds with a standard deviation of 20 pounds. Let's look at a fictional heavy (215 pound), average (195 pounds) and light (175 pounds) player:

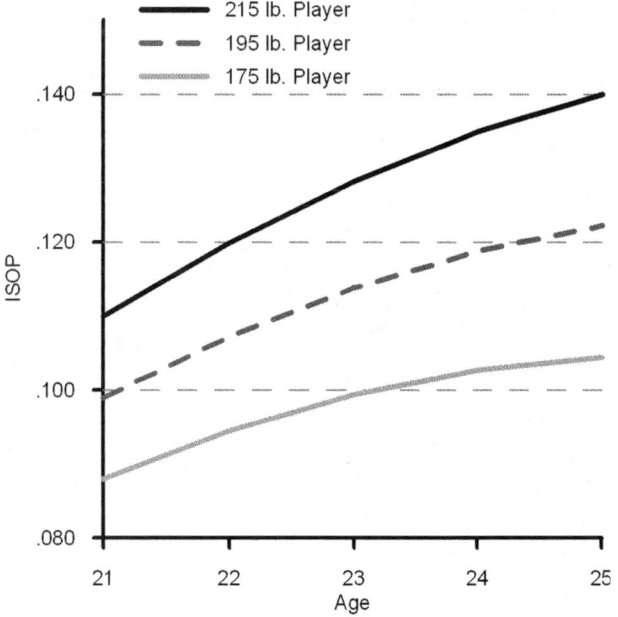

The rich get richer. Not only do heavy players typically enter their age-21 seasons with more power than the lightweights, but their power production increases at a higher rate than lighter hitters during the early part of their careers. This is just one reason why the 220-pound Joe Mauer is more likely to improve on his 13-home-run season than the 190-pound Josh Barfield, who also hit 13 home runs in 2006.

No other easy-to-measure physical characteristic has a significant relationship on a player's power development. Handedness does not matter. When controlling for all other variables included in this study, left-handed, right-handed and switch hitters are about equal in terms of power production. Their growth rates were not significantly different either, so this is not a useful characteristic to consider when evaluating a player's power potential.

Defensive Position

I hypothesized that a player's position on the defensive spectrum may inform his power development because his abilities with the glove may be a proxy for qualities of his athleticism that are not reflected in stolen base totals or physical characteristics. Additionally, the amount of attention needed to develop at each position varies and may affect the attention to improving performance at the plate. I suspected catchers in particular might develop differently at the plate due to the mental and physical demands of the position. It is not uncommon to hear player development personnel and young catchers explain away poor numbers at the plate by talking about how much focus is placed on learning how to call a game and become a good defensive catcher in the minor leagues.

As it turns out, defensive position matters very little when projecting players' power development. When controlling for all other variables in this model, corner infielders and outfielders do have a higher ISOP than other position players, but both of those effects are only marginally significant. Most importantly, the growth rates at each of these positions are not significantly different from one another. That means catchers, first basemen and other infielders and outfielders all develop power at about the same rate after the age of 21 when you control for other important characteristics of the players.

A player's position on the defensive spectrum might matter in other ways, such as forecasting playing time. After all, a light-hitting catcher or shortstop has a better chance of playing in some major league games than a first baseman without much pop in his bat. In terms of projecting future power, however, defense doesn't fit into the equation. This has special implications for forecasters who model their player projections on similar players from the past. It appears that we should not consider a player's defensive position when generating similarity scores for use with projections. There's nothing wrong with comparing a first baseman with a shortstop, at least when forecasting power development.

Pedigree

Teams' emphasis on drafting high school players, drafting college players or signing international players provides a lot of fodder for barroom debates. We actually know very little, however, about how players of these different backgrounds develop. In order to investigate the effects of a player's background on power development, I categorized each player in the data set as drafted out of high school or college or an international signing. Players drafted in the first two rounds of the first-year player draft were designated an "early pick" while every other draftee was labeled a "late pick."

The most obvious result is that hitters drafted out of high school have more power at the plate than hitters drafted out of college. This is especially true for high school hitters drafted in the early rounds of the draft.

The most interesting difference among these groups is a little more subtle. While hitters drafted out of high school and international signees have comparable rates of growth, college hitters' power develops at a much greater pace between the ages of 21 and 25.

The college players' higher growth rate could be explained by their part-time commitment to baseball prior to entering the professional ranks around 21 or 22 years of age. Players drafted out of high school simply play more baseball and have the benefit of a professional organization's resources year-round to improve their strength, conditioning and swing mechanics in their teenage years. For this reason, it's likely that players drafted out of high school or signed as teenagers are closer to their ceiling in terms of power production at age 21 than comparable players drafted out of college programs.

I don't think this evidence really informs whether or not teams are better off investing in young high school players or more experienced college players. It does, however, suggest that we should have different expectations for each type of player's growth past the age of 21. While all groups of players improve their power at the plate at this stage of their career, hitters drafted out of college will generally demonstrate more improvement than hitters who started playing professional baseball as teenagers.

Summary

Growth curve modeling is a powerful tool for analyzing player development. We learned that a player's size and pedigree can tell us something about his rate of growth in developing power at the plate. We also learned that a player's defensive position and other performance indicators are associated with more or less power production at age 21 but do not appear to influence players' rate of growth from age 21 to 25. Modeling the role of individual characteristics on growth over time may be the next frontier in understanding player development, and future work in this area could lead to important insights on a range of player qualities beyond isolated power.

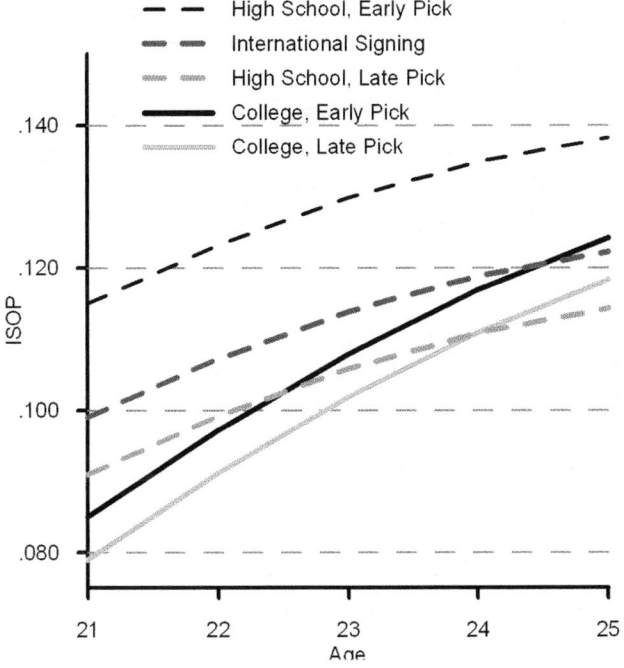

Batted Balls Redux

by Dave Studenmund

A New Run Table

In last year's *Annual,* I published a table that listed the number of runs each type of batted ball and batting event produces, on average. Actually, it didn't quite show that. To get technical, it showed the average number of runs each type of batted ball produces, relative to the overall average.

If you think that's confusing, so did some readers. For instance, the table showed that the relative run value of a ground ball is -0.16. In other words, the average ground ball is worth .16 runs less than the average batting event. I noticed during the season, however, that some bloggers cited that number as proof that ground balls are a negative event. Not true! Ground balls do produce runs; they just produce fewer runs than line drives and outfield flies.

Still confused? Well, allow me to post the following table for you, which shows the *absolute* number of runs each type of batted ball produced in 2006:

Event	Run Impact
Line Drive	0.391
HBP	0.355
Walk	0.355
Outfield Fly	0.192
IBB	0.075
Ground ball	0.045
Bunts	0.021
Infield Fly	-0.088
Strikeouts	-0.113

In other words, if you multiply these numbers by the average number of times each event occurred during a game last year, you'll get 4.8 runs, which was the average number of runs scored per game. If you were to follow the same math with last year's table, you'd get zero, because the numbers were calibrated around the average.

Some people like the average approach, while some like the absolute. Now you can choose between the

two. And, as you can see, ground balls do produce some runs.

To remind you, I developed these tables by calculating the "run impact" of each type of hit (such as a single, double, etc.) as well as the impact of strikeouts and other kinds of outs. I then applied those "run impact" figures to the specific number of times they occur for each type of batted ball.

For 2006, I used linear weights that were derived specifically from 2006 stats (thanks to David Gassko). Technically, actual run impact values will change slightly from year to year, but this table can serve as a good overall guide to the relative value of each batting event in just about any recent year.

The 2006 Batted Ball Champs

We've got something new in our stats section this year. For the first time, we've included comprehensive batted-ball statistics for every batter and pitcher with at least 100 plate appearances or batters faced. This is information you can't get anywhere else, and we think it's pretty interesting stuff. I could spend hours just staring at the stats. Let me run you through some of the details.

As you now know (you did read the previous section, right?), line drives are worth more than outfield flies, which are worth more than ground balls. So, in general, batters want to hit more line drives and outfield flies, while pitchers want to induce ground balls. As you can imagine, some players are good at this sort of thing, and others aren't. What's more, some players generate more runs (or prevent more runs) on their fly balls (for example) than the average player. This section examines how well individual batters and pitchers did each of these things.

Batters

For an average major league hitter, 20% of batted balls are line drives, but there were some big differences among individuals last year. Following is a list of the top 10 in most line drives hit and fewest line drives hit (as a percent of all batted balls; minimum of 502 plate appearances; figures not adjusted for ballpark).

Most Line Drives			Fewest Line Drives		
Player	Tm	LD%	Player	Tm	LD%
Sanchez F.	PIT	28	Inge B.	DET	14
Loretta M.	BOS	27	Bay J.	PIT	15
Kennedy A.	LAA	27	Iguchi T.	CHA	16
Young M.	TEX	25	Willingham J.	FLA	16
Mauer J.	MIN	25	Giambi J.	NYA	16
Konerko P.	CHA	25	Cedeno R.	CHN	16
Youkilis K.	BOS	24	Feliz P.	SF	16
Cabrera M.	FLA	24	Glaus T.	TOR	17
Kendall J.	OAK	24	Durham R.	SF	17
Helton T.	COL	24	Ortiz D.	BOS	17

The line drive leader was the National League batting champ, Pittsburgh's Freddy Sanchez. Also, AL batting champ Joe Mauer isn't far down the list. If you want to win a batting championship, it helps to hit line drives.

But there are some pretty good hitters on the "fewest line drives batted" list, too, such as Pittsburgh's Jason Bay, Yankee Jason Giambi, Troy Glaus of Toronto and Boston's David Ortiz. If these guys aren't hitting line drives, what are they hitting?

Well, since fly balls are the second-most valuable type of batted ball, let's draw a list of batters who hit the most and fewest fly balls, as a percentage of all batted balls. As you can see, a few players, such as Giambi and Glaus compensated for their lack of line drives by hitting lots of fly balls.

Most Fly Balls			Fewest Fly Balls		
Player	Tm	FB%	Player	Tm	FB%
Thomas F.	OAK	57	Jeter D.	NYA	18
Giambi J.	NYA	53	Castillo L.	MIN	21
Soriano A.	WAS	51	Pierre J.	CHN	24
Crede J.	CHA	51	Murton M.	CHN	24
Glaus T.	TOR	49	Grudzielanek M.	KC	25
Dunn A.	CIN	49	Roberts D.	SD	25
Hall B.	MIL	48	Jones J.	CHN	26
Swisher N.	OAK	48	Mauer J.	MIN	26
Barmes C.	COL	48	Kendall J.	OAK	26
Burrell P.	PHI	48	Young M.	TEX	27

Actually, the list of batters who hit the fewest fly balls is fascinating. For instance, players like Joe Mauer and the Rangers' Michael Young didn't hit many flies, but they did hit a lot of line drives so their low fly ball rate didn't hurt their productivity. But the MVP of the American League, Derek Jeter, hit the fewest fly balls of all. Admittedly, at a 22% line drive rate, he fell only a little behind the line drive leaders, but what's going on with that guy?

Let's fill out the picture by listing the players who hit the fewest and most ground balls.

Fewest Ground Balls			Most Ground Balls		
Player	Tm	GB%	Player	Tm	GB%
Thomas F.	OAK	24	Castillo L.	MIN	61
Dunn A.	CIN	28	Jeter D.	NYA	59
Soriano A.	WAS	29	Murton M.	CHN	58
Giambi J.	NYA	30	Jones J.	CHN	56
Youkilis K.	BOS	31	Roberts D.	SD	56
Burrell P.	PHI	31	Taveras W.	HOU	56
Crede J.	CHA	31	Pierre J.	CHN	55
Rolen S.	STL	33	Ausmus B.	HOU	53
Konerko P.	CHA	33	Berroa A.	KC	53
Swisher N.	OAK	33	Grudzielanek M.	KC	52

The fly ball and ground ball lists are almost mirror images of each other. Ground ball hitters hit fewer fly balls, and vice versa. Really, these two tables are completely redundant, but I thought you'd like to see the stats anyway.

If line drives are usually good, ground balls usually only a little good and fly balls in between, why do we see a mix of good and bad batters on all lists? The answer is that not every batter gets the same result from the same type of batted ball. In fact, there can be some big differences between them.

On the next page is a list of the number of runs generated by each batter's ground ball, based on the number of outs, , singles, doubles, etc. that he compiled on all his ground balls. There's not really a big difference between the most extreme hitters—only one-tenth of a run overall—but some of the differences are telling.

Most Runs per Ground Ball			Fewest Runs per Grounder		
Player	Tm	R	Player	Tm	R
Cameron M.	SD	.11	Dunn A.	CIN	-.02
Ramirez H.	FLA	.11	Kennedy A.	LAA	-.02
Crawford C.	TB	.11	Giles B.	SD	.00
Freel R.	CIN	.10	Millar K.	BAL	.00
Suzuki I.	SEA	.10	LaRoche A.	ATL	.00
Uggla D.	FLA	.09	Giambi J.	NYA	.00
Byrnes E.	ARI	.09	Gonzalez A.	SD	.00
Betancourt Y.	SEA	.09	Chavez E.	OAK	.00
Granderson C.	DET	.09	Ausmus B.	HOU	.00
Matthews Jr. G.	TEX	.08	Jacobs M.	FLA	.01

See how important speed can be? Speedsters like Mike Cameron of the Padres and Tampa Bay's Carl Crawford get the max out of their ground balls, but fly ball hitters like Adam Dunn of the Reds and Giambi hit fly balls for a reason. They're not fast enough to produce with their ground balls.

By the way, double plays are included in ground ball run values, too. For instance, Adrian Gonzalez of San Diego tied for the National League lead with 24 GIDPs, which decreased his ground ball run value by, well, a lot.

Let's look at a couple of other personalized run value lists. For instance, the average line drive is worth .39 runs. Which players got the most out of the line drives, and which got the fewest?

Most Runs per Line Drive			Fewest Runs per Liner		
Player	Tm	R	Player	Tm	R
Drew J.D.	LAN	.52	Figgins C.	LAA	.31
Hall B.	MIL	.49	Hatteberg S.	CIN	.32
Matthews Jr. G.	TEX	.49	Kendall J.	OAK	.32
Sizemore G.	CLE	.49	Phillips B.	CIN	.32
Cabrera M.	FLA	.49	Cedeno R.	CHN	.32
Dye J.	CHA	.48	Taveras W.	HOU	.32
Hawpe B.	COL	.48	Ausmus B.	HOU	.32
Ramirez H.	FLA	.47	Castillo J.	PIT	.33
Holliday M.	COL	.47	Berroa A.	KC	.33
Brown E.	KC	.47	Crawford C.	TB	.33

The Dodgers' J.D. Drew garnered over half a run for every line drive he hit because only 14% of his line drives were fielded for outs (the major league average was 31%). Unfortunately (for him) his line drive frequency was 19%, slightly below the major league average.

Conversely, 7% of Jermaine Dye's line drives were home runs, tied with Travis Hafner for the highest percentage in the majors. Among other notables, 8% of Hanley Ramirez's line drives were triples and 32% of Scott Rolen's line drives were doubles. Both figures led the majors.

You may have noticed that the difference between the best and worst line drive hitters is about 0.20 runs, while the difference between the best and worst ground ball hitters is about half that. The difference between fly balls hitters is even more dramatic.

When you hit a fly ball, the very first important thing to do is to get it out of the infield, because 99% of infield flies are caught for outs. Here are the batters who had the fewest and most infield flies as a percent of all flies (a fly is considered an infield fly if it falls inside the basepaths):

Fewest Infield Flies per Fly Ball			Most Infield Flies per Fly ball		
Player	Tm	IF/F	Player	Tm	IF/F
Mauer J.	MIN	.02	Byrnes E.	ARI	.26
Jones J.	CHN	.02	Francoeur J.	ATL	.21
Gonzalez A.	SD	.02	Lopez J.	SEA	.18
Jeter D.	NYA	.02	Encarnacion J.	STL	.18
Roberts B.	BAL	.03	Betancourt Y.	SEA	.17
Giles M.	ATL	.03	Everett A.	HOU	.17
Howard R.	PHI	.03	Vizquel O.	SF	.16
Hafner T.	CLE	.04	Thomas F.	OAK	.16
LaRoche A.	ATL	.04	Hunter T.	MIN	.16
Kennedy A.	LAA	.04	Chavez E.	OAK	.16

Already, you can pick up something that differentiates some of the league's best batters such as Joe Mauer and Derek Jeter: they avoid infield flies. The list of players with the highest rate of infield flies is a mixed one, including some poor hitters (such as Everett), great hitters (Thomas) and enigmas (Francoeur).

If a player manages to get a fly ball out of the infield, it's really nice (for the batter) if it clears the outfield fence altogether. In fact, there is probably no batted-ball stat that separates batters as much as the percentage of home runs per outfield fly. Check out the leaders and laggards:

Most Home Runs per Outfield Fly			Fewest Home Runs per Outfield Fly		
Player	Tm	HR/OF	Player	Tm	HR/OF
Howard R.	PHI	.39	Kendall J.	OAK	.01
Thome J.	CHA	.29	Punto N.	MIN	.01
Hafner T.	CLE	.28	Taveras W.	HOU	.01
Ortiz D.	BOS	.27	Eckstein D.	STL	.02
Berkman L.	HOU	.27	Ausmus B.	HOU	.02
Jones A.	ATL	.26	Roberts D.	SD	.02
Ramirez M.	BOS	.25	Pierre J.	CHN	.02
Pujols A.	STL	.24	Lofton K.	LAN	.02
Dye J.	CHA	.23	Vizquel O.	SF	.02
Dunn A.	CIN	.23	Loretta M.	BOS	.03

On average, 11% of outfield flies left the playing field, but a staggering 39% of Ryan Howard's outfield flies were home runs. You're probably not surprised by the other batters on these lists—they include some of the top sluggers in baseball, and some of the worst.

So when you compile the total runs produced by outfield flies, home run rate has the biggest impact. Really, the lists of most and fewest runs generated per outfield fly contain just about the same cast of characters as the homer lists...

Most Runs per Outfield Fly			Fewest Runs per Outfield Fly		
Player	Tm	R	Player	Tm	R
Howard R.	PHI	.58	Eckstein D.	STL	.00
Hafner T.	CLE	.47	Kendall J.	OAK	.01
Thome J.	CHA	.44	Punto N.	MIN	.04
Berkman L.	HOU	.42	Loretta M.	BOS	.05
Ortiz D.	BOS	.39	Pierre J.	CHN	.05
LaRoche A.	ATL	.39	Barmes C.	COL	.05
Ramirez M.	BOS	.38	Lofton K.	LAN	.06
Jones J.	CHN	.36	Wilson J.	PIT	.06
Beltran C.	NYN	.36	Vizquel O.	SF	.06
Dye J.	CHA	.36	Betancourt Y.	SEA	.06

Think about it: the top fly ball hitters generate half a run more than the worst for every single outfield fly they hit. Yes, there are differences between the best and worst ground ball and line drive hitters, but it is the fly ball that truly separates the best from the worst.

Well, okay, there is one other thing. There are times batters don't hit a pitch at all. For instance, Adam Dunn didn't hit the ball in 46% of his plate appearances. He struck out, he walked, he was hit by a pitch. No batted balls at all. So I ought to include those outcomes in the analysis too, don't you think?

Basically, it takes one walk to offset the damage of three strikeouts (as I showed in the run values table). Some batters use that ratio to their advantage, while others don't. Here's a table in a slightly different format: it ranks all batters according to how many runs they produced in total by striking out or walking, compared to the average batter. I've done it this way because this format captures both each batter's strikeout/walk ratio and how often he strikes out or walks in total:

Most Runs on Balls Not In Play			Fewest Runs on Balls Not in Play		
Player	Tm	R	Player	Tm	R
Giambi J.	NYA	24	Cedeno R.	CHN	-13
Johnson N.	WAS	23	Francoeur J.	ATL	-13
Giles B.	SD	21	Berroa A.	KC	-11
Ortiz D.	BOS	20	Feliz P.	SF	-10
Pujols A.	STL	19	Monroe C.	DET	-9
Helton T.	COL	18	Rodriguez I.	DET	-8
Hafner T.	CLE	17	Betancourt Y.	SEA	-8
Ramirez M.	BOS	16	Jones J.	CHN	-7
Hatteberg S.	CIN	15	Cano R.	NYA	-6
Beltran C.	NYN	15	Peralta J.	CLE	-6

There was almost a difference of 40 runs between the best players at controlling the plate, like Jason Giambi and Nick Johnson, and the worst, like Ronny Cedeno and Jeff Francoeur. I assume you're not surprised by the players on this list.

Now let's put it all together. Here is a table of the best major league batters last year, ranked by runs created above average. The "runs created" part of it is based on all of the batted-ball metrics I just described (basically, frequency of each batted ball times run value) and compared to the major league average. The overall results differ a bit from other metrics (such as Lee Sinins's Runs Created Above Average), but not by a lot.

Plus, with this approach you can see something you have never seen before: how much above or below average each batter ranks for each kind of batted ball. Like so…

Total Runs Above/Below Average

Player	Tm	NIP	GB	LD	Fly	Tot
Howard R.	PHI	11	0	-1	52	61
Pujols A.	STL	19	0	5	33	58
Ortiz D.	BOS	20	-7	-4	43	52
Hafner T.	CLE	17	-7	2	38	49
Berkman L.	HOU	15	2	-3	35	48
Cabrera M.	FLA	12	4	18	10	44
Ramirez M.	BOS	16	-3	2	29	44
Beltran C.	NYN	15	0	-6	33	42
Dye J.	CHA	1	2	8	31	42
Thome J.	CHA	14	-1	-5	33	41

Most of the top batters in the majors are pure sluggers, adept at controlling the plate and blasting fly balls. They tend to not get as much from ground balls and line drives. David Ortiz may be the most extreme example, because he's definitely below average on his ground balls and line drives. Among other types of hitters, Miguel Cabrera is much more of a line drive hitter. Jermaine Dye had a unique profile among the top 10 batters; he displayed top-notch fly ball and line drive power, but didn't control the plate any better than the average batter.

Let's look at a few unique batting profiles. Alfonso Soriano had a great year in Washington but, as you can see, he is all about the fly ball…

Player	Tm	NIP	GB	LD	Fly	Tot
Soriano A.	WAS	-2	1	-3	35	32

…and even his fine speed doesn't get him more than the major league average on ground balls. On the other hand, take a look at this fine all-around hitter…

Player	Tm	NIP	GB	LD	Fly	Tot
Utley C.	PHI	2	7	7	15	31

Philly Chase Utley can pretty much do it all, fly balls, line drives and ground balls. As pitchers give him

more respect over time, that NIP figure will probably increase, too.

Here are a couple of unique American League profiles:

Player	Tm	NIP	GB	LD	Fly	Tot
Mauer J.	MIN	13	3	12	-1	28
Jeter D.	NYA	7	12	10	-1	28

Joe Mauer and Derek Jeter are average fly ball hitters; Mauer gets more out of strikeouts and walks, while Derek Jeter is an extreme ground ball hitter. Few hitters are as successful as Jeter with such a heavy ground ball approach. For instance, compare Jeter to Ichiro Suzuki:

Player	Tm	NIP	GB	LD	Fly	Tot
Suzuki I.	SEA	1	21	5	-16	10

Suzuki is the best ground ball hitter in the majors, but he didn't fill in with line drives, fly ball power and plate discipline the way Jeter did last year.

Just for fun, here are two more unique batting profiles:

Player	Tm	NIP	GB	LD	Fly	Tot
Helton T.	COL	18	-6	17	-5	23
Matthews Jr. G.	TEX	1	13	10	-3	21

Todd Helton was all about plate discipline and line drives last year—not fly balls. And Gary Matthews's big year was the result of ground balls and line drives—a rare combination.

Finally, our change of scenery award goes to Bobby Abreu, who was a very different hitter with the Yankees compared to the first half of the year spent with the Phillies.

Player	Tm	NIP	GB	LD	Fly	Tot
Abreu B.	PHI	16	0	2	-5	13
Abreu B.	NYA	3	0	2	6	10

In 438 plate appearances with the Phillies, Abreu worked walks but was average, at best, at everything else. He was particularly below average with fly balls. Once he went to New York, however, he became more powerful and created six fly ball runs above average in only 248 plate appearances.

Pitchers

Want to do the same thing for pitchers? Of course, you do, but let's start at the most fundamental level for pitchers: strikeouts and walks. Here are the run value leaders and laggards for balls not in play last year (minimum of 502 batters faced):

Fewest Runs on Balls Not In Play			Most Runs on Balls Not In Play		
Player	Tm	NIP	Player	Tm	NIP
Santana J.	MIN	-22	Cabrera D.	BAL	11
Schilling C.	BOS	-21	Trachsel S.	NYN	9
Mussina M.	NYA	-16	Marquis J.	STL	9
Harang A.	CIN	-16	Zito B.	OAK	9
Oswalt R.	HOU	-16	Maholm P.	PIT	8
Smoltz J.	ATL	-15	Fossum C.	TB	8
Carpenter C.	STL	-14	Wright J.	SF	8
Webb B.	ARI	-14	Davis D.	MIL	7
Haren D.	OAK	-13	Zambrano C.	CHN	7
Halladay R.	TOR	-13	Marshall S.	CHN	7

The difference between the best strikeout/walk pitcher (Minnesota's Johan Santana) and the worst (Baltimore's Daniel Cabrera) is slightly less than that between the best and worst strikeout/walk batters, 33 vs. 37 runs. For all the attention spent on pitcher strikeout/walk ratios, the K/BB ratio of major league hitters can vary even more.

In "Tug of War," John Burnson shows that the outcome of a plate appearance tends to vary more with the batter than the pitcher, and we've uncovered the same dynamic with our strikeout and walk stats. Wondering about batted balls? Well, here are the pitching leader and laggards in percent of batted balls that are ground balls:

Most Ground Balls			Fewest Ground Balls		
Player	Tm	GB%	Player	Tm	GB%
Lowe D.	LAN	67	Young C.	SD	25
Webb B.	ARI	66	James C.	ATL	28
Wang C.	NYA	63	Milton E.	CIN	31
Westbrook J.	CLE	61	Lee C.	CLE	33

Most Ground Balls			Fewest Ground Balls		
Player	Tm	GB%	Player	Tm	GB%
Wright J.	SF	58	Williams W.	SD	36
Cook A.	COL	58	Cain M.	SF	36
Hernandez F.	SEA	58	Martinez P.	NYN	36
Hudson T.	ATL	58	Lowry N.	SF	36
Halladay R.	TOR	57	Schmidt J.	SF	37
Saarloos K.	OAK	54	Moyer J.	SEA	37

Thanks to Derek Lowe and Brandon Webb, there is a slightly larger difference between the most and least extreme ground ball pitchers. However, just like the batters, there are some pretty good pitchers among those who gave up the fewest ground balls. The two guys at the top, Chris Young and Chuck James, had pretty good years for San Diego and Atlanta, respectively. Let's see what else we can find out about them.

Here are the pitchers who gave up the most and fewest line drives, as a percent of their total batted balls:

Fewest Line Drives			Most Line Drives		
Player	Tm	LD%	Player	Tm	LD%
Lowe D.	LAN	16	Byrd P.	CLE	24
Johnson R.	NYA	16	Wright J.	NYA	24
Cain M.	SF	16	Pineiro J.	SEA	23
Contreras J.	CHA	16	Glavine T.	NYN	23
Wakefield T.	BOS	16	Shields J.	TB	23
Zito B.	OAK	17	Maddux G.	CHN	23
Hensley C.	SD	17	Verlander J.	DET	23
Wang C.	NYA	17	Hernandez R.	KC	23
Marquis J.	STL	17	Kim B.	COL	23
Webb B.	ARI	17	Suppan J.	STL	23

See, the good thing about being a ground ball pitcher is that you don't give up as many line drives and fly balls. The top ground ballers, Lowe, Webb and Chien-Ming Wang, are on the "least line drives" list...

Fewest Fly balls			Most Fly balls		
Player	**Tm**	**FB%**	**Player**	**Tm**	**FB%**
Webb B.	ARI	16	Young C.	SD	56
Lowe D.	LAN	17	James C.	ATL	53
Wang C.	NYA	20	Milton E.	CIN	50
Westbrook J.	CLE	22	Lee C.	CLE	48
Halladay R.	TOR	22	Cain M.	SF	48
Wright J.	SF	23	Lowry N.	SF	45
Cook A.	COL	24	Zito B.	OAK	45
Hudson T.	ATL	24	Martinez P.	NYN	44
Hernandez F.	SEA	25	Santana E.	LAA	44
Saarloos K.	OAK	25	Wakefield T.	BOS	44

...and they are also the leaders on the "fewest fly balls" list. Conversely, take a look at the pitchers who have given up the most fly balls. Yeah, it's guys like Young and James, who gave up the fewest ground balls. As I said before, when it comes to frequency, you really only need to know one batted-ball stat: ground ball percentage.

But do pitchers give up the same number of runs on each type of batted ball? Well, here's a look at runs given up per ground ball:

Fewest Runs per Ground ball			Most Runs per Ground ball		
Player	**Tm**	**R**	**Player**	**Tm**	**R**
Lidle C.	PHI	.00	Lee C.	CLE	.11
Glavine T.	NYN	.00	Madson R.	PHI	.11
Rogers K.	DET	.00	Kazmir S.	TB	.10
Halladay R.	TOR	.00	Byrd P.	CLE	.09
Robertson N.	DET	.00	Hernandez L.	WAS	.08
Suppan J.	STL	.01	Vargas C.	ARI	.08
Bush D.	MIL	.01	Milton E.	CIN	.08
Peavy J.	SD	.01	Snell I.	PIT	.07
Hensley C.	SD	.02	Harang A.	CIN	.06
Cook A.	COL	.02	Lopez R.	BAL	.06

Yes, pitchers do differ about as much (though slightly less) than batters in ground ball run values. This is actually a little surprising to me, because pitchers have better and worse infields behind them, while batters hit to all sorts of different infields. In fact, you can pick out some of the best infields on this list: there are two Detroit and San Diego pitchers on the "fewest runs" list, and two Cincinnati and Cleveland pitchers on the "most runs" list. That's partially a reflection of the quality of their respective infields.

Next up is the line drive list:

Fewest Runs per Line Drive			Most Runs per Line Drive		
Player	**Tm**	**R**	**Player**	**Tm**	**R**
Santana E.	LAA	.30	Lidle C.	PHI	.46
Fossum C.	TB	.31	Francis J.	COL	.46
Lee C.	CLE	.31	Nolasco C.	FLA	.46
Burnett A.	TOR	.32	Moehler B.	FLA	.46
Benson K.	BAL	.33	Schilling C.	BOS	.45
Mussina M.	NYA	.33	Bush D.	MIL	.45
Beckett J.	BOS	.33	Myers B.	PHI	.44
Arroyo B.	CIN	.34	Capuano C.	MIL	.44
Lowry N.	SF	.34	Davis D.	MIL	.44
James C.	ATL	.34	Meche G.	SEA	.44

Once again, the difference between the fewest and most runs per line drive is greater for batters than pitchers (.21 runs vs. .16). Simply put, line drive hitting (both in terms of frequency and getting hits out of line drives) changes more with batters than pitchers.

At this stage, I'm going to do you a favor and skip the infield flies and home run per outfield fly table. Let's go straight to those pitchers who gave up the fewest runs per outfield fly and those who gave up the most (which is, again, primarily driven by home run rates):

Least Runs per Outfield Fly			Most Runs per Outfield Fly		
Player	Tm	R	Player	Tm	R
Wright J.	NYA	.09	Saarloos K.	OAK	.34
Cabrera D.	BAL	.12	Lidle C.	PHI	.31
Schmidt J.	SF	.12	Pettitte A.	HOU	.29
Francis J.	COL	.12	Hernandez F.	SEA	.28
Lackey J.	LAA	.13	Silva C.	MIN	.28
Loewen A.	BAL	.13	Burnett A.	TOR	.28
Escobar K.	LAA	.13	Webb B.	ARI	.27
Bedard E.	BAL	.14	Snell I.	PIT	.27
Blanton J.	OAK	.15	Beckett J.	BOS	.26
Cain M.	SF	.15	Santos V.	PIT	.25

The difference in home run rates between Jaret Wright and Kirk Saarloos isn't nearly as great as that between Ryan Howard and David Eckstein. For pitchers, the best way to keep your home run rate down is to induce ground balls, because pitchers' rates of home runs per outfield fly tend to be much closer to the overall average.

And now we'll put it all together again. Here is the same "runs created vs. average" table, but this time the leaders are those pitchers who have given up fewer runs than average.

Total Runs Above/Below Average

Player	Tm	NIP	GB	LD	Fly	Tot
Santana J.	MIN	-22	-9	0	-8	-39
Carpenter C.	STL	-14	-7	-8	-5	-35
Webb B.	ARI	-14	-1	-5	-13	-32
Halladay R.	TOR	-13	-9	1	-8	-30
Mussina M.	NYA	-16	-1	-11	4	-25
Zambrano C.	CHN	7	-5	-16	-11	-24
Sabathia C.	CLE	-13	3	-5	-10	-24
Lackey J.	LAA	-6	5	-9	-14	-24
Lowe D.	LAN	-5	5	-8	-14	-23
Smoltz J.	ATL	-15	0	-6	-2	-22
Oswalt R.	HOU	-16	-4	2	-5	-22

There is a less consistent pattern among pitching leaders than batting leaders. This list includes strikeout pitchers (Santana), pitchers who "controlled" line drives (Carlos Zambrano and Mike Mussina) and those who "controlled" fly balls (John Lackey and Derek Lowe). The key to Lackey's performance was his home run rate (6% of outfield flies) while Lowe's key was his ground ball rate, as we have seen.

And what about those two youngsters with the low ground ball rates, Chris Young and Chuck James?

Player	Tm	NIP	GB	LD	Fly	Tot
Young C.	SD	-3	-8	-10	1	-20
James C.	ATL	1	-4	-5	2	-5

Young and James followed similar patterns, though James was less extreme. Neither one was terribly hurt by his high fly ball rates, primarily because 79% of their outfield flies were caught for outs vs. the major league average of 74%. Outfield defense?

Speaking of defense, look at the ground ball performance of these two Tigers hurlers:

Player	Tm	NIP	GB	LD	Fly	Tot
Rogers K.	DET	2	-12	3	-5	-12
Robertson N.	DET	-1	-12	1	7	-5

Both Kenny Rogers and Nate Robertson had relatively high ground ball rates last year. Usually, a higher rate will produce more runs, but these two Tigers hurlers actually yielded fewer overall runs on ground balls thanks to their fine infielders.

And our change of scenery award goes to Greg Maddux, who was traded from Chicago to Los Angeles at the trading deadline, with these results...

Player	Tm	NIP	GB	LD	Fly	Tot
Maddux G.	LAN	-3	-4	0	-2	-10
Maddux G.	CHN	-9	-5	12	-1	-3

In 572 plate appearances with the Cubs, Maddux was slightly better than average. But in just 290 plate appearances with the Dodgers, Maddux was outstanding. The difference was almost entirely in the line drive column. Fielders, skill, ballpark or just plain luck? Hmm.

As I said, these stats are available in our stats section for all players with at least 100 plate appearances/batters faced. I hope you enjoy them as much as we have.

Do Players Control Batted Balls? (Part Two)

by David Gassko

A large part of this book's statistical offering is the batted-ball data that The Hardball Times purchases from Baseball Info Solutions (BIS). The batted-ball data is collected by BIS scorers who classify each ball put into play as an infield or outfield fly, ground ball, line drive or bunt. Each batted-ball type is also broken into outcomes, e.g. singles on ground balls.

The data provide a wealth of previously unavailable information, as a player's batted-ball types are less likely to be influenced by luck and random chance than their outcomes. The data can also help identify stronger trends, help explain what we already know, and help identify players who have been lucky or unlucky. But before using batted-ball data, we have to ask an important question: Just how much control do players have over their batted-ball outcomes?

In last year's *Annual*, J.C. Bradbury and I looked into this question by examining the year-to-year correlations of various batted-ball types and outcomes using BIS data from 2002 to 2005. Correlation ("r") is continuous and ranges from -1 to +1, measuring the degree to which two variables move in relation to one another. A correlation of 1 indicates the variables correlate perfectly in the same direction, a correlation of 0 means there is no correlation between changes in the variables, and a correlation of -1 indicates the variables correlate perfectly in the opposite direction. The further away from zero the correlations are the more closely the variables are related.

We looked at the correlation between a player's performance in a given category in one year and the next, and also examined the *significance* of the correlation, also known as the "p-value." The significance test looks at the strength of the correlation and the sample size to determine the probability that the correlation could occur due to random chance alone. Generally, if that probability (p-value) is less than 5%, it is considered statistically significant.

Another year of data gives us reason to take another look. While the study is similar to last year's, some of the parameters have changed. First, I have discarded data from 2002, which was the first year BIS gathered data, and less reliable. With four years of data beyond that, the 2002 data is not necessary.

Second, instead of just calculating the year-to-year correlation coefficient for each event, I also calculate the spread in the data and compare it to the expected spread, using something known as the binomial distribution. Under a binomial model, each event has one of two possible outcomes (e.g., a coin flip, which either ends in heads or tails), there is a known probability of either of the events occurring (50% of coin flips land heads), and each event is independent (that a coin lands one way says nothing about the side it will land on next).

If the spread among players in a statistic is greater than the expected spread, that indicates that there is indeed a difference among players in that category—that they have control over it. For example, if there was no difference among players in their ability to hit home runs, we would expect the leader in the American League to hit a little over 30. Instead, David Ortiz hit 54 in 2006, so players almost certainly have control over their home run hitting ability, not a surprising conclusion. The dynamic between the expected spread and the actual spread determines the binomial correlation.

As in last year's *Annual*, I have looked only at pitchers with at least 350 batters faced per season and batters with at least 350 plate appearances. That yields a sample of 362 pitchers and 522 batters under the year-to-year correlation study, and 692 pitchers and 949 batters for the binomial study. This is another advantage of using the binomial—it increases the sample because you only need a single year's data. There are, however, drawbacks to that method as well, which I will discuss when they come up.

In the rest of this article, I will take a look at how much control both pitchers and hitters have over their batted balls, with the correlation based on the binomial test as well as the year-to-year correlation. I will discuss each category separately, explaining just what the numbers mean.

Batter Control Over Batted Balls

Batters have a great amount of control over all batted-ball types, as you can see in the following table:

Batted Balls

Batted Ball Types	Binomial Correlation	Year-to-Year Correlation
Infield flies per ball in play	0.46[1]	0.62[1]
Outfield flies per ball in play	0.60[1]	0.71[1]
Line drives per ball in play	0.32[1]	0.13[1]
Ground balls per ball in play	0.59[1]	0.73[1]
Bunts per ball in play	0.73[1]	0.86[1]
Infield flies per fly ball	0.35[1]	0.52[1]

[1] = Significant at the 1% level

Infield flies correlate well from year to year, independent of a hitter's total fly ball ability (meaning that a batter can be a fly ball hitter and still not pop up very often, for example). Ground balls and bunts correlate the best; how often a batter bunts, of course, is almost totally up to the player. (Even if most bunts are called for by managers, the player's proficiency at bunting and hitting ability are by far the two greatest variables in deciding whether or not to call a bunt.) We wouldn't expect bunt totals to change much from year to year.

The number for line drives is interesting. The year-to-year correlation (.13) is only slightly higher than what we found last year (.10), but the binomial correlation implies much more control. I think this actually makes a lot of sense.

It's hard to hit a line drive—it means hitting a tiny ball going 90 miles per hour on the nose. Some hitters clearly have more line drive skill than others, but because it's so hard to do, line drives are a relatively random event. So from year to year, there is so much "noise" in the data that much of the "signal" is blocked. Line drives in one year can be hit at a slightly different angle the next and become outfield flies. But the difference between players' line drive abilities is going to be great, greater than the simple correlation test will tell us.

Next, let's look at the outcome of each specific type of batted ball. First up is the outfield fly...

Outfield Flies

Outfield Flies	Binomial Correlation	Year-to-Year Correlation
Outfield flies per ball in play	0.60[1]	0.71[1]
Singles per outfield fly	0.23[1]	0.01
Doubles plus triples per outfield fly	0.24[1]	0.21[1]
Home runs per outfield fly	0.51[1]	0.74[1]
Batting average on outfield flies	0.44[1]	0.52[1]

[1] = Significant at the 1% level

Let's start out with the single biggest discrepancy: the correlation of singles per outfield fly. The spread in the statistic is highly significant; the year-to-year correlation is zero. I think this has to do with the difference between a line drive and an outfield fly—with some batted balls, it's hard to know the difference. Depending on how those balls are classified, a player might end up with many singles on outfield flies, if most of the questionable balls are called fly balls, or very few, if most of the questionable balls are labeled liners.

In fact, in 2006, BIS started tracking a new category, fliners, to adjust specifically to address that issue. When we have more years of data, we'll be able to look into the impact of fliners. Because of this, there will be a greater-than-random spread in the number of singles per outfield fly, but because the scorers are not biased, there is no year-to-year correlation. I doubt batters have much control over how many singles they hit on outfield flies, though obviously they do have control over the proportion of balls they hit in the air that become singles, as weaker hitters just don't hit the ball as far.

Batters *do* have plenty of control over the amount of power with which they hit an outfield fly—that should not be surprising.

Line Drives

Line Drives	Binomial Correlation	Year-to-Year Correlation
Line drives per ball in play	0.32[1]	0.13[1]
Singles per line drive	-0.01	0.12[1]
Doubles plus triples per line drive	0.02	0.22[1]
Home runs per line drive	0.10[1]	0.36[1]
Batting average on line drives	-0.05	0.13[1]

[1] = Significant at the 1% level

So how is it that we found no correlation for singles per outfield fly, but the singles per line drive have a highly significant correlation from year to year? Well, outfield flies that can land for singles are generally hit pretty softly, so whether or not a fly ball drops for a hit depends mostly on how far away from the fielder it's been hit—a matter of luck. Whether a line drive lands for a single, however, is largely dependent on how hard it is hit, which is something the batter has much more control over.

What's interesting is that while line drives are largely random from year to year, the outcomes of line drives are not any more random, though we would expect them to be. This suggests more batter control over line drives. Again, we see a higher correlation in the power categories (doubles plus triples, home runs) than anywhere else. This further advances the idea that power is one of the most consistent and important hitting skills.

I wouldn't pay much attention to the low correlations implied by the binomial test—it's just a case of the sample and true correlation being too small for the spread to be significant.

Ground balls

Ground Balls	Binomial Correlation	Year-to-Year Correlation
Ground balls per ball in play	0.59[1]	0.73[1]
Singles per ground ball	0.14[1]	0.20[1]
Doubles plus triples per ground ball	0.15[1]	0.11[1]
Reached on error per ground ball	0.04	0.10[5]
Batting average on ground balls	0.15[1]	0.22[1]

[1] = Significant at the 1% level

[5] = Significant at the 5% level

Though players clearly have some control over their rate of getting on-base via ground ball, it's much smaller than I would have expected. Most likely, there are some hitters who will have clearly high batting averages on grounders, like Ichiro, and some who will have very low batting averages on ground balls, like Frank Thomas, but most are just going to be clustered around average, bringing down the overall correlation. I would guess that the extreme hitters would regress less than these numbers suggest. The numbers also suggest that some hitters might have the ability to aim the ball "where

they ain't" when they hit a ground ball, resulting in more ground ball hits.

The correlation suggested by the binomial for reached on error is just barely insignificant, and it is clear that hitters have some ability to reach base on error. Faster batters probably cause more errors by forcing fielders to hurry throws and be more anxious in the field and also give fielders less of a chance to recover from a bobble.

Bunts

Bunts	Binomial Correlation	Year-to-Year Correlation
Bunts per ball in play	0.73[1]	0.86[1]
Batting average on bunts	0.14[1]	0.24[1]

[1] = Significant at the 1% level

I've included reached on error in batting average on bunts, since there aren't enough to find any significant year-to-year relationship, and because a reached on error on a bunt is clearly largely influenced by the batter's ability. And indeed, there is a large degree of skill involved in reaching base via bunt. This shouldn't be surprising; some batters are better bunters and have more speed down the line than others.

Overall, we see that batters have a large degree of control over all facets of their game, though power numbers are more consistent from year to year than singles and reached on error.

Pitcher Control Over Batted Balls

Batted Balls

Batted Ball Types	Binomial Correlation	Year-to-Year Correlation
Infield flies per ball in play	0.41[1]	0.51[1]
Outfield flies per ball in play	0.62[1]	0.71[1]
Line drives per ball in play	0.29[1]	-0.06
Ground balls per ball in play	0.67[1]	0.84[1]
Bunts per ball in play	0.29[1]	0.33[1]
Infield flies per fly ball	0.20[1]	0.21[1]

[1] = Significant at the 1% level

As we concluded last year, pitchers not only have the ability to force infield flies, which are pretty much automatic outs, but that ability is partially independent of their ability to force fly balls overall. Fly ball pitchers will allow more pop flies than ground ball pitchers, but the number they allow still varies on the individual level.

Ground balls and fly balls are subject to a very large degree of pitcher control—they pretty much don't change from year to year. Bunts are less consistent, but pitchers still have a large degree of control there. This is probably a function of the pitcher's league and quality. (Batters will bunt more against a good pitcher.)

Let's talk about line drives a bit. Last year, we made the shocking discovery that the number of line drives a pitcher allows from year to year is highly inconsistent. The results are no different this year—the correlation is actually slightly negative. However, when we look at the spread in line drives per ball in play, we find a highly significant correlation. So how can that be?

I think what's happening here is this: pitchers almost certainly *do* have differing abilities in terms of the number of line drives they allow. Some pitchers simply allow harder-hit balls than others. On the Hardball Times website, I wrote an article which found that there is an almost-perfect correlation between a pitcher's ground ball rate and the proportion of the balls hit in the air off of him that are line drives, which means that pitchers clearly do have a large degree of control over the number of line drives they allow. Because ground ball pitchers allow fewer balls in the air overall, however, those things cancel out, and ground ball pitchers allow roughly the same number of liners as do fly ball pitchers. So one year's worth of line drive data tells us nothing about a pitcher's ability. But pitchers *do* have a large amount of control over the number of line drives they will allow.

hit percentage on outfield flies, and I think the correlation predicted by the binomial is partially because of the issue of labeling those balls that aren't quite fly balls and aren't quite liners, as well as the quality of a pitcher's defense. In "DIPS Revisited," Mitchel Lichtman posted similar findings using different years of data and a different data source.

Last year, J.C. and I concluded that pitchers do not have much, if any, impact on the percentage of outfield flies that go over the fence. Further examination of the data shows this to be wrong. Pitchers clearly have some, though not much, impact on the number of home runs they allow per outfield fly. Some of this correlation is due to the park, but even adjusting for park effects, the correlation is still significant. These numbers also match the results Lichtman reported to me in a private e-mail. What this means is that we should pay attention to the numbers of home runs a pitcher allows per fly ball, but with one year of data, we should also be wary of pitchers with highly unusual numbers of home runs per outfield fly.

Line Drives

Line Drives	Binomial Correlation	Year-to-Year Correlation
Line drives per ball in play	0.29[1]	-0.06
Singles per line drive	0.08[5]	0.11[5]
Doubles plus triples per line drive	0.06	0.05
Home runs per line drive	0.04	0.21[1]
Batting average on line drives	0.06	0.09

[1] = *Significant at the 1% level*
[5] = *Significant at the 5% level*

The more granular line drive data gives more hints about whether pitchers have any control over liners, and the results are mixed. It seems clear that pitchers do have a relatively large impact on the percentage of line drives they allow that are home runs. They also seem to have some impact on the number of singles per line drive they allow (we found this effect last year as well). The correlation for batting average on line drives, using both methods, was just barely insignificant.

Again, the data are inconclusive. Pitchers do appear to have some very small degree of control over line drives, but it is so small—beyond home runs—that one

Outfield Flies

Outfield Flies	Binomial Correlation	Year-to-Year Correlation
Outfield flies per ball in play	0.62[1]	0.71[1]
Singles per outfield fly	0.23[1]	-0.04
Doubles plus triples per outfield fly	0.24[1]	0.03
Home runs per outfield fly	0.12[1]	0.17[1]
Batting average on outfield flies	0.27[1]	-0.01

[1] = *Significant at the 1% level*

Here's an effect similar to that of outfield flies for batters. I doubt pitchers have much control over their year's worth of line drive data does not appear to have any meaning whatsoever.

Ground Balls

Ground Balls	Binomial Correlation	Year-to-Year Correlation
Ground balls per ball in play	0.67[1]	0.84[1]
Singles per ground ball	0.08[5]	0.14[1]
Doubles plus triples per ground ball	0.09[1]	0.10[5]
Reached on error per ground ball	0.03	0.08
Batting average on ground balls	0.10[1]	0.15[1]

[1] = *Significant at the 1% level*

[5] = *Significant at the 5% level*

Pitchers control nothing like they control their ground ball rate. However, pitchers also appear to have some control over the outcomes of their ground balls as well. Even the reached-on-error correlations are barely insignificant. It is possible that these correlations can be attributed to the fielders or park, but it is also possible that pitchers have some ability to prevent hits on ground balls. There is a strong negative correlation ("r" = -.24) between the percentage of ground balls allowed by a pitcher and his batting average on ground balls, meaning that ground ball pitchers also allow easier-to-field ground balls.

Bunts

Bunts	Binomial Correlation	Year-to-Year Correlation
Bunts per ball in play	0.29[1]	0.33[1]
Batting average on bunts	0.05	0.09[5]

[1] = *Significant at the 1% level*

[5] = *Significant at the 5% level*

Any significant correlation is almost certainly due to the quality of a pitcher's defense, though the pitcher's fielding ability as well as his overall pitching ability (a bunt against a good pitcher might be more predictable) and league (a bunt in the National League might be more predictable, especially one by a pitcher hitting) might play some small role as well.

Conclusions

There is a lot of information in the preceding pages, a lot of data presented, so let's summarize it in bullet-point form:

- Both pitchers and hitters have much control over the types of batted balls they allow, though line drives tend to be more random than fly balls, grounders, or bunts, which are all highly stable from year-to-year.

- Pitchers and hitters also show some control over the outcomes of their batted balls, i.e. what percentage of their ground balls become singles, though the only outcomes that are very stable from year-to-year are power outcomes for hitters, i.e. home runs per fly ball.

- Pitchers do show some consistent skill in how many home runs they allow per outfield fly ball, though there is still quite a bit of randomness in that measurement. With one year of data, you're better off ignoring a pitcher's home run per outfield fly rate, and instead concentrating on the total number of outfield fly balls he allowed.

- Overall, batted ball data can give us more information about a player's performance and can then help us better evaluate his play. There is a a lot of luck in the outcome of an at-bat and that luck does not necessarily even out over the course of a season. But at the same time, it is dangerous to totally discount batted ball outcomes; some seasonal stats may be significant to understanding a player's talent.

Final Thoughts

Granular batted-ball data allow us to analyze baseball statistics in a whole new way, lending both a better understanding of the game and of the underlying numbers that might impact a player's future performance. Both hitters and pitchers have substantial influence over the distribution of batted balls they allow and some influence over their outcomes. However, one season's worth of data is not enough to tell us very much about their ability in certain categories, *i.e.* line drives.

Further studies of batted-ball data might lend us more knowledge about how the game works and what players can and cannot control.

Tug of War

by John Burnson

On June 6, 2006, New York Yankee starting pitcher Chien-Ming Wang faced off against Boston's David Ortiz. Wang is an inveterate inducer of ground balls—among pitchers in 2006, he had the third-highest ratio of ground balls to fly balls (G/F). At the other end is Ortiz, a fierce slugger who had the 13th-*lowest* G/F for hitters in 2006. So, what happened when Wang met Ortiz?

When trying to make sense of a player, we tend to dig deep into his statistics. Players do not exist in isolation, however—practically every one of their stats is the result not of a decision by one player but of a contest between two. The influence of "the other side" is ever-present.

One place to spot this influence is among pitchers. We have learned in recent years that pitchers have little control over three rates: the rate of hits on fieldable balls (roughly 30%); the rate of line drives on hit balls (roughly 20%); and the rate of home runs on fly balls (roughly 10%). (Note: be sure to read the previous article for David Gassko's analytic nuance to these "truisms.") These are *not* the rates for any ball of its type. We know, for example, that hit rate varies by the count at which the ball is struck, and recent research in this book and at BaseballHQ.com points to distinctions with the location of the pitch in the strike zone. Rather, these are the *aggregate* rates among major league batters. If a pitcher faces enough batters, and if he faces enough *different* batters, then his rates of these ratios should tend toward these figures. If major league hitters were generally stronger or weaker, or faster or slower, these figures would be different; however, they still would be largely independent of the pitcher.

And yet, pitchers are not helpless. They have characteristic rates of strikeouts and walks. Even in the matter of contact, pitchers have a say in whether a ball travels on the ground or in the air. (If this were not true, then all pitchers would have basically the same G/F, which they do not, and pitchers' year-to-year G/F's would not correlate, which they do.) Thus, at least one idiosyncrasy of a pitcher survives the collision of the ball with the bat—the hit ball "remembers" the pitcher.

However, batters also have dissimilar (and consistent) G/F's. Therefore, batters must also impart something of themselves to the hit ball. So who controls what?

Before tackling that question, let's first examine the goings-on at the rawest level of combat between hitter and pitcher: the count. Do changes in behavior from one count to another give an edge to one player? I tapped Retrosheet for all pitch sequences from 2003 to 2005, and I stepped through each sequence, pitch by pitch. For simplicity, I focused on five events: a ball, a called strike, a foul, a swinging strike, and a hit ball. These events are far and away the most common—they comprise more than 98% of Retrosheet's pitch events (excluding events that did not involve the batter, like pick-off attempts).

I focused on a single, easily trackable decision: whether, at a given count, the batter swings. Here are the numbers:

Odds of a Swing on the Pitch

Balls					
0	1	2	3		
28%	41%	40%	8%	0	
46%	53%	59%	56%	1	Strikes
49%	58%	65%	74%	2	

Batters do vary their propensity to swing by count. Curiously, for a given number of balls, batters swing most often when the consequences of a strike are most dire: at two strikes. Are batters right to expect something hittable? We can get a clue, and also get a bead on the initiative of pitchers, by looking at what happens if the batter does *not* swing. Is the pitch a ball or a strike?

Odds of a Called Strike if No Swing

Balls					
0	1	2	3		
42%	40%	47%	63%	0	
20%	23%	27%	36%	1	Strikes
8%	10%	13%	17%	2	

At least on those occasions when the batter does not swing, pitchers also adjust their behavior from count to count. Presumably the proportion of hittable pitches is similar when hitters *do* swing; however, these data don't say, and we ought not assume that the hitter's swinging is irrelevant. Regardless, contrary to hitters' inclinations, a count of two strikes seems to be the absolute worst time to swing. It appears that pitchers do not throw over the plate with more strikes after all; instead, they rely on batters' rashness to do their work for them. The conclusion that batters' judgment wanes with increasing strikes is reinforced by looking at the likelihood of a swinging strike at each count:

Odds of a Swinging Strike

Balls					
0	1	2	3		
20%	19%	15%	12%	0	
21%	20%	17%	13%	1	Strikes
23%	21%	18%	14%	2	

Whatever else batters are doing at two strikes, they are not being more discerning. There's that same agitation in the first chart, where batters go from swinging 41% of the time at 1-0 and 40% of the time at 2-0 to swinging only 8% of the time at 3-0. With only one more ball for a walk, batters are suddenly possessed by the prospect of surviving the plate appearance despite 3-0 being the best count for a good pitch (per the earlier table). But then add a strike to go to 3-1—with the batter still only one ball away from a walk, mind you—and batters' swing rate jumps back up to 56%!

Taken together, these tables paint a picture of cool pitchers and desperate hitters. But we can delve deeper. The state of the count—the number of balls and strikes—is not the end of the matter. Batters and pitchers care about the state; I've shown so above. But they don't care only about the state. Batters and pitchers do not just get plopped into the pitch count; as human beings, they have memory. And (as beings with memory) they behave differently at otherwise equivalent states based on the history.

Consider what happens at 3-2. In theory, a count of 3-2 can last indefinitely if the batter repeatedly fouls off pitches. However, batters do not behave consistently across the durations. It turns out that whether the batter swings depends on how long he has been waiting (as shown in the lower left-hand graph).

If batters did not reflect on how they got to 3-2, the odds of a swing would not change; instead, the probability rises as the at-bat lengthens. I'm not saying that batters' memory is *useful*—any way you slice it, 3-2 is 3-2—only that memory is at work.

Pitchers engage in their own hijinx:

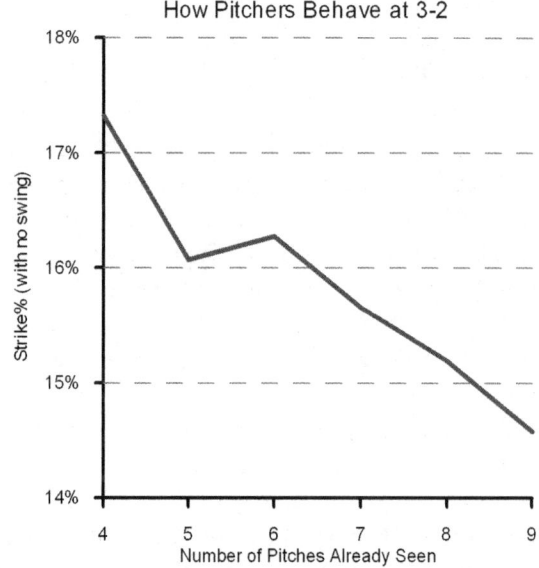

How Pitchers Behave at 3-2

Again, the pitchers sense the panic of their prey.

Why might batters become more restless in longer at-bats? I'll suggest a very human answer: embarrassment. Among all the outcomes, batters (in this hypothesis) most resent walking back to the bench after a called third strike. At least by swinging, batters can believe that they *did* something. (Recall the first chart: Batters swing more the closer that they get to a strikeout.) And as batters get deeper into 3-2, the pressure weighs more heavily. Yet the time already spent in the at-bat is a sunk cost; rationally, it should be dismissed.

But batters have a hard time dismissing memory; in fact, a batter's memory is strongly persistent. Consider the count of 2-2. There are six ways to reach this count. Let's look at two specific sequences, BBKK (when the

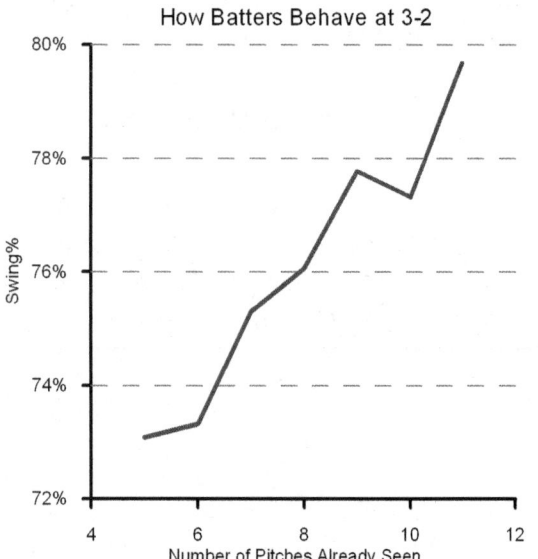

How Batters Behave at 3-2

batter gets the two strikes later) and KKBB (when the batter gets the two balls later). Do batters behave differently depending on which outcomes came later?

Yes. Strangely, batters swing more often at 2-2 if they more recently got two balls (swinging 67.4% of the time) than if they more recently got two strikes (swinging 62.9% of the time). The difference is statistically significant to a virtual certainty (p=.0000). As is the case at 3-2, the count itself is the same, but the path is different. This same effect is evident after only two pitches: At 1-1 batters swing 54.4% of the time if the ball comes second, only 51.2% of the time if the strike does (again, p=.0000).

Finally, batters even register the preceding plate appearance (that is, the appearance by the previous batter). Again demonstrating an expectation of a reversal by the pitcher, batters are less apt to swing on the first pitch after a strikeout (28.7%) than after a walk (30.1%).

The fact that batters and pitchers have memory is not terribly surprising, even if their rationale is not always clear. I've digressed on this topic to raise caution. We students of baseball often find it helpful to present our findings in tables; however, tables exult states. If baseball players have memory (and they seem to), then tables might hide a good deal of nuance.

Getting back to our original task: On casual inspection, pitchers seem to have the upper hand in their battle with batters. Both the tables and the graphs say that pitchers are accomplished at anticipating batters. Does this apparent command extend to the result after contact?

To find out, I moved beyond the count and looked at the results of historical meetings. From the data for 2003-05, I gathered all pairings of a batter and pitcher in which there were at least 18 encounters that ended in a ground ball or a fly ball. There were 303 such pairings.

For each match-up, I found the proportion of ground balls (GB%). I then looked to see where the outcome fell on the spectrum between the pitcher's GB% and the hitter's GB%. I set a line that had the pitcher's GB% at 0 and the hitter's GB% at 100. (For thoroughness, I calculated both ratios absent the at-bats in question, though they were too few to be consequential.) I then situated the GB% for the meeting along this axis.

If pitchers tend to dictate the course of the hit ball, I would expect more events closer to the 0 point. If batters dominate the match-up, I would expect more events closer to 100. If the two sides have equal pull, the result would be 50. (Note that the match-up GB% could extend below 0 or above 100 if the rate happens to not fall between the pitcher's and hitter's rates.)

Among the 303 cases, the match-up GB% favored the batter in 168 cases, versus 135 cases for the pitcher. The median rate landed on the axis at 71, indicating that batters have more sway than pitchers. Indeed, if I run a linear regression of match-up GB% against the hitters' and pitchers' individual rates, this is the result:

$$\text{Match-up GB\%} = 0.65 * \text{GB\%}_{\text{Hitters}} + 0.35 * \text{GB\%}_{\text{Pitchers}}$$

In terms of guiding a hit ball, hitters have nearly twice as much weight as pitchers! What if we look at only those pairs of hitters and pitchers whose rates of ground balls differ appreciably—say, by at least 10 percentage points? Our pool contains 87 such cases. The median match-up GB% (as defined by our axis) was still a healthy 64 in favor of batters, and the regression equation was essentially unchanged.

So a hit ball "listens" more to the batter than to the pitcher. The primacy of batters is plausible—although pitchers do their best to locate the ball, it is batters who react to the pitch and who determine the arc of the bat.

Maybe I am looking for pitching supremacy in the wrong place. Our earlier results suggested that pitchers outguess batters at the level of the count. Perhaps, then, pitchers triumph when it comes to strikeouts and walks.

We pulled all pairings of batters and pitchers who met at least 30 times from 2003 to 2005; there were 315 such pairs. We did the same analysis as before, this time looking at strikeouts per appearance (K/A) and walks per appearance (BB/A). Here are the results:

$$\text{Match-up K/A} = 0.66 * \text{KA}_{\text{Hitters}} + 0.29 * \text{KA}_{\text{Pitchers}}$$
$$\text{Match-up BB/A} = 0.63 * \text{BBA}_{\text{Hitters}} + 0.38 * \text{BBA}_{\text{Pitchers}}$$

A pitcher's walk rate is more influential than his strikeout rate, perhaps because the pitcher can serve up a pitch that is truly and obviously unworthy of a swing. But both his rates still play second fiddle to the batter's.

So here we have ground ball rate, strikeout rate, and walk rate—the three most defining traits of a pitcher!—and two-thirds of their magnitude derives from hitters.

Maybe we should have known that hitters would prevail. Remember the pitcher-independent rates that I mentioned before? To my knowledge, no one has identified an analogous rate for hitters—that is, there is no rate for hitters that relies largely on the skills of the mass of opposing pitchers. Hitters hold the reins of their destiny; pitchers are along for the ride.

If batters control the match-up, then pitchers' statistics should be more sensitive to the caliber of their opposition. Therefore, pitchers might experience a broader shift in fortunes from a trade to another team than do hitters. Furthermore, to flourish, it is critical that pitchers seize their chances—strike out the free-swingers (and, in the National League, the opposing pitchers) and induce grounders from the slappers.

Repeated failures on these occasions will haunt the pitcher.

I believe that the interaction between hitters and pitchers is a rich unplumbed vein in sabermetrics. Greater understanding of this area will help us to allot responsibility for a player's stats, as well as provide a fuller accounting of the events that unfold on the field.

Oh, and about that New York-Boston game? In three appearances against the GB-loving Wang, Ortiz hit... two fly balls. In the remaining appearance, Ortiz struck out. In 2006, Ortiz struck out 117 times. Wang struck out only 76 batters all year.

Who Will Break Out Next Year?

by David Gassko

Alfonso Soriano had one year to prove that he was the superstar everyone thought he would be when the Yankees parted with him to get Alex Rodriguez. In two years with the Texas Rangers, Soriano had averaged fewer than 90 runs and 100 RBIs per year. His numbers, adjusted for context, were only barely above average, and he was a year away from free agency.

The Rangers parted with him, trading Soriano to the Washington Nationals for Brad Wilkerson and assorted parts. It looked like the Rangers got the better deal: Soriano was a flashy 40/40 threat, but Wilkerson had been the better player over the past two years, and of course, he was cheaper as well. You probably know where the story goes from there: Wilkerson fell apart while Soriano hit 41 home runs, stole 41 bases, added 41 doubles, learned to walk, and received a huge contract in the offseason. (Well, as of this writing, that has yet to happen, but that's the type of prediction I feel safe making.) So here's the question: Could anyone have predicted that? This is a question that's interested me for a while now. Breakout seasons are supposed to be magical, unpredictable events when a player steps up and takes his game to the next level. We're not supposed to try to explain them, we're just supposed to marvel and watch. And maybe that is the right way to approach them, but I couldn't help but ask: Are there any indicators that might help predict a breakout year?

First, let's define a breakout. To me, a breakout year is punctuated by two things: the player has to have a good season in which he reaches a new level of play. If Mario Mendoza hit .250, that wouldn't make for a breakout season, because he would still suck. If Albert Pujols hits .350, that wouldn't make for a breakout season because he's already a great player. But if Mendoza hit .300, or Pujols hits .400, that would be a breakout year, because that would be a new plateau for each of them.

For the purposes of this study, I defined a player's performance as his weighted on-base average (wOBA) in a season. Bear with me getting technical for a moment: I used a player's wOBA with each component regressed and compared to the league average. For a season to be labeled a breakout year, a player's regressed wOBA had to be above average and had to have risen by more than 6% (which would be about one standard deviation for an average player).

My database consisted of all players, no older than 30 (because after 30, it's not so much a breakout as it is a fluke, or a freak accident) between 1955 and 2005 who had two consecutive years of at least 200 plate appearances, or more than 6,800 such data pairs overall. There were 913 seasons classified as breakouts, or about 13%. That means that if we were to just guess at a player's chances of having a breakout year, our guess would be 13%. Can we make a more accurate guess? I think so.

To figure out the answer, I added to my database a large number of variables that might be helpful in predicting a breakout season, everything from a player's handedness to his age to his eye color (okay, not his eye color). I then performed (technical stuff warning number two) a binary logistic regression on any number of combinations of the variables to predict whether or not the player had a breakout year. A binary regression is just like a normal regression, but the dependent variable (the one I'm trying to predict) can only be a 0 or a 1 (in this case, a 0 meant that the player did not have a breakout season, a 1 meant that he did). In a binary regression, the goal is to predict the dependent variable correctly as often as possible.

When all was said and done, I found a number of variables that affected a player's chances of having a breakout year. They were:

- **The player's handedness**. Lefties are more likely to have breakout seasons, likely because of the steeper learning curve they face adjusting to left-handed pitchers. While very good right-handed pitchers abound at all levels of play, thus giving right-handed batters plenty of experience facing quality same-handed pitchers, there are many fewer good lefties, especially at lower levels, which means that left-handed batters have a much greater adjustment to make when they come to the majors. When they make that adjustment, they break out.

- **Power**. Players who hit for power are more likely to have a breakout year. This makes sense: non-power components (singles, mainly) are much less predictable from year to year, so it's easier to improve on them. Also, players who demonstrate a lot of power are more likely to get more respect from pitchers the next year, which can result in more walks.

- **A player's combination of power and speed**. Many studies have shown that players with both power and speed age better than players who have skills in fewer dimensions, and accordingly, hitters with both power and speed are more likely to have a breakout year.

- **Patience at the plate**. Walks are positively correlated with breakout seasons, because, well, you can't teach patience. A player is more likely to have a breakout season by improving on his hitting than he is due to improving his walk total. Strikeouts, on the other hand, have a negative effect on a player's chances of having a breakout season because if a hitter doesn't put the ball in play that often, there is a very real cap to the numbers he can put up.

- **Weight**. Heavier players have better odds of having a breakout season because weight is generally correlated with improved future performance.

- **Age**. Generally speaking, younger players are more likely to have a breakout season. This one should be obvious. I should also add that hitters are less likely to have a breakout season at 29. I have no idea why that would be, but the effect is highly significant.

- **Performance**. It's easier to have a breakout year with a mediocre performance in the previous season, simply because it requires less improvement. A 10% increase in performance for Mendoza would have been 21 points of batting average; for Ted Williams it would have meant 35 points of batting average.

With these variables taken into account, we can improve our prediction rate remarkably. Among the players in my data set who actually had a breakout season, their average projected odds of doing so were 19%, almost 50% higher than the overall average. Among the 100 players given the best odds of having a breakout season, 34 actually did. If we look at the 500 hitters with the best odds (or 10 per season), we find that 152 actually did break out, which means that you can be reasonably confident that when I give you a list of the top 10 most likely players to have a breakout year in 2007, three of them actually will. And Soriano? His odds of stepping up to the next level last year were about 20%, which are pretty damn good odds.

So looking forward, which players have the best chance of breaking out in 2007?

2007 Batting Breakout Candidates

Last	First	Breakout%
Barmes	Clint	45%
Church	Ryan	42%
Alfonzo	Eliezer	41%
Pena	Wily Mo	37%
Abercrombie	Reggie	37%
Ross	Dave	32%
Shealy	Ryan	31%
Gross	Gabe	31%
Olivo	Miguel	31%
LaRue	Jason	30%

These guys are all likely to be undervalued by conventional projection systems, though then again, it's important to remember that what that percentage really signifies is the player's chances of having a breakout year *given that he accumulates 200 plate appearances*. Can we really be sure that any of those guys will get to the plate that often? If they do, that implies they won't be too bad. Also, as I mentioned earlier, poor players have an easier time breaking out than good players do. So what if we only look at those hitters who had an above-average performance in 2006?

Breakout Candidates: Above Average in 2006

Last	First	Breakout%
Ross	Dave	32%
Lee	Derrek	23%
Fielder	Prince	23%
Kearns	Austin	22%
Helms	Wes	22%
Pierzynski	A.J.	21%
Paulino	Ronny	19%
Crawford	Carl	18%
Hart	Corey	18%
Floyd	Cliff	17%

Fielder, Kearns, and Crawford are three guys I expected to be on this list—a sign that the system is working. Lee is a good catch as well. He had an .842 OPS this year, but it's likely that he will do much better next season. It wouldn't really be a breakout season, since Lee was injured last year and so good in 2005, but it would be a significant step up according to our criteria.

Now let's look at players that are no older than 25. Which young guys are poised to step up in 2007?

Top Breakout Candidates Under 26

Last	First	Breakout%
Pena	Wily Mo	37%
Weeks	Rickie	30%
Cedeno	Ronny	26%
Francoeur	Jeff	25%
Fielder	Prince	23%
Lopez	Jose	23%
McLouth	Nate	21%
Drew	Stephen	19%
Crawford	Carl	18%
Hart	Corey	18%

Maybe Francoeur's performance will finally match his reputation. Okay, one more list, this one out of pure, gleeful cruelty. Which below-average players are least likely to make significant improvements next year? That is, which players should be avoided at all costs because they are essentially hopeless? Here's the list:

Least Likely Breakout Batters

Last	First	Breakout%
Blum	Geoff	8%
Miller	Damian	8%
Bloomquist	Willie	8%
Boone	Aaron	8%
Amezaga	Alfredo	5%
Clayton	Royce	5%
Burnitz	Jeromy	3%
Ausmus	Brad	2%
Sanders	Reggie	2%
Castilla	Vinny	1%

Vinny Castilla? Brad Ausmus? Both had OPSs below .600 and both are almost 40. They sound like the perfect candidates to not break out ... ever.

Let's add some historical numbers here as well. The player with the greatest chance of breaking out since 1955 was Hee Seop Choi in 2004, and he did in fact have a breakout season going from a .306 wOBA to .345. The least likely breakout season of all time was Albert Pujols in 2003, because well, it's tough to do substantially better than a .955 OPS. Pujols had a 1.106 OPS in 2003 and would have won the MVP that year if not for he-who-shall-not-be-named. And the player most likely to have a breakout season who did not? That's Dave Kingman in 1974. Kingman had a

65% chance of breaking out that year, and instead, he declined slightly. Of course, in 1975, he doubled his home run total, so really the system was just one year off. (He had a 47% chance of breaking out that year, by the way.)

Now what about pitchers? To test whether or not we can predict breakout seasons for pitchers, I compiled a database of all pitchers with back-to-back seasons of at least 200 batters faced since 1946, over 6,500 pitchers in all. I then calculated their component run average in each season, with each component regressed (this is similar to what I did for hitters). If a pitcher's regressed component run average decreased by over 10% (about one standard deviation) from the previous year, that was labeled as a breakout season. There were 437 such seasons in all, or less than 7%. Can we do better than that? Yes, we can.

The test showed four components that had a significant effect on a pitcher's odds of breaking out. They were:

- **The pitcher's walk rate**. My guess is that when pitchers break out, it's often because they improve their control substantially and reduce the number of walks they issue, which is why the more wild a pitcher is, the more likely he is to have a breakout season.

- **Home run rate**. Pitchers with high home run rates are more likely to breakout. This one is a bit confounding, frankly. My best guess would be that pitchers with high home run rates pitch up in the zone a lot and are therefore more likely to substantially increase their strikeout rates.

- **Batting average on balls in play (BABIP)**. Again, the more hits a pitcher allows on balls in play, the more likely he is to break out the next season. This makes sense, actually, because we're only looking at pitchers with 200 batters faced in consecutive years. If a pitcher with a high BABIP is still given enough chances to pitch to 200 batters the next season, the team has to have high hopes for him, so he's more likely to have a breakout season. This has nothing to do with the fact that BABIP is highly inconsistent from year to year, because remember, each component is regressed the proper amount.

- **Performance**. This is roughly the same effect as for hitters, though not as great because while good pitchers are less likely to improve, they also have to improve a little bit less to have a breakout season. (For example, a pitcher with a 3.25

regressed component run average only has to lower it .30 points to have a breakout year, while a pitcher with a 4.75 regressed component run average has to lower it almost .45 points to have a breakout season.)

Pitchers are much harder to predict than hitters, but nevertheless, our method still adds some accuracy over randomly guessing. The average breakout pitcher was given an 8.9% chance of stepping up to the next level, versus a 6.7% overall average, which makes our method about 33% better than just randomly guessing. Of the 100 pitchers given the best chance to have a breakout season, 20 actually did.

The pitcher with the best historical odds of having a breakout season was Mark Clear in 1982, with a 47% chance. He came close, but alas he only improved by 5%. The player with the best odds of breaking out who actually did take that next step was David Riske in 2003—he was given a 39% shot at doing so. That year also witnessed the least likely breakout season of all time: Guillermo Mota, who had a less-than-2% shot at substantial improvement. Which player had the worst odds of having a breakout season ever (well, since 1946)? Paul Ortega in 1966, with a miniscule 0.3% chance.

Okay, let's turn our attention to next season. Which pitchers, no older than 30, have the best chance of having a breakout season next year?

2007 Pitching Breakout Candidates

Last	First	Breakout%
Cabrera	Fernando J	47%
Guzman	Angel M	43%
Burgos	Ambiorix	40%
Aquino	Greg	39%
Turnbow	Derrick	39%
Snyder	Kyle	35%
Valverde	Jose	32%
Lidge	Brad	26%
Bergmann	Jason C	23%
Gobble	Jimmy	22%

If Lidge improves that wouldn't be so much a break-out as a return to normalcy, but Astros fans must still be happy to see him on this list. What if we limit ourselves to 25-and-under players?

Top Breakout Candidates Under 26

Last	First	Breakout%
Cabrera	Fernando J	47%
Guzman	Angel M	43%
Burgos	Ambiorix	40%
Bergmann	Jason C	23%
Gobble	Jimmy	22%
Baker	Scott S	21%
Davies	Kyle K	20%
Snell	Ian D	20%
Hammel	Jason A	19%
Reyes	Anthony L	19%

And which pitchers are least likely to break out?

Least Likely Breakout Candidates

Last	First	Breakout%
Thompson	Mike P	2%
Silva	Carlos	2%
Gaudin	Chad	2%
Hennessey	Brad M	2%
Papelbon	Jonathan R	1%
Marquis	Jason	1%
Saarloos	Kirk	1%
McClung	Seth	1%
Hernandez	Runelvys	1%
Affeldt	Jeremy	1%

So what can we take from this exercise, beyond some fun lists that won't be worth the paper they're printed on a year from now? Well, I've found that breakout seasons are somewhat predictable; they are not totally random. Hitters are more predictable than pitchers, which always seems to be the case. We've discovered some very interesting variables that correlate with breakout seasons, and those effects deserve further investigation. I've tried to offer some explanations as to why, but they're just guesses, and frankly, I'm not a very good guesser. And if someone can explain those effects, that someone will also probably be able to improve on my system and do even better predicting this seemingly random event.

But of course, we can't be perfect. Sometimes, a player just busts out for no discernable reason, obliterating his track record and making believers out of fans. Whoever that guy is in 2007 or beyond, I look forward to watching him play, whether I predicted the breakout or not.

Statistics

Welcome to Our Stats

Enough with the words already. Let's talk numbers. Lots and lots of numbers. Baseball statistics are the inner language of the game, and the THT Annual has a slew of comprehensive stats, as well as some unique stats, for the 2006 season.

Inside these pages, you will find all of the standard baseball stats that baseball fans have been using for years: hits, wins, stolen bases, etc. We even have the much-maligned batting average.

We also have a few new "sabermetric" stats, such as Runs Created, Pitching Runs Created, Fielding-Independent Pitching and Gross Production Average. We don't like to invent new stats (aren't there enough acronyms already?) but the truth is that conventional baseball stats aren't robust enough to capture what really happened on the field. These advanced stats do, and you'll find definitions for them in the Glossary at the back of the book.

In addition, we have batted ball stats for all teams and batters and pitchers with at least 100 plate appearances. These aren't really new stats, but new ways of describing what happened on the field. We're tremendously excited about these figures, and you can read more about them in "Batted Balls Redux," in the Analysis section of the Annual.

Finally, we have two win-based stats, Win Probability Added and Win Shares, for all teams and players. These two unique stats, which assign credit for wins to individual players based on two entirely different methodologies, offer a unique view into who contributed the most to his team's wins. The fact that they sometimes arrive at different "answers" makes them even more fascinating. These are listed in a separate appendix, and described in the Analysis section as well as in the Glossary.

So most of the statistics you're about to see are pretty simple, some of them are kind of complex, but all of them are presented in a way that helps you easily see the big picture. Here's a little more info about each section...

League/Team Statistics

We've laid out graphs and stats that show the relative position of each team, separated into the American and National Leagues. Some people like graphs, others like numbers, but we like to combine them into a single presentation that gives you a lot of insight by uniquely juxtaposing them.

For instance, the first graph is a display of how many runs each team scored and allowed, and how that relates to the number of games it won.

Below the graph is a table that gives more detail regarding how each team scored runs, gave up runs and turned their run differential into victories.

In the far right column of that table, PWINS stands for "Projected Wins" or "Pythagorean Wins" depending on how technical you want to get. VAR stands for variance, the difference between each team's actual wins and its projected wins. You can read more about Pythagorean Wins in the Glossary.

On the next two pages, we repeat the graphs and stats format for runs scored and allowed. The graph and stats are pretty standard.

You'll find some unique statistics on the following two pages.

- Miscellaneous batting, base running, pitching and fielding stats. The definitions of all of these are contained in the Glossary.

- Win Stats. These include Win Probability Stats for batters, starters and relievers, as well as the Leverage Index for each bullpen. Plus, we've included Win Shares for batting, pitching and fielding, as well as some miscellaneous Win Share stats (average team age, weighted by Win Share contribution, and career Win Shares on the team).

- Batted Ball Stats. We have compiled one-of-a-kind batted ball information for all teams. For instance, you'll find that the Tigers scored 29 more runs than average on ground balls, but gave up 42 less runs than average on grounders. If you assume that 10 runs is enough to convert a loss to a win, then the Tigers were seven games better than their opponents on ground balls. Weird, but interesting, huh? These stats are explained in the "Batted Balls Redux" article.

League Leaderboards

Leaderboards are a popular item, so we've listed the top 10 players for a bunch of statistics. Once again, you can find the definition of all the leaderboard stats in our Glossary.

There are also complete player listings of all stats on our website, at http://www.hardballtimes.com/main/stats.

Team/Player Stats

Specific stats for players are laid out by team in alphabetical order. Each team section begins with a graphical review of that team's wins and losses during the year, shown as running 10-game running totals. The graphs also include each team's 10-game average in runs scored and allowed, so you can visualize how the team's batters and pitchers performed throughout the year. In addition, we've listed some of the season's highlights below the graph. There's also a table under the graph that displays the team's monthly vital stats (Wins, losses, OBP and SLG for the offense and FIP and DER for the defense).

On the following three or four pages, individual player stats are listed for batters, pitchers and fielders. Most of these are relatively straightforward stats, and you can find the definitions in the Glossary. If a statistic is italicized, that means it was adjusted for the home park.

Each team section also has detailed batted ball information for each batter who appeared in at least 100 plate appearances for that team, and each pitcher who faced at least 100 batters for that team.

As you can imagine, the different team statistics take up a lot of pages, 4-5 per team depending on the layout.

Appendices

We thought you'd like a little more information, so we've included two appendices of statistics. The first appendix contains the win stats (Win Shares and Win Probability Added) for most 2006 players, with instructions for dowloading the stats for all of them. We've included the basics in these tables: batting and pitching WPA, as well as batting, pitching and fielding Win Shares.

The second appendix contains 30 unique graphs contributed by John Burnson of *Heater Magazine*. These are called "Playing Time Constellations," and they are essentially graphical representations of who played which position for each team throughout the year. Yes, that's a mouthful, but if you check out the appendix, we think you'll be impressed.

That's the layout. We've had fun developing these graphs and tables for you, and we hope you find enough baseball stuff here to keep you occupied and happy the entire offseason.

American League Team Stats

Runs Scored and Allowed
(adjusted for ballpark factors)

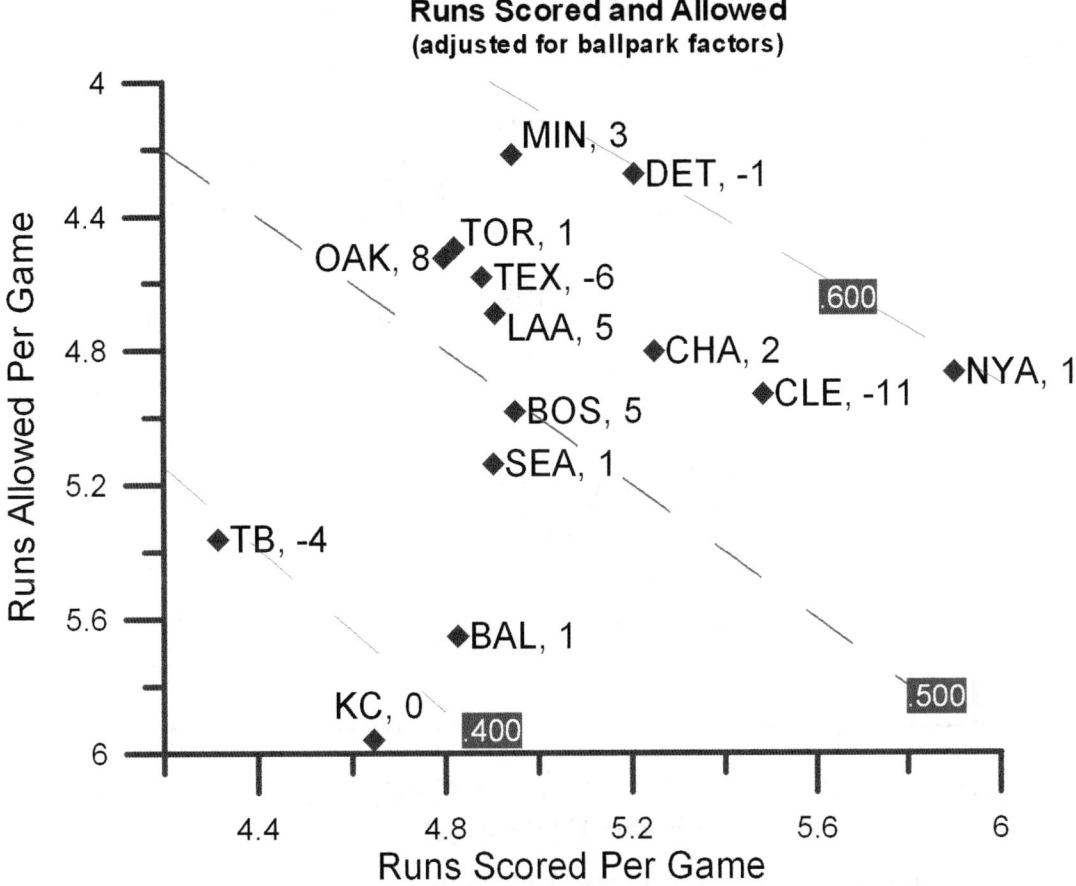

Notes: The dotted lines represent winning percentage based on run differential. The number after each team name represents the difference between the team's actual record and its run differential record.

	Team Record					Scoring Runs			Preventing Runs				Projection	
Team	W	L	RS	RA	RS-RA	AB/RSP	BA/RSP	HR	ERA	HRA	K	DER	PWINS	VAR
BAL	70	92	768	899	-131	1,459	.276	164	5.35	216	1,016	.681	69	1
BOS	86	76	820	825	-5	1,517	.258	192	4.83	181	1,070	.682	81	5
CHA	90	72	868	794	74	1,359	.307	236	4.61	200	1,012	.696	88	2
CLE	78	84	870	782	88	1,505	.290	196	4.41	166	948	.677	89	-11
DET	95	67	822	675	147	1,377	.277	203	3.84	160	1,003	.704	96	-1
KC	62	100	757	971	-214	1,445	.285	124	5.66	213	904	.677	62	0
LAA	89	73	766	732	34	1,404	.274	159	4.04	158	1,164	.693	84	5
MIN	96	66	801	683	118	1,441	.296	143	3.95	182	1,164	.687	93	3
NYA	97	65	930	767	163	1,582	.286	210	4.42	170	1,019	.697	96	1
OAK	93	69	771	727	44	1,389	.243	175	4.21	162	1,003	.690	85	8
SEA	78	84	756	792	-36	1,375	.265	172	4.60	183	1,067	.692	77	1
TB	61	101	689	856	-167	1,272	.240	190	4.96	180	979	.673	65	-4
TEX	80	82	835	784	51	1,381	.289	183	4.60	162	972	.681	86	-6
TOR	87	75	809	754	55	1,406	.277	199	4.37	185	1,076	.696	86	1
Average	83	79	804	789	16	1,422	.276	182	4.56	180	1,028	.688	81	2

Scoring Runs: OBP and Slugging

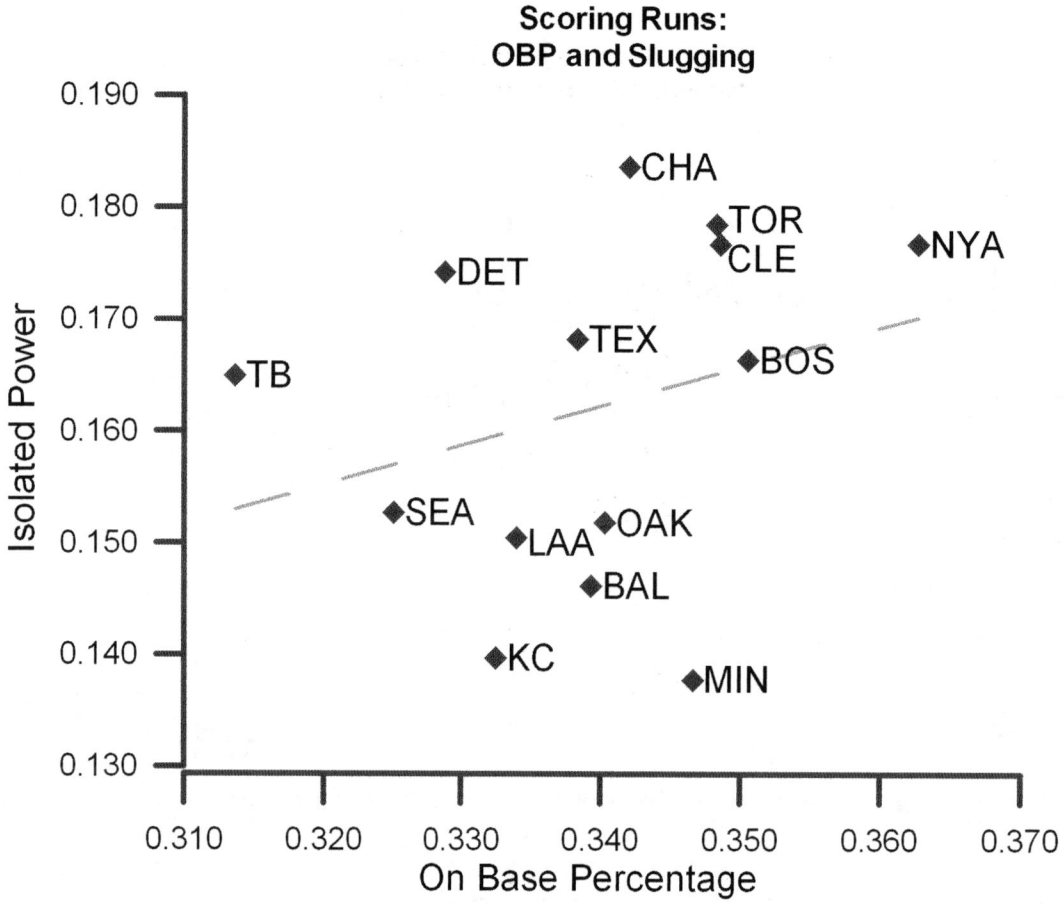

The dotted line shows the relationship between ISO and OBP.

Batting Statistics

Team	Runs	PA	H	1B	2B	3B	HR	TB	SO	BB	HBP	SH	SF	BA	OBP	SLG	GPA	ISO
BAL	768	6,240	1,556	1,084	288	20	164	2,376	878	474	73	40	41	.277	.339	.424	.259	.146
BOS	820	6,435	1,510	975	327	16	192	2,445	1,056	672	66	22	56	.269	.351	.435	.267	.166
CHA	868	6,318	1,586	1,039	291	20	236	2,625	1,056	502	58	44	57	.280	.342	.464	.270	.184
CLE	870	6,303	1,576	1,002	351	27	196	2,569	1,204	556	54	30	43	.280	.349	.457	.271	.177
DET	822	6,198	1,548	1,011	294	40	203	2,531	1,133	430	45	45	36	.274	.329	.449	.260	.174
KC	757	6,229	1,515	1,019	335	37	124	2,296	1,040	474	64	52	48	.271	.332	.411	.252	.140
LAA	766	6,221	1,539	1,042	309	29	159	2,383	914	486	42	31	53	.274	.334	.425	.256	.150
MIN	801	6,228	1,608	1,156	275	34	143	2,380	872	490	50	31	55	.287	.347	.425	.262	.138
NYA	930	6,455	1,608	1,050	327	21	210	2,607	1,053	649	72	34	49	.285	.363	.461	.279	.177
OAK	771	6,281	1,429	966	266	22	175	2,264	976	650	50	25	56	.260	.340	.412	.256	.152
SEA	756	6,213	1,540	1,060	266	42	172	2,406	974	404	63	38	38	.272	.325	.424	.252	.153
TB	689	6,041	1,395	905	267	33	190	2,298	1,106	441	47	35	43	.255	.314	.420	.246	.165
TEX	835	6,273	1,571	1,008	357	23	183	2,523	1,061	505	40	18	50	.278	.338	.446	.264	.168
TOR	809	6,241	1,591	1,017	348	27	199	2,590	906	514	63	16	52	.284	.348	.463	.272	.179
Average	804	6,263	1,541	1,024	307	28	182	2,450	1,016	518	56	33	48	.275	.342	.437	.263	.162

Preventing Runs:
Pitching and Fielding (sort of)

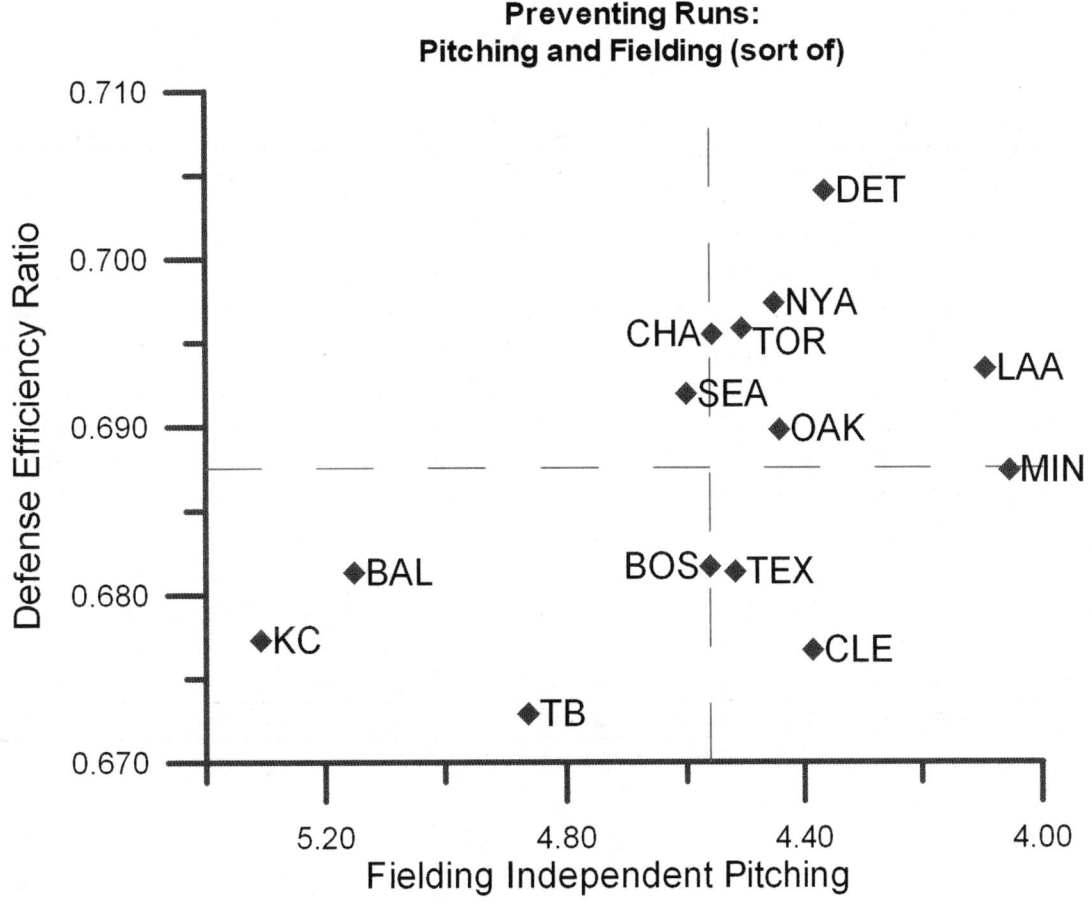

The dotted lines represent the league averages.

Pitching Statistics

Team	RA	IP	BFP	H	HRA	TBA	K	BB	ShO	Sv	Op	%Save	Holds	ERA	FIP	UERA	DER
BAL	899	1419.0	6,327	1,579	216	2,569	1,016	613	9	35	56	63%	58	5.35	5.15	0.36	.681
BOS	825	1441.0	6,292	1,570	181	2,517	1,070	509	6	46	69	67%	80	4.83	4.56	0.32	.682
CHA	794	1449.0	6,232	1,534	200	2,492	1,012	433	11	46	63	73%	64	4.61	4.55	0.32	.696
CLE	782	1423.0	6,190	1,583	166	2,420	948	429	13	24	47	51%	40	4.41	4.39	0.53	.677
DET	675	1448.0	6,145	1,420	160	2,239	1,003	489	16	46	62	74%	75	3.84	4.36	0.35	.704
KC	971	1426.0	6,434	1,648	213	2,682	904	637	5	35	66	53%	66	5.66	5.31	0.47	.677
LAA	732	1452.0	6,149	1,410	158	2,230	1,164	471	12	50	63	79%	50	4.04	4.09	0.50	.693
MIN	683	1439.0	6,066	1,490	182	2,362	1,164	356	6	40	50	80%	68	3.95	4.05	0.32	.687
NYA	767	1443.0	6,215	1,463	170	2,311	1,019	496	8	43	60	72%	83	4.42	4.45	0.36	.697
OAK	727	1451.0	6,279	1,525	162	2,368	1,003	529	11	54	74	73%	83	4.21	4.44	0.30	.690
SEA	792	1446.0	6,294	1,500	183	2,422	1,067	560	6	47	67	70%	72	4.60	4.60	0.33	.692
TB	856	1420.0	6,374	1,600	180	2,528	979	606	7	33	54	61%	47	4.96	4.86	0.47	.673
TEX	784	1431.0	6,237	1,558	162	2,377	972	496	8	42	65	65%	79	4.60	4.52	0.33	.681
TOR	754	1428.0	6,151	1,447	185	2,335	1,076	504	6	42	62	68%	87	4.37	4.51	0.38	.696
Average	789	1,436.9	6,242	1,523	180	2,418	1,028	509	9	42	61	68%	68	4.56	4.56	0.38	.688

Running and Miscellaneous Batting Stats

Team	SB	CS	SB%	GDP	P/PA	BABIP
BAL	121	32	79%	145	3.68	.305
BOS	51	23	69%	136	3.93	.302
CHA	93	48	66%	118	3.79	.309
CLE	55	23	71%	127	3.86	.327
DET	60	40	60%	120	3.74	.312
KC	65	34	66%	131	3.69	.314
LAA	148	57	72%	126	3.66	.304
MIN	101	42	71%	163	3.73	.319
NYA	139	35	80%	139	3.82	.319
OAK	61	20	75%	170	3.88	.288
SEA	106	37	74%	118	3.71	.302
TB	134	52	72%	101	3.70	.288
TEX	53	24	69%	148	3.78	.314
TOR	65	33	66%	166	3.78	.310
Average	89	36	71%	136	3.77	.308

Win Probability Added / Win Shares

Team	Bat	Starters	Bullpen	LI	Bat	Pitch	Field	WSAge	CWS
BAL	-3.4	-5.3	-2.3	0.90	118	59	32	29.3	1,789
BOS	5.6	-3.3	2.7	1.08	127	86	45	30.9	3,058
CHA	7.0	-0.1	2.2	1.08	132	96	42	29.6	1,874
CLE	3.2	0.5	-6.7	0.98	131	71	32	27.6	1,387
DET	0.2	9.0	4.8	1.10	127	109	50	29.1	1,905
KC	-2.2	-9.5	-7.4	1.02	107	47	32	29.3	1,417
LAA	-3.5	3.0	8.5	1.02	121	105	42	28.3	2,139
MIN	1.6	2.2	11.2	0.85	123	115	50	27.2	1,818
NYA	12.4	0.3	3.3	1.04	164	88	38	31.4	4,014
OAK	1.1	2.1	8.9	1.16	120	108	51	28.7	1,932
SEA	-8.0	-1.4	6.4	1.09	117	78	39	28.8	1,602
TB	-12.7	-3.6	-3.7	1.01	83	67	33	27.0	945
TEX	1.1	-2.2	0.2	0.94	109	91	40	28.6	1,869
TOR	2.4	-0.4	4.0	0.98	116	100	45	28.4	1,536
Average	0.3	-0.6	2.3	1.0	121	87	41	28.9	1,949

Leverage Index (LI) for bullpen only

Fielding and Miscellaneous Pitching Stats

Team	DER	Fld %	UER	SBA	CS	%CS	PO	E	TE	FE	DP	GIDP
BAL	.681	.983	56	130	50	38%	10	102	47	54	156	129
BOS	.682	.989	52	131	23	18%	13	66	27	37	174	148
CHA	.696	.985	51	150	34	23%	12	90	38	49	145	128
CLE	.677	.981	84	162	34	21%	10	118	44	69	165	143
DET	.704	.983	57	84	35	42%	14	106	45	61	162	140
KC	.677	.984	74	88	30	34%	9	98	39	59	189	161
LAA	.693	.979	80	117	40	34%	6	124	43	77	154	129
MIN	.687	.986	51	85	31	36%	9	84	43	40	134	110
NYA	.697	.983	58	139	47	34%	7	104	50	53	145	126
OAK	.690	.986	48	129	41	32%	12	84	39	43	173	150
SEA	.692	.985	53	110	38	35%	13	88	37	51	149	130
TB	.673	.981	74	154	46	30%	15	116	45	69	156	128
TEX	.681	.984	53	107	40	37%	7	98	41	55	174	145
TOR	.696	.984	60	162	32	20%	11	99	56	42	157	127
Average	.688	.984	61	125	37	30%	11	98	42	54	160	135

Batted Ball Stats for Batters

Team	PA	% of PA		% of Batted Balls					Runs Per Event				Total Runs vs. Avg.				
		K%	BB%	GB%	LD%	FB%	IF/F	HR/OF	NIP	GB	LD	OF	NIP	GB	LD	FB	Tot
BAL	6240	14	9	45	20	36	.10	.11	.06	.04	.38	.17	6	8	12	-33	-7
BOS	6435	16	11	40	20	40	.11	.11	.08	.04	.38	.18	49	-9	-6	10	44
CHA	6318	17	9	42	20	38	.11	.14	.05	.05	.39	.23	-11	16	7	60	73
CLE	6303	19	10	42	21	37	.08	.12	.04	.05	.39	.22	-10	9	8	57	64
DET	6198	18	8	42	19	39	.08	.13	.02	.06	.38	.22	-47	29	-20	66	27
KC	6229	17	9	48	20	33	.11	.09	.04	.05	.40	.16	-15	27	17	-77	-49
LAA	6221	15	8	44	19	37	.11	.10	.05	.05	.37	.17	-5	14	-19	-9	-18
MIN	6228	14	9	47	21	32	.09	.10	.06	.04	.38	.17	4	14	38	-57	0
NYA	6455	16	11	45	19	36	.10	.14	.07	.05	.40	.23	43	10	-2	54	106
OAK	6281	16	11	42	19	38	.12	.11	.08	.03	.39	.16	47	-27	-6	-44	-29
SEA	6213	16	8	44	19	37	.13	.11	.04	.06	.39	.18	-32	32	-0	-20	-20
TB	6041	18	8	44	19	37	.12	.13	.03	.05	.37	.19	-38	17	-36	-1	-57
TEX	6273	17	9	43	20	37	.12	.11	.04	.05	.40	.19	-16	17	28	4	33
TOR	6241	15	9	42	19	38	.08	.12	.07	.04	.40	.20	13	-14	24	45	69
MLB Average		17	9	44	20	37	.11	.11	.05	.04	.39	.19	-	-	-	-	-

Batted Ball Stats for Pitchers

Team	PA	% of PA		% of Batted Balls					Runs Per Event				Total Runs vs. Avg.				
		K%	BB%	GB%	LD%	FB%	IF/F	HR/OF	NIP	GB	LD	OF	NIP	GB	LD	FB	Tot
BAL	6327	16	10	42	20	37	.09	.13	.07	.06	.37	.21	28	30	-6	35	87
BOS	6292	17	9	44	20	37	.11	.12	.05	.04	.39	.22	-6	-12	6	37	25
CHA	6232	16	8	43	19	38	.11	.12	.04	.05	.38	.20	-28	11	-14	28	-4
CLE	6190	15	8	45	20	35	.11	.11	.04	.07	.36	.18	-24	55	-5	-24	3
DET	6145	16	9	45	19	35	.12	.11	.05	.02	.39	.19	-9	-42	1	-20	-70
KC	6434	14	11	42	21	37	.08	.13	.09	.05	.39	.20	52	21	31	29	133
LAA	6149	19	8	42	18	39	.10	.10	.03	.05	.38	.17	-34	11	-33	-20	-76
MIN	6066	19	6	44	20	36	.10	.12	.00	.05	.39	.19	-78	-0	10	5	-63
NYA	6215	16	9	43	18	39	.12	.11	.05	.04	.38	.18	-7	4	-30	-7	-39
OAK	6279	16	9	42	19	38	.12	.09	.06	.04	.39	.16	4	-4	8	-30	-21
SEA	6294	17	10	43	20	38	.11	.12	.05	.04	.41	.18	7	-6	15	-10	6
TB	6374	15	10	43	20	38	.11	.11	.07	.07	.41	.17	35	49	28	-27	85
TEX	6237	16	9	46	20	34	.10	.11	.06	.04	.38	.19	1	7	10	-22	-4
TOR	6151	17	9	46	20	34	.11	.13	.04	.04	.38	.21	-10	-8	-5	1	-22
MLB Average		17	9	44	20	37	.11	.11	.05	.04	.39	.19	-	-	-	-	-

American League Leaderboards
Batting Leaders

Italicized stats have been adjusted for home park.

Runs Created

1 D. Jeter	NYA	135
2 D. Ortiz	BOS	130
3 J. Thome	CHA	126
4 J. Dye	CHA	122
5 G. Sizemore	CLE	122
6 M. Young	TEX	122
7 J. Morneau	MIN	121
8 T. Hafner	CLE	119
9 M. Teixeira	TEX	116
10 P. Konerko	CHA	116
11 R. Ibanez	SEA	116

Runs Scored

1 G. Sizemore	CLE	134
2 D. Jeter	NYA	118
3 J. Damon	NYA	115
4 D. Ortiz	BOS	115
5 A. Rodriguez	NYA	113
6 I. Suzuki	SEA	110
7 J. Thome	CHA	108
8 N. Swisher	OAK	106
9 T. Glaus	TOR	105
10 R. Ibanez	SEA	103
11 J. Dye	CHA	103

Runs Batted In

1 D. Ortiz	BOS	137
2 J. Morneau	MIN	130
3 R. Ibanez	SEA	123
4 A. Rodriguez	NYA	121
5 J. Dye	CHA	120
6 T. Hafner	CLE	117
7 V. Guerrero	LAA	116
8 F. Thomas	OAK	114
9 P. Konerko	CHA	113
10 J. Giambi	NYA	113

Gross Production Average (GPA)

1 T. Hafner	CLE	.369
2 M. Ramirez	BOS	.344
3 D. Ortiz	BOS	.337
4 J. Giambi	NYA	.335
5 J. Thome	CHA	.331
6 J. Dye	CHA	.323
7 V. Guerrero	LAA	.321
8 J. Mauer	MIN	.320
9 C. Guillen	DET	.318
10 D. Jeter	NYA	.317

Batting Average

1 J. Mauer	MIN	.347
2 D. Jeter	NYA	.343
3 R. Cano	NYA	.342
4 M. Tejada	BAL	.330
5 V. Guerrero	LAA	.329
6 I. Suzuki	SEA	.322
7 J. Morneau	MIN	.321
8 M. Ramirez	BOS	.321
9 C. Guillen	DET	.320
10 R. Johnson	TOR	.319

On-Base Percentage

1 M. Ramirez	BOS	.439
2 T. Hafner	CLE	.439
3 J. Mauer	MIN	.429
4 D. Jeter	NYA	.417
5 J. Thome	CHA	.416
6 J. Giambi	NYA	.413
7 D. Ortiz	BOS	.413
8 C. Guillen	DET	.400
9 A. Rodriguez	NYA	.392
10 V. Martinez	CLE	.391

Slugging Percentage

1 T. Hafner	CLE	.659
2 D. Ortiz	BOS	.636
3 J. Dye	CHA	.622
4 M. Ramirez	BOS	.619
5 J. Thome	CHA	.598
6 J. Morneau	MIN	.559
7 J. Giambi	NYA	.558
8 V. Guerrero	LAA	.552
9 P. Konerko	CHA	.551
10 F. Thomas	OAK	.545

OPS (On-Base Plus Slugging)

1 T. Hafner	CLE	1.097
2 M. Ramirez	BOS	1.058
3 D. Ortiz	BOS	1.049
4 J. Thome	CHA	1.014
5 J. Dye	CHA	1.006
6 J. Giambi	NYA	.971
7 J. Mauer	MIN	.936
8 J. Morneau	MIN	.934
9 V. Guerrero	LAA	.934
10 P. Konerko	CHA	.932

Plate Appearances

1 I. Suzuki	SEA	752
2 G. Sizemore	CLE	751
3 M. Young	TEX	748
4 M. Teixeira	TEX	727
5 D. Jeter	NYA	715
6 M. Tejada	BAL	709
7 M. Mora	BAL	705
8 M. Loretta	BOS	703
9 R. Ibanez	SEA	699
10 G. Matthews Jr.	TEX	690

Outs

1 M. Young	TEX	512
2 A. Beltre	SEA	478
3 I. Suzuki	SEA	478
4 M. Loretta	BOS	478
5 G. Sizemore	CLE	478
6 C. Figgins	LAA	477
7 M. Mora	BAL	476
8 M. Teixeira	TEX	474
9 M. Tejada	BAL	470
10 2 tied with		469

Hits

1 I. Suzuki	SEA	224
2 M. Young	TEX	217
3 D. Jeter	NYA	214
4 M. Tejada	BAL	214
5 V. Guerrero	LAA	200
6 G. Matthews Jr.	TEX	194
7 J. Morneau	MIN	190
8 G. Sizemore	CLE	190
9 V. Wells	TOR	185
10 C. Crawford	TB	183

Total Bases

1 D. Ortiz	BOS	355
2 G. Sizemore	CLE	349
3 V. Guerrero	LAA	335
4 J. Dye	CHA	335
5 V. Wells	TOR	331
6 J. Morneau	MIN	331
7 R. Ibanez	SEA	323
8 M. Tejada	BAL	323
9 M. Teixeira	TEX	323
10 M. Young	TEX	317

Singles

1 I. Suzuki	SEA	186
2 D. Jeter	NYA	158
3 M. Tejada	BAL	153
4 M. Young	TEX	148
5 M. Loretta	BOS	143
6 L. Castillo	MIN	142
7 J. Kendall	OAK	139
8 V. Guerrero	LAA	132
9 M. Mora	BAL	130
10 C. Crawford	TB	129

Doubles

1 G. Sizemore	CLE	53
2 M. Young	TEX	52
3 M. Lowell	BOS	47
4 L. Overbay	TOR	46
5 O. Cabrera	LAA	45
6 M. Teixeira	TEX	45
7 G. Matthews Jr.	TEX	44
8 K. Youkilis	BOS	42
9 4 tied with		41

Triples

1 C. Crawford	TB	16
2 G. Sizemore	CLE	11
3 I. Suzuki	SEA	9
4 C. Granderson	DET	9
5 C. Figgins	LAA	8
6 J. Lopez	SEA	8
7 N. Punto	MIN	7
8 D. DeJesus	KC	7
9 M. Teahen	KC	7
10 8 tied with		6

Home Runs

1 D. Ortiz	BOS	54
2 J. Dye	CHA	44
3 J. Thome	CHA	42
4 T. Hafner	CLE	42
5 F. Thomas	OAK	39
6 T. Glaus	TOR	38
7 J. Giambi	NYA	37
8 4 tied with		35

Walks				Intentional Walks				Hit By Pitch				Pitches Per Plate Appearance			
1	D. Ortiz	BOS	119	1	V. Guerrero	LAA	25	1	R. Johnson	TOR	21	1	K. Youkilis	BOS	4.4
2	J. Giambi	NYA	110	2	D. Ortiz	BOS	23	2	J. Giambi	NYA	16	2	J. Giambi	NYA	4.4
3	J. Thome	CHA	107	3	J. Mauer	MIN	21	3	M. Mora	BAL	14	3	F. Thomas	OAK	4.4
4	M. Ramirez	BOS	100	4	M. Ramirez	BOS	16	4	G. Sizemore	CLE	13	4	J. Thome	CHA	4.3
5	T. Hafner	CLE	100	5	I. Suzuki	SEA	16	5	K. Johjima	SEA	13	5	T. Hafner	CLE	4.2
6	N. Swisher	OAK	97	6	T. Hafner	CLE	16	6	K. Millar	BAL	12	6	T. Glaus	TOR	4.2
7	K. Youkilis	BOS	91	7	R. Ibanez	SEA	15	7	D. Jeter	NYA	12	7	M. Ramirez	BOS	4.2
8	A. Rodriguez	NYA	90	8	J. Thome	CHA	12	8	J. Kendall	OAK	12	8	B. Inge	DET	4.1
9	M. Teixeira	TEX	89	9	J. Giambi	NYA	12	9	M. Loretta	BOS	12	9	J. Peralta	CLE	4.1
10	T. Glaus	TOR	86	10	M. Teixeira	TEX	12	10	D. DeJesus	KC	12	10	J. Dye	CHA	4.1

Stolen Bases				Caught Stealing				Net Stolen Bases				Grounded into Double Plays			
1	C. Crawford	TB	58	1	S. Podsednik	CHA	19	1	I. Suzuki	SEA	41	1	M. Tejada	BAL	28
2	C. Figgins	LAA	52	2	C. Figgins	LAA	16	2	C. Crawford	TB	40	2	V. Martinez	CLE	27
3	C. Patterson	BAL	45	3	L. Castillo	MIN	11	3	C. Patterson	BAL	27	3	M. Young	TEX	27
4	I. Suzuki	SEA	45	4	A. Kennedy	LAA	10	4	D. Jeter	NYA	24	4	T. Glaus	TOR	25
5	S. Podsednik	CHA	40	5	J. Damon	NYA	10	5	B. Roberts	BAL	22	5	P. Konerko	CHA	25
6	B. Roberts	BAL	36	6	C. Patterson	BAL	9	6	O. Cabrera	LAA	21	6	J. Mauer	MIN	24
7	D. Jeter	NYA	34	7	C. Guillen	DET	9	7	C. Figgins	LAA	20	7	M. Lowell	BOS	22
8	O. Cabrera	LAA	27	8	C. Crawford	TB	9	8	C. Crisp	BOS	14	8	A. Rodriguez	NYA	22
9	J. Damon	NYA	25	9	J. Gathright	TB/KC	9	9	M. Cairo	NYA	11	9	A. Berroa	KC	21
10	L. Castillo	MIN	25	10	Y. Betancourt	SEA	8	10	4 tied with		10	10	6 tied with		19

Isolated Power (ISO)				BA on Balls in Play (BABIP)				BA with RISP				Situational Hitting Runs			
1	T. Hafner	CLE	.350	1	D. Jeter	NYA	.394	1	M. Young	TEX	.412	1	M. Young	TEX	17
2	D. Ortiz	BOS	.349	2	J. Mauer	MIN	.370	2	D. Jeter	NYA	.383	2	H. Blalock	TEX	13
3	J. Thome	CHA	.310	3	R. Johnson	TOR	.367	3	P. Konerko	CHA	.366	3	P. Polanco	DET	11
4	J. Dye	CHA	.306	4	R. Cano	NYA	.363	4	J. Mauer	MIN	.360	4	A. Rios	TOR	10
5	J. Giambi	NYA	.305	5	C. Guillen	DET	.355	5	J. Dye	CHA	.354	5	C. Crawford	TB	9
6	M. Ramirez	BOS	.298	6	I. Suzuki	SEA	.350	6	C. Crawford	TB	.348	6	J. Lopez	SEA	8
7	F. Thomas	OAK	.275	7	M. Young	TEX	.349	7	K. Johjima	SEA	.344	7	M. Teahen	KC	8
8	T. Glaus	TOR	.261	8	M. Ramirez	BOS	.349	8	J. Crede	CHA	.343	8	A. Kennedy	LAA	8
9	G. Sizemore	CLE	.243	9	M. Tejada	BAL	.349	9	I. Rodriguez	DET	.341	9	R. Ibanez	SEA	8
10	R. Sexson	SEA	.240	10	G. Matthews Jr.	TEX	.349	10	A. Kennedy	LAA	.339	10	K. Johjima	SEA	8

Extra Base Hits				Sacrifice Hits				Sacrifice Flies				Strikeouts			
1	G. Sizemore	CLE	92	1	J. Lopez	SEA	12	1	J. Morneau	MIN	11	1	C. Granderson	DET	174
2	D. Ortiz	BOS	85	2	V. Wilson	DET	10	2	K. Youkilis	BOS	11	2	R. Sexson	SEA	154
3	M. Teixeira	TEX	79	3	N. Punto	MIN	10	3	O. Cabrera	LAA	11	3	G. Sizemore	CLE	153
4	V. Wells	TOR	77	4	J. Uribe	CHA	9	4	E. Brown	KC	10	4	N. Swisher	OAK	152
5	J. Dye	CHA	74	5	L. Castillo	MIN	9	5	A. Rios	TOR	10	5	J. Peralta	CLE	152
6	R. Sexson	SEA	74	6	A. Berroa	KC	9	6	V. Wells	TOR	9	6	J. Thome	CHA	147
7	T. Hafner	CLE	74	7	C. Crawford	TB	9	7	P. Konerko	CHA	9	7	A. Rodriguez	NYA	139
8	J. Morneau	MIN	72	8	J. Gathright	TB/KC	9	8	J. Gomes	TB	9	8	T. Glaus	TOR	134
9	R. Ibanez	SEA	71	9	B. Fahey	BAL	9	9	M. Young	TEX	8	9	M. Cuddyer	MIN	130
10	M. Cuddyer	MIN	70	10	4 tied with		8	10	G. Matthews Jr.	TEX	8	10	M. Teixeira	TEX	128
								11	M. Ramirez	BOS	8	11	B. Inge	DET	128

Pitching Leaders

Pitching Runs Created				Earned Run Average (ERA)				Runs Allowed Per 9 (RA)				Fielding Independent Pitching			
1	J. Santana	MIN	154	1	J. Santana	MIN	2.77	1	J. Santana	MIN	3.04	1	J. Santana	MIN	3.16
2	R. Halladay	TOR	118	2	R. Halladay	TOR	3.19	2	R. Halladay	TOR	3.35	2	J. Bonderman	DET	3.31
3	J. Lackey	LAA	108	3	C. Sabathia	CLE	3.22	3	J. Verlander	DET	3.77	3	C. Sabathia	CLE	3.37
4	B. Zito	OAK	104	4	M. Mussina	NYA	3.51	4	C. Wang	NYA	3.80	4	J. Lackey	LAA	3.41
4	C. Schilling	BOS	104	5	J. Lackey	LAA	3.56	5	C. Sabathia	CLE	3.88	5	M. Mussina	NYA	3.56
6	F. Liriano	MIN	101	6	K. Escobar	LAA	3.61	6	C. Schilling	BOS	3.97	6	R. Halladay	TOR	3.65
6	J. Bonderman	DET	101	7	J. Verlander	DET	3.63	7	M. Mussina	NYA	4.01	7	C. Schilling	BOS	3.69
8	D. Haren	OAK	100	8	C. Wang	NYA	3.63	8	B. Zito	OAK	4.03	8	K. Escobar	LAA	3.70
8	C. Sabathia	CLE	100	9	E. Bedard	BAL	3.76	9	J. Lackey	LAA	4.05	9	E. Bedard	BAL	3.71
10	M. Mussina	NYA	99	10	B. Zito	OAK	3.83	10	E. Bedard	BAL	4.22	10	K. Millwood	TEX	3.93

Innings Pitched				Batters Faced				Pitches				Pitches Per Plate Appearance			
1	J. Santana	MIN	233.7	1	B. Zito	OAK	945	1	B. Zito	OAK	3665	1	C. Silva	MIN	3.3
2	D. Haren	OAK	223.0	2	D. Haren	OAK	930	2	J. Lackey	LAA	3512	2	C. Wang	NYA	3.4
3	B. Zito	OAK	221.0	3	J. Santana	MIN	923	3	D. Haren	OAK	3487	3	R. Halladay	TOR	3.5
4	R. Halladay	TOR	220.0	4	J. Lackey	LAA	922	4	J. Santana	MIN	3450	4	N. Robertson	DET	3.5
5	C. Wang	NYA	218.0	5	F. Garcia	CHA	917	5	C. Lee	CLE	3361	5	M. Buehrle	CHA	3.5
6	J. Lackey	LAA	217.7	6	K. Millwood	TEX	907	6	J. Garland	CHA	3349	6	P. Byrd	CLE	3.6
7	F. Garcia	CHA	216.3	7	J. Westbrook	CLE	904	7	J. Vazquez	CHA	3317	7	B. Radke	MIN	3.6
8	K. Millwood	TEX	215.0	8	J. Bonderman	DET	903	7	F. Garcia	CHA	3317	8	R. Lopez	BAL	3.6
9	J. Bonderman	DET	214.0	9	J. Garland	CHA	900	9	K. Millwood	TEX	3306	9	F. Garcia	CHA	3.6
10	J. Garland	CHA	211.3	9	C. Wang	NYA	900	10	E. Bedard	BAL	3299	10	J. Westbrook	CLE	3.6
10	J. Westbrook	CLE	211.3												

Strikeouts				Walks (Most)				Strikeouts Per Game				Walks Per Game (Least)			
1	J. Santana	MIN	245	1	D. Cabrera	BAL	104	1	J. Santana	MIN	10.2	1	C. Schilling	BOS	1.3
2	J. Bonderman	DET	202	2	B. Zito	OAK	99	2	J. Bonderman	DET	8.6	2	R. Halladay	TOR	1.5
3	J. Lackey	LAA	190	3	G. Meche	SEA	84	3	C. Schilling	BOS	8.5	3	C. Silva	MIN	1.5
4	J. Vazquez	CHA	184	4	T. Lilly	TOR	81	4	F. Hernandez	SEA	8.3	4	M. Mussina	NYA	1.7
5	C. Schilling	BOS	183	5	J. Beckett	BOS	74	5	C. Sabathia	CLE	8.3	5	J. Garland	CHA	1.8
6	D. Haren	OAK	176	6	J. Lackey	LAA	72	6	M. Mussina	NYA	8.2	6	B. Radke	MIN	1.8
6	F. Hernandez	SEA	176	7	V. Padilla	TEX	70	7	J. Vazquez	CHA	8.1	7	P. Byrd	CLE	1.8
8	R. Johnson	NYA	172	7	E. Santana	LAA	70	8	J. Lackey	LAA	7.9	8	D. Haren	OAK	1.9
8	C. Sabathia	CLE	172	9	E. Bedard	BAL	69	9	E. Bedard	BAL	7.8	9	J. Santana	MIN	2.0
8	M. Mussina	NYA	172	10	S. McClung	TB	68	10	T. Lilly	TOR	7.7	10	F. Garcia	CHA	2.0

Wins				Losses				Shutouts				Games Started			
1	J. Santana	MIN	19	1	R. Lopez	BAL	18	1	C. Sabathia	CLE	2	1	K. Millwood	TEX	34
1	C. Wang	NYA	19	2	C. Silva	MIN	15	1	J. Westbrook	CLE	2	1	J. Santana	MIN	34
3	J. Garland	CHA	18	3	J. Washburn	SEA	14	1	J. Lackey	LAA	2	1	B. Zito	OAK	34
4	R. Johnson	NYA	17	3	K. Escobar	LAA	14	1	J. Sowers	CLE	2	1	J. Bonderman	DET	34
4	F. Garcia	CHA	17	3	F. Hernandez	SEA	14	5	Many tied with		1	1	D. Haren	OAK	34
4	K. Rogers	DET	17	6	5 tied with		13					6	10 tied with		33
4	J. Verlander	DET	17												
8	6 tied with		16												

Games				Saves				Save Opportunities				Holds			
1	S. Proctor	NYA	83	1	F. Rodriguez	LAA	47	1	F. Rodriguez	LAA	51	1	S. Shields	LAA	31
2	J. Rincon	MIN	75	2	B. Jenks	CHA	41	2	H. Street	OAK	48	2	J. Zumaya	DET	30
2	S. Camp	TB	75	3	B. Ryan	TOR	38	3	B. Jenks	CHA	45	3	J. Rincon	MIN	26
4	S. Shields	LAA	74	4	T. Jones	DET	37	4	T. Jones	DET	43	3	S. Proctor	NYA	26
5	K. Farnsworth	NYA	72	4	H. Street	OAK	37	4	J. Putz	SEA	43	5	J. Speier	TOR	25
5	J. Putz	SEA	72	6	J. Nathan	MIN	36	6	B. Ryan	TOR	42	6	K. Calero	OAK	23
5	G. Sherrill	SEA	72	6	J. Putz	SEA	36	7	J. Papelbon	BOS	41	7	M. Timlin	BOS	21
8	R. Villone	NYA	70	8	J. Papelbon	BOS	35	8	J. Nathan	MIN	38	8	K. Farnsworth	NYA	19
8	K. Calero	OAK	70	9	M. Rivera	NYA	34	8	C. Ray	BAL	38	9	5 tied with		18
8	N. Cotts	CHA	70	10	C. Ray	BAL	33	10	M. Rivera	NYA	37				

Home Runs Allowed				Home Runs Per Game				Total Bases Allowed				Slugging Average Against			
1	C. Silva	MIN	38	1	C. Wang	NYA	0.51	1	C. Silva	MIN	408	1	J. Santana	MIN	.360
2	M. Buehrle	CHA	36	2	J. Lackey	LAA	0.59	2	M. Buehrle	CHA	407	2	J. Lackey	LAA	.360
2	J. Beckett	BOS	36	3	J. Westbrook	CLE	0.64	3	R. Lopez	BAL	387	3	C. Sabathia	CLE	.363
4	K. Benson	BAL	33	4	E. Bedard	BAL	0.73	4	J. Garland	CHA	386	4	E. Bedard	BAL	.370
5	R. Lopez	BAL	32	5	J. Bonderman	DET	0.77	5	F. Garcia	CHA	380	5	R. Halladay	TOR	.374
5	F. Garcia	CHA	32	6	J. Blanton	OAK	0.77	6	D. Haren	OAK	372	6	M. Mussina	NYA	.374
7	D. Haren	OAK	31	7	C. Sabathia	CLE	0.82	7	C. Schilling	BOS	365	7	C. Wang	NYA	.375
8	N. Robertson	DET	29	8	K. Escobar	LAA	0.83	8	P. Byrd	CLE	362	8	K. Escobar	LAA	.393
8	C. Lee	CLE	29	9	R. Halladay	TOR	0.84	9	C. Lee	CLE	360	9	E. Santana	LAA	.395
10	4 tied with		28	10	J. Contreras	CHA	0.92	10	K. Millwood	TEX	351	10	J. Contreras	CHA	.398

Stolen Bases Allowed				Caught Stealing				Pick Offs				Net Stolen Bases			
1	F. Garcia	CHA	40	1	B. Zito	OAK	12	1	M. Buehrle	CHA	10	1	M. Buehrle	CHA	-30
2	T. Wakefield	BOS	24	2	C. Wang	NYA	11	2	J. Verlander	DET	8	2	J. Verlander	DET	-25
3	R. Johnson	NYA	21	3	R. Johnson	NYA	10	3	J. Lester	BOS	6	3	B. Zito	OAK	-20
3	J. Contreras	CHA	21	3	R. Lopez	BAL	10	4	S. Kazmir	TB	5	4	D. Reyes	MIN	-16
5	R. Halladay	TOR	20	3	K. Escobar	LAA	10	5	D. Reyes	MIN	4	5	C. Wang	NYA	-15
6	J. Johnson	CLE/BOS	19	6	E. Santana	LAA	9	5	J. Moyer	SEA	4	5	K. Rogers	DET	-15
7	A. Burnett	TOR	18	7	M. Buehrle	CHA	7	5	J. Shields	TB	4	5	J. Lester	BOS	-15
7	P. Byrd	CLE	18	7	J. Garland	CHA	7	8	8 tied with		3	8	J. Moyer	SEA	-14
9	J. Westbrook	CLE	16	7	G. Meche	SEA	7					9	E. Santana	LAA	-13
10	4 tied with		15	7	J. Moyer	SEA	7					9	G. Meche	SEA	-13
				7	A. Loewen	BAL	7					9	R. Lopez	BAL	-13

Defense Efficiency Ratio (DER)				Double Plays				Wild Pitches				Hit By Pitch			
1	K. Rogers	DET	.738	1	J. Westbrook	CLE	38	1	D. Cabrera	BAL	17	1	V. Padilla	TEX	17
2	J. Beckett	BOS	.737	2	C. Wang	NYA	36	2	J. Lackey	LAA	16	2	J. Vazquez	CHA	15
3	E. Santana	LAA	.735	3	B. Zito	OAK	33	2	J. Contreras	CHA	16	3	B. Zito	OAK	13
4	J. Santana	MIN	.731	4	N. Robertson	DET	32	4	M. Redman	KC	12	4	C. Fossum	TB	12
5	R. Halladay	TOR	.724	5	M. Redman	KC	29	5	F. Hernandez	SEA	11	5	E. Santana	LAA	11
6	N. Robertson	DET	.723	5	K. Rogers	DET	29	5	A. Burgos	KC	11	6	R. Johnson	NYA	10
7	K. Benson	BAL	.721	5	R. Halladay	TOR	29	5	J. Beckett	BOS	11	6	T. Wakefield	BOS	10
8	J. Washburn	SEA	.721	8	J. Tavarez	BOS	27	8	E. Santana	LAA	10	6	J. Beckett	BOS	10
9	B. Zito	OAK	.719	9	J. Garland	CHA	26	8	F. Rodriguez	LAA	10	6	J. Pineiro	SEA	10
10	R. Johnson	NYA	.719	9	J. Blanton	OAK	26	8	D. Haren	OAK	10	6	J. Contreras	CHA	10
												6	D. Haren	OAK	10

National League Team Stats

Runs Scored and Allowed
(adjusted for ballpark factors)

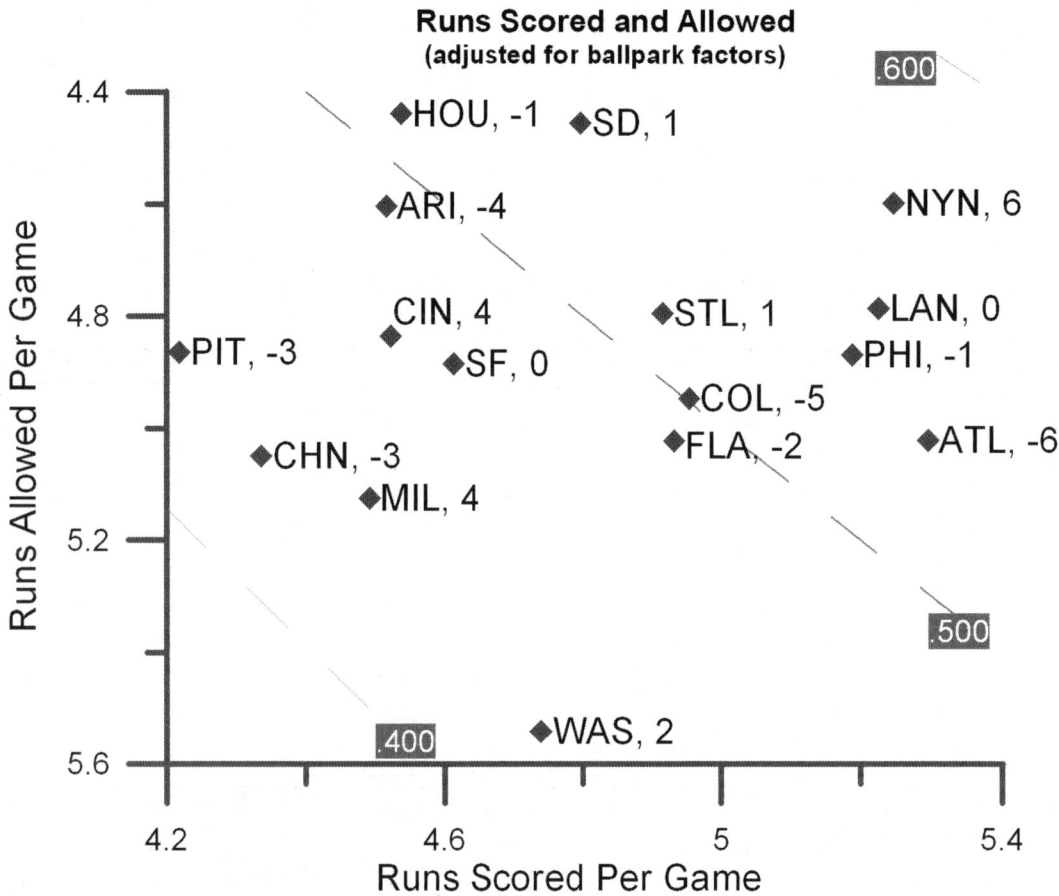

Notes: The dotted lines represent winning percentage based on run differential. The number after each team name represents the difference between the team's actual record and its run differential record.

	Team Record					Scoring Runs			Preventing Runs				Projection	
Team	W	L	RS	RA	RS-RA	AB/RSP	BA/RSP	HR	ERA	HRA	K	DER	PWINS	VAR
ARI	76	86	773	788	-15	1,456	.262	160	4.48	168	1,115	.688	80	-4
ATL	79	83	849	805	44	1,393	.275	222	4.60	183	1,049	.689	85	-6
CHN	66	96	716	834	-118	1,363	.262	166	4.74	210	1,250	.702	69	-3
CIN	80	82	749	801	-52	1,314	.244	217	4.52	213	1,053	.684	76	4
COL	76	86	813	812	1	1,518	.267	157	4.66	155	952	.685	81	-5
FLA	78	84	758	772	-14	1,405	.258	182	4.37	166	1,088	.688	80	-2
HOU	82	80	735	719	16	1,382	.253	174	4.08	182	1,160	.703	83	-1
LAN	88	74	820	751	69	1,474	.286	153	4.23	152	1,068	.683	88	0
MIL	75	87	730	833	-103	1,310	.263	180	4.83	177	1,145	.690	71	4
NYN	97	65	834	731	103	1,409	.274	200	4.15	180	1,161	.706	91	6
PHI	85	77	865	812	53	1,459	.255	216	4.60	211	1,138	.683	86	-1
PIT	67	95	691	797	-106	1,370	.266	141	4.52	156	1,060	.676	70	-3
STL	83	78	781	762	19	1,413	.271	184	4.54	193	970	.699	82	1
SD	88	74	731	679	52	1,425	.265	161	3.87	176	1,097	.714	87	1
SF	76	85	746	790	-44	1,363	.273	163	4.63	153	992	.703	76	0
WAS	71	91	746	872	-126	1,426	.250	164	5.03	193	960	.694	69	2
Average	79	83	771	785	-14	1,405	.264	178	4.49	179	1,079	.693	81	-2

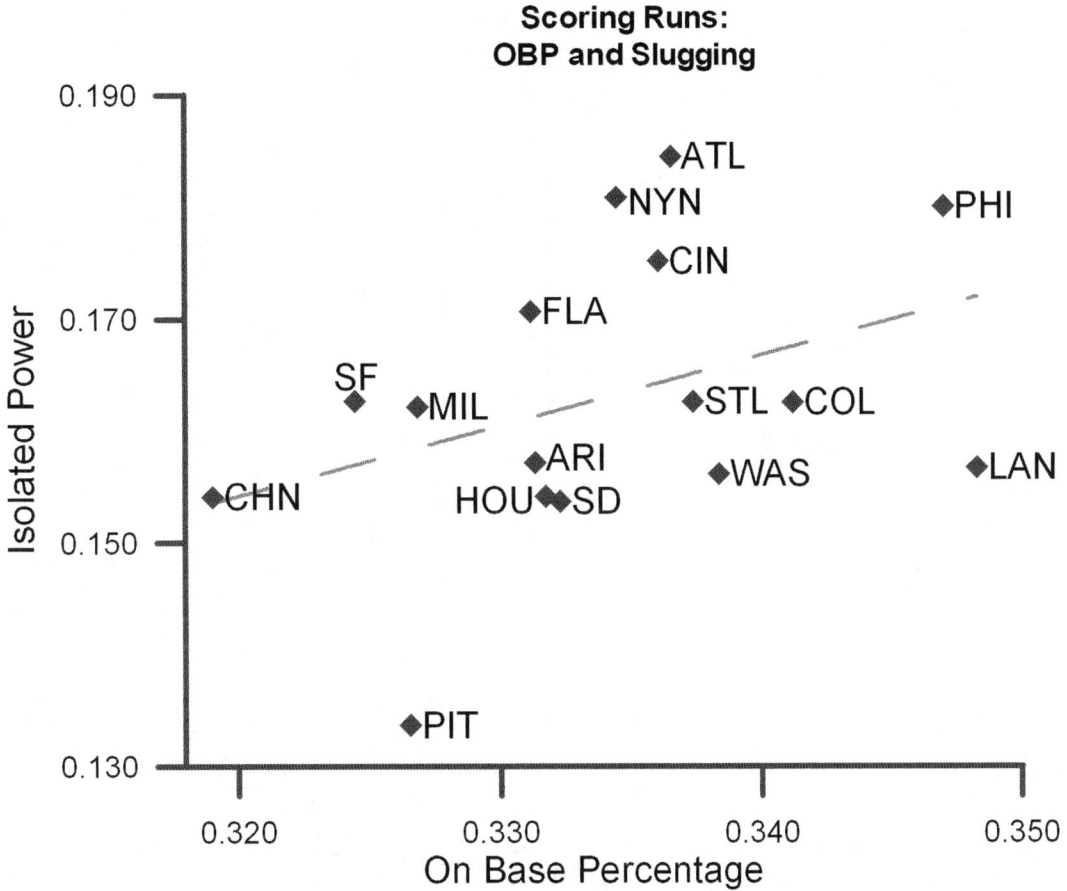

Scoring Runs:
OBP and Slugging

The dotted line shows the relationship between ISO and OBP.

Batting Statistics

Team	Runs	PA	H	1B	2B	3B	HR	TB	SO	BB	HBP	SH	SF	BA	OBP	SLG	GPA	ISO
ARI	773	6,330	1,506	977	331	38	160	2,393	965	504	67	61	53	.267	.331	.424	.255	.157
ATL	849	6,284	1,510	950	312	26	222	2,540	1,169	526	52	78	44	.270	.337	.455	.265	.184
CHN	716	6,147	1,496	1,013	271	46	166	2,357	928	395	43	84	37	.268	.319	.422	.249	.154
CIN	749	6,296	1,419	899	291	12	217	2,385	1,192	614	59	66	38	.257	.336	.432	.259	.175
COL	813	6,348	1,504	968	325	54	157	2,408	1,108	561	60	119	45	.270	.341	.433	.262	.163
FLA	758	6,191	1,454	921	309	42	182	2,393	1,249	497	74	76	42	.264	.331	.435	.258	.171
HOU	735	6,326	1,407	931	275	27	174	2,258	1,076	585	73	100	46	.255	.332	.409	.252	.154
LAN	820	6,394	1,552	1,034	307	58	153	2,434	959	601	51	66	48	.276	.348	.432	.265	.157
MIL	730	6,130	1,400	899	301	20	180	2,281	1,233	502	82	58	53	.258	.327	.420	.252	.162
NYN	834	6,291	1,469	905	323	41	200	2,474	1,071	547	62	77	47	.264	.334	.445	.262	.181
PHI	865	6,509	1,518	967	294	41	216	2,542	1,203	626	95	57	44	.267	.347	.447	.268	.180
PIT	691	6,218	1,462	1,018	286	17	141	2,205	1,200	459	89	62	49	.263	.327	.397	.246	.134
STL	781	6,225	1,484	981	292	27	184	2,382	922	531	61	71	40	.269	.337	.431	.260	.163
SD	731	6,287	1,465	968	298	38	161	2,322	1,104	564	40	59	47	.263	.332	.416	.254	.154
SF	746	6,136	1,418	906	297	52	163	2,308	891	494	53	80	37	.259	.324	.422	.251	.163
WAS	746	6,283	1,437	929	322	22	164	2,295	1,156	594	69	76	49	.262	.338	.418	.257	.156
Average	771	6,275	1,469	954	302	35	178	2,374	1,089	538	64	74	45	.264	.334	.427	.257	.163

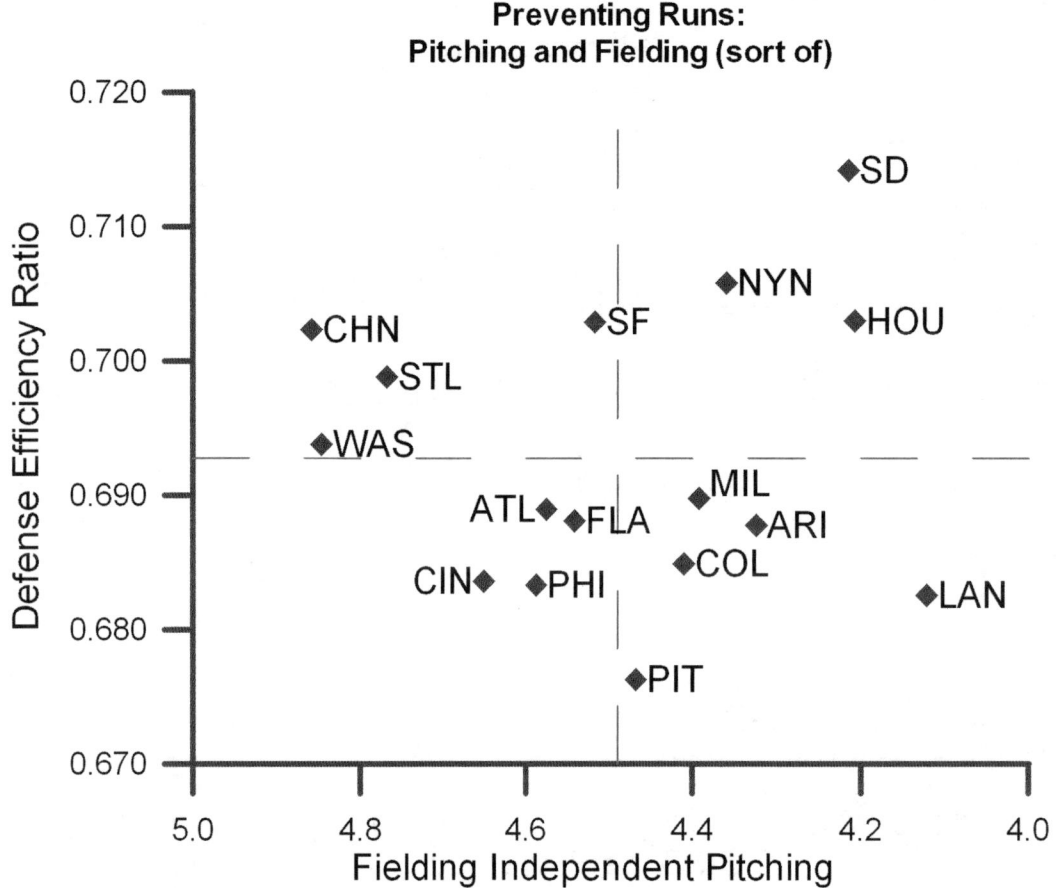

Preventing Runs:
Pitching and Fielding (sort of)

The dotted lines represent the league averages.

Pitching Statistics

Team	RA	IP	BFP	H	HR	TBA	K	BB	ShO	Sv	Op	%Save	Holds	ERA	FIP	UERA	DER
ARI	788	1459.0	6,341	1,503	168	2,430	1,115	536	9	34	54	63%	75	4.48	4.32	0.38	.688
ATL	805	1441.0	6,350	1,529	183	2,454	1,049	572	6	38	67	57%	56	4.60	4.57	0.43	.689
CHN	834	1439.0	6,366	1,396	210	2,366	1,250	687	7	29	46	63%	68	4.74	4.86	0.48	.702
CIN	801	1445.0	6,319	1,576	213	2,593	1,053	464	10	36	60	60%	49	4.52	4.65	0.47	.684
COL	812	1447.0	6,318	1,549	155	2,455	952	553	8	34	59	58%	76	4.66	4.41	0.39	.685
FLA	772	1433.0	6,294	1,465	166	2,325	1,088	622	6	41	68	60%	69	4.37	4.54	0.48	.688
HOU	719	1468.0	6,219	1,425	182	2,348	1,160	480	12	42	60	70%	75	4.08	4.21	0.32	.703
LAN	751	1460.0	6,289	1,524	152	2,363	1,068	492	10	40	61	66%	56	4.23	4.12	0.40	.683
MIL	833	1425.0	6,210	1,454	177	2,404	1,145	514	8	43	67	64%	59	4.83	4.39	0.44	.690
NYN	731	1461.0	6,240	1,402	180	2,252	1,161	527	12	43	58	74%	73	4.15	4.36	0.36	.706
PHI	812	1460.0	6,366	1,561	211	2,609	1,138	512	6	42	64	66%	85	4.60	4.59	0.40	.683
PIT	797	1435.0	6,354	1,545	156	2,375	1,060	620	10	39	60	65%	72	4.52	4.47	0.48	.676
STL	762	1429.0	6,196	1,475	193	2,432	970	504	9	38	57	67%	73	4.54	4.77	0.26	.699
SD	679	1463.0	6,175	1,385	176	2,247	1,097	468	11	50	71	70%	81	3.87	4.22	0.31	.714
SF	790	1429.0	6,225	1,422	153	2,262	992	584	9	37	59	63%	68	4.63	4.52	0.35	.703
WAS	872	1436.0	6,424	1,535	193	2,503	960	584	3	32	55	58%	62	5.03	4.85	0.43	.694
Average	785	1445.6	6,293	1,484	179	2,401	1,079	545	9	39	60	64%	69	4.49	4.49	0.40	.693

Miscellaneous Batting Stats

Team	SB	CS	SB%	GDP	P/PA	BABIP
ARI	76	30	72%	136	3.70	.298
ATL	52	35	60%	132	3.71	.307
CHN	121	49	71%	135	3.68	.296
CIN	124	33	79%	122	3.85	.293
COL	85	50	63%	119	3.79	.313
FLA	110	58	65%	109	3.78	.312
HOU	79	36	69%	123	3.79	.289
LAN	128	49	72%	140	3.72	.310
MIL	71	37	66%	134	3.78	.303
NYN	146	35	81%	114	3.81	.296
PHI	92	25	79%	115	3.82	.305
PIT	68	23	75%	153	3.77	.313
STL	59	32	65%	129	3.71	.294
SD	123	31	80%	128	3.80	.302
SF	58	25	70%	137	3.59	.284
WAS	123	62	66%	119	3.84	.305
Average	95	38	71%	128	3.76	.301

Win Probability Added / Win Shares

Team	Bat	Starters	Bullpen	LI	Bat	Pitch	Field	WSAge	CWS
ARI	-8.1	0.9	2.3	1.08	96	92	40	29.1	1,947
ATL	1.8	0.4	-4.2	0.91	128	73	36	28.3	2,046
CHN	-9.0	-5.7	-0.3	0.99	86	73	39	28.8	2,319
CIN	-0.3	0.2	-1.0	1.09	105	93	42	29.3	2,402
COL	-5.3	-0.9	1.2	1.08	103	86	39	28.2	1,284
FLA	-2.4	4.3	-4.9	1.07	121	76	37	24.9	533
HOU	-8.9	5.7	4.2	1.16	98	101	47	30.4	2,173
LAN	-1.2	4.8	3.4	1.06	129	96	39	30.3	3,055
MIL	-3.0	0.5	-3.5	1.12	109	80	36	28.8	1,567
NYN	4.6	0.3	11.1	1.06	146	98	46	30.0	3,399
PHI	3.3	-2.3	3.0	1.11	129	86	40	29.5	2,398
PIT	-15.4	-2.4	3.9	1.14	87	77	37	27.3	1,328
STL	-0.9	0.7	2.7	1.02	125	81	43	29.2	2,265
SD	-7.2	6.3	7.9	1.16	119	98	47	30.5	2,829
SF	-4.7	1.4	-1.2	1.06	107	81	40	33.2	3,115
WAS	-1.4	-7.0	-1.7	1.01	122	59	31	27.8	1,778
Average	-3.6	0.5	1.4	1.07	113	84	40	29.1	2,152

Leverage Index (LI) for bullpen only

Fielding and Miscellaneous Pitching Stats

Team	DER	Fld %	UER	SBA	CS	%CS	PO	E	TE	FE	DP	GIDP
ARI	.688	.983	61	135	45	33%	12	104	48	54	171	141
ATL	.689	.984	69	131	30	23%	6	99	44	53	146	132
CHN	.702	.982	76	157	39	25%	10	106	53	51	122	95
CIN	.684	.979	75	85	35	41%	5	128	66	60	139	112
COL	.685	.985	63	141	42	30%	12	91	35	56	190	166
FLA	.688	.979	76	115	46	40%	13	126	64	61	166	146
HOU	.703	.987	53	106	28	26%	10	80	26	51	163	144
LAN	.683	.982	65	148	38	26%	13	115	52	63	174	154
MIL	.690	.980	69	128	31	24%	14	117	59	58	127	111
NYN	.706	.983	58	151	40	26%	8	104	54	48	131	105
PHI	.683	.983	65	129	35	27%	8	104	52	50	153	136
PIT	.676	.983	77	154	52	34%	24	104	43	61	168	144
STL	.699	.984	41	95	32	34%	4	98	29	69	170	155
SD	.714	.985	50	176	26	15%	5	92	41	46	139	120
SF	.703	.985	55	138	40	29%	18	91	43	48	132	108
WAS	.694	.978	69	140	30	21%	6	131	61	64	123	90
Average	.693	.983	64	133	37	28%	11	106	48	56	151	129

185

Batted Ball Stats for Batters

Team	PA	% of PA K%	BB%	% of Batted Balls GB%	LD%	FB%	IF/F	HR/OF	Runs Per Event NIP	GB	LD	OF	Total Runs vs. Avg. NIP	GB	LD	FB	Tot
ARI	6330	15	9	44	19	37	.14	.10	.06	.05	.39	.17	3	2	3	-30	-22
ATL	6284	19	9	43	20	36	.09	.14	.04	.04	.38	.25	-17	-21	-3	76	35
CHN	6147	15	7	47	19	34	.10	.11	.03	.05	.38	.18	-36	23	-7	-25	-46
CIN	6296	19	11	43	19	37	.09	.14	.05	.03	.39	.21	13	-31	-20	30	-9
COL	6348	17	10	43	21	35	.08	.10	.05	.03	.41	.20	4	-33	32	-2	1
FLA	6191	20	9	44	19	37	.10	.12	.03	.06	.41	.20	-27	29	-9	2	-4
HOU	6326	17	10	43	19	38	.13	.11	.06	.04	.38	.17	21	-3	-36	-41	-59
LAN	6394	15	10	44	20	36	.09	.10	.07	.04	.41	.17	31	-5	22	-23	24
MIL	6130	20	10	43	20	38	.12	.12	.03	.04	.40	.20	-20	-15	-3	-3	-41
NYN	6291	17	10	43	19	38	.11	.12	.05	.04	.39	.22	5	-7	-23	42	17
PHI	6509	18	11	44	20	36	.12	.14	.06	.05	.39	.23	26	7	-7	32	58
PIT	6218	19	9	44	20	36	.11	.10	.03	.04	.39	.17	-29	-3	-5	-50	-88
SD	6287	18	10	42	19	38	.10	.10	.05	.04	.40	.18	-1	-22	-3	-13	-39
SF	6136	15	9	44	18	38	.13	.10	.06	.03	.40	.18	6	-35	-2	-11	-42
STL	6225	15	10	45	20	36	.12	.12	.07	.04	.39	.19	17	-7	8	-16	2
WAS	6283	18	11	44	20	37	.09	.10	.05	.03	.41	.18	14	-21	5	-25	-27
MLB Average		17	9	44	20	37	.11	.11	.05	.04	.39	.19	-	-	-	-	-

Batted Ball Stats for Pitchers

Team	PA	% of PA K%	BB%	% of Batted Balls GB%	LD%	FB%	IF/F	HR/OF	Runs Per Event NIP	GB	LD	OF	Total Runs vs. Avg. NIP	GB	LD	FB	Tot
ARI	6341	18	9	47	20	33	.10	.12	.05	.04	.42	.20	-5	-5	23	-19	-7
ATL	6350	17	10	45	21	34	.09	.12	.06	.05	.38	.19	13	13	1	-9	18
CHN	6366	20	12	42	20	39	.11	.14	.06	.05	.39	.21	34	-13	-27	17	12
CIN	6319	17	8	41	21	38	.10	.13	.04	.06	.39	.21	-23	14	15	46	52
COL	6318	15	10	46	20	35	.09	.10	.07	.03	.40	.20	21	-28	15	14	22
FLA	6294	17	11	43	19	38	.11	.11	.07	.05	.39	.19	33	0	-18	-13	2
HOU	6219	19	9	45	19	36	.10	.12	.03	.02	.40	.22	-30	-50	-7	26	-61
LAN	6289	17	8	48	18	34	.10	.10	.04	.05	.41	.19	-21	17	-15	-16	-35
MIL	6210	18	9	42	20	38	.11	.12	.04	.05	.43	.18	-10	8	24	-19	4
NYN	6240	19	9	43	19	37	.11	.12	.04	.04	.38	.19	-12	-25	-21	-13	-70
PHI	6366	18	9	44	21	36	.10	.13	.04	.05	.41	.22	-16	3	26	36	50
PIT	6354	17	11	46	20	34	.10	.11	.07	.05	.40	.20	33	2	5	-20	21
SD	6175	18	8	42	19	39	.12	.11	.03	.03	.37	.18	-28	-41	-28	-0	-97
SF	6225	16	11	42	20	39	.10	.09	.07	.04	.39	.16	30	-19	-3	-36	-28
STL	6196	16	9	46	19	34	.11	.13	.06	.03	.39	.22	9	-18	3	19	13
WAS	6424	15	11	40	19	41	.11	.11	.08	.06	.38	.18	39	23	-12	9	58
MLB Average		17	9	44	20	37	.11	.11	.05	.04	.39	.19	-	-	-	-	-

National League Leaderboards
Batting Leaders

Italicized stats have been adjusted for home park.

Runs Created				Runs Scored				Runs Batted In				Gross Production Average (GPA)			
1	A. Pujols	STL	150	1	C. Utley	PHI	131	1	R. Howard	PHI	149	1	A. Pujols	STL	.365
2	L. Berkman	HOU	141	2	C. Beltran	NYN	127	2	A. Pujols	STL	137	2	M. Cabrera	FLA	.354
2	M. Cabrera	FLA	141	3	J. Rollins	PHI	127	3	L. Berkman	HOU	136	3	R. Howard	PHI	.348
4	R. Howard	PHI	137	4	J. Reyes	NYN	122	4	A. Jones	ATL	129	4	L. Berkman	HOU	.344
5	C. Beltran	NYN	125	5	A. Soriano	WAS	119	5	G. Atkins	COL	120	5	N. Johnson	WAS	.335
6	J. Reyes	NYN	124	6	A. Pujols	STL	119	6	A. Ramirez	CHN	119	6	C. Beltran	NYN	.330
7	D. Wright	NYN	123	7	M. Holliday	COL	119	7	C. Beltran	NYN	116	7	D. Wright	NYN	.311
8	C. Utley	PHI	122	8	H. Ramirez	FLA	119	8	D. Wright	NYN	116	8	A. Soriano	WAS	.310
9	A. Soriano	WAS	121	9	G. Atkins	COL	117	9	C. Delgado	NYN	114	9	J. Drew	LAN	.309
10	G. Atkins	COL	119	10	R. Furcal	LAN	113	10	M. Cabrera	FLA	114	10	J. Bay	PIT	.308
11	R. Furcal	LAN	119					11	M. Holliday	COL	114				

Batting Average				On-Base Percentage				Slugging Percentage				OPS (On-Base Plus Slugging)			
1	F. Sanchez	PIT	.344	1	A. Pujols	STL	.431	1	A. Pujols	STL	.671	1	A. Pujols	STL	1.102
2	M. Cabrera	FLA	.339	2	M. Cabrera	FLA	.430	2	R. Howard	PHI	.659	2	R. Howard	PHI	1.084
3	A. Pujols	STL	.331	3	N. Johnson	WAS	.428	3	L. Berkman	HOU	.621	3	L. Berkman	HOU	1.041
4	G. Atkins	COL	.329	4	R. Howard	PHI	.425	4	C. Beltran	NYN	.594	4	M. Cabrera	FLA	.998
5	M. Holliday	COL	.326	5	L. Berkman	HOU	.420	5	M. Holliday	COL	.586	5	C. Beltran	NYN	.982
6	P. Lo Duca	NYN	.318	6	G. Atkins	COL	.409	6	M. Cabrera	FLA	.568	6	M. Holliday	COL	.973
7	L. Berkman	HOU	.315	7	T. Helton	COL	.404	7	A. LaRoche	ATL	.561	7	G. Atkins	COL	.965
8	R. Howard	PHI	.313	8	J. Bay	PIT	.396	8	A. Ramirez	CHN	.561	8	N. Johnson	WAS	.948
9	D. Wright	NYN	.311	9	J. Drew	LAN	.393	9	A. Soriano	WAS	.560	9	J. Bay	PIT	.928
10	C. Utley	PHI	.309	10	S. Hatteberg	CIN	.389	10	G. Atkins	COL	.556	10	A. LaRoche	ATL	.915

Plate Appearances				Outs				Hits				Total Bases			
1	J. Rollins	PHI	758	1	J. Pierre	CHN	532	1	J. Pierre	CHN	204	1	R. Howard	PHI	383
2	J. Pierre	CHN	750	2	J. Rollins	PHI	521	2	C. Utley	PHI	203	2	A. Soriano	WAS	362
3	C. Utley	PHI	739	3	J. Francoeur	ATL	507	3	F. Sanchez	PIT	200	3	A. Pujols	STL	359
4	R. Furcal	LAN	736	4	A. Soriano	WAS	493	4	G. Atkins	COL	198	4	M. Holliday	COL	353
5	A. Soriano	WAS	728	5	R. Furcal	LAN	486	5	R. Furcal	LAN	196	5	C. Utley	PHI	347
6	B. Giles	SD	717	6	F. Lopez	CIN/WAS	484	6	M. Holliday	COL	196	6	G. Atkins	COL	335
7	F. Lopez	CIN/WAS	714	7	P. Feliz	SF	482	7	M. Cabrera	FLA	195	7	L. Berkman	HOU	333
8	R. Howard	PHI	704	8	J. Reyes	NYN	478	8	J. Reyes	NYN	194	8	A. Ramirez	CHN	333
9	J. Reyes	NYN	703	9	H. Ramirez	FLA	477	9	J. Rollins	PHI	191	9	J. Rollins	PHI	329
10	H. Ramirez	FLA	700	10	C. Utley	PHI	472	10	H. Ramirez	FLA	185	10	M. Cabrera	FLA	327

Singles				Doubles				Triples				Home Runs			
1	J. Pierre	CHN	156	1	F. Sanchez	PIT	53	1	J. Reyes	NYN	17	1	R. Howard	PHI	58
2	R. Furcal	LAN	140	2	L. Gonzalez	ARI	52	2	J. Pierre	CHN	13	2	A. Pujols	STL	49
3	F. Sanchez	PIT	139	3	M. Cabrera	FLA	50	3	D. Roberts	SD	13	3	A. Soriano	WAS	46
4	O. Vizquel	SF	135	4	S. Rolen	STL	48	4	S. Finley	SF	12	4	L. Berkman	HOU	45
5	F. Lopez	CIN/WAS	128	5	G. Atkins	COL	48	5	K. Lofton	LAN	12	5	A. Jones	ATL	41
6	J. Reyes	NYN	128	6	R. Zimmerman	WAS	47	6	H. Ramirez	FLA	11	6	C. Beltran	NYN	41
7	C. Utley	PHI	127	7	N. Johnson	WAS	46	7	O. Vizquel	SF	10	7	A. Dunn	CIN	40
8	D. Eckstein	STL	125	8	H. Ramirez	FLA	46	8	C. Sullivan	COL	10	8	A. Ramirez	CHN	38
9	W. Taveras	HOU	122	9	J. Rollins	PHI	45	9	4 tied with		9	9	C. Delgado	NYN	38
10	G. Atkins	COL	120	10	M. Holliday	COL	45					10	B. Hall	MIL	35
												11	J. Bay	PIT	35

Walks

1	B. Bonds	SF	115
2	A. Dunn	CIN	112
3	N. Johnson	WAS	110
4	R. Howard	PHI	108
5	B. Giles	SD	104
6	J. Bay	PIT	102
7	M. Ensberg	HOU	101
8	L. Berkman	HOU	98
9	P. Burrell	PHI	98
10	C. Beltran	NYN	95

Intentional Walks

1	B. Bonds	SF	38
2	R. Howard	PHI	37
3	A. Pujols	STL	28
4	M. Cabrera	FLA	27
5	L. Berkman	HOU	22
6	A. Soriano	WAS	16
7	T. Helton	COL	15
8	N. Johnson	WAS	15
9	D. Wright	NYN	13
10	A. Dunn	CIN	12

Hit By Pitch

1	R. Weeks	MIL	19
2	A. Rowand	PHI	18
3	J. Bautista	PIT	16
4	D. Eckstein	STL	15
5	M. Holliday	COL	15
6	B. Clark	MIL	14
7	S. Victorino	PHI	14
8	C. Utley	PHI	14
9	C. Burke	HOU	14
10	3 tied with		13

Pitches Per Plate Appearance

1	P. Burrell	PHI	4.3
2	N. Johnson	WAS	4.3
3	C. Beltran	NYN	4.2
4	A. Dunn	CIN	4.2
5	J. Carroll	COL	4.2
6	B. Hall	MIL	4.2
7	F. Lopez	CIN/WAS	4.1
8	A. Kearns	CIN/WAS	4.1
9	R. Freel	CIN	4.1
10	M. Cameron	SD	4.1

Stolen Bases

1	J. Reyes	NYN	64
2	J. Pierre	CHN	58
3	H. Ramirez	FLA	51
4	D. Roberts	SD	49
5	F. Lopez	CIN/WAS	44
6	A. Soriano	WAS	41
7	R. Furcal	LAN	37
8	R. Freel	CIN	37
9	J. Rollins	PHI	36
10	W. Taveras	HOU	33

Caught Stealing

1	J. Pierre	CHN	20
2	A. Soriano	WAS	17
3	J. Reyes	NYN	17
4	H. Ramirez	FLA	15
5	R. Furcal	LAN	13
6	A. Amezaga	FLA	12
7	F. Lopez	CIN/WAS	12
8	J. Carroll	COL	12
9	R. Freel	CIN	11
10	M. Cameron	SD	9
11	B. Hall	MIL	9
12	W. Taveras	HOU	9

Net Stolen Bases

1	D. Roberts	SD	37
2	J. Reyes	NYN	30
3	J. Rollins	PHI	28
4	C. Duffy	PIT	24
5	K. Lofton	LAN	22
6	H. Ramirez	FLA	21
7	B. Phillips	CIN	21
8	F. Lopez	CIN/WAS	20
9	E. Byrnes	ARI	19
10	J. Pierre	CHN	18

Grounded into Double Plays

1	G. Atkins	COL	24
2	A. Gonzalez	SD	24
3	J. Castillo	PIT	22
4	M. Holliday	COL	22
5	B. Ausmus	HOU	21
6	P. Wilson	HOU/STL	20
7	A. Pujols	STL	20
8	B. Phillips	CIN	19
9	7 tied with		18

Isolated Power (ISO)

1	R. Howard	PHI	.346
2	A. Pujols	STL	.340
3	C. Beltran	NYN	.320
4	L. Berkman	HOU	.306
5	B. Hall	MIL	.283
6	A. Soriano	WAS	.283
7	C. Delgado	NYN	.282
8	A. LaRoche	ATL	.276
9	A. Ramirez	CHN	.269
10	A. Jones	ATL	.269

BA on Balls in Play (BABIP)

1	M. Cabrera	FLA	.382
2	F. Sanchez	PIT	.370
3	R. Howard	PHI	.363
4	M. Holliday	COL	.354
5	B. Hawpe	COL	.350
6	D. Wright	NYN	.350
7	C. Utley	PHI	.346
8	H. Ramirez	FLA	.344
9	A. Gonzalez	SD	.344
10	J. Carroll	COL	.342

BA with RISP

1	A. Pujols	STL	.397
2	F. Sanchez	PIT	.386
3	L. Berkman	HOU	.382
4	M. Cabrera	FLA	.378
5	N. Garciaparra	LAN	.368
6	D. Wright	NYN	.365
7	T. Helton	COL	.347
8	R. Furcal	LAN	.344
9	G. Atkins	COL	.341
10	J. Reyes	NYN	.336

Situational Hitting Runs

1	A. Pujols	STL	14
2	L. Berkman	HOU	13
3	B. Bonds	SF	12
4	J. Francoeur	ATL	12
5	T. Helton	COL	11
6	M. Cameron	SD	10
7	N. Garciaparra	LAN	10
8	J. Reyes	NYN	9
9	R. Zimmerman	WAS	9
10	D. Wright	NYN	9

Extra Base Hits

1	A. Soriano	WAS	89
2	R. Howard	PHI	84
3	M. Holliday	COL	84
4	A. Pujols	STL	83
5	C. Beltran	NYN	80
6	A. Ramirez	CHN	80
7	J. Rollins	PHI	79
8	M. Cabrera	FLA	78
9	G. Atkins	COL	78
10	B. Hall	MIL	78

Sacrifice Hits

1	C. Barmes	COL	19
2	C. Sullivan	COL	19
3	R. Cedeno	CHN	15
4	O. Vizquel	SF	13
5	E. Chavez	NYN	11
6	F. Lopez	CIN/WAS	11
7	W. Taveras	HOU	11
8	J. Pierre	CHN	10
9	A. Everett	HOU	10
10	4 tied with		9

Sacrifice Flies

1	C. Delgado	NYN	10
2	A. Jones	ATL	9
3	J. Bay	PIT	9
4	F. Sanchez	PIT	9
5	L. Berkman	HOU	8
6	D. Wright	NYN	8
7	S. Rolen	STL	8
8	P. Fielder	MIL	8
9	D. Uggla	FLA	8
10	J. Estrada	ARI	8

Strikeouts

1	A. Dunn	CIN	194
2	R. Howard	PHI	181
3	B. Hall	MIL	162
4	A. Soriano	WAS	160
5	J. Bay	PIT	156
6	M. Cameron	SD	142
7	A. Kearns	CIN/WAS	135
8	C. Utley	PHI	132
9	J. Francoeur	ATL	132
10	P. Burrell	PHI	131

Pitching Leaders

Pitching Runs Created			Earned Run Average (ERA)			Runs Allowed Per 9 (RA)			Fielding Independent Pitching (FIP)		
1 R. Oswalt	HOU	128	1 R. Oswalt	HOU	2.98	1 R. Oswalt	HOU	3.10	1 B. Webb	ARI	3.20
2 C. Carpenter	STL	125	2 C. Carpenter	STL	3.09	2 C. Carpenter	STL	3.29	2 R. Oswalt	HOU	3.32
3 B. Webb	ARI	124	3 B. Webb	ARI	3.10	3 B. Webb	ARI	3.49	3 J. Peavy	SD	3.42
3 J. Smoltz	ATL	124	4 B. Arroyo	CIN	3.29	4 J. Smoltz	ATL	3.61	4 J. Smoltz	ATL	3.46
5 B. Arroyo	CIN	122	5 C. Zambrano	CHN	3.41	5 C. Young	SD	3.61	5 C. Carpenter	STL	3.47
6 C. Zambrano	CHN	110	6 C. Young	SD	3.46	6 B. Arroyo	CIN	3.66	6 A. Harang	CIN	3.64
6 A. Harang	CIN	110	7 J. Smoltz	ATL	3.49	7 C. Zambrano	CHN	3.83	7 D. Lowe	LAN	3.72
8 J. Schmidt	SF	103	8 J. Schmidt	SF	3.59	8 C. Hensley	SD	3.95	8 G. Maddux	CHN/LAN	3.77
9 J. Peavy	SD	99	9 D. Lowe	LAN	3.63	9 J. Schmidt	SF	3.97	9 B. Penny	LAN	3.90
10 D. Willis	FLA	97	10 C. Hensley	SD	3.71	10 J. Jennings	COL	3.99	10 J. Schmidt	SF	3.94

Innings Pitched			Batters Faced			Pitches			Pitches Per Plate Appearance		
1 B. Arroyo	CIN	240.7	1 A. Harang	CIN	993	1 B. Arroyo	CIN	3852	1 G. Maddux	CHN/LAN	3.3
2 B. Webb	ARI	235.0	2 B. Arroyo	CIN	992	2 A. Harang	CIN	3740	2 A. Cook	COL	3.4
3 A. Harang	CIN	234.3	3 D. Willis	FLA	975	3 C. Zambrano	CHN	3626	3 D. Bush	MIL	3.5
4 J. Smoltz	ATL	232.0	4 J. Smoltz	ATL	960	4 D. Willis	FLA	3615	4 J. Lieber	PHI	3.5
5 D. Willis	FLA	223.3	5 T. Hudson	ATL	959	5 J. Smoltz	ATL	3535	5 Z. Duke	PIT	3.5
6 C. Carpenter	STL	221.7	5 L. Hernandez	WAS/ARI	959	6 L. Hernandez	WAS/ARI	3489	6 B. Webb	ARI	3.5
7 C. Capuano	MIL	221.3	7 B. Webb	ARI	950	7 A. Pettitte	HOU	3486	7 J. Marquis	STL	3.5
8 R. Oswalt	HOU	220.7	8 C. Capuano	MIL	936	7 D. Davis	MIL	3486	8 T. Hudson	ATL	3.6
9 T. Hudson	ATL	218.3	9 Z. Duke	PIT	935	9 J. Schmidt	SF	3461	9 M. Batista	ARI	3.6
10 D. Lowe	LAN	218.0	10 A. Pettitte	HOU	929	10 T. Hudson	ATL	3418	10 D. Lowe	LAN	3.6

Strikeouts			Walks (Most)			Strikeouts Per Game			Walks Per Game (Least)		
1 A. Harang	CIN	216	1 C. Zambrano	CHN	115	1 J. Peavy	SD	9.9	1 J. Lieber	PHI	1.3
2 J. Peavy	SD	215	2 D. Davis	MIL	102	2 O. Hernandez	ARI/NYN	9.1	2 R. Oswalt	HOU	1.6
3 J. Smoltz	ATL	211	3 M. Cain	SF	87	3 C. Zambrano	CHN	8.9	3 D. Bush	MIL	1.7
4 C. Zambrano	CHN	210	4 J. Jennings	COL	85	4 B. Myers	PHI	8.8	4 C. Carpenter	STL	1.9
5 B. Myers	PHI	189	5 M. Batista	ARI	84	5 C. Young	SD	8.7	5 C. Capuano	MIL	2.0
6 B. Arroyo	CIN	184	6 D. Willis	FLA	83	6 J. Smoltz	ATL	8.5	6 B. Webb	ARI	2.0
6 C. Carpenter	STL	184	7 P. Maholm	PIT	81	7 M. Cain	SF	8.5	7 A. Harang	CIN	2.2
8 J. Schmidt	SF	180	8 J. Schmidt	SF	80	8 S. Olsen	FLA	8.5	8 J. Smoltz	ATL	2.2
9 M. Cain	SF	179	9 T. Hudson	ATL	79	9 A. Harang	CIN	8.5	9 A. Cook	COL	2.3
10 A. Pettitte	HOU	178	10 S. Trachsel	NYN	78	10 I. Snell	PIT	8.1	10 D. Lowe	LAN	2.3
10 B. Webb	ARI	178	10 L. Hernandez	WAS/ARI	78						

Wins			Losses			Shutouts			Games Started		
1 J. Smoltz	ATL	16	1 R. Ortiz	WAS	16	1 C. Carpenter	STL	3	1 J. Smoltz	ATL	35
1 D. Lowe	LAN	16	1 J. Marquis	STL	16	1 B. Webb	ARI	3	1 A. Pettitte	HOU	35
1 C. Zambrano	CHN	16	3 M. Morris	SF	15	3 J. Jennings	COL	2	1 T. Hudson	ATL	35
1 B. Penny	LAN	16	3 A. Cook	COL	15	3 A. Harang	CIN	2	1 B. Arroyo	CIN	35
1 A. Harang	CIN	16	3 Z. Duke	PIT	15	3 C. Capuano	MIL	2	1 A. Harang	CIN	35
1 B. Webb	ARI	16	6 G. Maddux	CHN/LAN	14	3 D. Bush	MIL	2	6 7 tied with		34
7 5 tied with		15	6 J. Peavy	SD	14	7 Many with		1			
			8 4 tied with		13						

189

Games

1	S. Torres	PIT	94
2	J. Rauch	WAS	85
2	M. Capps	PIT	85
4	B. Howry	CHN	84
5	M. Stanton	WAS/SF	82
6	G. Geary	PHI	81
6	C. Qualls	HOU	81
6	T. Coffey	CIN	81
9	J. Mesa	COL	79
10	W. Ohman	CHN	78
10	B. Lidge	HOU	78

Saves

1	T. Hoffman	SD	46
2	B. Wagner	NYN	40
3	J. Borowski	FLA	36
4	T. Gordon	PHI	34
5	J. Isringhausen	STL	33
6	B. Lidge	HOU	32
7	B. Fuentes	COL	30
8	C. Cordero	WAS	29
9	R. Dempster	CHN	24
9	D. Turnbow	MIL	24
9	M. Gonzalez	PIT	24
9	T. Saito	LAN	24

Save Opportunities

1	T. Hoffman	SD	51
2	B. Wagner	NYN	45
3	J. Borowski	FLA	43
3	J. Isringhausen	STL	43
5	T. Gordon	PHI	39
6	B. Lidge	HOU	38
7	B. Fuentes	COL	36
8	R. Dempster	CHN	33
8	C. Cordero	WAS	33
10	D. Turnbow	MIL	32

Holds

1	S. Linebrink	SD	36
2	A. Heilman	NYN	27
3	L. Vizcaino	ARI	25
4	D. Wheeler	HOU	24
5	A. Rhodes	PHI	23
5	B. Lyon	ARI	23
5	C. Qualls	HOU	23
8	T. Tankersley	FLA	22
9	B. Howry	CHN	21
10	S. Torres	PIT	20

Home Runs Allowed

1	J. Marquis	STL	35
2	R. Ortiz	WAS	31
2	B. Arroyo	CIN	31
4	J. Sosa	ATL/STL	30
5	E. Milton	CIN	29
5	B. Myers	PHI	29
5	L. Hernandez	WAS/ARI	29
5	C. Capuano	MIL	29
5	I. Snell	PIT	29
10	A. Harang	CIN	28
10	C. Young	SD	28

Home Runs Per Game

1	D. Lowe	LAN	0.59
2	B. Webb	ARI	0.61
3	Z. Duke	PIT	0.71
4	A. Cook	COL	0.72
5	J. Jennings	COL	0.73
6	C. Hensley	SD	0.74
7	M. Batista	ARI	0.77
8	R. Oswalt	HOU	0.78
9	D. Davis	MIL	0.82
10	J. Francis	COL	0.83

Total Bases Allowed

1	A. Harang	CIN	390
2	J. Marquis	STL	389
3	L. Hernandez	WAS/ARI	388
4	C. Capuano	MIL	386
5	A. Pettitte	HOU	380
6	R. Ortiz	WAS	377
7	T. Hudson	ATL	374
8	Z. Duke	PIT	372
9	B. Arroyo	CIN	362
10	M. Morris	SF	356

Slugging Average Against

1	C. Zambrano	CHN	0.351
2	D. Lowe	LA	0.360
3	B. Webb	ARI	0.361
4	C. Carpenter	STL	0.364
5	M. Cain	SF	0.371
6	C. Hensley	SD	0.377
7	J. Schmidt	SF	0.379
8	C. Young	SD	0.382
9	J. Jennings	COL	0.386
10	J. Smoltz	ATL	0.393

Stolen Bases Allowed

1	C. Young	SD	41
2	D. Lowe	LAN	26
3	G. Maddux	CHN/LAN	25
3	J. Peavy	SD	25
5	B. Kim	COL	24
5	B. Webb	ARI	24
7	T. Hudson	ATL	23
8	J. Francis	COL	21
9	B. Penny	LAN	20
9	O. Hernandez	ARI/NYN	20

Caught Stealing

1	Z. Duke	PIT	12
2	P. Maholm	PIT	11
3	T. Glavine	NYN	9
3	B. Webb	ARI	9
5	7 tied with		8

Pick Offs

1	P. Maholm	PIT	9
2	Z. Duke	PIT	7
3	J. Wright	SF	6
3	J. Beimel	LAN	6
3	C. Capuano	MIL	6
6	J. Francis	COL	5
7	M. Stanton	WAS/SF	4
7	W. Rodriguez	HOU	4
9	6 tied with		3

Net Stolen Bases

1	P. Maholm	PIT	-27
2	Z. Duke	PIT	-25
3	J. Beimel	LAN	-17
3	C. Capuano	MIL	-17
5	T. Glavine	NYN	-16
6	J. Wright	SF	-15
7	S. Olsen	FLA	-14
7	W. Rodriguez	HOU	-14
9	M. Stanton	WAS/SF	-12
10	3 tied with		-11

Defense Efficiency Ratio (DER)

1	C. Young	SD	.774
2	C. Zambrano	CHN	.748
3	M. Cain	SF	.737
4	B. Arroyo	CIN	.730
5	J. Francis	COL	.730
6	C. Carpenter	STL	.729
7	J. Schmidt	SF	.723
8	C. Hensley	SD	.722
9	S. Olsen	FLA	.720
10	D. Bush	MIL	.718

Double Plays

1	B. Webb	ARI	36
2	M. Batista	ARI	35
3	D. Willis	FLA	33
4	A. Pettitte	HOU	31
4	Z. Duke	PIT	31
6	D. Lowe	LAN	30
6	C. Hensley	SD	30
8	A. Cook	COL	29
9	J. Jennings	COL	28
10	R. Oswalt	HOU	27

Wild Pitches

1	M. Batista	ARI	14
2	R. Madson	PHI	12
3	J. Schmidt	SF	11
3	B. Lidge	HOU	11
5	J. Jennings	COL	10
6	C. Zambrano	CHN	9
6	C. Vargas	FLA	9
6	J. Julio	NYN/ARI	9
6	M. Cain	SF	9
10	7 tied with		8

Hit By Pitch

1	D. Willis	FLA	19
2	R. Ortiz	WAS	18
2	D. Bush	MIL	18
4	J. Marquis	STL	16
5	M. Morris	SF	14
6	T. Armas Jr.	WAS	13
6	J. Francis	COL	13
8	O. Hernandez	ARI/NYN	12
8	P. Maholm	PIT	12
10	J. Cruz	ARI	11

Arizona Diamondbacks

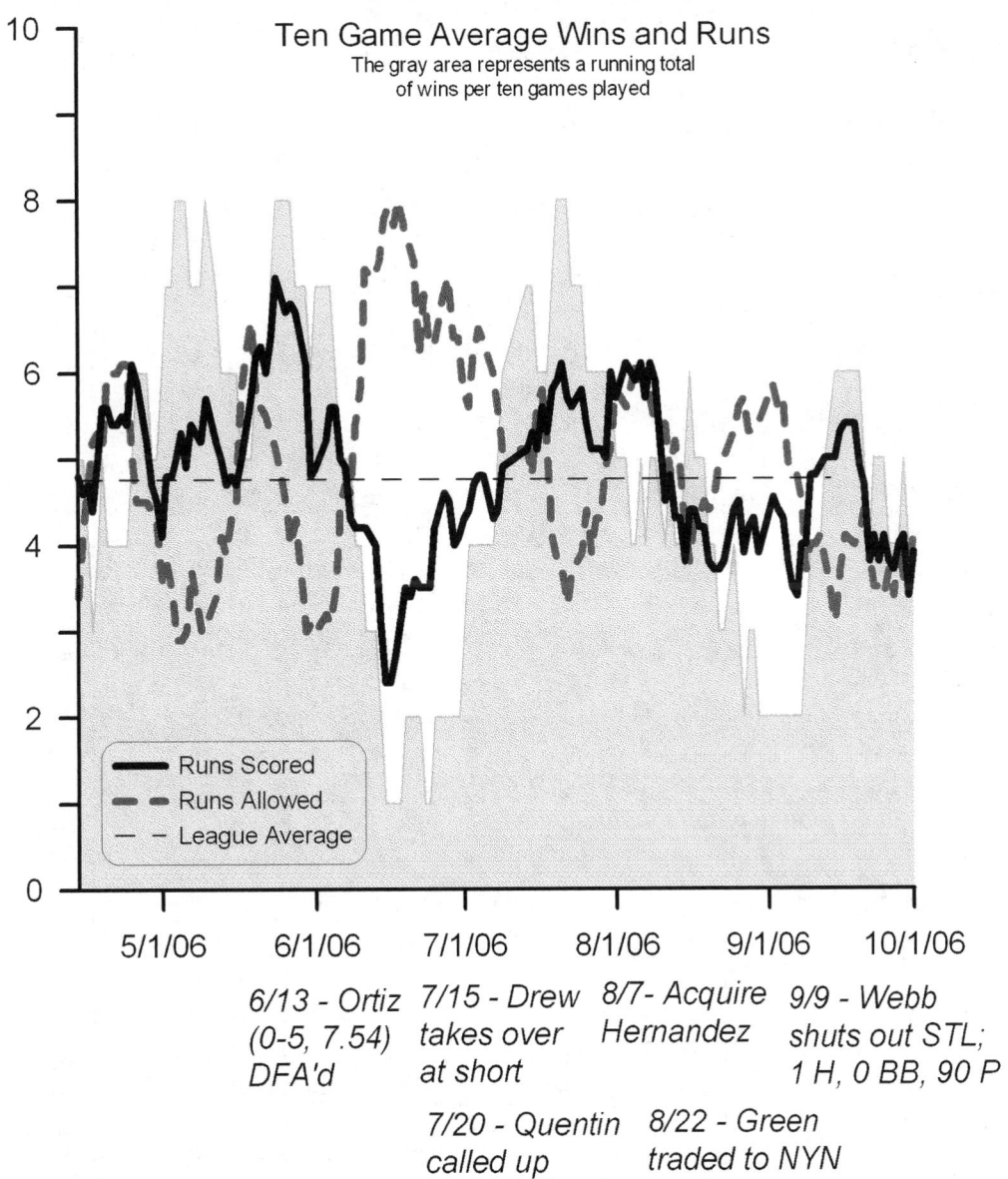

Ten Game Average Wins and Runs
The gray area represents a running total of wins per ten games played

- —— Runs Scored
- – – Runs Allowed
- – – League Average

6/13 - Ortiz (0-5, 7.54) DFA'd

7/15 - Drew takes over at short

7/20 - Quentin called up

8/7- Acquire Hernandez

8/22 - Green traded to NYN

9/9 - Webb shuts out STL; 1 H, 0 BB, 90 P

Team Batting and Pitching/Fielding Stats by Month						
	April	May	June	July	Aug	Sept/Oct
Wins	12	18	8	16	10	12
Losses	13	9	20	9	18	17
OBP	.336	.349	.319	.354	.321	.311
SLG	.415	.443	.392	.487	.402	.410
FIP	3.99	4.36	4.58	3.77	4.75	4.27
DER	.691	.684	.662	.682	.670	.741

Batting Stats

Player	RC	Runs	RBI	PA	Outs	P/PA	H	2B	3B	HR	TB	K	BB	IBB	HBP	SH	SF	SB	CS	GDP	BA	OBP	SLG	GPA
Hudson O.	84	87	67	650	436	3.83	166	34	9	15	263	78	61	5	2	4	4	9	6	17	.287	.354	.454	.257
Tracy C.	81	91	80	662	441	4.00	168	41	0	20	269	129	54	5	5	1	5	5	1	11	.281	.343	.451	.252
Gonzalez L.	76	93	73	668	442	3.80	159	52	2	15	260	58	69	10	7	0	6	0	1	14	.271	.352	.444	.254
Byrnes E.	74	82	79	606	427	3.60	150	37	3	26	271	88	34	2	5	2	3	25	3	12	.267	.313	.482	.246
Jackson C.	73	75	79	556	362	3.74	141	26	1	15	214	73	54	2	9	1	7	1	0	18	.291	.368	.441	.260
Estrada J.	56	43	71	443	306	3.19	125	26	0	11	184	40	13	7	7	1	8	0	0	17	.302	.328	.444	.244
Green S.	54	59	51	462	312	3.59	118	22	3	11	179	64	37	4	6	0	2	4	4	9	.283	.348	.429	.249
Counsell C.	43	56	30	415	286	3.77	95	14	4	4	129	47	31	0	9	2	1	15	8	1	.255	.327	.347	.220
DaVanon J.	39	38	35	256	167	3.88	64	12	4	5	99	42	31	0	0	0	4	10	4	6	.290	.371	.448	.263
Drew S.	29	27	23	226	144	3.69	66	13	7	5	108	50	14	4	0	2	1	2	0	1	.316	.357	.517	.273
Quentin C.	28	23	32	191	130	3.22	42	13	3	9	88	34	15	2	8	1	1	1	0	6	.253	.342	.530	.270
Easley D.	28	24	28	220	150	3.70	44	6	1	9	79	30	21	0	5	3	2	1	1	4	.233	.323	.418	.235
Snyder C.	25	19	32	213	138	4.00	51	9	0	6	78	39	22	4	1	1	5	0	0	5	.277	.349	.424	.248
Young C.	10	10	10	78	54	3.86	17	4	0	2	27	12	6	0	1	0	1	2	1	0	.243	.308	.386	.221
Clark T.	10	13	16	147	111	3.89	26	4	0	6	48	40	13	2	2	0	0	0	0	5	.197	.279	.364	.204
Green A.	7	15	6	102	70	3.86	16	4	0	1	23	20	13	0	0	3	0	1	0	0	.186	.293	.267	.187
Callaspo A.	5	2	6	47	33	3.83	10	1	1	0	13	6	4	0	0	0	1	0	1	0	.238	.298	.310	.199
Gonzalez E.	3	3	3	35	24	2.86	9	1	0	0	10	8	0	0	0	3	0	0	0	1	.281	.281	.313	.193
Hairston S.	2	2	2	16	10	3.81	6	2	0	0	8	5	1	0	0	0	0	0	0	1	.400	.438	.533	.311
Montero M.	2	0	3	17	12	3.59	4	1	0	0	5	3	1	0	0	0	0	0	0	0	.250	.294	.313	.198
Hernandez O.	1	0	0	14	8	2.86	3	1	0	0	4	0	1	0	0	2	0	0	0	0	.273	.333	.364	.227
Webb B.	1	4	9	86	63	3.57	11	2	0	0	13	33	2	0	0	10	1	0	0	1	.151	.171	.178	.115
Hammock R.	0	1	0	2	1	4.00	1	1	0	0	2	0	0	0	0	0	0	0	0	0	.500	.500	1.000	.448
Lyon B.	0	1	0	1	0	0.00	0	0	0	0	0	0	1	0	0	0	0	0	0	0	.000	1.000	.000	.424
Ortiz R.	-0	0	0	6	4	4.00	0	0	0	0	0	1	1	0	0	1	0	0	0	0	.000	.200	.000	.085
Koplove M.	-0	0	0	1	1	3.00	0	0	0	0	0	0	0	0	0	0	0	0	0	0	.000	.000	.000	.000
Daigle C.	-0	0	0	1	1	5.00	0	0	0	0	0	1	0	0	0	0	0	0	0	0	.000	.000	.000	.000
Pena T.	-0	0	0	2	2	1.50	0	0	0	0	0	0	0	0	0	0	0	0	0	0	.000	.000	.000	.000
Medders B.	-0	0	0	2	2	5.00	0	0	0	0	0	1	0	0	0	0	0	0	0	0	.000	.000	.000	.000
Nippert D.	-0	0	0	2	2	4.50	0	0	0	0	0	2	0	0	0	0	0	0	0	0	.000	.000	.000	.000
Grimsley J.	-0	1	0	4	4	2.75	0	0	0	0	0	2	0	0	0	0	0	0	0	0	.000	.000	.000	.000
Aquino G.	-0	0	0	1	2	6.00	0	0	0	0	0	0	0	0	0	0	0	0	0	1	.000	.000	.000	.000
Gonzalez E.	-1	0	0	13	12	2.92	1	0	0	0	1	4	0	0	0	0	0	0	0	0	.077	.077	.077	.051
Hernandez L.	-1	0	0	27	21	3.15	2	1	0	0	3	4	0	0	0	4	0	0	0	0	.087	.087	.130	.068
Cruz J.	-1	0	0	26	22	3.38	0	0	0	0	0	9	3	0	0	2	0	0	0	1	.000	.125	.000	.053
Vargas C.	-2	1	4	60	49	2.83	5	3	0	0	8	11	0	0	0	9	0	0	0	3	.098	.098	.157	.079
Batista M.	-3	3	4	72	56	3.39	6	1	0	0	7	31	2	0	0	9	1	0	0	2	.100	.127	.117	.081

Italicized stats have been adjusted for home park.

Batted Ball Batting Stats are listed at end of fielding stats

Pitching Stats

Player	PRC	IP	BFP	G	GS	P/PA	K	BB	IBB	HBP	H	HR	DP	DER	SB	CS	PO	W	L	Sv	Op	Hld	RA	ERA	FIP
Webb B.	124	235.0	950	33	33	3.51	178	50	4	6	216	15	36	.693	24	9	2	16	8	0	0	0	3.49	3.10	3.20
Batista M.	71	206.3	910	34	33	3.59	110	84	5	6	231	18	35	.681	15	7	2	11	8	0	0	0	5.06	4.58	4.52
Vargas C.	58	167.7	747	31	30	3.84	123	52	2	8	185	27	12	.683	12	5	3	12	10	0	0	0	5.42	4.83	4.88
Cruz J.	43	94.7	413	31	15	4.00	88	47	2	11	80	7	7	.715	7	3	0	5	6	0	0	0	4.28	4.18	4.09
Vizcaino L.	37	65.3	272	70	0	4.08	72	29	6	4	51	8	9	.723	2	2	0	4	6	0	2	25	3.58	3.58	3.85
Gonzalez E.	31	106.3	462	22	18	3.73	66	34	0	4	114	14	10	.701	2	6	0	3	7	0	0	0	6.01	5.67	4.76
Lyon B.	30	69.3	293	68	0	3.75	46	22	7	0	68	7	8	.711	2	0	0	2	4	0	7	23	4.15	3.89	3.85
Hernandez L.	30	69.3	298	10	10	3.55	39	26	2	2	70	7	5	.714	2	3	1	4	5	0	0	0	4.02	3.76	4.53
Medders B.	28	71.7	316	60	0	3.65	47	28	3	2	76	5	8	.688	4	1	0	5	3	0	1	10	4.65	3.64	3.94
Julio J.	23	44.7	189	44	0	4.12	55	25	1	0	31	6	2	.748	1	1	0	1	2	15	19	1	4.03	3.83	4.11
Aquino G.	19	48.3	220	42	0	3.88	51	24	2	4	54	8	9	.632	3	1	0	2	0	0	0	2	5.03	4.47	4.87
Gonzalez E.	18	42.7	182	11	5	3.49	28	9	0	3	45	7	4	.704	3	1	0	3	4	0	0	1	4.22	4.22	4.88
Valverde J.	18	49.3	223	44	0	4.14	69	22	3	2	50	6	0	.629	1	0	0	2	3	18	22	1	5.84	5.84	3.28
Hernandez O.	15	45.7	204	9	9	4.13	52	20	3	4	52	8	7	.633	3	3	0	2	4	0	0	0	6.31	6.11	4.60
Grimsley J.	9	27.7	118	19	0	3.33	10	8	2	0	30	4	5	.719	0	0	0	1	2	0	0	0	4.88	4.88	5.03
Pena T.	9	30.7	135	25	0	3.53	21	8	0	0	36	6	1	.670	0	1	0	3	4	1	1	2	6.16	5.58	5.17
Choate R.	6	16.0	75	30	0	3.69	12	3	0	3	21	0	2	.632	0	0	0	0	1	0	0	5	5.06	3.94	2.84
Daigle C.	6	12.3	52	10	0	3.71	7	6	0	0	14	1	5	.658	0	0	0	0	0	0	0	2	3.65	3.65	4.60
Ortiz R.	5	22.7	113	6	6	4.07	21	22	1	1	27	3	3	.621	4	2	3	0	5	0	0	0	8.34	7.54	6.00
Koplove M.	1	3.0	15	2	0	3.87	1	2	0	0	5	0	0	.583	2	0	0	0	0	0	0	0	3.00	3.00	4.55
Nippert D.	1	10.0	51	2	2	3.90	9	7	0	0	15	5	2	.633	1	0	0	0	2	0	0	0	11.70	11.70	10.02
Jarvis K.	1	11.3	58	5	1	3.26	6	5	0	1	18	2	0	.636	2	0	0	0	1	0	0	0	11.91	11.91	6.04
Mulholland T	0	3.0	17	5	0	3.24	1	1	0	0	7	1	0	.571	0	0	0	0	0	0	1	1	9.00	9.00	7.88
Bajenaru J.	0	1.0	7	1	0	2.86	0	0	0	0	4	3	0	.750	0	0	0	0	1	0	1	0	36.00	36.00	42.22
Slaten D.	0	5.7	21	9	0	3.33	3	2	1	0	3	0	1	.813	0	0	0	0	0	0	0	2	0.00	0.00	2.69

Batted Ball Pitching Stats

Player	PA	% of PA		% of Batted Balls			IF/F	HR/OF	Runs Per Event				Total Runs vs. Avg.				
		K%	BB%	GB%	LD%	FB%			NIP	GB	LD	OF	NIP	GB	LD	FB	Tot
Webb B.	950	19	6	66	17	16	.07	.13	-.00	.02	.40	.27	-14	-1	-5	-13	-32
Cruz J.	413	21	14	40	23	37	.10	.07	.07	.01	.47	.07	5	-5	5	-12	-8
Vizcaino L.	272	26	12	45	19	36	.08	.15	.03	.06	.41	.18	-0	0	-2	-2	-5
Julio J.	189	29	13	36	23	41	.00	.14	.03	-.01	.31	.22	-0	-3	-3	2	-4
Medders B.	316	15	9	42	20	38	.10	.06	.07	.06	.43	.07	1	1	3	-9	-4
Hernandez L.	298	13	9	33	21	45	.09	.08	.08	.04	.31	.13	1	-0	-2	-2	-3
Lyon B.	293	16	8	43	24	33	.08	.11	.04	.01	.41	.16	-2	-3	5	-2	-2
Valverde J.	223	31	11	35	24	41	.08	.10	.01	.10	.57	.11	-3	1	5	-5	-1
Gonzalez E.	462	14	8	44	19	37	.12	.12	.05	.04	.37	.21	-1	-1	-1	2	-1
Grimsley J.	118	8	7	57	18	26	.20	.15	.09	.02	.42	.25	0	-1	1	-1	-1
Batista M.	910	12	10	52	20	28	.10	.09	.09	.03	.40	.17	6	-0	5	-11	1
Gonzalez E.	182	15	7	38	15	47	.11	.12	.03	.07	.49	.20	-1	1	-0	3	2
Aquino G.	220	23	13	48	22	30	.10	.21	.05	.06	.38	.36	1	1	-0	4	5
Pena A.	135	16	6	39	22	39	.10	.17	.01	.09	.41	.29	-1	1	2	4	5
Ortiz R.	113	19	20	40	22	37	.00	.12	.13	.05	.44	.32	4	0	0	3	8
Hernandez O.	204	25	12	32	21	47	.24	.18	.03	.04	.52	.39	-0	-1	2	7	8
MLB Average		17	9	44	20	37	.11	.11	.05	.04	.39	.19	-	-	-	-	-

Fielding Stats

Name	POS	INN	SBA/G	CS%	ERA	WP+PB/G	PO	A	TE	FE
Estrada, J.	C	924.7	0.85	24%	4.45	0.350	686	47	2	0
Snyder, C.	C	495.0	0.62	38%	4.55	0.455	394	35	1	0
Montero, M.	C	40.0	0.90	25%	4.73	0.675	36	4	0	0

Name	POS	Inn	PO	A	TE	FE	FPct	RF	DPS	DPT
Jackson, C.	1B	1078.0	1107	81	3	9	.990	9.92	12	0
Clark, T.	1B	256.3	274	21	0	2	.993	10.36	4	1
Green, S.	1B	96.0	105	6	0	0	1.000	10.41	0	0
Tracy, C.	1B	21.3	23	1	0	1	.960	10.13	0	0
Easley, D.	1B	6.3	6	1	0	0	1.000	9.95	0	0
Hammock, R.	1B	1.0	2	0	0	0	1.000	18.00	0	0
Hudson, O.	2B	1349.0	311	510	7	6	.984	5.48	49	65
Easley, D.	2B	46.7	16	16	0	0	1.000	6.17	2	5
Callaspo, A.	2B	26.0	7	11	1	0	.947	6.23	3	0
Green, A.	2B	22.0	2	8	0	0	1.000	4.09	2	0
Counsell, C.	2B	16.0	5	7	0	0	1.000	6.75	0	0
Counsell, C.	SS	736.7	127	296	1	8	.979	5.17	36	36
Drew, S.	SS	480.3	73	150	1	4	.978	4.18	18	14
Easley, D.	SS	204.7	23	58	1	1	.976	3.56	7	1
Callaspo, A.	SS	34.0	4	9	1	0	.929	3.44	2	0
Green, A.	SS	4.0	0	1	1	0	.500	2.25	0	0
Tracy, C.	3B	1278.0	101	260	13	12	.935	2.54	26	1
Easley, D.	3B	121.7	10	18	1	2	.903	2.07	2	0
Green, A.	3B	32.0	1	8	0	0	1.000	2.53	0	0
Counsell, C.	3B	23.0	2	6	0	0	1.000	3.13	0	0
Callaspo, A.	3B	5.0	1	1	0	0	1.000	3.60	0	0

Name	POS	Inn	PO	A	TE	FE	FPct	RF	DPS	DPT
Gonzalez, L.	LF	1315.0	256	3	1	0	.996	1.77	2	0
Byrnes, E.	LF	43.3	10	0	0	0	1.000	2.08	0	0
Green, A.	LF	38.0	10	0	0	0	1.000	2.37	0	0
DaVanon, J.	LF	28.0	7	0	0	1	.875	2.25	0	0
Hairston, S.	LF	24.3	8	0	0	0	1.000	2.96	0	0
Quentin, C.	LF	11.0	1	0	0	0	1.000	0.82	0	0
Byrnes, E.	CF	1051.0	270	5	0	1	.996	2.35	2	0
DaVanon, J.	CF	259.3	62	0	0	1	.984	2.15	0	0
Young, C.	CF	149.3	50	1	0	0	1.000	3.07	0	0
Green, S.	RF	857.3	164	1	1	1	.988	1.73	2	0
Quentin, C.	RF	389.0	96	3	1	1	.980	2.29	0	0
DaVanon, J.	RF	120.3	23	0	0	0	1.000	1.72	0	0
Byrnes, E.	RF	86.0	17	0	0	0	1.000	1.78	0	0
Easley, D.	RF	7.0	0	0	0	0	0.000	0.00	0	0

Batted Ball Batting Stats

Player	PA	% of PA		% of Batted Balls					Runs Per Event				Total Runs vs. Avg.				
		K%	BB%	GB%	LD%	FB%	IF/F	HR/OF	NIP	GB	LD	OF	NIP	GB	LD	FB	Tot
Hudson O.	650	12	10	49	19	32	.10	.10	.09	.05	.41	.20	4	4	2	-0	10
Jackson C.	556	13	11	38	21	41	.09	.08	.10	.06	.37	.15	6	1	1	-0	8
Drew S.	226	22	6	36	24	40	.09	.09	-.01	.12	.42	.24	-4	3	3	4	7
Gonzalez L.	668	9	11	40	19	41	.15	.08	.15	.04	.39	.14	11	-0	3	-7	7
Byrnes E.	606	15	6	38	18	44	.26	.15	.03	.09	.40	.22	-5	7	1	2	6
Quentin C.	191	18	12	46	17	37	.26	.19	.07	.03	.41	.40	2	-1	-1	5	5
Tracy C.	662	19	9	36	21	43	.10	.09	.03	.04	.43	.18	-3	-4	6	5	5
DaVanon J.	256	16	12	51	20	29	.06	.10	.08	.06	.47	.17	2	2	3	-3	4
Green S.	462	14	9	56	19	25	.01	.13	.07	.05	.34	.23	1	3	-3	-0	2
Easley D.	220	14	12	45	15	40	.23	.18	.10	.08	.22	.25	3	2	-7	1	-0
Snyder C.	213	18	11	45	22	33	.10	.14	.06	.03	.40	.19	1	-1	1	-1	-1
Estrada J.	443	9	5	39	20	41	.04	.07	.04	.03	.39	.11	-4	-1	6	-3	-2
Green A.	102	20	13	45	15	40	.25	.06	.07	.07	.30	.09	1	2	-3	-3	-4
Clark T.	147	27	10	38	22	40	.11	.18	.01	-.05	.31	.25	-1	-4	-2	2	-5
Counsell C.	415	11	10	48	20	31	.24	.04	.10	.03	.38	.09	3	-1	1	-12	-9
MLB Average		17	9	44	20	37	.11	.11	.05	.04	.39	.19	-	-	-	-	-

Atlanta Braves

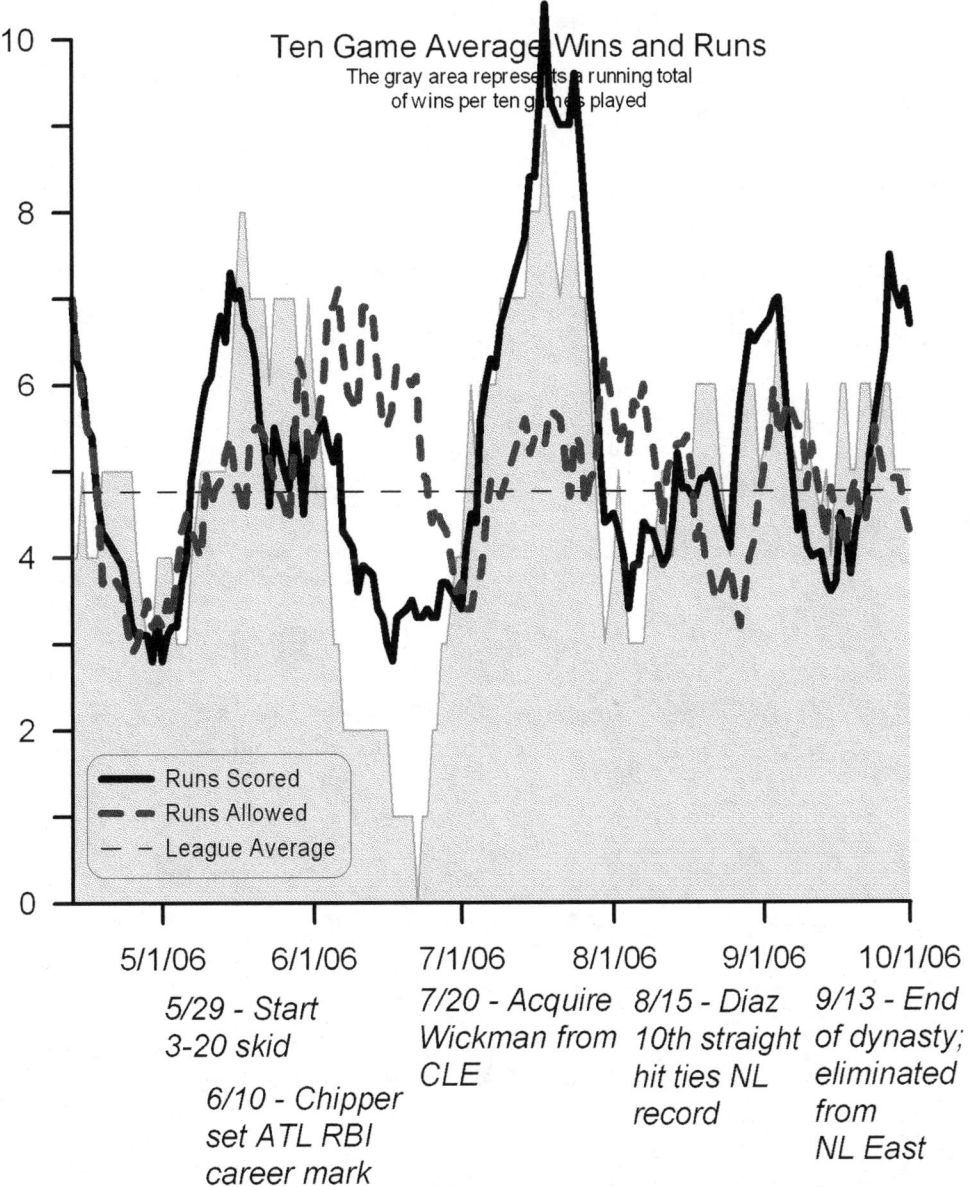

Ten Game Average Wins and Runs
The gray area represents a running total
of wins per ten games played

Runs Scored
Runs Allowed
League Average

5/1/06   6/1/06   7/1/06   8/1/06   9/1/06   10/1/06

5/29 - Start
3-20 skid

6/10 - Chipper
set ATL RBI
career mark

7/20 - Acquire
Wickman from
CLE

8/15 - Diaz
10th straight
hit ties NL
record

9/13 - End
of dynasty;
eliminated
from
NL East

Team Batting and Pitching/Fielding Stats by Month						
	April	May	June	July	Aug	Sept/Oct
Wins	10	18	6	14	15	16
Losses	14	11	21	10	13	14
OBP	.314	.352	.310	.368	.351	.322
SLG	.426	.453	.377	.553	.474	.451
FIP	4.58	4.29	5.47	4.71	3.93	4.43
DER	.699	.683	.704	.660	.701	.686

Batting Stats

Player	RC	Runs	RBI	PA	Outs	P/PA	H	2B	3B	HR	TB	K	BB	IBB	HBP	SH	SF	SB	CS	GDP	BA	OBP	SLG	GPA
Jones A.	107	107	129	669	431	3.91	148	29	0	41	300	127	82	9	13	0	9	4	1	13	.262	.363	.531	.299
McCann B.	94	61	93	492	307	3.64	147	34	0	24	253	54	41	8	3	0	6	2	0	12	.333	.388	.572	.320
Jones C.	93	87	86	477	291	3.74	133	28	3	26	245	73	61	4	1	0	4	6	1	12	.324	.409	.596	.336
Francoeur J.	91	83	103	686	504	3.32	169	24	6	29	292	132	23	6	9	0	3	1	6	16	.260	.293	.449	.246
Renteria E.	89	100	70	673	446	3.80	175	40	2	14	261	89	62	0	3	8	2	17	6	17	.293	.361	.436	.274
LaRoche A.	83	89	90	557	363	3.87	140	38	1	32	276	128	55	5	2	1	7	0	2	9	.285	.354	.561	.302
Giles M.	82	87	60	626	423	3.88	144	32	2	11	213	105	62	0	6	5	3	10	5	12	.262	.341	.387	.252
Langerhans R.	45	46	28	369	250	3.98	76	16	3	7	119	91	50	8	3	0	1	1	2	9	.241	.350	.378	.254
Diaz M.	40	37	32	323	214	3.45	97	15	4	7	141	49	11	3	9	1	4	5	5	9	.327	.364	.475	.285
Betemit W.	34	30	29	219	148	4.17	56	16	0	9	99	57	19	3	0	1	0	2	1	4	.281	.344	.497	.281
Orr P.	16	22	8	164	120	3.30	39	3	4	1	53	30	5	1	0	5	0	2	4	1	.253	.277	.344	.212
Aybar W.	14	17	8	127	83	3.39	36	6	0	1	45	19	10	0	1	1	0	0	2	2	.313	.373	.391	.268
Thorman S.	14	13	14	133	98	3.31	30	11	0	5	56	21	5	0	0	0	0	1	0	0	.234	.263	.438	.230
Pratt T.	12	14	19	152	111	4.14	28	6	0	4	46	43	12	0	1	1	3	1	0	4	.207	.272	.341	.209
Prado M.	9	3	9	49	33	4.04	11	1	1	1	17	7	5	0	0	2	0	0	0	2	.262	.340	.405	.256
Jordan B.	7	11	10	101	73	3.50	21	2	0	3	32	23	7	0	1	0	2	0	0	3	.231	.287	.352	.219
Ward D.	7	2	7	27	18	4.11	8	1	0	1	12	6	1	0	0	0	0	0	0	0	.308	.333	.462	.268
Pena B.	4	9	5	43	32	3.26	11	2	0	1	16	5	2	0	0	0	0	0	0	2	.268	.302	.390	.236
Thomson J.	3	1	4	32	22	3.78	8	2	0	0	10	10	0	0	0	2	0	0	0	0	.267	.267	.333	.205
Pena T.	3	12	3	46	35	3.70	10	2	0	1	15	10	2	1	0	0	0	0	0	1	.227	.261	.341	.204
Sosa J.	1	4	3	28	17	3.46	3	0	0	3	12	8	2	0	0	6	0	0	0	0	.150	.227	.600	.254
Shiell J.	-0	0	0	6	4	4.00	0	0	0	0	0	3	1	0	0	1	0	0	0	0	.000	.200	.000	.091
Ray K.	-0	0	0	1	1	4.00	0	0	0	0	0	0	0	0	0	0	0	0	0	0	.000	.000	.000	.000
Paronto C.	-0	0	0	1	1	4.00	0	0	0	0	0	1	0	0	0	0	0	0	0	0	.000	.000	.000	.000
Smith T.	-0	0	0	1	1	5.00	0	0	0	0	0	1	0	0	0	0	0	0	0	0	.000	.000	.000	.000
Barry K.	-0	0	0	2	2	5.00	0	0	0	0	0	1	0	0	0	0	0	0	0	0	.000	.000	.000	.000
Cormier L.	-1	0	0	14	11	3.36	1	0	0	0	1	4	0	0	0	2	0	0	0	0	.083	.083	.083	.059
Villarreal O.	-1	0	0	9	8	2.89	0	0	0	0	0	3	0	0	0	2	0	0	0	1	.000	.000	.000	.000
Ramirez H.	-1	2	0	28	21	3.79	3	0	0	0	3	2	1	0	0	3	0	0	0	0	.125	.160	.125	.104
Smoltz J.	-1	5	4	86	58	3.31	8	3	0	0	11	27	4	0	0	18	0	0	0	2	.125	.176	.172	.123
Hudson T.	-2	4	3	79	57	3.32	6	1	0	0	7	18	2	0	0	14	0	0	0	0	.095	.123	.111	.084
Davies K.	-2	1	1	24	22	3.67	1	0	0	1	4	8	0	0	0	1	0	0	0	0	.043	.043	.174	.064
James C.	-3	2	0	40	35	3.63	1	0	0	0	1	14	1	0	0	4	0	0	0	1	.029	.056	.029	.032

Italicized stats have been adjusted for home park.

Batted Ball Batting Stats are listed at end of fielding stats

Pitching Stats

Player	PRC	IP	BFP	G	GS	P/PA	K	BB	IBB	HBP	H	HR	DP	DER	SB	CS	PO	W	L	Sv	Op	Hld	RA	ERA	FIP
Smoltz J.	124	232.0	960	35	35	3.68	211	55	4	9	221	23	22	.690	10	4	0	16	9	0	0	0	3.61	3.49	3.46
Hudson T.	74	218.3	959	35	35	3.56	141	79	10	9	235	25	22	.689	23	4	2	13	12	0	0	0	5.32	4.86	4.49
James C.	55	119.0	504	25	18	3.88	91	47	2	6	101	20	6	.753	14	3	1	11	4	0	0	0	4.08	3.78	5.16
Villarreal O.	41	92.3	397	58	4	3.47	55	27	3	5	93	13	9	.714	4	1	1	9	1	0	4	2	4.00	3.61	4.80
Paronto C.	28	56.7	237	65	0	3.86	41	19	3	3	53	5	7	.698	2	4	1	2	3	0	2	8	3.65	3.18	3.92
Ray K.	26	67.7	299	69	0	3.95	50	38	4	0	66	9	6	.713	5	4	0	1	1	5	8	7	4.79	4.52	4.98
Ramirez H.	26	76.3	337	14	14	3.61	37	31	2	4	85	6	14	.680	5	1	0	5	5	0	0	0	4.95	4.48	4.57
Sosa J.	25	87.3	394	26	13	3.80	58	32	5	1	105	20	6	.696	1	1	0	3	10	3	6	0	6.29	5.46	5.83
McBride M.	24	56.7	249	71	0	3.84	46	32	4	1	53	2	8	.679	0	0	0	4	1	1	2	10	4.45	3.65	3.59
Cormier L.	24	73.7	333	29	9	3.67	43	39	7	2	90	8	16	.656	5	3	0	4	5	0	0	2	5.38	4.89	4.85
Yates T.	24	50.0	217	56	0	3.74	46	31	8	0	42	6	7	.716	2	0	0	2	5	1	6	12	4.14	3.96	4.32
Thomson J.	23	80.3	361	18	15	3.57	46	32	4	2	93	11	8	.685	11	4	0	2	7	0	0	1	6.16	4.82	4.97
Wickman B.	19	26.0	107	28	0	3.82	25	2	0	0	24	1	1	.671	1	0	0	0	2	18	19	0	2.42	1.04	2.03
Davies K.	13	63.3	312	14	14	3.97	51	33	0	3	90	14	5	.626	4	1	1	3	7	0	0	0	8.53	8.38	6.19
Remlinger M.	10	22.3	104	36	0	3.87	19	9	2	2	27	2	3	.639	0	0	0	2	4	2	5	2	4.43	4.03	3.89
Barry K.	9	25.7	115	19	1	3.82	19	14	0	1	24	2	0	.722	5	0	0	1	1	0	1	1	5.61	5.61	4.50
Moylan P.	6	15.0	68	15	0	3.60	14	5	1	0	18	1	1	.625	2	0	0	0	0	0	0	0	4.80	4.80	3.02
Reitsma C.	5	28.0	142	27	0	3.35	13	8	3	3	46	7	0	.649	1	0	0	1	2	8	12	3	8.68	8.68	6.40
Baez D.	4	10.0	44	11	0	4.30	10	6	1	1	7	0	0	.741	1	0	0	0	1	0	1	6	5.40	5.40	3.02
Stockman P.	3	4.0	19	4	0	4.74	4	4	2	0	3	0	0	.727	2	0	0	0	0	0	0	0	2.25	2.25	2.72
Shiell J.	3	15.7	80	4	3	4.01	9	5	1	1	23	5	1	.647	1	0	0	0	2	0	0	0	8.62	8.62	7.30
Franklin W.	2	7.7	35	11	0	4.03	3	6	2	0	8	2	2	.750	2	0	0	0	0	0	0	1	7.04	7.04	7.39
Devine J.	1	6.3	36	10	0	4.67	10	9	1	1	8	1	1	.533	0	0	0	0	0	0	1	0	9.95	9.95	6.38
Smith T.	1	4.3	19	1	1	3.63	1	1	0	0	5	0	1	.647	0	0	0	0	1	0	0	0	8.31	4.15	3.45
Lerew A.	0	2.0	15	1	0	3.93	1	3	0	1	5	0	0	.500	0	0	0	0	0	0	0	0	22.50	22.50	8.22
Boyer B.	0	0.7	7	2	0	4.00	0	1	0	0	4	0	0	.333	0	0	0	0	0	0	0	1	40.50	40.50	7.72

Batted Ball Pitching Stats

Player	PA	% of PA		% of Batted Balls			IF/F	HR/OF	Runs Per Event				Total Runs vs. Avg.				
		K%	BB%	GB%	LD%	FB%			NIP	GB	LD	OF	NIP	GB	LD	FB	Tot
Smoltz J.	960	22	7	46	20	33	.08	.11	-.01	.05	.34	.20	-15	0	-6	-2	-22
Wickman B.	107	23	2	47	21	32	.20	.05	-.08	.09	.34	.04	-4	2	-0	-4	-7
James C.	504	18	11	28	19	53	.10	.12	.06	.04	.34	.16	1	-4	-5	2	-5
Paronto C.	237	17	9	43	25	32	.06	.10	.05	.08	.24	.13	-0	2	-3	-4	-5
McBride M.	249	18	13	47	20	33	.13	.04	.08	.02	.47	.11	3	-2	2	-6	-4
Ramirez H.	337	11	10	54	20	26	.10	.10	.11	.02	.41	.14	3	-2	3	-7	-2
Villarreal O.	397	14	8	47	19	34	.07	.10	.06	.04	.37	.18	-0	-1	-0	0	-1
Ray K.	299	17	13	37	19	44	.11	.11	.08	.05	.34	.17	3	-1	-3	-1	-1
Yates T.	217	21	14	41	22	37	.04	.13	.07	.01	.35	.21	3	-3	-1	1	-1
Barry K.	115	17	13	33	17	50	.18	.06	.09	.09	.34	.20	1	0	-2	1	0
Remlinger M.	104	18	11	38	29	33	.09	.10	.06	.11	.36	.09	0	1	1	-3	0
Hudson T.	959	15	9	58	18	24	.10	.14	.06	.05	.43	.22	2	7	3	-9	3
Thomson J.	361	13	9	44	21	36	.05	.12	.08	.05	.35	.19	2	1	-1	1	3
Cormier L.	333	13	12	50	21	29	.06	.12	.11	.03	.39	.24	5	-0	2	1	8
Reitsma C.	142	9	8	50	20	30	.18	.25	.10	.09	.41	.42	0	3	2	5	11
Sosa J.	394	15	8	36	23	41	.11	.18	.05	.07	.37	.23	-0	2	4	7	12
Davies K.	312	16	12	37	24	39	.09	.17	.08	.11	.40	.28	2	5	4	7	19
MLB Average		17	9	44	20	37	.11	.11	.05	.04	.39	.19	-	-	-	-	-

Fielding Stats

Name	POS	INN	SBA/G	CS%	ERA	WP+PB/G	PO	A	TE	FE
McCann, B.	C	1016.3	0.80	22%	4.41	0.301	779	38	5	4
Pratt, T.	C	354.0	0.89	20%	5.19	0.331	279	11	3	0
Pena, B.	C	71.0	0.38	0%	4.31	0.000	30	2	0	0

Name	POS	Inn	PO	A	TE	FE	FPct	RF	DPS	DPT
LaRoche, A.	1B	1153.0	1116	96	1	4	.996	9.46	14	0
Jordan, B.	1B	142.7	137	9	1	1	.986	9.21	1	0
Thorman, S.	1B	118.3	111	9	0	1	.992	9.13	1	0
Ward, D.	1B	27.0	26	2	0	0	1.000	9.33	0	0
Giles, M.	2B	1149.0	259	368	7	4	.983	4.91	36	47
Orr, P.	2B	161.7	31	63	0	0	1.000	5.23	4	8
Betemit, W.	2B	69.0	26	20	0	0	1.000	6.00	1	6
Prado, M.	2B	61.0	15	26	0	1	.976	6.05	1	3
Renteria, E.	SS	1265.0	185	399	6	7	.978	4.15	39	34
Betemit, W.	SS	92.0	20	33	1	4	.914	5.18	3	6
Pena, T.	SS	84.0	14	28	0	1	.977	4.50	3	4
Jones, C.	3B	888.3	87	177	9	9	.936	2.67	21	2
Aybar, W.	3B	241.3	14	40	1	1	.947	2.01	4	1
Betemit, W.	3B	203.7	8	40	1	2	.941	2.12	8	1
Orr, P.	3B	64.0	5	15	0	0	1.000	2.81	1	0
Prado, M.	3B	38.0	2	4	0	1	.857	1.42	0	0
Pena, T.	3B	3.0	0	0	0	0	0.000	0.00	0	0
Pena, B.	3B	3.0	0	1	0	0	1.000	3.00	0	0

Name	POS	Inn	PO	A	TE	FE	FPct	RF	DPS	DPT
Langerhans, R.	LF	706.0	156	2	1	0	.994	2.01	0	0
Diaz, M.	LF	587.3	163	5	1	3	.977	2.57	2	0
Thorman, S.	LF	131.0	19	1	0	0	1.000	1.37	0	0
Jordan, B.	LF	14.0	3	0	0	0	1.000	1.93	0	0
Ward, D.	LF	3.0	1	0	0	0	1.000	3.00	0	0
Jones, A.	CF	1317.0	377	4	0	2	.995	2.60	2	0
Langerhans, R.	CF	116.0	40	0	0	0	1.000	3.10	0	0
Jordan, B.	CF	5.0	3	0	0	0	1.000	5.40	0	0
Francoeur, J.	CF	3.0	1	0	0	0	1.000	3.00	0	0
Francoeur, J.	RF	1421.0	317	12	3	6	.973	2.08	8	0
Diaz, M.	RF	13.0	3	0	0	0	1.000	2.08	0	0
Langerhans, R.	RF	5.0	0	0	0	0	0.000	0.00	0	0
Jordan, B.	RF	1.7	0	0	0	0	0.000	0.00	0	0

Batted Ball Batting Stats

Player	PA	% of PA		% of Batted Balls					Runs Per Event				Total Runs vs. Avg.				
		K%	BB%	GB%	LD%	FB%	IF/F	HR/OF	NIP	GB	LD	OF	NIP	GB	LD	FB	Tot
Jones C.	477	15	13	41	19	40	.03	.19	.10	.07	.45	.30	7	3	3	19	31
McCann B.	492	11	9	35	22	43	.10	.14	.09	.02	.44	.26	2	-5	11	17	26
Jones A.	669	19	14	39	19	42	.16	.26	.08	.02	.37	.36	10	-5	-6	25	23
LaRoche A.	557	23	10	38	21	41	.04	.22	.03	.00	.41	.39	-2	-8	2	31	23
Diaz M.	323	15	6	50	24	27	.06	.10	.02	.08	.37	.24	-3	5	4	1	6
Renteria E.	673	13	10	47	22	31	.08	.10	.08	.04	.42	.17	3	-1	10	-6	6
Betemit W.	219	26	9	38	23	39	.05	.15	.00	.03	.41	.34	-3	-2	1	9	5
Aybar W.	127	15	9	43	16	42	.05	.03	.06	.10	.35	.15	-0	2	-2	0	1
Thorman S.	133	16	4	40	17	43	.07	.12	-.02	.05	.33	.20	-2	0	-1	2	-1
Langerhans R.	369	25	14	41	21	38	.10	.08	.06	.05	.42	.15	3	0	-1	-5	-3
Francoeur J.	686	19	5	45	18	37	.21	.17	-.02	.05	.39	.27	-13	2	-1	8	-4
Jordan B.	101	23	8	40	14	46	.19	.12	.01	.03	.31	.18	-1	-0	-2	-0	-4
Giles M.	626	17	11	42	22	36	.03	.07	.07	.04	.36	.13	3	-1	-0	-8	-6
Pratt T.	152	28	9	41	18	41	.08	.08	-.01	.02	.39	.14	-2	-1	-2	-2	-7
Orr P.	164	18	3	53	23	25	.13	.04	-.05	.07	.25	.11	-4	3	-2	-4	-8
MLB Average		17	9	44	20	37	.11	.11	.05	.04	.39	.19	-	-	-	-	-

Baltimore Orioles

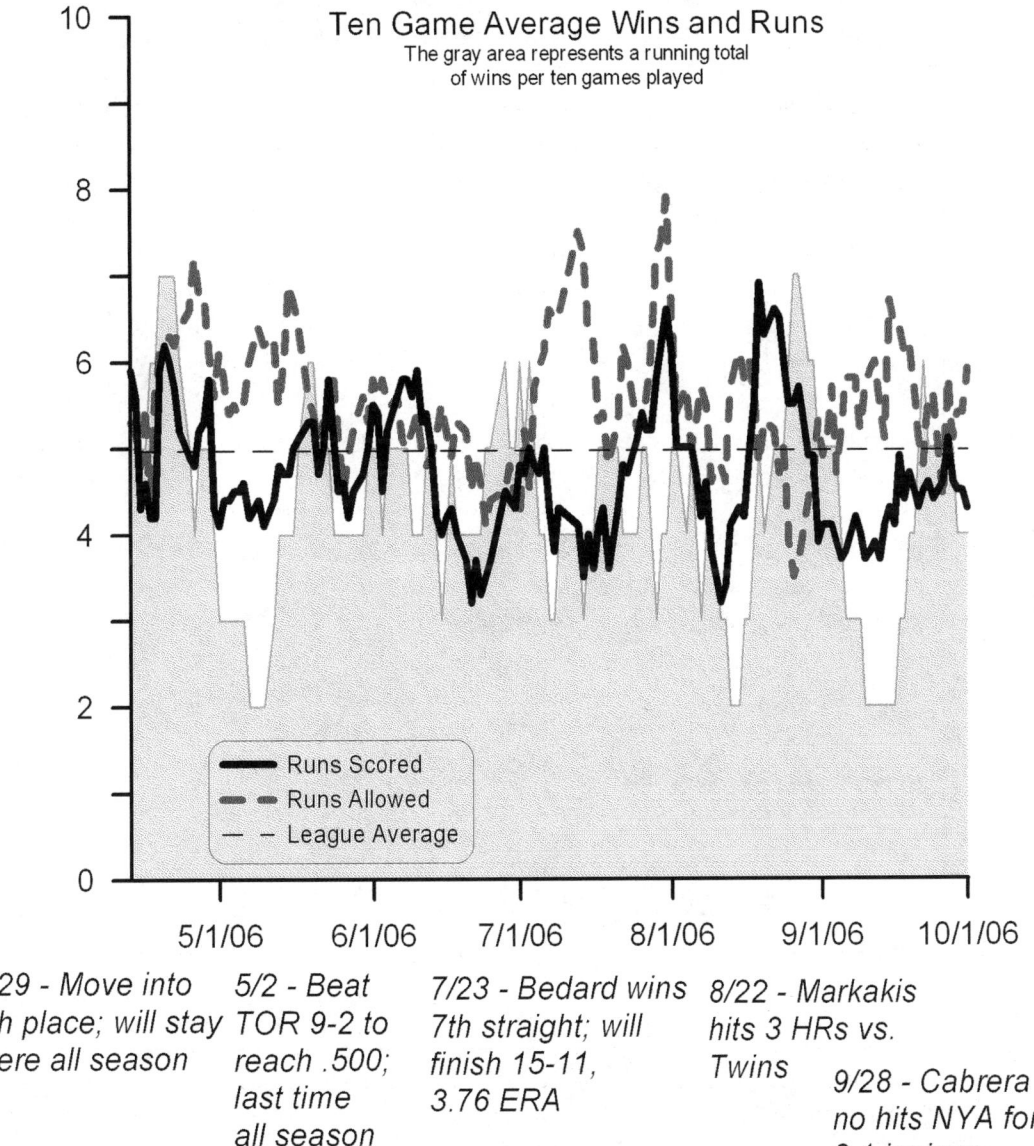

Ten Game Average Wins and Runs
The gray area represents a running total
of wins per ten games played

Legend:
- Runs Scored
- Runs Allowed
- League Average

4/29 - Move into 4th place; will stay there all season

5/2 - Beat TOR 9-2 to reach .500; last time all season

7/23 - Bedard wins 7th straight; will finish 15-11, 3.76 ERA

8/22 - Markakis hits 3 HRs vs. Twins

9/28 - Cabrera no hits NYA for 8.1 innings

Team Batting and Pitching/Fielding Stats by Month						
	April	May	June	July	Aug	Sept/Oct
Wins	13	12	12	11	12	10
Losses	13	15	16	15	14	19
OBP	.331	.334	.340	.356	.331	.343
SLG	.444	.418	.411	.417	.417	.435
FIP	5.47	5.35	4.77	5.35	4.65	4.98
DER	.694	.696	.693	.650	.693	.662

Batting Stats

Italicized stats have been adjusted for home park.

Player	RC	Runs	RBI	PA	Outs	P/PA	H	2B	3B	HR	TB	K	BB	IBB	HBP	SH	SF	SB	CS	GDP	BA	OBP	SLG	GPA
Tejada M.	104	99	100	709	464	3.51	214	37	0	24	323	79	46	10	9	0	6	6	2	28	.330	.379	.498	.301
Mora M.	97	96	83	705	463	3.97	171	25	0	16	244	99	54	1	14	6	7	11	1	9	.274	.342	.391	.257
Hernandez R.	86	66	91	560	376	3.70	138	29	2	23	240	79	43	2	11	0	5	1	0	13	.275	.343	.479	.280
Roberts B.	77	85	55	630	425	3.84	161	34	3	10	231	66	55	4	0	6	5	36	7	16	.286	.347	.410	.264
Millar K.	70	64	64	503	328	4.09	117	26	0	15	188	74	59	3	12	0	2	1	1	14	.272	.374	.437	.283
Markakis N.	70	72	62	542	363	3.69	143	25	2	16	220	72	43	3	3	3	2	2	0	15	.291	.351	.448	.275
Patterson C.	68	75	53	499	344	3.16	128	19	5	16	205	94	21	5	5	8	1	45	9	0	.276	.314	.443	.257
Gibbons J.	53	34	46	378	260	3.64	95	23	0	13	157	48	32	2	2	0	1	0	0	12	.277	.341	.458	.274
Conine J.	47	43	49	432	300	3.70	103	20	3	9	156	53	35	2	2	1	5	3	2	12	.265	.325	.401	.252
Lopez J.	35	30	31	299	210	3.58	74	15	1	8	115	60	18	0	2	0	0	0	0	5	.265	.314	.412	.250
Fahey B.	29	36	23	286	197	3.73	59	8	2	2	77	48	23	0	3	9	0	3	3	2	.235	.307	.307	.219
Gomez C.	22	14	17	142	96	3.51	45	7	0	2	58	11	7	1	3	0	0	1	2	7	.341	.387	.439	.290
Newhan D.	11	14	18	143	104	3.19	33	4	0	4	49	22	7	1	2	0	3	4	2	4	.252	.294	.374	.230
Tatis F.	9	7	8	64	44	3.75	14	6	1	2	28	17	6	1	0	0	2	0	0	2	.250	.313	.500	.271
Matos L.	7	14	5	134	99	3.57	25	7	1	2	40	21	10	0	2	1	0	7	0	3	.207	.278	.331	.212
Fiorentino J.	7	8	7	50	30	3.74	10	2	0	0	12	3	7	0	1	2	1	1	0	1	.256	.375	.308	.251
Terrero L.	3	4	6	42	35	3.69	8	1	0	1	12	7	1	0	1	0	0	0	3	0	.200	.238	.300	.186
Rogers E.	2	1	2	26	20	3.12	5	0	0	0	5	3	0	0	0	0	1	0	0	0	.200	.192	.200	.139
Ortiz R.	2	1	2	3	0	3.00	2	0	0	0	2	0	1	0	0	0	0	0	0	0	1.000	1.000	1.000	.715
Clark H.	1	1	0	10	6	3.90	1	0	0	0	1	2	2	0	0	1	0	0	0	0	.143	.333	.143	.190
Chen B.	1	0	0	1	0	4.00	1	0	0	0	1	0	0	0	0	0	0	0	0	0	1.000	1.000	1.000	.715
Widger C.	1	0	2	20	16	4.25	2	0	0	0	2	4	2	0	0	1	0	0	0	1	.118	.211	.118	.127
Chavez R.	0	1	0	29	23	3.17	5	0	0	0	5	4	1	0	0	0	0	0	0	0	.179	.207	.179	.141
Ardoin D.	0	2	1	15	13	4.20	1	0	0	0	1	6	1	0	1	0	0	0	0	1	.077	.200	.077	.111
Cabrera D.	-0	0	0	2	1	3.50	0	0	0	0	0	1	0	0	0	1	0	0	0	0	.000	.000	.000	.000
Lopez R.	-0	0	0	3	2	3.00	0	0	0	0	0	2	0	0	0	1	0	0	0	0	.000	.000	.000	.000
Bedard E.	-0	0	0	2	2	1.50	0	0	0	0	0	0	0	0	0	0	0	0	0	0	.000	.000	.000	.000
Loewen A.	-0	0	0	2	2	2.50	0	0	0	0	0	0	0	0	0	0	0	0	0	0	.000	.000	.000	.000
Benson K.	-1	1	2	9	8	3.11	1	0	0	1	4	3	0	0	0	0	0	0	0	0	.111	.111	.444	.164

Batted Ball Batting Stats

Player	PA	% of PA		% of Batted Balls			IF/F	HR/OF	Runs Per Event				Total Runs vs. Avg.				
		K%	BB%	GB%	LD%	FB%			NIP	GB	LD	OF	NIP	GB	LD	FB	Tot
Tejada M.	709	11	8	51	22	27	.08	.17	.08	.06	.35	.25	1	8	6	4	18
Hernandez R.	560	14	10	44	19	38	.14	.16	.07	.03	.44	.24	2	-3	4	7	10
Millar K.	503	15	14	35	22	42	.11	.11	.11	-.00	.35	.19	9	-8	-0	4	5
Gibbons J.	378	13	9	38	16	46	.17	.12	.08	.04	.46	.18	1	-1	1	2	3
Gomez C.	142	8	7	51	21	28	.06	.06	.11	.06	.44	.12	0	1	3	-3	2
Markakis N.	542	13	8	51	20	29	.08	.13	.07	.05	.37	.20	0	3	0	-2	2
Patterson C.	499	19	5	39	21	40	.18	.14	-.01	.08	.38	.20	-8	12	-0	-1	2
Lopez J.	299	20	7	43	23	34	.09	.12	.00	.04	.36	.23	-4	-1	1	2	-1
Roberts B.	630	10	9	44	21	35	.03	.06	.10	.06	.39	.07	3	4	7	-15	-2
Mora M.	705	14	10	39	20	41	.11	.08	.07	.05	.35	.13	3	2	-2	-7	-4
Newhan D.	143	15	6	50	17	34	.14	.13	.02	.04	.28	.17	-1	1	-3	-1	-5
Conine J.	432	12	9	47	18	35	.08	.08	.08	.01	.42	.15	1	-4	2	-3	-5
Matos L.	134	16	9	44	16	41	.05	.05	.05	.03	.31	.08	-0	-0	-3	-3	-6
Fahey B.	286	17	9	56	21	23	.09	.05	.05	.02	.39	.06	-0	-3	1	-10	-13
MLB Average		17	9	44	20	37	.11	.11	.05	.04	.39	.19	-	-	-	-	-

Pitching Stats

Player	PRC	IP	BFP	G	GS	P/PA	K	BB	IBB	HBP	H	HR	DP	DER	SB	CS	PO	W	L	Sv	Op	Hld	RA	ERA	FIP
Bedard E.	94	196.3	844	33	33	3.91	171	69	0	5	196	16	20	.676	4	2	0	15	11	0	0	0	4.22	3.76	3.71
Cabrera D.	63	148.0	662	26	26	4.05	157	104	1	5	130	11	20	.681	11	5	0	9	10	0	0	0	4.99	4.74	4.30
Benson K.	63	183.0	781	30	30	3.65	88	58	2	7	199	33	22	.714	12	6	0	11	12	0	0	0	5.16	4.82	5.68
Lopez R.	59	189.0	847	36	29	3.61	136	59	2	4	234	32	15	.662	9	10	1	9	18	0	0	0	6.14	5.90	4.99
Ray C.	41	66.0	267	61	0	3.92	51	27	2	1	45	10	4	.798	0	2	0	4	4	33	38	0	3.00	2.73	4.87
Loewen A.	39	112.3	504	22	19	3.94	98	62	0	8	111	8	10	.674	11	7	3	6	6	0	0	1	5.77	5.37	4.31
Britton C.	28	53.7	221	52	0	3.90	41	17	3	0	46	4	3	.723	6	1	0	0	2	1	3	6	3.69	3.35	3.49
Chen B.	25	98.7	453	40	12	4.03	70	35	3	0	137	28	7	.653	9	6	3	0	7	0	0	1	7.39	6.93	6.51
Hawkins L.	24	60.3	261	60	0	3.69	27	15	3	2	73	4	7	.670	7	2	0	3	2	0	4	16	4.48	4.48	3.83
Williams T.	17	57.0	260	62	0	3.63	24	19	3	2	76	8	14	.647	2	1	0	2	4	1	5	13	5.68	4.74	5.19
Rleal S.	17	46.7	203	42	0	3.62	19	23	1	0	48	10	8	.742	0	0	0	1	1	0	1	3	4.82	4.44	6.65
Birkins K.	11	31.0	136	35	0	3.85	27	16	0	3	25	4	3	.721	0	1	1	5	2	0	1	4	5.52	4.94	5.04
Halama J.	8	29.3	132	17	1	3.53	12	13	2	0	38	6	5	.673	1	2	2	3	1	0	1	0	6.14	6.14	6.23
Ortiz R.	8	40.3	190	20	5	3.94	23	18	0	2	59	15	6	.659	0	3	0	0	3	0	0	0	8.70	8.48	8.44
Manon J.	7	20.0	103	22	0	4.02	22	16	1	2	23	5	0	.655	1	1	0	0	1	0	1	2	5.85	5.40	6.86
Burres B.	6	8.0	31	11	0	4.48	6	1	0	0	6	1	0	.783	2	0	0	0	0	0	0	4	2.25	2.25	3.76
Rodriguez E.	3	15.0	72	9	0	4.00	11	10	0	0	17	5	1	.739	1	0	0	1	1	0	0	0	8.40	7.20	8.13
Hoey J.	1	9.7	49	12	0	3.90	6	5	0	2	14	1	1	.629	1	0	0	0	1	0	1	4	10.24	10.24	5.54
Penn H.	1	19.7	112	6	6	3.69	8	13	0	2	38	8	2	.605	2	0	0	0	4	0	0	0	15.10	15.10	10.03
Brower J.	1	12.3	71	12	0	3.89	9	13	1	3	21	1	2	.556	0	1	0	0	1	0	1	1	13.86	13.86	6.51
Abreu W.	1	8.0	42	7	0	4.24	6	6	1	1	10	1	0	.643	0	0	0	0	0	0	0	0	11.25	10.13	5.64
DuBose E.	1	4.7	23	2	0	4.57	2	3	0	0	10	2	4	.500	0	0	0	0	0	0	0	0	9.64	9.64	9.91
Byrdak T.	1	7.0	42	16	0	4.00	2	8	1	0	14	2	2	.600	0	0	0	1	0	0	0	3	12.86	12.86	9.41
Johnson J.	0	3.0	21	1	1	4.43	0	3	0	1	9	1	0	.500	1	0	0	0	1	0	0	0	24.00	24.00	11.60

Batted Ball Pitching Stats

Player	PA	% of PA		% of Batted Balls					Runs Per Event				Total Runs vs. Avg.				
		K%	BB%	GB%	LD%	FB%	IF/F	HR/OF	NIP	GB	LD	OF	NIP	GB	LD	FB	Tot
Bedard E.	844	20	9	49	21	30	.08	.09	.03	.04	.40	.14	-5	-1	3	-15	-18
Ray C.	267	19	10	35	16	48	.09	.12	.05	.01	.28	.14	0	-3	-6	-1	-11
Cabrera D.	662	24	16	41	22	37	.10	.08	.07	.05	.36	.12	11	0	-6	-14	-9
Britton C.	221	19	8	31	19	50	.06	.05	.02	.09	.25	.10	-2	1	-5	-2	-7
Loewen A.	504	19	14	48	21	31	.07	.09	.08	.06	.37	.13	6	2	-2	-10	-4
Birkins K.	136	20	14	43	12	45	.05	.11	.08	.10	.34	.15	2	1	-4	-1	-2
Hawkins L.	261	10	6	44	21	35	.12	.06	.05	.09	.32	.14	-1	4	0	-3	0
Rleal S.	203	9	11	40	18	42	.12	.17	.14	-.00	.43	.20	3	-2	1	2	4
Manon J.	103	21	17	31	15	54	.15	.18	.09	.18	.33	.31	2	2	-3	4	6
Halama J.	132	9	10	49	20	31	.09	.20	.13	.04	.32	.36	1	0	-1	5	6
Williams T.	260	9	8	58	18	25	.08	.15	.10	.05	.42	.27	1	4	1	1	7
Benson K.	781	11	8	41	19	39	.08	.15	.08	.03	.33	.22	2	1	-5	12	10
Penn H.	112	7	13	38	21	40	.11	.25	.19	.19	.38	.36	3	5	1	6	15
Ortiz R.	190	12	11	35	25	39	.10	.29	.10	.07	.38	.40	2	1	3	12	18
Lopez R.	847	16	7	43	22	35	.07	.15	.03	.06	.41	.23	-5	6	11	9	22
Chen B.	453	15	8	33	21	47	.09	.18	.04	.09	.41	.28	-2	3	4	20	26
MLB Average		17	9	44	20	37	.11	.11	.05	.04	.39	.19	-	-	-	-	-

Fielding Stats

Name	POS	INN	SBA/G	CS%	ERA	WP+PB/G	PO	A	TE	FE
Hernandez, R.	C	1094.3	0.74	39%	5.24	0.493	793	69	12	0
Lopez, J.	C	171.7	1.05	10%	5.09	0.419	123	10	0	0
Chavez, R.	C	75.0	0.48	50%	7.44	0.360	60	5	1	0
Widger, C.	C	43.0	1.05	20%	5.23	0.000	32	3	0	0
Ardoin, D.	C	35.0	0.26	0%	5.91	0.771	35	1	0	0

Name	POS	Inn	PO	A	TE	FE	FPct	RF	DPS	DPT
Millar, K.	1B	792.3	764	62	1	3	.995	9.38	2	2
Conine, J.	1B	446.7	422	30	0	2	.996	9.11	1	0
Gomez, C.	1B	138.0	116	7	0	0	1.000	8.02	1	1
Tatis, F.	1B	34.0	40	2	0	0	1.000	11.12	0	0
Hernandez, R.	1B	5.0	5	0	0	0	1.000	9.00	0	0
Newhan, D.	1B	3.0	3	1	0	0	1.000	12.00	0	0
Roberts, B.	2B	1167.0	214	375	2	7	.985	4.54	50	49
Gomez, C.	2B	118.3	37	33	1	0	.986	5.32	1	8
Fahey, B.	2B	106.0	29	34	0	0	1.000	5.35	5	6
Rogers, E.	2B	22.0	3	5	0	0	1.000	3.27	0	2
Mora, M.	2B	3.0	0	2	0	0	1.000	6.00	0	0
Tatis, F.	2B	2.0	0	0	0	0	0.000	0.00	0	0
Tejada, M.	SS	1293.0	239	417	8	11	.972	4.57	60	45
Fahey, B.	SS	97.3	11	32	1	2	.935	3.98	11	2
Gomez, C.	SS	27.0	5	7	0	0	1.000	4.00	1	1
Rogers, E.	SS	1.0	0	0	0	0	0.000	0.00	0	0
Mora, M.	3B	1323.0	100	296	8	9	.959	2.69	19	1
Gomez, C.	3B	37.3	3	10	0	2	.867	3.13	1	0
Tatis, F.	3B	30.0	1	8	0	0	1.000	2.70	0	0
Rogers, E.	3B	18.0	1	1	0	1	.667	1.00	1	0
Fahey, B.	3B	5.7	1	1	0	0	1.000	3.18	0	0
Conine, J.	3B	3.0	0	0	0	0	0.000	0.00	0	0
Clark, H.	3B	2.0	0	0	0	0	0.000	0.00	0	0

Name	POS	Inn	PO	A	TE	FE	FPct	RF	DPS	DPT
Conine, J.	LF	429.3	84	5	0	1	.989	1.87	2	0
Fahey, B.	LF	372.0	101	2	2	3	.954	2.49	2	0
Markakis, N.	LF	197.3	59	1	0	1	.984	2.74	0	0
Matos, L.	LF	123.3	21	0	0	0	1.000	1.53	0	0
Newhan, D.	LF	120.0	25	0	0	2	.926	1.88	0	0
Fiorentino, J.	LF	104.0	28	3	0	0	1.000	2.68	2	0
Terrero, L.	LF	38.0	12	2	0	0	1.000	3.32	0	0
Tatis, F.	LF	22.0	3	1	0	0	1.000	1.64	0	0
Rogers, E.	LF	13.0	3	0	1	0	.750	2.08	0	0
Patterson, C.	CF	1078.0	345	7	0	4	.989	2.94	8	0
Newhan, D.	CF	161.3	34	0	0	0	1.000	1.90	0	0
Matos, L.	CF	73.0	18	0	0	0	1.000	2.22	0	0
Markakis, N.	CF	62.0	15	0	0	0	1.000	2.18	0	0
Terrero, L.	CF	43.0	16	1	0	1	.944	3.56	2	0
Fiorentino, J.	CF	1.0	0	0	0	0	0.000	0.00	0	0
Markakis, N.	RF	917.3	240	7	0	1	.996	2.42	0	0
Gibbons, J.	RF	348.7	97	1	0	2	.980	2.53	0	0
Matos, L.	RF	94.0	28	0	0	0	1.000	2.68	0	0
Terrero, L.	RF	25.0	5	0	0	0	1.000	1.80	0	0
Newhan, D.	RF	16.0	6	0	0	0	1.000	3.38	0	0
Tatis, F.	RF	8.0	4	0	0	0	1.000	4.50	0	0
Fahey, B.	RF	5.0	0	0	0	0	0.000	0.00	0	0
Conine, J.	RF	2.0	1	0	0	0	1.000	4.50	0	0
Fiorentino, J.	RF	2.0	0	0	0	0	0.000	0.00	0	0
Rogers, E.	RF	1.0	0	0	0	0	0.000	0.00	0	0

Boston Red Sox

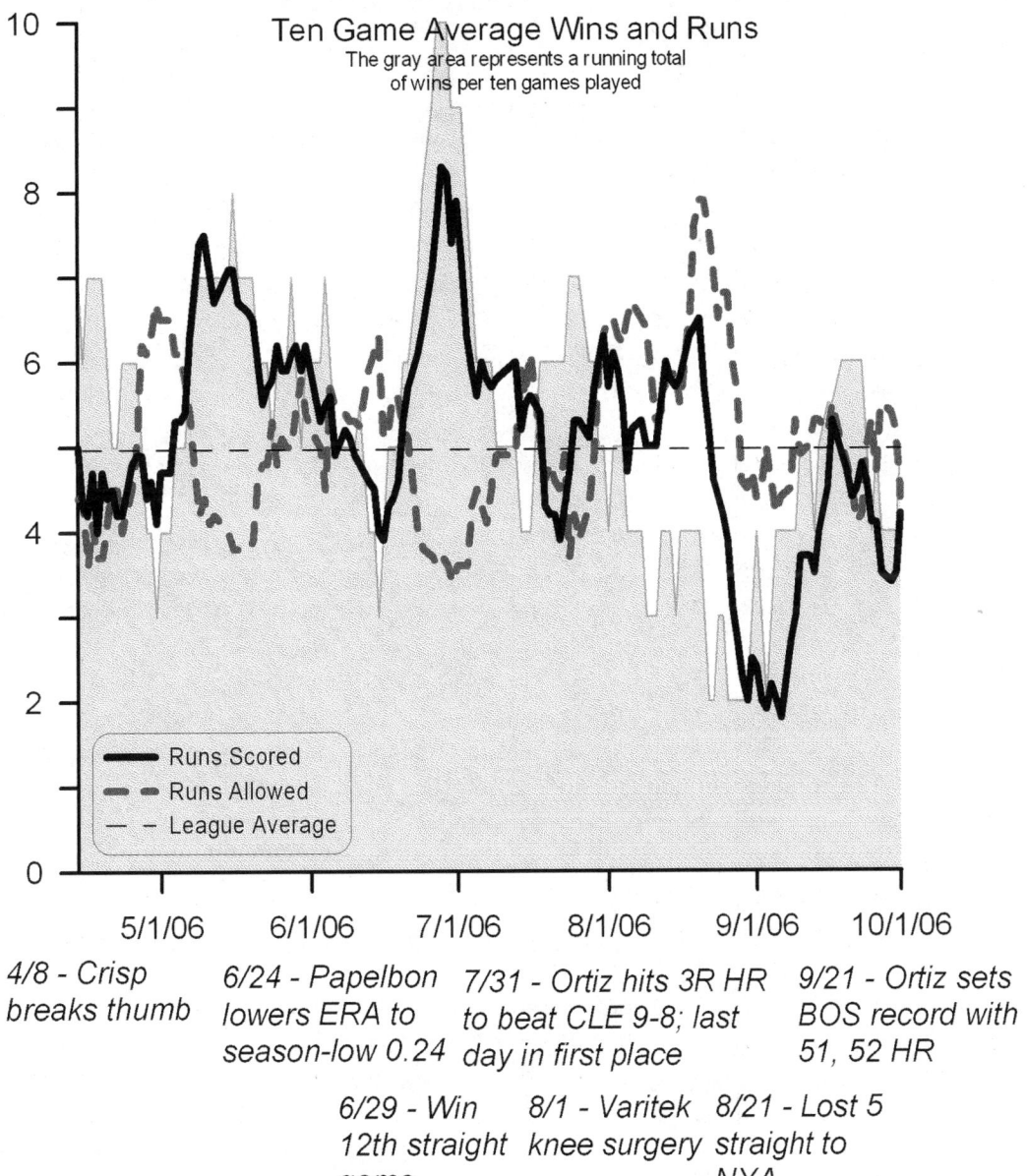

Ten Game Average Wins and Runs

The gray area represents a running total
of wins per ten games played

- Runs Scored
- Runs Allowed
- League Average

4/8 - Crisp breaks thumb

6/24 - Papelbon lowers ERA to season-low 0.24

6/29 - Win 12th straight game

7/31 - Ortiz hits 3R HR to beat CLE 9-8; last day in first place

8/1 - Varitek knee surgery

8/21 - Lost 5 straight to NYA

9/21 - Ortiz sets BOS record with 51, 52 HR

Team Batting and Pitching/Fielding Stats by Month						
	April	May	June	July	Aug	Sept/Oct
Wins	14	17	17	15	9	14
Losses	11	9	9	12	21	14
OBP	.353	.385	.371	.344	.332	.321
SLG	.416	.483	.462	.468	.409	.373
FIP	4.55	4.86	4.19	4.51	4.74	4.13
DER	.695	.706	.698	.680	.645	.675

Batting Stats

Player	RC	Runs	RBI	PA	Outs	P/PA	H	2B	3B	HR	TB	K	BB	IBB	HBP	SH	SF	SB	CS	GDP	BA	OBP	SLG	GPA
Ortiz D.	127	115	137	686	410	4.07	160	29	2	54	355	117	119	23	4	0	5	1	0	12	.287	.413	.636	.337
Ramirez M.	112	79	102	558	319	4.16	144	27	1	35	278	102	100	16	1	0	8	0	1	13	.321	.439	.619	.344
Youkilis K.	102	100	72	680	424	4.43	159	42	2	13	244	120	91	0	9	0	11	5	2	12	.279	.381	.429	.272
Loretta M.	79	75	59	703	471	3.67	181	33	0	5	229	63	49	1	12	2	5	4	1	16	.285	.345	.361	.240
Lowell M.	76	79	80	631	434	3.83	163	47	1	20	272	61	47	5	4	0	7	2	2	22	.284	.339	.475	.265
Nixon T.	54	59	52	453	291	3.73	102	24	0	8	150	56	60	1	7	0	5	0	2	10	.268	.373	.394	.260
Crisp C.	50	58	36	452	313	3.85	109	22	2	8	159	67	31	1	1	7	0	22	4	5	.264	.317	.385	.233
Varitek J.	45	46	55	416	290	4.02	87	19	2	12	146	87	46	7	2	1	2	1	2	10	.238	.325	.400	.241
Gonzalez A.	39	48	50	429	295	3.68	99	24	2	9	154	67	22	1	5	7	7	1	0	6	.255	.299	.397	.228
Pena W.	38	36	42	304	201	3.55	83	15	2	11	135	90	20	0	3	0	5	0	1	7	.301	.349	.489	.273
Cora A.	24	31	18	264	185	3.80	56	7	2	1	70	29	19	1	6	4	0	6	2	4	.238	.312	.298	.210
Mirabelli D.	16	12	25	176	132	4.11	31	6	0	6	55	54	11	0	4	0	0	0	0	2	.193	.261	.342	.198
Kapler G.	14	21	12	147	103	3.89	33	7	0	2	46	15	14	0	3	0	0	1	1	5	.254	.340	.354	.236
Hinske E.	10	8	5	88	60	4.34	23	8	0	1	34	30	8	0	0	0	0	1	1	2	.288	.352	.425	.259
Snow J.	5	5	4	53	36	4.34	9	0	0	0	9	8	8	0	1	0	0	0	0	1	.205	.340	.205	.199
Pena C.	3	3	3	37	25	3.65	9	2	0	1	14	10	4	0	0	0	0	0	0	1	.273	.351	.424	.258
Pedroia D.	3	5	7	98	74	4.02	17	4	0	2	27	7	7	0	1	1	0	0	1	1	.191	.258	.303	.187
Beckett J.	3	2	3	7	4	3.71	3	0	0	1	6	2	0	0	0	0	0	0	0	0	.429	.429	.857	.398
Murphy D.	2	4	2	26	18	3.88	5	1	0	1	9	4	4	0	0	0	0	0	0	1	.227	.346	.409	.252
Mohr D.	2	5	3	43	33	3.81	7	1	0	2	14	20	3	0	0	0	0	0	0	0	.175	.233	.350	.188
Bard J.	2	2	0	21	13	3.57	5	1	0	0	6	3	3	0	0	0	0	0	0	0	.278	.381	.333	.249
Stern A.	2	3	4	21	17	3.05	3	1	0	0	4	4	0	0	1	0	0	1	0	0	.150	.190	.200	.133
Harris W.	1	17	1	52	41	3.90	7	2	0	0	9	11	4	0	2	0	1	6	3	0	.156	.250	.200	.159
Lopez J.	0	6	4	65	56	3.29	12	5	0	0	17	16	2	0	0	0	0	0	0	5	.190	.215	.270	.161
Clement M.	0	1	0	3	2	4.67	1	0	0	0	1	2	0	0	0	0	0	0	0	0	.333	.333	.333	.228
Schilling C.	-0	0	0	2	1	4.50	1	0	0	0	1	1	0	0	0	0	0	0	0	0	.500	.500	.500	.342
Johnson J.	-0	0	0	1	1	5.00	0	0	0	0	0	1	0	0	0	0	0	0	0	0	.000	.000	.000	.000
DiNardo L.	-0	0	0	1	1	4.00	0	0	0	0	0	1	0	0	0	0	0	0	0	0	.000	.000	.000	.000
Alvarez A.	-0	0	0	1	1	3.00	0	0	0	0	0	1	0	0	0	0	0	0	0	0	.000	.000	.000	.000
Miller C.	-0	0	0	4	4	5.75	0	0	0	0	0	1	0	0	0	0	0	0	0	0	.000	.000	.000	.000
Wakefield T.	-0	0	0	4	4	3.50	0	0	0	0	0	3	0	0	0	0	0	0	0	0	.000	.000	.000	.000
Lester J.	-0	0	0	4	4	4.00	0	0	0	0	0	3	0	0	0	0	0	0	0	0	.000	.000	.000	.000
Huckaby K.	-1	0	1	5	5	3.40	1	0	0	0	1	0	0	0	0	0	0	0	0	1	.200	.200	.200	.137

Italicized stats have been adjusted for home park.
Batted Ball Batting Stats are listed after fielding stats

Pitching Stats

Player	PRC	IP	BFP	G	GS	P/PA	K	BB	IBB	HBP	H	HR	DP	DER	SB	CS	PO	W	L	Sv	Op	Hld	RA	ERA	FIP
Schilling C.	104	204.0	834	31	31	3.89	183	28	1	3	220	28	19	.676	6	5	3	15	7	0	0	0	3.97	3.97	3.69
Papelbon J.	95	68.3	257	59	0	4.00	75	13	2	1	40	3	1	.776	4	1	0	4	2	35	41	1	1.05	0.92	2.17
Beckett J.	77	204.7	868	33	33	3.73	158	74	1	10	191	36	23	.729	15	1	0	16	11	0	0	0	5.28	5.01	5.22
Wakefield T.	52	140.0	610	23	23	3.69	90	51	0	10	135	19	7	.734	24	4	2	7	11	0	0	0	5.14	4.63	5.05
Tavarez J.	37	98.7	431	58	6	3.70	56	44	3	6	110	10	27	.673	2	0	0	5	4	1	3	2	4.93	4.47	4.87
Lester J.	33	81.3	367	15	15	4.11	60	43	1	5	91	7	11	.667	9	6	6	7	2	0	0	0	4.76	4.76	4.64
Timlin M.	24	64.0	280	68	0	3.66	30	16	4	2	78	7	6	.671	4	1	0	6	6	9	17	21	4.64	4.36	4.40
Foulke K.	22	49.7	205	44	0	3.77	36	7	0	2	52	9	5	.715	1	0	0	3	1	0	0	14	4.35	4.35	4.71
Delcarmen M.	20	53.3	243	50	0	3.98	45	17	2	2	68	2	4	.621	5	0	0	2	0	0	4	14	5.40	5.06	3.02
Seanez R.	18	46.7	216	41	0	3.92	48	26	1	1	51	6	2	.659	7	0	0	2	1	0	1	3	5.40	4.82	4.55
Snyder K.	18	58.3	268	16	10	3.75	55	19	3	2	77	11	7	.613	6	2	0	4	5	0	0	1	6.48	6.02	4.75
Clement M.	17	65.3	310	12	12	3.74	43	38	0	6	77	8	6	.670	1	1	0	5	5	0	0	0	6.89	6.61	5.56
Wells D.	15	47.0	206	8	8	3.45	24	8	0	0	64	10	6	.659	3	0	1	2	3	0	0	0	5.74	4.98	5.52
Gabbard K.	12	25.7	111	7	4	3.95	15	16	0	0	24	0	7	.675	1	1	0	1	3	0	0	0	3.86	3.51	3.96
Hansen C.	9	38.0	176	38	0	3.83	30	15	0	4	46	5	4	.656	4	0	0	2	2	0	2	8	7.58	6.63	4.89
Corey B.	9	21.7	91	16	0	3.73	15	7	0	2	20	1	4	.712	1	0	0	1	0	0	0	3	4.57	4.57	3.72
DiNardo L.	8	39.0	190	13	6	3.73	17	20	1	1	61	6	10	.616	0	1	0	1	2	0	0	1	8.08	7.85	5.93
Hansack D.	7	10.0	36	2	2	3.94	8	1	0	0	6	2	1	.840	0	0	0	1	1	0	0	0	2.70	2.70	4.56
Breslow C.	7	12.0	55	13	0	4.04	12	6	1	1	12	0	0	.667	2	0	0	0	2	0	0	3	3.75	3.75	2.76
Johnson J.	6	29.3	141	6	6	3.72	18	13	0	2	41	3	5	.629	6	0	0	0	4	0	0	0	7.98	7.36	4.90
Lopez J.	6	16.7	69	27	0	3.41	11	10	1	2	13	1	6	.711	2	0	0	1	0	1	1	6	5.40	2.70	4.70
Riske D.	5	9.7	42	8	0	3.57	5	3	0	2	8	2	0	.800	0	0	0	0	1	0	0	0	3.72	3.72	6.47
Jarvis K.	4	16.7	77	4	3	3.55	7	6	1	1	22	1	3	.629	0	0	1	0	1	0	0	0	6.48	4.86	4.28
Pauley D.	4	16.0	82	3	3	3.57	10	6	1	2	31	1	5	.508	0	0	0	0	2	0	0	0	7.88	7.88	4.14
Burns M.	3	7.7	34	7	0	3.41	7	1	1	0	10	0	1	.577	0	0	0	0	0	0	0	0	4.70	4.70	1.44
Van Buren J.	2	13.0	65	10	0	4.58	8	15	1	0	14	1	3	.683	5	0	0	1	0	0	0	2	11.77	11.77	6.26
Alvarez A.	0	3.0	15	1	0	3.93	2	2	0	0	5	2	1	.667	0	0	0	0	0	0	0	0	12.00	12.00	12.60
Holtz M.	0	1.7	13	3	0	4.54	2	4	0	1	3	0	0	.500	0	0	0	0	0	0	0	1	16.20	16.20	9.86

Batted Ball Pitching Stats are listed after fielding stats

Fielding Stats

Name	POS	INN	SBA/G	CS%	ERA	WP+PB/G	PO	A	TE	FE
Varitek, J.	C	822.3	0.61	18%	4.84	0.274	648	27	2	2
Mirabelli, D.	C	400.0	0.92	15%	4.55	0.698	298	18	2	0
Lopez, J.	C	137.0	1.05	6%	5.58	0.591	98	5	1	0
Bard, J.	C	53.0	2.21	8%	5.26	1.868	35	4	0	0
Huckaby, K.	C	20.0	0.00	0%	3.60	0.000	11	0	0	0
Miller, C.	C	9.0	0.00	0%	5.00	0.000	6	0	0	0

Name	POS	Inn	PO	A	TE	FE	FPct	RF	DPS	DPT
Youkilis, K.	1B	1030.0	1033	70	0	5	.995	9.64	8	0
Snow, J.	1B	102.3	84	9	0	1	.989	8.18	2	0
Hinske, E.	1B	86.0	91	6	0	1	.990	10.15	2	0
Pena, C.	1B	80.0	81	5	0	1	.989	9.68	0	0
Loretta, M.	1B	75.0	74	9	0	0	1.000	9.96	4	0
Ortiz, D.	1B	68.0	62	6	0	1	.971	9.00	0	0
Loretta, M.	2B	1172.0	246	389	0	4	.994	4.88	37	63
Pedroia, D.	2B	172.0	45	73	0	3	.975	6.17	7	10
Cora, A.	2B	95.3	18	24	0	1	.977	3.97	2	4
Harris, W.	2B	2.0	0	0	0	0	0.000	0.00	0	0
Gonzalez, A.	SS	966.3	163	305	3	4	.985	4.36	39	27
Cora, A.	SS	434.0	66	166	3	2	.975	4.81	24	21
Pedroia, D.	SS	41.0	7	13	1	0	.952	4.39	3	1
Lowell, M.	3B	1298.0	143	313	3	3	.987	3.16	35	2
Youkilis, K.	3B	92.0	11	27	1	2	.927	3.72	1	0
Cora, A.	3B	50.7	3	7	0	0	1.000	1.78	3	0

Name	POS	Inn	PO	A	TE	FE	FPct	RF	DPS	DPT
Ramirez, M.	LF	1031.0	175	7	0	2	.989	1.59	0	0
Youkilis, K.	LF	134.0	36	3	0	0	1.000	2.62	0	0
Pena, W.	LF	113.0	24	3	1	0	.964	2.15	0	0
Kapler, G.	LF	63.0	18	2	0	0	1.000	2.86	0	0
Harris, W.	LF	33.0	10	1	0	0	1.000	3.00	0	0
Hinske, E.	LF	23.0	5	0	0	0	1.000	1.96	0	0
Murphy, D.	LF	20.0	1	0	0	0	1.000	0.45	0	0
Mohr, D.	LF	13.0	3	0	0	0	1.000	2.08	0	0
Pena, C.	LF	7.0	0	0	0	0	0.000	0.00	0	0
Stern, A.	LF	4.0	2	0	0	0	1.000	4.50	0	0
Crisp, C.	CF	900.7	246	3	0	1	.996	2.49	6	0
Pena, W.	CF	194.0	59	0	0	0	1.000	2.74	0	0
Kapler, G.	CF	95.0	17	0	0	0	1.000	1.61	0	0
Harris, W.	CF	91.7	27	0	0	0	1.000	2.65	0	0
Mohr, D.	CF	77.0	25	0	0	0	1.000	2.92	0	0
Stern, A.	CF	47.0	16	1	0	0	1.000	3.26	0	0
Murphy, D.	CF	36.0	9	0	0	0	1.000	2.25	0	0
Nixon, T.	RF	891.3	212	6	0	1	.995	2.20	4	0
Pena, W.	RF	282.0	63	2	0	2	.970	2.07	0	0
Kapler, G.	RF	177.7	48	2	0	0	1.000	2.53	2	0
Hinske, E.	RF	61.0	10	1	0	0	1.000	1.62	0	0
Mohr, D.	RF	11.0	2	0	0	0	1.000	1.64	0	0
Murphy, D.	RF	9.3	2	0	0	0	1.000	1.93	0	0
Harris, W.	RF	9.0	1	0	0	0	1.000	1.00	0	0

Batted Ball Batting Stats

Player	PA	% of PA		% of Batted Balls					Runs Per Event				Total Runs vs. Avg.				
		K%	BB%	GB%	LD%	FB%	IF/F	HR/OF	NIP	GB	LD	OF	NIP	GB	LD	FB	Tot
Ortiz D.	686	17	18	36	17	47	.08	.27	.12	.01	.46	.39	20	-7	-4	43	52
Ramirez M.	558	18	18	36	22	42	.05	.25	.11	.04	.42	.38	16	-3	2	29	44
Lowell M.	631	10	8	38	22	41	.11	.11	.10	.02	.39	.17	2	-6	9	4	10
Youkilis K.	680	18	15	31	24	45	.07	.07	.10	.07	.34	.15	12	-1	0	-2	10
Pena W.	305	30	8	40	21	39	.17	.16	-.02	.11	.49	.32	-6	4	3	5	6
Nixon T.	452	12	15	39	17	44	.09	.06	.14	.03	.40	.13	11	-3	-2	-4	2
Kapler G.	147	10	12	47	14	38	.14	.05	.13	.10	.36	.06	2	5	-2	-5	0
Varitek J.	416	21	12	45	17	38	.08	.11	.05	.04	.37	.20	1	-1	-6	1	-5
Crisp C.	452	15	7	48	16	36	.12	.08	.04	.08	.36	.12	-3	9	-6	-8	-7
Gonzalez A.	429	16	6	37	20	43	.15	.08	.02	.07	.35	.13	-4	2	-1	-6	-8
Mirabelli D.	176	31	9	41	12	47	.16	.14	-.01	.01	.42	.22	-3	-2	-4	1	-8
Cora A.	264	11	9	51	16	32	.17	.02	.10	.05	.36	-.02	2	3	-3	-13	-11
Loretta M.	703	9	9	35	27	38	.12	.03	.11	.02	.33	.05	5	-6	13	-24	-13
MLB Average		17	9	44	20	37	.11	.11	.05	.04	.39	.19	-	-	-	-	-

Batted Ball Pitching Stats

Player	PA	% of PA		% of Batted Balls					Runs Per Event				Total Runs vs. Avg.				
		K%	BB%	GB%	LD%	FB%	IF/F	HR/OF	NIP	GB	LD	OF	NIP	GB	LD	FB	Tot
Papelbon J.	257	29	5	37	17	46	.17	.03	-.04	-.01	.41	.06	-7	-5	-3	-8	-23
Schilling C.	834	22	4	40	20	40	.11	.12	-.05	.03	.45	.23	-21	-3	8	10	-6
Wakefield T.	610	15	10	39	16	44	.14	.10	.07	.03	.41	.16	3	-4	-3	-1	-5
Gabbard K.	111	14	14	58	18	24	.11	.00	.12	.06	.32	.01	2	1	-2	-5	-3
Beckett J.	868	18	10	45	17	38	.10	.17	.05	.04	.33	.26	-1	-2	-12	15	-0
Foulke K.	205	18	4	24	20	56	.09	.11	-.02	-.01	.44	.18	-4	-3	2	5	0
Delcarmen M.	243	19	8	45	26	30	.10	.04	.02	.06	.32	.24	-2	1	1	1	0
Seanez R.	216	22	13	29	24	46	.09	.10	.05	.08	.35	.18	1	-0	-0	0	1
Lester J.	367	16	13	41	22	38	.14	.08	.09	.03	.41	.18	5	-3	3	-2	3
Timlin M.	280	11	7	40	21	39	.11	.09	.06	.03	.36	.19	-1	-0	2	2	3
Hansen C.	176	17	11	44	22	35	.12	.11	.07	.06	.33	.27	1	1	-1	2	3
Johnson J.	141	13	11	58	19	24	.08	.13	.10	.11	.28	.22	1	5	-2	-1	3
Tavarez J.	431	13	12	57	17	26	.06	.13	.10	.00	.36	.35	5	-6	-4	8	4
Clement M.	310	14	14	49	16	35	.18	.13	.12	.05	.44	.26	6	0	-2	2	6
Wells D.	206	12	4	48	19	33	.04	.18	.00	.05	.37	.33	-3	1	1	9	8
Snyder K.	268	21	8	40	25	35	.08	.18	.01	.12	.41	.23	-3	6	5	2	10
DiNardo L.	190	9	11	61	20	19	.00	.21	.14	.04	.54	.31	3	2	6	1	11
MLB Average		17	9	44	20	37	.11	.11	.05	.04	.39	.19	-	-	-	-	-

Chicago Cubs

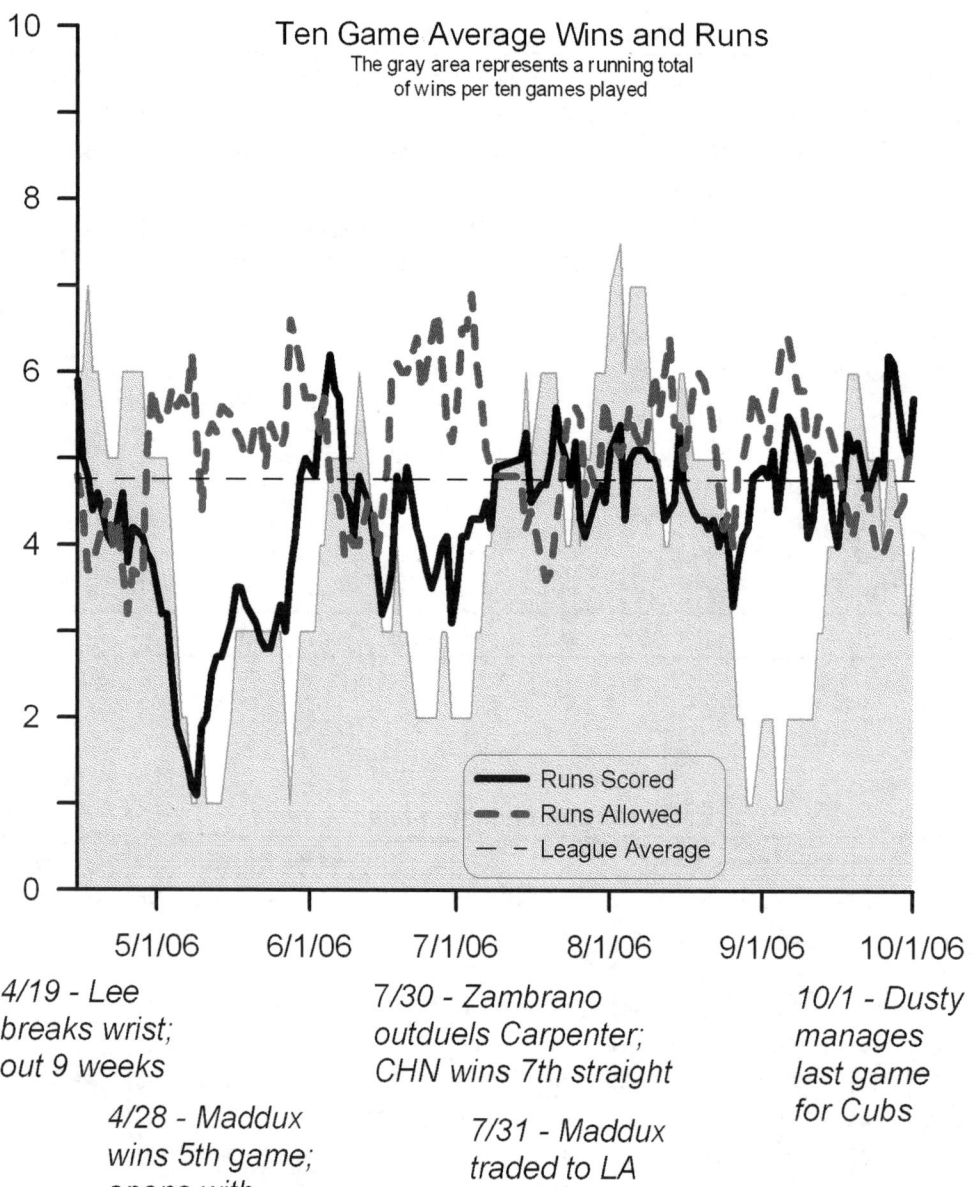

Ten Game Average Wins and Runs
The gray area represents a running total
of wins per ten games played

Legend:
- Runs Scored
- - Runs Allowed
- – – League Average

X-axis: 5/1/06, 6/1/06, 7/1/06, 8/1/06, 9/1/06, 10/1/06

4/19 - Lee breaks wrist; out 9 weeks

4/28 - Maddux wins 5th game; opens with 1.35 ERA

7/30 - Zambrano outduels Carpenter; CHN wins 7th straight

7/31 - Maddux traded to LA

10/1 - Dusty manages last game for Cubs

Team Batting and Pitching/Fielding Stats by Month						
	April	May	June	July	Aug	Sept/Oct
Wins	13	7	9	14	11	12
Losses	10	22	18	12	17	17
OBP	.316	.296	.324	.341	.319	.319
SLG	.401	.359	.418	.484	.427	.442
FIP	5.24	4.77	4.79	5.06	4.76	4.52
DER	.735	.704	.694	.696	.684	.711

Batting Stats

Player	RC	Runs	RBI	PA	Outs	P/PA	H	2B	3B	HR	TB	K	BB	IBB	HBP	SH	SF	SB	CS	GDP	BA	OBP	SLG	GPA
Ramirez A.	109	93	119	660	437	3.72	173	38	4	38	333	63	50	4	9	0	7	2	1	15	.291	.352	.561	.291
Pierre J.	84	87	40	750	521	3.49	204	32	13	3	271	38	32	0	8	10	1	58	20	6	.292	.330	.388	.240
Jones J.	82	73	81	578	399	3.66	152	31	1	27	266	116	35	6	5	2	2	9	1	17	.285	.334	.499	.269
Murton M.	68	70	62	508	338	3.72	135	22	3	13	202	62	45	1	5	1	2	5	2	16	.297	.365	.444	.269
Barrett M.	58	54	53	418	273	3.56	115	25	3	16	194	41	33	2	5	2	3	0	1	12	.307	.368	.517	.288
Cedeno R.	41	51	41	572	421	3.50	131	18	7	6	181	109	17	4	3	15	3	8	8	10	.245	.271	.339	.202
Walker T.	40	38	40	362	238	3.88	88	16	1	6	124	27	38	1	1	1	4	0	1	7	.277	.352	.390	.250
Theriot R.	31	34	16	159	97	3.69	44	11	3	3	70	18	17	0	2	6	0	13	2	5	.328	.412	.522	.308
Nevin P.	29	26	33	197	134	4.09	49	4	0	12	89	52	17	0	0	0	1	0	0	4	.274	.335	.497	.269
Lee D.	27	30	30	204	140	4.45	50	9	0	8	83	41	25	1	0	0	4	8	4	11	.286	.368	.474	.277
Blanco H.	26	23	37	261	185	3.84	64	15	2	6	101	38	14	1	0	4	2	0	0	8	.266	.304	.419	.236
Mabry J.	24	16	25	237	172	3.77	43	8	1	5	68	57	23	0	1	0	3	0	0	5	.205	.283	.324	.203
Perez N.	24	27	24	246	180	3.17	60	13	1	2	81	21	5	2	0	2	3	0	1	3	.254	.266	.343	.201
Pagan A.	21	28	18	187	133	3.67	42	6	2	5	67	28	15	0	0	1	1	4	2	3	.247	.306	.394	.231
Bynum F.	18	20	12	148	107	3.98	35	5	5	4	62	44	9	0	1	2	0	8	4	2	.257	.308	.456	.247
Zambrano C.	6	9	11	80	64	3.46	11	0	0	6	29	27	1	0	0	5	1	1	0	2	.151	.160	.397	.167
Hairston J.	5	8	4	92	66	3.97	17	3	0	0	20	14	4	2	1	5	0	3	0	1	.207	.253	.244	.171
Moore S.	5	6	5	42	29	3.57	10	2	0	2	18	10	2	0	1	1	0	0	0	1	.263	.317	.474	.255
Izturis C.	4	4	6	79	60	3.51	17	2	0	0	19	8	5	0	0	1	0	0	1	3	.233	.282	.260	.187
Womack T.	4	6	2	57	37	4.16	14	1	0	1	18	4	4	0	0	3	0	1	1	0	.280	.333	.360	.234
Wood K.	3	0	2	6	3	2.17	3	1	0	0	4	0	0	0	0	0	0	0	0	0	.500	.500	.667	.382
Restovich M.	1	0	1	13	10	4.15	2	1	0	0	3	5	1	0	0	0	0	0	0	0	.167	.231	.250	.162
Marmol C.	1	3	1	24	18	3.38	6	1	0	1	10	7	0	0	0	1	0	0	0	1	.261	.261	.435	.221
Reyes J.	1	0	2	5	4	5.40	1	0	0	0	1	3	0	0	0	0	0	0	0	0	.200	.200	.200	.137
Novoa R.	1	0	1	5	5	2.80	1	1	0	0	2	2	0	0	0	0	0	0	0	1	.200	.200	.400	.186
Guzman A.	1	0	2	16	11	3.38	2	1	0	0	3	4	0	0	0	4	0	0	0	1	.167	.167	.250	.134
Howry B.	1	0	0	1	0	2.00	1	0	0	0	1	0	0	0	0	0	0	0	0	0	1.000	1.000	1.000	.683
Ohman W.	1	0	0	1	0	4.00	1	0	0	0	1	0	0	0	0	0	0	0	0	0	1.000	1.000	1.000	.683
Rusch G.	0	1	0	18	12	3.33	3	1	0	0	4	4	0	0	0	3	0	0	0	0	.200	.200	.267	.153
Soto G.	0	1	2	26	20	3.38	5	1	0	0	6	5	0	0	1	0	0	0	0	0	.200	.231	.240	.160
Coats B.	0	2	1	18	16	3.00	3	1	0	1	7	6	0	0	0	0	0	0	0	1	.167	.167	.389	.168
Prior M.	0	0	0	14	12	3.86	1	0	0	0	1	5	0	0	0	1	0	0	0	0	.077	.077	.077	.053
Wuertz M.	0	0	0	1	0	0.00	0	0	0	0	0	0	0	0	0	1	0	0	0	0	.000	.000	.000	.000
Eyre S.	-0	0	0	1	1	2.00	0	0	0	0	0	0	0	0	0	0	0	0	0	0	.000	.000	.000	.000
Ryu J.	-0	0	0	1	1	4.00	0	0	0	0	0	1	0	0	0	0	0	0	0	0	.000	.000	.000	.000
Aardsma D.	-0	0	0	3	2	3.00	0	0	0	0	0	0	0	0	0	1	0	0	0	0	.000	.000	.000	.000
Walrond L.	-0	0	0	3	2	2.67	0	0	0	0	0	1	0	0	0	1	0	0	0	0	.000	.000	.000	.000
Williams J.	-0	0	0	2	2	2.50	0	0	0	0	0	1	0	0	0	0	0	0	0	0	.000	.000	.000	.000
Dempster R.	-0	0	0	2	2	5.50	0	0	0	0	0	2	0	0	0	0	0	0	0	0	.000	.000	.000	.000
Miller W.	-0	0	0	7	6	4.71	1	0	0	0	1	5	0	0	0	0	0	0	0	0	.143	.143	.143	.098
O'Malley R.	-0	0	0	4	4	3.50	0	0	0	0	0	3	0	0	0	0	0	0	0	0	.000	.000	.000	.000
Maddux G.	-1	2	4	48	39	3.15	4	1	0	0	5	17	2	0	0	3	0	1	0	0	.093	.133	.116	.087
Mateo J.	-1	1	0	14	12	3.79	0	0	0	0	0	9	0	0	0	2	0	0	0	0	.000	.000	.000	.000
Hill R.	-1	0	0	34	27	3.12	3	1	0	0	4	11	1	0	0	3	0	0	0	0	.100	.129	.133	.089
Marshall S.	-1	3	2	43	35	4.19	5	0	0	1	8	19	0	0	0	3	0	0	0	0	.125	.125	.200	.104

Italicized stats have been adjusted for home park.

Batted Ball Batting Stats are listed after fielding stats

Pitching Stats

Player	PRC	IP	BFP	G	GS	P/PA	K	BB	IBB	HBP	H	HR	DP	DER	SB	CS	PO	W	L	Sv	Op	Hld	RA	ERA	FIP
Zambrano C.	110	214.0	917	33	33	3.95	210	115	4	9	162	20	19	.734	2	3	1	16	7	0	0	0	3.83	3.41	4.15
Maddux G.	47	136.3	572	22	22	3.29	81	23	3	0	153	14	13	.685	19	4	1	9	11	0	0	0	5.15	4.69	3.80
Howry B.	44	76.7	314	84	0	4.16	71	17	4	3	70	8	4	.702	4	5	0	4	5	5	9	21	3.29	3.17	3.35
Hill R.	42	99.3	417	17	16	3.93	90	39	1	2	83	16	7	.741	10	3	1	6	7	0	0	0	4.62	4.17	4.71
Marshall S.	36	125.7	563	24	24	3.66	77	59	3	7	132	20	16	.703	12	5	2	6	9	0	0	0	6.09	5.59	5.57
Eyre S.	34	61.3	266	74	0	4.28	73	30	4	0	61	11	7	.664	4	1	0	1	3	0	3	18	3.67	3.38	4.44
Ohman W.	32	65.3	286	78	0	3.88	74	34	2	5	51	6	2	.719	4	0	0	1	1	0	0	9	4.13	4.13	3.85
Dempster R.	26	75.0	342	74	0	3.94	67	36	3	3	77	5	6	.662	5	0	0	1	9	24	33	2	5.64	4.80	3.74
Wuertz M.	25	40.7	175	41	0	3.86	42	16	2	1	35	5	2	.703	4	0	0	3	1	0	1	6	3.10	2.66	3.86
Novoa R.	25	76.0	336	66	0	3.83	53	32	5	6	77	15	9	.717	10	0	0	2	1	0	0	4	5.57	4.26	5.69
Aardsma D.	24	53.0	225	45	0	4.28	49	28	0	1	41	9	3	.761	5	0	0	3	0	0	0	5	4.25	4.08	5.22
Marmol C.	22	77.0	356	19	13	3.94	59	59	2	5	71	14	5	.740	11	5	2	5	7	0	0	0	6.31	6.08	6.46
Rusch G.	15	66.3	311	25	9	4.29	59	33	2	1	86	21	8	.665	3	3	1	3	8	0	0	0	7.73	7.46	7.00
Mateo J.	14	45.7	210	11	10	3.84	35	23	1	3	51	6	6	.657	1	1	0	1	3	0	0	0	6.11	5.32	5.04
Guzman A.	14	56.0	272	15	10	4.08	60	37	1	6	68	9	4	.631	5	3	0	0	6	0	0	0	7.71	7.39	5.41
Williamson S.	11	28.3	127	31	0	3.72	32	16	1	1	27	2	2	.658	8	1	1	2	3	0	0	3	5.40	5.08	3.57
Prior M.	10	43.7	211	9	9	3.96	38	28	2	8	46	9	4	.703	5	2	0	1	6	0	0	0	8.04	7.21	6.49
Miller W.	9	21.7	103	5	5	4.16	20	18	1	1	19	4	0	.733	2	0	0	0	2	0	0	0	4.98	4.57	6.26
O'Malley R.	8	12.7	55	2	2	3.36	4	7	0	1	10	0	0	.767	0	1	1	1	1	0	0	0	2.13	2.13	4.48
Wood K.	6	19.7	86	4	4	3.69	13	8	0	1	19	5	2	.746	2	1	0	1	2	0	0	0	5.95	4.12	6.57
Walrond L.	5	17.3	84	10	2	3.83	21	12	1	0	19	2	0	.653	1	0	0	0	1	0	0	0	6.75	6.23	4.20
Ryu J.	3	15.0	77	10	1	3.62	17	6	1	2	23	7	0	.644	0	0	0	0	1	0	0	0	8.40	8.40	8.42
Williams J.	2	12.3	61	5	2	3.84	5	11	1	1	15	2	3	.667	1	1	0	0	2	0	0	0	8.76	7.30	7.19

Batted Ball Pitching Stats are listed after fielding stats

Fielding Stats

Name	POS	INN	SBA/G	CS%	ERA	WP+PB/G	PO	A	TE	FE
Barrett, M.	C	852.0	1.11	15%	4.60	0.581	729	40	4	0
Blanco, H.	C	526.0	0.67	38%	4.94	0.394	468	33	1	0
Soto, G.	C	55.0	0.82	0%	5.24	0.327	66	4	1	0
Reyes, J.	C	5.0	0.00	0%	3.60	0.000	7	0	0	0
Nevin, P.	C	1.0	0.00	0%	0.00	0.000	1	0	0	0

Name	POS	Inn	PO	A	TE	FE	FPct	RF	DPS	DPT
Lee, D.	1B	393.7	369	26	0	5	.988	9.03	7	0
Mabry, J.	1B	352.3	312	29	0	2	.994	8.71	1	0
Walker, T.	1B	311.7	272	19	2	1	.990	8.40	0	0
Nevin, P.	1B	282.0	250	17	0	0	1.000	8.52	3	0
Blanco, H.	1B	47.0	34	3	0	0	1.000	7.09	1	0
Moore, S.	1B	46.0	43	2	0	1	.978	8.80	0	0
Hairston, J.	1B	6.3	4	0	0	0	1.000	5.68	0	0
Walker, T.	2B	329.3	76	93	2	2	.977	4.62	8	14
Perez, N.	2B	327.0	72	107	3	2	.973	4.93	15	10
Theriot, R.	2B	281.7	62	59	2	0	.984	3.87	6	3
Hairston, J.	2B	152.7	30	33	0	0	1.000	3.71	2	3
Cedeno, R.	2B	126.7	35	37	0	2	.973	5.12	4	3
Bynum, F.	2B	117.7	34	32	1	4	.930	5.05	3	4
Womack, T.	2B	104.0	27	39	0	0	1.000	5.71	3	5
Cedeno, R.	SS	1129.0	148	356	14	9	.956	4.02	36	26
Izturis, C.	SS	160.7	33	44	1	1	.975	4.31	4	3
Perez, N.	SS	131.7	24	36	1	1	.968	4.10	3	4
Theriot, R.	SS	17.0	3	3	0	1	.857	3.18	1	0
Ramirez, A.	3B	1353.0	110	252	6	7	.965	2.41	13	2
Perez, N.	3B	51.0	3	9	0	0	1.000	2.12	0	0
Moore, S.	3B	32.0	3	4	0	0	1.000	1.97	0	0
Mabry, J.	3B	2.0	0	1	0	0	1.000	4.50	0	0
Theriot, R.	3B	1.0	0	0	0	0	0.000	0.00	0	0

Name	POS	Inn	PO	A	TE	FE	FPct	RF	DPS	DPT
Murton, M.	LF	1049.0	240	3	0	3	.988	2.08	4	0
Pagan, A.	LF	211.3	44	2	1	0	.979	1.96	0	0
Bynum, F.	LF	80.7	19	0	0	2	.905	2.12	0	0
Nevin, P.	LF	64.0	7	0	0	0	1.000	0.98	0	0
Mabry, J.	LF	17.0	8	0	0	0	1.000	4.24	0	0
Hairston, J.	LF	12.0	3	0	0	0	1.000	2.25	0	0
Restovich, M.	LF	5.0	0	0	0	0	0.000	0.00	0	0
Pierre, J.	CF	1426.0	379	5	0	0	1.000	2.42	0	0
Bynum, F.	CF	6.0	2	0	0	0	1.000	3.00	0	0
Coats, B.	CF	4.0	1	0	0	0	1.000	2.25	0	0
Pagan, A.	CF	3.0	1	0	0	0	1.000	3.00	0	0
Jones, J.	RF	1205.0	275	5	4	3	.976	2.09	4	0
Pagan, A.	RF	134.7	41	0	0	0	1.000	2.74	0	0
Bynum, F.	RF	26.0	6	0	0	0	1.000	2.08	0	0
Mabry, J.	RF	25.7	4	0	0	0	1.000	1.40	0	0
Hairston, J.	RF	21.3	6	0	0	0	1.000	2.53	0	0
Nevin, P.	RF	13.0	2	0	0	0	1.000	1.38	0	0
Coats, B.	RF	8.3	2	0	0	0	1.000	2.16	0	0
Restovich, M.	RF	5.0	1	0	0	0	1.000	1.80	0	0

Batted Ball Batting Stats

Player	PA	% of PA		% of Batted Balls					Runs Per Event				Total Runs vs. Avg.				
		K%	BB%	GB%	LD%	FB%	IF/F	HR/OF	NIP	GB	LD	OF	NIP	GB	LD	FB	Tot
Ramirez A.	660	10	9	35	18	47	.12	.17	.11	.06	.37	.25	4	2	-1	23	29
Barrett M.	418	10	9	45	20	36	.08	.14	.11	.04	.39	.25	3	-0	3	8	14
Jones J.	578	20	7	56	19	26	.02	.22	.00	.04	.46	.36	-7	1	3	13	10
Theriot R.	159	11	12	50	27	24	.08	.08	.12	.04	.45	.23	2	2	4	-2	7
Murton M.	508	12	10	58	18	24	.13	.13	.09	.05	.42	.24	3	4	2	-3	6
Nevin P.	197	26	9	41	23	36	.11	.29	-.00	.04	.39	.39	-3	-1	0	7	4
Lee D.	204	20	12	41	20	38	.04	.16	.06	.04	.32	.25	1	-0	-2	4	2
Bynum F.	148	30	7	45	25	30	.04	.16	-.03	-.04	.53	.36	-4	-4	3	2	-1
Pagan A.	187	15	8	51	15	34	.08	.11	.05	.05	.29	.22	-1	2	-4	1	-1
Walker T.	362	7	11	38	20	42	.09	.05	.16	.03	.36	.09	6	-2	1	-6	-1
Blanco H.	261	15	5	38	24	38	.10	.07	.01	.05	.39	.10	-3	-0	5	-5	-4
Pierre J.	750	5	5	55	21	24	.09	.02	.12	.05	.38	.05	-1	13	8	-26	-6
Perez N.	246	9	2	37	19	43	.16	.03	-.02	.08	.35	.03	-4	4	1	-10	-9
Mabry J.	237	24	10	41	14	45	.11	.08	.02	.02	.30	.17	-1	-2	-7	-0	-10
Cedeno R.	572	19	3	47	16	37	.11	.04	-.04	.08	.32	.07	-13	10	-9	-16	-29
MLB Average		*17*	*9*	*44*	*20*	*37*	*.11*	*.11*	*.05*	*.04*	*.39*	*.19*	*-*	*-*	*-*	*-*	*-*

Batted Ball Pitching Stats

Player	PA	% of PA		% of Batted Balls					Runs Per Event				Total Runs vs. Avg.				
		K%	BB%	GB%	LD%	FB%	IF/F	HR/OF	NIP	GB	LD	OF	NIP	GB	LD	FB	Tot
Zambrano C.	917	23	14	47	17	36	.12	.11	.06	.03	.36	.18	7	-5	-16	-11	-24
Howry B.	314	23	6	38	18	44	.14	.10	-.01	.08	.37	.14	-5	1	-3	-3	-10
Ohman W.	286	26	14	34	23	44	.09	.07	.05	.08	.40	.05	1	0	-0	-9	-8
Hill R.	417	22	10	30	18	52	.13	.12	.03	.05	.41	.16	-2	-2	-2	1	-6
Aardsma D.	225	22	13	37	19	44	.08	.14	.06	.01	.35	.15	1	-3	-3	-1	-4
Dempster R.	342	20	11	52	18	30	.09	.08	.06	.05	.43	.15	1	2	-1	-6	-4
Wuertz M.	175	24	10	54	16	30	.12	.14	.02	.08	.43	.21	-1	2	-2	-2	-3
Maddux G.	572	14	4	50	23	27	.11	.13	-.01	.02	.41	.23	-9	-5	12	-1	-3
Williamson S.	127	25	13	51	19	30	.09	.10	.05	.08	.41	.17	1	1	-1	-2	-1
Miller W.	103	19	18	32	18	50	.06	.14	.11	.08	.35	.16	3	-0	-2	0	1
Eyre S.	266	27	11	42	20	38	.07	.20	.02	.10	.36	.26	-1	3	-3	4	1
Novoa R.	336	16	11	43	18	39	.09	.17	.08	.02	.37	.26	3	-2	-2	7	5
Mateo J.	210	17	12	41	26	33	.19	.13	.08	.06	.39	.24	2	-0	3	-0	5
Prior M.	211	18	17	37	21	43	.14	.18	.11	.03	.30	.30	5	-1	-3	5	6
Marshall S.	563	14	12	47	17	36	.10	.14	.10	.05	.37	.21	7	2	-5	3	6
Marmol C.	356	17	18	29	18	53	.13	.13	.13	.04	.44	.19	11	-3	-2	3	9
Guzman A.	272	22	16	32	28	40	.09	.15	.08	.07	.40	.27	4	-1	3	4	10
Rusch G.	311	19	11	35	22	43	.10	.25	.06	.04	.44	.40	1	-2	3	18	19
MLB Average		*17*	*9*	*44*	*20*	*37*	*.11*	*.11*	*.05*	*.04*	*.39*	*.19*	*-*	*-*	*-*	*-*	*-*

Chicago White Sox

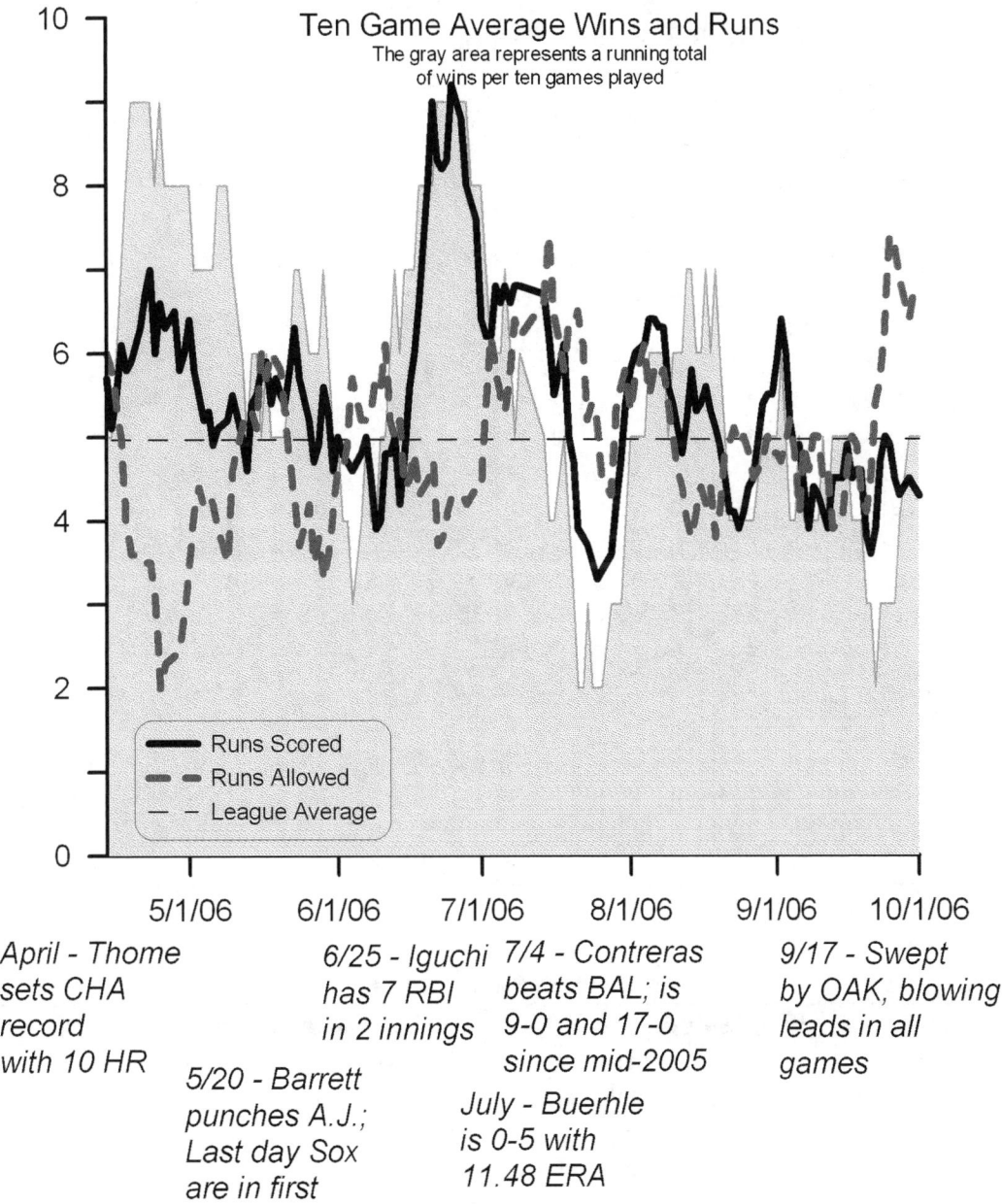

Ten Game Average Wins and Runs
The gray area represents a running total
of wins per ten games played

- Runs Scored
- Runs Allowed
- League Average

*April - Thome
sets CHA
record
with 10 HR*

*6/25 - Iguchi
has 7 RBI
in 2 innings*

*7/4 - Contreras
beats BAL; is
9-0 and 17-0
since mid-2005*

*9/17 - Swept
by OAK, blowing
leads in all
games*

*5/20 - Barrett
punches A.J.;
Last day Sox
are in first*

*July - Buerhle
is 0-5 with
11.48 ERA*

Team Batting and Pitching/Fielding Stats by Month						
	April	May	June	July	Aug	Sept/Oct
Wins	17	16	19	10	16	12
Losses	7	12	8	15	13	17
OBP	.358	.347	.352	.338	.335	.325
SLG	.467	.472	.464	.499	.453	.432
FIP	4.39	4.65	4.59	4.80	4.51	4.03
DER	.723	.706	.695	.677	.697	.679

Batting Stats

Player	RC	Runs	RBI	PA	Outs	P/PA	H	2B	3B	HR	TB	K	BB	IBB	HBP	SH	SF	SB	CS	GDP	BA	OBP	SLG	GPA
Thome J.	124	108	109	610	353	4.31	141	26	0	42	293	147	107	12	6	0	7	0	0	4	.288	.416	.598	.331
Dye J.	120	103	120	611	387	4.11	170	27	3	44	335	118	59	4	6	0	7	7	3	15	.315	.385	.622	.323
Konerko P.	114	97	113	643	414	3.90	177	30	0	35	312	104	60	3	8	0	9	1	0	25	.313	.381	.551	.304
Iguchi T.	90	97	67	627	411	3.93	156	24	0	18	234	110	59	0	3	8	2	11	5	7	.281	.352	.422	.259
Crede J.	87	76	94	586	410	3.67	154	31	0	30	275	58	28	1	7	0	7	0	2	18	.283	.323	.506	.267
Pierzynski A.	71	65	64	543	369	3.36	150	24	0	16	222	72	22	6	8	3	1	1	0	10	.295	.333	.436	.254
Podsednik S.	68	86	45	592	413	4.10	137	27	6	3	185	96	54	1	2	8	4	40	19	7	.261	.330	.353	.233
Uribe J.	54	53	71	495	365	3.41	109	28	2	21	204	82	13	1	3	9	7	1	1	10	.235	.257	.441	.222
Mackowiak R.	37	31	23	290	184	3.80	74	12	1	5	103	59	28	3	3	2	2	5	2	1	.290	.365	.404	.260
Cintron A.	34	35	41	304	219	3.28	82	10	3	5	113	35	10	0	2	1	3	10	3	10	.285	.310	.392	.233
Anderson B.	33	46	33	405	293	3.47	82	23	1	8	131	90	30	2	5	2	3	4	7	3	.225	.290	.359	.216
Ozuna P.	31	25	17	203	136	3.23	62	12	2	2	84	16	7	0	4	3	0	6	6	3	.328	.365	.444	.270
Gload R.	25	22	18	167	108	3.68	51	8	2	3	72	15	6	0	1	3	1	6	0	3	.327	.354	.462	.270
Widger C.	4	6	7	87	63	4.16	14	3	0	1	20	20	9	0	0	0	2	0	0	1	.184	.264	.263	.181
Alomar Jr. S.	3	5	8	51	36	3.92	10	3	0	1	16	7	3	0	0	0	2	0	0	0	.217	.255	.348	.198
Sweeney R.	1	1	5	35	28	3.37	8	0	0	0	8	7	0	0	0	0	0	0	0	1	.229	.229	.229	.157
Garland J.	1	2	2	7	4	3.14	1	0	0	1	4	3	0	0	0	2	0	0	0	0	.200	.200	.800	.285
Owens J.	1	4	0	9	6	4.22	3	1	0	0	4	2	0	0	0	0	0	1	0	0	.333	.333	.444	.256
Fields J.	1	4	2	25	17	4.44	3	2	0	1	8	8	5	0	0	0	0	0	0	0	.150	.320	.400	.240
Vazquez J.	1	1	0	2	0	4.00	1	0	0	0	1	0	0	0	0	1	0	0	0	0	1.000	1.000	1.000	.687
Contreras J.	0	1	0	6	4	3.33	0	0	0	0	0	2	2	0	0	0	0	0	0	0	.000	.333	.000	.147
Garcia F.	-0	0	0	6	4	2.17	1	0	0	0	1	2	0	0	0	1	0	0	0	0	.200	.200	.200	.137
McCarthy B.	-0	0	0	1	1	7.00	0	0	0	0	0	0	0	0	0	0	0	0	0	0	.000	.000	.000	.000
Buehrle M.	-0	0	0	5	4	3.00	0	0	0	0	0	1	0	0	0	1	0	0	0	0	.000	.000	.000	.000
Stewart C.	-1	0	0	8	8	4.25	0	0	0	0	0	2	0	0	0	0	0	0	0	0	.000	.000	.000	.000

Italicized stats have been adjusted for home park.

Batted Ball Batting Stats

Player	PA	% of PA		% of Batted Balls					Runs Per Event				Total Runs vs. Avg.				
		K%	BB%	GB%	LD%	FB%	IF/F	HR/OF	NIP	GB	LD	OF	NIP	GB	LD	FB	Tot
Dye J.	611	19	11	39	20	40	.06	.23	.05	.06	.48	.36	1	2	8	31	42
Thome J.	610	24	19	37	20	43	.08	.29	.09	.06	.41	.44	14	-1	-5	33	41
Konerko P.	643	16	11	33	25	42	.09	.19	.07	.04	.38	.26	3	-4	8	18	26
Crede J.	586	10	6	31	18	51	.14	.13	.06	.04	.38	.19	-2	-2	1	12	8
Ozuna P.	203	8	5	49	19	32	.15	.05	.08	.11	.33	.15	-1	9	-1	-3	4
Gload R.	167	9	4	51	21	27	.05	.08	.03	.06	.46	.15	-2	1	5	-2	3
Iguchi T.	627	18	10	51	16	34	.07	.13	.05	.06	.38	.24	1	5	-8	5	2
Mackowiak R.	290	20	11	54	17	29	.09	.10	.05	.13	.42	.14	0	9	-2	-6	2
Pierzynski A.	543	13	6	44	23	33	.14	.13	.02	.05	.34	.20	-5	2	4	-1	0
Cintron A.	304	12	4	46	23	31	.12	.07	.00	-.02	.41	.15	-4	-6	7	-4	-7
Anderson B.	406	22	9	44	21	35	.12	.09	.01	.06	.38	.14	-4	2	-1	-7	-9
Uribe J.	495	17	3	38	17	45	.16	.14	-.04	.06	.32	.20	-10	1	-6	5	-11
Podsednik S.	591	16	9	49	23	28	.09	.03	.06	.04	.37	.09	1	0	2	-17	-13
MLB Average		17	9	44	20	37	.11	.11	.05	.04	.39	.19	-	-	-	-	-

Pitching Stats

Player	PRC	IP	BFP	G	GS	P/PA	K	BB	IBB	HBP	H	HR	DP	DER	SB	CS	PO	W	L	Sv	Op	Hld	RA	ERA	FIP
Garcia F.	85	216.3	917	33	33	3.62	135	48	3	7	228	32	16	.711	40	2	0	17	9	0	0	0	4.83	4.53	4.66
Contreras J.	81	196.0	833	30	30	3.65	134	55	4	10	194	20	16	.705	21	6	0	13	9	0	0	0	4.64	4.27	4.16
Vazquez J.	81	202.7	872	33	32	3.80	184	56	2	15	206	23	18	.677	10	4	2	11	12	0	0	0	5.15	4.84	3.94
Garland J.	81	211.3	900	33	32	3.72	112	41	4	6	247	26	26	.683	6	7	0	18	7	0	0	0	4.77	4.51	4.41
Buehrle M.	66	204.0	876	32	32	3.54	98	48	5	6	247	36	24	.689	4	7	10	12	13	0	0	0	5.47	4.99	5.32
McCarthy B.	36	84.7	354	53	2	4.10	69	33	9	0	77	17	9	.736	8	3	0	4	7	0	1	11	4.68	4.68	5.09
Jenks B.	36	69.7	300	67	0	3.57	80	31	10	2	66	5	9	.654	11	2	0	3	4	41	45	0	4.13	4.00	2.89
Thornton M.	32	54.0	227	63	0	3.75	49	21	4	1	46	5	5	.722	4	0	0	5	3	2	5	18	3.33	3.33	3.65
MacDougal M.	22	25.0	97	25	0	3.67	19	6	0	1	19	1	5	.729	2	0	0	1	1	0	1	11	1.80	1.80	3.10
Cotts N.	19	54.0	251	70	0	4.11	43	24	6	3	64	12	3	.686	2	0	0	1	2	1	4	14	5.50	5.17	5.73
Riske D.	16	34.3	147	33	0	3.81	23	14	1	1	32	4	3	.724	3	1	0	1	1	0	1	2	4.19	3.93	4.66
Haeger C.	8	18.3	79	7	1	4.35	19	13	0	0	12	0	3	.745	2	1	0	1	1	1	1	0	4.91	3.44	3.32
Politte C.	5	30.0	151	30	0	3.72	15	15	7	1	47	9	2	.658	3	0	0	2	2	0	2	4	9.00	8.70	7.06
Tracey S.	4	8.0	34	7	0	3.38	3	5	0	1	4	2	1	.870	0	0	0	0	0	0	0	0	3.38	3.38	8.01
Montero A.	4	14.0	59	11	0	3.47	7	2	0	0	15	3	2	.702	0	0	0	1	0	0	0	2	6.43	5.14	5.48
Logan B.	3	17.3	93	21	0	3.71	15	15	2	3	21	2	2	.603	0	0	0	0	0	1	2	2	9.35	8.31	5.80
Hermanson D.	3	6.7	27	6	0	3.74	5	1	1	1	6	2	1	.778	0	0	0	0	0	0	0	0	4.05	4.05	6.11
Nelson J.	2	2.7	15	6	0	3.60	2	5	1	0	3	1	0	.714	0	1	0	0	1	0	1	0	3.38	3.38	11.14

Batted Ball Pitching Stats

Player	PA	% of PA		% of Batted Balls					Runs Per Event				Total Runs vs. Avg.				
		K%	BB%	GB%	LD%	FB%	IF/F	HR/OF	NIP	GB	LD	OF	NIP	GB	LD	FB	Tot
Contreras J.	833	16	8	45	16	39	.12	.09	.04	.04	.37	.18	-4	1	-9	-0	-12
Thornton M.	227	22	10	49	19	32	.10	.09	.03	.04	.43	.11	-1	-1	-1	-5	-8
Vazquez J.	872	21	8	40	20	41	.13	.11	.02	.05	.40	.19	-8	-0	-0	1	-8
Jenks B.	300	27	11	59	19	22	.10	.14	.02	.04	.41	.30	-2	-0	-2	-3	-7
Garcia F.	917	15	6	41	18	41	.08	.11	.02	.05	.36	.17	-9	4	-3	5	-3
Riske D.	147	16	10	34	25	41	.14	.11	.07	.04	.28	.12	1	-0	-0	-2	-2
McCarthy B.	354	19	9	38	15	47	.14	.17	.04	.06	.35	.23	-1	-0	-7	6	-2
Garland J.	900	12	5	42	20	38	.09	.09	.02	.06	.39	.16	-9	4	8	-1	3
Cotts N.	251	17	11	42	21	37	.11	.19	.06	.06	.47	.27	1	0	3	5	9
Politte C.	151	10	11	31	22	47	.09	.18	.12	.12	.45	.24	2	2	3	5	13
Buehrle M.	876	11	6	44	19	37	.13	.14	.05	.04	.39	.24	-4	2	3	17	17
MLB Average		17	9	44	20	37	.11	.11	.05	.04	.39	.19	-	-	-	-	-

215

Fielding Stats

Name	POS	INN	SBA/G	CS%	ERA	WP+PB/G	PO	A	TE	FE
Pierzynski, A.	C	1125.0	0.89	19%	4.47	0.432	800	57	2	1
Widger, C.	C	183.0	0.98	15%	5.36	0.393	102	5	1	2
Alomar Jr., S.	C	126.0	0.71	20%	4.79	0.143	96	4	1	0
Stewart, C.	C	15.0	1.80	67%	4.80	0.000	17	2	0	0

Name	POS	Inn	PO	A	TE	FE	FPct	RF	DPS	DPT
Konerko, P.	1B	1181.0	1168	67	2	4	.995	9.41	20	2
Gload, R.	1B	247.3	266	13	2	1	.986	10.15	0	0
Thome, J.	1B	20.0	21	0	0	0	1.000	9.45	0	0
Iguchi, T.	2B	1209.0	270	371	4	4	.988	4.77	27	51
Cintron, A.	2B	203.7	43	59	1	0	.990	4.51	3	5
Ozuna, P.	2B	36.0	5	12	0	1	.944	4.25	1	0
Uribe, J.	SS	1130.0	217	373	6	6	.977	4.70	43	39
Cintron, A.	SS	319.0	50	94	0	4	.973	4.06	8	11
Crede, J.	3B	1260.0	114	339	4	6	.978	3.24	36	1
Ozuna, P.	3B	65.0	5	11	0	0	1.000	2.22	0	0
Cintron, A.	3B	63.0	8	20	0	3	.903	4.00	0	1
Fields, J.	3B	36.0	5	12	0	0	1.000	4.25	0	0
Mackowiak, R.	3B	25.0	0	4	0	0	1.000	1.44	0	0

Name	POS	Inn	PO	A	TE	FE	FPct	RF	DPS	DPT
Podsednik, S.	LF	1086.0	245	4	1	7	.969	2.06	1	0
Ozuna, P.	LF	272.0	45	3	0	0	1.000	1.59	0	0
Mackowiak, R.	LF	65.3	11	1	0	0	1.000	1.65	0	0
Gload, R.	LF	12.0	2	0	0	0	1.000	1.50	0	0
Sweeney, R.	LF	12.0	2	0	0	0	1.000	1.50	0	0
Fields, J.	LF	1.0	0	0	0	0	0.000	0.00	0	0
Anderson, B.	CF	966.0	305	3	0	2	.994	2.87	2	0
Mackowiak, R.	CF	436.0	119	0	2	2	.967	2.46	0	0
Sweeney, R.	CF	35.0	8	0	0	0	1.000	2.06	0	0
Owens, J.	CF	12.0	5	0	0	0	1.000	3.75	0	0
Dye, J.	RF	1245.0	305	4	0	6	.981	2.23	3	0
Mackowiak, R.	RF	100.0	19	1	0	0	1.000	1.80	0	0
Gload, R.	RF	73.0	14	0	0	0	1.000	1.73	0	0
Sweeney, R.	RF	28.0	13	0	0	0	1.000	4.18	0	0
Ozuna, P.	RF	2.0	0	0	0	0	0.000	0.00	0	0
Owens, J.	RF	1.0	1	0	0	0	1.000	9.00	0	0

Cincinnati Reds

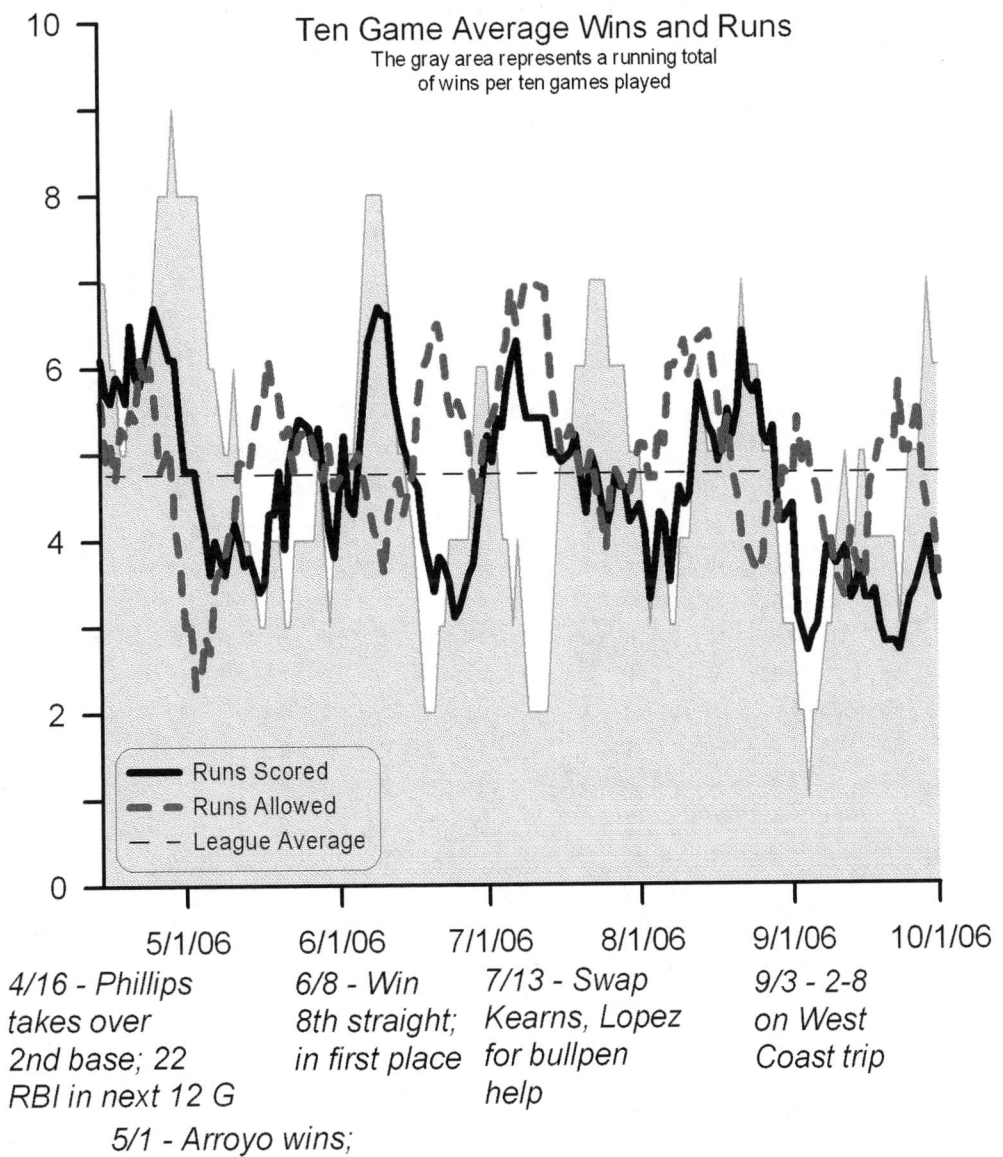

Ten Game Average Wins and Runs
The gray area represents a running total
of wins per ten games played

— Runs Scored
- - Runs Allowed
- - League Average

5/1/06   6/1/06   7/1/06   8/1/06   9/1/06   10/1/06

*4/16 - Phillips
takes over
2nd base; 22
RBI in next 12 G*

*6/8 - Win
8th straight;
in first place*

*7/13 - Swap
Kearns, Lopez
for bullpen
help*

*9/3 - 2-8
on West
Coast trip*

*5/1 - Arroyo wins;
is 5-0, 2.06 ERA*

Team Batting and Pitching/Fielding Stats by Month						
	April	May	June	July	Aug	Sept/Oct
Wins	17	12	15	11	12	13
Losses	8	16	12	14	17	15
OBP	.362	.325	.345	.353	.326	.307
SLG	.468	.404	.486	.444	.443	.350
FIP	5.17	4.12	4.78	4.35	5.10	4.26
DER	.687	.678	.698	.666	.669	.705

Batting Stats

Player	RC	Runs	RBI	PA	Outs	P/PA	H	2B	3B	HR	TB	K	BB	IBB	HBP	SH	SF	SB	CS	GDP	BA	OBP	SLG	GPA
Dunn A.	98	99	92	683	438	4.20	131	24	0	40	275	194	112	12	6	1	3	7	0	8	.234	.365	.490	.280
Hatteberg S.	78	62	51	539	339	3.98	132	28	0	13	199	41	74	3	3	2	4	2	2	13	.289	.389	.436	.278
Phillips B.	75	65	75	587	409	3.66	148	28	1	17	229	88	35	3	6	4	6	25	2	19	.276	.324	.427	.247
Aurilia R.	74	61	70	481	318	3.60	132	25	1	23	228	51	34	1	1	2	4	3	0	10	.300	.349	.518	.280
Encarnacion E.	67	60	72	467	306	3.84	112	33	1	15	192	78	41	3	13	0	3	6	3	9	.276	.359	.473	.273
Freel R.	61	67	27	523	347	4.09	123	30	2	8	181	98	57	0	9	3	0	37	11	5	.271	.363	.399	.257
Griffey Jr. K.	56	62	72	472	333	3.69	108	19	0	27	208	78	39	6	2	0	3	0	0	13	.252	.316	.486	.258
Lopez F.	49	55	30	394	263	4.09	92	14	1	9	135	66	47	1	0	3	1	23	6	6	.268	.355	.394	.253
Kearns A.	47	53	50	368	251	4.13	89	21	1	16	160	85	35	2	5	0	3	7	1	14	.274	.351	.492	.275
Ross D.	44	37	52	296	188	3.95	63	15	1	21	143	75	37	7	3	4	5	0	0	4	.255	.353	.579	.297
Valentin J.	18	24	27	201	141	3.28	50	6	1	8	82	29	13	3	0	0	2	0	0	5	.269	.313	.441	.246
LaRue J.	18	22	21	230	157	3.76	37	5	0	8	66	51	27	9	8	3	1	1	0	3	.194	.317	.346	.224
Castro J.	16	8	14	100	69	3.71	27	5	1	2	40	13	5	0	0	0	0	0	1	0	.284	.320	.421	.244
Denorfia C.	14	14	7	120	78	4.02	30	6	0	1	39	21	11	1	1	2	0	1	1	1	.283	.356	.368	.247
Clayton R.	11	13	13	164	120	3.79	35	8	0	2	49	32	11	0	1	2	1	6	3	3	.235	.290	.329	.208
Hollandsworth T	10	6	8	74	52	3.73	18	6	0	1	27	19	6	0	0	0	0	0	1	1	.265	.324	.397	.240
Hopper N.	8	6	5	47	28	3.45	14	1	0	1	18	4	6	0	0	1	1	2	2	1	.359	.435	.462	.304
Milton E.	5	8	3	58	39	3.64	11	3	1	0	16	24	2	0	0	6	1	0	0	1	.224	.250	.327	.190
Womack T.	4	1	3	23	14	3.87	4	2	0	0	6	3	4	1	0	1	0	0	0	0	.222	.364	.333	.241
Olmedo R.	4	5	4	48	35	4.17	9	2	0	1	14	4	4	0	0	0	0	1	0	0	.205	.271	.318	.197
McCracken Q.	3	5	2	60	43	3.73	11	1	1	1	17	9	4	0	0	3	0	2	0	1	.208	.263	.321	.194
Lohse K.	2	2	3	24	19	3.04	4	1	0	0	5	10	0	0	0	1	0	0	0	0	.174	.174	.217	.130
Ramirez E.	2	2	3	29	21	3.17	5	1	0	0	6	9	1	0	0	2	0	0	0	0	.192	.222	.231	.154
Ross C.	1	0	0	5	4	3.80	1	0	0	0	1	2	0	0	0	0	0	0	0	0	.200	.200	.200	.137
Mays J.	1	0	3	10	7	3.10	2	1	0	0	3	4	0	0	0	1	0	0	0	0	.222	.222	.333	.179
Michalak C.	1	0	0	11	6	3.73	2	1	0	0	3	5	1	0	0	2	0	0	0	0	.250	.333	.375	.238
Harris B.	1	2	1	11	9	5.27	2	0	0	1	5	4	1	0	0	0	0	0	0	1	.200	.273	.500	.242
Abad A.	0	0	0	5	3	3.80	0	0	0	0	0	0	2	0	0	0	0	0	0	0	.000	.400	.000	.176
Wise D.	-0	3	1	40	33	3.45	7	2	0	0	9	6	0	0	0	2	0	0	0	2	.184	.184	.237	.139
Kim S.	-0	0	0	1	1	5.00	0	0	0	0	0	0	0	0	0	0	0	0	0	0	.000	.000	.000	.000
Weathers D.	-0	0	0	1	1	5.00	0	0	0	0	0	1	0	0	0	0	0	0	0	0	.000	.000	.000	.000
Germano J.	-0	0	0	3	2	3.00	0	0	0	0	0	2	0	0	0	1	0	0	0	0	.000	.000	.000	.000
Franklin R.	-0	0	0	2	2	3.50	0	0	0	0	0	2	0	0	0	0	0	0	0	0	.000	.000	.000	.000
Williams D.	-0	0	0	13	11	4.54	1	0	0	0	1	5	1	0	0	0	0	0	0	0	.083	.154	.083	.088
Belisle M.	-0	0	0	7	5	4.00	0	0	0	0	0	2	0	0	0	2	0	0	0	0	.000	.000	.000	.000
Claussen B.	-1	1	1	24	19	3.54	2	0	0	0	2	11	0	0	0	3	0	0	0	0	.095	.095	.095	.065
Arroyo B.	-2	5	6	94	73	3.20	9	3	0	2	18	31	3	0	0	10	0	0	0	1	.111	.143	.222	.117
Harang A.	-3	1	2	81	67	3.26	8	0	0	0	8	35	1	0	1	5	0	0	0	1	.108	.132	.108	.084

Italicized stats have been adjusted for home park.

Batted Ball Batting Stats are listed after fielding stats

Pitching Stats

Player	PRC	IP	BFP	G	GS	P/PA	K	BB	IBB	HBP	H	HR	DP	DER	SB	CS	PO	W	L	Sv	Op	Hld	RA	ERA	FIP
Arroyo B.	122	240.7	992	35	35	3.88	184	64	7	5	222	31	19	.723	5	5	0	14	11	0	0	0	3.66	3.29	4.14
Harang A.	110	234.3	993	36	35	3.77	216	56	8	8	242	28	25	.672	16	8	1	16	11	0	0	0	4.19	3.76	3.64
Milton E.	49	152.7	662	26	26	3.59	90	42	4	5	163	29	7	.720	3	2	0	8	8	0	0	0	5.54	5.19	5.35
Coffey T.	37	78.0	339	81	0	3.66	60	27	5	2	85	7	10	.658	0	2	0	6	7	8	12	15	3.92	3.58	3.77
Weathers D.	35	73.7	314	67	0	3.67	50	34	4	2	61	12	7	.750	3	1	0	4	4	12	19	9	3.79	3.54	5.28
Ramirez E.	31	104.0	465	21	19	3.66	69	29	2	8	123	14	8	.667	2	3	0	4	9	0	0	0	6.06	5.37	4.65
Lohse K.	26	63.0	272	12	11	3.73	51	19	2	0	70	7	6	.672	2	1	0	3	5	0	0	0	4.71	4.57	3.85
Schoeneweis	24	14.3	60	16	0	3.93	11	8	1	1	9	1	2	.769	1	0	0	2	0	3	3	1	0.63	0.63	4.26
Claussen B.	21	77.0	351	14	14	3.79	57	28	1	6	93	14	6	.663	7	3	2	3	8	0	0	0	6.55	6.19	5.39
Belisle M.	18	40.0	180	30	2	3.80	26	19	1	3	43	5	6	.693	1	0	0	2	0	0	1	0	4.05	3.60	5.12
Mercker K.	11	28.3	123	37	0	3.85	17	11	1	0	28	6	4	.719	1	0	0	1	1	1	3	6	4.76	4.13	5.83
Bray B.	10	27.7	123	29	0	3.72	23	9	1	0	33	3	4	.636	0	0	0	2	1	2	3	2	5.20	4.23	3.83
Michalak C.	10	35.0	162	8	6	3.33	10	16	2	3	42	6	6	.685	2	2	2	2	4	0	0	0	5.40	4.89	6.33
Franklin R.	9	24.3	111	20	0	3.60	18	16	6	0	27	3	3	.662	2	2	0	5	2	0	2	0	5.18	4.44	4.57
Guardado E.	9	14.0	58	15	0	4.24	17	2	1	1	15	2	3	.611	0	0	0	0	0	8	10	0	3.21	1.29	3.08
Williams D.	8	40.0	194	8	8	3.53	16	16	0	4	54	9	2	.671	2	2	0	2	3	0	0	0	7.65	7.20	6.84
Hammond C.	7	28.7	125	29	0	3.62	23	5	0	0	36	5	3	.652	0	0	0	1	1	0	2	6	7.22	6.91	4.40
Yan E.	6	15.0	63	14	0	3.33	8	7	2	0	13	4	2	.773	0	1	0	1	0	1	1	0	4.20	3.60	6.62
White R.	6	27.3	118	26	0	3.34	17	5	1	1	34	5	3	.667	1	0	0	1	0	1	2	2	7.57	6.26	4.90
Mays J.	6	27.0	130	7	4	3.49	16	12	2	0	40	4	2	.612	1	0	0	0	1	0	0	0	7.67	7.33	5.07
Standridge J.	5	18.7	86	21	0	3.87	18	14	0	1	17	2	2	.667	1	0	0	1	1	0	0	1	6.75	4.82	5.09
Cormier R.	5	14.0	66	21	0	3.45	6	4	0	0	21	3	1	.660	0	0	0	0	1	0	0	2	4.50	4.50	6.00
Shackelford B.	4	16.3	79	26	0	3.51	15	10	0	2	18	4	0	.708	0	0	0	1	0	0	0	2	7.16	7.16	6.77
Majewski G.	3	15.0	79	19	0	3.39	9	4	2	3	30	1	1	.516	0	2	0	1	2	0	2	2	8.40	8.40	3.88
Johnson J.	3	8.7	38	4	0	3.29	4	0	0	1	11	1	1	.656	0	0	0	0	0	0	0	0	5.19	3.12	4.14
Germano J.	3	6.7	31	2	1	3.65	8	3	1	1	8	1	2	.556	0	0	0	0	1	0	0	0	5.40	5.40	4.12
Burns M.	2	13.3	70	11	0	3.46	9	3	1	2	30	2	4	.463	0	1	0	0	0	0	0	1	8.78	8.78	4.72
Kim S.	2	6.7	28	2	1	3.32	4	0	0	0	7	3	0	.810	0	0	0	0	1	0	0	0	5.40	5.40	7.87
Gosling M.	0	1.3	7	1	0	3.00	1	1	0	1	1	1	0	1.000	0	0	0	0	0	0	0	0	13.50	13.50	15.97

Batted Ball Pitching Stats are listed after fielding stats

Fielding Stats

Name	POS	INN	SBA/G	CS%	ERA	WP+PB/G	PO	A	TE	FE
Ross, D.	C	620.7	0.42	41%	4.26	0.392	480	33	5	3
LaRue, J.	C	512.3	0.60	32%	4.43	0.264	376	36	1	1
Valentin, J.	C	312.7	0.49	41%	5.24	0.201	247	17	5	1

Name	POS	Inn	PO	A	TE	FE	FPct	RF	DPS	DPT
Hatteberg, S.	1B	1088.0	997	69	1	2	.996	8.82	10	1
Aurilia, R.	1B	329.7	301	26	1	1	.994	8.93	9	0
Dunn, A.	1B	17.0	15	1	0	1	.941	8.47	0	0
Encarnacion, E.	1B	9.0	9	0	0	0	1.000	9.00	0	0
Valentin, J.	1B	1.3	2	0	0	0	1.000	13.50	0	0
Phillips, B.	2B	1216.0	331	334	8	8	.977	4.92	33	47
Freel, R.	2B	91.0	23	25	1	0	.980	4.75	0	2
Aurilia, R.	2B	41.0	13	14	0	0	1.000	5.93	1	1
Olmedo, R.	2B	40.3	5	13	0	2	.900	4.02	0	2
Womack, T.	2B	40.0	11	17	0	0	1.000	6.30	0	2
Harris, B.	2B	12.0	4	3	0	0	1.000	5.25	2	1
Castro, J.	2B	5.0	0	2	0	0	1.000	3.60	0	0
Lopez, F.	SS	735.7	98	227	9	5	.959	3.98	26	15
Clayton, R.	SS	334.7	61	100	3	4	.958	4.33	6	10
Aurilia, R.	SS	198.7	37	68	0	1	.991	4.76	5	10
Castro, J.	SS	140.7	23	42	0	1	.985	4.16	4	5
Olmedo, R.	SS	21.0	4	6	0	1	.909	4.29	2	0
Phillips, B.	SS	15.0	1	3	0	1	.800	2.40	0	0
Encarnacion, E.	3B	931.3	74	196	16	9	.915	2.61	16	0
Aurilia, R.	3B	356.0	24	78	3	2	.953	2.58	7	0
Freel, R.	3B	88.3	7	25	0	0	1.000	3.26	2	0
Castro, J.	3B	64.0	4	16	0	0	1.000	2.81	2	0
Olmedo, R.	3B	6.0	0	0	0	0	0.000	0.00	0	0

Name	POS	Inn	PO	A	TE	FE	FPct	RF	DPS	DPT
Dunn, A.	LF	1321.0	279	7	4	8	.960	1.95	2	0
Freel, R.	LF	41.7	10	1	0	0	1.000	2.38	0	0
Denorfia, C.	LF	27.0	4	0	0	0	1.000	1.33	0	0
Wise, D.	LF	22.0	4	0	0	0	1.000	1.64	0	0
McCracken, Q.	LF	14.0	3	0	0	0	1.000	1.93	0	0
Ross, C.	LF	9.0	1	0	0	0	1.000	1.00	0	0
Hollandsworth, T.	LF	8.0	1	1	0	0	1.000	2.25	0	0
Hopper, N.	LF	3.0	1	0	0	0	1.000	3.00	0	0
Griffey Jr., K.	CF	870.3	229	6	3	2	.979	2.43	0	0
Freel, R.	CF	400.0	127	4	0	0	1.000	2.95	0	0
Denorfia, C.	CF	85.3	20	0	0	0	1.000	2.11	0	0
McCracken, Q.	CF	40.0	15	0	0	1	.938	3.38	0	0
Wise, D.	CF	36.0	14	1	0	1	.938	3.75	0	0
Hopper, N.	CF	14.0	1	1	0	0	1.000	1.29	0	0
Kearns, A.	RF	746.3	207	5	2	0	.991	2.56	2	0
Freel, R.	RF	360.7	101	7	1	4	.956	2.70	2	0
Hollandsworth, T.	RF	118.3	22	0	0	0	1.000	1.67	0	0
Denorfia, C.	RF	118.3	34	2	0	1	1.000	2.74	2	0
Hopper, N.	RF	70.0	25	1	0	0	1.000	3.34	2	0
Wise, D.	RF	21.0	0	0	0	0	0.000	0.00	0	0
McCracken, Q.	RF	10.0	3	0	0	0	1.000	2.70	0	0
Olmedo, R.	RF	1.0	0	0	0	0	0.000	0.00	0	0

Batted Ball Batting Stats

Player	PA	% of PA		% of Batted Balls					Runs Per Event				Total Runs vs. Avg.				
		K%	BB%	GB%	LD%	FB%	IF/F	HR/OF	NIP	GB	LD	OF	NIP	GB	LD	FB	Tot
Dunn A.	683	28	17	28	24	49	.08	.23	.06	-.02	.41	.32	10	-12	-2	21	17
Aurilia R.	481	11	7	38	20	42	.15	.16	.07	.05	.38	.23	-0	1	3	9	13
Ross D.	296	25	14	32	17	51	.13	.27	.05	-.01	.46	.40	1	-4	-3	17	11
Hatteberg S.	539	8	14	46	21	33	.09	.10	.19	.04	.32	.17	15	0	-2	-3	9
Encarnacion E.	467	17	12	41	21	37	.14	.13	.08	.06	.40	.22	4	1	2	2	9
Kearns A.	368	23	11	43	21	36	.05	.19	.03	.02	.48	.27	-1	-3	4	6	6
Griffey Jr. K.	472	17	9	42	15	43	.09	.18	.04	.01	.40	.27	-1	-5	-5	15	4
Freel R.	523	19	13	44	21	35	.09	.06	.07	.10	.42	.10	5	8	2	-13	2
Castro J.	100	13	5	40	23	37	.13	.08	.01	.02	.41	.17	-1	-1	2	-0	-0
Lopez F.	394	17	12	50	18	32	.07	.11	.08	.05	.49	.12	3	1	2	-8	-1
Valentin J.	201	14	6	33	23	43	.04	.12	.03	.00	.34	.15	-2	-3	1	1	-2
Denorfia C.	120	18	10	59	17	24	.10	.00	.05	.09	.41	.08	0	3	-1	-4	-2
Phillips B.	587	15	7	46	19	35	.06	.12	.03	.03	.32	.21	-4	-2	-5	5	-6
Clayton R.	164	20	7	55	19	26	.06	.07	.01	.06	.23	.18	-2	1	-4	-2	-6
LaRue J.	230	22	15	44	20	36	.08	.17	.07	-.01	.30	.20	3	-5	-4	-1	-6
MLB Average		17	9	44	20	37	.11	.11	.05	.04	.39	.19	-	-	-	-	-

Batted Ball Pitching Stats

Player	PA	% of PA		% of Batted Balls					Runs Per Event				Total Runs vs. Avg.				
		K%	BB%	GB%	LD%	FB%	IF/F	HR/OF	NIP	GB	LD	OF	NIP	GB	LD	FB	Tot
Arroyo B.	992	19	7	38	21	41	.12	.12	.01	.02	.34	.17	-10	-7	-3	-1	-22
Harang A.	993	22	6	39	22	40	.13	.11	-.01	.06	.40	.22	-16	-0	3	6	-7
Weathers D.	314	16	11	45	17	38	.10	.16	.08	.05	.31	.18	3	1	-6	-0	-3
Lohse K.	272	19	7	48	19	33	.13	.13	.01	.07	.40	.20	-3	3	-1	-1	-2
Coffey T.	339	18	8	52	21	27	.09	.11	.03	.06	.41	.21	-2	2	2	-3	-0
Belisle M.	180	14	12	48	17	35	.04	.12	.10	.05	.32	.20	2	1	-3	1	1
Bray B.	123	19	7	40	29	31	.07	.08	.02	.03	.44	.14	-1	-1	5	-2	1
Hammond C.	125	18	4	54	14	33	.16	.19	-.03	.12	.35	.31	-3	4	-2	2	1
Mercker K.	123	14	9	36	22	42	.03	.14	.07	.02	.29	.25	0	-1	-1	4	2
White R.	118	14	5	58	16	26	.04	.23	.01	.05	.51	.29	-1	2	1	1	3
Franklin R.	111	16	15	46	20	34	.08	.13	.11	.10	.40	.20	2	1	-0	-0	3
Michalak C.	162	6	12	51	17	32	.10	.14	.19	.02	.41	.28	3	-0	0	3	6
Mays J.	130	12	9	48	20	31	.03	.13	.08	.10	.37	.29	1	3	0	3	6
Milton E.	662	14	7	31	19	50	.08	.11	.04	.08	.38	.16	-3	2	0	8	7
Ramirez E.	465	15	8	44	23	33	.13	.14	.05	.06	.39	.25	-1	1	5	4	9
Williams D.	194	8	10	32	25	43	.12	.12	.14	.04	.45	.19	3	-0	6	2	11
Claussen B.	351	16	10	36	20	44	.15	.14	.06	.06	.48	.24	1	1	4	6	11
MLB Average		17	9	44	20	37	.11	.11	.05	.04	.39	.19	-	-	-	-	-

Cleveland Indians

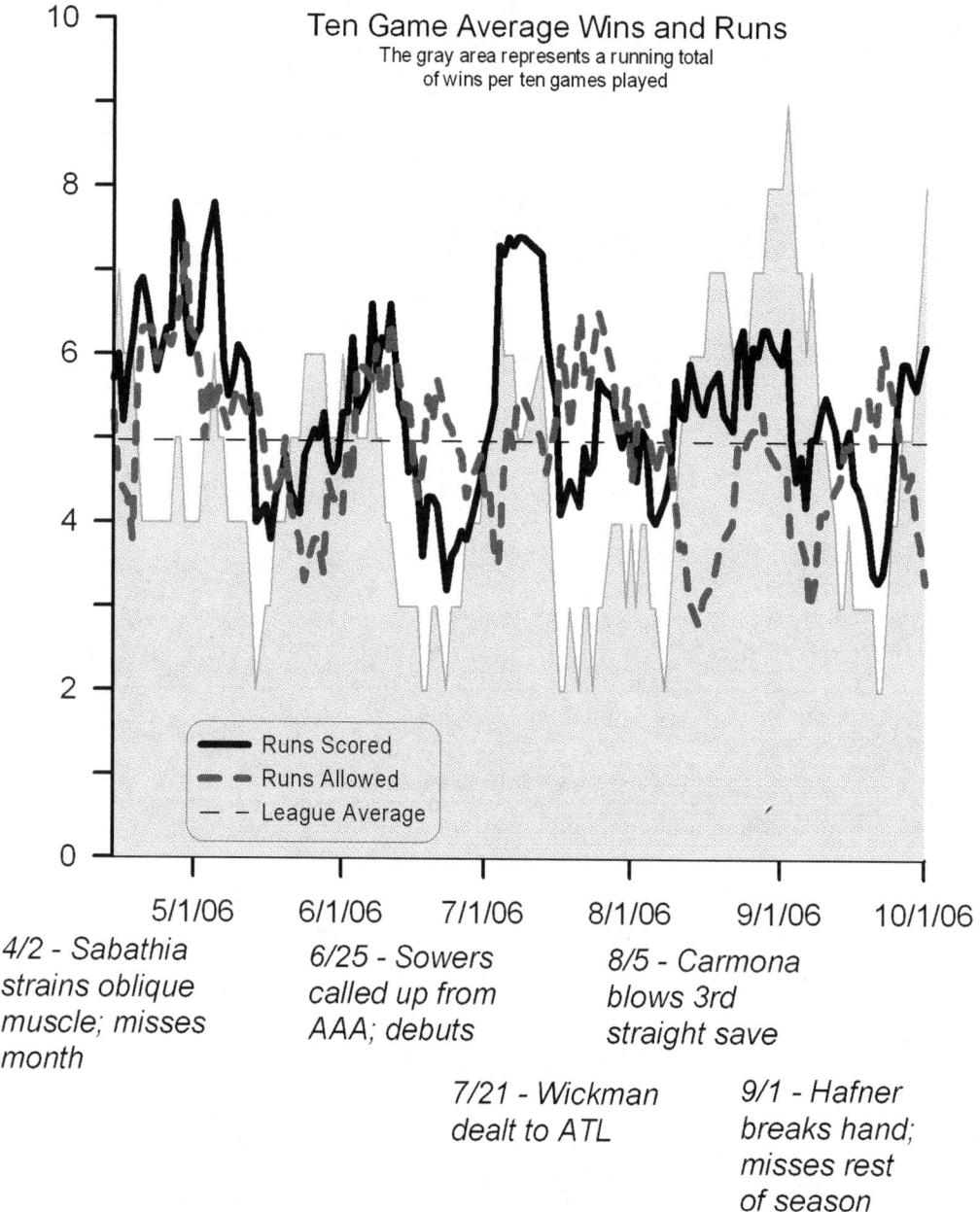

Ten Game Average Wins and Runs

The gray area represents a running total
of wins per ten games played

Runs Scored
Runs Allowed
League Average

4/2 - Sabathia
strains oblique
muscle; misses
month

6/25 - Sowers
called up from
AAA; debuts

8/5 - Carmona
blows 3rd
straight save

7/21 - Wickman
dealt to ATL

9/1 - Hafner
breaks hand;
misses rest
of season

Team Batting and Pitching/Fielding Stats by Month						
	April	May	June	July	Aug	Sept/Oct
Wins	13	13	9	10	18	15
Losses	12	14	17	16	10	15
OBP	.368	.355	.327	.351	.356	.335
SLG	.473	.449	.446	.481	.482	.415
FIP	4.58	3.95	4.92	4.39	3.86	4.30
DER	.694	.681	.686	.655	.667	.679

Batting Stats

Player	RC	Runs	RBI	PA	Outs	P/PA	H	2B	3B	HR	TB	K	BB	IBB	HBP	SH	SF	SB	CS	GDP	BA	OBP	SLG	GPA
Sizemore G.	124	134	76	751	473	4.02	190	53	11	28	349	153	78	8	13	1	4	22	6	2	.290	.375	.533	.307
Hafner T.	121	100	117	564	324	4.21	140	31	1	42	299	111	100	16	7	0	2	0	0	10	.308	.439	.659	.369
Martinez V.	99	82	93	652	418	3.65	181	37	0	16	266	78	71	8	3	0	6	0	0	27	.316	.391	.465	.298
Peralta J.	68	84	68	632	443	4.12	146	28	3	13	219	152	56	0	1	3	3	0	1	19	.257	.323	.385	.246
Blake C.	64	63	68	456	299	4.07	113	20	1	19	192	93	45	5	4	1	5	6	0	11	.282	.356	.479	.285
Michaels J.	63	77	55	548	373	3.93	132	32	1	9	193	101	43	0	3	2	6	9	5	6	.267	.326	.391	.249
Broussard B.	50	44	46	288	188	3.57	86	14	0	13	139	58	17	1	1	0	2	0	1	5	.321	.361	.519	.297
Belliard R.	49	43	44	379	256	3.36	102	21	0	8	147	45	21	0	4	2	2	2	0	8	.291	.337	.420	.261
Boone A.	47	50	46	392	273	3.59	89	19	1	7	131	62	27	1	6	4	1	5	4	4	.251	.314	.370	.238
Garko R.	33	28	45	209	136	4.26	54	12	0	7	87	37	14	0	7	0	3	0	0	5	.292	.359	.470	.284
Inglett J.	29	26	21	222	146	3.55	57	8	3	2	77	39	14	0	1	5	1	5	1	1	.284	.332	.383	.249
Choo S.	25	23	22	167	108	4.03	43	11	3	3	69	46	18	2	1	1	1	5	3	2	.295	.373	.473	.291
Marte A.	22	20	23	178	130	3.88	37	15	1	5	69	38	13	0	1	0	0	0	0	3	.226	.287	.421	.238
Hollandsworth	21	21	27	162	122	3.57	37	12	1	6	69	33	4	1	0	0	2	0	1	2	.237	.253	.442	.228
Perez E.	19	16	22	108	74	3.59	30	9	0	8	63	11	5	0	2	0	2	0	0	5	.303	.343	.636	.319
Luna H.	14	14	17	134	97	3.48	35	7	1	2	50	26	6	0	0	0	1	0	1	4	.276	.306	.394	.240
Shoppach K.	13	7	16	120	85	3.85	27	6	0	3	42	45	8	0	0	2	0	0	0	2	.245	.297	.382	.233
Gutierrez F.	13	21	8	141	103	3.79	37	9	0	1	49	28	3	0	0	2	0	0	0	4	.272	.288	.360	.224
Kouzmanoff K.	7	4	11	61	47	3.74	12	2	0	3	23	12	5	0	0	0	0	0	0	3	.214	.279	.411	.232
Vazquez R.	7	11	8	77	56	3.77	14	2	0	1	19	18	6	0	0	2	2	0	0	3	.209	.267	.284	.194
Laker T.	2	1	2	13	9	3.77	4	1	0	0	5	4	0	0	0	0	0	0	0	0	.308	.308	.385	.239
Merloni L.	1	1	1	23	16	3.78	4	1	0	0	5	5	2	0	0	2	0	1	0	1	.211	.286	.263	.198
Sabathia C.	1	0	2	9	7	3.33	2	0	0	0	2	5	0	0	0	0	0	0	0	0	.222	.222	.222	.158
Lee C.	1	0	0	6	5	3.50	1	0	0	0	1	3	0	0	0	0	0	0	0	0	.167	.167	.167	.119
Westbrook J.	1	0	1	5	2	4.20	2	1	0	0	3	1	0	0	0	1	0	0	0	0	.500	.500	.750	.420
Byrd P.	1	0	0	6	3	2.00	1	0	0	0	1	0	0	0	0	2	0	0	0	0	.250	.250	.250	.178

Italicized stats have been adjusted for home park.

Batted Ball Batting Stats are listed after fielding stats

Pitching Stats

Player	PRC	IP	BFP	G	GS	P/PA	K	BB	IBB	HBP	H	HR	DP	DER	SB	CS	PO	W	L	Sv	Op	Hld	RA	ERA	FIP
Sabathia C.	100	192.7	802	28	28	3.65	172	44	3	7	182	17	18	.687	14	5	0	12	11	0	0	0	3.88	3.22	3.37
Westbrook J.	84	211.3	904	32	32	3.62	109	55	4	4	247	15	38	.666	16	3	3	15	10	0	0	0	4.51	4.17	3.93
Lee C.	75	200.7	882	33	33	3.81	129	58	3	8	224	29	15	.691	7	3	1	14	11	0	0	0	5.11	4.40	4.80
Byrd P.	52	179.0	805	31	31	3.55	88	38	3	6	232	26	15	.662	18	5	1	10	9	0	0	0	6.03	4.88	4.85
Sowers J.	40	88.3	360	14	14	3.54	35	20	1	2	85	10	15	.730	6	3	0	7	4	0	0	0	3.67	3.57	4.66
Betancourt R.	28	56.7	231	50	0	3.91	48	11	5	0	52	7	2	.709	8	2	0	3	4	3	6	7	3.97	3.81	3.49
Carmona F.	27	74.7	340	38	7	3.67	58	31	3	7	88	9	9	.655	10	2	1	1	10	0	3	10	5.54	5.42	4.68
Cabrera F.	25	60.7	256	51	0	3.91	71	32	2	1	53	12	5	.693	11	6	2	3	3	0	4	6	5.34	5.19	5.03
Davis J.	23	55.3	246	39	0	3.43	37	14	2	3	67	1	6	.639	4	1	0	3	2	1	3	6	4.55	3.74	2.97
Johnson J.	20	77.0	348	14	14	3.50	32	22	0	2	108	10	15	.638	13	0	0	3	8	0	0	0	6.43	5.96	5.05
Mujica E.	11	18.3	78	10	0	3.62	12	0	0	1	25	1	1	.609	0	1	1	0	1	0	0	0	2.95	2.95	2.83
Mota G.	11	37.7	173	34	0	4.14	27	19	3	0	45	9	4	.686	6	0	0	1	3	0	0	5	6.45	6.21	6.21
Wickman B.	11	28.0	126	29	0	3.76	17	11	0	1	29	1	2	.677	3	0	0	1	4	15	18	0	4.82	4.18	3.80
Sikorski B.	9	19.7	82	17	0	4.01	24	4	0	1	20	4	0	.673	3	1	1	2	1	0	1	2	4.58	4.58	4.23
Miller M.	9	15.7	65	14	0	3.71	12	9	0	2	11	2	5	.750	0	0	0	1	0	0	0	1	3.45	3.45	5.50
Perez R.	6	12.3	56	18	0	3.77	15	6	1	0	10	2	0	.727	3	0	0	0	0	0	1	1	4.38	4.38	4.15
Mastny T.	6	16.3	73	15	0	3.74	14	8	1	1	17	1	1	.673	0	0	0	0	1	5	7	0	5.51	5.51	3.81
Slocum B.	6	17.7	85	8	2	4.09	11	9	0	1	27	3	5	.607	1	1	0	0	0	0	0	0	5.60	5.60	5.92
Brown A.	5	10.0	44	9	0	3.75	7	8	1	1	6	0	1	.786	0	0	0	0	0	0	0	0	3.60	3.60	4.26
Guthrie J.	5	19.3	93	9	1	3.85	14	15	1	2	24	2	3	.633	2	1	0	0	0	0	0	0	6.98	6.98	5.64
Sauerbeck S.	4	13.0	57	24	0	3.86	11	9	1	1	9	2	1	.794	0	0	0	0	1	0	2	2	6.23	6.23	5.65
Graves D.	3	14.0	65	13	0	3.52	3	5	1	0	18	3	2	.685	1	0	0	2	1	0	1	0	7.71	5.79	6.48
Lara J.	2	5.0	19	9	0	3.47	2	1	0	0	4	0	2	.688	2	0	0	0	0	0	1	0	3.60	1.80	3.06

Batted Ball Pitching Stats are listed after fielding stats

Fielding Stats

Name	POS	INN	SBA/G	CS%	ERA	WP+PB/G	PO	A	TE	FE
Martinez, V.	C	1110.0	0.95	15%	4.51	0.308	755	44	3	4
Shoppach, K.	C	280.3	0.93	34%	4.11	0.449	208	20	1	1
Laker, T.	C	33.0	2.45	0%	4.64	0.273	24	1	0	0

Name	POS	Inn	PO	A	TE	FE	FPct	RF	DPS	DPT
Broussard, B.	1B	569.7	577	51	2	5	.989	9.92	7	0
Garko, R.	1B	396.0	398	30	1	4	.986	9.73	5	1
Perez, E.	1B	196.0	209	14	1	1	.991	10.24	3	0
Martinez, V.	1B	166.3	149	5	0	0	1.000	8.33	1	0
Blake, C.	1B	62.0	62	1	0	1	.984	9.15	0	0
Hafner, T.	1B	33.3	18	4	0	0	1.000	5.94	0	0
Belliard, R.	2B	768.3	169	252	5	3	.981	4.93	22	32
Inglett, J.	2B	417.3	112	142	2	1	.984	5.48	14	28
Luna, H.	2B	169.3	39	50	0	5	.947	4.73	8	7
Vazquez, R.	2B	43.0	8	20	0	0	1.000	5.86	2	3
Merloni, L.	2B	23.0	3	3	0	0	1.000	2.35	0	0
Boone, A.	2B	2.3	1	1	0	0	1.000	7.71	0	0
Peralta, J.	SS	1275.0	235	459	8	8	.977	4.90	51	43
Luna, H.	SS	87.0	15	34	0	0	1.000	5.07	7	3
Vazquez, R.	SS	43.0	8	15	0	3	.885	4.81	0	3
Merloni, L.	SS	9.0	0	4	0	0	1.000	4.00	1	0
Inglett, J.	SS	9.0	3	1	0	0	1.000	4.00	0	0
Boone, A.	3B	842.7	56	186	3	12	.938	2.58	16	1
Marte, A.	3B	428.0	32	118	1	5	.962	3.15	16	0
Vazquez, R.	3B	93.0	4	20	1	0	.960	2.32	1	0
Merloni, L.	3B	17.3	1	3	0	0	1.000	2.08	2	0
Luna, H.	3B	17.0	0	0	0	0	0.000	0.00	0	0
Kouzmanoff, K.	3B	16.0	2	4	0	1	.857	3.38	0	0
Belliard, R.	3B	9.3	1	1	0	0	1.000	1.93	0	0

Name	POS	Inn	PO	A	TE	FE	FPct	RF	DPS	DPT
Michaels, J.	LF	1009.0	214	6	0	2	.991	1.96	4	0
Hollandsworth, T.	LF	212.3	56	4	0	0	1.000	2.54	0	0
Gutierrez, F.	LF	83.0	21	0	1	0	.955	2.28	0	0
Choo, S.	LF	77.7	14	0	0	1	.933	1.62	0	0
Inglett, J.	LF	41.0	8	0	0	0	1.000	1.76	0	0
Sizemore, G.	CF	1379.0	409	7	2	1	.993	2.72	2	0
Gutierrez, F.	CF	27.0	14	0	0	0	1.000	4.67	0	0
Inglett, J.	CF	11.0	6	0	0	0	1.000	4.91	0	0
Hollandsworth, T.	CF	6.0	0	0	0	0	0.000	0.00	0	0
Blake, C.	RF	814.3	210	6	0	3	.986	2.39	0	0
Choo, S.	RF	256.7	67	2	1	0	.986	2.42	2	0
Gutierrez, F.	RF	212.0	50	1	0	2	.962	2.17	0	0
Hollandsworth, T.	RF	93.0	20	0	0	2	.909	1.94	0	0
Perez, E.	RF	30.3	4	2	0	0	1.000	1.78	0	0
Michaels, J.	RF	9.0	2	0	0	0	1.000	2.00	0	0
Luna, H.	RF	8.0	0	0	0	0	0.000	0.00	0	0

Batted Ball Batting Stats

Player	PA	% of PA		% of Batted Balls					Runs Per Event				Total Runs vs. Avg.				
		K%	BB%	GB%	LD%	FB%	IF/F	HR/OF	NIP	GB	LD	OF	NIP	GB	LD	FB	Tot
Hafner T.	564	20	19	39	21	40	.04	.28	.11	.01	.45	.47	17	-7	2	38	49
Sizemore G.	751	20	12	33	20	47	.06	.12	.06	.06	.49	.25	4	-1	7	22	33
Martinez V.	652	12	11	44	22	34	.06	.10	.11	.01	.37	.24	8	-7	3	9	14
Broussard B.	288	20	6	45	20	35	.11	.19	-0.00	.12	.31	.33	-4	7	-3	9	9
Blake C.	456	20	11	40	23	37	.09	.17	.05	.05	.41	.24	0	0	4	4	9
Perez E.	108	10	6	48	17	36	.16	.22	.07	.01	.40	.45	-0	-1	-0	7	5
Choo S.	167	28	11	58	22	20	0.00	.15	.02	.11	.39	.40	-1	4	-1	1	4
Garko R.	209	18	10	42	17	41	.08	.12	.05	.08	.38	.21	0	2	-2	2	3
Belliard R.	379	12	7	42	18	39	.05	.06	.05	.07	.37	.12	-2	3	0	-3	-2
Luna H.	134	19	4	43	25	32	.06	.06	-.03	.06	.37	.12	-3	1	2	-2	-2
Hollandsworth T.	162	20	2	47	18	35	.09	.15	-.06	.05	.24	.29	-5	1	-4	4	-3
Marte A.	178	21	8	34	17	48	.13	.09	.01	.01	.56	.12	-2	-2	3	-2	-3
Inglett J.	222	18	7	47	24	29	.04	.05	.01	.02	.43	.10	-2	0	4	-5	-3
Shoppach K.	120	38	7	43	15	42	0.00	.11	-.04	.13	.37	.24	-4	2	-3	1	-3
Gutierrez F.	141	20	2	43	23	34	.17	.03	-.07	.09	.29	.11	-4	2	-1	-3	-6
Michaels J.	548	18	8	40	23	38	.10	.06	.03	.07	.38	.11	-3	4	4	-11	-6
Boone A.	392	16	8	36	25	40	.17	.07	.05	.01	.32	.14	-1	-5	1	-5	-10
Peralta J.	632	24	9	48	19	34	.06	.09	.01	.08	.40	.16	-6	6	-4	-7	-11
MLB Average		*17*	*9*	*44*	*20*	*37*	*.11*	*.11*	*.05*	*.04*	*.39*	*.19*	-	-	-	-	-

Batted Ball Pitching Stats

Player	PA	% of PA		% of Batted Balls					Runs Per Event				Total Runs vs. Avg.				
		K%	BB%	GB%	LD%	FB%	IF/F	HR/OF	NIP	GB	LD	OF	NIP	GB	LD	FB	Tot
Sabathia C.	802	21	6	45	19	36	.12	.10	-.01	.06	.36	.15	-13	3	-5	-10	-24
Westbrook J.	904	12	7	61	17	22	.05	.10	.05	.04	.41	.17	-4	8	2	-14	-9
Sowers J.	360	10	6	48	21	30	.10	.12	.06	.01	.29	.20	-1	-4	-2	-0	-7
Betancourt R.	231	21	5	23	25	51	.12	.09	-.03	.10	.30	.12	-5	1	-0	-2	-6
Davis J.	246	15	7	49	20	32	.10	.02	.03	.12	.43	.04	-2	7	2	-9	-2
Wickman B.	126	13	10	37	27	36	.21	.04	.08	.01	.43	.09	1	-2	4	-3	-1
Cabrera F.	256	28	13	33	23	43	.12	.21	.03	.11	.37	.25	-0	1	-1	2	2
Carmona F.	340	17	11	60	13	27	.08	.15	.07	.06	.34	.35	2	4	-8	6	4
Lee C.	882	15	7	33	19	48	.14	.10	.04	.11	.31	.16	-4	12	-9	4	4
Mota G.	173	16	11	30	20	50	.03	.15	.08	.02	.48	.21	1	-2	2	5	7
Johnson J.	348	9	7	60	17	24	.12	.17	.08	.08	.43	.27	-0	10	2	1	12
Byrd P.	805	11	5	39	24	37	.11	.12	.04	.09	.35	.17	-6	12	12	-0	18
MLB Average		*17*	*9*	*44*	*20*	*37*	*.11*	*.11*	*.05*	*.04*	*.39*	*.19*	-	-	-	-	-

Colorado Rockies

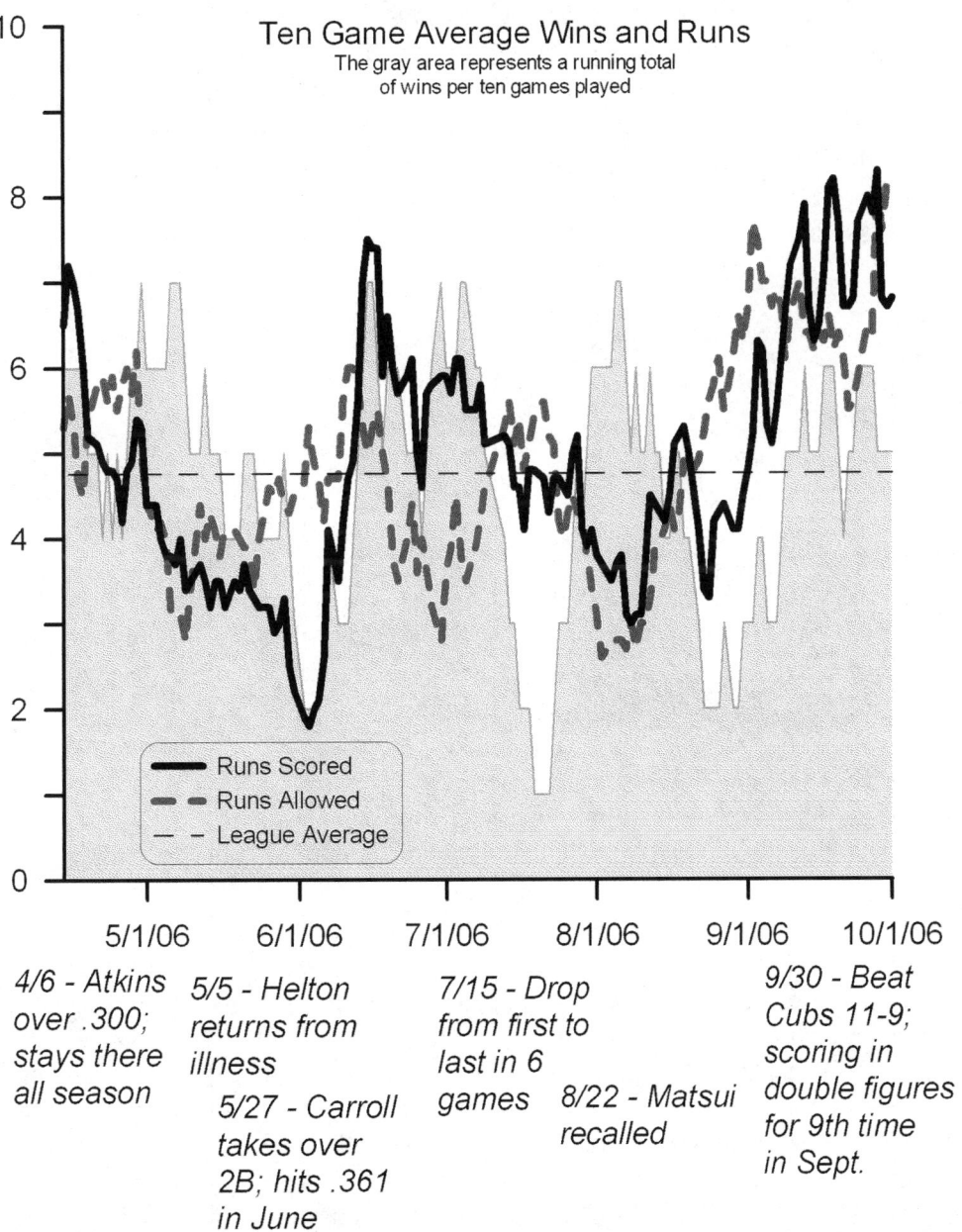

Ten Game Average Wins and Runs
The gray area represents a running total
of wins per ten games played

- Runs Scored
- Runs Allowed
- League Average

4/6 - Atkins over .300; stays there all season

5/5 - Helton returns from illness

5/27 - Carroll takes over 2B; hits .361 in June

7/15 - Drop from first to last in 6 games

8/22 - Matsui recalled

9/30 - Beat Cubs 11-9; scoring in double figures for 9th time in Sept.

Team Batting and Pitching/Fielding Stats by Month						
	April	May	June	July	Aug	Sept/Oct
Wins	15	12	14	10	11	14
Losses	10	16	12	16	17	15
OBP	.359	.299	.355	.329	.335	.365
SLG	.479	.369	.443	.421	.413	.468
FIP	4.29	3.75	4.18	4.83	4.33	4.93
DER	.684	.697	.689	.702	.687	.656

Batting Stats

Player	RC	Runs	RBI	PA	Outs	P/PA	H	2B	3B	HR	TB	K	BB	IBB	HBP	SH	SF	SB	CS	GDP	BA	OBP	SLG	GPA
Atkins G.	120	117	120	695	428	3.82	198	48	1	29	335	76	79	6	7	0	7	4	0	24	.329	.409	.556	.303
Helton T.	109	94	81	649	393	3.94	165	40	5	15	260	64	91	15	6	0	6	3	2	10	.302	.404	.476	.282
Holliday M.	103	119	114	667	433	3.62	196	45	5	34	353	110	47	3	15	0	3	10	5	22	.326	.387	.586	.300
Hawpe B.	78	67	84	575	366	3.96	146	33	6	22	257	123	74	11	0	0	2	5	5	8	.293	.383	.515	.282
Carroll J.	60	84	36	534	346	4.16	139	23	5	5	187	66	56	1	3	9	3	10	12	10	.300	.377	.404	.254
Sullivan C.	44	47	30	443	294	3.86	103	26	10	2	155	100	32	3	1	19	5	10	6	5	.267	.321	.402	.229
Barmes C.	43	57	56	535	379	3.45	105	26	4	7	160	72	22	6	9	19	7	5	4	2	.220	.264	.335	.189
Torrealba Y.	28	23	43	241	178	3.66	55	16	3	7	98	49	11	1	4	2	1	4	3	7	.247	.293	.439	.226
Matsui K.	21	22	19	126	75	4.07	39	6	3	2	57	27	10	0	0	1	2	8	1	0	.345	.392	.504	.283
Spilborghs R.	20	26	21	186	128	3.78	48	6	3	4	72	30	14	0	0	2	3	5	2	7	.287	.337	.431	.243
Freeman C.	20	24	18	191	139	3.83	41	6	3	2	59	42	14	2	1	3	0	5	6	1	.237	.298	.341	.205
Baker J.	15	13	21	58	36	3.14	21	7	2	5	47	14	1	0	0	0	0	2	0	0	.368	.379	.825	.353
Smith J.	14	9	13	108	74	3.59	26	1	0	5	42	29	7	1	2	0	0	3	0	1	.263	.324	.424	.236
Gonzalez L.	11	7	14	158	117	3.27	36	9	1	2	53	27	4	0	2	2	1	1	1	3	.242	.269	.356	.197
Salazar J.	10	13	8	67	38	4.34	15	4	0	1	22	16	11	2	1	1	1	2	0	0	.283	.409	.415	.270
Marrero E.	9	7	10	72	48	4.11	13	3	0	4	28	16	11	1	1	0	0	3	0	1	.217	.347	.467	.256
Tulowitzki T.	9	15	6	108	74	3.67	23	2	0	1	28	25	10	3	1	1	0	3	0	1	.240	.318	.292	.202
Iannetta C.	8	12	10	93	59	4.06	20	4	0	2	30	17	13	2	1	1	1	0	1	1	.260	.370	.390	.247
Ojeda M.	8	5	11	82	63	3.95	17	3	0	2	26	16	8	2	0	0	0	0	0	6	.230	.305	.351	.211
Closser J.	8	10	11	112	80	3.80	19	3	1	2	30	23	12	2	1	1	1	0	1	1	.196	.288	.309	.194
Francis J.	3	3	6	80	54	3.48	7	0	0	0	7	20	8	0	0	9	2	0	0	0	.115	.211	.115	.116
Quintanilla O.	2	3	3	38	30	4.79	6	1	1	0	9	9	3	1	0	1	0	1	1	1	.176	.243	.265	.165
Castilla V.	2	2	4	22	19	3.45	4	0	0	1	7	3	0	0	1	0	0	0	0	2	.190	.227	.333	.174
Ardoin D.	1	12	2	120	90	3.88	21	5	1	0	28	27	8	2	2	1	0	0	0	2	.193	.261	.257	.170
Piedra J.	1	4	10	64	51	3.94	10	2	0	3	21	22	3	0	1	0	0	1	0	2	.169	.222	.356	.177
Kim B.	1	4	4	57	44	3.26	8	1	0	0	9	15	1	0	0	6	0	0	0	2	.160	.176	.180	.117
Ramirez R.	1	0	0	5	2	2.60	2	0	0	0	2	2	0	0	0	1	0	0	0	0	.500	.500	.500	.328
Kim S.	1	0	0	1	0	2.00	1	1	0	0	2	0	0	0	0	0	0	0	0	0	1.000	1.000	2.000	.890
Colina A.	1	0	1	5	4	3.60	1	0	0	0	1	1	0	0	0	0	0	0	0	0	.200	.200	.200	.131
Jimenez U.	0	1	0	3	2	3.00	1	0	0	0	1	1	0	0	0	0	0	0	0	0	.333	.333	.333	.219
Hampson J.	0	2	0	5	3	3.60	0	0	0	0	0	1	1	0	0	1	0	0	0	0	.000	.250	0.000	.105
Shealy R.	0	2	1	9	7	3.78	2	2	0	0	4	4	0	0	0	0	0	0	0	0	.222	.222	.444	.198
Affeldt J.	-0	0	0	1	1	3.00	0	0	0	0	0	0	0	0	0	0	0	0	0	0	.000	.000	.000	.000
Mesa J.	-0	0	0	1	1	5.00	0	0	0	0	0	0	0	0	0	0	0	0	0	0	.000	.000	.000	.000
Bautista D.	-0	0	0	1	1	5.00	0	0	0	0	0	0	0	0	0	0	0	0	0	0	.000	.000	.000	.000
Morillo J.	-0	0	0	1	1	3.00	0	0	0	0	0	0	0	0	0	0	0	0	0	0	.000	.000	.000	.000
King R.	-0	0	0	1	1	3.00	0	0	0	0	0	1	0	0	0	0	0	0	0	0	.000	.000	.000	.000
Dohmann S.	-0	0	0	1	1	4.00	0	0	0	0	0	1	0	0	0	0	0	0	0	0	.000	.000	.000	.000
Asencio M.	-0	0	0	3	3	4.00	0	0	0	0	0	2	0	0	0	0	0	0	0	0	.000	.000	.000	.000
Fogg J.	-0	5	2	70	46	3.33	5	1	0	0	6	20	3	0	1	15	0	0	0	0	.098	.164	.118	.097
Martin T.	-0	0	0	4	4	2.50	0	0	0	0	0	1	0	0	0	0	0	0	0	0	.000	.000	.000	.000
Day Z.	-0	0	0	6	5	3.33	0	0	0	0	0	3	0	0	0	1	0	0	0	0	.000	.000	.000	.000
Jennings J.	-1	3	2	75	54	3.07	8	1	0	0	9	12	3	0	0	10	0	0	0	0	.129	.169	.145	.105
Cook A.	-3	1	0	75	55	3.45	3	0	0	0	3	21	4	0	0	13	0	0	0	0	.052	.113	.052	.060

Italicized stats have been adjusted for home park.

Batted Ball Batting Stats are listed after fielding stats

Pitching Stats

Player	PRC	IP	BFP	G	GS	P/PA	K	BB	IBB	HBP	H	HR	DP	DER	SB	CS	PO	W	L	Sv	Op	Hld	RA	ERA	FIP
Jennings J.	96	212.0	902	32	32	3.64	142	85	7	3	206	17	28	.702	16	7	0	9	13	0	0	0	3.99	3.78	4.07
Cook A.	78	212.7	915	32	32	3.40	92	55	11	7	242	17	29	.685	7	5	2	9	15	0	0	0	4.53	4.23	4.11
Francis J.	77	199.0	843	32	32	3.77	117	69	15	13	187	18	24	.714	21	7	5	13	11	0	0	0	4.57	4.16	4.23
Fogg J.	49	172.0	765	31	31	3.61	93	60	13	6	206	24	19	.679	8	6	2	11	9	0	0	0	6.02	5.49	4.87
Kim B.	49	155.0	689	27	27	3.68	129	61	8	8	179	18	20	.649	24	7	2	8	12	0	0	0	5.98	5.57	4.24
Fuentes B.	38	65.3	274	66	0	3.88	73	26	4	6	50	8	4	.733	3	1	0	3	4	30	36	0	3.44	3.44	3.86
Ramirez R.	35	67.7	285	61	0	3.84	61	27	3	1	58	5	4	.717	2	0	0	4	3	0	2	10	3.72	3.46	3.48
Mesa J.	31	72.3	314	79	0	3.59	39	36	6	5	73	9	16	.702	0	3	0	1	5	1	8	19	3.98	3.86	5.21
Martin T.	20	60.3	266	68	0	3.65	46	25	5	4	62	4	8	.663	2	2	1	2	0	0	1	11	5.52	5.07	3.75
Corpas M.	17	32.3	136	35	0	3.49	27	8	1	2	36	3	5	.656	3	1	0	1	2	0	2	7	3.62	3.62	3.59
King R.	15	44.7	200	67	0	3.53	23	20	0	2	56	6	15	.651	2	1	0	1	4	1	2	15	5.24	4.43	5.41
Cortes D.	12	29.3	124	30	0	3.35	14	6	1	1	35	3	6	.680	0	0	0	3	1	0	1	3	4.30	4.30	4.21
Dohmann S.	7	24.7	114	27	0	3.94	22	15	2	2	26	4	3	.690	1	1	0	1	1	1	2	3	6.57	6.20	5.37
Affeldt J.	6	27.3	128	27	0	3.63	20	13	3	1	31	4	2	.656	3	0	0	4	2	1	3	3	7.57	6.91	4.86
Field N.	5	9.0	40	14	0	4.58	14	5	1	0	9	2	1	.632	0	0	0	1	1	0	1	4	4.00	4.00	4.33
Hampson J.	3	12.0	60	5	1	3.87	9	5	0	1	19	3	1	.595	1	0	0	1	0	0	1	0	7.50	7.50	6.47
Jimenez U.	3	7.7	30	2	1	3.73	3	3	0	0	5	1	0	.826	2	1	0	0	0	0	0	0	4.70	3.52	5.30
Venafro M.	2	3.7	15	7	0	3.27	2	3	0	0	3	0	2	.700	0	0	0	1	0	0	0	0	2.45	2.45	4.58
Day Z.	1	13.3	71	3	3	3.46	6	10	1	1	22	3	1	.627	3	0	0	1	2	0	0	0	11.48	10.80	7.49
Asencio M.	1	7.7	37	3	1	3.59	7	4	0	1	9	1	1	.625	1	0	0	1	0	0	0	0	9.39	4.70	5.04
Bautista D.	1	6.7	33	4	1	3.79	5	4	0	0	9	0	1	.625	0	0	0	0	1	0	0	0	13.50	5.40	3.52
Morillo J.	0	4.0	24	1	1	4.17	4	3	0	1	8	3	0	.615	0	0	0	0	0	0	0	0	15.75	15.75	13.97
Kim S.	0	7.0	45	6	0	4.02	4	8	0	1	17	2	0	.500	0	0	0	0	0	0	0	0	19.29	19.29	9.65
DeJean M.	0	1.7	8	2	0	4.00	0	2	0	0	1	0	0	.833	0	0	0	1	0	0	0	1	0.00	0.00	6.82

Batted Ball Pitching Stats are listed after fielding stats

Fielding Stats

Name	POS	INN	SBA/G	CS%	ERA	WP+PB/G	PO	A	TE	FE
Torrealba, Y.	C	530.0	0.80	34%	4.70	0.187	336	35	3	2
Ardoin, D.	C	288.3	0.84	26%	3.87	0.250	205	14	1	2
Closser, J.	C	239.7	0.86	26%	4.06	0.225	173	13	2	0
Iannetta, C.	C	191.7	0.99	14%	6.10	0.704	139	8	0	0
Ojeda, M.	C	174.7	0.62	8%	4.84	0.412	126	9	0	1
Marrero, E.	C	14.0	1.29	0%	5.14	1.286	11	1	0	0
Colina, A.	C	9.0	0.00	0%	8.00	1.000	8	0	0	0

Name	POS	Inn	PO	A	TE	FE	FPct	RF	DPS	DPT
Helton, T.	1B	1272.0	1365	86	3	1	.997	10.27	7	0
Marrero, E.	1B	61.0	58	8	0	0	1.000	9.74	0	0
Smith, J.	1B	43.0	34	3	0	0	1.000	7.74	0	0
Gonzalez, L.	1B	32.0	40	1	0	0	1.000	11.53	0	0
Castilla, V.	1B	21.0	19	0	0	0	1.000	8.14	0	0
Shealy, R.	1B	10.0	13	0	0	0	1.000	11.70	0	0
Atkins, G.	1B	5.0	5	0	0	0	1.000	9.00	0	0
Baker, J.	1B	3.0	4	0	0	0	1.000	12.00	0	0
Carroll, J.	2B	894.7	187	396	0	3	.995	5.86	45	53
Gonzalez, L.	2B	217.0	51	69	0	2	.984	4.98	2	5
Matsui, K.	2B	187.0	48	73	0	2	.984	5.82	12	15
Smith, J.	2B	115.7	32	46	0	2	.975	6.07	7	7
Quintanilla, O.	2B	19.0	8	4	0	0	1.000	5.68	0	2
Barmes, C.	2B	14.0	2	9	0	0	1.000	7.07	0	1
Barmes, C.	SS	1072.0	192	372	11	7	.969	4.74	49	44
Tulowitzki, T.	SS	220.3	47	69	0	2	.983	4.74	10	13
Quintanilla, O.	SS	62.7	10	26	0	0	1.000	5.17	3	4
Carroll, J.	SS	62.0	9	24	0	1	.971	4.79	4	3
Matsui, K.	SS	26.0	4	1	0	0	1.000	1.73	0	1
Smith, J.	SS	3.7	0	1	0	0	1.000	2.45	0	0
Atkins, G.	3B	1381.0	98	286	6	13	.953	2.50	36	0
Carroll, J.	3B	28.0	3	8	0	1	.917	3.54	2	0
Smith, J.	3B	18.0	2	4	0	0	1.000	3.00	0	0
Gonzalez, L.	3B	11.0	2	1	0	0	1.000	2.45	0	0
Castilla, V.	3B	9.0	1	3	0	0	1.000	4.00	0	0

Name	POS	Inn	PO	A	TE	FE	FPct	RF	DPS	DPT
Holliday, M.	LF	1334.0	277	8	1	5	.979	1.92	2	1
Spilborghs, R.	LF	50.3	14	1	0	0	1.000	2.68	2	0
Marrero, E.	LF	21.0	6	1	0	1	.875	3.00	0	0
Freeman, C.	LF	18.0	6	0	0	0	1.000	3.00	0	0
Baker, J.	LF	10.0	1	0	0	0	1.000	0.90	0	0
Piedra, J.	LF	7.0	2	0	0	0	1.000	2.57	0	0
Gonzalez, L.	LF	6.7	4	0	0	0	1.000	5.40	0	0
Sullivan, C.	CF	841.0	225	4	0	1	.996	2.45	0	0
Freeman, C.	CF	321.0	101	0	0	1	.990	2.83	0	0
Spilborghs, R.	CF	167.0	43	2	0	0	1.000	2.43	2	0
Salazar, J.	CF	111.3	25	0	0	0	1.000	2.02	0	0
Piedra, J.	CF	7.0	2	0	0	0	1.000	2.57	0	0
Hawpe, B.	RF	1197.0	280	16	1	3	.987	2.23	6	0
Spilborghs, R.	RF	99.3	18	1	0	1	.950	1.72	0	0
Baker, J.	RF	77.3	10	1	0	0	1.000	1.28	0	0
Gonzalez, L.	RF	37.0	6	0	0	0	1.000	1.46	0	0
Marrero, E.	RF	23.0	7	0	0	0	1.000	2.74	0	0
Piedra, J.	RF	10.0	3	0	0	0	1.000	2.70	0	0
Freeman, C.	RF	2.0	0	0	0	0	0.000	0.00	0	0
Salazar, J.	RF	1.0	0	0	0	0	0.000	0.00	0	0

Batted Ball Batting Stats

Player	PA	% of PA		% of Batted Balls					Runs Per Event				Total Runs vs. Avg.				
		K%	BB%	GB%	LD%	FB%	IF/F	HR/OF	NIP	GB	LD	OF	NIP	GB	LD	FB	Tot
Holliday M.	667	16	9	45	21	34	.06	.19	.05	.07	.47	.31	0	5	12	20	38
Atkins G.	695	11	12	37	22	41	.05	.13	.13	.05	.38	.24	12	-1	6	19	36
Helton T.	649	10	15	35	24	41	.08	.08	.16	.02	.46	.13	18	-6	17	-5	23
Hawpe B.	575	21	13	42	22	36	.07	.17	.06	.03	.48	.31	4	-4	8	13	21
Matsui K.	126	21	8	47	24	29	.00	.08	.01	.15	.47	.23	-1	4	3	0	6
Carroll J.	534	12	11	49	23	29	.11	.05	.10	.07	.35	.14	6	4	2	-10	2
Smith J.	108	27	8	43	19	38	.00	.19	-.00	.01	.30	.32	-2	-1	-2	4	-1
Spilborghs R.	186	16	8	51	21	29	.05	.05	.03	.04	.43	.15	-1	-0	2	-3	-2
Torrealba Y.	241	20	6	63	13	25	.14	.19	-.01	.05	.44	.38	-4	2	-4	3	-2
Tulowitzki T.	108	23	10	49	21	30	.10	.05	.03	.08	.39	.06	-0	1	-0	-4	-3
Freeman R.	191	22	8	54	22	24	.03	.07	.01	.10	.40	.02	-2	4	1	-8	-5
Closser J.	112	21	12	36	23	41	.13	.08	.05	-.04	.30	.13	0	-3	-1	-2	-5
Gonzalez L.	158	17	4	46	17	37	.07	.05	-.03	.02	.41	.13	-3	-1	-0	-2	-6
Ardoin D.	120	23	8	50	14	36	.17	.00	.01	-.04	.35	.17	-1	-3	-3	-1	-8
Sullivan C.	443	23	7	36	32	33	.02	.02	.00	.01	.33	.22	-6	-7	4	-0	-10
Barmes C.	535	13	6	34	18	48	.12	.04	.03	.02	.42	.05	-5	-3	1	-16	-23
MLB Average		*17*	*9*	*44*	*20*	*37*	*.11*	*.11*	*.05*	*.04*	*.39*	*.19*	-	-	-	-	-

Batted Ball Pitching Stats

Player	PA	% of PA		% of Batted Balls					Runs Per Event				Total Runs vs. Avg.				
		K%	BB%	GB%	LD%	FB%	IF/F	HR/OF	NIP	GB	LD	OF	NIP	GB	LD	FB	Tot
Jennings J.	902	16	10	44	19	37	.11	.08	.06	.02	.36	.16	2	-5	-4	-7	-14
Francis J.	843	14	10	45	19	36	.14	.09	.08	.02	.46	.12	4	-6	8	-15	-9
Ramirez R.	285	21	10	41	14	45	.11	.06	.03	.01	.35	.21	-1	-4	-6	3	-8
Fuentes B.	274	27	12	35	16	50	.11	.11	.03	-.00	.40	.21	-1	-4	-5	3	-7
Cook A.	915	10	7	58	18	24	.06	.10	.07	.02	.41	.23	-1	-7	6	-2	-4
Cortes D.	124	11	6	39	24	38	.05	.08	.04	.08	.34	.07	-1	1	1	-3	-1
Corpas M.	136	20	7	45	20	34	.03	.09	.01	.04	.46	.17	-1	0	2	-0	-0
Mesa J.	314	12	13	46	17	37	.12	.11	.12	.03	.28	.24	5	-2	-6	3	0
Martin T.	266	17	11	49	22	28	.13	.09	.06	.05	.41	.18	1	1	3	-4	1
Affeldt J.	128	16	11	53	18	29	.04	.15	.08	.06	.37	.30	1	1	-1	2	3
Dohmann S.	114	19	15	32	20	48	.06	.13	.09	.08	.39	.22	2	0	-1	2	3
King R.	200	12	12	53	22	25	.08	.17	.12	.01	.44	.28	3	-2	4	1	5
Kim B.	689	19	10	42	23	35	.05	.11	.05	.02	.42	.23	0	-6	8	7	9
Fogg J.	765	12	9	43	20	37	.10	.12	.08	.05	.38	.23	2	1	4	12	19
MLB Average		*17*	*9*	*44*	*20*	*37*	*.11*	*.11*	*.05*	*.04*	*.39*	*.19*	-	-	-	-	-

Detroit Tigers

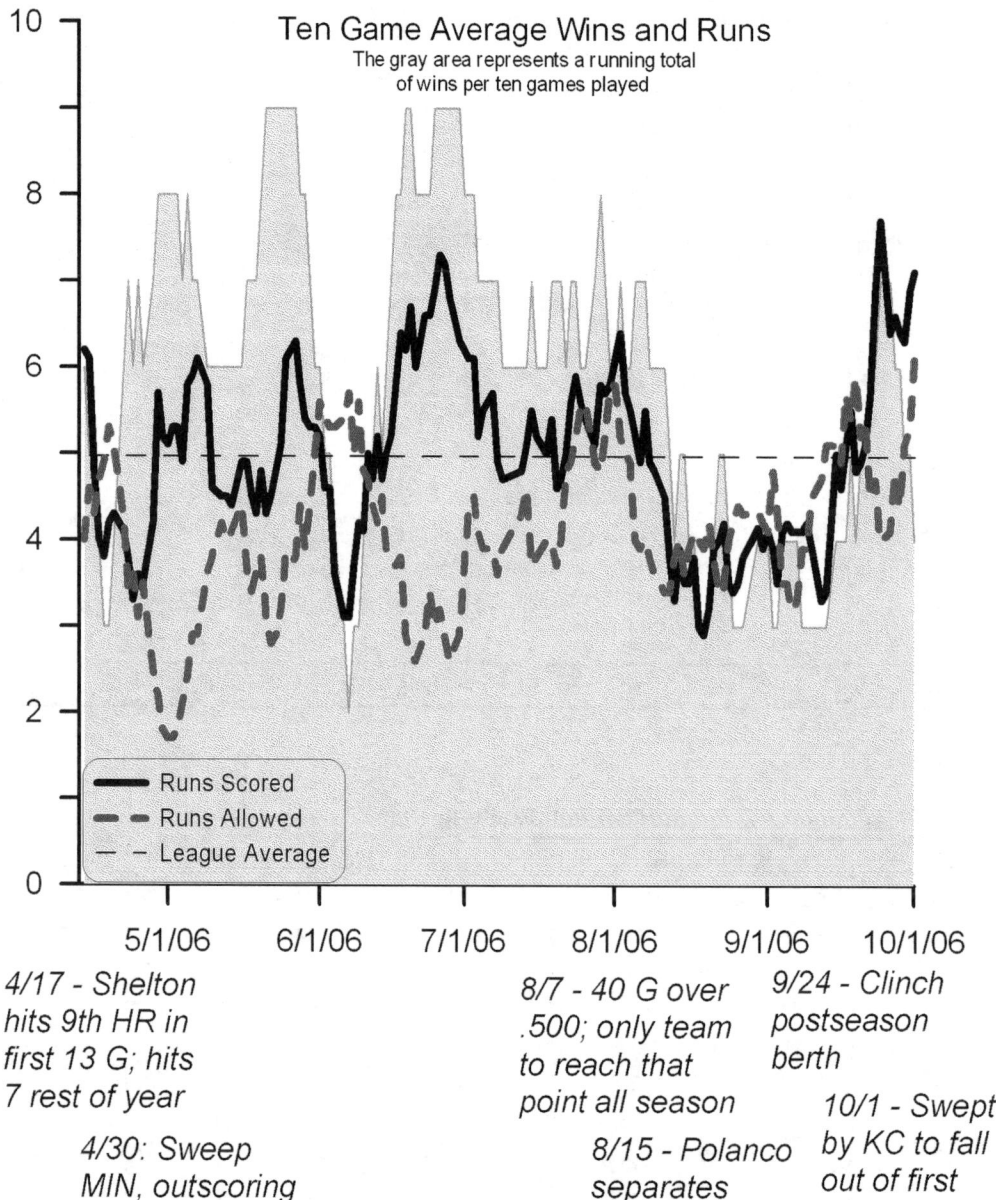

Ten Game Average Wins and Runs
The gray area represents a running total
of wins per ten games played

- ▬▬ Runs Scored
- ▬ ▬ Runs Allowed
- — — League Average

4/17 - Shelton
hits 9th HR in
first 13 G; hits
7 rest of year

4/30: Sweep
MIN, outscoring
them 33-1

8/7 - 40 G over
.500; only team
to reach that
point all season

8/15 - Polanco
separates
shoulder

9/24 - Clinch
postseason
berth

10/1 - Swept
by KC to fall
out of first

Team Batting and Pitching/Fielding Stats by Month						
	April	May	June	July	Aug	Sept/Oct
Wins	16	19	20	15	13	12
Losses	9	9	7	10	16	16
OBP	.344	.319	.329	.341	.310	.332
SLG	.489	.436	.455	.442	.417	.456
FIP	3.88	4.63	4.18	4.17	4.03	4.84
DER	.745	.696	.727	.686	.698	.680

Batting Stats

Player	RC	Runs	RBI	PA	Outs	P/PA	H	2B	3B	HR	TB	K	BB	IBB	HBP	SH	SF	SB	CS	GDP	BA	OBP	SLG	GPA
Guillen C.	107	100	85	622	394	3.81	174	41	5	19	282	87	71	10	4	0	4	20	9	16	.320	.400	.519	.318
Ordonez M.	97	82	104	646	433	3.54	177	32	1	24	283	87	45	3	4	0	4	1	4	13	.298	.350	.477	.284
Granderson C.	89	90	68	679	450	4.09	155	31	9	19	261	174	66	0	4	7	6	8	5	4	.260	.335	.438	.267
Rodriguez I.	82	74	69	580	402	3.39	164	28	4	13	239	86	26	4	1	4	2	8	3	16	.300	.332	.437	.265
Inge B.	80	83	83	601	421	4.13	137	29	2	27	251	128	43	2	7	4	5	7	4	12	.253	.313	.463	.263
Monroe C.	76	89	92	585	419	3.68	138	35	2	28	261	126	37	3	1	0	6	2	2	14	.255	.301	.482	.262
Polanco P.	66	58	52	495	345	3.29	136	18	1	4	168	27	17	0	7	8	2	1	2	18	.295	.329	.364	.245
Thames M.	60	61	60	390	260	4.04	89	20	2	26	191	92	37	0	4	0	1	1	1	0	.256	.333	.549	.295
Shelton C.	50	50	47	412	283	4.17	102	16	4	16	174	107	34	1	4	0	1	1	2	10	.273	.340	.466	.276
Infante O.	26	35	25	245	169	3.47	62	11	4	4	93	45	14	0	3	2	2	3	2	5	.277	.325	.415	.256
Casey S.	24	17	30	196	143	3.34	45	7	0	5	67	21	10	4	1	0	1	0	1	3	.245	.286	.364	.225
Young D.	20	19	23	184	133	3.70	43	4	1	7	70	39	11	0	0	0	1	1	1	3	.250	.293	.407	.240
Wilson V.	17	18	18	168	114	3.55	43	9	0	5	67	33	2	0	3	10	1	0	4	1	.283	.304	.441	.253
Gomez A.	14	17	6	111	76	3.54	28	5	2	1	40	21	6	0	1	1	0	4	0	1	.272	.318	.388	.246
Stairs M.	6	5	8	44	32	4.34	10	3	0	2	19	12	3	0	0	0	0	0	0	1	.244	.295	.463	.255
Clevlen B.	6	9	6	42	28	3.81	11	1	2	3	25	15	2	0	0	1	0	0	0	0	.282	.317	.641	.311
Santiago R.	3	9	3	86	63	3.34	18	1	1	0	21	14	1	0	1	4	0	2	0	1	.225	.244	.263	.180
Perez N.	3	4	5	70	54	3.21	13	1	0	0	14	4	3	0	0	2	0	1	0	2	.200	.235	.215	.164
Hooper K.	0	1	0	5	3	3.00	0	0	0	0	0	1	1	0	0	1	0	0	0	0	.000	.250	.000	.115
Robertson N.	0	0	1	6	5	4.50	1	0	0	0	1	3	0	0	0	0	0	0	0	0	.167	.167	.167	.120
Miner Z.	0	1	0	6	5	3.33	1	1	0	0	2	3	0	0	0	0	0	0	0	0	.167	.167	.333	.162
Verlander J.	-0	0	0	2	1	3.00	0	0	0	0	0	0	0	0	0	1	0	0	0	0	.000	.000	.000	.000
Rodney F.	-0	0	0	1	1	4.00	0	0	0	0	0	0	0	0	0	0	0	0	0	0	.000	.000	.000	.000
Rabelo M.	-0	0	0	1	1	3.00	0	0	0	0	0	1	0	0	0	0	0	0	0	0	.000	.000	.000	.000
Rogers K.	-0	0	0	7	6	4.00	1	1	0	0	2	2	0	0	0	0	0	0	0	0	.143	.143	.286	.139
Bonderman J.	-0	0	0	4	4	5.00	0	0	0	0	0	4	0	0	0	0	0	0	0	0	.000	.000	.000	.000
Hannahan J.	-1	0	0	10	9	3.70	0	0	0	0	0	1	1	0	0	0	0	0	0	0	.000	.100	.000	.046

Italicized stats have been adjusted for home park.

Batted Ball Batting Stats

Player	PA	% of PA		% of Batted Balls					Runs Per Event				Total Runs vs. Avg.				
		K%	BB%	GB%	LD%	FB%	IF/F	HR/OF	NIP	GB	LD	OF	NIP	GB	LD	FB	Tot
Guillen C.	622	14	12	42	20	38	.06	.11	.10	.04	.42	.27	8	-0	4	17	29
Thames M.	390	24	11	26	15	59	.17	.21	.03	.10	.41	.32	-1	1	-6	21	14
Ordonez M.	646	13	8	45	18	38	.10	.14	.05	.07	.39	.22	-2	6	-1	8	12
Inge B.	601	21	8	40	14	46	.11	.15	.02	.08	.41	.25	-5	6	-9	14	5
Monroe C.	585	22	6	38	18	44	.04	.15	-.01	.06	.39	.23	-9	1	-3	15	4
Shelton C.	412	26	9	33	20	48	.10	.14	.01	.06	.37	.27	-4	-1	-3	12	4
Granderson C.	679	26	10	39	22	39	.06	.12	.02	.09	.34	.25	-5	4	-6	8	1
Rodriguez I.	580	15	5	50	21	28	.05	.11	-0.00	.05	.40	.18	-8	5	7	-3	-0
Infante O.	245	18	7	38	19	43	.09	.06	.01	.08	.40	.15	-2	2	-0	-1	-1
Gomez A.	111	19	6	37	28	35	.11	.04	0.00	.01	.37	.09	-1	0	2	-2	-2
Wilson V.	168	20	3	43	21	36	.10	.13	-.05	.02	.42	.27	-4	-1	1	2	-2
Young D.	184	21	6	52	14	34	0.00	.16	-.01	.07	.26	.26	-3	2	-5	4	-2
Casey S.	196	11	6	43	23	34	.05	.09	.04	.02	.29	.10	-1	-1	-0	-3	-6
Polanco P.	495	5	5	51	21	28	.08	.04	.10	.07	.33	.02	-1	8	3	-20	-10
MLB Average		17	9	44	20	37	.11	.11	.05	.04	.39	.19	-	-	-	-	-

Pitching Stats

Player	PRC	IP	BFP	G	GS	P/PA	K	BB	IBB	HBP	H	HR	DP	DER	SB	CS	PO	W	L	Sv	Op	Hld	RA	ERA	FIP
Bonderman J.	101	214.0	903	34	34	3.64	202	64	7	3	214	18	24	.675	14	2	1	14	8	0	0	0	4.37	4.08	3.31
Robertson N.	94	208.7	881	32	32	3.53	137	67	2	8	206	29	32	.705	9	5	1	13	13	0	0	0	4.23	3.84	4.81
Verlander J.	93	186.0	776	30	30	3.83	124	60	1	6	187	21	25	.699	1	5	8	17	9	0	0	0	3.77	3.63	4.45
Rogers K.	85	204.0	849	34	33	3.68	99	62	2	9	195	23	29	.724	1	6	2	17	8	0	0	0	4.28	3.84	4.77
Zumaya J.	73	83.3	350	62	0	4.07	97	42	2	2	56	6	5	.744	4	1	0	6	3	1	6	30	2.16	1.94	3.38
Miner Z.	34	93.0	398	27	16	4.11	59	32	1	0	100	11	9	.682	8	5	1	7	6	0	0	1	5.13	4.84	4.53
Rodney F.	32	71.7	304	63	0	3.94	65	34	4	8	51	6	4	.743	5	4	1	7	4	7	11	18	4.52	3.52	4.13
Walker J.	31	48.0	196	56	0	3.51	37	8	3	0	47	8	3	.720	2	1	0	0	1	0	0	11	2.81	2.81	4.20
Ledezma W.	27	60.3	264	24	7	3.58	39	23	0	2	60	5	4	.697	2	1	0	3	3	0	1	2	4.18	3.58	4.29
Jones T.	25	64.0	272	62	0	3.42	28	11	3	3	70	4	8	.690	0	0	0	2	6	37	43	0	4.36	3.94	3.72
Grilli J.	25	62.0	270	51	0	3.58	31	25	3	5	61	6	5	.724	2	1	0	2	3	0	0	9	4.50	4.21	4.83
Maroth M.	21	53.7	234	13	9	3.68	24	16	1	1	64	11	6	.698	1	1	0	5	2	0	0	0	4.36	4.19	5.93
Colon R.	15	38.7	170	20	1	3.44	25	14	2	1	46	6	3	.677	0	2	0	2	0	1	1	3	4.89	4.89	5.00
Spurling C.	6	11.3	49	9	0	3.45	4	4	2	0	13	2	2	.692	0	1	0	0	0	0	0	0	3.18	3.18	5.38
Durbin C.	6	6.0	24	3	0	3.46	3	0	0	0	6	1	0	.750	0	0	0	0	0	0	0	0	1.50	1.50	4.43
Seay B.	5	15.3	71	14	0	3.92	12	9	1	3	14	1	1	.717	0	0	0	0	0	0	0	0	6.46	6.46	4.70
Tata J.	4	14.7	65	8	0	3.66	6	7	1	0	14	1	1	.745	0	0	0	0	0	0	0	0	6.75	6.14	4.56
Miller A.	2	10.3	51	8	0	3.76	6	10	0	2	8	0	1	.727	0	0	0	0	1	0	0	1	7.84	6.10	5.59
Lewis C.	2	3.0	18	2	0	4.22	5	1	0	0	8	1	0	.364	0	0	0	0	0	0	0	0	3.00	3.00	5.26

Batted Ball Pitching Stats

Player	PA	% of PA		% of Batted Balls			IF/F	HR/OF	Runs Per Event				Total Runs vs. Avg.				
		K%	BB%	GB%	LD%	FB%			NIP	GB	LD	OF	NIP	GB	LD	FB	Tot
Zumaya J.	350	28	13	34	21	45	.20	.07	.03	.07	.33	.05	-0	-0	-5	-13	-19
Bonderman J.	903	22	7	48	20	32	.10	.09	.00	.03	.41	.22	-12	-4	0	-0	-15
Rogers K.	849	12	8	50	18	32	.08	.11	.08	.00	.41	.17	2	-12	3	-5	-12
Rodney F.	304	21	14	57	12	31	.12	.11	.07	.04	.42	.13	3	-0	-7	-7	-11
Verlander J.	776	16	9	42	23	35	.13	.11	.05	.03	.36	.17	-2	-5	5	-6	-8
Jones T.	272	10	5	53	18	29	.12	.07	.04	.04	.40	.13	-2	1	0	-5	-6
Robertson N.	881	16	9	47	20	33	.10	.14	.05	.00	.37	.24	-1	-12	1	7	-5
Ledezma W.	264	15	9	34	21	46	.16	.05	.07	.08	.38	.11	1	1	1	-5	-3
Walker J.	196	19	4	31	20	49	.21	.12	-.03	-.02	.50	.19	-4	-4	4	1	-2
Grilli J.	270	11	11	47	15	38	.11	.09	.11	-.00	.37	.22	3	-4	-4	3	-1
Miner Z.	398	15	8	47	21	32	.08	.12	.05	.03	.45	.17	-1	-2	6	-3	1
Colon R.	170	15	9	40	17	43	.18	.13	.06	.07	.34	.28	0	1	-2	4	4
Maroth M.	234	10	7	42	18	40	.05	.15	.08	-.00	.37	.29	0	-4	0	11	7
MLB Average		17	9	44	20	37	.11	.11	.05	.04	.39	.19	-	-	-	-	-

Fielding Stats

Name	POS	INN	SBA/G	CS%	ERA	WP+PB/G	PO	A	TE	FE
Rodriguez, I.	C	1054.3	0.39	46%	3.83	0.324	747	53	1	1
Wilson, V.	C	393.7	0.73	25%	3.91	0.274	285	27	1	0

Name	POS	Inn	PO	A	TE	FE	FPct	RF	DPS	DPT
Shelton, C.	1B	913.0	994	55	0	6	.994	10.34	7	1
Casey, S.	1B	413.0	467	14	0	2	.996	10.48	0	1
Rodriguez, I.	1B	55.0	56	6	0	1	.984	10.15	1	0
Guillen, C.	1B	39.0	30	4	0	0	1.000	7.85	1	0
Young, D.	1B	20.0	19	5	1	2	.889	10.80	0	0
Hannahan, J.	1B	8.0	6	0	0	0	1.000	6.75	0	0
Polanco, P.	2B	943.0	224	325	3	3	.989	5.24	40	43
Infante, O.	2B	307.3	65	108	1	3	.977	5.07	10	17
Perez, N.	2B	119.0	34	42	0	0	1.000	5.75	2	9
Santiago, R.	2B	70.7	14	19	0	0	1.000	4.20	2	2
Hooper, K.	2B	6.0	0	3	0	0	1.000	4.50	1	0
Rodriguez, I.	2B	2.0	1	0	0	0	1.000	4.50	0	0
Guillen, C.	SS	1235.0	178	427	13	15	.956	4.41	47	38
Santiago, R.	SS	133.0	17	48	0	0	1.000	4.40	3	3
Perez, N.	SS	40.0	9	17	1	0	.963	5.85	5	2
Infante, O.	SS	40.0	7	16	0	1	.958	5.18	2	3
Inge, B.	3B	1392.0	135	397	10	12	.960	3.44	33	1
Infante, O.	3B	51.0	3	8	0	0	1.000	1.94	0	0
Santiago, R.	3B	2.0	0	2	0	0	1.000	9.00	0	0
Hooper, K.	3B	2.0	0	2	0	0	1.000	9.00	0	0
Perez, N.	3B	1.0	0	0	0	0	0.000	0.00	0	0

Name	POS	Inn	PO	A	TE	FE	FPct	RF	DPS	DPT
Monroe, C.	LF	927.3	168	12	0	3	.984	1.75	4	0
Thames, M.	LF	400.7	70	1	0	2	.973	1.59	0	0
Gomez, A.	LF	103.0	25	1	0	0	1.000	2.27	0	0
Clevlen, B.	LF	17.0	6	0	0	0	1.000	3.18	0	0
Granderson, C.	CF	1312.0	385	3	1	0	.997	2.66	0	0
Clevlen, B.	CF	70.0	19	2	0	0	1.000	2.70	2	0
Monroe, C.	CF	47.0	13	0	0	1	.929	2.49	0	0
Infante, O.	CF	19.0	1	0	0	0	1.000	0.47	0	0
Ordonez, M.	RF	1268.0	258	9	0	7	.974	1.90	2	0
Gomez, A.	RF	113.0	19	1	0	0	1.000	1.59	0	0
Thames, M.	RF	44.0	14	0	0	0	1.000	2.86	0	0
Clevlen, B.	RF	23.0	4	1	0	0	1.000	1.96	0	0

Florida Marlins

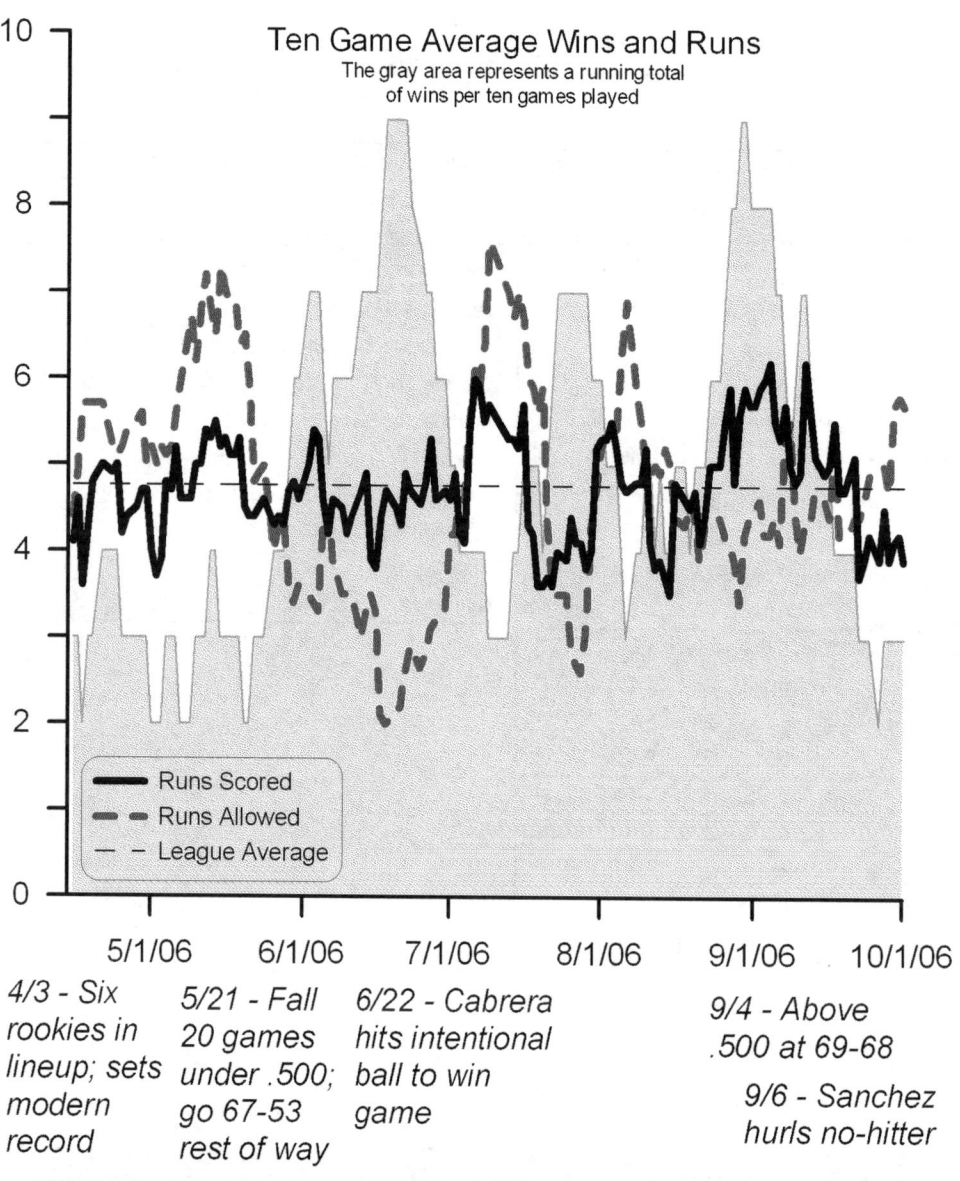

Ten Game Average Wins and Runs
The gray area represents a running total
of wins per ten games played

— Runs Scored
– – Runs Allowed
– – League Average

5/1/06   6/1/06   7/1/06   8/1/06   9/1/06   10/1/06

4/3 - Six rookies in lineup; sets modern record

5/21 - Fall 20 games under .500; go 67-53 rest of way

6/22 - Cabrera hits intentional ball to win game

9/4 - Above .500 at 69-68

9/6 - Sanchez hurls no-hitter

Team Batting and Pitching/Fielding Stats by Month						
	April	May	June	July	Aug	Sept/Oct
Wins	6	11	18	14	16	13
Losses	16	18	7	15	12	16
OBP	.322	.336	.339	.330	.332	.328
SLG	.405	.409	.454	.457	.438	.443
FIP	4.86	4.46	3.88	4.96	4.48	4.50
DER	.699	.676	.689	.694	.684	.690

Batting Stats

Player	RC	Runs	RBI	PA	Outs	P/PA	H	2B	3B	HR	TB	K	BB	IBB	HBP	SH	SF	SB	CS	GDP	BA	OBP	SLG	GPA
Cabrera M.	142	112	114	676	405	3.92	195	50	2	26	327	108	86	27	10	0	4	9	6	18	.339	.430	.568	.354
Ramirez H.	108	119	59	700	470	4.01	185	46	11	17	304	128	56	0	4	5	2	51	15	7	.292	.353	.480	.294
Uggla D.	104	105	90	683	450	3.73	172	26	7	27	293	123	48	1	9	7	8	6	6	5	.282	.339	.480	.287
Willingham J.	80	62	74	573	376	4.01	139	28	2	26	249	109	54	2	11	0	6	2	0	13	.277	.356	.496	.300
Jacobs M.	71	54	77	520	362	3.69	123	37	1	20	222	105	45	2	1	0	5	3	0	16	.262	.325	.473	.279
Olivo M.	53	52	58	452	329	3.42	113	22	3	16	189	103	9	4	7	3	3	2	3	9	.263	.287	.440	.252
Helms W.	48	30	47	278	172	3.62	79	19	5	10	138	55	21	1	6	6	5	0	4	7	.329	.390	.575	.337
Hermida J.	41	37	28	348	237	4.00	77	19	1	5	113	70	33	3	5	2	1	4	1	6	.251	.332	.368	.255
Amezaga A.	34	42	19	378	264	3.78	87	9	3	3	111	46	33	4	3	7	1	20	12	5	.260	.332	.332	.245
Ross C.	32	30	37	279	206	3.89	53	11	1	11	99	61	22	0	4	1	2	0	1	8	.212	.284	.396	.239
Borchard J.	28	30	28	261	184	3.84	53	7	1	10	92	66	28	3	3	0	0	0	2	5	.230	.322	.400	.258
Abercrombie R.	26	39	24	281	208	3.52	54	12	2	5	85	78	18	2	3	4	1	6	5	2	.212	.271	.333	.216
Treanor M.	17	12	14	185	126	3.90	36	6	1	2	50	34	19	4	5	2	2	0	1	4	.229	.328	.318	.240
Aguila C.	8	5	7	104	76	3.79	22	8	1	0	32	26	9	1	0	0	0	2	1	2	.232	.298	.337	.230
Willis D.	6	8	10	76	53	3.16	11	0	1	3	22	13	6	0	0	6	0	0	0	0	.172	.243	.344	.206
Olsen S.	4	3	8	64	47	3.08	11	2	0	0	13	18	0	0	0	6	0	0	0	0	.190	.190	.224	.149
Wood J.	4	3	1	14	7	3.93	6	2	0	0	8	2	1	0	0	0	0	1	0	0	.462	.500	.615	.400
Vargas J.	3	1	1	17	11	3.59	5	1	0	0	6	2	1	0	0	0	0	0	0	0	.313	.353	.375	.266
Nolasco R.	2	2	5	49	34	3.78	7	0	0	1	10	19	2	0	0	6	0	0	0	0	.171	.209	.244	.164
Hoover P.	1	0	1	5	3	3.00	2	0	0	0	2	0	0	0	0	0	0	0	0	0	.400	.400	.400	.295
Mitre S.	1	2	1	14	10	2.86	2	1	0	0	3	4	0	0	0	2	0	0	0	0	.167	.167	.250	.145
Petit Y.	1	1	1	5	4	5.00	1	0	0	0	1	2	0	0	0	0	0	0	0	0	.200	.200	.200	.148
Garcia J.	1	0	0	2	1	3.00	1	0	0	0	1	1	0	0	0	0	0	0	0	0	.500	.500	.500	.369
Sanchez A.	0	1	2	38	32	3.53	4	0	0	0	4	14	0	0	0	3	0	0	0	1	.114	.114	.114	.084
Andino R.	0	0	2	28	20	3.21	4	1	0	0	5	6	1	0	0	1	2	1	0	0	.167	.185	.208	.143
Moehler B.	0	1	2	40	29	3.20	2	0	0	0	2	15	1	0	1	7	0	0	0	0	.065	.121	.065	.075
Pinto R.	-0	0	0	1	1	3.00	0	0	0	0	0	0	0	0	0	0	0	0	0	0	.000	.000	.000	.000
Kensing L.	-0	0	0	1	1	3.00	0	0	0	0	0	1	0	0	0	0	0	0	0	0	.000	.000	.000	.000
Messenger R.	-0	0	0	2	2	3.50	0	0	0	0	0	1	0	0	0	0	0	0	0	0	.000	.000	.000	.000
Tankersley T	-0	0	0	2	2	5.00	0	0	0	0	0	2	0	0	0	0	0	0	0	0	.000	.000	.000	.000
Reed E.	-0	6	0	47	39	3.30	4	0	0	0	4	10	2	1	2	2	0	3	1	1	.098	.178	.098	.110
Cepicky M.	-1	0	0	19	16	3.79	2	0	0	0	2	4	1	0	0	0	0	0	0	0	.111	.158	.111	.104
Johnson J.	-1	1	3	49	38	3.67	4	2	0	0	6	23	1	0	0	6	0	0	0	0	.095	.116	.143	.093

Italicized stats have been adjusted for home park.

Batted Ball Batting Stats are listed at end of fielding stats

Florida Marlins

Pitching Stats

Player	PRC	IP	BFP	G	GS	P/PA	K	BB	IBB	HBP	H	HR	DP	DER	SB	CS	PO	W	L	Sv	Op	Hld	RA	ERA	FIP
Willis D.	97	223.3	975	34	34	3.71	160	83	6	19	234	21	33	.679	6	5	2	12	12	0	0	0	4.27	3.87	4.30
Johnson J.	82	157.0	659	31	24	3.92	133	68	6	4	136	14	18	.716	9	8	2	12	7	0	1	0	3.61	3.10	3.94
Olsen S.	76	180.7	761	31	31	3.78	166	75	1	7	160	23	15	.708	8	8	3	12	10	0	0	0	4.68	4.04	4.38
Sanchez A.	64	114.3	469	18	17	3.77	72	46	1	4	90	9	13	.751	6	1	0	10	3	0	0	0	3.07	2.83	4.27
Nolasco R.	47	140.0	613	35	22	3.65	99	41	5	10	157	20	15	.677	6	6	0	11	11	0	0	2	5.53	4.82	4.65
Borowski J.	34	69.7	304	72	0	4.03	64	33	7	2	63	7	3	.712	4	1	0	3	3	36	43	0	4.00	3.75	3.89
Moehler B.	28	122.0	556	29	21	3.50	58	38	3	5	164	19	16	.651	5	6	2	7	11	0	1	0	7.01	6.57	5.28
Tankersley T.	26	41.0	178	49	0	3.91	46	26	5	1	33	4	4	.693	1	0	3	2	1	3	7	22	3.07	2.85	3.85
Herges M.	23	71.0	328	66	0	3.53	36	28	5	3	94	5	14	.633	0	2	0	2	3	0	4	9	5.32	4.31	4.22
Messenger R.	18	60.3	275	59	0	3.75	45	24	2	1	72	8	7	.655	6	1	0	2	7	0	1	9	6.27	5.67	4.59
Kensing L.	17	37.7	161	37	0	4.25	45	19	2	3	30	6	1	.727	3	1	0	1	3	1	7	14	4.54	4.54	4.49
Pinto R.	17	29.7	135	27	0	4.02	36	27	0	1	20	3	6	.721	0	0	0	0	0	1	1	3	3.64	3.03	4.94
Mitre S.	12	41.0	189	15	7	3.56	31	20	3	6	44	7	5	.680	5	2	1	1	5	0	1	2	6.15	5.71	5.61
Martinez C.	10	10.3	44	12	0	4.34	11	6	0	0	9	0	1	.667	1	2	0	0	1	0	0	5	1.74	1.74	2.83
Resop C.	9	21.3	101	22	0	3.83	10	16	5	1	26	1	5	.630	3	1	0	1	2	0	1	2	3.80	3.38	4.58
Vargas J.	8	43.0	213	12	5	3.86	25	30	3	4	50	9	3	.697	6	0	0	1	2	0	0	0	8.16	7.33	6.94
Wellemeyer T.	7	21.3	97	18	0	4.06	17	13	1	2	20	1	2	.703	0	0	0	0	2	0	0	0	5.48	5.48	4.20
German F.	7	12.0	57	12	0	4.19	6	14	2	1	7	1	0	.829	0	0	0	0	0	0	1	1	3.00	3.00	6.55
Petit Y.	4	26.3	129	15	1	3.77	20	9	1	0	46	7	5	.581	0	2	0	1	1	0	0	0	9.57	9.57	6.07
Garcia J.	4	11.0	48	5	0	4.00	8	5	0	0	10	1	0	.735	0	0	0	0	0	0	0	0	4.91	4.91	4.31
Fulchino J.	0	0.3	2	1	0	5.50	0	1	0	0	0	0	0	1.000	0	0	0	0	0	0	0	0	0.00	0.00	12.22

Batted Ball Pitching Stats

Player	PA	% of PA		% of Batted Balls			IF/F	HR/OF	Runs Per Event				Total Runs vs. Avg.				
		K%	BB%	GB%	LD%	FB%			NIP	GB	LD	OF	NIP	GB	LD	FB	Tot
Sanchez A.	469	15	11	44	14	41	.13	.07	.08	.04	.35	.10	3	-2	-9	-10	-17
Johnson J.	659	20	11	46	19	36	.09	.09	.05	.04	.36	.15	1	-2	-7	-8	-16
Willis D.	975	16	10	47	19	33	.10	.10	.07	.03	.36	.20	4	-4	-5	-3	-8
Olsen S.	761	22	11	45	18	37	.12	.13	.04	.04	.36	.23	-1	-2	-9	4	-8
Borowski J.	304	21	12	33	18	50	.15	.08	.05	.09	.33	.14	1	2	-5	-3	-5
Tankersley T.	178	26	15	44	16	40	.23	.13	.06	.03	.43	.24	2	-2	-3	-1	-4
Pinto R.	135	27	21	45	16	39	.11	.13	.09	-.01	.28	.24	4	-2	-4	-0	-3
Kensing L.	161	28	14	29	24	47	.12	.16	.04	.03	.28	.27	0	-2	-3	3	-1
Mitre S.	189	16	14	52	20	28	.11	.22	.10	.07	.29	.29	3	2	-3	1	3
Resop C.	101	10	17	41	23	36	.19	.05	.18	.06	.53	.08	3	0	3	-3	4
Messenger R.	275	16	9	38	19	43	.15	.10	.05	.08	.39	.24	-0	1	-1	4	5
Nolasco C.	613	16	8	39	21	40	.08	.10	.04	.04	.46	.16	-2	0	9	-2	6
Herges M.	328	11	9	47	22	31	.14	.07	.10	.07	.41	.16	2	4	5	-4	6
Vargas J.	213	12	16	32	17	51	.14	.14	.15	.10	.39	.23	6	2	-2	5	11
Petit Y.	129	16	7	29	24	46	.11	.17	.03	.15	.55	.26	-1	2	6	4	12
Moehler B.	556	10	8	45	22	33	.10	.13	.08	.04	.46	.24	1	2	13	6	22
MLB Average		17	9	44	20	37	.11	.11	.05	.04	.39	.19	-	-	-	-	-

Fielding Stats

Name	POS	INN	SBA/G	CS%	ERA	WP+PB/G	PO	A	TE	FE
Olivo, M.	C	971.3	0.68	34%	4.41	0.435	733	64	5	2
Treanor, M.	C	439.7	0.63	42%	4.20	0.225	375	25	2	1
Willingham, J.	C	14.0	1.29	0%	7.71	0.643	11	1	0	0
Hoover, P.	C	8.3	1.08	0%	3.24	2.160	7	0	1	0

Name	POS	Inn	PO	A	TE	FE	FPct	RF	DPS	DPT
Jacobs, M.	1B	972.0	930	57	1	5	.993	9.14	9	4
Helms, W.	1B	432.3	375	25	0	0	1.000	8.33	3	0
Wood, J.	1B	13.0	16	1	0	0	1.000	11.77	0	0
Olivo, M.	1B	9.0	4	1	0	0	1.000	5.00	0	0
Willingham, J.	1B	3.0	5	0	0	0	1.000	15.00	0	0
Amezaga, A.	1B	2.0	4	0	0	0	1.000	18.00	0	0
Borchard, J.	1B	2.0	2	0	0	0	1.000	9.00	0	0
Uggla, D.	2B	1304.0	313	423	5	10	.980	5.08	42	65
Amezaga, A.	2B	127.0	33	41	2	0	.974	5.24	9	8
Wood, J.	2B	2.0	0	0	0	0	0.000	0.00	0	0
Ramirez, H.	SS	1323.0	258	410	11	15	.963	4.54	52	52
Andino, R.	SS	55.7	7	20	1	0	.964	4.37	1	1
Amezaga, A.	SS	54.3	5	21	0	0	1.000	4.31	3	2
Cabrera, M.	3B	1334.0	114	266	11	6	.957	2.56	30	3
Helms, W.	3B	94.3	7	23	2	0	.938	2.86	1	0
Amezaga, A.	3B	5.0	1	0	0	0	1.000	1.80	0	0

Name	POS	Inn	PO	A	TE	FE	FPct	RF	DPS	DPT
Willingham, J.	LF	1069.0	206	5	2	5	.968	1.78	0	0
Ross, C.	LF	205.0	40	0	0	0	1.000	1.76	0	0
Borchard, J.	LF	77.0	17	1	0	0	1.000	2.10	0	0
Aguila, C.	LF	43.3	5	1	0	0	1.000	1.25	0	0
Amezaga, A.	LF	28.3	11	0	0	0	1.000	3.49	0	0
Abercrombie, R.	LF	5.0	0	0	0	0	0.000	0.00	0	0
Helms, W.	LF	2.0	1	0	0	0	1.000	4.50	0	0
Reed, E.	LF	2.0	0	0	0	0	0.000	0.00	0	0
Cepicky, M.	LF	1.0	0	0	0	0	0.000	0.00	0	0
Abercrombie, R.	CF	590.3	172	3	1	4	.972	2.67	0	0
Amezaga, A.	CF	530.0	155	2	2	2	.975	2.67	0	0
Ross, C.	CF	145.0	40	1	0	1	.976	2.54	0	0
Reed, E.	CF	112.0	33	1	0	0	1.000	2.73	2	0
Hermida, J.	CF	53.0	20	0	0	0	1.000	3.40	0	0
Aguila, C.	CF	3.0	1	0	0	0	1.000	3.00	0	0
Hermida, J.	RF	683.7	157	1	1	7	.952	2.08	0	0
Borchard, J.	RF	332.3	84	6	0	2	.978	2.44	3	0
Ross, C.	RF	216.7	45	2	0	1	.979	1.95	0	0
Aguila, C.	RF	135.3	33	1	0	0	1.000	2.26	0	0
Cepicky, M.	RF	32.0	8	0	0	0	1.000	2.25	0	0
Abercrombie, R.	RF	24.3	4	0	0	0	1.000	1.48	0	0
Amezaga, A.	RF	9.0	0	0	0	0	0.000	0.00	0	0

Batted Ball Batting Stats

Player	PA	% of PA		% of Batted Balls					Runs Per Event				Total Runs vs. Avg.				
		K%	BB%	GB%	LD%	FB%	IF/F	HR/OF	NIP	GB	LD	OF	NIP	GB	LD	FB	Tot
Cabrera M.	676	16	14	40	24	35	.07	.16	.10	.07	.49	.26	12	4	18	10	44
Willingham J.	573	19	11	43	16	41	.10	.18	.06	.08	.37	.29	2	6	-8	17	17
Ramirez H.	700	18	9	44	21	35	.13	.10	.03	.11	.47	.16	-3	14	11	-7	15
Helms W.	278	20	10	38	26	36	.06	.16	.04	.05	.43	.32	-1	-1	6	8	13
Uggla D.	683	18	8	41	17	42	.07	.14	.03	.09	.40	.20	-3	10	-5	8	9
Jacobs M.	520	20	9	40	20	40	.09	.15	.03	.01	.44	.24	-3	-7	4	9	2
Borchard J.	261	25	12	48	18	34	.13	.18	.03	.03	.43	.27	-0	-2	-2	1	-3
Treanor M.	185	18	13	44	18	38	.15	.03	.08	.07	.40	.08	2	1	-2	-5	-4
Aguila C.	104	25	9	37	19	44	.10	.00	.00	.02	.52	.05	-1	-0	1	-4	-4
Olivo M.	452	23	4	42	19	39	.15	.12	-.05	.05	.40	.24	-12	0	0	5	-7
Hermida J.	348	20	11	45	20	35	.07	.07	.05	.04	.45	.09	1	-1	2	-8	-7
Ross C.	279	22	9	36	21	42	.06	.14	.03	-.01	.29	.18	-2	-4	-4	2	-8
Abercrombie R.	281	28	7	54	12	34	.15	.08	-.02	.10	.36	.20	-5	7	-8	-3	-10
Amezaga A.	378	12	10	51	17	33	.14	.04	.09	.09	.29	.06	2	7	-7	-13	-11
MLB Average		17	9	44	20	37	.11	.11	.05	.04	.39	.19	-	-	-	-	-

Houston Astros

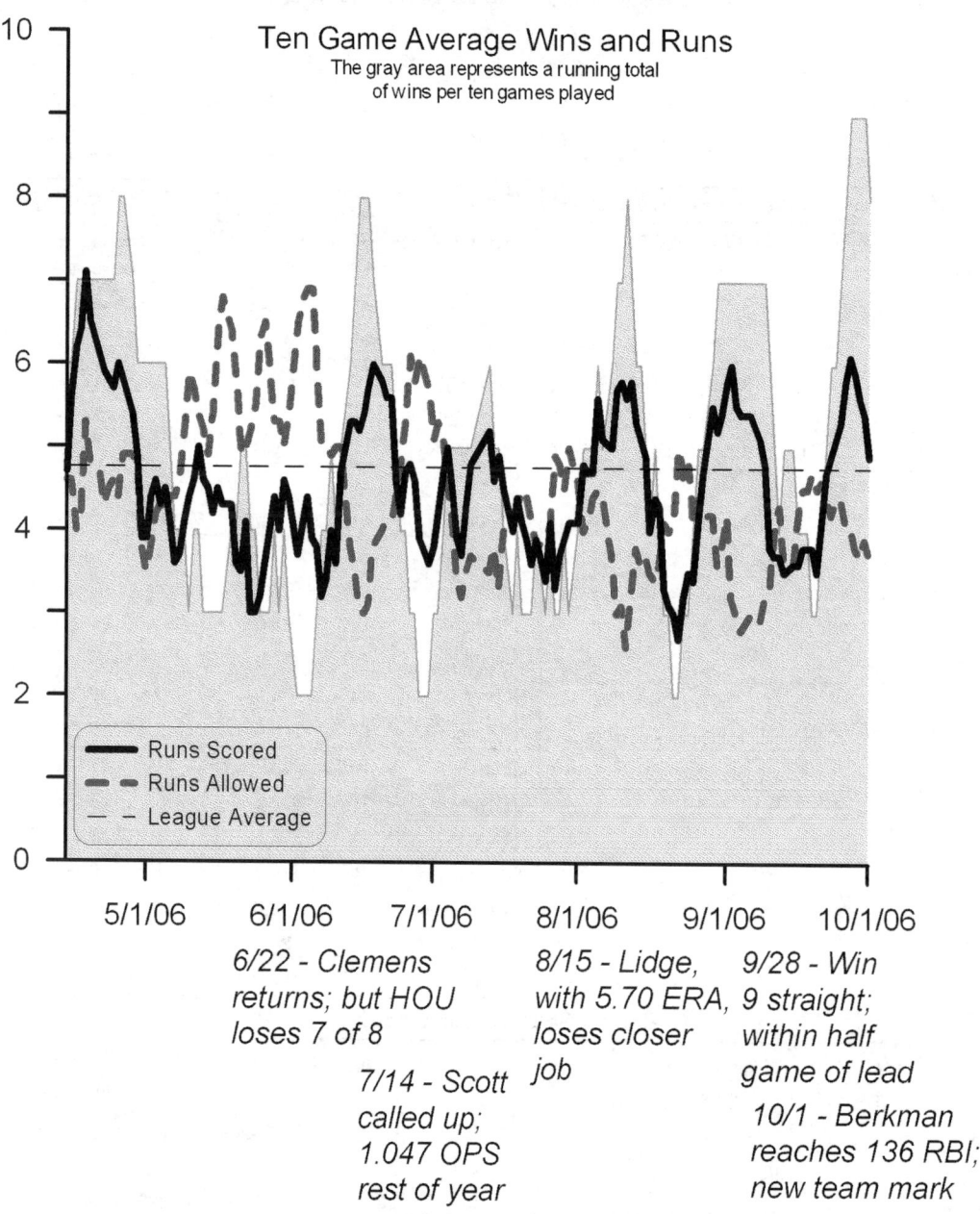

Ten Game Average Wins and Runs
The gray area represents a running total
of wins per ten games played

Runs Scored
Runs Allowed
League Average

6/22 - Clemens returns; but HOU loses 7 of 8

7/14 - Scott called up; 1.047 OPS rest of year

8/15 - Lidge, with 5.70 ERA, loses closer job

9/28 - Win 9 straight; within half game of lead

10/1 - Berkman reaches 136 RBI; new team mark

Team Batting and Pitching/Fielding Stats by Month						
	April	May	June	July	Aug	Sept/Oct
Wins	16	11	11	11	17	16
Losses	8	19	15	14	12	12
OBP	.355	.314	.322	.335	.340	.327
SLG	.457	.365	.404	.399	.426	.412
FIP	4.42	4.70	4.29	4.05	3.55	4.14
DER	.695	.693	.697	.707	.697	.730

Batting Stats

Player	RC	Runs	RBI	PA	Outs	P/PA	H	2B	3B	HR	TB	K	BB	IBB	HBP	SH	SF	SB	CS	GDP	BA	OBP	SLG	GPA
Berkman L.	142	95	136	646	380	3.89	169	29	0	45	333	106	98	22	4	0	8	3	2	11	.315	.420	.621	.344
Ensberg M.	75	67	58	495	303	4.24	91	17	1	23	179	96	101	7	4	0	3	1	4	3	.235	.396	.463	.294
Taveras W.	65	83	30	587	397	3.92	147	19	5	1	179	88	34	0	11	11	2	33	9	6	.278	.333	.338	.234
Biggio C.	64	79	62	607	431	3.55	135	33	0	21	231	84	40	1	9	5	5	3	2	16	.246	.306	.422	.243
Lamb M.	53	70	45	422	278	3.88	117	22	3	12	181	55	35	6	0	0	5	2	4	10	.307	.361	.475	.281
Everett A.	52	52	59	566	402	3.44	123	28	6	6	181	71	34	5	4	10	4	9	6	5	.239	.290	.352	.218
Burke C.	51	58	40	413	272	3.86	101	23	1	9	153	77	27	0	14	4	2	11	1	6	.276	.347	.418	.260
Scott L.	49	31	37	249	145	3.60	72	19	6	10	133	43	30	4	4	0	1	2	1	2	.336	.426	.621	.347
Wilson P.	45	40	55	417	305	3.71	105	22	2	9	158	94	22	2	2	0	3	6	2	18	.269	.309	.405	.240
Lane J.	40	44	45	345	238	4.02	58	10	0	15	113	75	49	0	2	2	4	1	2	6	.201	.318	.392	.241
Ausmus B.	37	37	39	502	360	3.64	101	16	1	2	125	71	45	2	6	9	3	3	1	21	.230	.308	.285	.210
Huff A.	28	31	38	261	175	3.76	56	10	1	13	107	39	26	3	7	0	4	0	0	7	.250	.341	.478	.273
Bruntlett E.	15	11	10	136	89	4.26	33	8	0	0	41	21	13	1	1	2	1	3	1	2	.277	.351	.345	.244
Palmeiro O.	13	12	17	128	92	4.15	30	6	1	0	38	17	6	0	1	2	0	0	1	2	.252	.294	.319	.212
Munson E.	13	10	19	156	115	3.71	28	6	0	5	49	32	11	1	3	0	1	0	0	2	.199	.269	.348	.208
Pettitte A.	4	4	5	73	50	3.71	12	3	0	1	18	19	1	0	0	10	0	0	0	0	.194	.206	.290	.165
Oswalt R.	4	3	8	90	58	3.76	10	1	0	1	14	15	4	0	0	20	0	0	0	2	.152	.200	.212	.143
Quintero H.	2	2	2	22	16	3.41	7	2	0	0	9	3	1	0	0	0	0	0	0	2	.333	.364	.429	.270
Jimerson C.	1	2	1	6	4	3.00	2	0	0	1	5	3	0	0	0	0	0	2	0	0	.333	.333	.833	.358
Nieve F.	1	0	1	23	14	3.30	2	0	0	0	2	8	2	0	0	5	0	0	0	0	.125	.222	.125	.131
Gallo M.	-0	0	0	1	1	3.00	0	0	0	0	0	1	0	0	0	0	0	0	0	0	.000	.000	.000	.000
Clemens R.	-0	0	0	38	25	3.42	2	1	0	0	3	11	3	0	1	7	0	0	0	0	.074	.194	.111	.115
Gimenez H.	-0	0	0	2	2	4.00	0	0	0	0	0	1	0	0	0	0	0	0	0	0	.000	.000	.000	.000
Albers M.	-0	0	0	4	4	3.25	0	0	0	0	0	3	0	0	0	0	0	0	0	0	.000	.000	.000	.000
Sampson C.	-0	0	0	7	5	3.00	0	0	0	0	0	2	0	0	0	2	0	0	0	0	.000	.000	.000	.000
Borkowski D.	-1	0	0	5	5	3.60	0	0	0	0	0	1	0	0	0	0	0	0	0	0	.000	.000	.000	.000
Backe B.	-1	0	0	15	13	4.60	2	0	0	0	2	6	1	0	0	0	0	0	0	1	.143	.200	.143	.126
McEwing J.	-1	0	0	6	6	4.17	0	0	0	0	0	2	0	0	0	0	0	0	0	0	.000	.000	.000	.000
Rodriguez W.	-1	4	1	43	34	3.49	3	0	0	0	3	10	1	0	0	5	0	0	0	0	.081	.105	.081	.068
House J.	-1	0	0	9	10	2.89	0	0	0	0	0	2	0	0	0	0	0	0	0	1	.000	.000	.000	.000
Hirsh J.	-2	0	0	17	15	3.65	0	0	0	0	0	9	0	0	0	2	0	0	0	0	.000	.000	.000	.000
Buchholz T.	-2	0	0	35	29	3.43	1	0	0	0	1	11	1	0	0	4	0	0	0	0	.033	.065	.033	.037

Italicized stats have been adjusted for home park.

Batted Ball Batting Stats are listed after fielding stats

Pitching Stats

Player	PRC	IP	BFP	G	GS	P/PA	K	BB	IBB	HBP	H	HR	DP	DER	SB	CS	PO	W	L	Sv	Op	Hld	RA	ERA	FIP
Oswalt R.	128	220.7	896	33	32	3.63	166	38	4	6	220	18	27	.692	5	6	1	15	8	0	0	0	3.10	2.98	3.32
Pettitte A.	86	214.3	929	36	35	3.75	178	70	9	2	238	27	31	.664	10	3	3	14	13	0	0	0	4.79	4.20	4.08
Clemens R.	76	113.3	451	19	19	4.04	102	29	1	4	89	7	12	.722	14	2	0	7	6	0	0	0	2.70	2.30	3.07
Wheeler D.	48	71.3	295	75	0	3.97	68	24	8	2	58	5	3	.719	3	1	0	3	5	9	12	24	2.78	2.52	2.98
Nieve F.	42	96.3	411	40	11	3.80	70	41	5	2	87	18	9	.746	4	1	0	3	3	0	0	0	4.30	4.20	5.38
Qualls C.	41	88.7	356	81	0	3.33	56	28	6	6	76	10	17	.730	3	4	1	7	3	0	6	23	3.86	3.76	4.37
Rodriguez W.	39	135.7	611	30	24	3.72	98	63	7	6	154	17	22	.660	6	6	4	9	10	0	0	0	6.37	5.64	4.77
Miller T.	33	50.7	207	70	0	3.92	56	13	2	4	42	7	4	.724	2	1	0	2	3	1	3	12	3.02	3.02	3.69
Buchholz T.	32	113.0	479	22	19	3.67	77	34	4	3	107	21	11	.735	11	1	0	6	10	0	0	0	6.37	5.89	5.15
Springer R.	32	59.7	240	72	0	4.20	46	16	1	4	46	10	3	.780	7	1	0	1	1	0	0	9	3.47	3.47	4.81
Lidge B.	28	75.0	340	78	0	3.97	104	36	4	6	69	10	2	.641	7	0	0	1	5	32	38	6	5.64	5.28	3.70
Borkowski D.	28	71.0	299	40	0	3.70	52	23	7	0	70	8	6	.713	1	0	0	3	2	0	0	1	4.82	4.69	3.89
Sampson C.	20	34.0	130	12	3	3.32	15	5	1	1	25	3	4	.783	0	0	0	2	1	0	0	0	2.65	2.12	3.92
Backe B.	19	43.0	189	8	8	3.53	19	18	0	3	43	4	3	.724	0	1	1	3	2	0	0	0	3.77	3.77	5.01
Hirsh J.	12	44.7	206	9	9	3.75	29	22	2	3	48	11	2	.723	2	1	0	3	4	0	0	0	6.45	6.04	6.67
Albers M.	5	15.0	66	4	2	3.73	11	7	0	0	17	1	3	.660	1	0	0	0	2	0	0	0	6.00	6.00	4.02
Gallo M.	4	16.3	82	23	0	3.39	7	7	1	2	28	3	4	.603	1	0	0	1	2	0	1	0	6.06	6.06	6.22
Astacio E.	1	5.7	30	6	0	3.83	6	6	3	0	7	2	0	.688	1	0	0	2	0	0	0	0	11.12	11.12	7.28
Barzilla P.	0	0.3	2	1	0	4.00	0	0	0	0	1	0	0	.500	0	0	0	0	0	0	0	0	0.00	0.00	3.22

Batted Ball Pitching Stats are listed after fielding stats

Fielding Stats

Name	POS	INN	SBA/G	CS%	ERA	WP+PB/G	PO	A	TE	FE
Ausmus, B.	C	1124.7	0.58	18%	3.82	0.208	933	61	2	0
Munson, E.	C	275.3	0.59	17%	4.90	0.654	198	9	1	0
Quintero, H.	C	56.7	0.79	60%	5.56	0.476	42	6	0	0
House, J.	C	12.0	0.75	0%	4.50	1.500	10	1	0	0

Name	POS	Inn	PO	A	TE	FE	FPct	RF	DPS	DPT
Berkman, L.	1B	923.0	962	69	1	4	.994	10.05	12	0
Lamb, M.	1B	503.0	473	41	2	3	.990	9.20	5	0
Munson, E.	1B	25.0	29	1	0	0	1.000	10.80	0	0
House, J.	1B	8.0	8	0	0	0	1.000	9.00	0	0
Huff, A.	1B	8.0	6	3	0	0	1.000	10.13	0	0
Lane, J.	1B	1.0	3	0	0	0	1.000	27.00	0	0
Ausmus, B.	1B	0.7	0	0	0	0	0.000	0.00	0	0
Biggio, C.	2B	1062.0	218	334	0	6	.989	4.68	35	40
Burke, C.	2B	345.7	68	117	2	3	.974	4.82	10	16
Bruntlett, E.	2B	48.0	13	17	0	2	.938	5.63	1	4
Lamb, M.	2B	7.0	2	1	0	0	1.000	3.86	1	0
Ausmus, B.	2B	3.0	0	1	0	0	1.000	3.00	0	0
McEwing, J.	2B	3.0	1	2	0	0	1.000	9.00	0	0
Everett, A.	SS	1292.0	202	479	2	4	.990	4.74	44	60
Bruntlett, E.	SS	144.7	20	57	0	4	.951	4.79	3	6
Burke, C.	SS	31.7	2	8	1	0	.909	2.84	0	1
Ensberg, M.	3B	975.0	81	230	8	4	.963	2.87	24	1
Lamb, M.	3B	263.7	24	70	1	5	.940	3.21	8	0
Huff, A.	3B	220.0	23	47	1	1	.972	2.86	3	0
Bruntlett, E.	3B	10.0	1	2	0	0	1.000	2.70	0	0
Wilson, P.	LF	823.0	147	2	0	0	1.000	1.63	0	0
Scott, L.	LF	417.0	81	1	0	0	1.000	1.77	2	0
Burke, C.	LF	119.0	14	0	0	0	1.000	1.06	0	0
Palmeiro, O.	LF	42.7	8	0	0	0	1.000	1.69	0	0
Berkman, L.	LF	25.7	5	0	0	0	1.000	1.75	0	0
Lane, J.	LF	23.0	6	0	0	0	1.000	2.35	0	0
Bruntlett, E.	LF	18.3	3	0	0	0	1.000	1.47	0	0
Taveras, W.	CF	1116.0	335	9	1	4	.986	2.77	5	0
Burke, C.	CF	284.3	72	2	0	1	.987	2.34	0	0
Bruntlett, E.	CF	39.0	10	1	0	0	1.000	2.54	0	0
Lane, J.	CF	17.0	5	0	0	0	1.000	2.65	0	0
Wilson, P.	CF	9.7	2	0	0	0	1.000	1.86	0	0
Jimerson, C.	CF	1.0	0	0	0	0	0.000	0.00	0	0
Scott, L.	CF	1.0	0	0	0	0	0.000	0.00	0	0
Lane, J.	RF	679.3	155	1	0	0	1.000	2.07	0	0
Berkman, L.	RF	305.7	56	3	0	3	.952	1.74	4	0
Huff, A.	RF	270.7	40	1	1	1	.953	1.36	0	0
Scott, L.	RF	78.3	15	1	0	0	1.000	1.84	0	0
Palmeiro, O.	RF	45.0	7	0	0	0	1.000	1.40	0	0
Burke, C.	RF	31.7	10	0	0	0	1.000	2.84	0	0
Wilson, P.	RF	30.3	6	0	0	0	1.000	1.78	0	0
Jimerson, C.	RF	14.0	6	0	0	0	1.000	3.86	0	0
Bruntlett, E.	RF	13.7	5	0	0	0	.833	3.29	0	0

Batted Ball Batting Stats

Player	PA	% of PA		% of Batted Balls					Runs Per Event				Total Runs vs. Avg.				
		K%	BB%	GB%	LD%	FB%	IF/F	HR/OF	NIP	GB	LD	OF	NIP	GB	LD	FB	Tot
Berkman L.	646	16	16	39	19	42	.15	.27	.11	.07	.39	.42	15	2	-3	35	48
Scott L.	249	17	14	36	24	40	.07	.14	.09	.13	.50	.24	4	4	7	4	19
Ensberg M.	495	19	21	38	15	48	.09	.16	.13	.02	.40	.26	19	-5	-10	10	14
Lamb M.	422	13	8	40	20	39	.09	.10	.07	.08	.38	.16	0	5	2	0	7
Huff A.	261	15	13	41	20	39	.07	.17	.10	.03	.35	.21	4	-2	-1	3	3
Burke C.	413	19	10	36	23	41	.16	.07	.05	.09	.41	.11	0	5	3	-9	-1
Bruntlett E.	136	15	10	41	20	38	.16	.00	.07	.11	.39	.04	1	2	0	-5	-2
Lane J.	345	22	15	28	14	58	.14	.13	.07	-.00	.42	.17	4	-5	-6	1	-6
Munson E.	156	21	9	39	17	44	.10	.12	.03	.01	.46	.08	-1	-2	0	-4	-6
Palmeiro O.	128	13	5	41	28	30	.17	.00	.02	.05	.32	-.07	-1	1	2	-8	-6
Biggio C.	607	14	8	39	19	41	.11	.11	.06	.04	.37	.13	-1	-1	-0	-6	-8
Wilson P.	417	23	6	57	18	24	.13	.11	-.02	.03	.43	.27	-8	-1	1	-0	-8
Taveras W.	587	15	8	56	18	27	.16	.01	.04	.07	.32	.08	-2	15	-9	-19	-16
Everett A.	566	13	7	37	20	43	.17	.04	.05	.05	.35	.08	-3	1	-0	-15	-17
Ausmus B.	502	14	10	53	19	28	.07	.02	.08	.00	.32	.07	3	-7	-5	-16	-26
MLB Average		17	9	44	20	37	.11	.11	.05	.04	.39	.19	-	-	-	-	-

Batted Ball Pitching Stats

Player	PA	% of PA		% of Batted Balls					Runs Per Event				Total Runs vs. Avg.				
		K%	BB%	GB%	LD%	FB%	IF/F	HR/OF	NIP	GB	LD	OF	NIP	GB	LD	FB	Tot
Clemens R.	451	23	7	49	16	35	.12	.06	-.00	.01	.42	.16	-6	-6	-4	-6	-23
Oswalt R.	896	19	5	49	20	31	.15	.10	-.02	.03	.39	.21	-16	-4	2	-5	-22
Wheeler D.	295	23	9	37	20	44	.13	.05	.01	.01	.46	.12	-3	-4	1	-5	-10
Qualls C.	356	16	10	60	14	26	.03	.15	.06	-.00	.30	.30	1	-6	-8	4	-10
Sampson C.	130	12	5	53	24	22	.04	.13	.02	-.06	.25	.19	-1	-5	-1	-1	-9
Springer R.	240	19	8	27	15	58	.10	.11	.03	.01	.32	.16	-1	-3	-5	3	-7
Miller T.	207	27	8	33	18	49	.08	.12	-.01	.10	.27	.17	-3	1	-5	1	-6
Borkowski D.	299	17	8	47	17	36	.06	.11	.03	-.01	.38	.26	-2	-4	-2	6	-2
Backe B.	189	10	11	36	20	44	.11	.05	.13	.02	.45	.08	3	-2	3	-4	-1
Nieve F.	411	17	10	41	15	44	.13	.16	.06	-.01	.44	.24	1	-6	-3	7	-1
Lidge B.	340	31	12	44	23	33	.13	.15	.02	.05	.54	.24	-2	-1	4	-2	-0
Buchholz T.	479	16	8	44	18	38	.11	.16	.04	.03	.39	.24	-2	-3	-1	7	1
Pettitte A.	929	19	8	50	22	29	.04	.15	.02	.03	.39	.29	-8	-3	4	11	3
Hirsh J.	206	14	12	30	18	52	.17	.17	.10	.03	.39	.25	3	-1	-1	6	6
Rodriguez W.	611	16	11	45	22	33	.06	.12	.08	.04	.42	.22	5	-2	7	3	13
MLB Average		17	9	44	20	37	.11	.11	.05	.04	.39	.19	-	-	-	-	-

Kansas City Royals

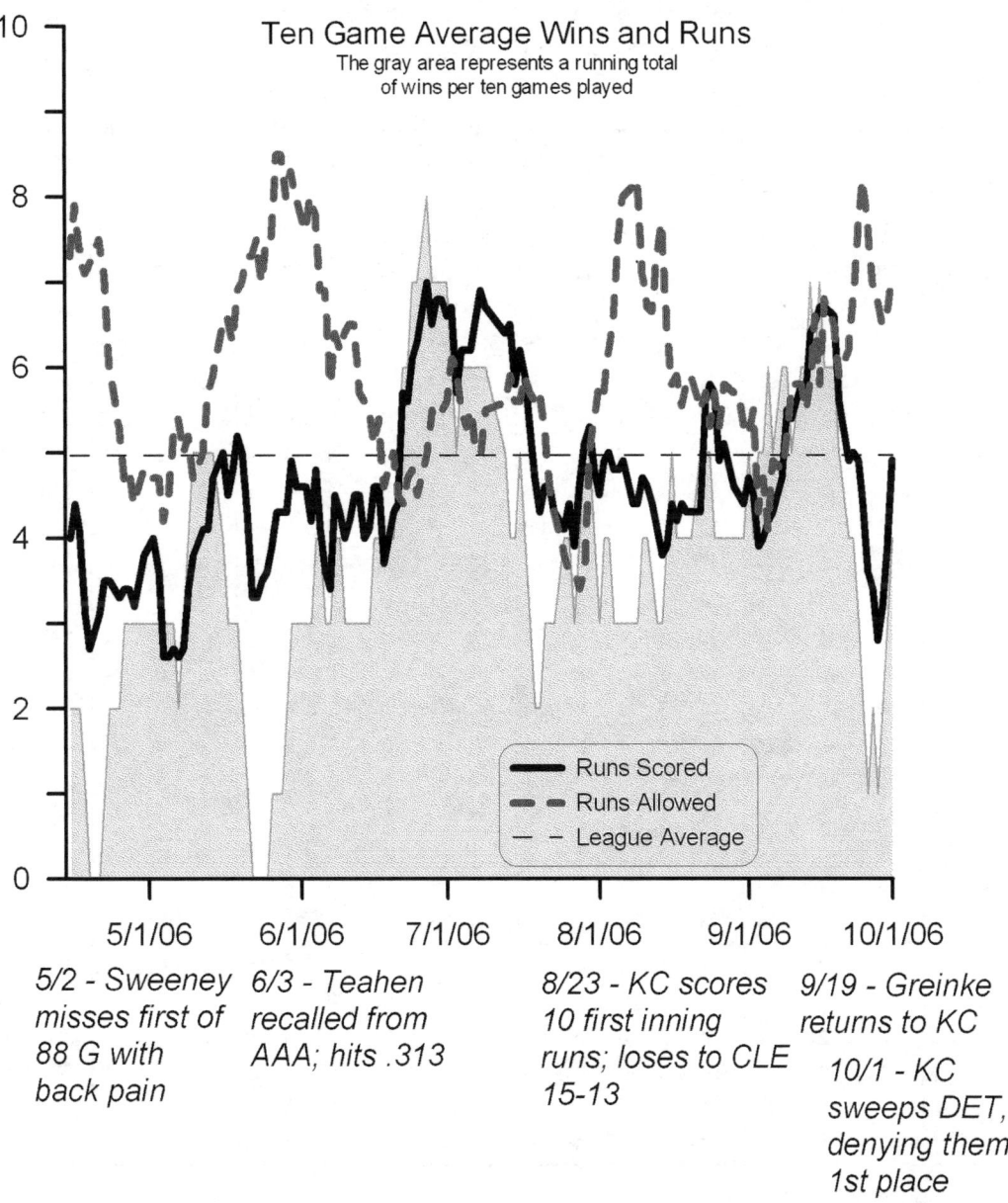

Ten Game Average Wins and Runs
The gray area represents a running total
of wins per ten games played

Legend:
— Runs Scored
- - Runs Allowed
- - League Average

5/2 - Sweeney misses first of 88 G with back pain

6/3 - Teahen recalled from AAA; hits .313

8/23 - KC scores 10 first inning runs; loses to CLE 15-13

9/19 - Greinke returns to KC

10/1 - KC sweeps DET, denying them 1st place

Team Batting and Pitching/Fielding Stats by Month						
	April	May	June	July	Aug	Sept/Oct
Wins	5	8	13	11	12	13
Losses	17	21	14	16	18	14
OBP	.303	.324	.338	.354	.335	.333
SLG	.378	.408	.405	.405	.429	.429
FIP	5.52	6.06	5.04	4.91	5.14	4.85
DER	.686	.688	.681	.684	.677	.651

Batting Stats

Player	RC	Runs	RBI	PA	Outs	P/PA	H	2B	3B	HR	TB	K	BB	IBB	HBP	SH	SF	SB	CS	GDP	BA	OBP	SLG	GPA
Teahen M.	80	70	69	439	284	3.92	114	21	7	18	203	85	40	2	2	2	2	10	0	5	.290	.357	.517	.288
Brown E.	80	77	81	601	394	3.71	151	41	2	15	241	95	59	3	5	0	10	6	3	15	.287	.358	.457	.274
DeJesus D.	77	83	56	552	359	3.68	145	36	7	8	219	70	43	4	12	2	4	6	3	10	.295	.364	.446	.274
Grudzielanek, M	70	85	52	586	399	3.46	163	32	4	7	224	69	28	4	2	3	5	3	2	12	.297	.331	.409	.250
German E.	55	44	34	331	199	4.10	91	18	5	3	128	49	40	0	6	6	0	7	3	8	.326	.422	.459	.303
Mientkiewicz D.	48	37	43	361	231	3.83	89	24	2	4	129	50	35	1	5	1	5	3	0	6	.283	.359	.411	.263
Buck J.	44	37	50	409	290	3.49	91	21	1	11	147	84	26	2	7	4	1	0	2	8	.245	.306	.396	.235
Sanders R.	40	45	49	358	262	3.70	80	23	1	11	138	86	28	3	1	0	4	7	7	10	.246	.304	.425	.242
Stairs M.	35	31	32	262	172	4.33	59	14	0	8	97	52	31	2	2	0	2	0	0	5	.261	.352	.429	.264
Sweeney M.	33	23	33	252	166	3.54	56	15	0	8	95	48	28	5	4	0	3	2	0	5	.258	.349	.438	.265
Berroa A.	33	45	54	503	385	3.39	111	18	1	9	158	88	14	1	3	9	3	3	1	21	.234	.259	.333	.199
Shealy R.	32	29	36	210	145	4.09	54	10	1	7	87	50	15	1	2	0	0	1	1	5	.280	.338	.451	.263
Gathright J.	32	34	28	263	177	3.75	60	6	3	1	75	45	22	0	4	4	4	10	6	2	.262	.332	.328	.230
Graffanino T.	31	34	32	250	169	3.96	59	16	0	5	90	31	25	1	1	4	0	3	4	4	.268	.346	.409	.256
Costa S.	26	23	23	252	177	3.31	65	20	1	3	96	29	6	2	5	2	2	2	0	5	.274	.304	.405	.237
Blanco A.	9	9	9	96	69	3.64	21	4	1	0	27	14	5	0	1	3	0	0	1	2	.241	.290	.310	.207
Bako P.	9	7	10	167	124	3.60	32	3	0	0	35	46	11	0	0	2	1	0	0	3	.209	.261	.229	.173
Phillips P.	9	8	5	69	47	2.86	18	3	0	1	24	8	1	0	0	2	1	0	0	0	.277	.284	.369	.219
Keppinger J.	8	11	8	67	46	3.43	16	2	0	2	24	6	5	1	0	2	0	0	0	2	.267	.323	.400	.244
Guiel A.	7	9	7	59	40	3.88	11	3	0	3	23	11	7	0	2	0	0	0	0	1	.220	.339	.460	.266
Robinson K.	5	8	5	67	49	3.52	17	2	1	0	21	7	1	0	0	2	0	1	1	1	.266	.277	.328	.205
Huber J.	2	1	1	11	8	4.73	2	1	0	0	3	4	1	0	0	0	0	1	0	0	.200	.273	.300	.197
Elarton S.	1	1	0	4	2	2.25	1	1	0	0	2	0	0	0	0	1	0	0	0	0	.333	.333	.667	.315
Redman M.	0	0	0	3	1	6.33	0	0	0	0	0	1	1	0	0	1	0	0	0	0	.000	.500	.000	.224
Sanchez A.	0	2	1	28	21	3.50	6	0	0	0	6	4	0	0	0	0	1	0	0	0	.222	.214	.222	.151
Gobble J.	0	0	0	1	0	0.00	0	0	0	0	0	0	0	0	0	1	0	0	0	0	.000	.000	.000	.000
Duckworth B.	-0	1	0	4	2	3.50	1	1	0	0	2	0	0	0	0	1	0	0	0	0	.333	.333	.667	.315
Maier M.	-0	3	0	15	12	3.33	2	0	0	0	2	4	2	0	0	0	0	0	0	1	.154	.267	.154	.158
Affeldt J.	-0	0	0	2	2	5.00	0	0	0	0	0	1	0	0	0	0	0	0	0	0	.000	.000	.000	.000
Wellemeyer T.	-0	0	0	2	2	5.00	0	0	0	0	0	1	0	0	0	0	0	0	0	0	.000	.000	.000	.000
Keppel R.	-0	0	0	2	2	2.00	0	0	0	0	0	1	0	0	0	0	0	0	0	0	.000	.000	.000	.000
Wood M.	-0	0	0	3	3	2.67	0	0	0	0	0	1	0	0	0	0	0	0	0	0	.000	.000	.000	.000

Italicized stats have been adjusted for home park.

Batted Ball Batting Stats are listed after fielding stats

Pitching Stats

Player	PRC	IP	BFP	G	GS	P/PA	K	BB	IBB	HBP	H	HR	DP	DER	SB	CS	PO	W	L	Sv	Op	Hld	RA	ERA	FIP
Redman M.	49	167.0	740	29	29	3.73	76	63	1	8	202	19	29	.672	5	6	1	11	10	0	0	0	5.93	5.71	5.09
Hudson L.	35	102.0	440	26	15	3.79	64	38	1	4	109	7	19	.673	1	2	0	7	6	0	1	1	5.47	5.12	4.11
Elarton S.	34	114.7	501	20	20	3.79	49	52	1	6	117	26	12	.747	4	3	2	4	9	0	0	0	5.73	5.34	6.85
Peralta J.	32	73.7	304	64	0	3.81	57	17	2	2	74	10	10	.697	4	1	0	1	3	1	3	17	4.52	4.40	4.17
Gobble J.	32	84.0	370	60	6	3.94	80	29	1	1	95	12	9	.645	4	2	1	4	6	2	4	11	5.46	5.14	4.25
Wellemeyer T.	27	57.0	248	28	0	3.89	37	37	2	2	48	5	11	.725	6	1	1	1	2	1	1	3	3.95	3.63	5.05
Hernandez R.	26	109.7	508	21	21	3.70	50	48	0	6	145	22	16	.675	2	2	0	6	10	0	0	0	7.14	6.48	6.44
Burgos A.	25	73.3	336	68	1	4.02	72	37	4	6	83	16	10	.663	5	0	0	4	5	18	30	5	6.01	5.52	5.73
Perez O.	22	67.0	298	12	12	3.70	48	18	1	1	80	9	2	.667	0	3	1	2	4	0	0	0	5.91	5.64	4.38
Nelson J.	21	44.7	193	43	0	4.12	44	24	4	1	37	5	4	.706	2	1	0	1	1	9	10	5	4.43	4.43	4.16
Dessens E.	20	54.0	234	43	0	3.76	36	13	6	1	63	4	8	.656	2	1	0	5	7	2	7	12	5.17	4.50	3.34
de la Rosa J.	18	48.7	221	10	10	3.87	36	32	0	1	49	10	7	.725	5	0	0	3	4	0	0	0	5.36	5.18	6.49
Affeldt J.	18	70.0	320	27	9	3.80	28	42	0	1	71	9	6	.733	5	0	0	4	6	0	0	2	6.56	5.91	5.98
Sisco A.	16	58.3	278	65	0	3.97	52	40	6	1	66	8	5	.650	5	1	0	1	3	1	5	5	7.25	7.10	5.06
Wood M.	15	64.7	307	23	7	3.67	29	23	3	7	86	10	7	.651	0	2	0	3	3	0	0	1	7.10	5.71	5.63
Bernero A.	15	13.0	53	3	2	4.09	12	0	0	0	15	0	1	.634	0	0	0	1	0	0	0	0	1.38	1.38	1.42
Keppel R.	12	34.3	157	8	6	3.62	20	15	2	1	45	6	4	.661	1	1	1	0	4	0	0	0	5.50	5.50	5.59
Duckworth B.	11	45.7	216	10	8	3.99	27	24	4	2	62	3	6	.625	0	1	1	1	5	0	0	0	7.09	6.11	4.38
Bautista D.	11	35.0	161	8	7	3.95	22	17	0	4	38	5	2	.699	2	2	1	0	2	0	0	0	6.17	5.66	5.66
Dohmann S.	6	23.7	117	21	0	3.75	22	18	5	2	33	5	5	.600	3	0	0	1	3	0	1	3	7.99	7.99	6.05
Nunez L.	5	13.3	58	7	0	3.43	7	5	0	2	15	2	6	.643	0	0	0	0	0	0	0	0	4.73	4.73	5.74
Greinke Z.	3	6.3	28	3	0	3.36	5	3	2	0	7	1	1	.684	0	0	0	1	0	0	0	0	4.26	4.26	4.21
Braun R.	3	10.7	46	9	0	3.85	6	3	0	0	13	2	1	.657	0	1	0	0	1	0	2	0	6.75	6.75	5.42
Mays J.	2	23.7	120	6	6	3.76	9	14	0	0	38	7	5	.633	0	0	0	0	4	0	0	0	12.55	10.27	8.12
Etherton S.	1	7.7	40	2	2	4.38	4	6	0	0	10	3	0	.741	0	0	0	1	1	0	0	0	10.57	9.39	9.65
Andrade S.	1	4.7	23	4	0	3.70	5	4	0	0	5	0	0	.643	1	0	0	0	0	0	0	1	9.64	9.64	3.69
Diaz J.	1	6.7	38	4	0	3.71	3	8	0	1	10	2	1	.667	0	0	0	0	0	0	0	0	10.80	10.80	10.31
Snyder K.	0	2.0	19	1	1	2.79	2	1	0	0	10	1	0	.267	0	0	0	0	0	0	0	0	40.50	22.50	9.26
MacDougal M.	0	4.0	13	4	0	2.69	2	0	0	0	2	0	1	.818	0	0	0	0	0	1	1	0	0.00	0.00	2.26
Booker C.	0	1.0	11	1	0	3.91	0	3	0	0	5	3	0	.600	0	0	0	0	0	0	0	0	54.00	54.00	51.26
Stemle S.	0	6.0	36	5	0	3.36	0	3	0	0	15	1	1	.563	1	0	1	0	1	0	1	0	15.00	15.00	6.93

Batted Ball Pitching Stats are listed after fielding stats

Fielding Stats

Name	POS	INN	SBA/G	CS%	ERA	WP+PB/G	PO	A	TE	FE
Buck, J.	C	930.3	0.45	28%	5.71	0.590	616	36	6	0
Bako, P.	C	392.0	0.64	29%	5.74	0.551	258	19	2	0
Phillips, P.	C	104.0	0.78	44%	5.11	0.865	75	8	1	0

Name	POS	Inn	PO	A	TE	FE	FPct	RF	DPS	DPT
Mientkiewicz, D.	1B	724.7	748	42	0	3	.996	9.81	8	0
Shealy, R.	1B	453.0	417	26	0	3	.993	8.80	4	1
Graffanino, T.	1B	99.0	96	6	0	2	.981	9.27	3	0
Stairs, M.	1B	76.3	67	1	0	0	1.000	8.02	0	0
Phillips, P.	1B	34.3	34	0	0	0	1.000	8.91	0	0
Keppinger, J.	1B	30.0	37	1	0	0	1.000	11.40	0	0
German, E.	1B	9.0	8	1	0	0	1.000	9.00	0	0
Grudzielanek, M.	2B	1111.0	261	372	1	3	.994	5.13	36	77
German, E.	2B	164.0	36	41	0	1	.987	4.23	2	9
Graffanino, T.	2B	78.3	19	24	0	0	1.000	4.94	1	6
Sanchez, A.	2B	38.0	13	22	0	0	1.000	8.29	0	2
Blanco, A.	2B	27.0	5	8	0	0	1.000	4.33	2	1
Keppinger, J.	2B	8.0	3	3	0	0	1.000	6.75	1	1
Berroa, A.	SS	1117.0	188	367	3	15	.969	4.47	58	42
Blanco, A.	SS	200.0	30	77	3	2	.955	4.82	14	10
Graffanino, T.	SS	75.0	10	15	0	1	.962	3.00	3	0
Sanchez, A.	SS	20.3	2	9	0	0	1.000	4.87	2	0
Grudzielanek, M.	SS	11.7	0	1	0	0	1.000	0.77	0	0
German, E.	SS	2.0	0	0	0	0	0.000	0.00	0	0
Teahen, M.	3B	923.7	80	235	8	6	.957	3.07	31	2
Graffanino, T.	3B	215.3	15	63	1	1	.975	3.26	2	0
German, E.	3B	181.0	9	43	1	3	.929	2.59	4	0
Keppinger, J.	3B	106.3	7	30	0	2	.949	3.13	3	0

Name	POS	Inn	PO	A	TE	FE	FPct	RF	DPS	DPT
Brown, E.	LF	719.3	163	7	0	1	.994	2.13	4	0
DeJesus, D.	LF	544.7	138	5	1	1	.986	2.36	0	0
German, E.	LF	78.3	17	1	0	1	.947	2.07	2	0
Costa, S.	LF	42.0	10	0	0	0	1.000	2.14	0	0
Guiel, A.	LF	17.0	3	0	0	0	1.000	1.59	0	0
Stairs, M.	LF	14.0	4	0	0	0	1.000	2.57	0	0
Maier, M.	LF	8.0	0	0	0	0	0.000	0.00	0	0
Robinson, K.	LF	2.0	1	0	0	0	1.000	4.50	0	0
Keppinger, J.	LF	1.0	0	0	0	0	0.000	0.00	0	0
Gathright, J.	CF	578.7	186	4	1	1	.990	2.96	4	0
DeJesus, D.	CF	479.7	149	7	1	0	.994	2.93	4	0
Costa, S.	CF	159.0	49	0	0	1	.980	2.77	0	0
Robinson, K.	CF	120.7	37	1	0	0	1.000	2.83	0	0
German, E.	CF	71.3	19	0	0	2	.905	2.40	0	0
Guiel, A.	CF	17.0	6	0	0	0	1.000	3.18	0	0
Sanders, R.	RF	601.0	170	4	1	1	.989	2.61	0	0
Brown, E.	RF	414.0	110	3	0	2	.983	2.46	0	0
Costa, S.	RF	307.0	83	0	1	4	.943	2.43	0	0
Guiel, A.	RF	77.7	21	1	0	0	1.000	2.55	0	0
Maier, M.	RF	21.3	4	0	1	0	.800	1.69	0	0
Robinson, K.	RF	5.3	2	0	0	0	1.000	3.38	0	0

Batted Ball Batting Stats

Player	PA	% of PA		% of Batted Balls					Runs Per Event				Total Runs vs. Avg.				
		K%	BB%	GB%	LD%	FB%	IF/F	HR/OF	NIP	GB	LD	OF	NIP	GB	LD	FB	Tot
Teahen M.	439	19	10	49	16	35	.06	.18	.04	.09	.41	.32	-1	7	-5	13	15
German E.	331	15	14	58	18	24	.04	.06	.11	.12	.40	.23	6	10	-2	-3	11
Brown E.	601	16	11	44	18	38	.10	.09	.07	.04	.47	.18	3	-1	5	-1	7
DeJesus D.	552	13	10	49	22	29	.09	.07	.09	.07	.38	.13	4	8	5	-11	6
Sweeney M.	252	19	13	35	21	44	.11	.12	.07	.02	.39	.19	2	-2	0	1	1
Stairs M.	262	20	13	43	19	38	.07	.13	.07	.02	.44	.21	2	-2	-0	1	1
Shealy R.	210	24	8	37	17	45	.09	.12	.00	.07	.46	.20	-3	1	0	2	0
Mientkiewicz D.	361	14	11	41	22	37	.10	.04	.09	.06	.43	.08	3	1	5	-9	0
Graffanino T.	250	12	10	43	19	38	.17	.05	.10	.09	.44	.08	2	3	2	-7	-0
Sanders R.	358	24	8	43	19	39	.15	.14	.00	.04	.47	.22	-5	-2	1	1	-4
Costa S.	252	12	4	43	24	33	.13	.05	.01	-.00	.42	.08	-3	-2	7	-7	-6
Grudzielanek M.	586	12	5	52	23	25	.05	.04	.03	.04	.39	.10	-5	2	11	-14	-6
Gathright J.	263	17	10	70	15	15	.15	.05	.06	.10	.35	.02	0	10	-6	-11	-7
Buck J.	409	21	8	45	20	35	.15	.12	.02	.04	.39	.19	-4	-1	-0	-3	-8
Bako P.	167	28	7	56	19	24	.04	.00	-.02	.09	.32	-.09	-4	3	-3	-10	-13
Berroa A.	503	17	3	53	17	30	.14	.09	-.04	.02	.33	.14	-11	-2	-6	-9	-28
MLB Average		*17*	*9*	*44*	*20*	*37*	*.11*	*.11*	*.05*	*.04*	*.39*	*.19*	-	-	-	-	-

Batted Ball Pitching Stats

Player	PA	% of PA		% of Batted Balls					Runs Per Event				Total Runs vs. Avg.				
		K%	BB%	GB%	LD%	FB%	IF/F	HR/OF	NIP	GB	LD	OF	NIP	GB	LD	FB	Tot
Hudson L.	440	15	10	49	23	28	.04	.08	.07	.04	.37	.12	1	0	4	-9	-3
Wellemeyer T.	248	15	16	51	13	37	.10	.09	.12	.04	.41	.12	6	0	-5	-4	-3
Dessens E.	234	15	6	45	25	30	.06	.08	.02	.03	.37	.14	-2	-1	4	-3	-3
Peralta J.	304	19	6	32	22	46	.12	.10	.00	.04	.46	.14	-4	-2	6	-1	-1
Nelson J.	193	23	13	34	23	43	.08	.11	.05	.04	.33	.22	1	-1	-2	1	-0
Affeldt J.	320	9	13	49	17	35	.06	.11	.16	.02	.32	.17	7	-2	-5	-0	1
Bautista D.	161	14	13	50	17	32	.05	.14	.11	.04	.34	.26	3	0	-2	2	3
de la Rosa J.	221	16	15	40	21	38	.09	.19	.11	.02	.31	.24	4	-2	-2	3	3
Keppel R.	157	13	10	44	23	33	.15	.15	.09	.06	.45	.19	1	1	4	-1	5
Gobble J.	370	22	8	38	22	40	.09	.13	.01	.09	.39	.22	-4	4	1	4	5
Sisco A.	278	19	15	39	17	44	.06	.11	.09	.12	.42	.15	5	4	-2	-1	6
Duckworth B.	216	13	12	47	21	32	.10	.06	.11	.10	.40	.15	3	4	2	-3	6
Perez O.	298	16	6	40	24	36	.06	.12	.02	.04	.39	.23	-3	0	5	4	6
Dohmann S.	117	19	17	47	25	29	.05	.25	.11	.10	.41	.31	3	2	1	1	6
Burgos A.	336	21	13	43	18	39	.06	.19	.06	.08	.44	.26	2	4	-2	6	10
Wood M.	307	9	10	52	16	32	.05	.14	.12	.10	.39	.22	3	8	-2	3	12
Mays J.	120	8	12	45	20	35	.03	.18	.17	.06	.45	.39	2	1	2	7	13
Elarton S.	501	10	12	29	18	52	.09	.13	.14	.03	.40	.17	8	-3	1	8	13
Redman M.	740	10	10	44	20	35	.10	.10	.11	.04	.38	.20	6	3	3	2	14
Hernandez R.	508	10	11	39	23	38	.11	.16	.13	.04	.40	.20	6	1	9	4	19
MLB Average		*17*	*9*	*44*	*20*	*37*	*.11*	*.11*	*.05*	*.04*	*.39*	*.19*	-	-	-	-	-

Los Angeles Angels of Anaheim

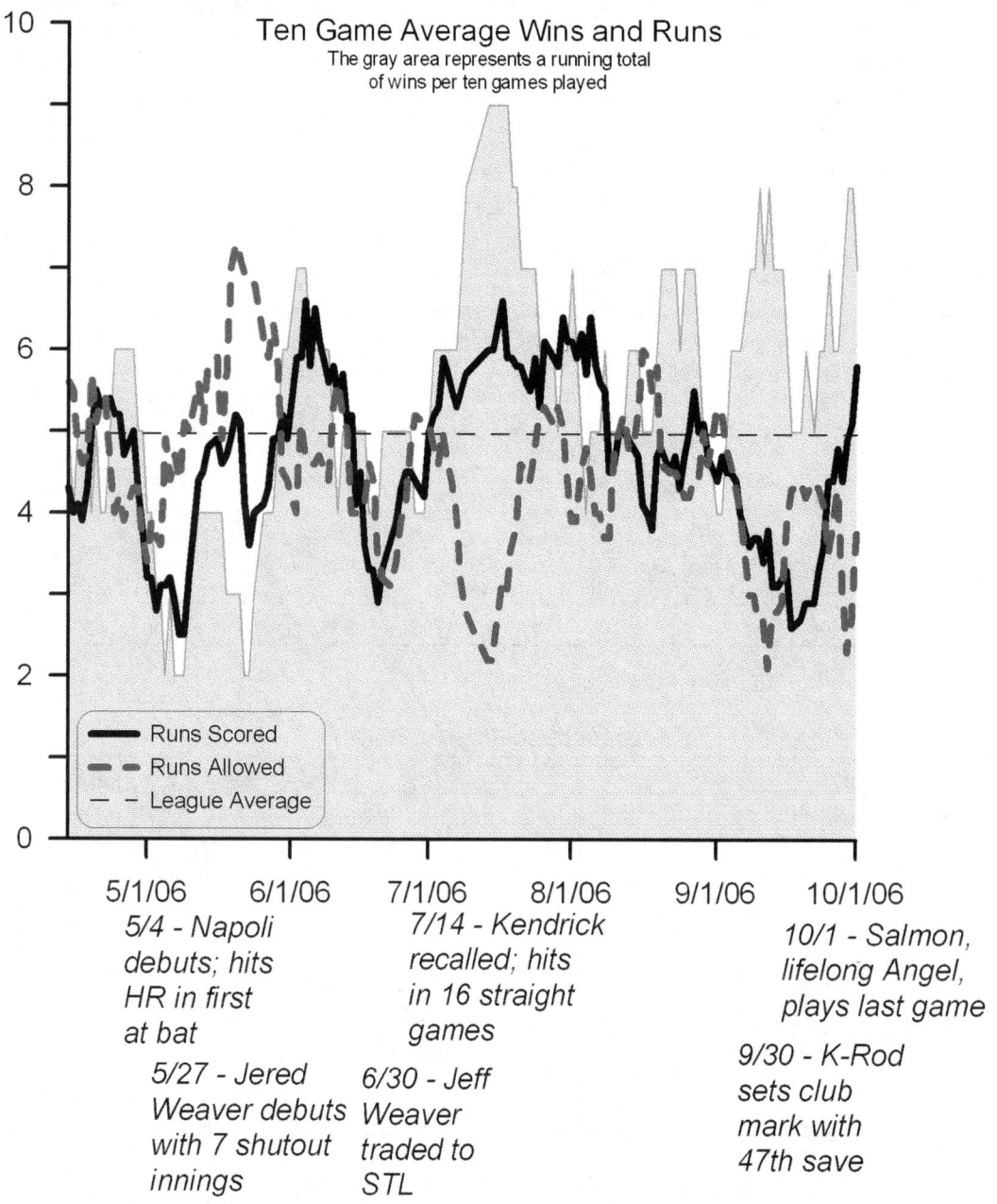

Ten Game Average Wins and Runs
The gray area represents a running total
of wins per ten games played

- Runs Scored
- Runs Allowed
- League Average

5/1/06   6/1/06   7/1/06   8/1/06   9/1/06   10/1/06

5/4 - Napoli
debuts; hits
HR in first
at bat

5/27 - Jered
Weaver debuts
with 7 shutout
innings

7/14 - Kendrick
recalled; hits
in 16 straight
games

6/30 - Jeff
Weaver
traded to
STL

10/1 - Salmon,
lifelong Angel,
plays last game

9/30 - K-Rod
sets club
mark with
47th save

Team Batting and Pitching/Fielding Stats by Month						
	April	May	June	July	Aug	Sept/Oct
Wins	12	11	12	19	16	19
Losses	13	17	14	7	13	9
OBP	.302	.315	.329	.366	.349	.338
SLG	.404	.375	.410	.494	.445	.420
FIP	4.49	4.41	4.03	3.37	4.38	3.53
DER	.709	.680	.699	.700	.670	.706

Batting Stats

Player	RC	Runs	RBI	PA	Outs	P/PA	H	2B	3B	HR	TB	K	BB	IBB	HBP	SH	SF	SB	CS	GDP	BA	OBP	SLG	GPA
Guerrero V.	116	92	116	665	428	3.16	200	34	1	33	335	68	50	25	4	0	4	15	5	16	.329	.382	.552	.321
Figgins C.	90	93	62	683	465	3.89	161	23	8	9	227	100	65	1	2	5	7	52	16	6	.267	.336	.376	.254
Rivera J.	85	65	85	494	327	3.56	139	27	0	23	235	59	33	0	7	0	6	0	4	14	.310	.362	.525	.305
Cabrera O.	82	95	72	675	451	3.64	171	45	1	9	245	58	51	0	3	3	11	27	3	12	.282	.335	.404	.261
Anderson G.	79	63	85	588	399	3.39	152	28	2	17	235	95	38	11	0	0	7	1	0	8	.280	.323	.433	.263
Kennedy A.	66	50	55	503	353	3.63	123	26	6	4	173	72	39	5	5	3	5	16	10	15	.273	.334	.384	.255
Izturis M.	60	64	44	399	262	3.96	103	21	3	5	145	35	38	1	3	5	1	14	6	7	.293	.365	.412	.277
Napoli M.	43	47	42	325	212	4.54	61	13	0	16	122	90	51	0	5	0	1	2	3	2	.228	.360	.455	.286
Quinlan R.	39	28	32	244	166	3.66	75	11	1	9	115	28	7	1	2	0	1	2	1	6	.321	.344	.491	.288
Kendrick H.	34	25	30	283	196	3.29	76	21	1	4	111	44	9	2	4	0	3	6	0	5	.285	.314	.416	.254
Salmon T.	29	30	27	244	165	3.96	56	8	2	9	95	44	29	1	3	0	1	0	2	8	.265	.361	.450	.285
Molina J.	23	18	22	245	177	3.37	54	17	0	4	83	49	9	0	2	7	2	1	0	6	.240	.273	.369	.223
Morales K.	21	21	22	215	163	3.64	46	10	1	5	73	28	17	1	0	0	1	1	1	11	.234	.293	.371	.233
McPherson D.	17	16	13	121	88	3.95	30	4	0	7	55	40	6	0	0	0	0	1	0	3	.261	.298	.478	.263
Murphy T.	7	12	6	77	55	3.32	16	4	1	1	25	21	5	0	0	1	1	4	1	0	.229	.276	.357	.221
Willits R.	6	12	2	58	36	4.19	12	1	0	0	13	10	11	0	0	2	0	4	3	0	.267	.411	.289	.266
Erstad D.	6	8	5	105	77	3.84	21	8	1	0	31	18	6	0	2	1	1	1	1	2	.221	.279	.326	.215
Mathis J.	4	9	6	63	47	3.86	8	2	0	2	16	14	7	1	0	0	1	0	0	0	.145	.238	.291	.186
Aybar E.	4	5	2	40	31	3.78	10	1	1	0	13	8	0	0	0	0	0	1	0	1	.250	.250	.325	.201
Pride C.	4	6	2	33	22	4.36	6	2	0	1	11	8	6	0	0	0	0	0	0	1	.222	.364	.407	.275
Kotchman C.	1	6	6	88	70	3.50	12	2	0	1	17	13	7	0	0	2	0	0	1	2	.152	.221	.215	.159
Weaver J.	1	0	0	4	2	2.75	1	0	0	0	1	0	0	0	0	1	0	0	0	0	.333	.333	.333	.242
Santana E.	-0	0	0	4	3	4.50	1	0	0	0	1	3	0	0	0	0	0	0	0	0	.250	.250	.250	.181
Colon B.	-0	0	0	2	1	3.50	0	0	0	0	0	1	0	0	0	1	0	0	0	0	.000	.000	.000	.000
Shields S.	-0	0	0	1	1	5.00	0	0	0	0	0	0	0	0	0	0	0	0	0	0	.000	.000	.000	.000
Lackey J.	-0	0	0	3	3	4.00	0	0	0	0	0	0	0	0	0	0	0	0	0	0	.000	.000	.000	.000
Gregg K.	-0	0	0	3	3	3.00	0	0	0	0	0	2	0	0	0	0	0	0	0	0	.000	.000	.000	.000
Escobar K.	-0	0	0	4	4	3.75	0	0	0	0	0	3	0	0	0	0	0	0	0	0	.000	.000	.000	.000
Alfonzo E.	-2	1	1	52	46	3.87	5	1	0	0	6	3	2	0	0	0	0	0	0	1	.100	.135	.120	.094

Italicized stats have been adjusted for home park.
Batted Ball Batting Stats are listed after fielding stats

Pitching Stats

Player	PRC	IP	BFP	G	GS	P/PA	K	BB	IBB	HBP	H	HR	DP	DER	SB	CS	PO	W	L	Sv	Op	Hld	RA	ERA	FIP
Lackey J.	108	217.7	922	33	33	3.81	190	72	4	9	203	14	21	.688	12	4	0	13	11	0	0	0	4.05	3.56	3.41
Weaver Jer.	87	123.0	490	19	19	3.94	105	33	1	3	94	15	8	.751	11	3	0	11	2	0	0	0	2.63	2.56	3.99
Escobar K.	85	189.3	789	30	30	3.69	147	50	2	4	192	17	19	.674	14	10	0	11	14	0	0	0	4.42	3.61	3.70
Santana E.	84	204.0	846	33	33	3.80	141	70	2	11	181	21	23	.723	5	9	0	16	8	0	0	0	4.68	4.28	4.38
Rodriguez F.	70	73.0	296	69	0	4.11	98	28	5	1	52	6	4	.712	2	1	1	2	3	47	51	0	1.97	1.73	2.63
Shields S.	56	87.7	351	74	0	3.75	84	24	4	1	70	8	10	.718	10	0	0	7	7	2	8	31	3.08	2.87	3.25
Carrasco H.	51	100.3	417	56	3	3.64	72	27	1	5	93	10	14	.713	2	0	0	7	3	1	2	1	3.77	3.41	4.05
Gregg K.	34	78.3	341	32	3	4.19	71	21	0	2	88	10	6	.658	5	0	1	3	4	0	0	0	4.71	4.14	3.99
Donnelly B.	29	64.0	278	62	0	3.94	53	28	3	4	58	8	6	.724	1	0	0	6	0	0	1	11	4.50	3.94	4.59
Saunders J.	26	70.7	302	13	13	3.85	51	29	1	1	71	6	12	.670	1	3	1	7	3	0	0	0	5.35	4.71	4.15
Weaver Jef.	24	88.7	397	16	16	3.73	62	21	0	4	114	18	9	.651	6	5	2	3	10	0	0	0	6.90	6.29	5.35
Colon B.	16	56.3	251	10	10	3.40	31	11	0	3	71	11	4	.667	1	3	0	1	5	0	0	0	6.23	5.11	5.45
Romero J.	12	48.3	226	65	0	3.94	31	28	2	1	57	3	5	.663	2	1	1	1	2	0	1	7	7.45	6.70	4.46
Yan E.	6	22.3	98	13	0	4.05	16	13	2	1	19	4	4	.734	2	1	0	0	0	0	0	0	7.25	6.85	5.77
Moseley D.	2	11.0	54	3	2	3.93	3	2	0	0	22	3	4	.587	2	0	0	1	0	0	0	0	9.00	9.00	6.81
Bootcheck C.	2	10.3	54	7	0	3.72	7	9	0	0	16	3	4	.571	0	0	0	0	1	0	0	0	10.45	10.45	8.29
Jones G.	1	6.0	28	5	0	3.46	1	2	0	0	8	1	1	.667	1	0	0	0	0	0	0	0	7.50	6.00	6.10
Bulger J.	0	1.7	9	2	0	4.56	1	3	0	0	1	0	0	.800	0	0	0	0	0	0	0	0	16.20	16.20	7.46

Batted Ball Pitching Stats are listed after fielding stats

Fielding Stats

Name	POS	INN	SBA/G	CS%	ERA	WP+PB/G	PO	A	TE	FE
Napoli, M.	C	716.3	0.68	30%	3.76	0.490	576	47	4	3
Molina, J.	C	603.3	0.69	41%	3.98	0.701	504	48	3	5
Mathis, J.	C	133.0	0.95	14%	5.82	0.474	92	6	1	1

Name	POS	Inn	PO	A	TE	FE	FPct	RF	DPS	DPT
Morales, K.	1B	453.7	422	37	1	3	.989	9.11	6	1
Quinlan, R.	1B	384.0	351	24	1	2	.992	8.79	4	1
Kendrick, H.	1B	351.3	330	29	1	1	.994	9.20	7	1
Kotchman, C.	1B	197.0	180	15	0	0	1.000	8.91	0	1
McPherson, D.	1B	30.7	32	0	0	0	1.000	9.39	0	0
Erstad, D.	1B	28.0	31	1	0	0	1.000	10.29	0	0
Molina, J.	1B	5.0	4	0	0	0	1.000	7.20	0	0
Alfonzo, E.	1B	3.0	0	1	0	0	1.000	3.00	0	0
Kennedy, A.	2B	1140.0	205	361	2	7	.984	4.47	32	43
Kendrick, H.	2B	220.0	48	67	0	0	1.000	4.70	10	13
Figgins, C.	2B	62.0	9	19	0	1	.966	4.06	3	4
Izturis, M.	2B	24.0	3	8	0	0	1.000	4.13	1	1
Aybar, E.	2B	6.0	1	3	0	0	1.000	6.00	0	0
Cabrera, O.	SS	1321.0	253	377	6	10	.975	4.29	46	52
Aybar, E.	SS	75.3	13	22	3	1	.897	4.18	2	4
Izturis, M.	SS	53.0	9	13	0	1	.957	3.74	4	2
Figgins, C.	SS	3.0	0	1	0	0	1.000	3.00	0	0
Izturis, M.	3B	707.3	45	145	3	9	.936	2.42	13	0
Figgins, C.	3B	280.3	22	50	4	6	.878	2.31	4	0
McPherson, D.	3B	228.3	13	49	1	2	.954	2.44	4	0
Quinlan, R.	3B	130.0	11	24	0	1	.972	2.42	1	0
Alfonzo, E.	3B	100.7	5	20	0	0	1.000	2.24	1	0
Kendrick, H.	3B	6.0	0	0	0	0	0.000	0.00	0	0

Name	POS	Inn	PO	A	TE	FE	FPct	RF	DPS	DPT
Anderson, G.	LF	812.7	192	1	0	0	1.000	2.14	0	0
Rivera, J.	LF	478.3	126	7	1	2	.978	2.50	2	0
Figgins, C.	LF	90.7	16	1	0	0	1.000	1.69	0	0
Pride, C.	LF	36.0	8	0	0	0	1.000	2.00	0	0
Quinlan, R.	LF	26.0	11	0	0	0	1.000	3.81	0	0
Salmon, T.	LF	7.0	2	0	0	0	1.000	2.57	0	0
Murphy, T.	LF	2.0	1	0	0	0	1.000	4.50	0	0
Figgins, C.	CF	829.0	242	7	0	5	.980	2.70	6	0
Erstad, D.	CF	219.7	71	1	0	0	1.000	2.95	0	0
Murphy, T.	CF	145.7	50	2	0	0	1.000	3.21	4	0
Rivera, J.	CF	143.3	34	3	0	2	.949	2.32	0	0
Willits, R.	CF	115.0	36	1	1	0	.974	2.90	0	0
Guerrero, V.	RF	1090.0	251	7	4	7	.959	2.13	4	0
Rivera, J.	RF	242.0	50	3	0	1	.981	1.97	0	0
Murphy, T.	RF	39.0	13	0	0	0	1.000	3.00	0	0
Figgins, C.	RF	37.7	7	0	0	0	1.000	1.67	0	0
Salmon, T.	RF	19.0	1	0	0	0	1.000	0.47	0	0
Pride, C.	RF	12.0	4	0	0	0	1.000	3.00	0	0
Quinlan, R.	RF	11.0	2	0	0	0	1.000	1.64	0	0
Willits, R.	RF	2.0	0	0	0	0	0.000	0.00	0	0

Batted Ball Batting Stats

Player	PA	% of PA		% of Batted Balls					Runs Per Event				Total Runs vs. Avg.				
		K%	BB%	GB%	LD%	FB%	IF/F	HR/OF	NIP	GB	LD	OF	NIP	GB	LD	FB	Tot
Guerrero V.	665	10	8	44	19	37	.12	.18	.09	.03	.40	.31	2	-1	3	26	29
Rivera J.	494	12	8	51	16	33	.12	.20	.07	.06	.40	.30	1	6	-2	12	17
Napoli M.	325	28	17	34	14	52	.20	.22	.06	.09	.42	.32	5	1	-8	8	6
Quinlan R.	244	11	4	53	17	30	.16	.15	-.00	.09	.34	.25	-3	7	-2	3	5
Salmon T.	244	18	13	34	20	46	.10	.12	.08	.04	.46	.18	3	-1	2	1	5
Izturis M.	399	9	10	49	19	32	.12	.06	.13	.08	.35	.12	5	7	-2	-8	2
McPherson D.	121	33	5	40	21	39	.07	.22	-.05	.12	.32	.30	-4	2	-2	4	1
Kendrick H.	283	16	5	52	15	32	.04	.06	-.01	.07	.41	.18	-4	4	-2	0	-2
Anderson G.	588	16	6	41	22	37	.07	.10	.02	.02	.36	.19	-6	-4	3	3	-3
Cabrera O.	675	9	8	39	17	44	.14	.04	.11	.08	.40	.07	3	7	1	-16	-5
Erstad D.	105	17	8	51	12	37	.21	.00	.03	.01	.43	.16	-1	-1	-2	-1	-5
Morales K.	215	13	8	52	15	34	.12	.10	.06	.02	.38	.11	-0	-2	-2	-4	-8
Figgins C.	683	15	10	44	21	36	.07	.06	.07	.07	.31	.11	3	7	-6	-12	-9
Kennedy A.	503	14	9	41	27	33	.04	.03	.06	-.02	.37	.09	0	-10	10	-10	-10
Molina J.	245	20	4	42	18	39	.09	.06	-.03	-.01	.42	.14	-5	-4	-0	-2	-12
MLB Average		*17*	*9*	*44*	*20*	*37*	*.11*	*.11*	*.05*	*.04*	*.39*	*.19*	-	-	-	-	-

Batted Ball Pitching Stats

Player	PA	% of PA		% of Batted Balls					Runs Per Event				Total Runs vs. Avg.				
		K%	BB%	GB%	LD%	FB%	IF/F	HR/OF	NIP	GB	LD	OF	NIP	GB	LD	FB	Tot
Lackey J.	922	21	9	43	18	39	.09	.06	.02	.06	.36	.13	-6	5	-9	-14	-24
Weaver Jer.	490	21	7	30	18	52	.14	.10	.00	.06	.30	.13	-6	-0	-9	-3	-18
Shields S.	351	24	7	52	15	33	.05	.11	-.01	.01	.46	.18	-6	-4	-4	-2	-16
Santana E.	846	17	10	38	17	44	.10	.09	.05	.06	.30	.15	1	1	-15	-2	-14
Rodriguez F.	296	33	10	39	14	47	.14	.07	-.01	.03	.49	.18	-5	-3	-4	-1	-14
Escobar K.	789	19	7	45	19	36	.06	.08	.01	.05	.44	.13	-9	2	4	-9	-11
Carrasco H.	417	17	8	50	19	31	.05	.11	.03	.01	.36	.16	-3	-2	-2	-4	-11
Donnelly B.	278	19	12	44	19	37	.26	.12	.06	.03	.38	.17	1	-1	-2	-5	-6
Saunders J.	302	17	10	48	20	32	.03	.09	.06	.02	.40	.17	1	-3	1	-2	-3
Gregg K.	341	21	7	36	18	46	.09	.10	-.00	.14	.32	.15	-5	8	-5	-0	-1
Romero J.	226	14	13	57	16	27	.13	.05	.11	.06	.45	.20	3	3	-1	-2	4
Colon B.	251	12	6	41	22	37	.16	.18	.03	.06	.39	.27	-2	1	4	5	8
Weaver Jef.	397	16	6	39	23	38	.05	.15	.02	.08	.37	.28	-4	3	4	13	17
MLB Average		*17*	*9*	*44*	*20*	*37*	*.11*	*.11*	*.05*	*.04*	*.39*	*.19*	-	-	-	-	-

Los Angeles Dodgers

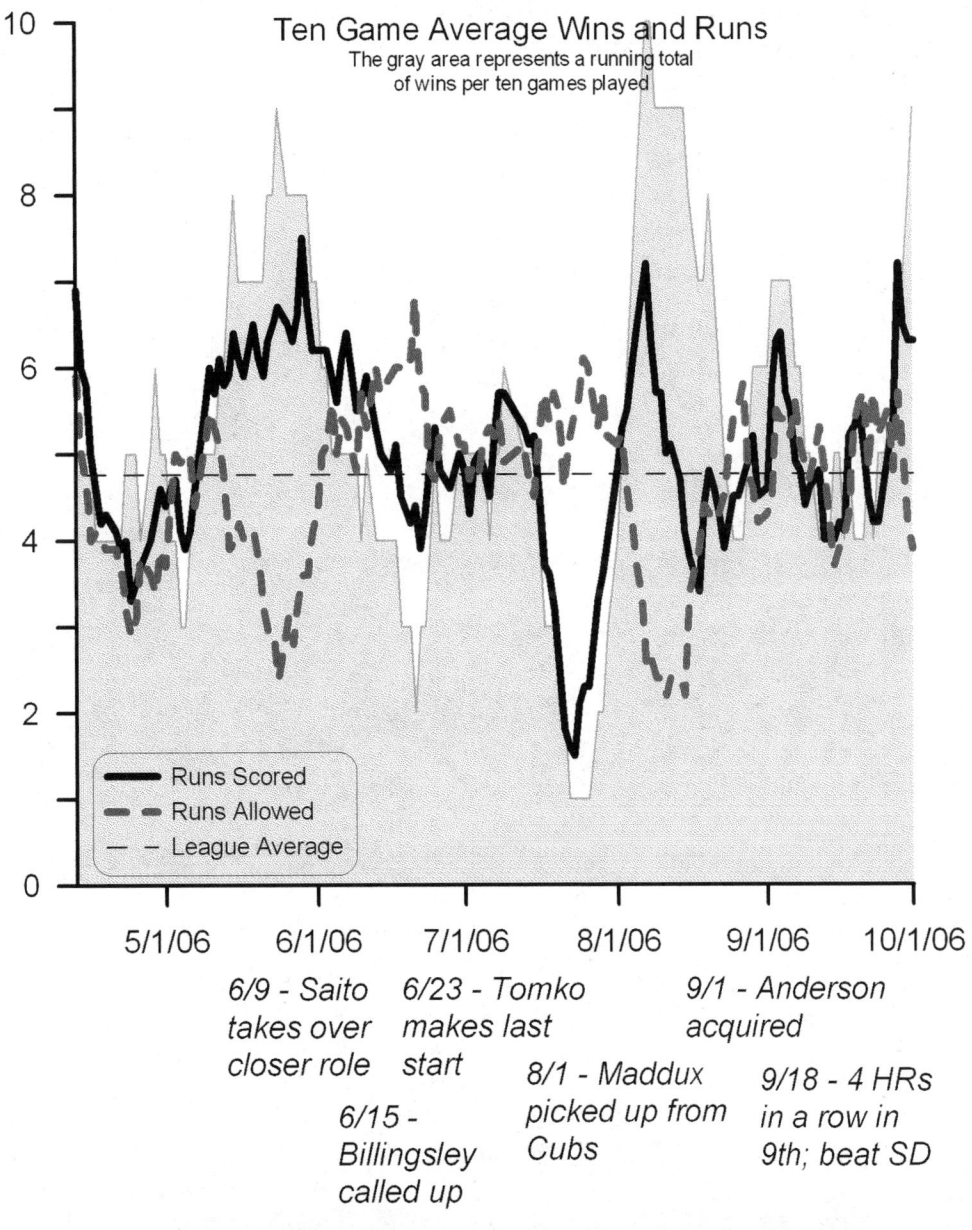

Ten Game Average Wins and Runs
The gray area represents a running total
of wins per ten games played

- Runs Scored
- Runs Allowed
- League Average

6/9 - Saito takes over closer role

6/23 - Tomko makes last start

6/15 - Billingsley called up

8/1 - Maddux picked up from Cubs

9/1 - Anderson acquired

9/18 - 4 HRs in a row in 9th; beat SD

Team Batting and Pitching/Fielding Stats by Month						
	April	May	June	July	Aug	Sept/Oct
Wins	12	18	11	9	21	17
Losses	13	10	15	17	7	12
OBP	.341	.376	.343	.335	.344	.348
SLG	.385	.468	.434	.407	.440	.453
FIP	4.18	4.25	4.31	4.73	3.76	3.50
DER	.705	.682	.677	.676	.705	.653

Batting Stats

Player	RC	Runs	RBI	PA	Outs	P/PA	H	2B	3B	HR	TB	K	BB	IBB	HBP	SH	SF	SB	CS	GDP	BA	OBP	SLG	GPA
Furcal R.	119	113	63	736	478	3.84	196	32	9	15	291	98	73	3	1	5	3	37	13	7	.300	.369	.445	.284
Drew J.	100	84	100	594	361	3.97	140	34	6	20	246	106	89	8	4	1	6	2	3	4	.283	.393	.498	.309
Garciaparra N.	94	82	93	523	342	3.21	142	31	2	20	237	30	42	9	8	0	4	3	0	15	.303	.367	.505	.299
Kent J.	77	61	68	473	299	3.73	119	27	3	14	194	69	55	8	8	0	3	1	2	9	.292	.385	.477	.300
Lofton K.	74	79	41	522	349	3.64	141	15	12	3	189	42	45	1	0	6	2	32	5	16	.301	.360	.403	.269
Ethier A.	67	50	55	441	290	3.59	122	20	7	11	189	77	34	2	5	0	6	5	5	11	.308	.365	.477	.291
Martin R.	62	65	65	468	320	3.77	117	26	4	10	181	57	45	8	4	1	3	10	5	17	.282	.355	.436	.276
Saenz O.	35	30	48	204	130	3.79	53	15	0	11	101	47	14	1	7	0	4	0	0	4	.296	.363	.564	.312
Cruz J.	29	34	17	273	175	3.99	52	16	1	5	85	54	43	2	0	4	3	5	1	3	.233	.353	.381	.260
Martinez R.	24	20	24	194	136	3.82	49	7	1	2	64	20	15	1	1	2	0	0	0	9	.278	.339	.364	.249
Repko J.	23	21	16	150	103	4.09	33	5	1	3	49	24	15	1	3	2	0	10	4	2	.254	.345	.377	.255
Kemp M.	22	30	23	166	116	3.94	39	7	1	7	69	53	9	0	0	0	3	6	0	1	.253	.289	.448	.248
Aybar W.	21	15	22	151	101	3.99	32	12	0	3	53	17	18	0	3	2	0	1	0	5	.250	.356	.414	.270
Betemit W.	19	19	24	193	139	3.88	42	7	0	9	76	45	17	3	0	0	2	1	0	7	.241	.306	.437	.253
Loney J.	18	20	18	111	81	3.82	29	6	5	4	57	10	8	1	1	0	0	1	0	8	.284	.342	.559	.301
Mueller B.	18	12	15	126	82	3.58	27	7	0	3	43	9	17	3	1	0	1	1	1	1	.252	.357	.402	.268
Anderson M.	15	12	15	73	45	4.03	24	3	2	7	52	8	7	0	0	1	1	2	2	3	.375	.431	.813	.407
Izturis C.	11	10	12	129	93	3.68	30	7	1	1	42	6	7	3	2	0	1	1	3	1	.252	.302	.353	.230
Alomar Jr. S.	10	3	9	62	45	3.19	20	5	0	0	25	7	0	0	0	0	0	0	0	3	.323	.323	.403	.252
Lugo J.	10	16	10	164	121	3.86	32	5	1	0	39	29	12	0	1	2	3	6	5	2	.219	.278	.267	.196
Navarro D.	9	5	8	86	55	3.86	21	2	0	2	29	18	11	4	0	0	0	1	0	1	.280	.372	.387	.271
Hall T.	8	2	8	60	38	3.40	21	4	0	0	25	5	2	2	0	0	1	0	0	2	.368	.383	.439	.289
Ross C.	7	4	9	14	7	3.57	7	1	1	2	16	2	0	0	0	0	0	1	0	0	.500	.500	1.143	.523
Ledee R.	5	4	8	55	43	3.84	13	5	0	1	21	10	2	0	0	0	0	1	0	3	.245	.273	.396	.227
Guzman J.	3	2	3	23	18	3.48	4	0	0	0	4	2	3	0	1	0	0	0	0	3	.211	.348	.211	.214
Penny B.	2	3	5	70	53	2.84	12	3	0	0	15	16	0	0	0	5	0	0	0	0	.185	.185	.231	.144
Maddux G.	2	1	3	29	20	2.52	5	1	0	0	6	5	0	0	0	3	1	1	0	0	.200	.192	.240	.150
Diaz E.	1	0	0	3	1	4.00	2	0	0	0	2	0	0	0	0	0	0	0	0	0	.667	.667	.667	.478
Robles O.	1	6	0	39	28	4.36	5	0	1	0	7	5	5	0	0	1	0	0	0	0	.152	.263	.212	.176
Stults E.	1	1	0	6	2	3.00	3	0	0	0	3	1	0	0	0	1	0	0	0	0	.600	.600	.600	.430
Tomko B.	0	2	0	31	22	2.97	3	0	0	0	3	13	1	0	0	5	0	0	0	0	.120	.154	.120	.102
Broxton J.	0	0	0	4	2	5.50	0	0	0	0	0	2	1	0	0	1	0	0	0	0	.000	.333	.000	.154
Billingsley C.	-0	2	2	28	22	3.71	2	0	0	0	2	15	2	0	1	1	0	0	0	0	.083	.185	.083	.107
Kuo H.	-0	1	0	11	7	3.55	1	1	0	0	2	6	0	0	0	3	0	0	0	0	.125	.125	.250	.122
Dessens E.	-0	0	0	1	1	4.00	0	0	0	0	0	0	0	0	0	0	0	0	0	0	.000	.000	.000	.000
Hamulack T.	-0	0	0	1	1	4.00	0	0	0	0	0	0	0	0	0	0	0	0	0	0	.000	.000	.000	.000
Beimel J.	-0	0	0	1	1	7.00	0	0	0	0	0	1	0	0	0	0	0	0	0	0	.000	.000	.000	.000
Osoria F.	-0	0	0	2	2	3.50	0	0	0	0	0	2	0	0	0	0	0	0	0	0	.000	.000	.000	.000
Young D.	-1	0	0	5	5	3.00	0	0	0	0	0	1	0	0	0	0	0	0	0	0	.000	.000	.000	.000
Sele A.	-1	2	0	33	22	3.21	5	1	0	0	6	7	1	0	0	6	0	0	0	1	.192	.222	.231	.162
Perez O.	-1	3	0	17	14	2.35	1	0	0	0	1	1	1	0	0	1	0	0	0	0	.067	.125	.067	.075
Seo J.	-1	0	0	20	17	3.50	2	0	0	0	2	6	1	0	0	1	0	0	0	1	.111	.158	.111	.101
Hendrickson M	-1	1	0	23	19	3.61	0	0	0	0	0	14	2	0	0	2	0	0	0	0	.000	.095	.000	.044
Lowe D.	-2	5	3	79	59	3.46	6	2	0	0	8	19	4	0	0	10	1	0	0	1	.094	.145	.125	.099

Italicized stats have been adjusted for home park.

Batted Ball Batting Stats are listed after fielding stats

Pitching Stats

Player	PRC	IP	BFP	G	GS	P/PA	K	BB	IBB	HBP	H	HR	DP	DER	SB	CS	PO	W	L	Sv	Op	Hld	RA	ERA	FIP
Lowe D.	95	218.0	913	35	34	3.59	123	55	2	5	221	14	30	.690	26	4	1	16	8	0	0	0	4.00	3.63	3.72
Penny B.	80	189.0	813	34	33	3.98	148	54	4	9	206	19	25	.669	20	8	2	16	9	0	0	1	4.48	4.33	3.90
Saito T.	68	78.3	303	72	0	4.32	107	23	3	2	48	3	6	.726	5	0	0	6	2	24	26	7	2.18	2.07	1.83
Broxton J.	52	76.3	320	68	0	4.09	97	33	6	1	61	7	8	.676	5	2	0	4	1	3	7	12	2.95	2.59	2.97
Tomko B.	38	112.3	491	44	15	3.92	76	29	0	2	123	17	6	.698	4	1	0	8	7	0	3	5	5.37	4.73	4.66
Billingsley C.	38	90.0	403	18	16	3.97	59	58	3	3	92	7	14	.685	5	5	1	7	4	0	0	0	4.30	3.80	4.85
Sele A.	36	103.3	451	28	15	3.74	57	30	2	2	120	11	13	.681	6	2	0	8	6	0	1	0	4.96	4.53	4.37
Beimel J.	34	70.0	295	62	0	3.66	30	21	3	0	70	7	10	.696	3	4	6	2	1	2	2	10	3.34	2.96	4.43
Maddux G.	33	73.7	290	12	12	3.17	36	14	4	0	66	6	9	.735	6	2	0	6	3	0	0	0	3.79	3.30	3.71
Kuo H.	27	59.7	258	28	5	3.91	71	33	5	1	54	3	8	.660	5	4	2	1	5	0	0	2	4.53	4.22	2.95
Hendrickson M	25	75.0	342	18	12	3.65	48	28	0	2	92	7	5	.650	5	2	1	2	7	0	0	1	5.40	4.68	4.35
Seo J.	20	67.0	296	19	10	3.70	49	25	1	1	75	14	6	.691	1	1	0	2	4	0	0	0	6.04	5.78	5.59
Baez D.	17	49.7	213	46	0	3.66	29	11	2	6	53	3	6	.683	4	2	0	5	5	9	16	6	5.26	4.35	3.74
Perez O.	13	59.3	275	20	8	3.57	33	13	1	2	89	9	8	.624	9	0	0	4	4	0	1	0	7.43	6.83	4.79
Carrara G.	12	27.7	116	25	0	4.02	25	7	0	1	27	5	3	.705	4	0	0	0	1	1	2	2	4.55	4.55	4.63
Dessens E.	9	23.0	100	19	0	3.70	16	9	2	0	23	4	2	.704	1	1	0	0	1	0	0	6	4.70	4.70	5.00
Hamulack T.	9	34.0	161	33	0	3.99	34	22	1	2	36	7	5	.667	0	0	0	0	3	0	0	4	7.41	6.35	5.92
Osoria F.	4	17.7	86	12	0	3.50	13	9	1	1	27	4	4	.610	0	0	0	0	2	0	0	0	7.13	7.13	6.22
Stults E.	4	17.7	73	6	2	3.55	5	7	0	0	17	4	5	.754	0	0	0	1	0	0	0	0	6.11	5.60	6.78
Carter L.	2	11.7	59	10	0	3.85	5	8	0	0	17	1	1	.622	0	0	0	0	1	0	1	0	8.49	8.49	5.53
Brazoban Y.	2	5.0	23	5	0	3.91	4	2	0	0	7	0	0	.588	1	0	0	0	0	0	1	0	5.40	5.40	2.82
Gagne E.	0	2.0	8	2	0	4.00	3	1	0	1	0	0	0	1.000	0	0	0	0	0	1	1	0	0.00	0.00	3.22

Batted Ball Pitching Stats are listed after fielding stats

Fielding Stats

Name	POS	INN	SBA/G	CS%	ERA	WP+PB/G	PO	A	TE	FE
Martin, R.	C	1015.0	0.85	26%	3.93	0.408	789	61	5	1
Navarro, D.	C	195.0	0.74	0%	3.88	0.415	149	3	1	0
Hall, T.	C	134.0	0.87	31%	5.44	0.134	84	8	0	1
Alomar Jr., S.	C	115.3	1.17	7%	6.09	0.312	80	2	1	0
Diaz, E.	C	1.0	0.00	0%	0.00	0.000	0	0	0	0

Name	POS	Inn	PO	A	TE	FE	FPct	RF	DPS	DPT
Garciaparra, N.	1B	1017.0	1058	61	0	4	.996	9.90	14	0
Loney, J.	1B	228.7	212	15	0	1	.996	8.93	1	0
Saenz, O.	1B	164.3	173	7	1	1	.989	9.86	5	0
Kent, J.	1B	46.3	52	0	0	0	1.000	10.10	0	0
Martinez, R.	1B	3.0	5	0	0	0	1.000	15.00	0	0
Guzman, J.	1B	1.0	1	0	0	0	1.000	9.00	0	0
Kent, J.	2B	887.7	217	313	2	6	.985	5.37	24	50
Martinez, R.	2B	259.3	55	79	0	0	1.000	4.65	7	7
Lugo, J.	2B	159.3	37	63	1	1	.980	5.65	6	5
Aybar, W.	2B	98.3	25	42	0	1	.985	6.13	7	4
Robles, O.	2B	44.7	9	10	0	0	1.000	3.83	2	2
Izturis, C.	2B	9.0	4	8	0	0	1.000	12.00	1	1
Anderson, M.	2B	2.0	0	1	0	0	1.000	4.50	0	0
Furcal, R.	SS	1371.0	269	492	15	12	.966	5.00	59	56
Martinez, R.	SS	50.0	6	17	0	0	1.000	4.14	1	4
Lugo, J.	SS	27.3	3	11	0	2	.875	4.61	1	0
Izturis, C.	SS	12.0	1	5	0	0	1.000	4.50	2	0
Betemit, W.	3B	398.3	24	83	1	3	.964	2.42	8	1
Mueller, B.	3B	256.0	15	60	6	2	.904	2.64	7	0
Izturis, C.	3B	252.0	12	73	1	3	.955	3.04	3	0
Aybar, W.	3B	214.3	9	50	0	5	.922	2.48	2	0
Lugo, J.	3B	115.0	10	29	1	0	.975	3.05	3	0
Martinez, R.	3B	86.7	8	20	0	2	.933	2.91	4	0
Saenz, O.	3B	78.0	6	24	2	0	.938	3.46	0	0
Guzman, J.	3B	43.7	0	7	0	0	1.000	1.44	1	0
Robles, O.	3B	16.3	0	6	1	0	.857	3.31	1	0

Name	POS	Inn	PO	A	TE	FE	FPct	RF	DPS	DPT
Ethier, A.	LF	895.7	172	9	1	5	.968	1.82	2	0
Cruz, J.	LF	279.7	60	0	0	0	1.000	1.93	0	0
Anderson, M.	LF	115.7	19	0	0	1	.950	1.48	0	0
Kemp, M.	LF	72.3	18	1	0	1	.950	2.36	2	0
Repko, J.	LF	48.7	12	0	1	0	.923	2.22	0	0
Ledee, R.	LF	37.7	3	0	0	0	1.000	0.72	0	0
Lugo, J.	LF	7.0	0	0	0	0	0.000	0.00	0	0
Young, D.	LF	2.0	0	0	0	0	0.000	0.00	0	0
Guzman, J.	LF	1.0	0	0	0	0	0.000	0.00	0	0
Ross, C.	LF	0.7	0	0	0	0	0.000	0.00	0	0
Lofton, K.	CF	961.0	241	4	2	1	.988	2.29	0	0
Repko, J.	CF	217.0	52	4	0	1	.982	2.32	4	0
Kemp, M.	CF	189.7	37	0	2	1	.925	1.76	0	0
Cruz, J.	CF	92.7	32	0	0	0	1.000	3.11	0	0
Drew, J.	RF	1118.0	284	3	1	4	.983	2.31	0	0
Cruz, J.	RF	144.3	37	0	0	0	1.000	2.31	0	0
Kemp, M.	RF	71.7	8	1	0	1	.900	1.13	0	0
Repko, J.	RF	64.0	18	0	0	0	1.000	2.53	0	0
Ross, C.	RF	18.0	4	0	0	0	1.000	2.00	0	0
Lugo, J.	RF	13.0	1	0	0	0	1.000	0.69	0	0
Ledee, R.	RF	10.3	1	0	0	0	1.000	0.87	0	0
Anderson, M.	RF	7.0	2	0	0	0	1.000	2.57	0	0
Martinez, R.	RF	6.0	1	0	0	0	1.000	1.50	0	0
Loney, J.	RF	6.0	0	0	0	0	0.000	0.00	0	0
Young, D.	RF	2.0	0	0	0	0	0.000	0.00	0	0

Batted Ball Batting Stats

Player	PA	% of PA		% of Batted Balls					Runs Per Event				Total Runs vs. Avg.				
		K%	BB%	GB%	LD%	FB%	IF/F	HR/OF	NIP	GB	LD	OF	NIP	GB	LD	FB	Tot
Drew D.	594	18	16	45	19	36	.13	.16	.10	.03	.52	.26	12	-3	5	6	21
Garciaparra N.	523	6	10	38	20	42	.09	.11	.17	.04	.38	.17	7	-1	5	4	15
Kent J.	473	15	13	34	23	43	.07	.10	.11	.05	.35	.20	8	-1	1	7	14
Furcal R.	736	13	10	50	21	29	.06	.10	.08	.08	.38	.16	5	14	2	-9	12
Saenz O.	204	23	10	37	19	44	.07	.20	.03	.06	.48	.32	-1	-0	1	9	9
Ethier A.	441	17	9	41	22	37	.03	.09	.04	.06	.45	.16	-1	2	8	0	9
Loney J.	111	9	8	49	12	39	.08	.12	.10	.05	.49	.26	0	1	-1	3	4
Martin R.	468	12	10	50	20	30	.07	.09	.10	-.01	.49	.17	4	-8	9	-4	1
Mueller B.	126	7	14	49	15	35	.03	.09	.19	.00	.40	.16	4	-2	-1	-0	1
Aybar W.	151	11	14	45	14	41	.11	.07	.14	.00	.40	.22	3	-2	-2	2	0
Lofton K.	522	8	9	45	22	33	.05	.02	.12	.07	.36	.06	4	8	4	-16	0
Betemit W.	193	23	9	47	20	34	.07	.22	.01	.03	.23	.38	-2	-1	-5	7	-1
Cruz J.	273	20	16	36	14	50	.16	.07	.09	.08	.53	.12	5	1	-2	-4	-1
Repko J.	150	16	12	43	21	35	.24	.11	.08	.08	.36	.14	2	1	-0	-3	-1
Kemp M.	166	32	5	40	24	36	.08	.18	-.05	.02	.42	.32	-5	-1	1	4	-1
Izturis C.	129	5	7	50	15	35	.15	.03	.16	.09	.23	.11	1	4	-3	-2	-1
Martinez R.	194	10	8	44	19	37	.07	.04	.09	-.00	.44	.08	1	-3	2	-4	-4
Lugo J.	164	18	8	39	22	38	.16	.00	.03	.02	.44	-.06	-1	-1	2	-10	-10
MLB Average		17	9	44	20	37	.11	.11	.05	.04	.39	.19	-	-	-	-	-

Batted Ball Pitching Stats

Player	PA	% of PA		% of Batted Balls					Runs Per Event				Total Runs vs. Avg.				
		K%	BB%	GB%	LD%	FB%	IF/F	HR/OF	NIP	GB	LD	OF	NIP	GB	LD	FB	Tot
Saito T.	303	35	8	36	16	49	.10	.04	-.03	.05	.36	.07	-8	-2	-7	-8	-24
Lowe D.	913	13	7	67	16	17	.09	.11	.04	.04	.38	.23	-5	5	-8	-14	-23
Maddux G.	290	12	5	52	18	30	.09	.09	.02	.00	.38	.17	-3	-4	-0	-2	-10
Broxton J.	320	30	11	39	20	40	.08	.10	.01	.07	.35	.18	-4	0	-4	-2	-10
Kuo H.	258	28	13	44	21	34	.10	.07	.04	.09	.39	.10	0	2	-2	-6	-6
Penny B.	813	18	8	43	20	36	.08	.10	.02	.05	.40	.19	-6	0	3	-0	-3
Baez D.	213	14	8	40	17	43	.10	.05	.06	.08	.44	.08	-0	2	1	-5	-2
Beimel J.	295	10	7	57	11	32	.09	.09	.08	.04	.37	.25	-0	2	-6	3	-1
Billingsley C.	403	15	15	48	16	36	.07	.08	.12	.04	.44	.13	9	-0	-3	-6	-0
Dessens E.	100	16	9	45	19	36	.08	.17	.05	.06	.38	.18	-0	0	-0	-0	0
Carrara G.	116	22	7	34	24	41	.15	.17	-.00	.00	.27	.34	-2	-1	-1	4	1
Tomko B.	491	15	6	37	18	45	.08	.10	.02	.08	.38	.18	-4	4	-2	5	3
Sele A.	451	13	7	46	15	39	.07	.09	.05	.06	.44	.18	-1	3	-1	3	3
Hendrickson M.	342	14	9	47	22	31	.16	.09	.06	.07	.44	.15	0	3	6	-6	4
Hamulack T.	161	21	15	48	21	31	.16	.26	.08	.04	.32	.46	2	-0	-2	5	5
Seo J.	296	17	9	40	17	43	.12	.16	.05	.03	.49	.27	-1	-1	1	9	8
Perez O.	275	12	5	48	21	31	.15	.14	.03	.09	.47	.24	-2	6	7	1	11
MLB Average		17	9	44	20	37	.11	.11	.05	.04	.39	.19	-	-	-	-	-

Milwaukee Brewers

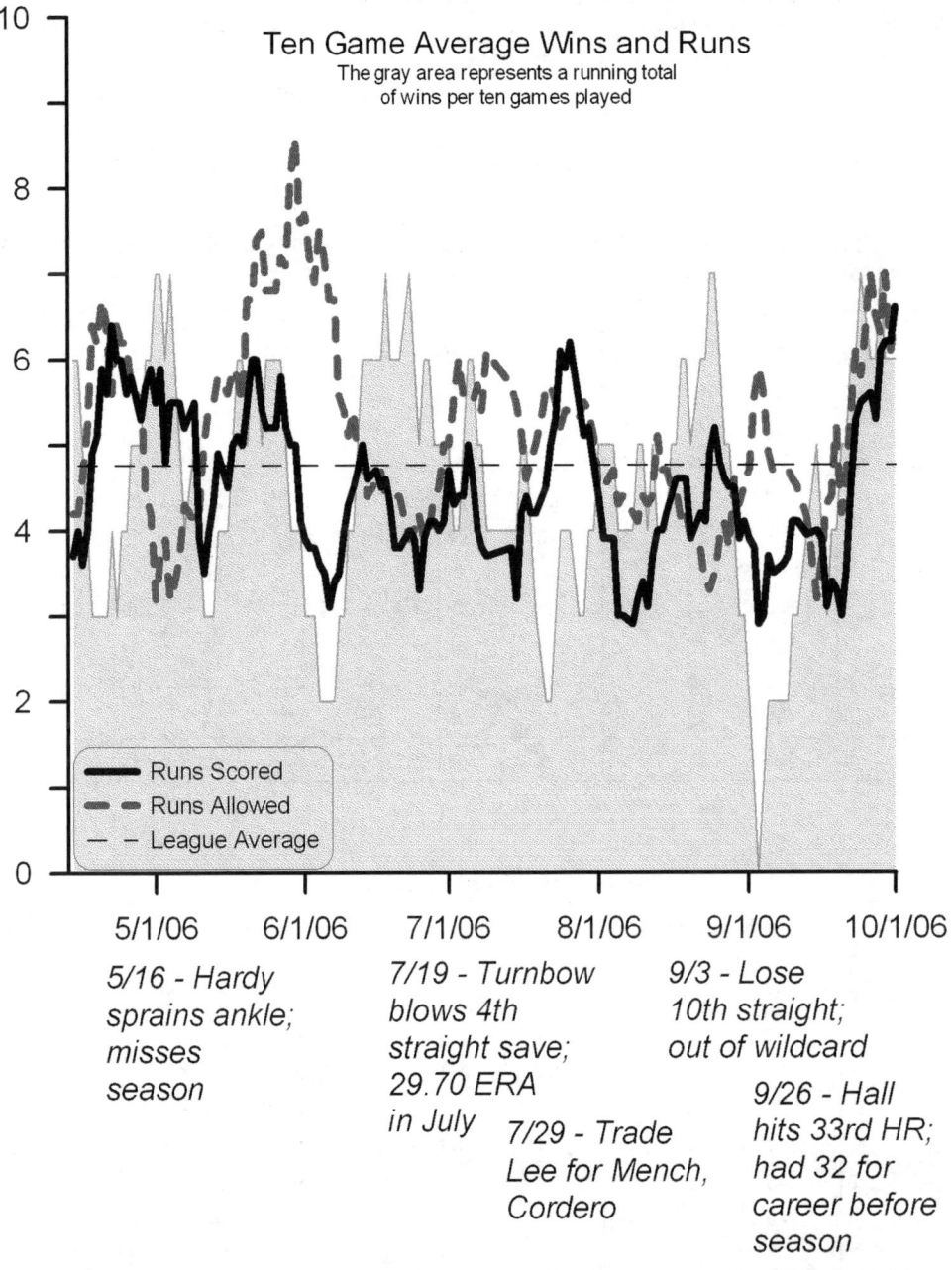

Ten Game Average Wins and Runs
The gray area represents a running total
of wins per ten games played

Legend:
— Runs Scored
– – Runs Allowed
– – League Average

5/1/06   6/1/06   7/1/06   8/1/06   9/1/06   10/1/06

5/16 - Hardy sprains ankle; misses season

7/19 - Turnbow blows 4th straight save; 29.70 ERA in July

7/29 - Trade Lee for Mench, Cordero

9/3 - Lose 10th straight; out of wildcard

9/26 - Hall hits 33rd HR; had 32 for career before season

Team Batting and Pitching/Fielding Stats by Month						
	April	May	June	July	Aug	Sept/Oct
Wins	14	12	14	10	12	13
Losses	11	16	14	15	16	15
OBP	.354	.328	.310	.331	.319	.321
SLG	.475	.452	.388	.410	.369	.427
FIP	4.39	4.72	4.03	4.64	4.35	4.16
DER	.716	.654	.676	.674	.719	.703

Batting Stats

Player	RC	Runs	RBI	PA	Outs	P/PA	H	2B	3B	HR	TB	K	BB	IBB	HBP	SH	SF	SB	CS	GDP	BA	OBP	SLG	GPA
Hall B.	88	101	85	608	413	4.16	145	39	4	35	297	162	63	6	1	3	4	8	9	12	.270	.345	.553	.293
Fielder P.	85	82	81	648	435	3.61	154	35	1	28	275	125	59	5	12	0	8	7	2	18	.271	.347	.483	.276
Jenkins G.	78	62	70	555	363	3.99	131	26	1	17	210	129	56	8	11	0	4	4	1	9	.271	.357	.434	.268
Lee C.	76	60	81	435	292	3.61	111	18	0	28	213	39	38	4	2	0	7	12	2	13	.286	.347	.549	.292
Weeks R.	54	73	34	413	270	3.89	100	15	3	8	145	92	30	1	19	2	3	19	5	6	.279	.363	.404	.263
Clark B.	48	51	29	483	319	3.71	109	14	2	4	139	60	43	4	14	5	5	3	4	9	.263	.348	.335	.240
Gross G.	43	42	38	252	154	4.12	57	15	0	9	99	60	36	3	2	3	3	1	0	3	.274	.382	.476	.290
Koskie C.	41	29	33	289	199	4.10	67	23	0	12	126	58	29	3	3	0	0	1	2	7	.261	.343	.490	.276
Miller D.	39	34	38	376	259	3.67	83	28	0	6	129	86	33	7	4	3	5	0	0	11	.251	.322	.390	.241
Cirillo J.	39	33	23	290	188	3.59	84	16	0	3	109	33	21	0	1	3	2	1	1	8	.319	.369	.414	.269
Graffanino T.	37	34	27	261	176	3.88	66	17	3	2	95	37	20	0	4	0	1	2	0	6	.280	.345	.403	.255
Hart C.	31	32	33	256	185	3.71	67	13	2	9	111	58	17	1	0	0	2	5	8	7	.283	.328	.468	.264
Bell D.	25	21	29	201	142	3.85	46	10	2	4	72	30	18	1	1	0	2	2	1	7	.256	.323	.400	.245
Rivera M.	19	16	24	158	107	3.84	38	9	0	6	65	21	10	5	3	1	2	0	0	3	.268	.325	.458	.260
Hardy J.	13	13	14	139	102	4.12	31	5	0	5	51	23	10	0	0	0	1	1	1	4	.242	.295	.398	.232
Mench K.	9	9	18	133	101	3.25	29	6	1	1	40	17	4	0	0	0	3	0	0	4	.230	.248	.317	.190
Gwynn A.	5	5	4	80	60	3.44	20	2	1	0	24	15	2	0	0	0	1	3	1	2	.260	.275	.312	.201
Moeller C.	3	9	5	104	83	3.91	18	3	0	2	27	26	4	0	2	0	0	0	0	3	.184	.231	.276	.172
Bush D.	3	6	9	72	52	2.74	11	3	0	0	14	25	0	0	1	9	0	0	0	1	.177	.190	.226	.142
Ohka T.	3	0	6	36	26	3.53	5	1	0	0	6	15	1	0	0	3	0	0	0	0	.161	.188	.194	.132
Nix L.	3	2	6	36	28	3.72	8	1	0	1	12	11	0	0	1	0	0	0	0	1	.229	.250	.343	.198
Rottino V.	1	1	1	15	11	4.00	3	1	0	0	4	2	1	0	0	0	0	1	0	0	.214	.267	.286	.191
Capuano C.	-0	3	3	75	60	3.39	8	1	0	0	9	35	2	0	0	5	0	0	0	0	.118	.143	.132	.097
Hendrickson B	-0	0	0	4	3	5.00	0	0	0	0	0	3	1	0	0	0	0	0	0	0	.000	.250	.000	.112
Wise M.	-0	0	0	1	1	3.00	0	0	0	0	0	1	0	0	0	0	0	0	0	0	.000	.000	.000	.000
Turnbow D.	-0	0	0	1	1	5.00	0	0	0	0	0	1	0	0	0	0	0	0	0	0	.000	.000	.000	.000
Villanueva C.	-0	0	1	17	14	3.12	1	0	0	0	1	9	0	0	0	2	0	0	0	0	.067	.067	.067	.047
Capellan J.	-0	0	0	2	2	4.00	0	0	0	0	0	2	0	0	0	0	0	0	0	0	.000	.000	.000	.000
Helling R.	-0	0	0	3	3	4.67	0	0	0	0	0	2	0	0	0	0	0	0	0	0	.000	.000	.000	.000
Jackson Z.	-0	1	0	13	8	2.15	1	0	0	0	1	2	0	0	0	4	0	0	0	0	.111	.111	.111	.078
Gonzalez J.	-1	0	0	5	5	1.80	0	0	0	0	0	1	0	0	0	0	0	0	0	0	.000	.000	.000	.000
Anderson D.	-1	3	0	10	8	3.60	1	0	0	0	1	4	1	0	0	0	0	0	0	0	.111	.200	.111	.117
de la Rosa J	-1	0	0	5	5	3.40	0	0	0	0	0	4	0	0	0	0	0	0	0	0	.000	.000	.000	.000
Eveland D.	-1	0	0	8	7	3.50	0	0	0	0	0	4	0	0	0	1	0	0	0	0	.000	.000	.000	.000
Barnwell C.	-1	2	1	31	28	3.45	2	0	0	0	2	6	1	0	0	0	0	1	0	0	.067	.097	.067	.060
Sheets B.	-2	1	0	37	32	3.30	1	0	0	0	1	13	1	0	0	3	0	0	0	0	.030	.059	.030	.034
Davis D.	-3	5	2	78	62	3.19	3	0	0	0	3	22	1	0	1	11	0	0	0	0	.046	.075	.046	.045

Italicized stats have been adjusted for home park.

Batted Ball Batting Stats are listed after fielding stats

Pitching Stats

Player	PRC	IP	BFP	G	GS	P/PA	K	BB	IBB	HBP	H	HR	DP	DER	SB	CS	PO	W	L	Sv	Op	Hld	RA	ERA	FIP
Capuano C.	95	221.3	936	34	34	3.61	174	47	4	9	229	29	19	.690	1	3	6	11	12	0	0	0	4.39	4.03	4.05
Bush D.	84	210.0	869	34	32	3.49	166	38	2	18	201	26	10	.710	18	8	1	12	11	0	0	1	4.76	4.41	4.02
Davis D.	74	203.3	904	34	34	3.86	159	102	1	5	206	19	25	.685	15	4	2	11	11	0	0	0	5.22	4.91	4.43
Sheets B.	54	106.0	430	17	17	3.65	116	11	1	2	105	9	3	.671	10	2	2	6	7	0	0	0	3.99	3.82	2.47
Ohka T.	31	97.0	421	18	18	3.69	50	35	1	5	98	12	11	.715	4	2	1	4	5	0	0	0	5.38	4.82	5.00
Capellan J.	29	71.7	310	61	0	3.60	58	31	7	3	65	11	2	.734	10	3	0	4	2	0	2	16	4.65	4.40	4.72
Villanueva C.	27	53.7	215	10	6	3.75	39	11	1	4	43	8	7	.752	2	0	0	2	2	0	0	0	3.69	3.69	4.49
Cordero F.	26	26.7	112	28	0	4.07	30	16	1	0	20	2	6	.703	1	0	0	3	1	16	18	1	1.69	1.69	3.63
Wise M.	16	44.3	188	40	0	3.99	27	14	2	2	45	6	7	.698	1	1	0	5	6	0	4	14	4.87	3.86	4.71
Kolb D.	16	48.3	213	53	0	3.65	26	20	1	1	53	4	9	.673	2	0	0	2	2	1	3	6	5.21	4.84	4.46
Helling R.	16	35.0	142	20	2	3.96	32	15	0	0	25	6	3	.775	2	0	0	0	2	0	1	2	4.37	4.11	4.90
Shouse B.	14	34.0	154	59	0	3.68	20	17	4	6	34	3	3	.704	2	2	0	1	3	2	4	14	4.24	3.97	4.87
Turnbow D.	13	56.3	266	64	0	4.10	69	39	2	4	56	8	5	.651	3	1	0	4	9	24	32	4	8.15	6.87	4.80
Gonzalez J.	12	42.0	193	21	1	3.96	36	17	1	2	50	6	1	.659	1	2	0	4	2	0	1	0	6.64	5.14	4.65
Jackson Z.	11	38.3	178	8	7	3.70	22	14	0	4	48	6	6	.659	4	0	0	2	2	0	0	0	6.10	5.40	5.51
Eveland D.	6	27.7	141	9	5	3.86	32	16	2	5	39	4	2	.571	5	2	1	0	3	0	1	0	8.13	8.13	4.84
de la Rosa J.	6	30.3	146	18	3	3.76	31	22	1	1	32	4	2	.648	5	1	1	2	2	0	0	1	8.90	8.60	5.06
Sarfate D.	4	8.3	38	8	0	4.24	11	4	1	0	9	0	0	.609	1	0	0	0	0	0	0	0	4.32	4.32	1.66
Demaria C.	3	13.7	63	10	0	4.16	11	9	0	2	10	4	0	.811	0	0	0	0	1	0	0	0	7.24	5.93	7.83
Lehr J.	3	15.7	75	16	0	3.97	12	7	1	1	24	2	4	.566	4	0	0	2	1	0	0	0	9.19	8.62	4.69
Spurling C.	2	10.0	46	7	0	3.59	3	4	1	0	12	3	0	.750	0	0	0	0	0	0	1	0	7.20	7.20	7.42
Winkelsas J.	1	7.0	35	7	0	3.74	4	6	0	0	9	1	2	.625	0	0	0	0	1	0	0	0	9.00	7.71	6.50
Hendrickson B	1	12.0	65	4	3	4.06	8	9	0	0	21	0	0	.563	5	0	0	0	2	0	0	0	12.75	12.00	4.13
Simpson A.	1	2.7	14	2	0	4.64	5	4	0	0	1	0	0	.600	0	0	0	0	0	0	0	0	6.75	3.38	3.97
Fernandez J.	1	6.3	31	4	0	3.45	1	1	0	0	11	2	0	.667	0	0	0	0	0	0	0	0	9.95	9.95	7.48
Adams M.	0	2.3	13	2	0	3.85	1	2	0	0	4	1	0	.667	1	0	0	0	0	0	0	0	11.57	11.57	10.50
Mabeus C.	0	1.7	12	1	0	3.67	2	3	0	0	4	1	0	.500	0	0	0	0	0	0	0	0	21.60	21.60	14.02

Batted Ball Pitching Stats are listed after fielding stats

Fielding Stats

Name	POS	INN	SBA/G	CS%	ERA	WP+PB/G	PO	A	TE	FE
Miller, D.	C	840.0	0.53	27%	4.58	0.396	649	43	2	0
Rivera, M.	C	352.7	1.20	17%	5.03	0.357	299	31	2	2
Moeller, C.	C	231.0	0.97	12%	5.42	0.312	193	14	0	1
Rottino, V.	C	2.0	0.00	0%	9.00	4.500	3	0	0	0

Name	POS	Inn	PO	A	TE	FE	FPct	RF	DPS	DPT
Fielder, P.	1B	1319.0	1258	87	0	11	.992	9.18	10	1
Cirillo, J.	1B	98.3	110	5	0	0	1.000	10.53	1	0
Hart, C.	1B	8.0	8	0	0	1	.889	9.00	0	0
Weeks, R.	2B	794.0	177	261	12	10	.952	4.96	22	45
Graffanino, T.	2B	486.3	111	119	0	3	.987	4.26	11	9
Cirillo, J.	2B	91.7	20	30	0	0	1.000	4.91	7	2
Hall, B.	2B	34.0	6	9	0	0	1.000	3.97	1	0
Barnwell, C.	2B	19.7	3	4	1	0	.875	3.20	0	1
Hall, B.	SS	1090.0	173	321	9	8	.967	4.08	35	21
Hardy, J.	SS	257.7	51	90	1	1	.986	4.92	10	15
Graffanino, T.	SS	29.3	4	13	0	0	1.000	5.22	1	2
Barnwell, C.	SS	29.3	13	11	1	0	.960	7.36	0	3
Cirillo, J.	SS	19.0	4	3	0	0	1.000	3.32	1	1
Koskie, C.	3B	603.3	54	150	5	2	.967	3.04	12	1
Bell, D.	3B	434.7	27	110	1	4	.965	2.84	5	0
Cirillo, J.	3B	274.0	27	64	1	1	.978	2.99	8	0
Hall, B.	3B	86.0	5	15	2	0	.909	2.09	2	0
Rottino, V.	3B	14.0	2	3	0	0	1.000	3.21	0	0
Barnwell, C.	3B	13.7	2	3	0	0	1.000	3.29	0	0
Lee, C.	LF	835.3	145	4	0	4	.974	1.61	0	0
Mench, K.	LF	277.0	64	1	1	0	.985	2.11	0	0
Hart, C.	LF	164.3	37	1	0	1	.974	2.08	0	0
Gross, G.	LF	124.0	36	4	1	0	.976	2.90	0	0
Rottino, V.	LF	10.7	3	0	0	0	1.000	2.53	0	0
Anderson, D.	LF	7.3	0	0	0	0	0.000	0.00	0	0
Clark, B.	LF	7.0	3	0	0	0	1.000	3.86	0	0
Clark, B.	CF	910.7	250	2	2	2	.984	2.49	1	0
Gross, G.	CF	253.7	72	2	0	1	.987	2.63	2	0
Gwynn, A.	CF	129.7	42	1	0	0	1.000	2.98	0	0
Nix, L.	CF	76.7	20	0	0	0	1.000	2.35	0	0
Hall, B.	CF	32.0	11	1	0	0	1.000	3.38	0	0
Hart, C.	CF	23.0	3	0	0	0	1.000	1.17	0	0
Jenkins, G.	RF	1101.0	247	6	2	4	.977	2.07	4	0
Hart, C.	RF	266.0	63	2	0	0	1.000	2.20	0	0
Gross, G.	RF	38.3	13	0	0	0	1.000	3.05	0	0
Clark, B.	RF	18.3	4	0	0	0	1.000	1.96	0	0
Anderson, D.	RF	2.0	1	0	0	0	1.000	4.50	0	0

Batted Ball Batting Stats

Player	PA	% of PA		% of Batted Balls					Runs Per Event				Total Runs vs. Avg.				
		K%	BB%	GB%	LD%	FB%	IF/F	HR/OF	NIP	GB	LD	OF	NIP	GB	LD	FB	Tot
Hall B.	608	27	11	33	19	48	.07	.20	.02	.07	.49	.31	-4	0	2	24	22
Lee C.	435	9	9	40	19	41	.10	.20	.12	.06	.33	.24	4	2	-2	11	16
Fielder P.	648	19	11	42	18	39	.12	.17	.05	.02	.42	.29	2	-5	-1	15	10
Koskie C.	289	20	11	47	17	35	.16	.19	.05	.03	.53	.32	1	-1	2	5	7
Gross G.	252	24	15	34	23	42	.14	.16	.06	.08	.38	.26	3	1	-1	2	6
Jenkins G.	555	23	12	44	22	34	.11	.14	.04	.04	.41	.26	1	-2	1	3	3
Weeks R.	413	22	12	46	20	33	.15	.11	.05	.11	.44	.15	1	9	1	-8	3
Cirillo J.	290	11	8	46	20	34	.14	.04	.07	.08	.41	.12	-0	5	3	-5	3
Hart C.	256	23	7	42	17	41	.09	.13	-.01	.10	.56	.16	-4	3	3	-1	2
Rivera M.	158	13	8	38	14	48	.25	.14	.06	.08	.44	.20	0	1	-1	0	1
Graffanino T.	261	14	9	39	19	42	.12	.03	.07	.06	.45	.10	1	1	2	-5	-1
Bell D.	201	15	9	45	26	30	.18	.11	.06	.01	.27	.27	0	-2	-1	0	-2
Hardy J.	139	17	7	47	19	34	.17	.17	.03	.07	.34	.16	-1	1	-1	-2	-3
Mench K.	133	13	3	45	21	35	.23	.03	-.03	.04	.32	.04	-2	-0	0	-5	-8
Moeller C.	104	25	6	35	25	40	.10	.08	-.03	-.08	.28	.13	-2	-3	-1	-1	-8
Miller D.	376	23	10	44	21	35	.05	.07	.03	-.01	.44	.18	-2	-7	2	-1	-8
Clark B.	483	12	12	40	23	37	.09	.03	.11	.02	.32	.07	7	-4	0	-13	-11
MLB Average		*17*	*9*	*44*	*20*	*37*	*.11*	*.11*	*.05*	*.04*	*.39*	*.19*	-	-	-	-	-

Batted Ball Pitching Stats

Player	PA	% of PA		% of Batted Balls					Runs Per Event				Total Runs vs. Avg.				
		K%	BB%	GB%	LD%	FB%	IF/F	HR/OF	NIP	GB	LD	OF	NIP	GB	LD	FB	Tot
Bush D.	869	19	6	47	19	34	.11	.13	.00	.01	.45	.22	-11	-9	6	2	-12
Sheets B.	430	27	3	40	19	40	.14	.09	-.07	.10	.50	.13	-14	6	4	-7	-11
Davis D.	904	18	12	44	20	36	.08	.09	.07	.03	.44	.15	7	-5	5	-10	-4
Villanueva C.	215	18	7	43	16	41	.08	.13	.01	.05	.34	.18	-2	-0	-3	1	-4
Cordero F.	112	27	14	33	22	44	.11	.08	.05	-.08	.45	.18	1	-3	0	-1	-3
Capuano C.	936	19	6	40	20	40	.10	.11	-.00	.04	.44	.18	-13	-1	9	2	-3
Helling R.	142	23	11	30	15	55	.06	.13	.03	.08	.37	.15	-0	-0	-3	1	-2
Ohka T.	421	12	10	39	21	40	.13	.11	.09	.05	.36	.12	3	2	1	-6	-1
Wise M.	188	14	9	45	18	37	.08	.13	.06	.05	.36	.17	-0	1	-1	-1	-1
Kolb D.	213	12	10	51	17	32	.10	.09	.09	.08	.30	.17	1	4	-3	-2	0
Capellan J.	310	19	11	32	24	44	.16	.13	.06	.08	.34	.18	1	-0	-0	-1	0
Shouse B.	154	13	15	53	17	29	.13	.11	.13	.05	.41	.13	4	1	-1	-3	0
de la Rosa J.	146	21	16	42	19	39	.09	.13	.08	.06	.42	.20	2	1	-1	-0	3
Turnbow D.	266	26	16	42	25	33	.16	.19	.06	.08	.41	.28	3	2	1	-1	5
Gonzalez J.	193	19	10	32	24	44	.09	.09	.05	.11	.49	.14	-0	2	5	-2	5
Jackson Z.	178	12	10	46	19	35	.11	.14	.09	.03	.41	.30	1	-1	0	5	6
Eveland D.	141	23	15	44	27	29	.17	.15	.07	.11	.53	.26	2	2	4	-1	7
MLB Average		*17*	*9*	*44*	*20*	*37*	*.11*	*.11*	*.05*	*.04*	*.39*	*.19*	-	-	-	-	-

Minnesota Twins

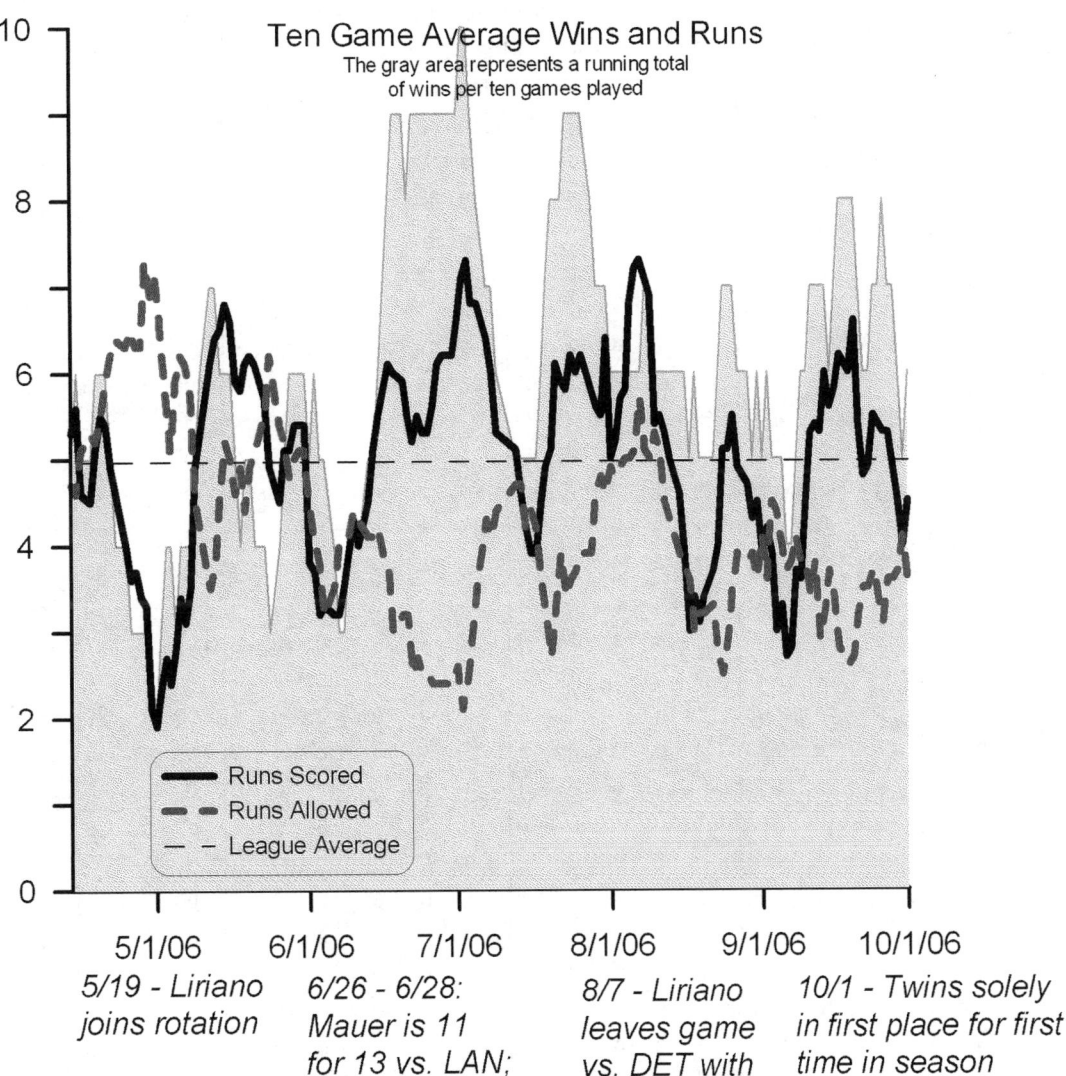

Ten Game Average Wins and Runs

The gray area represents a running total of wins per ten games played

- —— Runs Scored
- – – Runs Allowed
- – – League Average

5/1/06   6/1/06   7/1/06   8/1/06   9/1/06   10/1/06

5/19 - Liriano joins rotation

6/26 - 6/28: Mauer is 11 for 13 vs. LAN; batting .392

8/7 - Liriano leaves game vs. DET with elbow injury

10/1 - Twins solely in first place for first time in season

6/14 - Bartlett replaces Castro at SS

June and July: Morneau slugs .718

Team Batting and Pitching/Fielding Stats by Month						
	April	May	June	July	Aug	Sept/Oct
Wins	9	15	19	18	16	19
Losses	15	13	7	8	12	11
OBP	.311	.342	.360	.363	.352	.347
SLG	.365	.429	.433	.474	.425	.417
FIP	5.00	3.80	3.53	3.81	3.92	4.03
DER	.649	.646	.724	.694	.700	.710

Batting Stats

Player	RC	Runs	RBI	PA	Outs	P/PA	H	2B	3B	HR	TB	K	BB	IBB	HBP	SH	SF	SB	CS	GDP	BA	OBP	SLG	GPA
Morneau J.	121	97	130	661	415	3.59	190	37	1	34	331	93	53	9	5	0	11	3	3	10	.321	.375	.559	.309
Mauer J.	106	86	84	608	367	3.90	181	36	4	13	264	54	79	21	1	0	7	8	3	24	.347	.429	.507	.320
Cuddyer M.	104	102	109	635	410	4.06	158	41	5	24	281	130	62	5	10	0	6	6	0	11	.284	.362	.504	.289
Hunter T.	84	86	98	611	427	3.56	155	21	2	31	273	108	45	2	5	0	4	12	6	19	.278	.336	.490	.274
Castillo L.	82	84	49	652	436	4.00	173	22	6	3	216	58	56	0	1	9	2	25	11	14	.296	.358	.370	.254
Punto N.	61	73	45	524	339	3.74	133	21	7	1	171	68	47	0	1	10	7	17	5	8	.290	.352	.373	.252
Bartlett J.	51	44	32	372	243	3.71	103	18	2	2	131	46	22	1	11	1	5	10	5	8	.309	.367	.393	.264
Tyner J.	31	29	18	232	157	3.48	68	5	2	0	77	18	11	2	1	0	2	4	2	5	.312	.345	.353	.244
White R.	28	32	38	355	266	3.44	83	17	1	7	123	54	11	2	4	0	3	1	1	11	.246	.276	.365	.216
Stewart S.	26	21	21	190	131	3.53	51	5	1	2	64	19	14	0	1	0	1	3	1	7	.293	.347	.368	.249
Batista T.	24	24	21	195	142	3.91	42	12	0	5	69	27	15	1	2	0	0	0	1	5	.236	.303	.388	.233
Ford L.	22	40	18	255	187	4.08	53	6	1	4	73	43	16	0	4	1	0	9	1	5	.226	.287	.312	.208
Redmond M.	22	20	23	190	127	3.08	61	13	0	0	74	18	4	0	4	1	2	0	0	9	.341	.365	.413	.268
Kubel J.	21	23	26	235	180	3.59	53	8	0	8	85	45	12	0	0	2	1	2	0	13	.241	.279	.386	.222
Castro J.	11	10	14	164	127	3.23	36	5	2	1	48	23	6	0	0	1	1	1	1	6	.231	.258	.308	.193
Rodriguez L.	8	11	6	132	91	3.82	27	4	0	2	37	16	14	1	0	2	1	0	0	3	.235	.315	.322	.223
Rabe J.	6	8	7	51	39	3.86	14	1	0	3	24	11	2	0	0	0	0	0	1	3	.286	.314	.490	.264
Tiffee T.	6	4	6	49	37	3.06	11	1	0	2	18	8	4	1	0	0	0	0	1	2	.244	.306	.400	.238
Nevin P.	4	2	4	54	34	4.17	8	1	0	1	12	15	10	1	0	1	1	0	0	0	.190	.340	.286	.224
Sierra R.	2	3	4	33	23	4.03	5	1	0	0	6	7	4	0	0	0	1	0	0	0	.179	.273	.214	.176
Liriano F.	1	0	1	7	4	3.86	1	0	0	0	1	3	1	0	0	1	0	0	0	0	.200	.333	.200	.200
Casilla A.	1	1	0	6	3	4.17	1	0	0	0	1	1	2	0	0	0	0	0	0	0	.250	.500	.250	.288
Radke B.	-0	0	0	2	1	2.00	0	0	0	0	0	0	0	0	0	1	0	0	0	0	.000	.000	.000	.000
Heintz C.	-0	0	0	1	1	4.00	0	0	0	0	0	0	0	0	0	0	0	0	0	0	.000	.000	.000	.000
Nathan J.	-0	0	0	1	1	4.00	0	0	0	0	0	1	0	0	0	0	0	0	0	0	.000	.000	.000	.000
Eyre W.	-0	0	0	1	1	4.00	0	0	0	0	0	1	0	0	0	0	0	0	0	0	.000	.000	.000	.000
Santana J.	-0	0	0	2	2	4.00	0	0	0	0	0	2	0	0	0	0	0	0	0	0	.000	.000	.000	.000
Bonser B.	-0	1	0	4	3	1.50	0	0	0	0	0	0	0	0	0	1	0	0	0	0	.000	.000	.000	.000
Silva C.	-0	0	0	3	2	2.00	1	0	0	0	1	0	0	0	0	0	0	0	0	0	.333	.333	.333	.234
Baker S.	-0	0	0	3	3	5.67	0	0	0	0	0	3	0	0	0	0	0	0	0	0	.000	.000	.000	.000

Italicized stats have been adjusted for home park.

Batted Ball Batting Stats are listed at end of fielding stats

Pitching Stats

Player	PRC	IP	BFP	G	GS	P/PA	K	BB	IBB	HBP	H	HR	DP	DER	SB	CS	PO	W	L	Sv	Op	Hld	RA	ERA	FIP
Santana J.	154	233.7	923	34	34	3.74	245	47	0	4	186	24	14	.720	4	5	0	19	6	0	0	0	3.04	2.77	3.16
Liriano F.	101	121.0	473	28	16	3.80	144	32	0	1	89	9	19	.704	9	0	0	12	3	1	1	1	2.31	2.16	2.67
Nathan J.	77	68.3	262	64	0	4.09	95	16	4	1	38	3	0	.755	2	0	0	7	0	36	38	0	1.58	1.58	1.62
Radke B.	61	162.3	689	28	28	3.60	83	32	3	1	197	24	22	.676	6	5	0	12	9	0	0	0	4.82	4.32	4.72
Reyes D.	56	50.7	194	66	0	3.60	49	15	2	0	35	3	8	.732	0	4	4	5	0	0	1	16	1.42	0.89	2.87
Silva C.	46	180.3	811	36	31	3.32	70	32	4	7	246	38	20	.675	10	2	0	11	15	0	0	2	6.49	5.94	5.81
Bonser B.	45	100.3	419	18	18	3.74	84	24	0	1	104	18	9	.692	4	3	2	7	6	0	0	0	4.49	4.22	4.67
Crain J.	41	76.7	325	68	0	3.52	60	18	2	2	79	6	4	.690	4	1	0	4	5	1	4	10	3.64	3.52	3.42
Rincon J.	41	74.3	315	75	0	3.90	65	24	3	3	76	2	11	.656	3	0	0	3	1	1	3	26	3.63	2.91	2.83
Neshek P.	33	37.0	138	32	0	4.02	53	6	0	0	23	6	1	.767	3	2	0	4	2	0	2	10	2.19	2.19	2.99
Guerrier M.	33	69.7	300	39	1	3.58	37	21	0	0	78	9	6	.695	1	3	1	1	0	1	1	2	3.75	3.36	4.78
Baker S.	23	83.3	377	16	16	3.82	62	16	1	3	114	17	6	.638	5	3	0	5	8	0	0	0	6.80	6.37	5.07
Eyre W.	19	59.3	275	42	0	3.76	26	22	4	6	75	8	5	.676	1	1	0	1	0	0	0	0	5.46	5.31	5.35
Lohse K.	17	63.7	295	22	8	3.69	46	25	2	6	80	8	5	.652	0	2	2	2	5	0	0	0	7.07	7.07	4.82
Garza M.	16	50.0	232	10	9	3.84	38	23	0	0	62	6	4	.655	2	0	0	3	6	0	0	0	5.94	5.76	4.68
Perkins G.	6	5.7	20	4	0	4.10	6	0	0	0	3	0	0	.786	0	0	0	0	0	0	0	1	1.59	1.59	1.15
Smith M.	0	3.0	18	1	1	4.44	1	3	0	1	5	1	0	.667	0	0	0	0	0	0	0	0	12.00	12.00	10.93

Batted Ball Pitching Stats

Player	PA	% of PA		% of Batted Balls			IF/F	HR/OF	Runs Per Event				Total Runs vs. Avg.				
		K%	BB%	GB%	LD%	FB%			NIP	GB	LD	OF	NIP	GB	LD	FB	Tot
Santana J.	923	27	6	41	20	40	.13	.10	-.03	.02	.42	.16	-22	-9	0	-8	-39
Liriano F.	473	30	7	55	21	23	.09	.13	-.03	.01	.35	.19	-11	-5	-4	-9	-29
Nathan J.	262	36	6	36	22	42	.18	.04	-.04	.00	.40	.05	-8	-4	-2	-10	-24
Reyes D.	194	25	8	69	11	20	.12	.13	-.01	.03	.30	.22	-3	-0	-6	-4	-13
Rincon J.	315	21	9	51	22	28	.03	.03	.02	.07	.37	.06	-2	3	-0	-10	-10
Neshek P.	138	38	4	32	14	54	.05	.15	-.07	.05	.27	.19	-6	-1	-5	1	-10
Crain J.	325	18	6	55	21	24	.07	.09	.00	.05	.41	.11	-4	2	3	-8	-8
Guerrier M.	300	12	7	45	18	37	.08	.10	.05	.05	.40	.15	-1	1	1	-2	-1
Bonser B.	419	20	6	42	15	43	.08	.15	-.01	.09	.37	.22	-7	5	-6	8	0
Garza M.	232	16	10	35	25	40	.12	.10	.06	.06	.35	.22	1	-0	2	3	5
Lohse K.	295	16	11	38	21	41	.08	.09	.07	.11	.36	.14	2	5	-0	-2	5
Eyre W.	275	9	10	46	18	36	.10	.10	.13	.04	.41	.24	3	0	1	4	8
Radke B.	689	12	5	42	20	38	.11	.11	.02	.05	.42	.19	-7	1	9	6	8
Baker T.	377	16	5	34	19	47	.10	.13	-.01	.12	.42	.25	-6	6	3	13	16
Silva C.	811	9	5	44	22	34	.07	.16	.05	.02	.39	.28	-5	-5	14	25	29
MLB Average		17	9	44	20	37	.11	.11	.05	.04	.39	.19	-	-	-	-	-

Fielding Stats

Name	POS	INN	SBA/G	CS%	ERA	WP+PB/G	PO	A	TE	FE
Mauer, J.	C	1059.3	0.45	32%	3.92	0.306	868	42	2	1
Redmond, M.	C	378.0	0.62	31%	4.05	0.214	317	21	0	0
Heintz, C.	C	2.0	0.00	0%	4.50	0.000	0	0	0	0

Name	POS	Inn	PO	A	TE	FE	FPct	RF	DPS	DPT
Morneau, J.	1B	1346.0	1295	111	1	7	.994	9.40	11	1
Cuddyer, M.	1B	52.0	48	3	0	0	1.000	8.83	0	0
Nevin, P.	1B	32.7	29	1	0	0	1.000	8.27	0	0
Tiffee, T.	1B	7.3	8	0	0	1	.889	9.82	0	0
Rodriguez, L.	1B	1.0	1	0	0	0	1.000	9.00	0	0
Castillo, L.	2B	1239.0	268	378	4	2	.991	4.69	25	52
Punto, N.	2B	114.7	21	50	0	2	.973	5.57	4	5
Rodriguez, L.	2B	72.3	11	26	1	0	.974	4.60	4	2
Casilla, A.	2B	13.0	5	8	0	0	1.000	9.00	1	3
Bartlett, J.	SS	879.7	131	298	7	6	.971	4.39	29	17
Castro, J.	SS	408.0	66	148	3	4	.968	4.72	9	18
Punto, N.	SS	146.7	14	50	2	0	.970	3.93	4	3
Rodriguez, L.	SS	3.0	0	1	1	0	.500	3.00	0	0
Casilla, A.	SS	2.0	1	2	0	0	1.000	13.50	1	1
Punto, N.	3B	766.0	53	176	5	4	.962	2.69	18	0
Batista, T.	3B	434.0	27	97	3	3	.954	2.57	5	1
Rodriguez, L.	3B	188.3	18	41	0	0	1.000	2.82	8	1
Tiffee, T.	3B	51.0	3	13	0	1	.941	2.82	2	0

Name	POS	Inn	PO	A	TE	FE	FPct	RF	DPS	DPT
Ford, L.	LF	321.3	72	1	0	0	1.000	2.04	0	0
White, R.	LF	286.0	57	0	0	0	1.000	1.79	0	0
Stewart, S.	LF	286.0	58	3	0	1	.984	1.92	2	0
Tyner, J.	LF	281.0	86	4	1	0	.989	2.88	2	0
Kubel, J.	LF	204.0	33	1	1	1	.944	1.50	0	0
Rabe, J.	LF	55.0	22	0	2	0	.917	3.60	0	0
Punto, N.	LF	4.0	1	0	0	0	1.000	2.25	0	0
Cuddyer, M.	LF	2.0	0	0	0	0	0.000	0.00	0	0
Hunter, T.	CF	1232.0	343	8	0	4	.989	2.56	8	0
Tyner, J.	CF	150.0	43	0	0	0	1.000	2.58	0	0
Ford, L.	CF	41.0	7	0	1	0	.875	1.54	0	0
Punto, N.	CF	16.0	5	0	0	0	1.000	2.81	0	0
Cuddyer, M.	RF	1227.0	244	11	3	2	.981	1.87	4	0
Ford, L.	RF	169.0	53	3	0	1	.982	2.98	4	0
Kubel, J.	RF	40.0	7	0	0	0	1.000	1.58	0	0
Tyner, J.	RF	2.0	0	0	0	0	0.000	0.00	0	0
Rabe, J.	RF	1.0	0	0	0	0	0.000	0.00	0	0

Batted Ball Batting Stats

Player	PA	% of PA		% of Batted Balls					Runs Per Event				Total Runs vs. Avg.				
		K%	BB%	GB%	LD%	FB%	IF/F	HR/OF	NIP	GB	LD	OF	NIP	GB	LD	FB	Tot
Morneau J.	661	14	9	36	24	41	.09	.15	.06	.08	.42	.22	1	4	14	12	30
Mauer J.	608	9	13	49	25	26	.02	.10	.16	.04	.40	.22	13	3	12	-1	28
Cuddyer M.	635	20	11	44	21	35	.10	.17	.05	.06	.42	.30	2	2	2	12	18
Hunter T.	611	18	8	45	18	37	.16	.21	.03	.04	.41	.30	-3	-1	-1	14	9
Bartlett J.	372	12	9	44	22	34	.07	.02	.08	.04	.39	.11	1	0	4	-7	-1
Redmond M.	191	10	4	46	27	27	.02	.00	.02	.06	.36	.05	-2	2	5	-6	-1
Stewart S.	190	10	8	48	14	39	.08	.04	.09	.03	.44	.14	0	-1	-1	-1	-2
Tyner J.	232	8	5	52	27	21	.00	.00	.07	.04	.31	.01	-1	5	3	-10	-3
Batista T.	195	14	9	40	22	38	.11	.06	.06	-.01	.39	.10	0	-3	2	-4	-5
Rodriguez L.	132	12	11	46	19	34	.03	.06	.10	.01	.36	.04	1	-2	-0	-4	-5
Castillo L.	652	9	9	61	18	21	.14	.03	.11	.07	.37	.06	4	14	-2	-24	-7
Punto N.	524	13	9	46	24	30	.08	.01	.08	.06	.37	.04	2	5	5	-19	-8
Kubel J.	235	19	5	49	21	31	.06	.16	-.02	-.02	.33	.23	-4	-6	-1	1	-10
Castro J.	164	14	4	55	20	25	.12	.03	-.02	-.04	.46	.06	-3	-6	3	-6	-11
White R.	355	15	4	44	21	34	.16	.07	-.01	.05	.30	.14	-6	1	-1	-6	-12
Ford L.	255	17	8	52	16	32	.08	.05	.03	.03	.33	.09	-1	-1	-4	-6	-12
MLB Average		17	9	44	20	37	.11	.11	.05	.04	.39	.19	-	-	-	-	-

New York Mets

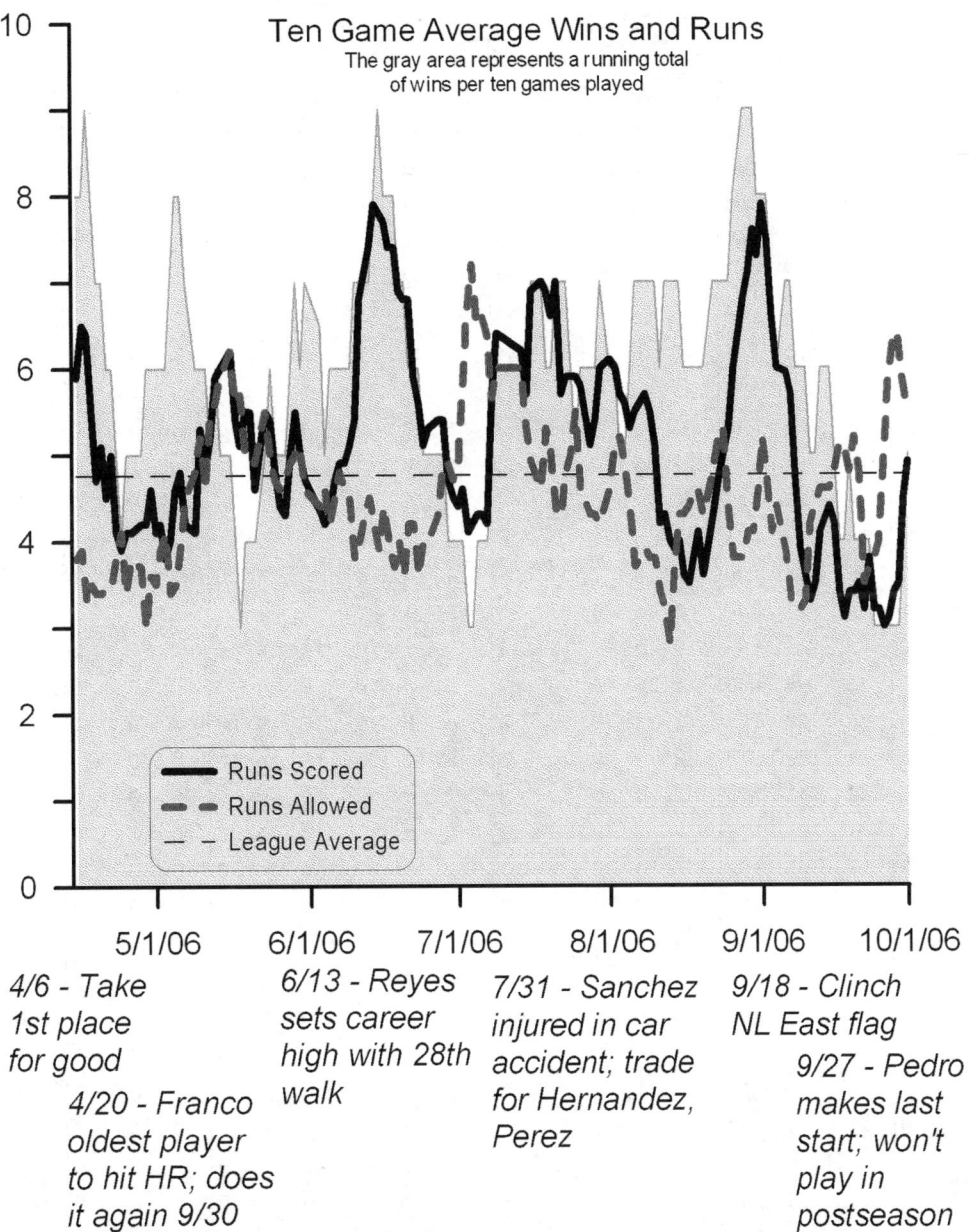

Ten Game Average Wins and Runs

The gray area represents a running total
of wins per ten games played

— Runs Scored
- - Runs Allowed
— — League Average

5/1/06   6/1/06   7/1/06   8/1/06   9/1/06   10/1/06

4/6 - Take
1st place
for good

6/13 - Reyes
sets career
high with 28th
walk

7/31 - Sanchez
injured in car
accident; trade
for Hernandez,
Perez

9/18 - Clinch
NL East flag

4/20 - Franco
oldest player
to hit HR; does
it again 9/30

9/27 - Pedro
makes last
start; won't
play in
postseason

Team Batting and Pitching/Fielding Stats by Month						
	April	May	June	July	Aug	Sept/Oct
Wins	16	16	15	16	19	15
Losses	8	12	11	10	9	15
OBP	.329	.332	.339	.344	.342	.321
SLG	.448	.433	.500	.450	.452	.393
FIP	4.07	4.15	4.84	4.41	4.54	4.07
DER	.719	.700	.711	.681	.728	.699

Batting Stats

Player	RC	Runs	RBI	PA	Outs	P/PA	H	2B	3B	HR	TB	K	BB	IBB	HBP	SH	SF	SB	CS	GDP	BA	OBP	SLG	GPA
Beltran C.	125	127	116	617	379	4.20	140	38	1	41	303	99	95	6	4	1	7	18	3	6	.275	.388	.594	.330
Reyes J.	125	122	81	703	476	3.61	194	30	17	19	315	81	53	6	1	2	0	64	17	6	.300	.354	.487	.287
Wright D.	123	96	116	661	421	3.93	181	40	5	26	309	113	66	13	5	0	8	20	5	15	.311	.381	.531	.311
Delgado C.	105	89	114	618	397	3.82	139	30	2	38	287	120	74	11	10	0	10	0	0	12	.265	.361	.548	.306
Lo Duca P.	74	80	49	551	364	3.45	163	39	1	5	219	38	24	0	6	7	2	3	0	15	.318	.355	.428	.272
Valentin J.	58	56	62	432	287	3.94	104	24	3	18	188	71	37	5	0	5	6	6	2	5	.271	.330	.490	.277
Chavez E.	56	48	42	390	255	3.62	108	22	5	4	152	44	24	3	0	11	2	12	3	7	.306	.348	.431	.270
Floyd C.	46	45	44	376	256	3.53	81	19	1	11	135	58	29	3	12	0	3	6	0	5	.244	.324	.407	.253
Nady X.	37	37	40	292	203	3.66	70	15	1	14	129	51	19	4	6	1	1	2	1	7	.264	.326	.487	.274
Franco J.	22	14	26	179	132	4.11	45	10	0	2	61	49	13	2	1	0	0	6	1	11	.273	.330	.370	.246
Milledge L.	22	14	22	185	132	3.96	40	7	2	4	63	39	12	4	5	1	1	1	2	4	.241	.310	.380	.239
Woodward C.	18	25	25	253	177	3.95	48	10	1	3	69	55	23	2	1	4	3	1	1	2	.216	.289	.311	.212
Green S.	12	14	15	126	92	3.79	29	9	0	4	50	18	8	1	4	0	1	0	0	8	.257	.325	.442	.263
Castro R.	12	13	12	144	98	4.03	30	7	0	4	49	40	15	2	1	1	1	0	0	2	.238	.322	.389	.247
Tucker M.	9	3	6	74	46	4.25	11	4	0	1	18	14	16	0	1	0	1	2	0	2	.196	.378	.321	.256
Matsui K.	5	10	7	139	105	3.99	26	6	0	1	35	19	6	1	0	3	0	2	0	1	.200	.235	.269	.177
Marrero E.	5	4	5	41	27	4.41	6	1	0	2	13	15	4	0	1	2	1	2	0	0	.182	.282	.394	.230
Glavine T.	3	6	2	70	46	3.96	9	1	0	0	10	18	7	0	0	10	0	0	0	2	.170	.267	.189	.171
Bannister B.	2	2	2	13	8	4.00	4	3	0	0	7	3	0	0	0	1	0	0	0	0	.333	.333	.583	.302
DiFelice M.	1	3	1	30	23	3.97	2	1	0	0	3	10	5	0	0	0	0	0	0	0	.080	.233	.120	.138
Diaz V.	1	0	2	11	9	3.73	2	1	0	0	3	5	0	0	0	0	0	0	0	0	.182	.182	.273	.153
Oliver D.	1	2	2	16	13	3.63	2	1	0	0	3	7	1	0	0	0	0	0	0	0	.133	.188	.200	.137
Williams D.	0	1	0	11	7	5.18	2	0	0	0	2	4	2	0	0	0	0	0	0	0	.222	.364	.222	.224
Trachsel S.	0	4	2	59	43	3.92	7	1	0	1	11	13	4	0	1	4	0	0	0	0	.140	.218	.220	.157
Sanchez D.	0	1	0	2	1	3.00	0	0	0	0	0	1	0	0	1	0	0	0	0	0	.000	.500	.000	.230
Gonzalez J.	0	1	0	6	3	3.67	0	0	0	0	0	1	1	0	0	2	0	0	0	0	.000	.250	.000	.115
Julio J.	-0	0	0	1	1	3.00	0	0	0	0	0	1	0	0	0	0	0	0	0	0	.000	.000	.000	.000
Bell H.	-0	0	0	1	1	4.00	0	0	0	0	0	1	0	0	0	0	0	0	0	0	.000	.000	.000	.000
Zambrano V.	-0	0	0	6	5	2.67	0	0	0	0	0	1	0	0	1	0	0	0	0	0	.000	.167	.000	.077
Ledee R.	-0	4	1	36	29	3.78	3	1	0	1	7	6	4	0	0	0	0	0	0	0	.094	.194	.219	.145
Feliciano P.	-0	0	0	3	3	2.33	0	0	0	0	0	1	0	0	0	0	0	0	0	0	.000	.000	.000	.000
Lima J.	-1	0	0	6	5	2.33	0	0	0	0	0	3	0	0	0	1	0	0	0	0	.000	.000	.000	.000
Hernandez O.	-1	4	2	40	30	3.48	5	0	1	0	7	10	0	0	0	5	0	1	0	0	.143	.143	.200	.117
Martinez P.	-1	2	1	49	34	3.63	4	1	0	0	5	16	2	0	0	9	0	0	0	0	.105	.150	.132	.103
Stinnett K.	-1	0	0	12	11	3.92	1	0	0	0	1	4	0	0	0	0	0	0	0	0	.083	.083	.083	.060
Perez O.	-1	0	0	15	13	4.27	1	0	0	0	1	4	2	0	0	0	0	0	0	1	.077	.200	.077	.112
Soler A.	-1	0	0	15	10	3.20	1	0	0	0	1	6	0	0	0	4	0	0	0	0	.091	.091	.091	.065
Pelfrey M.	-1	0	0	9	9	4.11	0	0	0	0	0	4	0	0	0	0	0	0	0	0	.000	.000	.000	.000
Hernandez A.	-2	4	3	67	59	3.54	10	1	1	1	16	12	1	0	0	0	0	0	0	3	.152	.164	.242	.137
Maine J.	-2	3	0	32	27	3.66	1	1	0	0	2	16	0	0	1	3	0	0	0	0	.036	.069	.071	.050

Italicized stats have been adjusted for home park.
Batted Ball Batting Stats are listed at end of fielding stats

Pitching Stats

Player	PRC	IP	BFP	G	GS	P/PA	K	BB	IBB	HBP	H	HR	DP	DER	SB	CS	PO	W	L	Sv	Op	Hld	RA	ERA	FIP
Glavine T.	84	198.0	842	32	32	3.88	131	62	7	6	202	22	20	.694	6	9	2	15	7	0	0	0	4.27	3.82	4.26
Martinez P.	55	132.7	550	23	23	3.84	137	39	2	10	108	19	8	.730	13	1	0	9	8	0	0	0	4.88	4.48	4.08
Trachsel S.	54	164.7	736	30	30	3.83	79	78	1	4	185	23	12	.705	12	7	1	15	8	0	0	0	5.14	4.97	5.55
Wagner B.	52	72.3	297	70	0	4.18	94	21	1	4	59	7	5	.678	5	4	1	3	2	40	45	0	2.74	2.24	2.87
Hernandez O.	52	116.7	495	20	20	4.05	112	41	2	8	103	14	8	.713	17	4	1	9	7	0	0	0	4.47	4.09	4.07
Feliciano P.	47	60.3	256	64	0	3.74	54	20	1	3	56	4	7	.674	0	1	0	7	2	0	3	10	2.24	2.09	3.38
Heilman A.	43	87.0	356	74	0	3.97	73	28	2	3	73	5	8	.721	9	0	0	4	5	0	5	27	3.83	3.62	3.29
Maine J.	42	90.0	365	16	15	4.14	71	33	1	2	69	15	5	.775	6	3	0	6	5	0	0	0	4.00	3.60	4.94
Oliver D.	41	81.0	333	45	0	3.81	60	21	2	3	70	13	7	.750	3	1	0	4	1	0	0	3	3.67	3.44	4.64
Bradford C.	35	62.0	252	70	0	3.58	45	13	4	0	59	1	6	.694	3	0	0	4	2	2	3	10	3.19	2.90	2.41
Sanchez D.	33	55.3	229	49	0	3.72	44	24	6	4	43	3	12	.708	3	0	1	5	1	0	1	14	3.09	2.60	3.53
Mota G.	25	18.0	68	18	0	4.15	19	5	1	0	10	2	0	.810	3	1	0	3	0	0	0	4	1.00	1.00	3.22
Bannister B.	15	38.0	171	8	6	3.95	19	22	2	2	34	4	1	.750	7	1	0	2	1	0	0	0	4.26	4.26	5.32
Bell H.	12	37.0	166	22	0	4.01	35	11	2	0	51	6	6	.596	2	2	0	0	0	0	0	0	6.08	5.11	4.16
Perez O.	12	36.7	165	7	7	3.98	41	17	0	3	41	7	6	.649	1	0	0	1	3	0	0	0	6.38	6.38	5.10
Soler A.	11	45.0	208	8	8	3.78	23	21	1	1	50	2	2	.705	5	0	0	2	3	0	0	0	6.60	6.00	5.62
Hernandez R.	11	20.7	83	22	0	3.98	15	8	1	0	15	2	3	.759	3	1	0	0	0	0	0	3	3.48	3.48	4.04
Ring R.	9	12.7	48	11	0	3.96	8	3	0	0	7	2	0	.857	0	0	0	0	0	0	0	2	2.13	2.13	4.72
Williams D.	9	29.0	126	6	5	3.69	16	4	1	2	39	5	4	.657	0	2	2	3	1	0	0	0	5.59	5.59	4.87
Julio J.	7	21.3	96	18	0	4.56	33	10	1	1	21	4	2	.625	4	1	0	1	2	1	1	0	6.33	5.06	3.97
Pelfrey M.	6	21.3	99	4	4	3.83	13	12	0	3	25	1	4	.643	2	1	0	2	1	0	0	0	5.91	5.48	4.72
Zambrano V.	6	21.3	97	5	5	3.76	15	11	0	0	25	5	1	.697	2	1	0	1	2	0	0	0	6.75	6.75	6.41
Gonzalez J.	3	14.0	67	3	3	3.57	8	6	1	0	21	4	1	.653	2	0	0	0	0	0	0	0	7.71	7.71	6.86
Lima J.	2	17.3	91	4	4	4.03	12	10	0	2	25	3	1	.625	1	0	0	0	4	0	0	0	11.42	9.87	6.16
Owens H.	1	4.0	19	3	0	4.68	2	4	0	0	4	0	1	.692	1	0	0	0	0	0	0	0	9.00	9.00	5.22
Fortunato B.	0	3.0	18	2	0	3.39	0	2	0	1	7	2	1	.615	0	0	0	1	0	0	0	0	27.00	27.00	14.88
Humber P.	0	2.0	7	2	0	4.29	2	1	0	0	0	0	0	1.000	1	0	0	0	0	0	0	0	0.00	0.00	2.72

Batted Ball Pitching Stats

Player	PA	% of PA		% of Batted Balls			IF/F	HR/OF	Runs Per Event				Total Runs vs. Avg.				
		K%	BB%	GB%	LD%	FB%			NIP	GB	LD	OF	NIP	GB	LD	FB	Tot
Heilman A.	356	21	9	45	17	38	.15	.06	.02	.00	.40	.14	-2	-5	-3	-6	-16
Martinez P.	550	25	9	36	19	44	.10	.13	.01	.04	.35	.18	-6	-3	-7	1	-15
Wagner B.	297	32	8	53	16	31	.02	.11	-.02	.06	.42	.18	-6	1	-5	-3	-13
Bradford C.	252	18	5	63	16	21	.05	.03	-.01	.03	.42	.10	-4	-0	-1	-7	-12
Sanchez D.	229	19	12	52	13	34	.23	.08	.07	.03	.52	.07	2	0	-2	-8	-9
Maine J.	365	19	10	38	15	47	.14	.15	.04	-.00	.45	.18	-1	-6	-2	1	-8
Feliciano P.	256	21	9	49	21	29	.10	.09	.02	.06	.35	.11	-2	1	-1	-6	-8
Hernandez O.	495	23	10	35	19	47	.08	.10	.03	.06	.37	.17	-2	-2	-5	2	-7
Oliver D.	333	18	7	48	17	35	.06	.16	.02	-.02	.35	.27	-3	-7	-4	7	-7
Glavine T.	842	16	8	44	23	32	.11	.12	.04	.00	.38	.22	-3	-12	8	2	-5
Bannister B.	171	11	14	40	15	45	.18	.09	.14	.10	.38	.08	4	2	-2	-5	-1
Perez O.	165	25	12	30	24	46	.06	.16	.04	.07	.28	.27	0	0	-2	5	3
Williams D.	126	13	5	35	26	38	.21	.17	.01	.15	.31	.21	-1	3	1	0	3
Bell H.	166	21	7	51	26	23	.00	.22	-.00	.02	.40	.43	-2	-1	3	4	4
Soler A.	208	11	11	42	18	41	.05	.10	.11	.09	.35	.18	2	2	-2	2	5
Trachsel S.	736	11	11	42	18	40	.12	.12	.12	.04	.41	.18	9	-1	2	2	12
MLB Average		17	9	44	20	37	.11	.11	.05	.04	.39	.19	-	-	-	-	-

Fielding Stats

Name	POS	INN	SBA/G	CS%	ERA	WP+PB/G	PO	A	TE	FE
Lo Duca, P.	C	1027.0	0.93	21%	4.34	0.351	802	59	9	1
Castro, R.	C	307.3	0.76	35%	4.22	0.205	267	16	1	0
DiFelice, M.	C	84.0	0.86	13%	2.46	0.000	71	3	2	0
Stinnett, K.	C	40.0	1.35	50%	2.93	0.000	35	5	1	0
Marrero, E.	C	3.0	0.00	0%	0.00	0.000	1	0	0	0

Name	POS	Inn	PO	A	TE	FE	FPct	RF	DPS	DPT
Delgado, C.	1B	1246.0	1199	70	1	7	.994	9.17	6	1
Franco, J.	1B	194.0	197	5	1	0	.995	9.37	2	0
Tucker, M.	1B	9.0	8	0	0	0	1.000	8.00	0	0
Nady, X.	1B	4.0	3	0	0	0	1.000	6.75	0	0
Valentin, J.	1B	3.0	3	0	0	0	1.000	9.00	0	0
Green, S.	1B	2.0	2	0	0	0	1.000	9.00	0	0
Woodward, C.	1B	2.0	2	0	0	0	1.000	9.00	0	0
Marrero, E.	1B	1.0	1	0	0	0	1.000	9.00	0	0
Valentin, J.	2B	782.3	194	286	2	4	.988	5.52	15	33
Woodward, C.	2B	292.0	72	93	0	4	.976	5.09	4	17
Matsui, K.	2B	276.0	72	85	0	1	.994	5.12	10	12
Hernandez, A.	2B	111.0	26	27	0	0	1.000	4.30	0	3
Reyes, J.	SS	1320.0	176	390	9	8	.971	3.86	44	29
Woodward, C.	SS	97.0	13	34	1	0	.979	4.36	5	5
Hernandez, A.	SS	44.0	3	7	0	0	1.000	2.05	0	0
Wright, D.	3B	1365.0	107	288	11	7	.954	2.60	29	3
Woodward, C.	3B	66.0	4	17	0	0	1.000	2.86	1	1
Franco, J.	3B	20.0	0	6	0	0	1.000	2.70	0	0
Valentin, J.	3B	8.0	1	1	0	0	1.000	2.25	0	0
Marrero, E.	3B	2.0	0	1	0	0	1.000	4.50	0	0

Name	POS	Inn	PO	A	TE	FE	FPct	RF	DPS	DPT
Floyd, C.	LF	768.3	148	3	0	2	.987	1.77	0	0
Chavez, E.	LF	239.7	55	4	0	0	1.000	2.22	0	0
Milledge, L.	LF	194.0	42	3	0	1	.978	2.09	0	0
Tucker, M.	LF	115.0	22	2	0	0	1.000	1.88	0	0
Valentin, J.	LF	47.3	12	1	0	0	1.000	2.47	0	0
Woodward, C.	LF	40.7	10	0	0	0	1.000	2.21	0	0
Marrero, E.	LF	27.0	3	0	0	0	1.000	1.00	0	0
Diaz, V.	LF	20.0	4	0	0	1	.800	1.80	0	0
Ledee, R.	LF	9.3	0	0	0	0	0.000	0.00	0	0
Beltran, C.	CF	1184.0	357	13	1	1	.995	2.81	12	0
Chavez, E.	CF	264.3	83	2	0	0	1.000	2.89	4	0
Marrero, E.	CF	13.0	3	0	0	1	.750	2.08	0	0
Nady, X.	RF	620.7	137	5	1	3	.973	2.06	0	0
Chavez, E.	RF	310.7	71	3	0	0	1.000	2.14	2	0
Green, S.	RF	264.0	56	0	1	2	.949	1.91	0	0
Milledge, L.	RF	205.3	38	1	0	1	.975	1.71	0	0
Ledee, R.	RF	18.3	5	0	0	0	1.000	2.45	0	0
Woodward, C.	RF	13.0	2	0	0	0	1.000	1.38	0	0
Tucker, M.	RF	10.0	4	0	0	0	1.000	3.60	0	0
Marrero, E.	RF	10.0	4	0	0	0	1.000	3.60	0	0
Valentin, J.	RF	9.3	1	1	0	0	1.000	1.93	0	0

Batted Ball Batting Stats

Player	PA	% of PA		% of Batted Balls					Runs Per Event				Total Runs vs. Avg.				
		K%	BB%	GB%	LD%	FB%	IF/F	HR/OF	NIP	GB	LD	OF	NIP	GB	LD	FB	Tot
Beltran C.	617	16	16	37	17	47	.11	.23	.12	.05	.40	.36	15	0	-6	33	42
Wright D.	661	17	11	36	19	44	.10	.13	.06	.05	.44	.27	3	-2	4	20	25
Delgado C.	618	19	14	42	18	40	.05	.22	.08	.01	.47	.31	7	-7	0	22	23
Reyes J.	703	12	8	45	21	34	.12	.10	.07	.05	.41	.23	0	5	8	5	18
Valentin J.	432	16	9	31	16	53	.17	.13	.04	.10	.47	.20	-1	3	-1	6	7
Nady X.	292	17	9	46	15	40	.06	.16	.04	.04	.40	.25	-1	1	-3	7	3
Lo Duca P.	551	7	5	45	21	34	.09	.03	.09	.05	.39	.11	-1	4	9	-10	2
Chavez E.	390	11	6	55	20	25	.10	.06	.05	.04	.31	.25	-2	7	-3	-1	0
Green S.	126	14	10	45	16	40	.11	.12	.07	-.01	.39	.23	0	-2	-1	2	-1
Castro R.	144	28	11	36	22	42	.16	.13	.02	.06	.43	.19	-1	-0	0	-1	-2
Milledge L.	185	21	9	44	22	34	.16	.11	.03	.11	.29	.12	-1	4	-2	-4	-4
Floyd C.	376	15	11	42	18	40	.12	.11	.08	.06	.28	.17	3	1	-7	-1	-4
Franco J.	179	27	8	55	27	18	.05	.10	-.01	0.00	.38	.26	-3	-2	2	-3	-6
Matsui K.	139	14	4	50	17	33	.14	.03	-0.00	.01	.31	.04	-2	-2	-2	-5	-11
Woodward C.	253	22	9	44	18	38	.09	.03	.03	.08	.38	.02	-1	2	-2	-10	-12
MLB Average		17	9	44	20	37	.11	.11	.05	.04	.39	.19	-	-	-	-	-

New York Yankees

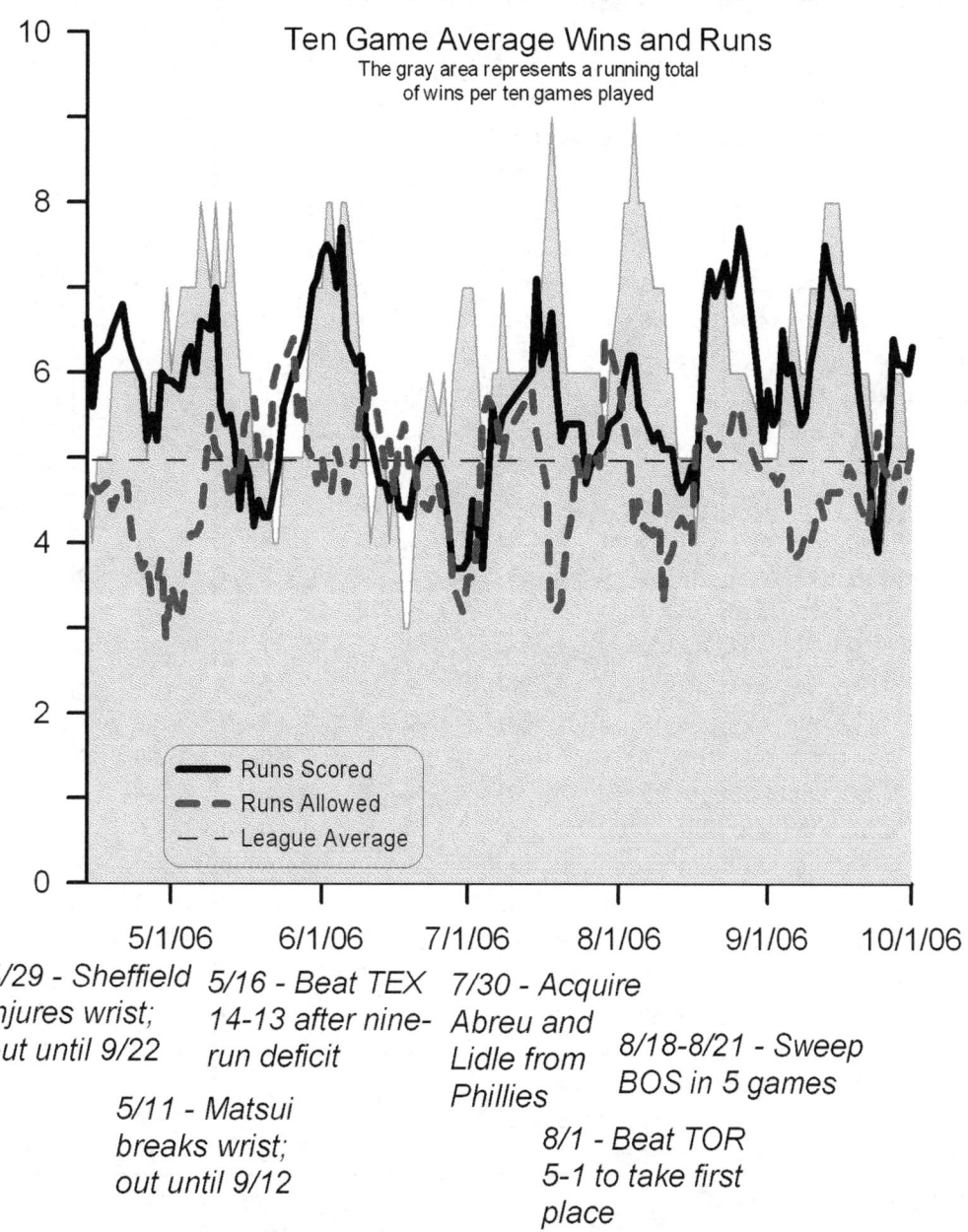

Ten Game Average Wins and Runs
The gray area represents a running total
of wins per ten games played

Legend:
— Runs Scored
– – Runs Allowed
– – League Average

4/29 - Sheffield injures wrist; out until 9/22

5/11 - Matsui breaks wrist; out until 9/12

5/16 - Beat TEX 14-13 after nine-run deficit

7/30 - Acquire Abreu and Lidle from Phillies

8/1 - Beat TOR 5-1 to take first place

8/18-8/21 - Sweep BOS in 5 games

Team Batting and Pitching/Fielding Stats by Month						
	April	May	June	July	Aug	Sept/Oct
Wins	13	18	13	17	18	18
Losses	10	10	12	9	12	12
OBP	.395	.354	.355	.335	.375	.364
SLG	.495	.408	.451	.443	.493	.478
FIP	3.71	4.68	4.32	4.46	4.51	4.50
DER	.707	.698	.700	.683	.698	.698

273

Batting Stats

Player	RC	Runs	RBI	PA	Outs	P/PA	H	2B	3B	HR	TB	K	BB	IBB	HBP	SH	SF	SB	CS	GDP	BA	OBP	SLG	GPA
Jeter D.	139	118	97	715	427	3.78	214	39	3	14	301	102	69	4	12	7	4	34	5	13	.343	.417	.483	.317
Rodriguez A.	118	113	121	674	432	3.82	166	26	1	35	299	139	90	8	8	0	4	15	4	22	.290	.392	.523	.316
Giambi J.	111	92	113	579	343	4.38	113	25	0	37	249	106	110	12	16	0	7	2	0	10	.253	.413	.558	.335
Damon J.	104	115	80	671	438	4.10	169	35	5	24	286	85	67	1	4	2	5	25	10	4	.285	.359	.482	.290
Posada J.	93	65	93	545	346	3.72	129	27	2	23	229	97	64	1	11	0	5	3	0	10	.277	.374	.492	.300
Cano R.	78	62	78	508	338	3.22	165	41	1	15	253	54	18	3	2	1	5	5	2	19	.342	.365	.525	.304
Cabrera M.	71	75	50	524	345	3.66	129	26	2	7	180	59	56	3	2	5	1	12	5	9	.280	.360	.391	.268
Williams B.	55	65	61	462	316	3.43	118	29	0	12	183	53	33	5	2	1	6	2	0	14	.281	.332	.436	.266
Abreu B.	49	37	42	248	147	4.44	69	16	0	7	106	52	33	1	1	2	3	10	2	5	.330	.419	.507	.324
Matsui H.	32	32	29	201	126	4.06	52	9	0	8	85	23	27	2	0	0	2	1	0	6	.302	.393	.494	.309
Cairo M.	27	28	30	244	174	3.61	53	12	3	0	71	31	13	0	1	5	3	13	1	4	.239	.280	.320	.212
Phillips A.	23	30	29	263	198	3.57	59	11	3	7	97	56	15	0	0	0	2	3	2	9	.240	.281	.394	.232
Sheffield G.	22	22	25	166	113	3.76	45	5	0	6	68	16	13	2	1	0	1	5	1	6	.298	.355	.450	.280
Green N.	10	8	4	82	58	3.87	18	5	0	2	29	29	5	0	1	1	0	1	1	0	.240	.296	.387	.237
Guiel A.	9	16	11	92	64	4.01	21	3	0	4	36	20	7	0	3	0	0	2	1	2	.256	.337	.439	.269
Stinnett K.	7	6	9	87	61	4.15	18	3	0	1	24	29	5	1	1	2	0	0	0	0	.228	.282	.304	.209
Crosby B.	7	9	6	96	70	3.46	18	3	1	1	26	21	4	0	2	3	0	3	1	0	.207	.258	.299	.196
Thompson K.	6	5	6	37	21	4.68	9	3	0	1	15	9	6	0	0	1	0	2	0	0	.300	.417	.500	.322
Wilson C.	5	15	8	109	86	3.81	22	4	0	4	38	34	4	0	1	0	0	0	0	4	.212	.248	.365	.209
Fasano S.	3	3	5	57	43	3.74	7	4	0	1	14	14	2	0	3	3	0	0	0	1	.143	.222	.286	.176
Reese K.	3	2	1	14	7	3.29	5	0	0	0	5	1	1	0	1	0	0	1	0	0	.417	.500	.417	.339
Long T.	2	6	2	40	30	4.20	6	1	0	0	7	8	4	0	0	0	0	0	0	0	.167	.250	.194	.166
Cannizaro A.	1	5	1	9	7	4.11	2	0	0	1	5	1	1	0	0	0	0	0	0	1	.250	.333	.625	.315
Johnson R.	0	0	0	6	5	3.50	1	0	0	0	1	4	0	0	0	0	0	0	0	0	.167	.167	.167	.120
Chacon S.	0	1	0	3	2	4.00	0	0	0	0	0	1	1	0	0	0	0	0	0	0	.000	.333	.000	.154
Wright J.	0	0	1	5	3	4.00	0	0	0	0	0	1	1	0	0	0	1	0	0	0	.000	.200	.000	.093
Small A.	-0	0	0	2	1	3.00	0	0	0	0	0	1	0	0	0	1	0	0	0	0	.000	.000	.000	.000
Rivera M.	-0	0	0	1	1	3.00	0	0	0	0	0	1	0	0	0	0	0	0	0	0	.000	.000	.000	.000
Beam T.	-0	0	0	1	1	5.00	0	0	0	0	0	1	0	0	0	0	0	0	0	0	.000	.000	.000	.000
Mussina M.	-0	0	0	4	4	3.25	0	0	0	0	0	1	0	0	0	0	0	0	0	0	.000	.000	.000	.000
Wang C.	-0	0	0	4	4	3.50	0	0	0	0	0	3	0	0	0	0	0	0	0	0	.000	.000	.000	.000
Nieves W.	-1	0	0	6	6	4.33	0	0	0	0	0	1	0	0	0	0	0	0	0	0	.000	.000	.000	.000

Italicized stats have been adjusted for home park.

Batted Ball Batting Stats are listed after fielding stats

Pitching Stats

Player	PRC	IP	BFP	G	GS	P/PA	K	BB	IBB	HBP	H	HR	DP	DER	SB	CS	PO	W	L	Sv	Op	Hld	RA	ERA	FIP
Mussina M.	99	197.3	804	32	32	3.78	172	35	1	5	184	22	20	.698	15	4	0	15	7	0	0	0	4.01	3.51	3.56
Wang C.	93	218.0	900	34	33	3.39	76	52	4	2	233	12	36	.699	9	11	1	19	6	1	1	0	3.80	3.63	3.97
Johnson R.	75	205.0	860	33	33	3.79	172	60	1	10	194	28	16	.705	21	10	1	17	11	0	0	0	5.49	5.00	4.37
Rivera M.	64	75.0	293	63	0	3.76	55	11	4	5	61	3	10	.721	3	3	0	5	5	34	37	0	1.92	1.80	2.80
Proctor S.	56	102.3	426	83	0	3.74	89	33	6	2	89	12	7	.717	7	2	0	6	4	1	8	26	3.61	3.52	3.90
Wright J.	54	140.3	625	30	27	3.77	84	57	0	7	157	10	16	.670	3	4	0	11	7	0	0	1	4.87	4.49	4.36
Bruney B.	33	20.7	90	19	0	4.30	25	15	0	1	14	1	2	.708	1	1	0	1	1	0	0	4	0.87	0.87	3.79
Farnsworth K.	31	66.0	289	72	0	3.82	75	28	3	1	62	8	2	.684	6	2	0	3	6	6	10	19	4.64	4.36	3.75
Villone R.	31	80.3	365	70	0	4.06	72	51	9	4	75	9	3	.703	1	3	3	3	3	0	1	6	5.38	5.04	4.64
Lidle C.	17	45.3	203	10	9	3.80	32	19	1	3	49	11	3	.710	3	4	0	4	3	0	0	0	5.16	5.16	6.40
Karstens J.	17	42.7	178	8	6	3.39	16	11	2	1	40	6	2	.750	2	0	0	2	1	0	0	0	4.22	3.80	5.04
Myers M.	14	30.7	133	62	0	3.98	22	10	1	3	29	3	2	.716	4	2	1	1	2	0	1	18	4.11	3.23	4.27
Chacon S.	14	63.0	306	17	11	3.83	35	36	2	5	77	11	5	.680	5	0	0	5	3	0	0	0	7.71	7.00	6.28
Rasner D.	8	20.3	83	6	3	4.02	11	5	0	1	18	2	2	.750	0	0	0	3	1	0	0	0	4.43	4.43	4.34
Veras E.	5	10.0	39	11	0	4.33	5	5	0	0	7	2	2	.815	1	1	0	0	0	1	1	1	3.60	3.60	6.36
Small A.	4	27.7	137	11	3	3.47	12	12	1	1	42	9	4	.650	1	0	0	0	3	0	0	0	9.43	8.46	7.93
Henn S.	4	9.3	44	4	1	3.93	7	5	0	1	11	2	1	.690	0	0	0	0	1	0	0	0	4.82	4.82	6.48
Beam T.	4	18.0	85	20	0	4.01	12	6	2	2	26	5	3	.650	1	0	0	2	0	0	1	2	8.50	8.50	6.54
Ponson S.	2	16.3	81	5	3	3.81	15	7	0	0	26	3	1	.554	3	0	1	0	1	0	0	0	11.02	10.47	5.10
Sturtze T.	2	10.7	56	18	0	4.00	6	6	0	1	17	3	1	.650	1	0	0	0	0	0	0	3	8.44	7.59	7.76
Wilson K.	2	8.3	42	5	1	3.83	6	4	0	0	14	4	1	.643	0	0	0	0	0	0	0	0	8.64	8.64	9.50
Erickson S.	1	11.3	57	9	0	4.21	2	7	2	3	13	2	2	.721	2	0	0	0	0	0	0	2	9.53	7.94	7.32
Dotel O.	1	10.0	59	14	0	4.07	7	11	1	0	18	2	1	.590	1	0	0	0	0	0	0	1	11.70	10.80	7.46
Bean C.	0	2.0	10	2	0	4.70	1	2	0	1	2	0	1	.667	1	0	0	0	0	0	0	0	9.00	9.00	6.76
Veras J.	0	1.0	4	1	0	4.25	1	0	0	0	1	0	0	.667	1	0	0	0	0	0	0	0	9.00	9.00	1.26
Smith M.	0	12.0	46	12	0	4.30	9	8	1	0	4	0	2	.862	0	0	0	0	0	0	0	0	0.00	0.00	3.51

Batted Ball Pitching Stats are listed after fielding stats

Fielding Stats

Name	POS	INN	SBA/G	CS%	ERA	WP+PB/G	PO	A	TE	FE
Posada, J.	C	1050.7	0.84	35%	4.37	0.428	789	66	8	1
Stinnett, K.	C	221.7	0.97	17%	4.38	0.244	169	10	2	0
Fasano, S.	C	152.3	0.53	33%	4.84	0.236	104	9	1	0
Nieves, W.	C	19.0	1.42	33%	4.74	1.421	15	1	0	0

Name	POS	Inn	PO	A	TE	FE	FPct	RF	DPS	DPT
Phillips, A.	1B	533.0	536	27	2	4	.988	9.51	5	2
Giambi, J.	1B	480.0	457	11	4	3	.985	8.78	1	1
Wilson, C.	1B	228.0	226	8	0	2	.992	9.24	1	0
Cairo, M.	1B	71.7	60	5	0	0	1.000	8.16	0	0
Guiel, A.	1B	68.0	69	1	0	0	1.000	9.26	0	0
Sheffield, G.	1B	57.0	56	3	0	1	.983	9.32	0	0
Posada, J.	1B	3.0	2	0	0	0	1.000	6.00	0	0
Damon, J.	1B	2.0	3	0	0	0	1.000	13.50	0	0
Green, N.	1B	1.0	1	1	0	0	1.000	18.00	0	0
Cano, R.	2B	1009.0	230	333	3	6	.984	5.02	34	39
Cairo, M.	2B	323.7	79	116	0	2	.990	5.42	7	19
Green, N.	2B	103.0	37	29	0	1	.985	5.77	2	4
Cannizaro, A.	2B	6.0	0	0	0	0	0.000	0.00	0	0
Phillips, A.	2B	2.0	0	1	0	0	1.000	4.50	0	0
Jeter, D.	SS	1292.0	214	381	8	7	.975	4.14	46	33
Cairo, M.	SS	99.3	18	28	0	1	.979	4.17	4	4
Green, N.	SS	35.0	10	11	1	1	.913	5.40	2	2
Cannizaro, A.	SS	17.0	5	5	1	0	.909	5.29	0	0
Rodriguez, A.	3B	1287.0	96	261	14	10	.937	2.50	22	0
Green, N.	3B	80.0	7	18	2	0	.926	2.81	4	0
Cairo, M.	3B	41.0	3	8	0	0	1.000	2.41	0	0
Phillips, A.	3B	26.0	1	6	0	0	1.000	2.42	1	0
Cannizaro, A.	3B	9.0	0	0	0	0	0.000	0.00	0	0

Name	POS	Inn	PO	A	TE	FE	FPct	RF	DPS	DPT
Cabrera, M.	LF	998.7	217	12	0	1	.996	2.06	2	0
Matsui, H.	LF	289.0	82	1	0	1	.988	2.58	2	0
Crosby, B.	LF	45.0	11	1	0	0	1.000	2.40	0	0
Williams, B.	LF	41.0	12	0	0	0	1.000	2.63	0	0
Guiel, A.	LF	18.0	3	0	0	0	1.000	1.50	0	0
Long, T.	LF	17.0	2	1	0	0	1.000	1.59	0	0
Thompson, K.	LF	15.0	6	0	0	0	1.000	3.60	0	0
Cairo, M.	LF	11.0	3	0	0	0	1.000	2.45	0	0
Reese, K.	LF	9.0	1	0	0	1	.500	1.00	0	0
Damon, J.	CF	1086.0	306	3	1	2	.990	2.56	2	0
Williams, B.	CF	200.0	44	0	0	0	1.000	1.98	0	0
Crosby, B.	CF	117.0	34	0	0	0	1.000	2.62	0	0
Cabrera, M.	CF	23.0	8	0	0	0	1.000	3.13	0	0
Guiel, A.	CF	7.0	3	0	0	0	1.000	3.86	0	0
Abreu, B.	CF	4.0	1	0	0	0	1.000	2.25	0	0
Long, T.	CF	3.0	2	0	0	0	1.000	6.00	0	0
Thompson, K.	CF	3.0	1	0	0	0	1.000	3.00	0	0
Abreu, B.	RF	447.0	113	6	0	2	.983	2.40	1	0
Williams, B.	RF	425.3	98	1	0	1	.990	2.09	0	0
Sheffield, G.	RF	165.0	39	1	0	1	.976	2.18	0	0
Guiel, A.	RF	109.0	26	1	0	0	1.000	2.23	0	0
Crosby, B.	RF	91.3	19	0	0	0	1.000	1.87	0	0
Cabrera, M.	RF	69.7	20	0	0	1	.952	2.58	0	0
Thompson, K.	RF	64.0	15	0	0	0	1.000	2.11	0	0
Long, T.	RF	54.3	18	0	0	1	.947	2.98	0	0
Reese, K.	RF	11.0	1	0	0	0	1.000	0.82	0	0
Wilson, C.	RF	7.0	2	0	0	0	1.000	2.57	0	0

Batted Ball Batting Stats

Player	PA	% of PA		% of Batted Balls					Runs Per Event				Total Runs vs. Avg.				
		K%	BB%	GB%	LD%	FB%	IF/F	HR/OF	NIP	GB	LD	OF	NIP	GB	LD	FB	Tot
Giambi J.	579	18	22	30	16	53	.11	.22	.14	.00	.37	.33	24	-8	-11	28	32
Jeter D.	715	14	11	59	22	18	.02	.15	.09	.07	.43	.32	7	12	10	-1	28
Rodriguez A.	674	21	15	42	18	40	.12	.22	.08	.06	.41	.35	9	1	-5	22	27
Posada J.	544	18	14	38	20	42	.05	.14	.09	.04	.38	.25	8	-2	-2	13	17
Damon J.	671	13	11	41	19	40	.15	.14	.10	.05	.39	.23	6	2	0	7	16
Cano R.	508	11	4	52	20	28	.13	.14	.01	.07	.43	.26	-6	8	9	4	15
Abreu B.	248	21	14	38	28	34	.02	.13	.07	.06	.35	.31	3	-0	2	6	10
Matsui H.	201	11	13	39	17	44	.03	.09	.13	.06	.53	.12	4	1	3	-1	6
Sheffield G.	166	10	8	49	15	37	.12	.11	.10	.09	.42	.16	1	3	-1	-1	3
Cabrera M.	525	11	11	49	17	33	.13	.06	.11	.06	.42	.13	6	4	-1	-9	1
Williams B.	462	11	8	50	18	32	.08	.11	.07	.02	.39	.19	-0	-4	1	1	-2
Wilson C.	109	31	5	49	17	34	.08	.18	-.05	-.00	.47	.25	-4	-2	-0	1	-5
Phillips G.	263	21	6	44	20	35	.03	.11	-.02	.01	.37	.20	-5	-3	-0	2	-7
Cairo M.	244	13	6	53	16	31	.08	.00	.03	.07	.43	-.03	-2	4	-0	-13	-11
MLB Average		17	9	44	20	37	.11	.11	.05	.04	.39	.19	-	-	-	-	-

Batted Ball Pitching Stats

Player	PA	% of PA		% of Batted Balls					Runs Per Event				Total Runs vs. Avg.				
		K%	BB%	GB%	LD%	FB%	IF/F	HR/OF	NIP	GB	LD	OF	NIP	GB	LD	FB	Tot
Mussina M.	804	21	5	42	17	40	.16	.11	-.03	.04	.33	.21	-16	-1	-11	4	-25
Wang C.	900	8	6	63	17	20	.05	.07	.08	.02	.35	.18	-2	-1	-4	-14	-21
Rivera M.	293	19	5	54	16	30	.14	.05	-.01	-.00	.38	.13	-5	-5	-3	-6	-19
Proctor S.	426	21	8	33	18	49	.10	.09	.02	.08	.40	.10	-4	2	-3	-7	-11
Johnson R.	860	20	8	42	16	43	.12	.12	.02	.06	.41	.18	-7	4	-8	2	-9
Farnsworth K.	289	26	10	34	22	44	.19	.13	.01	.12	.30	.18	-2	4	-4	-3	-5
Karstens J.	178	9	6	33	16	51	.07	.08	.07	.09	.33	.08	-0	2	-2	-2	-2
Myers M.	133	17	11	47	14	38	.14	.09	.07	.05	.36	.16	1	0	-2	-1	-2
Villone R.	365	20	15	31	21	48	.10	.07	.09	.08	.43	.10	6	1	1	-7	-0
Wright J.	625	13	10	38	24	38	.15	.05	.09	.05	.42	.09	4	1	13	-16	2
Lidle C.	203	16	11	51	15	34	.08	.23	.07	.02	.39	.37	1	-2	-3	9	6
Small A.	137	9	9	45	25	30	.06	.29	.13	.05	.25	.51	1	2	-1	10	12
Chacon S.	306	11	13	34	16	50	.08	.10	.13	.10	.41	.20	6	3	-2	7	14
MLB Average		17	9	44	20	37	.11	.11	.05	.04	.39	.19	-	-	-	-	-

Oakland Athletics

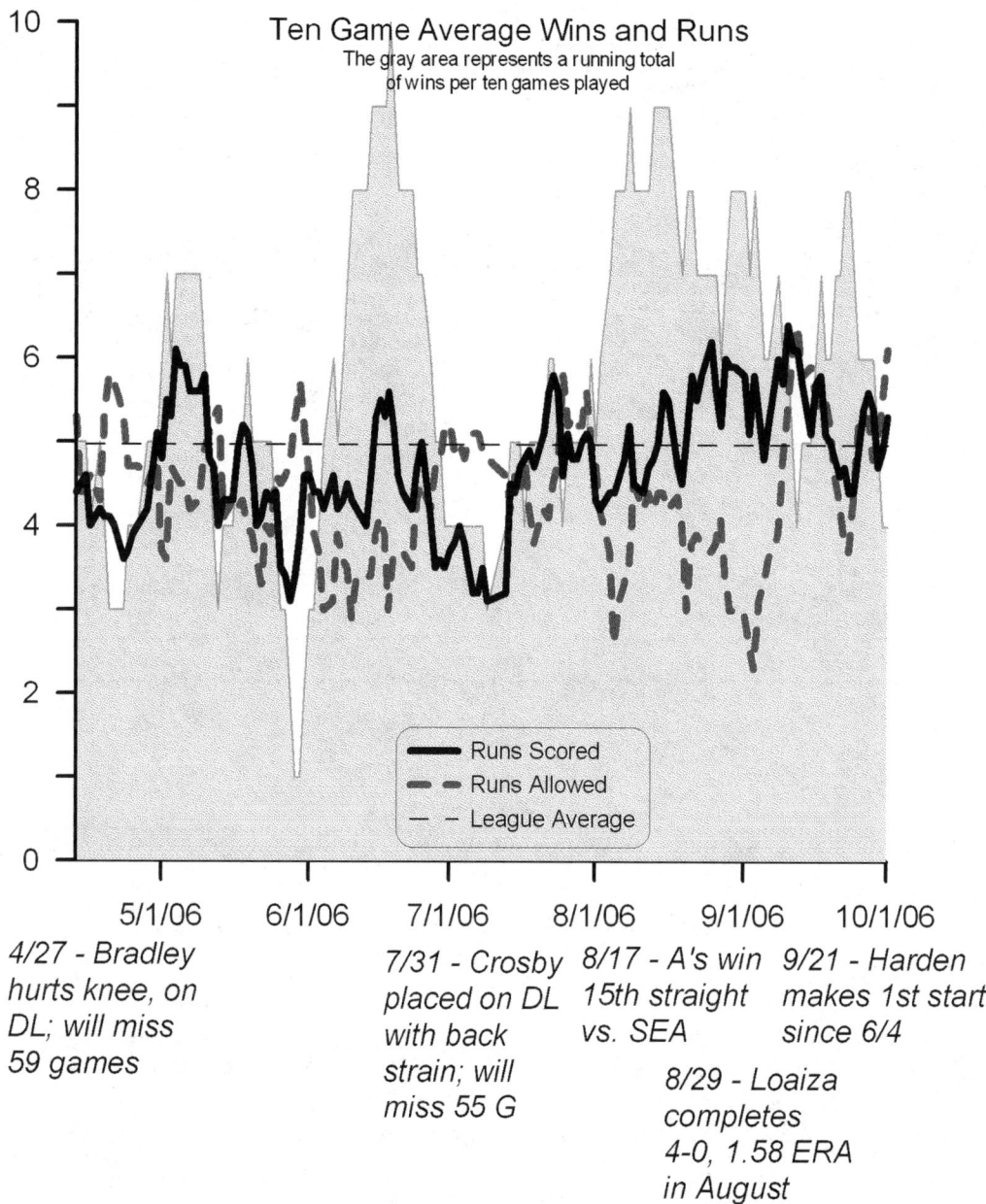

Ten Game Average Wins and Runs
The gray area represents a running total
of wins per ten games played

- Runs Scored
- Runs Allowed
- League Average

4/27 - Bradley hurts knee, on DL; will miss 59 games

7/31 - Crosby placed on DL with back strain; will miss 55 G

8/17 - A's win 15th straight vs. SEA

8/29 - Loaiza completes 4-0, 1.58 ERA in August

9/21 - Harden makes 1st start since 6/4

Team Batting and Pitching/Fielding Stats by Month						
	April	May	June	July	Aug	Sept/Oct
Wins	12	12	18	14	21	16
Losses	12	17	8	13	6	13
OBP	.316	.340	.331	.321	.367	.360
SLG	.408	.404	.384	.378	.442	.449
FIP	4.65	4.88	4.24	4.38	3.65	4.47
DER	.686	.703	.720	.688	.679	.664

Batting Stats

Player	RC	Runs	RBI	PA	Outs	P/PA	H	2B	3B	HR	TB	K	BB	IBB	HBP	SH	SF	SB	CS	GDP	BA	OBP	SLG	GPA
Thomas F.	96	77	114	559	353	4.36	126	11	0	39	254	81	81	3	6	0	6	0	0	13	.270	.381	.545	.311
Swisher N.	92	106	95	672	430	4.11	141	24	2	35	274	152	97	7	11	2	6	1	2	13	.254	.372	.493	.293
Kendall J.	78	76	50	626	413	4.08	163	23	0	1	189	54	53	2	12	4	5	11	5	19	.295	.367	.342	.253
Payton J.	74	78	59	588	408	3.13	165	32	3	10	233	52	22	1	4	0	5	8	4	12	.296	.325	.418	.253
Chavez E.	68	74	72	576	387	3.93	117	24	2	22	211	100	84	6	1	0	6	3	0	19	.241	.351	.435	.269
Kotsay M.	61	57	59	558	385	3.54	138	29	3	7	194	55	44	1	2	4	6	6	3	18	.275	.332	.386	.249
Bradley M.	59	53	52	405	269	3.75	97	14	2	14	157	65	51	1	2	0	1	10	2	13	.276	.370	.447	.281
Ellis M.	51	64	52	500	344	3.97	110	25	1	11	170	76	40	1	8	4	7	4	0	13	.249	.319	.385	.242
Scutaro M.	46	52	41	423	285	3.97	97	21	6	5	145	66	50	0	0	3	5	5	1	16	.266	.350	.397	.259
Kielty B.	39	35	36	297	206	3.57	73	20	1	8	119	49	22	0	2	2	1	2	0	9	.270	.329	.441	.261
Crosby B.	37	42	40	398	288	3.95	82	12	0	9	121	76	36	1	0	2	2	8	1	11	.229	.298	.338	.221
Johnson D.	32	30	37	331	225	4.04	67	13	1	9	109	45	40	2	0	0	5	0	0	6	.234	.323	.381	.243
Melhuse A.	9	10	18	139	107	3.64	28	8	0	4	48	34	9	1	1	0	1	0	1	6	.219	.273	.375	.219
Rouse M.	3	2	2	26	18	4.19	7	3	0	0	10	4	1	0	1	0	0	1	0	1	.292	.346	.417	.263
Perez A.	2	10	8	109	89	4.07	10	5	1	1	20	44	10	0	0	1	0	0	1	0	.102	.185	.204	.136
Bocachica H.	1	3	0	16	10	4.25	3	0	0	0	3	4	3	0	0	0	0	1	0	0	.231	.375	.231	.229
Brown J.	1	1	0	11	7	4.55	3	2	0	0	5	1	1	0	0	0	0	0	0	0	.300	.364	.500	.292
Jimenez D.	0	1	0	20	14	4.60	1	0	0	0	1	7	6	2	0	0	0	0	0	1	.071	.350	.071	.177
Clark D.	0	0	0	6	5	4.17	1	0	0	0	1	3	0	0	0	0	0	1	0	0	.167	.167	.167	.118
Flores R.	-0	0	0	1	1	4.00	0	0	0	0	0	0	0	0	0	0	0	0	0	0	.000	.000	.000	.000
Blanton J.	-0	0	0	3	2	2.67	0	0	0	0	0	1	0	0	0	1	0	0	0	0	.000	.000	.000	.000
Zito B.	-0	0	0	4	3	2.50	0	0	0	0	0	2	0	0	0	1	0	0	0	0	.000	.000	.000	.000
Loaiza E.	-1	0	0	6	5	4.00	0	0	0	0	0	3	0	0	0	1	0	0	0	0	.000	.000	.000	.000
Haren D.	-1	0	0	7	7	3.71	0	0	0	0	0	2	0	0	0	0	0	0	0	0	.000	.000	.000	.000

Italicized stats have been adjusted for home park.

Batted Ball Batting Stats

Player	PA	% of PA		% of Batted Balls					Runs Per Event				Total Runs vs. Avg.				
		K%	BB%	GB%	LD%	FB%	IF/F	HR/OF	NIP	GB	LD	OF	NIP	GB	LD	FB	Tot
Thomas F.	559	14	16	24	19	57	.16	.20	.12	.03	.37	.24	13	-5	-3	20	25
Swisher N.	672	23	16	33	19	48	.12	.19	.08	.03	.45	.27	11	-6	-1	14	19
Bradley M.	405	16	13	52	15	33	.09	.16	.09	.06	.40	.23	5	4	-5	2	7
Chavez E.	576	17	15	39	18	44	.16	.14	.10	.00	.44	.18	10	-8	-1	-1	0
Kielty B.	297	16	8	49	17	34	.07	.12	.04	-.02	.54	.21	-1	-5	4	1	-1
Payton J.	588	9	4	45	21	34	.15	.07	.04	.06	.35	.13	-5	6	6	-9	-2
Scutaro M.	423	16	12	44	21	36	.17	.06	.08	.05	.36	.14	4	1	-0	-7	-3
Melhuse A.	139	24	7	45	26	28	.11	.17	-.01	.01	.26	.28	-2	-2	-1	0	-5
Johnson D.	331	13	12	49	15	35	.08	.10	.11	-.00	.47	.13	4	-5	-1	-4	-6
Kotsay M.	558	10	8	46	19	35	.08	.05	.10	.02	.37	.09	2	-3	1	-10	-10
Perez A.	109	40	9	36	11	53	.11	.04	-.03	-.04	.39	.14	-3	-2	-4	-1	-11
Kendall J.	626	9	10	50	24	26	.10	.01	.14	.05	.32	.01	8	5	3	-27	-11
Ellis M.	500	15	10	39	19	42	.14	.07	.06	.04	.39	.09	1	-1	0	-11	-11
Crosby B.	398	19	9	47	18	35	.05	.09	.03	.03	.36	.11	-2	-1	-4	-7	-13
MLB Average		17	9	44	20	37	.11	.11	.05	.04	.39	.19	-	-	-	-	-

Pitching Stats

Player	PRC	IP	BFP	G	GS	P/PA	K	BB	IBB	HBP	H	HR	DP	DER	SB	CS	PO	W	L	Sv	Op	Hld	RA	ERA	FIP
Zito B.	104	221.0	945	34	34	3.88	151	99	5	13	211	27	33	.713	8	12	2	16	10	0	0	0	4.03	3.83	4.94
Haren D.	100	223.0	930	34	34	3.75	176	45	6	10	224	31	17	.698	10	4	1	14	13	0	0	0	4.40	4.12	4.15
Blanton J.	69	194.3	856	32	31	3.70	107	58	4	5	241	17	26	.658	13	5	1	16	12	0	0	0	5.14	4.82	4.21
Loaiza E.	54	154.7	679	26	26	3.51	97	40	3	5	179	17	13	.675	10	3	0	11	9	0	0	0	5.35	4.89	4.25
Saarloos K.	40	121.3	548	35	16	3.59	52	53	3	3	149	19	18	.682	7	5	0	7	7	2	3	0	5.19	4.75	5.75
Street H.	40	70.7	290	69	0	3.75	67	13	3	2	64	4	3	.696	5	1	0	4	4	37	48	1	3.57	3.31	2.61
Duchscherer J.	37	55.7	224	53	0	4.05	51	9	0	1	52	4	4	.692	5	1	2	2	1	9	11	17	2.91	2.91	2.90
Calero K.	36	58.0	241	70	0	4.22	67	24	3	0	50	4	4	.685	6	3	3	3	2	2	5	23	3.41	3.41	2.94
Halsey B.	34	94.3	431	52	7	3.69	53	46	7	5	108	11	12	.677	10	3	3	5	4	0	0	8	5.06	4.67	5.05
Gaudin C.	34	64.0	276	55	0	3.95	36	42	2	1	51	3	10	.753	6	0	0	4	2	2	3	11	3.38	3.09	4.67
Kennedy J.	25	35.0	148	39	0	3.80	29	13	3	1	34	1	6	.673	0	0	0	4	1	1	3	14	2.57	2.31	2.92
Harden R.	23	46.7	191	9	9	4.19	49	26	0	1	31	5	4	.764	2	3	0	4	0	0	0	0	4.24	4.24	4.29
Flores R.	16	29.7	122	25	0	3.76	20	10	2	0	28	3	6	.708	1	0	0	1	2	1	1	1	3.34	3.34	4.04
Witasick J.	7	22.7	111	20	0	3.89	23	21	2	1	25	3	4	.651	1	0	0	1	0	0	0	2	6.75	6.75	5.60
Keisler R.	4	10.0	42	11	0	3.86	5	2	1	0	14	3	4	.656	0	1	0	0	0	0	0	1	4.50	4.50	6.46
Sauerbeck S.	4	12.3	64	22	0	3.70	6	9	0	6	13	1	2	.690	1	0	0	0	0	0	0	3	5.84	3.65	6.99
Karsay S.	3	9.3	43	9	0	3.09	5	3	1	1	13	4	2	.700	0	0	0	1	0	0	0	2	5.79	5.79	8.73
Windsor J.	3	13.7	65	4	3	3.88	6	5	0	0	21	2	3	.615	2	0	0	0	1	0	0	0	7.90	6.59	5.38
Komine S.	2	9.0	45	2	2	3.76	1	8	1	0	10	3	1	.758	0	0	0	0	0	0	0	0	5.00	5.00	9.71
Casilla S.	0	2.3	10	2	0	3.20	2	2	0	0	2	0	1	.667	1	0	0	0	0	0	0	0	11.57	11.57	4.12
Roney M.	0	4.0	18	3	0	3.33	0	1	1	0	5	0	0	.706	0	0	0	0	1	0	0	0	4.50	4.50	3.26

Batted Ball Pitching Stats

Player	PA	% of PA		% of Batted Balls					Runs Per Event				Total Runs vs. Avg.				
		K%	BB%	GB%	LD%	FB%	IF/F	HR/OF	NIP	GB	LD	OF	NIP	GB	LD	FB	Tot
Street H.	290	23	5	37	21	42	.12	.05	-.03	.04	.35	.11	-6	-1	-1	-4	-12
Duchscherer J.	224	23	4	37	26	38	.10	.06	-.04	.05	.32	.08	-5	-0	1	-6	-11
Calero K.	241	28	10	35	21	44	.18	.07	.01	.13	.37	.07	-3	3	-2	-8	-9
Haren D.	930	19	6	45	19	36	.12	.12	-.00	.06	.42	.18	-13	4	4	-3	-8
Harden R.	191	26	14	43	24	32	.11	.06	.05	-.05	.44	.05	1	-5	2	-5	-8
Gaudin C.	276	13	16	39	16	45	.13	.04	.14	.00	.38	.07	7	-3	-3	-8	-7
Zito B.	945	16	12	38	17	45	.13	.09	.08	.04	.43	.15	9	-5	-5	-5	-6
Kennedy J.	148	20	9	49	20	31	.09	.03	.04	.06	.24	.16	-0	1	-3	-2	-5
Flores R.	122	16	8	31	12	57	.10	.07	.04	-.00	.39	.17	-0	-1	-2	2	-2
Loaiza E.	679	14	7	42	20	38	.07	.09	.03	.06	.39	.16	-5	4	4	-1	2
Witasick J.	111	21	20	45	24	30	.25	.13	.11	.05	.40	.18	4	0	0	-1	3
Halsey B.	431	12	12	44	18	38	.17	.10	.11	.05	.42	.15	6	1	1	-3	5
Blanton J.	856	13	7	43	19	37	.16	.08	.06	.06	.42	.15	-2	6	8	-5	7
Saarloos K.	548	9	10	54	21	25	.05	.18	.12	.02	.35	.34	6	-3	1	11	15
MLB Average		17	9	44	20	37	.11	.11	.05	.04	.39	.19	-	-	-	-	-

Fielding Stats

Name	POS	INN	SBA/G	CS%	ERA	WP+PB/G	PO	A	TE	FE
Kendall, J.	C	1254.0	0.68	25%	4.09	0.344	924	54	4	0
Melhuse, A.	C	196.7	1.14	32%	4.99	0.229	131	12	0	0
Brown, J.	C	1.0	0.00	0%	9.00	0.000	2	0	0	0

Name	POS	Inn	PO	A	TE	FE	FPct	RF	DPS	DPT
Johnson, D.	1B	714.7	686	63	2	2	.995	9.43	12	0
Swisher, N.	1B	700.0	665	42	2	3	.993	9.09	5	0
Kotsay, M.	1B	24.0	28	0	1	1	.933	10.50	1	0
Melhuse, A.	1B	10.0	9	0	0	0	1.000	8.10	1	0
Ellis, M.	1B	3.0	1	0	0	0	1.000	3.00	0	0
Ellis, M.	2B	1070.0	273	357	1	1	.997	5.30	20	70
Scutaro, M.	2B	301.7	73	93	1	0	.994	4.95	11	21
Rouse, M.	2B	60.0	9	16	0	0	1.000	3.75	5	1
Jimenez, D.	2B	11.0	2	1	0	0	1.000	2.45	0	0
Perez, A.	2B	9.0	1	1	0	0	1.000	2.00	1	0
Crosby, B.	SS	828.0	145	268	4	8	.972	4.49	31	25
Scutaro, M.	SS	572.7	87	168	4	5	.966	4.01	25	11
Jimenez, D.	SS	26.0	3	7	0	0	1.000	3.46	0	0
Perez, A.	SS	25.0	6	8	0	0	1.000	5.04	2	0
Chavez, E.	3B	1165.0	105	281	2	3	.987	2.98	46	1
Perez, A.	3B	187.0	20	47	1	3	.944	3.22	3	0
Scutaro, M.	3B	78.0	4	21	1	1	.893	2.88	1	0
Melhuse, A.	3B	12.0	0	2	0	0	1.000	1.50	0	0
Jimenez, D.	3B	9.0	1	1	1	0	.667	2.00	0	0

Name	POS	Inn	PO	A	TE	FE	FPct	RF	DPS	DPT
Swisher, N.	LF	654.7	170	5	0	3	.983	2.41	6	0
Payton, J.	LF	454.0	118	3	0	2	.984	2.40	0	0
Kielty, B.	LF	335.7	80	0	1	0	.988	2.14	0	0
Scutaro, M.	LF	6.0	1	0	0	0	1.000	1.50	0	0
Bocachica, H.	LF	1.0	1	0	0	0	1.000	9.00	0	0
Clark, D.	LF	0.3	0	0	0	0	0.000	0.00	0	0
Kotsay, M.	CF	1047.0	281	6	0	2	.993	2.47	4	0
Payton, J.	CF	380.7	105	1	1	2	.972	2.51	0	0
Bocachica, H.	CF	22.0	2	0	0	0	1.000	0.82	0	0
Swisher, N.	CF	2.0	3	0	0	0	1.000	13.50	0	0
Bradley, M.	RF	802.7	191	4	2	2	.980	2.19	0	0
Payton, J.	RF	377.0	89	1	0	2	.978	2.15	0	0
Kielty, B.	RF	255.0	56	3	0	0	1.000	2.08	2	0
Bocachica, H.	RF	14.0	2	0	0	0	1.000	1.29	0	0
Swisher, N.	RF	3.0	1	0	0	0	1.000	3.00	0	0

Philadelphia Phillies

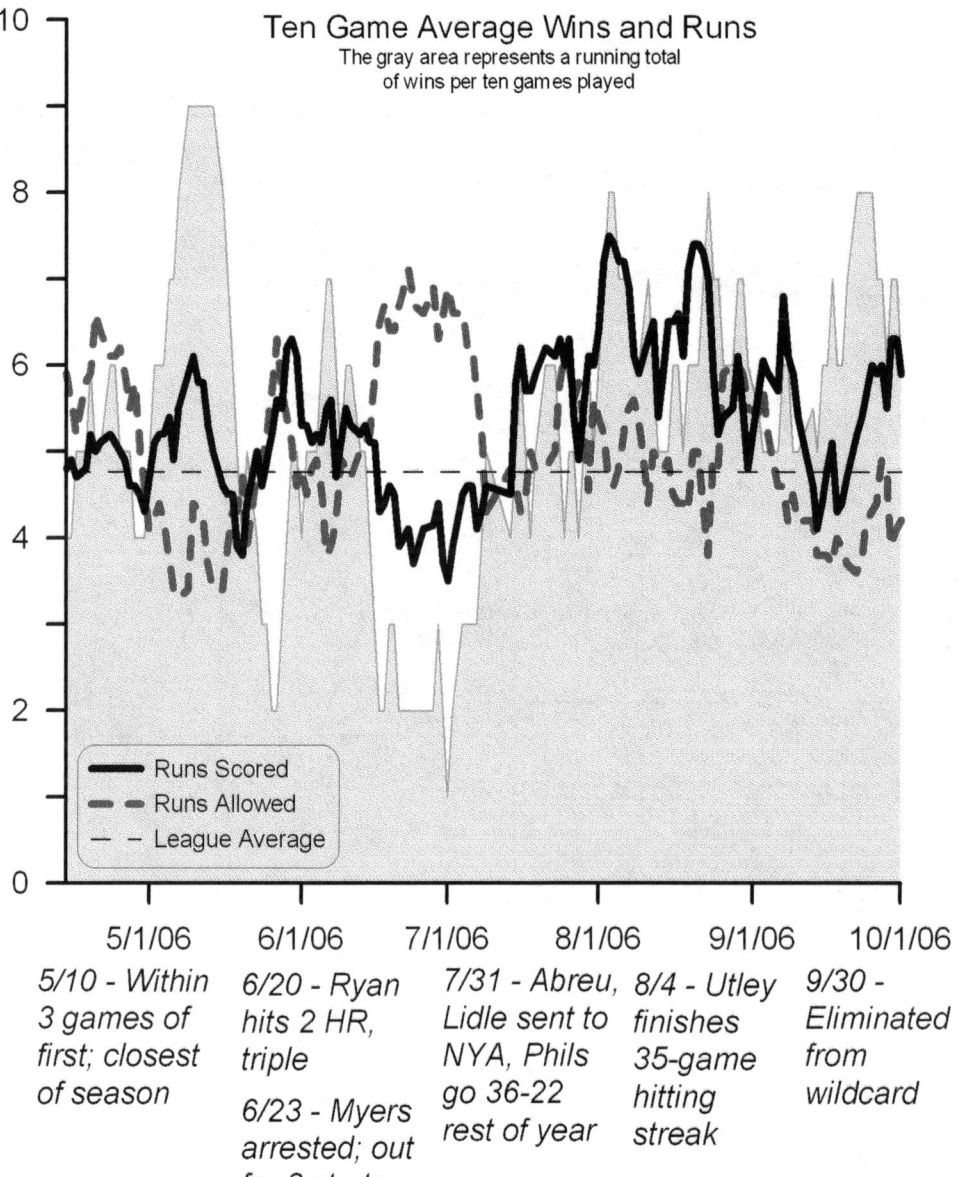

Ten Game Average Wins and Runs
The gray area represents a running total
of wins per ten games played

Legend:
— Runs Scored
- - Runs Allowed
– – League Average

5/1/06   6/1/06   7/1/06   8/1/06   9/1/06   10/1/06

5/10 - Within 3 games of first; closest of season

6/20 - Ryan hits 2 HR, triple

6/23 - Myers arrested; out for 3 starts

7/31 - Abreu, Lidle sent to NYA, Phils go 36-22 rest of year

8/4 - Utley finishes 35-game hitting streak

9/30 - Eliminated from wildcard

Team Batting and Pitching/Fielding Stats by Month						
	April	May	June	July	Aug	Sept/Oct
Wins	10	17	9	13	18	18
Losses	14	11	18	12	11	11
OBP	.330	.343	.315	.361	.361	.365
SLG	.427	.453	.414	.469	.457	.459
FIP	4.37	4.55	5.12	4.93	4.21	4.30
DER	.651	.704	.662	.692	.682	.707

Batting Stats

Player	RC	Runs	RBI	PA	Outs	P/PA	H	2B	3B	HR	TB	K	BB	IBB	HBP	SH	SF	SB	CS	GDP	BA	OBP	SLG	GPA
Howard R.	138	104	149	704	406	4.07	182	25	1	58	383	181	108	37	9	0	6	0	0	7	.313	.425	.659	.348
Utley C.	122	131	102	739	468	3.96	203	40	4	32	347	132	63	1	14	0	4	15	4	9	.309	.379	.527	.296
Rollins J.	114	127	83	758	514	3.70	191	45	9	25	329	80	57	2	5	0	7	36	4	12	.277	.334	.478	.264
Burrell P.	81	80	95	567	354	4.32	119	24	1	29	232	131	98	5	3	0	4	0	0	11	.258	.388	.502	.294
Abreu B.	76	61	65	438	257	4.47	94	25	2	8	147	86	91	5	2	0	6	20	4	8	.277	.427	.434	.294
Victorino S.	58	70	46	462	304	3.42	119	19	8	6	172	54	24	0	14	8	1	4	3	5	.287	.346	.414	.254
Rowand A.	47	59	47	445	316	3.40	106	24	3	12	172	76	18	2	18	2	2	10	4	13	.262	.321	.425	.245
Dellucci D.	43	41	39	301	191	4.00	77	14	5	13	140	62	28	0	6	0	3	1	3	1	.292	.369	.530	.292
Bell D.	42	39	34	365	245	3.67	90	17	2	6	129	38	32	2	3	3	3	1	0	11	.278	.345	.398	.249
Coste C.	36	25	32	213	139	3.77	65	14	0	7	100	31	10	1	5	0	0	0	0	6	.328	.376	.505	.289
Lieberthal M.	28	22	36	230	157	3.21	57	14	0	9	98	19	8	0	6	5	2	0	0	5	.273	.316	.469	.253
Nunez A.	27	42	32	369	261	3.69	68	10	2	2	88	58	41	8	2	3	1	1	0	7	.211	.303	.273	.200
Conine J.	14	11	17	107	73	3.38	28	6	1	1	39	12	5	2	2	0	0	0	0	1	.280	.327	.390	.239
Ruiz C.	10	5	10	78	54	3.49	18	1	1	3	30	8	5	2	1	2	1	0	0	3	.261	.316	.435	.245
Fasano S.	9	9	10	149	111	3.59	34	8	0	4	54	47	5	0	3	1	0	0	1	4	.243	.284	.386	.219
Hernandez J.	5	4	7	34	25	3.82	8	2	0	1	13	11	1	0	0	1	0	0	0	1	.250	.273	.406	.219
Sandoval D.	4	1	4	43	32	3.16	8	1	0	0	9	3	4	0	0	0	1	0	0	2	.211	.279	.237	.181
Roberson C.	2	9	1	43	33	3.74	8	0	1	0	10	9	0	0	1	1	0	3	0	0	.195	.214	.244	.154
Wolf R.	2	2	4	25	17	3.76	4	2	0	0	6	8	2	0	0	0	2	0	0	0	.190	.240	.286	.175
Simon R.	2	0	2	23	16	3.78	5	0	0	0	5	6	2	0	0	0	0	0	0	0	.238	.304	.238	.192
Madson R.	1	3	2	38	28	4.05	6	1	0	0	7	13	1	0	0	4	0	0	0	1	.182	.206	.212	.142
Geary G.	1	2	1	6	4	4.00	1	1	0	0	2	3	1	0	0	0	0	0	0	0	.200	.333	.400	.244
Thurston J.	1	3	0	20	14	3.30	4	1	0	0	5	2	1	0	1	0	0	0	0	0	.222	.300	.278	.200
Bourn M.	0	2	0	11	9	2.91	1	0	0	0	1	3	1	0	0	2	0	1	2	0	.125	.222	.125	.128
Hamels C.	0	4	3	53	40	3.51	5	0	0	0	5	24	6	0	0	2	1	0	0	1	.114	.216	.114	.123
Santana J.	-0	0	0	2	1	5.50	0	0	0	0	0	1	0	0	0	1	0	0	0	0	.000	.000	.000	.000
Lidle C.	-0	3	0	40	32	3.48	3	0	1	0	5	14	2	0	0	4	0	0	0	1	.088	.139	.147	.097
Condrey C.	-0	0	0	2	2	5.00	0	0	0	0	0	1	0	0	0	0	0	0	0	0	.000	.000	.000	.000
Franklin R.	-0	0	0	2	2	4.00	0	0	0	0	0	2	0	0	0	0	0	0	0	0	.000	.000	.000	.000
Mathieson S.	-0	0	0	9	6	2.44	1	0	0	0	1	4	0	0	0	2	0	0	0	0	.143	.143	.143	.098
Brito E.	-0	0	0	7	6	4.57	0	0	0	0	0	4	1	0	0	0	0	0	0	0	.000	.143	.000	.063
Fultz A.	-0	0	0	4	4	3.50	0	0	0	0	0	0	0	0	0	0	0	0	0	0	.000	.000	.000	.000
Castro F.	-1	0	0	2	3	5.00	0	0	0	0	0	1	0	0	0	0	0	0	0	1	.000	.000	.000	.000
Moyer J.	-1	1	0	22	17	3.59	1	0	0	0	1	5	1	0	0	3	0	0	0	0	.056	.105	.056	.060
Gonzalez A.	-2	4	1	38	35	3.79	4	0	0	0	4	10	2	0	0	0	0	0	0	3	.111	.158	.111	.097
Floyd G.	-2	0	0	23	22	3.35	1	0	0	0	1	12	0	0	0	0	0	0	0	0	.043	.043	.043	.030
Lieber J.	-3	0	0	63	49	3.79	5	0	0	0	5	28	4	0	0	6	0	0	0	1	.094	.158	.094	.093
Myers B.	-4	1	1	74	62	4.05	2	0	0	0	2	24	4	0	0	7	0	0	0	1	.032	.090	.032	.047

Italicized stats have been adjusted for home park.

Batted Ball Batting Stats are listed at end of fielding stats

Pitching Stats

Player	PRC	IP	BFP	G	GS	P/PA	K	BB	IBB	HBP	H	HR	DP	DER	SB	CS	PO	W	L	Sv	Op	Hld	RA	ERA	FIP
Myers B.	92	198.0	833	31	31	3.86	189	63	3	3	194	29	20	.689	13	5	2	12	7	0	0	0	4.23	3.91	4.17
Hamels C.	60	132.3	558	23	23	3.90	145	48	4	3	117	19	7	.700	9	2	0	9	8	0	0	0	4.49	4.08	3.96
Lieber J.	56	168.0	714	27	27	3.49	100	24	3	6	196	27	14	.680	8	3	0	9	11	0	0	0	5.36	4.93	4.60
Geary G.	48	91.3	390	81	0	3.77	60	20	4	6	103	6	17	.664	4	2	0	7	1	1	4	15	3.35	2.96	3.48
Lidle C.	45	125.3	542	21	21	3.68	98	39	4	8	132	19	12	.688	5	4	0	8	7	0	0	0	5.31	4.74	4.68
Madson R.	40	134.3	620	50	17	3.55	99	50	4	10	176	20	16	.630	14	6	1	11	9	2	4	6	6.16	5.69	4.93
Gordon T.	34	59.3	253	59	0	3.81	68	22	4	1	53	9	4	.706	6	0	0	3	4	34	39	0	3.49	3.34	3.86
Fultz A.	28	71.3	317	66	1	3.95	62	28	8	2	80	7	7	.651	5	2	0	3	1	0	2	9	4.92	4.54	3.68
Cormier R.	27	34.0	139	43	0	3.47	13	13	3	3	27	2	6	.759	1	0	0	2	2	0	4	12	1.59	1.59	4.37
Castro F.	21	23.3	88	16	0	3.99	13	6	0	2	12	1	3	.818	1	0	0	0	1	1	2	0	1.54	1.54	3.69
Moyer J.	20	51.3	209	8	8	3.54	26	7	2	2	49	8	7	.735	3	1	1	5	2	0	0	0	4.38	4.03	4.64
Franklin R.	19	53.0	233	46	0	3.55	25	17	4	4	59	10	6	.712	2	1	1	1	5	0	1	8	4.75	4.58	5.69
Wolf R.	18	56.7	261	12	12	4.05	44	33	2	2	63	13	3	.704	3	2	0	4	0	0	0	0	5.88	5.56	6.39
Rhodes A.	17	45.7	213	55	0	4.16	48	30	7	2	47	2	4	.649	2	0	0	0	5	4	7	23	5.32	5.32	3.33
Condrey C.	14	28.7	122	21	0	3.34	16	9	2	0	35	3	6	.649	1	1	1	2	2	0	1	1	3.45	3.14	4.19
White R.	13	37.3	158	38	0	3.76	23	15	0	0	38	3	8	.678	2	2	0	3	1	0	0	5	5.06	4.34	4.40
Floyd G.	11	54.3	264	11	11	3.78	34	32	3	3	70	14	6	.674	11	2	1	4	3	0	0	0	7.95	7.29	7.08
Smith M.	8	8.7	31	14	0	4.90	12	4	0	1	3	0	1	.800	1	1	1	0	1	0	0	6	2.08	2.08	1.83
Sanches B.	7	21.3	99	18	0	4.14	22	13	3	0	23	5	1	.678	0	1	0	0	0	0	0	0	5.91	5.91	5.61
Mathieson S.	7	37.3	177	9	8	3.82	28	16	1	1	48	8	2	.661	1	0	0	1	4	0	0	0	8.68	7.47	5.79
Brito E.	4	18.3	87	5	2	3.47	9	12	2	1	21	2	2	.698	1	0	0	1	2	0	0	0	7.36	7.36	5.45
Santana J.	1	8.3	43	7	0	3.95	4	9	1	1	8	1	1	.714	0	0	0	0	0	0	0	0	9.72	7.56	7.06
Bernero A.	0	2.0	15	1	1	4.07	0	2	0	0	7	3	0	.600	1	0	0	0	1	0	0	0	36.00	36.00	25.72

Batted Ball Pitching Stats

Player	PA	% of PA		% of Batted Balls			IF/F	HR/OF	Runs Per Event				Total Runs vs. Avg.				
		K%	BB%	GB%	LD%	FB%			NIP	GB	LD	OF	NIP	GB	LD	FB	Tot
Myers B.	833	23	8	46	18	36	.09	.14	.01	.05	.44	.21	-10	2	-0	1	-7
Geary G.	390	15	7	50	19	31	.04	.06	.03	.05	.40	.12	-3	2	1	-7	-7
Hamels C.	558	26	9	39	18	43	.08	.13	.01	.05	.38	.24	-6	-1	-7	9	-6
Cormier R.	139	9	12	47	19	34	.08	.06	.14	-.04	.36	.11	2	-5	-1	-3	-6
Gordon F.	253	27	9	45	23	31	.04	.19	.00	.04	.26	.30	-3	-1	-4	4	-5
White R.	158	15	11	63	17	20	.04	.14	.08	.02	.34	.31	1	-1	-2	-0	-2
Moyer J.	209	12	4	49	23	28	.19	.13	.01	-.00	.48	.17	-3	-3	7	-3	-2
Rhodes A.	213	23	15	36	22	41	.11	.04	.07	.10	.35	.15	2	2	-2	-3	-0
Condrey C.	122	13	7	48	29	23	.23	.18	.05	.03	.39	.28	-0	-1	4	-1	1
Fultz A.	317	20	9	38	23	39	.09	.08	.04	.07	.49	.14	-1	1	7	-4	4
Lidle C.	542	18	9	49	18	32	.06	.16	.04	-.00	.46	.31	-2	-9	3	13	5
Franklin R.	233	11	9	47	17	35	.09	.17	.10	.04	.45	.23	1	2	1	3	7
Lieber J.	714	14	4	43	22	35	.13	.15	-.01	.05	.36	.25	-11	3	5	10	7
Mathieson S.	177	16	10	35	24	41	.12	.13	.06	.11	.42	.26	0	2	3	4	9
Wolf R.	261	17	13	37	19	44	.21	.15	.09	.06	.51	.25	4	1	3	3	10
Floyd G.	264	13	13	39	24	37	.08	.17	.12	.10	.37	.27	5	4	3	6	17
Madson R.	620	16	10	43	22	35	.08	.13	.06	.11	.38	.24	1	12	2	8	23
MLB Average		17	9	44	20	37	.11	.11	.05	.04	.39	.19	-	-	-	-	-

Fielding Stats

Name	POS	INN	SBA/G	CS%	ERA	WP+PB/G	PO	A	TE	FE
Lieberthal, M.	C	484.0	0.80	33%	4.74	0.446	429	32	2	2
Coste, C.	C	434.3	0.64	19%	4.46	0.269	328	12	2	2
Fasano, S.	C	365.7	0.89	19%	4.85	0.517	267	24	2	0
Ruiz, C.	C	176.3	0.66	15%	4.13	0.561	148	10	1	2

Name	POS	Inn	PO	A	TE	FE	FPct	RF	DPS	DPT
Howard, R.	1B	1412.0	1369	91	6	8	.991	9.31	7	0
Gonzalez, A.	1B	23.0	17	4	0	0	1.000	8.22	1	0
Utley, C.	1B	18.0	15	0	0	0	1.000	7.50	0	0
Coste, C.	1B	4.3	3	0	0	0	1.000	6.23	0	0
Hernandez, J.	1B	3.0	2	0	0	0	1.000	6.00	0	0
Utley, C.	2B	1367.0	357	425	8	9	.978	5.15	42	73
Nunez, A.	2B	49.7	7	13	0	0	1.000	3.62	2	0
Sandoval, D.	2B	33.0	7	7	0	0	1.000	3.82	0	0
Thurston, J.	2B	10.3	6	2	0	0	1.000	6.97	1	0
Rollins, J.	SS	1378.0	213	446	8	3	.984	4.30	54	42
Sandoval, D.	SS	33.3	5	9	0	1	.933	3.78	3	2
Gonzalez, A.	SS	21.0	2	4	0	0	1.000	2.57	0	0
Nunez, A.	SS	21.0	0	4	0	0	1.000	1.71	1	0
Hernandez, J.	SS	7.0	1	4	0	0	1.000	6.43	0	1
Bell, D.	3B	781.3	55	186	7	7	.945	2.78	18	3
Nunez, A.	3B	632.0	36	151	5	3	.959	2.66	11	0
Hernandez, J.	3B	38.3	2	11	0	0	1.000	3.05	3	0
Gonzalez, A.	3B	8.7	1	0	0	1	.500	1.04	0	0

Name	POS	Inn	PO	A	TE	FE	FPct	RF	DPS	DPT
Burrell, P.	LF	987.7	204	8	1	2	.986	1.93	2	0
Dellucci, D.	LF	279.7	59	1	0	0	1.000	1.93	0	0
Victorino, S.	LF	101.0	22	2	0	0	1.000	2.14	0	0
Roberson, C.	LF	49.0	6	0	0	0	1.000	1.10	0	0
Conine, J.	LF	26.0	4	0	0	1	.800	1.38	1	0
Thurston, J.	LF	14.0	4	1	0	0	1.000	3.21	0	0
Bourn, M.	LF	2.0	0	0	0	0	0.000	0.00	0	0
Gonzalez, A.	LF	1.0	0	0	0	0	0.000	0.00	0	0
Rowand, A.	CF	900.7	251	6	2	3	.981	2.57	4	0
Victorino, S.	CF	557.7	161	6	0	0	1.000	2.70	4	0
Abreu, B.	CF	2.0	0	0	0	0	0.000	0.00	0	0
Abreu, B.	RF	846.0	178	5	1	0	.995	1.95	0	0
Dellucci, D.	RF	188.0	36	0	0	1	.973	1.72	0	0
Conine, J.	RF	171.3	32	0	0	0	1.000	1.68	0	0
Victorino, S.	RF	156.0	38	3	0	0	1.000	2.37	2	0
Roberson, C.	RF	54.7	13	0	0	0	1.000	2.14	0	0
Bourn, M.	RF	34.3	8	0	0	0	1.000	2.10	0	0
Hernandez, J.	RF	9.0	2	0	0	0	1.000	2.00	0	0
Thurston, J.	RF	1.0	1	0	0	0	1.000	9.00	0	0

Batted Ball Batting Stats

Player	PA	% of PA		% of Batted Balls					Runs Per Event				Total Runs vs. Avg.				
		K%	BB%	GB%	LD%	FB%	IF/F	HR/OF	NIP	GB	LD	OF	NIP	GB	LD	FB	Tot
Howard R.	704	26	17	42	22	36	.03	.39	.07	.06	.43	.58	11	-0	-1	52	61
Utley C.	739	18	10	37	20	43	.14	.15	.06	.08	.46	.26	2	7	7	15	31
Burrell P.	567	23	18	31	21	48	.13	.19	.09	.05	.39	.30	12	-3	-4	15	20
Abreu B.	438	20	21	49	25	26	.00	.10	.13	.05	.40	.20	16	-0	2	-5	13
Dellucci D.	301	21	11	37	19	44	.07	.14	.05	.08	.46	.27	1	2	1	9	13
Rollins J.	758	11	8	44	19	37	.11	.11	.09	.04	.44	.17	2	1	10	-1	12
Coste C.	213	15	7	40	29	31	.06	.14	.04	.06	.38	.20	-1	1	6	1	7
Lieberthal M.	230	8	6	38	17	45	.14	.11	.08	.05	.40	.19	-0	0	0	3	3
Conine J.	107	11	7	44	22	34	.17	.04	.06	.08	.32	.12	-0	1	0	-2	-1
Victorino S.	462	12	8	45	21	34	.23	.06	.08	.10	.36	.10	1	9	2	-13	-1
Rowand A.	445	17	8	44	22	34	.11	.12	.04	.04	.33	.23	-2	-1	-1	2	-1
Bell D.	365	10	10	44	22	34	.17	.06	.11	.05	.29	.15	3	1	-2	-5	-4
Fasano S.	149	32	5	46	13	41	.16	.13	-.05	.08	.52	.22	-5	1	-2	0	-5
Nunez A.	369	16	12	62	15	23	.12	.04	.08	.04	.37	.03	3	0	-6	-15	-17
MLB Average		17	9	44	20	37	.11	.11	.05	.04	.39	.19	-	-	-	-	-

Pittsburgh Pirates

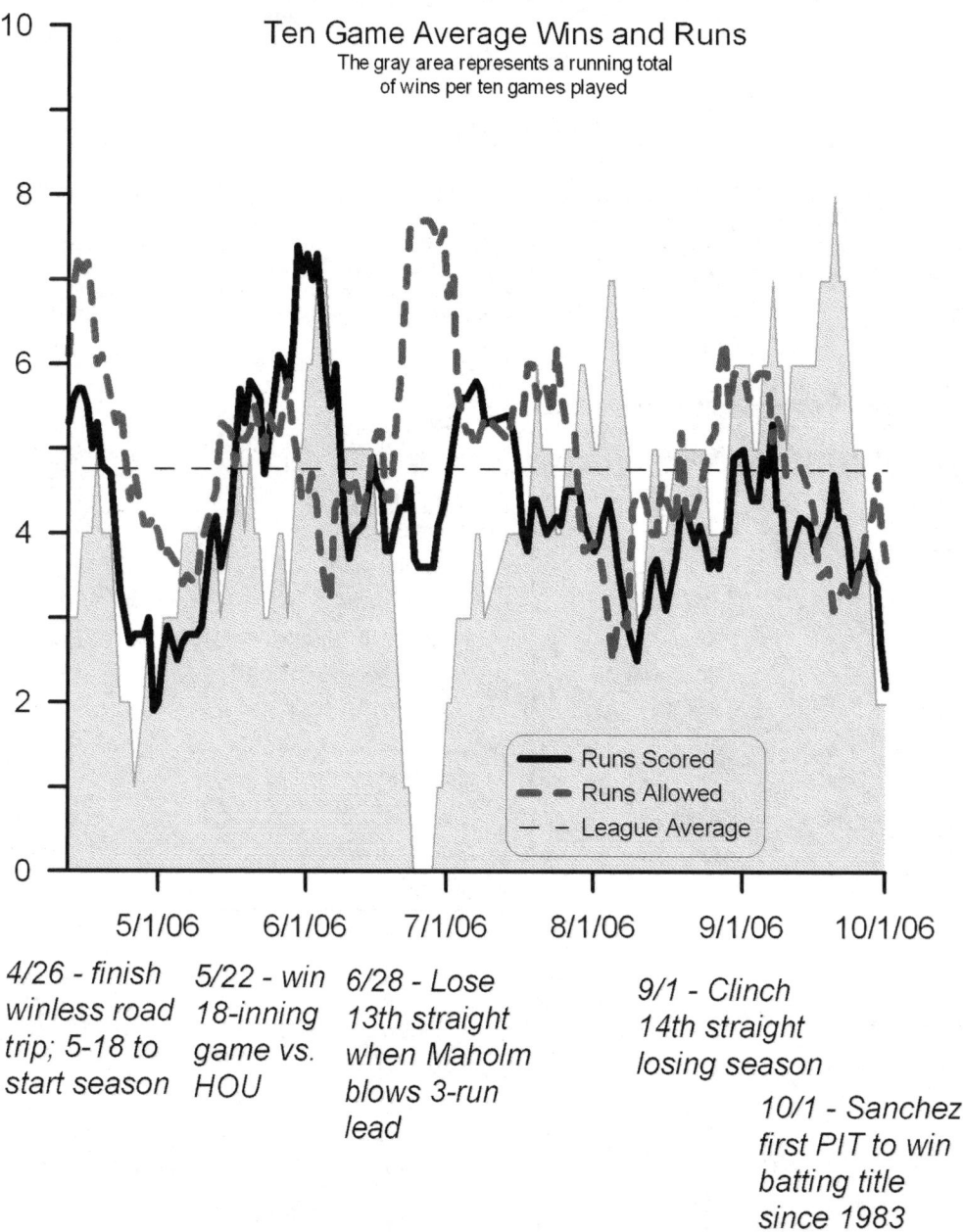

Ten Game Average Wins and Runs
The gray area represents a running total
of wins per ten games played

Legend:
— Runs Scored
- - Runs Allowed
- - League Average

4/26 - finish winless road trip; 5-18 to start season

5/22 - win 18-inning game vs. HOU

6/28 - Lose 13th straight when Maholm blows 3-run lead

9/1 - Clinch 14th straight losing season

10/1 - Sanchez first PIT to win batting title since 1983

Team Batting and Pitching/Fielding Stats by Month						
	April	May	June	July	Aug	Sept/Oct
Wins	7	12	8	13	13	14
Losses	19	15	20	12	15	14
OBP	.311	.345	.319	.350	.328	.304
SLG	.410	.445	.405	.398	.377	.344
FIP	5.30	4.08	4.29	4.18	4.46	4.44
DER	.670	.677	.643	.669	.680	.719

Batting Stats

Player	RC	Runs	RBI	PA	Outs	P/PA	H	2B	3B	HR	TB	K	BB	IBB	HBP	SH	SF	SB	CS	GDP	BA	OBP	SLG	GPA
Bay J.	105	101	109	689	424	4.02	163	29	3	35	303	156	102	9	8	0	9	11	2	15	.286	.396	.532	.308
Sanchez F.	103	85	85	632	396	3.43	200	53	2	6	275	52	31	6	7	3	9	3	2	12	.344	.378	.473	.285
Paulino R.	61	37	55	481	322	3.86	137	19	0	6	174	79	34	5	2	1	2	0	0	17	.310	.360	.394	.258
Wilson J.	59	70	35	594	413	3.80	148	27	1	8	201	65	33	0	4	9	5	4	3	15	.273	.316	.370	.232
Bautista J.	56	58	51	469	322	4.19	94	20	3	16	168	110	46	2	16	3	4	2	4	12	.235	.335	.420	.253
Castillo J.	54	54	65	562	413	3.53	131	25	0	14	198	98	32	8	5	1	6	6	4	22	.253	.299	.382	.228
Wilson C.	44	38	41	286	193	3.79	68	11	2	13	122	88	24	2	5	0	2	1	0	6	.267	.339	.478	.269
Duffy C.	37	46	18	348	236	3.75	80	14	3	2	106	71	19	1	10	4	1	26	1	1	.255	.317	.338	.225
Burnitz J.	36	35	49	343	250	3.82	72	12	0	16	132	74	22	4	5	0	2	1	1	8	.230	.289	.422	.233
Casey S.	33	30	29	244	157	3.67	63	15	0	3	87	22	23	5	6	0	2	0	0	7	.296	.377	.408	.269
Nady X.	27	20	23	220	149	3.56	61	13	0	3	83	34	11	3	5	1	0	1	2	5	.300	.352	.409	.258
McLouth N.	25	50	16	297	215	3.86	63	16	2	7	104	59	18	0	5	3	1	10	1	7	.233	.293	.385	.226
Randa J.	22	23	28	227	163	3.74	55	13	0	4	80	26	16	2	0	2	3	0	0	12	.267	.316	.388	.237
Doumit R.	17	15	17	178	121	3.84	31	9	0	6	58	42	15	1	11	1	2	0	0	3	.208	.322	.389	.240
Hernandez J.	12	8	12	132	91	3.73	32	2	1	2	42	29	11	0	0	1	0	0	0	3	.267	.328	.350	.233
Duke Z.	4	2	7	78	55	3.27	13	3	0	0	16	32	1	0	0	9	0	0	0	0	.191	.203	.235	.149
Cota H.	3	5	5	110	84	3.59	19	1	0	0	20	26	8	0	0	1	1	0	0	3	.190	.248	.200	.160
Youman S.	1	0	1	7	4	3.29	3	0	0	0	3	3	0	0	0	0	0	0	0	0	.429	.429	.429	.297
Perez O.	1	0	3	26	22	3.54	3	0	0	0	3	8	0	0	0	1	0	1	0	0	.120	.120	.120	.083
Vogelsong R.	1	1	0	5	2	4.20	1	0	0	0	1	2	2	0	0	0	0	0	0	0	.333	.600	.333	.350
Chacon S.	0	1	1	15	12	3.20	1	1	0	0	2	5	0	0	0	2	0	0	0	0	.077	.077	.154	.072
Edwards M.	0	1	0	18	14	3.50	3	0	0	0	3	5	1	0	0	1	0	0	0	1	.188	.235	.188	.151
Capps M.	0	1	0	3	2	3.33	0	0	0	0	0	1	1	0	0	0	0	0	0	0	.000	.333	.000	.148
Gonzalez M.	-0	0	0	1	1	4.00	0	0	0	0	0	0	0	0	0	0	0	0	0	0	.000	.000	.000	.000
Grabow J.	-0	0	0	1	1	4.00	0	0	0	0	0	1	0	0	0	0	0	0	0	0	.000	.000	.000	.000
Marte D.	-0	0	0	2	2	2.50	0	0	0	0	0	0	0	0	0	0	0	0	0	0	.000	.000	.000	.000
De Caster Y.	-0	0	0	2	2	4.00	0	0	0	0	0	2	0	0	0	0	0	0	0	0	.000	.000	.000	.000
Torres S.	-0	0	0	5	4	3.00	1	0	0	0	1	3	0	0	0	0	0	0	0	0	.200	.200	.200	.139
McLeary M.	-1	0	0	5	5	4.20	0	0	0	0	0	3	0	0	0	0	0	0	0	0	.000	.000	.000	.000
Santos V.	-1	4	1	44	33	3.36	6	1	0	0	7	13	0	0	0	6	0	0	0	1	.158	.158	.184	.116
Davis R.	-1	1	0	17	15	4.06	2	1	0	0	3	3	2	0	0	1	0	1	3	0	.143	.250	.214	.164
Maldonado C.	-1	0	0	20	17	3.85	2	0	0	0	2	10	1	1	0	0	0	1	0	0	.105	.150	.105	.093
Wells K.	-1	0	0	12	10	3.92	1	0	0	0	1	8	0	0	0	1	0	0	0	0	.091	.091	.091	.063
Maholm P.	-1	3	2	59	51	4.10	6	0	0	0	6	31	3	0	0	1	0	0	0	2	.109	.155	.109	.096
Gorzelanny T.	-2	0	1	21	19	3.76	0	0	0	0	0	11	1	0	0	1	0	0	0	0	.000	.050	.000	.022
Snell I.	-2	2	2	65	52	3.66	3	1	0	0	4	28	2	0	0	9	0	0	0	1	.056	.089	.074	.058

Italicized stats have been adjusted for home park.

Batted Ball Batting Stats are listed at end of fielding stats

Pitching Stats

Player	PRC	IP	BFP	G	GS	P/PA	K	BB	IBB	HBP	H	HR	DP	DER	SB	CS	PO	W	L	Sv	Op	Hld	RA	ERA	FIP
Duke Z.	78	215.3	935	34	34	3.50	117	68	6	7	255	17	31	.663	13	12	7	10	15	0	0	0	4.85	4.47	4.12
Snell I.	72	186.0	813	32	32	3.73	169	74	4	2	198	29	19	.677	16	5	0	14	11	0	0	0	5.03	4.74	4.59
Maholm P.	64	176.0	788	30	30	3.70	117	81	6	12	202	19	25	.665	13	11	9	8	10	0	0	0	5.01	4.76	4.77
Gonzalez M.	45	54.0	234	54	0	4.07	64	31	2	2	42	1	2	.699	3	0	0	3	4	24	24	3	2.17	2.17	2.81
Torres S.	43	93.3	411	94	0	3.59	72	38	9	6	98	6	13	.661	5	3	1	3	6	12	15	20	4.05	3.28	3.64
Capps M.	36	80.7	329	85	0	3.47	56	12	5	3	81	12	10	.707	3	3	0	9	1	1	10	13	4.13	3.79	4.14
Santos V.	33	115.3	522	25	19	3.90	81	42	3	4	150	16	14	.636	8	4	2	5	9	0	0	0	6.24	5.70	4.74
Grabow J.	31	69.7	303	72	0	3.52	66	30	3	3	68	7	7	.675	2	1	0	4	2	0	2	11	4.39	4.13	3.92
Gorzelanny T.	26	61.7	267	11	11	3.80	40	31	2	4	50	3	7	.730	4	2	2	2	5	0	0	0	4.23	3.79	4.16
Marte D.	26	58.3	255	75	0	4.02	63	31	6	4	51	5	5	.678	4	2	2	1	7	0	4	13	4.63	3.70	3.66
Perez O.	18	76.0	364	15	15	4.02	61	51	0	3	88	13	8	.665	4	1	1	2	10	0	0	0	7.58	6.63	5.97
Hernandez R.	16	43.0	202	46	0	4.05	33	24	7	1	46	3	4	.652	3	1	0	0	3	2	5	9	5.02	2.93	3.85
Chacon S.	13	46.0	210	9	9	3.62	27	27	1	4	47	12	6	.743	4	2	0	2	3	0	0	0	6.26	5.48	7.39
Sharpless J.	11	12.0	53	14	0	3.91	7	11	1	0	7	0	0	.800	5	1	0	0	0	0	0	2	1.50	1.50	4.55
Vogelsong R.	11	38.0	178	20	0	3.64	27	16	2	7	44	1	2	.659	6	1	0	0	0	0	0	0	6.39	6.39	4.14
McLeary M.	11	17.7	73	5	2	3.84	8	6	1	0	17	1	3	.724	4	0	0	2	0	0	0	0	2.55	2.04	3.90
Youman S.	10	21.7	88	5	3	3.86	5	10	0	0	15	1	2	.806	0	0	0	0	2	0	0	0	2.91	2.91	4.74
Wells K.	9	36.3	168	7	7	3.71	16	18	1	4	46	3	6	.661	2	3	0	1	5	0	0	0	6.69	6.69	5.14
Bayliss J.	7	14.7	69	11	0	3.54	15	11	2	1	13	1	0	.707	2	0	0	1	1	0	0	1	4.30	4.30	4.10
Rogers B.	2	8.7	38	10	0	3.58	7	2	0	1	11	2	2	.654	0	0	0	0	0	0	0	0	8.31	8.31	5.64
Reames B.	1	7.3	37	6	0	3.62	6	5	1	0	11	2	1	.625	1	0	0	0	0	0	0	0	9.82	9.82	6.76
Perez J.	1	3.3	17	7	0	3.24	3	1	0	2	5	1	1	.600	0	0	0	0	1	0	0	0	8.10	8.10	8.02

Batted Ball Pitching Stats

Player	PA	% of PA		% of Batted Balls					Runs Per Event				Total Runs vs. Avg.				
		K%	BB%	GB%	LD%	FB%	IF/F	HR/OF	NIP	GB	LD	OF	NIP	GB	LD	FB	Tot
Gonzalez M.	234	27	14	37	27	36	.13	.02	.04	.03	.36	-0.00	1	-2	0	-11	-12
Gorzelanny T.	267	15	13	49	18	33	.17	.06	.10	.01	.37	.13	4	-3	-3	-6	-8
Torres S.	411	18	11	55	19	26	.13	.09	.06	.05	.43	.15	2	2	-0	-9	-5
Marte D.	255	25	14	34	25	41	.14	.08	.05	.04	.41	.12	2	-1	1	-6	-4
Capps M.	329	17	5	41	20	40	.11	.14	-.02	.03	.35	.23	-6	-2	-1	5	-4
Grabow J.	303	22	11	49	18	34	.12	.09	.04	.07	.49	.18	-0	1	-0	-3	-2
Vogelsong R.	178	15	13	38	23	39	.09	.05	.10	.12	.41	.05	3	2	2	-6	0
Hernandez R.	202	16	12	49	18	33	.00	.07	.08	.05	.39	.19	2	1	-1	-0	2
Wells K.	168	10	13	52	20	29	.11	.09	.15	.01	.37	.28	4	-1	-0	2	4
Duke Z.	935	13	8	51	20	29	.07	.08	.07	.05	.44	.17	0	3	11	-9	5
Snell I.	813	21	9	43	21	36	.08	.16	.03	.07	.35	.27	-4	3	-5	12	6
Chacon S.	210	13	15	31	20	49	.10	.19	.13	.03	.38	.25	5	-2	-1	6	8
Maholm P.	788	15	12	53	20	27	.09	.13	.09	.04	.42	.23	8	2	4	-4	10
Perez O.	364	17	15	30	23	47	.12	.13	.10	.07	.38	.20	7	-0	0	4	11
Santos V.	522	16	9	44	22	35	.07	.12	.05	.05	.42	.25	-0	2	6	9	16
MLB Average		17	9	44	20	37	.11	.11	.05	.04	.39	.19	-	-	-	-	-

Fielding Stats

Name	POS	INN	SBA/G	CS%	ERA	WP+PB/G	PO	A	TE	FE
Paulino, R.	C	1047.0	0.79	27%	4.19	0.464	804	68	10	1
Cota, H.	C	242.3	0.85	22%	6.09	0.594	179	16	0	0
Doumit, R.	C	91.7	1.28	15%	6.09	0.589	66	12	1	0
Maldonado, C.	C	54.0	1.17	14%	1.83	0.167	27	3	1	0

Name	POS	Inn	PO	A	TE	FE	FPct	RF	DPS	DPT
Casey, S.	1B	461.3	470	20	0	0	1.000	9.56	4	0
Wilson, C.	1B	360.3	344	19	0	1	.997	9.07	3	0
Nady, X.	1B	236.3	247	32	1	1	.993	10.62	8	0
Doumit, R.	1B	208.3	212	12	0	3	.987	9.68	0	0
Hernandez, J.	1B	99.3	96	11	0	1	.991	9.69	1	0
Randa, J.	1B	69.3	69	4	1	0	.986	9.48	0	0
Castillo, J.	2B	1235.0	343	351	3	15	.975	5.06	39	69
Sanchez, F.	2B	165.3	39	39	0	0	1.000	4.25	7	7
Bautista, J.	2B	21.7	9	9	0	0	1.000	7.48	1	2
Hernandez, J.	2B	13.0	1	6	0	0	1.000	4.85	1	0
Wilson, J.	SS	1130.0	198	425	9	9	.972	4.96	52	34
Sanchez, F.	SS	240.0	47	88	2	2	.971	5.06	12	12
Hernandez, J.	SS	65.0	12	25	0	0	1.000	5.12	3	3
Sanchez, F.	3B	821.7	59	243	3	3	.981	3.31	23	0
Randa, J.	3B	312.0	31	70	1	3	.962	2.91	9	0
Bautista, J.	3B	267.3	22	56	0	6	.929	2.63	6	0
Edwards, M.	3B	19.0	2	3	0	0	1.000	2.37	0	0
Hernandez, J.	3B	15.0	0	7	0	0	1.000	4.20	0	0

Name	POS	Inn	PO	A	TE	FE	FPct	RF	DPS	DPT
Bay, J.	LF	1373.0	316	10	0	3	.991	2.14	1	0
Bautista, J.	LF	50.0	9	0	0	0	1.000	1.62	0	0
McLouth, N.	LF	8.0	2	0	0	0	1.000	2.25	0	0
Hernandez, J.	LF	4.0	1	0	0	0	1.000	2.25	0	0
Duffy, C.	CF	671.7	166	4	1	2	.983	2.28	4	0
Bautista, J.	CF	418.3	114	5	0	2	.983	2.56	2	0
McLouth, N.	CF	345.0	84	1	1	0	.988	2.22	2	0
Burnitz, J.	RF	643.0	120	1	0	2	.984	1.69	1	0
Nady, X.	RF	234.0	50	1	0	0	1.000	1.96	0	0
Wilson, C.	RF	194.0	37	2	0	0	1.000	1.81	0	0
Bautista, J.	RF	172.7	31	1	0	0	1.000	1.67	0	0
McLouth, N.	RF	164.3	23	0	0	1	.958	1.26	0	0
Hernandez, J.	RF	24.0	9	0	0	0	1.000	3.38	0	0
Davis, R.	RF	3.0	0	0	0	0	0.000	0.00	0	0

Batted Ball Batting Stats

Player	PA	% of PA		% of Batted Balls					Runs Per Event				Total Runs vs. Avg.				
		K%	BB%	GB%	LD%	FB%	IF/F	HR/OF	NIP	GB	LD	OF	NIP	GB	LD	FB	Tot
Bay J.	689	23	16	41	15	44	.04	.19	.08	.05	.46	.32	11	-2	-8	28	29
Sanchez F.	632	8	6	37	28	36	.10	.03	.08	.05	.41	.10	-1	2	25	-11	15
Wilson C.	286	31	10	34	17	50	.11	.17	.00	.16	.38	.29	-4	5	-5	9	5
Casey S.	244	9	12	45	23	32	.08	.05	.15	.02	.43	.09	4	-2	5	-6	2
Nady X.	220	15	7	47	20	33	.16	.06	.03	.08	.39	.14	-1	3	1	-4	-1
Doumit R.	178	24	15	46	17	38	.17	.15	.06	.03	.53	.15	2	-1	-0	-3	-3
Bautista J.	469	23	13	40	13	47	.18	.14	.05	.07	.44	.22	3	1	-10	3	-3
Hernandez J.	132	22	8	49	20	30	.11	.08	.01	.09	.42	.05	-1	2	0	-5	-4
Paulino R.	481	16	7	47	23	31	.09	.05	.03	.05	.38	.14	-3	1	4	-7	-4
Randa J.	227	11	7	37	20	43	.14	.06	.06	.01	.40	.11	-0	-3	2	-3	-5
Burnitz J.	343	22	8	43	15	41	.13	.17	.01	.02	.41	.24	-4	-3	-4	5	-6
Duffy C.	348	20	8	58	19	23	.08	.04	.02	.10	.34	.13	-3	8	-4	-9	-8
McLouth N.	297	20	8	39	25	35	.08	.10	.02	.01	.29	.18	-3	-3	-1	-1	-8
Cota H.	110	24	7	55	16	29	.36	.00	-.01	.06	.27	-.06	-2	1	-3	-6	-10
Wilson J.	594	11	6	47	23	30	.15	.06	.05	.03	.39	.06	-3	-1	9	-21	-15
Castillo J.	562	17	7	46	19	34	.06	.09	.01	.02	.33	.17	-6	-5	-4	-1	-16
MLB Average		17	9	44	20	37	.11	.11	.05	.04	.39	.19	-	-	-	-	-

San Diego Padres

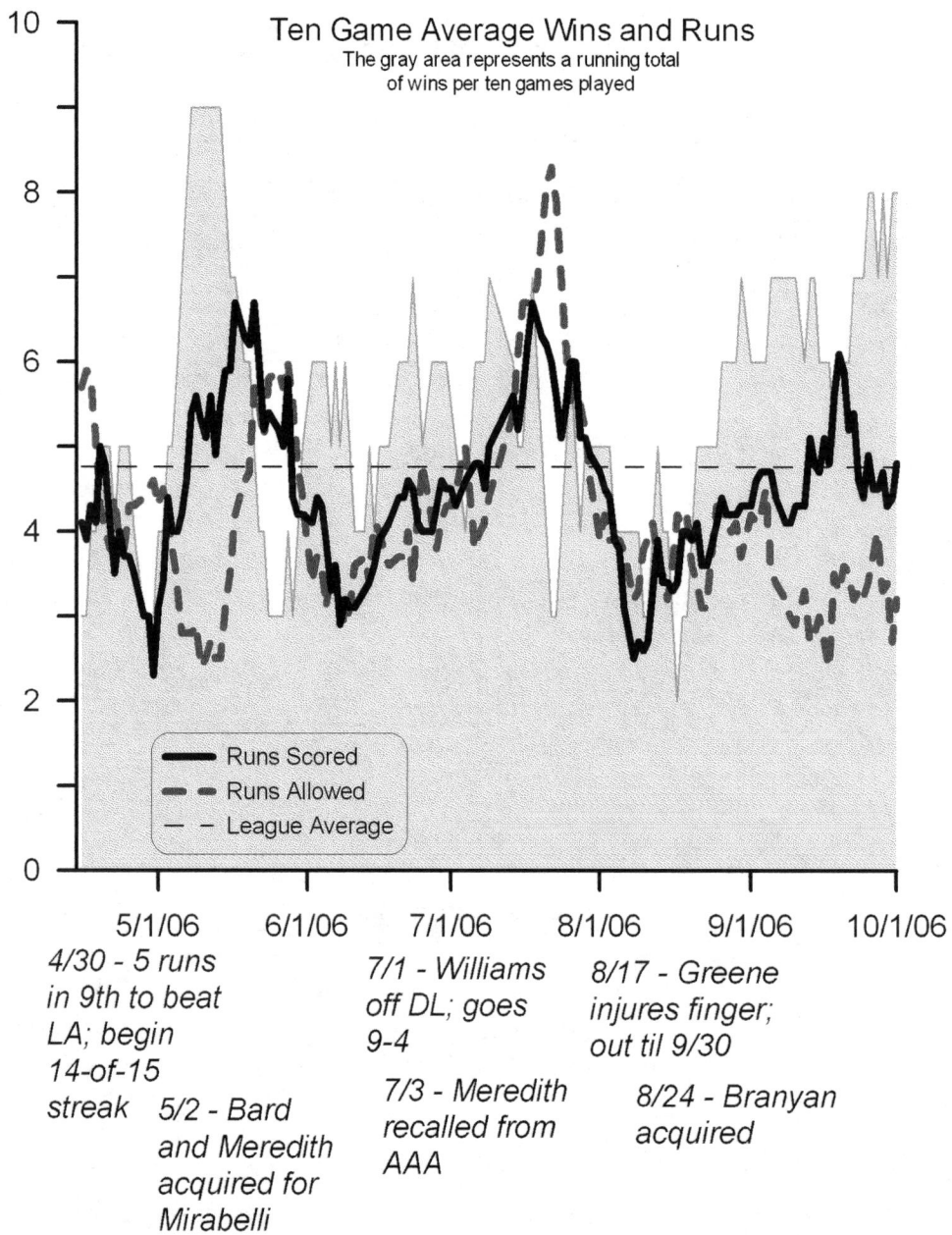

Ten Game Average Wins and Runs
The gray area represents a running total
of wins per ten games played

- Runs Scored
- Runs Allowed
- League Average

4/30 - 5 runs in 9th to beat LA; begin 14-of-15 streak

5/2 - Bard and Meredith acquired for Mirabelli

7/1 - Williams off DL; goes 9-4

7/3 - Meredith recalled from AAA

8/17 - Greene injures finger; out til 9/30

8/24 - Branyan acquired

Team Batting and Pitching/Fielding Stats by Month						
	April	May	June	July	Aug	Sept/Oct
Wins	9	19	14	13	13	20
Losses	15	10	12	13	15	9
OBP	.301	.337	.331	.356	.326	.337
SLG	.338	.422	.436	.482	.385	.425
FIP	4.34	4.19	4.01	4.79	3.80	4.09
DER	.715	.728	.723	.680	.707	.732

Batting Stats

Player	RC	Runs	RBI	PA	Outs	P/PA	H	2B	3B	HR	TB	K	BB	IBB	HBP	SH	SF	SB	CS	GDP	BA	OBP	SLG	GPA
Cameron M.	109	88	83	634	421	4.09	148	34	9	22	266	142	71	2	6	0	5	25	9	8	.268	.355	.482	.294
Giles B.	106	87	83	717	467	3.69	159	37	1	14	240	60	104	6	5	0	4	9	4	18	.263	.374	.397	.281
Gonzalez A.	92	83	82	631	422	3.90	173	38	1	24	285	113	52	9	3	1	5	0	1	24	.304	.362	.500	.302
Roberts D.	90	80	44	567	364	3.95	146	18	13	2	196	61	51	2	4	7	5	49	6	5	.293	.360	.393	.273
Barfield J.	76	72	58	578	401	3.51	151	32	3	13	228	81	30	7	2	2	5	21	5	8	.280	.318	.423	.261
Piazza M.	62	39	68	439	299	3.83	113	19	1	22	200	66	34	2	3	0	3	0	0	13	.283	.342	.501	.293
Greene K.	54	56	55	460	328	3.91	101	26	2	15	176	87	39	0	7	0	2	5	1	16	.245	.320	.427	.263
Bard J.	47	28	40	263	162	3.72	78	19	0	9	124	39	27	1	1	2	2	1	0	9	.338	.406	.537	.333
Blum G.	29	27	34	299	212	3.63	70	17	1	4	101	51	17	1	0	2	4	0	1	5	.254	.293	.366	.235
Bellhorn M.	26	26	27	288	208	4.16	48	11	2	8	87	90	32	0	2	0	1	0	0	3	.190	.285	.344	.225
Walker T.	23	18	13	142	90	4.01	35	6	1	3	52	11	17	1	0	0	1	2	0	1	.282	.366	.419	.283
Castilla V.	18	24	23	269	200	3.03	59	10	0	4	81	46	9	0	2	0	4	0	0	5	.232	.260	.319	.207
Bowen R.	14	22	13	110	73	4.15	23	5	0	3	37	26	13	0	1	1	1	0	1	1	.245	.339	.394	.264
Branyan R.	13	14	9	89	51	4.16	21	1	0	6	40	27	15	1	1	0	1	0	0	0	.292	.416	.556	.342
Johnson B.	11	19	12	135	93	4.04	30	5	2	4	51	36	14	2	1	0	0	3	0	3	.250	.333	.425	.269
Young E.	9	19	13	147	110	3.95	26	5	0	3	40	16	13	1	2	1	3	8	2	6	.203	.281	.313	.215
Peavy J.	8	6	9	69	50	3.45	10	3	0	2	19	19	1	0	0	8	0	0	0	0	.167	.180	.317	.168
Sledge T.	6	7	7	78	55	4.29	16	3	0	2	25	17	8	0	0	0	0	0	0	1	.229	.308	.357	.239
Williams W.	4	3	4	62	43	3.68	11	1	0	0	12	13	2	0	0	6	0	0	0	0	.204	.232	.222	.168
McAnulty P.	4	3	3	15	10	4.07	3	1	0	1	7	4	2	0	0	0	0	0	0	0	.231	.333	.538	.299
Park C.	3	0	5	48	32	2.71	11	0	0	0	11	12	0	0	0	7	0	0	0	2	.268	.268	.268	.197
Klesko R.	3	0	2	6	1	4.00	3	1	0	0	4	0	2	0	0	0	0	0	0	0	.750	.833	1.000	.656
Alexander M.	1	2	4	39	29	3.38	6	1	1	0	9	5	2	2	0	2	1	0	1	0	.176	.216	.265	.172
Mirabelli D.	1	1	0	26	18	3.35	4	1	0	0	5	5	4	0	0	0	0	0	0	0	.182	.308	.227	.205
Linebrink S.	1	0	0	1	0	1.00	1	0	0	0	1	0	0	0	0	0	0	0	0	0	1.000	1.000	1.000	.735
Brazelton D.	1	0	1	4	3	4.00	1	1	0	0	2	2	0	0	0	0	0	0	0	0	.250	.250	.500	.249
Stauffer T.	1	0	0	2	1	4.50	1	0	0	0	1	1	0	0	0	0	0	0	0	0	.500	.500	.500	.368
Cust J.	0	1	0	3	2	2.33	1	0	0	0	1	1	0	0	0	0	0	0	0	0	.333	.333	.333	.245
Wells D.	0	0	0	8	4	2.38	1	0	0	0	1	2	0	0	0	3	0	0	0	0	.200	.200	.200	.147
Estes S.	0	0	0	2	1	5.50	0	0	0	0	0	0	1	0	0	0	0	0	0	0	.000	.500	.000	.236
Young C.	0	2	4	62	47	3.52	7	2	1	0	11	26	0	0	0	8	0	0	0	0	.130	.130	.204	.115
Meredith C.	0	0	0	1	0	0.00	0	0	0	0	0	0	0	0	0	1	0	0	0	0	.000	.000	.000	.000
Leone J.	-0	0	0	1	1	3.00	0	0	0	0	0	0	0	0	0	0	0	0	0	0	.000	.000	.000	.000
Embree A.	-0	0	0	1	1	5.00	0	0	0	0	0	1	0	0	0	0	0	0	0	0	.000	.000	.000	.000
Cassidy S.	-0	0	0	1	1	3.00	0	0	0	0	0	1	0	0	0	0	0	0	0	0	.000	.000	.000	.000
Adkins J.	-0	0	0	1	1	5.00	0	0	0	0	0	1	0	0	0	0	0	0	0	0	.000	.000	.000	.000
Sweeney B.	-0	0	0	1	1	7.00	0	0	0	0	0	1	0	0	0	0	0	0	0	0	.000	.000	.000	.000
Thompson M.	-0	2	0	29	21	3.79	4	0	0	0	4	12	1	0	0	3	0	0	0	0	.160	.192	.160	.133
Knott J.	-0	0	0	3	3	3.67	0	0	0	0	0	1	0	0	0	0	0	0	0	0	.000	.000	.000	.000
Hensley C.	-2	2	2	56	44	3.52	4	1	0	0	5	28	3	0	0	5	0	0	0	0	.083	.137	.104	.092

Italicized stats have been adjusted for home park.

Batted Ball Batting Stats are listed at end of fielding stats

Pitching Stats

Player	PRC	IP	BFP	G	GS	P/PA	K	BB	IBB	HBP	H	HR	DP	DER	SB	CS	PO	W	L	Sv	Op	Hld	RA	ERA	FIP
Peavy J.	99	202.3	846	32	32	3.96	215	62	11	6	187	23	13	.691	25	6	0	11	14	0	0	0	4.14	4.09	3.42
Young C.	95	179.3	735	31	31	4.12	164	69	4	6	134	28	12	.765	41	4	1	11	5	0	0	0	3.61	3.46	4.61
Hensley C.	85	187.0	787	37	29	3.70	122	76	7	3	174	15	30	.708	12	4	1	11	12	0	1	1	3.95	3.71	4.11
Meredith C.	61	50.7	185	45	0	3.63	37	6	3	2	30	3	4	.803	4	1	0	5	1	0	2	16	1.07	1.07	2.82
Williams W.	59	145.3	624	25	24	3.66	72	35	3	7	152	21	14	.720	10	0	0	12	5	0	0	0	4.21	3.65	4.91
Park C.	47	136.7	606	24	21	3.61	96	44	7	10	146	20	11	.702	9	0	0	7	7	0	0	0	5.33	4.81	4.75
Hoffman T.	47	63.0	248	65	0	3.72	50	13	1	1	48	6	5	.753	2	0	0	0	2	46	51	0	2.29	2.14	3.49
Linebrink S.	39	75.7	314	73	0	3.95	68	22	3	1	70	9	3	.715	8	1	0	7	4	2	11	36	3.69	3.57	3.76
Embree A.	29	52.3	221	73	0	3.72	53	15	2	0	50	4	4	.671	12	1	0	4	3	0	0	16	3.61	3.27	2.93
Thompson M.	27	92.0	405	19	16	3.48	35	30	4	7	103	13	12	.709	6	0	0	4	5	0	0	0	5.48	4.99	5.37
Sweeney B.	26	56.3	237	37	0	3.82	23	16	5	1	53	6	7	.728	3	0	0	2	0	2	3	0	3.51	3.20	4.43
Cassidy S.	23	42.7	182	42	0	4.47	49	19	4	1	39	8	3	.686	1	4	1	6	4	0	2	4	3.80	2.53	4.62
Adkins J.	22	54.3	232	55	0	3.59	30	20	4	2	55	3	8	.701	2	1	0	2	1	0	0	8	4.31	3.98	3.83
Wells D.	14	28.3	118	5	5	3.31	14	4	0	0	33	1	4	.677	4	0	0	1	2	0	0	0	3.49	3.49	3.11
Brocail D.	10	28.3	119	25	0	3.47	19	8	2	0	27	1	2	.714	1	0	0	2	2	0	0	0	5.08	4.76	2.97
Sikorski B.	5	14.3	60	13	0	4.33	14	3	1	0	16	4	1	.667	0	1	1	1	1	0	0	0	5.65	5.65	5.31
Stauffer T.	3	6.0	21	1	1	3.14	2	1	0	0	3	0	0	.833	0	1	0	1	0	0	0	0	3.00	1.50	3.05
Williamson S.	3	11.0	49	11	0	3.94	10	6	0	0	14	2	1	.613	6	2	1	0	1	0	0	0	7.36	7.36	5.40
Estes S.	2	6.0	27	1	1	3.00	4	3	0	1	5	0	1	.684	0	0	0	0	1	0	0	0	4.50	4.50	3.88
Seanez R.	2	6.3	33	8	0	4.45	6	6	3	0	7	2	0	.737	0	0	0	1	2	0	1	0	5.68	5.68	6.85
Brazelton D.	2	18.0	91	9	2	3.36	9	9	1	0	28	6	1	.657	3	0	0	0	2	0	0	0	12.50	12.00	7.88
Brower J.	1	7.7	35	6	0	3.60	5	1	0	2	11	1	2	.615	1	0	0	0	0	0	0	0	9.39	9.39	4.78

Batted Ball Pitching Stats

Player	PA	% of PA		% of Batted Balls					Runs Per Event				Total Runs vs. Avg.				
		K%	BB%	GB%	LD%	FB%	IF/F	HR/OF	NIP	GB	LD	OF	NIP	GB	LD	FB	Tot
Young C.	735	22	10	25	18	56	.16	.12	.03	.02	.35	.16	-3	-8	-10	1	-20
Meredith C.	185	20	4	69	16	15	.14	.17	-.03	-.02	.30	.16	-4	-5	-4	-5	-18
Hensley C.	787	16	10	54	17	30	.10	.10	.07	.02	.38	.19	3	-4	-8	-7	-16
Peavy J.	846	25	8	38	18	44	.09	.10	-.00	.01	.39	.25	-12	-9	-8	15	-14
Hoffman T.	248	20	6	32	22	45	.18	.06	-.01	-.01	.36	.03	-4	-4	1	-7	-14
Linebrink S.	314	22	7	39	19	42	.15	.10	.00	.09	.31	.14	-4	3	-4	-4	-9
Sweeney B.	237	10	7	39	20	40	.12	.07	.08	-.02	.38	.12	0	-5	2	-3	-6
Embree A.	221	24	7	43	20	37	.11	.06	-.01	.08	.41	.13	-4	2	0	-4	-6
Wells D.	118	12	3	51	15	34	.18	.04	-.01	.04	.43	.08	-2	0	-0	-4	-5
Brocail D.	119	16	7	40	26	33	.17	.04	.02	-.02	.38	.06	-1	-2	2	-4	-5
Adkins J.	232	13	9	41	18	41	.08	.05	.08	.03	.36	.14	1	-2	-2	-1	-4
Williams W.	624	12	7	36	21	43	.20	.11	.06	.03	.34	.18	-2	-5	2	2	-3
Cassidy S.	182	27	11	36	26	38	.05	.18	.02	.06	.42	.27	-1	-1	2	3	2
Thompson M.	405	9	9	49	18	33	.06	.13	.12	.02	.35	.22	3	-3	-2	4	3
Park C.	606	16	9	43	18	38	.07	.13	.05	.05	.40	.20	-0	0	-1	4	3
MLB Average		17	9	44	20	37	.11	.11	.05	.04	.39	.19	-	-	-	-	-

Fielding Stats

Name	POS	INN	SBA/G	CS%	ERA	WP+PB/G	PO	A	TE	FE
Piazza, M.	C	718.0	1.38	12%	3.52	0.238	554	33	6	0
Bard, J.	C	494.7	0.91	18%	4.28	0.200	385	31	2	0
Bowen, R.	C	202.0	0.40	11%	3.39	0.624	145	13	0	0
Mirabelli, D.	C	49.0	0.92	20%	7.16	0.184	37	2	0	0

Name	POS	Inn	PO	A	TE	FE	FPct	RF	DPS	DPT
Gonzalez, A.	1B	1341.0	1240	115	1	6	.995	9.09	14	0
Bellhorn, M.	1B	97.3	90	6	0	2	.980	8.88	1	0
Walker, T.	1B	22.0	26	1	0	0	1.000	11.05	0	0
Blum, G.	1B	2.3	4	0	0	0	1.000	15.43	0	0
Bowen, R.	1B	1.0	1	0	0	0	1.000	9.00	0	0
Barfield, J.	2B	1259.0	294	381	4	5	.987	4.83	29	54
Walker, T.	2B	108.3	21	32	1	0	.981	4.40	4	5
Bellhorn, M.	2B	84.3	22	33	0	0	1.000	5.87	2	2
Blum, G.	2B	9.0	3	6	0	0	1.000	9.00	1	0
Young, E.	2B	3.0	0	0	0	0	0.000	0.00	0	0
Greene, K.	SS	997.7	139	309	2	7	.980	4.04	36	24
Blum, G.	SS	391.0	72	129	3	3	.971	4.63	15	13
Alexander, M.	SS	75.0	12	27	1	0	.975	4.68	6	1
Castilla, V.	3B	575.0	54	111	1	4	.971	2.58	8	0
Bellhorn, M.	3B	323.7	28	66	1	2	.959	2.61	5	1
Blum, G.	3B	200.3	18	36	0	0	1.000	2.43	1	0
Branyan, R.	3B	181.7	14	28	2	1	.933	2.08	3	0
Walker, T.	3B	149.7	12	31	4	1	.896	2.59	2	0
Alexander, M.	3B	33.3	2	7	1	0	.900	2.43	1	0

Name	POS	Inn	PO	A	TE	FE	FPct	RF	DPS	DPT
Roberts, D.	LF	970.0	239	0	0	0	1.000	2.22	0	0
Young, E.	LF	242.3	48	0	0	1	.980	1.78	0	0
Johnson, B.	LF	167.3	48	1	0	0	1.000	2.64	0	0
Sledge, T.	LF	82.0	23	0	0	1	.958	2.52	0	0
Cust, J.	LF	2.0	0	0	0	0	0.000	0.00	0	0
Cameron, M.	CF	1244.0	367	6	3	3	.984	2.70	4	0
Johnson, B.	CF	110.7	40	0	0	0	1.000	3.25	0	0
Roberts, D.	CF	104.0	34	1	0	0	1.000	3.03	0	0
Young, E.	CF	5.0	2	0	0	0	1.000	3.60	0	0
Giles, B.	RF	1398.0	299	7	0	7	.978	1.97	4	0
Sledge, T.	RF	43.0	9	1	0	0	1.000	2.09	0	0
Johnson, B.	RF	11.0	0	0	0	0	0.000	0.00	0	0
Blum, G.	RF	4.0	1	0	0	0	1.000	2.25	0	0
Bellhorn, M.	RF	3.0	0	0	0	0	0.000	0.00	0	0
Young, E.	RF	2.0	0	0	0	0	0.000	0.00	0	0
McAnulty, P.	RF	2.0	0	0	0	0	0.000	0.00	0	0

Batted Ball Batting Stats

Player	PA	% of PA		% of Batted Balls					Runs Per Event				Total Runs vs. Avg.				
		K%	BB%	GB%	LD%	FB%	IF/F	HR/OF	NIP	GB	LD	OF	NIP	GB	LD	FB	Tot
Cameron M.	634	22	12	38	17	45	.09	.13	.05	.11	.44	.23	2	8	-4	9	16
Gonzalez A.	631	18	9	44	23	33	.02	.15	.04	.00	.43	.27	-2	-7	11	12	13
Bard J.	263	15	11	52	20	28	.04	.17	.08	.06	.41	.32	2	2	1	6	11
Piazza M.	439	15	8	40	21	38	.09	.19	.05	.04	.36	.26	-1	-1	2	10	10
Giles B.	717	8	15	40	17	43	.11	.06	.18	-.00	.41	.13	21	-11	0	-7	3
Walker T.	142	8	12	41	19	39	.04	.07	.17	.05	.36	.12	3	0	-0	-1	2
Johnson B.	135	27	11	46	17	37	.23	.17	.02	.08	.53	.24	-1	1	0	-1	-0
Bowen R.	110	24	13	48	25	28	.05	.17	.05	.01	.32	.29	0	-1	-1	0	-1
Roberts D.	567	11	10	56	19	25	.11	.02	.10	.06	.39	.12	4	8	0	-14	-1
Barfield J.	578	14	6	39	19	42	.06	.07	.02	.06	.39	.14	-6	2	2	-0	-2
Greene K.	460	19	10	35	19	46	.10	.11	.05	.02	.44	.16	-0	-5	2	0	-3
Young E.	147	11	10	44	20	37	.17	.09	.11	-.08	.36	.08	1	-5	-0	-4	-8
Blum G.	299	17	6	36	23	41	.16	.05	.00	.03	.35	.11	-4	-2	2	-6	-10
Bellhorn M.	288	31	12	35	15	50	.18	.12	.01	.09	.35	.18	-2	1	-7	-2	-10
Castilla V.	269	17	4	41	20	39	.10	.05	-.02	.02	.34	.06	-5	-2	-0	-7	-15
MLB Average		17	9	44	20	37	.11	.11	.05	.04	.39	.19	-	-	-	-	-

San Francisco Giants

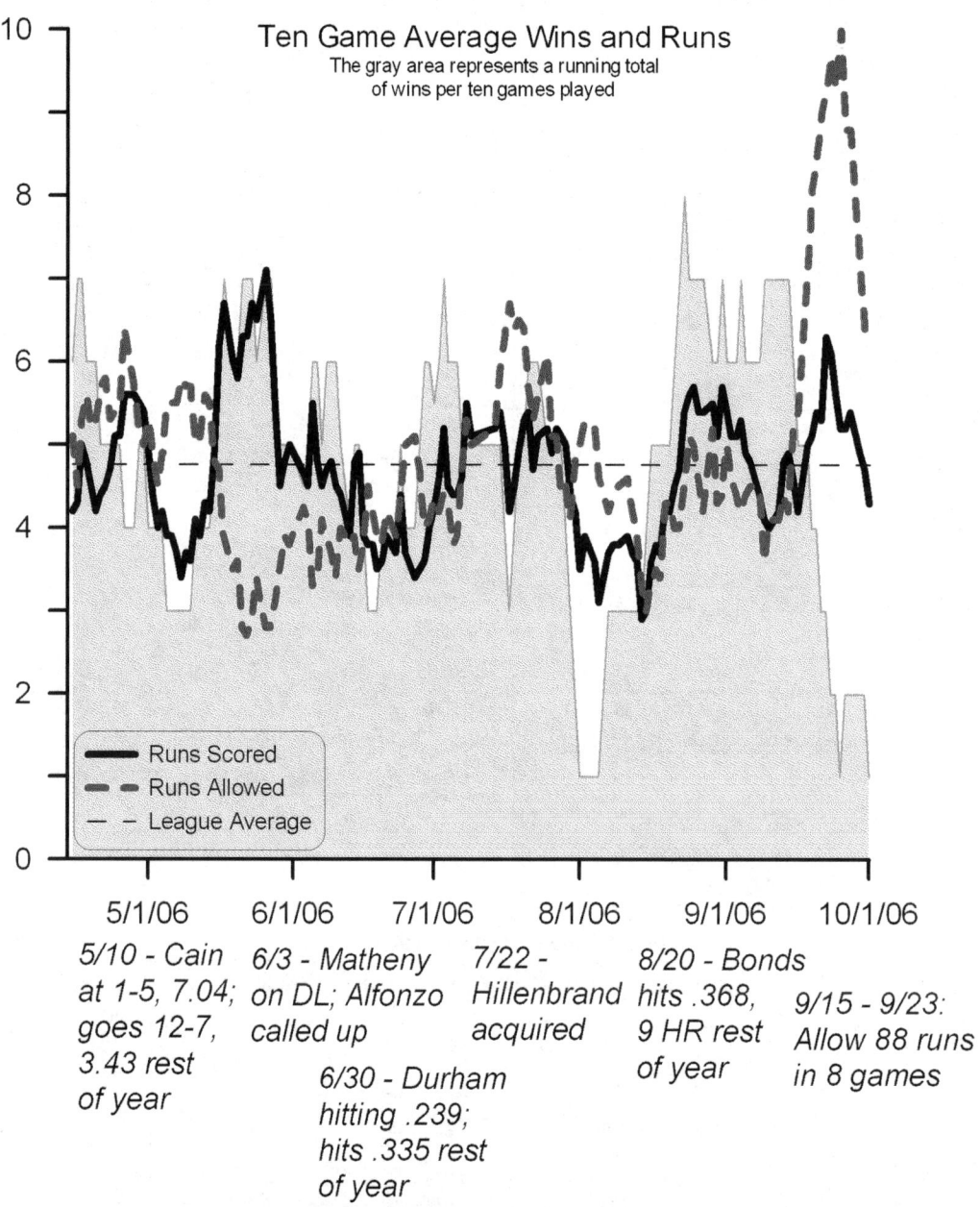

Ten Game Average Wins and Runs
The gray area represents a running total
of wins per ten games played

— Runs Scored
— — Runs Allowed
— - League Average

5/1/06   6/1/06   7/1/06   8/1/06   9/1/06   10/1/06

5/10 - Cain at 1-5, 7.04; goes 12-7, 3.43 rest of year

6/3 - Matheny on DL; Alfonzo called up

6/30 - Durham hitting .239; hits .335 rest of year

7/22 - Hillenbrand acquired

8/20 - Bonds hits .368, 9 HR rest of year

9/15 - 9/23: Allow 88 runs in 8 games

Team Batting and Pitching/Fielding Stats by Month						
	April	May	June	July	Aug	Sept/Oct
Wins	13	14	13	11	15	10
Losses	11	15	13	16	13	17
OBP	.343	.332	.321	.328	.327	.297
SLG	.402	.422	.419	.430	.429	.426
FIP	5.17	4.32	4.29	4.60	3.98	4.73
DER	.709	.725	.710	.681	.707	.685

Batting Stats

Player	RC	Runs	RBI	PA	Outs	P/PA	H	2B	3B	HR	TB	K	BB	IBB	HBP	SH	SF	SB	CS	GDP	BA	OBP	SLG	GPA
Bonds B.	102	74	77	493	277	4.00	99	23	0	26	200	51	115	38	10	0	1	3	0	9	.270	.454	.545	.337
Durham R.	91	79	93	555	371	3.73	146	30	7	26	268	61	51	6	2	2	2	7	2	17	.293	.360	.538	.293
Vizquel O.	88	88	58	659	428	3.76	171	22	10	4	225	51	56	3	6	13	5	24	7	13	.295	.361	.389	.257
Feliz P.	70	75	98	644	475	3.36	147	35	5	22	258	112	33	4	1	1	6	1	1	18	.244	.281	.428	.231
Winn R.	69	82	56	635	438	3.50	150	34	5	11	227	63	48	3	7	3	4	10	8	7	.262	.324	.396	.242
Alou M.	64	52	74	378	257	3.29	104	25	1	22	197	31	28	2	1	0	4	2	1	15	.301	.352	.571	.298
Finley S.	51	66	40	481	327	3.78	105	21	12	6	168	55	46	2	2	3	4	7	0	6	.246	.320	.394	.240
Alfonzo E.	36	27	39	309	221	3.29	76	17	2	12	133	74	9	7	7	4	3	1	0	11	.266	.302	.465	.249
Sweeney M.	33	32	37	291	201	3.87	65	15	2	5	99	50	28	3	3	0	1	0	1	6	.251	.330	.382	.241
Hillenbrand S.	23	33	29	247	183	3.75	58	12	0	9	97	40	7	0	3	0	3	0	0	7	.248	.275	.415	.225
Greene T.	22	16	17	170	113	3.55	46	12	2	2	68	45	10	3	1	0	0	0	0	0	.289	.335	.428	.255
Niekro L.	21	27	31	210	157	3.54	49	9	2	5	77	32	11	0	0	0	0	0	0	7	.246	.286	.387	.223
Matheny M.	13	10	18	177	130	3.62	37	8	0	3	54	30	9	2	2	3	3	0	0	7	.231	.276	.338	.206
Vizcaino J.	10	16	5	136	99	3.42	25	3	0	1	31	10	16	3	0	1	0	0	2	3	.210	.304	.261	.200
Linden T.	10	15	5	89	58	3.57	21	4	2	2	35	20	9	0	1	2	0	1	0	2	.273	.356	.455	.271
Frandsen K.	7	12	7	102	77	3.18	20	4	0	2	30	14	3	0	6	0	0	0	1	3	.215	.284	.323	.206
Ellison J.	4	14	4	91	68	3.38	18	5	1	2	31	14	5	0	1	3	1	2	2	3	.222	.273	.383	.216
Ishikawa T.	4	1	4	25	18	3.44	7	3	1	0	12	6	1	0	0	0	0	0	0	1	.292	.320	.500	.266
Morris M.	4	2	6	75	48	3.39	12	4	0	0	16	21	1	0	0	14	0	0	0	0	.200	.213	.267	.161
Lewis F.	4	5	2	11	6	3.82	5	1	0	0	6	3	0	0	0	0	0	0	0	0	.455	.455	.545	.337
Santos C.	3	2	2	8	4	3.38	3	0	0	1	6	2	1	0	0	0	0	0	0	0	.429	.500	.857	.434
Ortmeier D.	2	0	2	12	9	3.50	3	1	0	0	4	4	0	0	0	0	0	0	0	0	.250	.250	.333	.194
Delarosa T.	1	1	1	17	11	4.06	5	0	0	0	5	3	1	0	0	0	0	0	0	0	.313	.353	.313	.234
Hennessey B.	1	1	0	30	21	2.83	6	1	0	0	7	9	0	0	0	3	0	0	0	0	.222	.222	.259	.163
Munter S.	1	1	1	1	0	2.00	1	1	0	0	2	0	0	0	0	0	0	0	0	0	1.000	1.000	2.000	.939
Lowry N.	1	2	2	57	39	3.60	7	0	0	1	10	10	3	0	0	8	0	0	0	0	.152	.204	.217	.145
Wright J.	0	4	1	52	36	3.35	12	2	0	0	14	11	0	0	0	5	0	0	0	1	.255	.255	.298	.187
Fassero J.	0	2	0	5	3	3.60	1	0	0	0	1	1	0	0	0	1	0	0	0	0	.250	.250	.250	.173
Walker T.	0	0	0	1	0	0.00	0	0	0	0	0	0	1	0	0	0	0	0	0	0	.000	1.000	.000	.445
Stanton M.	-0	0	0	1	1	3.00	0	0	0	0	0	0	0	0	0	0	0	0	0	0	.000	.000	.000	.000
Worrell T.	-0	0	0	1	1	1.00	0	0	0	0	0	0	0	0	0	0	0	0	0	0	.000	.000	.000	.000
Chulk V.	-0	0	0	1	1	2.00	0	0	0	0	0	0	0	0	0	0	0	0	0	0	.000	.000	.000	.000
Knoedler J.	-0	0	0	7	6	3.71	1	0	0	0	1	1	0	0	0	0	0	0	0	0	.143	.143	.143	.099
Wilson B.	-0	0	0	2	2	3.00	0	0	0	0	0	1	0	0	0	0	0	0	0	0	.000	.000	.000	.000
Sanchez J.	-0	1	0	8	7	3.50	0	0	0	0	0	4	1	0	0	0	0	0	0	0	.000	.125	.000	.056
Accardo J.	-1	0	0	5	5	2.60	0	0	0	0	0	1	0	0	0	0	0	0	0	0	.000	.000	.000	.000
Correia K.	-1	1	0	12	11	2.92	1	0	0	0	1	7	0	0	0	0	0	0	0	0	.083	.083	.083	.058
Cain M.	-1	1	1	66	49	3.68	8	2	0	0	10	28	1	0	0	8	0	0	0	0	.140	.155	.175	.112
Schmidt J.	-1	4	1	72	58	3.53	9	3	0	1	15	26	0	0	0	6	0	0	0	1	.136	.136	.227	.117

Italicized stats have been adjusted for home park.

Batted Ball Batting Stats are listed at end of fielding stats

Pitching Stats

Player	PRC	IP	BFP	G	GS	P/PA	K	BB	IBB	HBP	H	HR	DP	DER	SB	CS	PO	W	L	Sv	Op	Hld	RA	ERA	FIP
Schmidt J.	103	213.3	894	32	32	3.87	180	80	6	6	189	21	15	.713	12	8	2	11	9	0	0	0	3.97	3.59	3.94
Cain M.	86	190.7	818	32	31	4.04	179	87	1	6	157	18	7	.729	15	3	0	13	12	0	0	0	4.39	4.15	4.02
Morris M.	68	207.7	903	33	33	3.62	117	63	9	14	218	22	18	.702	13	3	3	10	15	0	0	0	5.33	4.98	4.45
Lowry N.	55	159.3	689	27	27	3.80	84	56	2	6	166	21	17	.713	6	4	0	7	10	0	0	0	5.03	4.74	5.01
Wright J.	49	156.0	676	34	21	3.53	79	64	4	10	167	16	26	.702	13	8	6	6	10	0	0	0	5.48	5.19	4.88
Correia K.	37	69.7	295	48	0	3.85	57	22	0	3	64	5	2	.707	3	3	1	2	0	0	1	10	3.49	3.49	3.59
Hennessey B.	34	99.3	428	34	12	3.68	42	42	1	10	92	12	15	.730	11	3	2	5	6	1	1	2	4.80	4.26	5.48
Kline S.	22	51.7	227	72	0	3.63	33	26	3	7	53	3	7	.689	0	1	1	4	3	1	1	18	4.18	3.66	4.09
Benitez A.	20	38.3	171	41	0	4.17	31	21	2	0	39	6	4	.708	6	0	0	4	2	17	25	1	3.52	3.52	5.12
Accardo J.	16	40.3	170	38	0	4.23	40	11	3	1	38	2	1	.690	1	0	0	1	3	3	6	8	5.13	4.91	2.55
Stanton M.	14	23.3	94	26	0	3.36	18	6	0	1	23	1	2	.676	0	1	2	4	2	8	11	5	3.09	3.09	3.13
Sanchez J.	13	40.0	185	27	4	3.99	33	23	0	4	39	2	3	.683	9	0	0	3	1	0	0	5	5.85	4.95	4.24
Wilson B.	10	30.0	141	31	0	4.13	23	21	2	1	32	1	3	.663	2	2	0	2	3	1	2	4	5.70	5.40	4.12
Chulk V.	9	22.3	98	28	0	4.20	25	15	2	1	17	2	1	.727	1	0	0	0	3	0	1	5	5.24	5.24	4.02
Worrell T.	4	20.3	99	23	0	3.60	12	7	0	1	28	9	1	.686	1	0	0	3	2	6	8	1	7.97	7.52	8.97
Munter S.	4	22.7	110	27	0	3.17	7	18	2	2	30	1	6	.634	2	1	0	0	1	0	0	5	8.74	8.74	5.56
Fassero J.	3	15.0	73	10	1	3.73	7	8	0	0	23	4	2	.648	0	1	1	1	1	0	0	0	7.80	7.80	7.35
Taschner J.	3	19.3	101	24	0	3.79	15	7	0	2	31	4	1	.562	2	1	0	0	1	0	1	3	10.71	8.38	5.75
Sadler W.	1	4.0	20	5	0	4.60	6	2	0	1	5	2	0	.667	0	0	0	0	0	0	0	0	6.75	6.75	8.97
Walker T.	0	5.3	28	6	0	4.04	3	5	0	0	9	1	1	.579	1	1	0	0	1	0	2	1	15.19	15.19	7.34
Misch P.	0	1.0	5	1	0	3.60	1	0	0	0	2	0	0	.500	0	0	0	0	0	0	0	0	0.00	0.00	1.22

Batted Ball Pitching Stats

Player	PA	% of PA		% of Batted Balls					Runs Per Event				Total Runs vs. Avg.				
		K%	BB%	GB%	LD%	FB%	IF/F	HR/OF	NIP	GB	LD	OF	NIP	GB	LD	FB	Tot
Cain M.	818	22	11	36	16	48	.16	.09	.04	.05	.40	.15	1	-3	-11	-6	-19
Schmidt J.	894	20	10	37	19	43	.09	.08	.04	.06	.38	.12	-3	0	-5	-12	-19
Accardo J.	170	24	7	41	24	35	.02	.05	-.01	.01	.39	.08	-3	-2	2	-4	-7
Correia K.	295	19	8	34	22	44	.15	.04	.03	.06	.47	.05	-2	-0	5	-10	-6
Kline S.	227	15	12	47	19	34	.04	.06	.09	.01	.40	.16	3	-3	-1	-1	-2
Wright J.	676	12	11	58	18	23	.09	.15	.11	.02	.37	.25	8	-4	-2	-2	-2
Sanchez J.	185	18	15	36	20	45	.11	.02	.09	.09	.44	.06	3	1	0	-6	-1
Wilson B.	141	16	16	45	26	29	.07	.04	.11	.03	.42	.04	3	-1	3	-5	-0
Benitez A.	171	18	12	32	21	47	.07	.12	.07	.04	.32	.17	1	-1	-1	1	-0
Hennessey B.	428	10	12	44	19	37	.09	.10	.14	.03	.37	.15	8	-2	-1	-3	1
Lowry N.	689	12	9	36	18	45	.11	.09	.08	.03	.34	.20	3	-5	-5	11	2
Morris M.	903	13	9	46	21	33	.07	.10	.07	.03	.42	.16	1	-4	10	-6	2
Munter S.	110	6	18	53	28	19	.07	.08	.23	.03	.35	.27	5	-1	1	-1	4
Taschner J.	101	15	9	27	29	44	.18	.11	.06	.12	.55	.17	0	1	6	-0	8
MLB Average		17	9	44	20	37	.11	.11	.05	.04	.39	.19	-	-	-	-	-

Fielding Stats

Name	POS	INN	SBA/G	CS%	ERA	WP+PB/G	PO	A	TE	FE
Alfonzo, E.	C	700.3	0.84	20%	4.50	0.437	568	30	3	2
Matheny, M.	C	391.3	0.74	25%	4.23	0.276	252	17	1	0
Greene, T.	C	326.0	0.77	29%	5.38	0.221	196	14	1	0
Knoedler, J.	C	12.0	1.50	0%	6.00	0.750	11	0	0	0

Name	POS	Inn	PO	A	TE	FE	FPct	RF	DPS	DPT
Hillenbrand, S.	1B	453.0	422	35	0	1	.998	9.08	4	0
Niekro, L.	1B	431.3	418	36	5	0	.989	9.47	4	0
Sweeney, M.	1B	395.3	362	36	0	2	.995	9.06	4	0
Vizcaino, J.	1B	63.3	77	1	0	2	.975	11.08	2	0
Ishikawa, T.	1B	55.0	50	8	0	0	1.000	9.49	2	0
Santos, C.	1B	19.7	17	1	0	1	.947	8.24	2	0
Greene, T.	1B	12.0	10	3	0	0	1.000	9.75	0	0
Durham, R.	2B	1138.0	271	341	4	7	.982	4.84	28	52
Frandsen, K.	2B	177.0	35	51	2	0	.977	4.37	1	6
Vizcaino, J.	2B	109.0	30	41	0	0	1.000	5.86	2	5
Delarosa, T.	2B	5.0	0	2	0	0	1.000	3.60	1	0
Vizquel, O.	SS	1281.0	205	389	1	3	.993	4.17	46	37
Vizcaino, J.	SS	88.3	15	34	1	1	.961	4.99	2	1
Delarosa, T.	SS	33.0	7	7	0	1	.933	3.82	0	0
Frandsen, K.	SS	17.0	3	5	0	1	.889	4.24	0	1
Feliz, P.	SS	10.0	4	0	0	0	1.000	3.60	0	0
Feliz, P.	3B	1372.0	117	330	5	16	.955	2.93	32	0
Hillenbrand, S.	3B	53.3	4	8	1	0	.923	2.03	1	0
Vizcaino, J.	3B	2.0	0	1	0	0	1.000	4.50	0	0
Delarosa, T.	3B	2.0	0	0	0	0	0.000	0.00	0	0

Name	POS	Inn	PO	A	TE	FE	FPct	RF	DPS	DPT
Bonds, B.	LF	875.0	188	6	0	3	.985	2.00	1	0
Linden, T.	LF	128.0	31	1	0	0	1.000	2.25	0	0
Sweeney, M.	LF	113.3	24	0	0	1	.960	1.91	0	0
Ellison, J.	LF	112.7	26	1	1	1	.931	2.16	0	0
Winn, R.	LF	100.7	27	0	0	0	1.000	2.41	0	0
Alou, M.	LF	79.0	19	0	0	0	1.000	2.16	0	0
Lewis, F.	LF	18.0	7	0	1	0	.875	3.50	0	0
Feliz, P.	LF	3.0	1	0	0	0	1.000	3.00	0	0
Finley, S.	CF	973.3	287	5	0	1	.997	2.70	2	0
Winn, R.	CF	441.0	137	2	0	0	1.000	2.84	0	0
Ellison, J.	CF	14.3	3	0	0	0	1.000	1.88	0	0
Lewis, F.	CF	1.0	1	0	0	0	1.000	9.00	0	0
Winn, R.	RF	652.7	184	6	3	0	.984	2.62	2	0
Alou, M.	RF	646.7	154	1	1	3	.975	2.16	0	0
Ellison, J.	RF	72.7	17	1	0	0	1.000	2.23	0	0
Linden, T.	RF	45.7	9	0	0	0	1.000	1.77	0	0
Ortmeier, D.	RF	12.0	4	0	0	0	1.000	3.00	0	0

Batted Ball Batting Stats

Player	PA	% of PA		% of Batted Balls					Runs Per Event				Total Runs vs. Avg.				
		K%	BB%	GB%	LD%	FB%	IF/F	HR/OF	NIP	GB	LD	OF	NIP	GB	LD	FB	Tot
Bonds B.	493	10	25	30	20	50	.10	.18	.21	-.03	.39	.27	31	-10	-3	15	33
Durham R.	555	11	10	46	17	37	.10	.17	.10	.05	.44	.26	4	2	1	13	20
Alou M.	378	8	8	40	20	40	.06	.18	.11	.03	.35	.27	1	-2	1	15	16
Greene T.	170	26	6	36	18	46	.15	.04	-.02	.14	.59	.14	-4	3	2	-2	0
Alfonzo E.	309	24	5	41	19	40	.13	.16	-.03	.05	.43	.29	-7	-1	0	7	-0
Sweeney M.	291	17	11	42	22	36	.05	.07	.06	-.03	.34	.23	1	-7	-0	3	-3
Frandsen K.	102	14	9	48	13	39	.17	.08	.07	.04	.25	.14	0	-0	-3	-1	-5
Niekro L.	210	15	5	45	17	38	.17	.09	.00	-.02	.43	.21	-3	-4	0	1	-6
Finley S.	481	11	10	46	15	38	.19	.04	.10	.04	.48	.11	4	0	1	-11	-6
Vizquel O.	659	8	9	40	22	38	.16	.02	.14	.04	.39	.06	7	0	9	-22	-6
Hillenbrand S.	247	16	4	46	21	33	.18	.15	-.02	.00	.44	.16	-4	-3	5	-3	-6
Winn R.	635	10	9	50	17	33	.13	.07	.10	.05	.37	.14	3	3	-4	-9	-6
Vizcaino J.	136	7	12	61	12	27	.10	.04	.17	.02	.37	.02	3	-1	-3	-6	-7
Matheny M.	177	17	6	39	20	41	.09	.06	.01	-.01	.38	.08	-2	-3	0	-4	-9
Feliz P.	644	17	5	40	16	43	.15	.11	-.01	.03	.44	.18	-10	-4	0	2	-11
MLB Average		17	9	44	20	37	.11	.11	.05	.04	.39	.19	-	-	-	-	-

Seattle Mariners

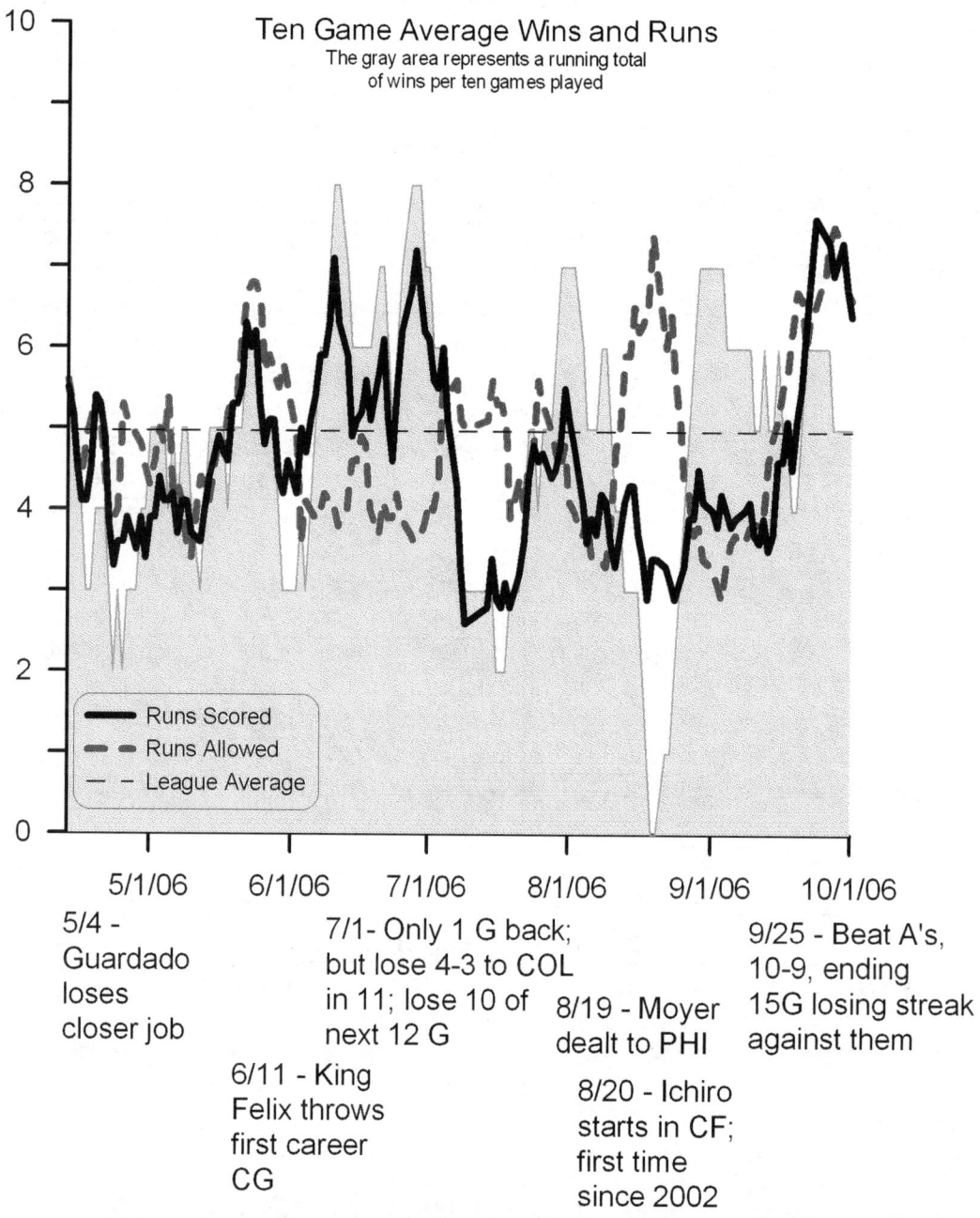

Ten Game Average Wins and Runs
The gray area represents a running total
of wins per ten games played

Runs Scored
Runs Allowed
League Average

5/1/06   6/1/06   7/1/06   8/1/06   9/1/06   10/1/06

5/4 - Guardado loses closer job

7/1- Only 1 G back; but lose 4-3 to COL in 11; lose 10 of next 12 G

8/19 - Moyer dealt to PHI

9/25 - Beat A's, 10-9, ending 15G losing streak against them

6/11 - King Felix throws first career CG

8/20 - Ichiro starts in CF; first time since 2002

Team Batting and Pitching/Fielding Stats by Month						
	April	May	June	July	Aug	Sept/Oct
Wins	11	12	18	11	11	15
Losses	15	17	8	13	17	14
OBP	.315	.321	.343	.311	.308	.347
SLG	.389	.397	.497	.399	.406	.454
FIP	4.83	4.61	4.09	4.51	4.52	4.66
DER	.688	.707	.698	.685	.685	.688

Italicized stats have been adjusted for home park.

Batting Stats

Player	RC	Runs	RBI	PA	Outs	P/PA	H	2B	3B	HR	TB	K	BB	IBB	HBP	SH	SF	SB	CS	GDP	BA	OBP	SLG	GPA
Ibanez R.	*121*	103	123	699	462	4.01	181	33	5	33	323	115	65	15	1	0	7	2	4	13	.289	.353	.516	*.301*
Suzuki I.	*113*	110	49	752	475	3.75	224	20	9	9	289	71	49	16	5	1	2	45	2	2	.322	.370	.416	*.283*
Sexson R.	*97*	75	107	663	453	3.95	156	40	0	34	298	154	64	5	4	0	4	1	1	17	.264	.338	.504	*.291*
Beltre A.	*90*	88	89	681	474	3.78	166	39	4	25	288	118	47	4	10	1	3	11	5	15	.268	.328	.465	*.276*
Lopez J.	*88*	78	79	655	452	3.63	170	28	8	10	244	80	26	1	9	12	5	5	2	17	.282	.319	.405	*.256*
Johjima K.	*84*	61	76	542	375	3.37	147	25	1	18	228	46	20	1	13	0	3	3	1	15	.291	.332	.451	*.274*
Betancourt Y.	*64*	68	47	584	415	3.27	161	28	6	8	225	54	17	0	1	7	1	11	8	10	.289	.310	.403	*.252*
Everett C.	*29*	37	33	343	248	3.84	70	8	0	11	111	57	29	2	3	0	3	1	3	7	.227	.297	.360	*.234*
Bloomquist W.	*28*	36	15	283	195	3.68	62	6	2	1	75	40	24	0	4	2	2	16	3	3	.247	.320	.299	*.229*
Broussard B.	*17*	17	17	177	128	3.79	39	7	0	8	70	45	9	2	2	0	2	2	0	3	.238	.282	.427	*.245*
Reed J.	*14*	27	17	229	174	3.42	46	6	5	6	80	31	11	1	2	2	2	2	3	5	.217	.260	.377	*.221*
Snelling C.	*12*	14	8	119	73	4.13	24	6	1	3	41	38	13	0	4	5	1	2	1	0	.250	.360	.427	*.281*
Perez E.	*9*	6	11	102	74	3.80	17	1	0	1	21	22	13	2	1	0	1	0	1	3	.195	.304	.241	*.206*
Morse M.	*9*	5	11	48	29	3.77	16	5	0	0	21	7	3	0	0	0	2	1	0	2	.372	.396	.488	*.314*
Dobbs G.	*5*	4	3	28	18	3.46	10	3	1	0	15	4	0	0	1	0	0	0	1	0	.370	.393	.556	*.330*
Rivera R.	*4*	8	4	106	86	3.46	15	4	0	2	25	29	3	0	1	3	0	1	0	2	.152	.184	.253	*.153*
Jones A.	*4*	6	8	76	62	3.83	16	4	0	1	23	22	2	0	0	0	0	3	1	3	.216	.237	.311	*.193*
Lawton M.	*4*	5	1	29	20	3.59	7	0	0	0	7	2	2	0	0	0	0	0	0	0	.259	.310	.259	*.214*
Navarro O.	*2*	0	0	4	1	2.75	2	0	0	0	2	1	0	0	0	1	0	0	0	0	.667	.667	.667	*.488*
Moyer J.	*1*	0	1	3	2	4.67	1	0	0	0	1	1	0	0	0	0	0	0	0	0	.333	.333	.333	*.244*
Bohn T.	*1*	2	2	16	12	4.88	2	0	0	1	5	8	2	0	0	0	0	0	0	0	.143	.250	.357	*.211*
Petagine R.	*1*	3	2	32	22	4.44	5	2	0	1	10	10	4	0	1	0	0	0	0	0	.185	.313	.370	*.244*
Washburn J.	*0*	0	0	4	2	3.50	0	0	0	0	0	1	1	0	0	1	0	0	0	0	.000	.333	.000	*.157*
Quiroz G.	*-0*	0	0	2	2	7.50	0	0	0	0	0	2	0	0	0	0	0	0	0	0	.000	.000	.000	*.000*
Pineiro J.	*-0*	0	0	6	4	3.17	0	0	0	0	0	3	0	0	0	2	0	0	0	0	.000	.000	.000	*.000*
Hernandez F.	*-0*	0	0	5	4	3.20	0	0	0	0	0	3	0	0	0	1	0	0	0	0	.000	.000	.000	*.000*
Borchard J.	*-0*	3	0	9	8	4.00	2	0	0	0	2	3	0	0	0	0	0	0	1	0	.222	.222	.222	*.163*
Meche G.	*-0*	0	0	4	4	4.25	0	0	0	0	0	3	0	0	0	0	0	0	0	0	.000	.000	.000	*.000*
Choo S.	*-1*	0	0	12	11	2.92	1	1	0	0	2	4	0	0	1	0	0	0	0	1	.091	.167	.182	*.126*

Batted Ball Batting Stats

Player	PA	% of PA		% of Batted Balls			IF/F	HR/OF	Runs Per Event				Total Runs vs. Avg.				
		K%	BB%	GB%	LD%	FB%			NIP	GB	LD	OF	NIP	GB	LD	FB	Tot
Ibanez R.	699	16	9	42	19	39	.11	.17	.05	.07	.45	.23	0	5	6	9	21
Sexson R.	663	23	10	42	18	40	.11	.21	.03	.03	.41	.34	-3	-5	-4	23	12
Suzuki I.	752	9	7	51	22	28	.13	.06	.09	.10	.35	.12	1	21	5	-16	10
Beltre A.	681	17	8	37	21	42	.14	.14	.04	.05	.35	.24	-3	-1	-1	12	7
Johjima K.	542	8	6	45	19	36	.13	.12	.08	.03	.40	.21	-1	-2	5	5	7
Snelling C.	119	32	14	38	21	41	.08	.14	.03	.09	.56	.23	0	0	0	0	1
Broussard B.	177	25	6	32	18	50	.12	.15	-.02	.06	.42	.19	-4	-0	-0	2	-3
Perez E.	102	22	14	50	21	29	.21	.07	.07	.02	.30	.00	1	-1	-1	-5	-6
Betancourt Y.	584	9	3	46	18	36	.17	.05	.00	.09	.42	.06	-8	13	5	-19	-9
Lopez J.	655	12	5	49	18	33	.18	.06	.03	.06	.44	.12	-6	4	6	-14	-9
Rivera R.	106	27	4	44	11	44	.16	.08	-.06	.06	.27	.11	-3	-0	-4	-2	-9
Bloomquist W.	283	14	10	46	17	37	.11	.01	.08	.07	.30	.05	1	3	-5	-9	-10
Reed J.	229	14	6	51	13	37	.03	.10	.02	.01	.24	.18	-2	-1	-7	1	-10
Everett C.	343	17	9	37	16	46	.08	.09	.05	.02	.35	.12	0	-3	-5	-3	-10
MLB Average		*17*	*9*	*44*	*20*	*37*	*.11*	*.11*	*.05*	*.04*	*.39*	*.19*	-	-	-	-	-

Pitching Stats

Player	PRC	IP	BFP	G	GS	P/PA	K	BB	IBB	HBP	H	HR	DP	DER	SB	CS	PO	W	L	Sv	Op	Hld	RA	ERA	FIP
Hernandez F.	80	191.0	816	31	31	3.75	176	60	2	6	195	23	20	.675	14	5	1	12	14	0	0	0	4.95	4.52	3.99
Meche G.	74	186.7	811	32	32	4.07	156	84	2	8	183	24	19	.694	5	7	2	11	8	0	0	0	5.11	4.48	4.71
Washburn J.	69	187.0	809	31	31	3.80	103	55	2	7	198	25	16	.712	5	5	2	8	14	0	0	0	4.96	4.67	4.86
Putz J.	67	78.3	303	72	0	4.02	104	13	1	2	59	4	5	.683	7	0	0	4	1	36	43	5	2.30	2.30	1.81
Moyer J.	60	160.0	685	25	25	3.70	82	44	3	3	179	25	16	.699	8	7	4	6	12	0	0	0	4.78	4.39	5.09
Soriano R.	50	60.0	241	53	0	4.09	65	21	0	2	44	6	5	.735	7	2	0	1	2	2	6	18	2.25	2.25	3.55
Woods J.	45	105.0	473	37	8	3.90	66	53	5	2	115	12	11	.691	4	2	0	7	4	1	1	2	4.37	4.20	4.92
Pineiro J.	44	165.7	753	40	25	3.65	87	64	13	10	209	23	24	.666	8	3	0	8	13	1	2	4	6.68	6.36	5.12
Mateo J.	22	53.7	241	48	0	3.47	31	22	8	3	62	6	6	.676	4	1	0	9	4	0	3	7	4.53	4.19	4.51
Sherrill G.	20	40.0	174	72	0	4.24	42	27	4	0	30	0	3	.695	4	2	2	2	4	1	1	17	4.28	4.28	2.89
Lowe M.	17	18.7	75	15	0	4.08	20	9	1	2	12	1	4	.721	0	0	0	1	0	0	0	6	1.93	1.93	3.42
Baek C.	17	34.3	140	6	6	4.11	23	13	0	2	26	6	2	.781	1	1	0	4	1	0	0	0	3.93	3.67	5.51
Huber J.	16	16.7	66	16	0	3.47	11	6	1	0	10	0	2	.755	0	1	0	2	1	0	0	6	1.62	1.08	2.84
Green S.	13	32.0	139	24	0	3.98	15	13	1	2	34	2	6	.692	1	0	0	0	0	0	1	3	4.50	4.50	4.45
Fruto E.	12	36.0	165	23	0	3.88	34	24	1	2	34	4	3	.683	3	0	1	2	2	1	2	1	6.00	5.50	4.90
Guardado E.	9	23.0	108	28	0	4.18	22	11	1	0	29	8	0	.687	0	1	0	1	3	5	8	2	5.48	5.48	7.18
Feierabend R.	9	17.0	73	4	2	3.79	11	7	0	0	15	3	2	.712	0	1	1	0	1	0	0	0	3.71	3.71	5.50
O'Flaherty E.	3	11.0	57	15	0	3.60	6	6	3	0	18	2	1	.605	0	0	0	0	0	0	0	1	7.36	4.09	5.35
Harris J.	1	3.3	12	3	0	3.33	1	0	0	0	3	0	1	.727	0	0	0	0	0	0	0	0	5.40	5.40	2.66
Cruceta F.	1	6.7	34	4	1	3.94	2	6	0	0	10	2	1	.667	0	0	0	0	0	0	0	0	10.80	10.80	9.26
Jimenez C.	1	7.3	38	4	1	3.76	3	4	0	0	13	4	1	.667	0	0	0	0	0	0	0	0	14.73	14.73	11.17
Chick T.	0	5.0	31	3	0	4.61	2	10	0	0	7	0	1	.632	0	0	0	0	0	0	0	0	12.60	12.60	8.46
Livingston B.	0	5.0	32	3	0	3.50	3	6	1	2	9	2	0	.632	0	0	0	0	0	0	0	0	18.00	18.00	11.46
Campillo J.	0	2.3	11	1	0	4.18	1	0	0	0	4	0	0	.600	0	0	0	0	0	0	0	0	15.43	15.43	2.41
Nageotte C.	0	1.0	7	1	0	4.29	1	2	1	0	2	1	0	.667	1	0	0	0	0	0	0	0	27.00	27.00	17.26

Batted Ball Pitching Stats

Player	PA	% of PA		% of Batted Balls			IF/F	HR/OF	Runs Per Event				Total Runs vs. Avg.				
		K%	BB%	GB%	LD%	FB%			NIP	GB	LD	OF	NIP	GB	LD	FB	Tot
Putz J.	303	34	5	51	16	33	.08	.05	-.06	.05	.48	.08	-11	1	-2	-9	-21
Soriano R.	241	27	10	27	19	54	.15	.09	.01	.08	.26	.14	-3	-0	-6	-2	-11
Hernandez F.	816	22	8	58	18	25	.08	.17	.01	.05	.39	.28	-8	5	-6	0	-9
Sherrill G.	174	24	16	30	19	51	.10	.00	.07	.03	.49	.02	2	-2	-0	-7	-8
Baek C.	140	16	11	43	17	40	.12	.17	.07	.02	.28	.20	1	-1	-3	1	-3
Green S.	139	11	11	58	19	24	.04	.08	.12	.02	.30	.24	2	-1	-2	-0	-1
Fruto E.	165	21	16	37	21	42	.07	.10	.09	.03	.41	.14	3	-1	-0	-2	-0
Washburn J.	809	13	8	40	18	42	.13	.10	.06	.06	.40	.15	-1	3	1	-3	0
Meche G.	811	19	11	43	18	38	.08	.12	.06	.06	.44	.16	3	3	0	-6	2
Mateo J.	241	13	10	24	25	51	.16	.08	.09	.08	.42	.09	2	0	6	-5	3
Woods J.	473	14	12	42	20	38	.08	.09	.10	.02	.41	.18	5	-3	2	1	5
Guardado E.	108	20	10	33	13	54	.21	.26	.04	.11	.39	.43	-0	1	-2	8	6
Moyer J.	685	12	7	37	20	43	.12	.12	.05	.02	.43	.19	-2	-5	9	8	9
Pineiro J.	753	12	10	47	23	29	.08	.13	.10	.02	.43	.23	6	-5	18	3	21
MLB Average		17	9	44	20	37	.11	.11	.05	.04	.39	.19	-	-	-	-	-

Fielding Stats

Name	POS	INN	SBA/G	CS%	ERA	WP+PB/G	PO	A	TE	FE
Johjima, K.	C	1172.7	0.61	28%	4.81	0.376	881	59	5	2
Rivera, R.	C	266.0	0.68	25%	3.62	0.474	223	11	3	0
Quiroz, G.	C	8.0	0.00	0%	5.63	0.000	5	0	0	0

Name	POS	Inn	PO	A	TE	FE	FPct	RF	DPS	DPT
Sexson, R.	1B	1310.0	1233	110	1	3	.997	9.23	14	1
Broussard, B.	1B	72.0	74	8	2	0	.976	10.25	1	1
Petagine, R.	1B	25.0	23	4	0	0	1.000	9.72	1	0
Perez, E.	1B	15.3	10	2	0	0	1.000	7.04	0	0
Morse, M.	1B	10.0	11	0	0	0	1.000	9.90	0	0
Dobbs, G.	1B	8.3	10	0	0	0	1.000	10.80	0	0
Bloomquist, W.	1B	5.7	6	0	0	0	1.000	9.53	0	0
Lopez, J.	2B	1322.0	282	416	4	12	.978	4.75	43	55
Bloomquist, W.	2B	123.7	20	31	1	1	.962	3.71	2	5
Beltre, A.	2B	1.0	0	0	0	0	0.000	0.00	0	0
Betancourt, Y.	SS	1374.0	251	430	10	10	.971	4.46	44	46
Bloomquist, W.	SS	65.3	9	23	0	0	1.000	4.41	1	2
Navarro, O.	SS	6.0	0	3	1	0	.750	4.50	1	0
Morse, M.	SS	1.0	0	0	0	0	0.000	0.00	0	0
Beltre, A.	3B	1358.0	136	323	4	11	.968	3.04	29	3
Bloomquist, W.	3B	70.0	5	15	0	0	1.000	2.57	3	0
Morse, M.	3B	16.7	0	3	0	0	1.000	1.62	1	0
Dobbs, G.	3B	2.0	1	0	0	0	1.000	4.50	0	0

Name	POS	Inn	PO	A	TE	FE	FPct	RF	DPS	DPT
Ibanez, R.	LF	1396.0	301	11	1	1	.994	2.01	0	0
Bloomquist, W.	LF	10.0	2	0	0	0	1.000	1.80	0	0
Morse, M.	LF	10.0	1	0	0	0	1.000	0.90	0	0
Lawton, M.	LF	9.0	0	0	0	0	0.000	0.00	0	0
Everett, C.	LF	9.0	1	0	0	0	1.000	1.00	0	0
Snelling, C.	LF	9.0	2	0	0	0	1.000	2.00	0	0
Bohn, T.	LF	3.0	0	0	0	1	0.000	0.00	1	0
Reed, J.	CF	507.3	129	3	0	1	.992	2.34	0	0
Suzuki, I.	CF	338.0	114	1	0	1	.991	3.06	0	0
Bloomquist, W.	CF	320.3	89	2	0	0	1.000	2.56	0	0
Jones, A.	CF	193.0	67	5	0	3	.960	3.36	2	0
Choo, S.	CF	36.0	16	1	0	1	.944	4.25	0	0
Lawton, M.	CF	35.0	10	0	0	0	1.000	2.57	0	0
Borchard, J.	CF	16.0	4	1	0	0	1.000	2.81	0	0
Snelling, C.	CF	1.0	0	0	0	0	0.000	0.00	0	0
Suzuki, I.	RF	1061.0	250	8	0	2	.992	2.19	6	0
Snelling, C.	RF	235.0	43	2	1	0	.978	1.72	2	0
Bloomquist, W.	RF	52.0	13	0	0	0	1.000	2.25	0	0
Bohn, T.	RF	44.0	7	0	0	0	1.000	1.43	0	0
Morse, M.	RF	36.0	8	1	0	0	1.000	2.25	0	0
Everett, C.	RF	9.0	2	0	0	0	1.000	2.00	0	0
Lawton, M.	RF	5.0	1	0	0	0	1.000	1.80	0	0
Dobbs, G.	RF	4.0	1	0	0	0	1.000	2.25	0	0

St. Louis Cardinals

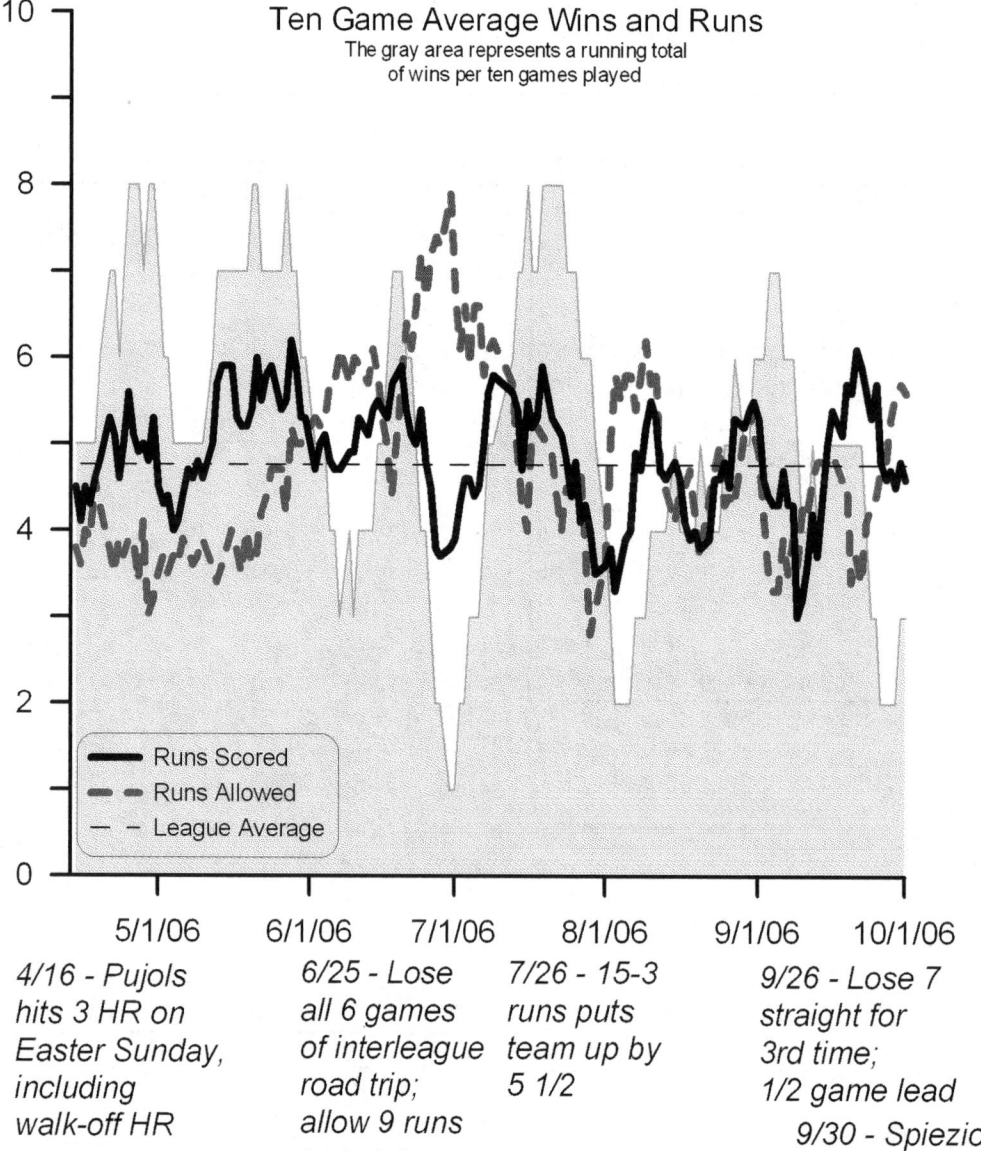

Ten Game Average Wins and Runs
The gray area represents a running total
of wins per ten games played

Legend:
— Runs Scored
- - Runs Allowed
- - League Average

4/16 - Pujols hits 3 HR on Easter Sunday, including walk-off HR

6/25 - Lose all 6 games of interleague road trip; allow 9 runs per game

7/26 - 15-3 runs puts team up by 5 1/2

9/26 - Lose 7 straight for 3rd time; 1/2 game lead

9/30 - Spiezio hits triple to beat MIL 3-2; clinch title

Team Batting and Pitching/Fielding Stats by Month						
	April	May	June	July	Aug	Sept/Oct
Wins	17	17	9	15	13	12
Losses	8	11	16	11	15	17
OBP	.346	.351	.339	.334	.340	.315
SLG	.432	.424	.412	.433	.465	.422
FIP	4.72	4.53	5.21	4.72	5.29	4.09
DER	.736	.721	.666	.698	.693	.681

Batting Stats

Player	RC	Runs	RBI	PA	Outs	P/PA	H	2B	3B	HR	TB	K	BB	IBB	HBP	SH	SF	SB	CS	GDP	BA	OBP	SLG	GPA
Pujols A.	150	119	137	634	380	3.78	177	33	1	49	359	50	92	28	4	0	3	7	2	20	.331	.431	.671	.365
Rolen S.	91	94	95	594	381	3.91	154	48	1	22	270	69	56	7	9	0	8	7	4	10	.296	.369	.518	.298
Encarnacion J.	81	74	79	598	418	3.63	155	25	5	19	247	86	30	6	4	1	6	6	5	11	.278	.317	.443	.256
Eckstein D.	61	68	23	552	367	3.75	146	18	1	2	172	41	31	0	15	3	3	7	6	7	.292	.350	.344	.246
Spiezio S.	54	44	52	321	202	3.85	75	15	4	13	137	66	37	1	5	1	2	1	0	1	.272	.366	.496	.291
Edmonds J.	52	52	70	408	271	4.07	90	18	0	19	165	101	53	7	0	0	5	4	0	11	.257	.350	.471	.278
Miles A.	51	48	30	471	323	3.52	112	20	5	2	148	42	38	9	2	2	3	2	1	8	.263	.324	.347	.235
Duncan C.	49	60	43	314	202	4.09	82	11	3	22	165	69	30	0	2	0	2	0	0	4	.293	.363	.589	.314
Taguchi S.	36	46	31	361	244	3.69	84	19	1	2	111	48	32	1	2	9	2	11	3	9	.266	.335	.351	.241
Molina Y.	36	29	49	461	344	3.40	90	26	0	6	134	41	26	2	8	8	2	1	2	15	.216	.274	.321	.205
Luna H.	33	27	21	245	164	3.61	65	14	1	4	93	34	21	1	1	0	0	5	3	3	.291	.355	.417	.267
Rodriguez J.	30	31	19	212	137	3.99	55	12	3	2	79	45	21	1	3	1	4	0	0	9	.301	.374	.432	.279
Wilson P.	16	18	17	120	86	3.61	27	3	0	8	54	27	7	1	2	0	0	6	0	2	.243	.300	.486	.259
Belliard R.	15	20	23	211	160	3.25	46	9	1	5	72	36	15	2	1	1	0	0	3	9	.237	.295	.371	.228
Bennett G.	13	13	22	170	125	3.48	35	5	0	4	52	30	11	2	0	2	0	0	0	3	.223	.274	.331	.208
Suppan J.	7	4	6	70	44	3.57	12	1	0	0	13	11	5	0	1	9	0	0	1	0	.218	.295	.236	.194
Vizcaino J.	6	3	3	25	17	4.04	8	3	0	1	14	4	1	0	0	1	0	0	0	2	.348	.375	.609	.324
Mulder M.	6	5	5	36	18	3.81	7	2	0	1	12	8	5	0	0	6	0	0	0	0	.280	.400	.480	.303
Perez T.	3	3	3	35	25	3.49	6	1	0	1	10	4	3	1	1	0	0	0	0	0	.194	.286	.323	.211
Bigbie L.	3	2	1	28	20	3.57	6	1	0	0	7	9	3	0	0	0	0	0	0	1	.240	.321	.280	.217
Ponson S.	2	1	1	21	11	3.19	3	0	0	0	3	6	3	0	0	5	0	0	1	0	.231	.375	.231	.229
Gall J.	2	1	1	12	9	3.75	3	0	0	0	3	5	0	0	0	0	0	0	0	0	.250	.250	.250	.177
Schumaker J.	2	3	2	60	46	3.13	10	1	0	1	14	6	5	1	0	1	0	2	1	1	.185	.254	.259	.181
Marquis J.	2	8	5	85	66	2.95	14	4	1	0	20	14	2	0	1	4	0	0	0	2	.179	.210	.256	.160
Wainwright A	1	2	1	6	3	2.50	3	1	0	1	7	0	0	0	0	0	0	0	0	0	.500	.500	1.167	.522
Thompson B.	1	0	0	2	1	4.00	1	0	0	0	1	1	0	0	0	0	0	0	0	0	.500	.500	.500	.353
Weaver J.	1	1	3	35	25	4.20	3	1	0	0	4	12	3	0	0	5	0	0	0	1	.111	.200	.148	.128
Looper B.	1	0	0	2	1	3.00	1	1	0	0	2	0	0	0	0	0	0	0	0	0	.500	.500	1.000	.480
Rose M.	0	0	1	9	7	4.22	2	0	0	0	2	4	0	0	0	0	0	0	0	0	.222	.222	.222	.157
Falkenborg B.	-0	0	0	1	1	5.00	0	0	0	0	0	1	0	0	0	0	0	0	0	0	.000	.000	.000	.000
Narveson C.	-0	0	0	1	1	5.00	0	0	0	0	0	1	0	0	0	0	0	0	0	0	.000	.000	.000	.000
Johnson T.	-0	0	0	1	1	5.00	0	0	0	0	0	1	0	0	0	0	0	0	0	0	.000	.000	.000	.000
Hancock J.	-0	0	0	8	6	4.75	0	0	0	0	0	6	1	0	0	1	0	0	0	0	.000	.143	.000	.065
Sosa J.	-0	0	0	4	4	4.50	0	0	0	0	0	3	0	0	0	0	0	0	0	0	.000	.000	.000	.000
Nelson J.	-1	2	0	5	5	4.40	0	0	0	0	0	4	0	0	0	0	0	0	0	0	.000	.000	.000	.000
Reyes A.	-1	1	0	27	22	3.81	3	0	0	0	3	10	0	0	0	2	0	0	0	0	.120	.120	.120	.085
Carpenter C.	-1	2	2	80	62	3.33	9	0	0	0	9	27	0	0	0	9	0	0	0	0	.127	.127	.127	.090

Italicized stats have been adjusted for home park.

Batted Ball Batting Stats are listed after fielding stats

Pitching Stats

Player	PRC	IP	BFP	G	GS	P/PA	K	BB	IBB	HBP	H	HR	DP	DER	SB	CS	PO	W	L	Sv	Op	Hld	RA	ERA	FIP
Carpenter C.	125	221.7	896	32	32	3.63	184	43	3	10	194	21	20	.721	3	7	0	15	8	0	0	0	3.29	3.09	3.47
Suppan J.	70	190.0	837	32	32	3.66	104	69	6	8	207	21	26	.690	12	3	1	12	7	0	0	0	4.74	4.12	4.68
Marquis J.	52	194.3	870	33	33	3.54	96	75	2	16	221	35	21	.704	10	5	0	14	16	0	0	0	6.30	6.02	5.95
Wainwright A.	46	75.0	309	61	0	3.86	72	22	2	4	64	6	5	.712	3	0	0	2	1	3	5	17	3.12	3.12	3.30
Looper B.	34	73.3	308	69	0	3.64	41	20	5	2	76	3	10	.694	3	1	0	9	3	0	2	15	3.68	3.56	3.33
Reyes A.	32	85.3	370	17	17	3.89	72	34	0	7	84	17	8	.713	5	2	0	5	8	0	0	0	5.06	5.06	5.56
Hancock J.	32	77.0	323	62	0	3.61	50	23	2	1	70	9	10	.708	4	0	0	3	3	1	3	5	4.32	4.09	4.30
Isringhausen J	29	58.3	257	59	0	4.12	52	38	3	3	47	10	5	.740	5	1	0	4	8	33	43	0	3.86	3.55	5.62
Weaver J.	27	83.3	373	15	15	3.75	45	26	1	6	99	16	10	.689	3	3	0	5	4	0	0	0	5.29	5.18	5.75
Thompson B.	27	56.7	245	43	1	3.49	32	20	3	5	58	4	10	.696	1	1	0	1	2	0	0	3	3.65	3.34	4.17
Ponson S.	21	68.7	303	14	13	3.67	33	29	1	4	82	7	15	.661	2	3	1	4	4	0	0	0	5.50	5.24	4.98
Mulder M.	21	93.3	430	17	17	3.45	50	35	1	5	124	19	16	.664	5	1	0	6	7	0	0	0	7.43	7.14	6.05
Kinney J.	14	25.0	99	21	0	3.84	22	8	0	1	17	3	3	.769	1	0	0	0	0	0	0	2	3.24	3.24	4.10
Johnson T.	14	36.3	164	56	0	3.79	37	23	2	4	33	5	4	.705	3	0	0	2	4	0	2	11	5.20	4.95	5.03
Flores R.	13	41.7	196	65	0	3.81	40	22	3	1	49	5	3	.617	1	2	1	1	1	0	1	18	6.26	5.62	4.30
Sosa J.	10	30.7	130	19	0	3.59	17	8	1	0	33	10	3	.758	1	1	1	0	1	1	1	0	5.28	5.28	7.03
Narveson C.	4	9.3	40	5	1	4.40	12	5	0	1	6	1	1	.714	1	1	0	0	0	0	0	0	4.82	4.82	3.97
Falkenborg B.	4	6.3	25	5	0	4.48	5	0	0	1	5	0	0	.684	0	1	0	0	1	0	0	0	2.84	2.84	2.11
Rincon R.	1	3.3	21	5	0	4.62	6	4	0	1	6	1	0	.444	0	0	0	0	0	0	0	2	10.80	10.80	8.02

Batted Ball Pitching Stats are listed after fielding stats

Fielding Stats

Name	POS	INN	SBA/G	CS%	ERA	WP+PB/G	PO	A	TE	FE
Molina, Y.	C	1037.3	0.55	41%	4.53	0.278	736	77	3	1
Bennett, G.	C	385.3	0.68	10%	4.58	0.234	243	14	2	1
Rose, M.	C	7.0	0.00	0%	3.86	1.286	10	0	0	0

Name	POS	Inn	PO	A	TE	FE	FPct	RF	DPS	DPT
Pujols, A.	1B	1244.0	1345	110	1	5	.996	10.53	18	2
Duncan, C.	1B	61.3	54	3	0	0	1.000	8.36	0	0
Spiezio, S.	1B	55.0	57	3	0	0	1.000	9.82	0	0
Edmonds, J.	1B	40.7	43	2	0	0	1.000	9.96	0	0
Luna, H.	1B	19.7	25	1	0	0	1.000	11.90	0	0
Molina, Y.	1B	5.0	5	0	0	1	.833	9.00	0	0
Bennett, G.	1B	1.0	0	0	0	0	0.000	0.00	0	0
Vizcaino, J.	1B	1.0	1	0	0	0	1.000	9.00	0	0
Nelson, J.	1B	1.0	1	0	0	0	1.000	9.00	0	0
Gall, J.	1B	0.7	0	0	0	0	0.000	0.00	0	0
Miles, A.	2B	649.7	165	232	2	8	.975	5.50	18	38
Belliard, R.	2B	448.0	98	151	1	2	.988	5.00	21	24
Luna, H.	2B	300.3	69	94	2	2	.976	4.88	5	16
Spiezio, S.	2B	26.7	7	13	0	0	1.000	6.75	1	3
Vizcaino, J.	2B	3.0	0	1	0	0	1.000	3.00	0	0
Taguchi, S.	2B	2.0	1	1	0	0	1.000	9.00	0	0
Eckstein, D.	SS	1029.0	178	363	4	2	.989	4.73	42	42
Miles, A.	SS	298.0	55	108	3	4	.959	4.92	16	10
Luna, H.	SS	68.0	9	17	0	0	1.000	3.44	1	3
Vizcaino, J.	SS	32.7	9	10	2	0	.905	5.23	3	1
Nelson, J.	SS	2.0	1	1	0	0	1.000	9.00	0	0
Rolen, S.	3B	1215.0	93	318	4	11	.965	3.04	36	0
Spiezio, S.	3B	202.7	10	45	1	3	.932	2.44	4	0
Luna, H.	3B	9.0	1	4	0	0	1.000	5.00	0	0
Miles, A.	3B	2.3	0	0	0	0	0.000	0.00	0	0

Name	POS	Inn	PO	A	TE	FE	FPct	RF	DPS	DPT
Taguchi, S.	LF	361.7	87	1	0	1	.989	2.19	0	0
Duncan, C.	LF	327.3	66	2	0	3	.958	1.87	0	0
Rodriguez, J.	LF	227.7	47	1	0	0	1.000	1.90	0	0
Spiezio, S.	LF	216.0	34	1	0	1	.972	1.46	0	0
Luna, H.	LF	111.3	24	0	0	1	.960	1.94	0	0
Schumaker, J.	LF	63.0	13	0	0	0	1.000	1.86	0	0
Wilson, P.	LF	50.0	9	0	0	0	1.000	1.62	0	0
Bigbie, L.	LF	44.3	8	0	0	0	1.000	1.62	0	0
Perez, T.	LF	13.7	3	0	0	0	1.000	1.98	0	0
Gall, J.	LF	8.7	2	0	0	0	1.000	2.08	0	0
Encarnacion, J.	LF	6.0	0	0	0	0	0.000	0.00	0	0
Edmonds, J.	CF	792.3	223	4	0	3	.987	2.58	0	0
Taguchi, S.	CF	353.3	90	2	1	4	.948	2.34	0	0
Encarnacion, J.	CF	230.7	46	0	0	2	.958	1.79	0	0
Wilson, P.	CF	28.3	8	0	0	1	.889	2.54	0	0
Schumaker, J.	CF	25.0	10	0	0	0	1.000	3.60	0	0
Encarnacion, J.	RF	983.3	219	4	0	4	.982	2.04	0	0
Duncan, C.	RF	151.3	41	0	0	3	.932	2.44	0	0
Wilson, P.	RF	150.7	31	0	0	1	.969	1.85	0	0
Rodriguez, J.	RF	74.3	21	0	0	1	.955	2.54	0	0
Schumaker, J.	RF	26.0	4	0	0	0	1.000	1.38	0	0
Perez, T.	RF	21.3	3	0	0	0	1.000	1.27	0	0
Taguchi, S.	RF	19.7	5	0	0	0	1.000	2.29	0	0
Bigbie, L.	RF	2.0	1	0	0	0	1.000	4.50	0	0
Luna, H.	RF	1.0	0	0	0	0	0.000	0.00	0	0

Batted Ball Batting Stats

Player	PA	% of PA		% of Batted Balls					Runs Per Event				Total Runs vs. Avg.				
		K%	BB%	GB%	LD%	FB%	IF/F	HR/OF	NIP	GB	LD	OF	NIP	GB	LD	FB	Tot
Pujols A.	634	8	15	37	18	45	.16	.24	.19	.05	.46	.35	19	0	5	33	58
Rolen S.	594	12	11	33	20	48	.12	.11	.11	.07	.40	.19	7	2	4	9	21
Duncan C.	314	22	10	44	21	35	.09	.32	.03	.07	.33	.46	-1	2	-3	17	16
Spiezio S.	321	21	13	34	20	46	.10	.14	.07	.03	.48	.24	3	-1	2	6	10
Edmonds J.	408	25	13	35	20	44	.06	.18	.04	.02	.39	.27	1	-5	-2	10	5
Wilson P.	120	23	8	48	17	36	.13	.31	.00	.02	.23	.47	-2	-1	-3	7	1
Luna H.	245	14	9	44	22	34	.11	.05	.07	.09	.40	.08	0	4	3	-7	1
Rodriguez J.	212	21	11	52	18	29	.05	.05	.05	.07	.40	.22	0	2	-1	-1	1
Encarnacion J.	598	14	6	45	20	35	.18	.12	.02	.06	.43	.17	-6	3	8	-5	0
Bennett G.	170	18	6	48	20	31	.08	.11	.01	.03	.28	.19	-2	-1	-2	-1	-6
Taguchi S.	361	13	9	48	21	30	.05	.03	.08	.06	.40	.03	1	3	3	-13	-6
Belliard R.	211	17	8	53	19	28	.24	.15	.03	.01	.37	.20	-1	-2	-1	-3	-7
Eckstein D.	552	7	8	49	22	29	.12	.02	.13	.07	.35	-.00	4	9	4	-25	-9
Miles A.	471	9	8	55	20	25	.12	.02	.11	.02	.37	.06	3	-1	2	-16	-12
Molina Y.	461	9	7	42	18	39	.15	.05	.10	-.01	.34	.07	1	-10	-2	-14	-24
MLB Average		*17*	*9*	*44*	*20*	*37*	*.11*	*.11*	*.05*	*.04*	*.39*	*.19*	-	-	-	-	-

Batted Ball Pitching Stats

Player	PA	% of PA		% of Batted Balls					Runs Per Event				Total Runs vs. Avg.				
		K%	BB%	GB%	LD%	FB%	IF/F	HR/OF	NIP	GB	LD	OF	NIP	GB	LD	FB	Tot
Carpenter C.	896	21	6	53	18	28	.07	.12	-.01	.02	.35	.21	-14	-7	-8	-5	-35
Wainwright A.	309	23	8	48	17	35	.15	.10	.01	.03	.46	.15	-3	-2	-1	-5	-12
Looper B.	308	13	7	49	20	30	.17	.05	.05	.07	.29	.11	-1	3	-3	-8	-9
Thompson B.	245	13	10	55	21	24	.18	.11	.09	.00	.32	.30	2	-3	-1	-0	-3
Hancock J.	323	15	7	40	19	40	.07	.09	.04	.04	.33	.17	-2	0	-2	1	-3
Isringhausen J.	257	20	16	44	18	38	.13	.15	.09	.01	.47	.18	5	-3	-0	-2	-1
Johnson T.	164	23	16	39	19	42	.07	.11	.08	.00	.51	.16	3	-2	1	-1	0
Sosa J.	130	13	6	34	14	52	.13	.21	.03	.08	.30	.28	-1	1	-3	7	4
Suppan J.	837	12	9	47	23	31	.16	.12	.08	.01	.43	.20	4	-9	16	-6	5
Flores R.	196	20	12	39	22	39	.04	.10	.05	.13	.35	.21	1	4	-1	1	5
Ponson S.	303	11	11	53	19	29	.12	.10	.12	.11	.36	.14	4	9	-1	-6	5
Reyes A.	370	19	11	35	20	46	.10	.17	.05	.02	.46	.24	1	-3	3	7	8
Weaver J.	373	12	9	39	22	39	.12	.15	.08	.01	.35	.28	1	-4	2	10	9
Mulder M.	430	12	9	55	22	24	.03	.23	.09	.05	.39	.39	2	2	4	10	18
Marquis J.	870	11	10	43	17	40	.09	.14	.11	.05	.43	.22	9	0	1	15	24
MLB Average		*17*	*9*	*44*	*20*	*37*	*.11*	*.11*	*.05*	*.04*	*.39*	*.19*	-	-	-	-	-

Tampa Bay Devil Rays

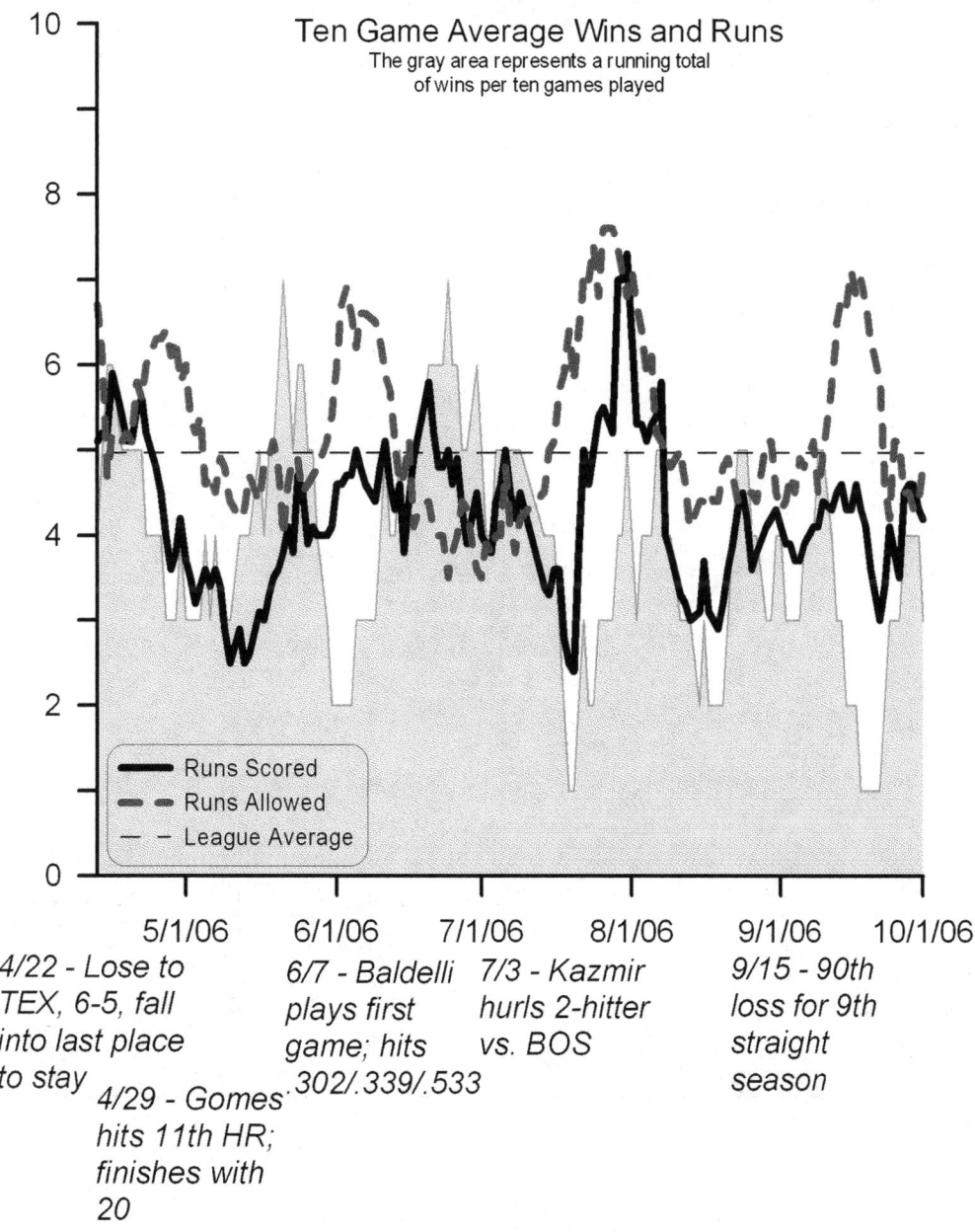

Ten Game Average Wins and Runs

The gray area represents a running total
of wins per ten games played

Legend:
- Runs Scored
- Runs Allowed
- League Average

4/22 - Lose to
TEX, 6-5, fall
into last place
to stay

4/29 - Gomes
hits 11th HR;
finishes with
20

6/7 - Baldelli
plays first
game; hits
.302/.339/.533

7/3 - Kazmir
hurls 2-hitter
vs. BOS

9/15 - 90th
loss for 9th
straight
season

Team Batting and Pitching/Fielding Stats by Month						
	April	May	June	July	Aug	Sept/Oct
Wins	11	10	14	9	9	8
Losses	14	18	13	17	19	20
OBP	.323	.286	.330	.307	.331	.303
SLG	.431	.379	.453	.432	.400	.427
FIP	5.58	4.83	4.09	4.69	4.72	4.98
DER	.682	.683	.681	.645	.677	.668

Batting Stats

Player	RC	Runs	RBI	PA	Outs	P/PA	H	2B	3B	HR	TB	K	BB	IBB	HBP	SH	SF	SB	CS	GDP	BA	OBP	SLG	GPA
Crawford C.	115	89	77	653	434	3.55	183	20	16	18	289	85	37	3	4	9	2	58	9	8	.305	.348	.482	.281
Wigginton T.	70	55	79	486	336	3.84	122	25	1	24	221	97	32	3	6	1	3	4	3	11	.275	.330	.498	.277
Baldelli R.	66	59	57	387	257	3.40	110	24	6	16	194	70	14	1	7	0	2	10	1	2	.302	.339	.533	.290
Norton G.	54	47	45	335	214	3.81	87	15	0	17	153	69	35	2	3	1	2	1	5	2	.296	.374	.520	.303
Gomes J.	54	53	59	461	317	3.84	83	21	1	20	166	116	61	2	6	0	9	1	5	10	.216	.325	.431	.258
Lugo J.	53	53	27	322	211	3.97	89	17	1	12	144	47	27	0	3	3	0	18	4	7	.308	.373	.498	.297
Cantu J.	42	40	62	448	327	3.71	103	18	2	14	167	91	26	2	3	0	6	1	1	16	.249	.295	.404	.237
Lee T.	33	35	31	388	276	3.93	77	11	2	11	125	73	42	1	2	0	1	5	2	8	.224	.312	.364	.235
Hollins D.	33	37	33	355	264	3.85	76	20	0	15	141	64	19	1	0	2	1	3	3	4	.228	.269	.423	.230
Huff A.	28	26	28	256	169	3.71	65	15	1	8	106	25	24	3	0	0	2	0	0	4	.283	.348	.461	.276
Branyan R.	22	23	27	193	136	4.06	34	10	0	12	80	62	19	0	2	1	2	2	0	1	.201	.286	.473	.251
Navarro D.	20	23	20	216	153	3.85	47	7	0	4	66	33	20	2	1	1	1	1	1	6	.244	.316	.342	.231
Hall T.	18	15	23	234	180	3.11	51	13	0	8	88	17	8	2	2	0	3	0	2	8	.231	.261	.398	.220
Upton B.	17	20	10	189	136	3.74	43	5	0	1	51	40	13	0	1	0	0	11	3	1	.246	.302	.291	.212
Paul J.	17	15	8	165	112	3.99	38	9	0	1	50	39	14	0	1	3	1	1	2	2	.260	.327	.342	.236
Young D.	16	16	10	131	88	2.85	40	9	1	3	60	24	1	0	3	0	1	2	2	0	.317	.336	.476	.274
Gathright J.	15	25	13	182	127	3.74	31	6	0	0	37	30	20	0	3	5	0	12	3	1	.201	.305	.240	.200
Zobrist B.	13	10	18	198	147	3.68	41	6	2	2	57	26	10	1	0	2	3	2	3	2	.224	.260	.311	.198
Perez T.	11	31	16	254	193	3.34	51	12	0	2	69	44	5	0	0	4	4	1	0	3	.212	.224	.286	.175
Burroughs S.	2	3	1	25	18	4.36	4	1	0	0	5	7	4	0	0	0	0	1	0	1	.190	.320	.238	.206
Witt K.	1	5	5	61	53	3.64	9	2	0	2	17	21	0	0	0	0	0	0	0	1	.148	.148	.279	.138
Riggans S.	0	3	1	33	25	3.52	5	1	0	0	6	7	4	0	0	0	0	0	0	1	.172	.273	.207	.177
Shields J.	0	2	0	8	5	3.38	3	0	0	0	3	3	0	0	0	0	0	0	0	0	.375	.375	.375	.266
Seo J.	-0	0	0	2	1	3.50	0	0	0	0	0	0	0	0	0	1	0	0	0	0	.000	.000	.000	.000
McClung S.	-0	0	0	2	1	2.00	0	0	0	0	0	0	0	0	0	1	0	0	0	0	.000	.000	.000	.000
Fossum C.	-0	0	0	2	2	2.00	0	0	0	0	0	0	0	0	0	0	0	0	0	0	.000	.000	.000	.000
Ordaz L.	-0	0	0	2	2	2.50	0	0	0	0	0	0	0	0	0	0	0	0	0	0	.000	.000	.000	.000
Kazmir S.	-0	0	0	3	3	3.67	0	0	0	0	0	2	0	0	0	0	0	0	0	0	.000	.000	.000	.000
Corcoran T.	-0	0	0	5	4	4.20	0	0	0	0	0	3	0	0	0	1	0	0	0	0	.000	.000	.000	.000
Green N.	-3	4	0	45	41	3.87	3	0	0	0	3	11	6	0	0	0	0	0	3	2	.077	.200	.077	.111

Italicized stats have been adjusted for home park.
Batted Ball Batting Stats are listed after fielding stats

Pitching Stats

Player	PRC	IP	BFP	G	GS	P/PA	K	BB	IBB	HBP	H	HR	DP	DER	SB	CS	PO	W	L	Sv	Op	Hld	RA	ERA	FIP
Kazmir S.	83	144.7	610	24	24	3.99	163	52	3	2	132	15	12	.661	15	3	5	10	8	0	0	0	3.67	3.24	3.41
Shields J.	50	124.7	540	21	21	3.69	104	38	5	5	141	18	12	.664	7	4	4	6	8	0	0	0	4.98	4.84	4.39
Fossum C.	40	130.0	594	25	25	3.68	88	63	3	12	136	18	11	.690	12	3	2	6	6	0	0	0	6.16	5.33	5.37
Hendrickson M.	39	89.7	377	13	13	3.61	51	34	0	2	81	10	11	.736	4	1	1	4	8	0	0	0	4.22	3.81	4.78
Lugo R.	38	85.0	363	64	0	3.85	48	37	0	5	75	4	12	.725	2	3	0	2	4	0	0	8	4.13	3.81	4.23
Corcoran T.	36	90.3	396	21	16	3.82	59	48	3	4	92	10	15	.687	10	6	0	5	9	0	0	0	4.78	4.38	5.02
Camp S.	28	75.0	328	75	0	3.38	53	19	3	7	93	9	15	.633	6	2	0	7	4	4	6	12	5.16	4.68	4.33
Seo J.	28	90.0	411	17	16	3.60	39	31	3	3	122	17	15	.664	4	6	1	1	8	0	0	1	5.60	5.00	5.88
McClung S.	27	103.0	489	39	15	3.97	59	68	5	3	120	14	7	.681	15	5	1	6	12	6	7	0	6.73	6.29	5.81
Meadows B.	22	69.7	312	53	0	3.53	35	15	4	0	90	14	6	.677	5	1	0	3	6	8	10	4	5.56	5.17	5.34
Howell J.	16	42.3	187	8	8	3.80	33	14	0	3	52	4	7	.632	3	1	0	1	3	0	0	0	5.31	5.10	4.14
Harper T.	14	42.0	196	30	0	3.57	32	13	1	2	62	6	6	.587	1	1	0	2	0	0	2	5	5.79	4.93	4.60
Harville C.	13	41.0	184	32	0	3.70	30	22	2	0	44	5	5	.685	7	1	0	0	2	1	2	2	5.93	5.93	4.85
Waechter D.	13	53.0	249	11	10	3.44	25	19	1	5	67	6	1	.675	1	2	0	1	4	0	0	0	6.79	6.62	5.09
Miceli D.	12	32.0	142	33	0	3.96	18	20	3	1	25	4	1	.768	2	1	0	1	2	4	7	6	4.78	3.94	5.45
Switzer J.	12	33.7	157	40	0	3.75	18	19	3	1	38	5	4	.702	1	1	0	2	2	0	3	5	5.08	4.54	5.64
Jackson E.	10	36.3	174	23	1	3.96	27	25	0	1	42	2	4	.655	3	0	0	0	0	0	0	0	6.69	5.45	4.64
Hammel J.	10	44.0	208	9	9	3.85	32	21	0	1	61	7	3	.633	1	2	1	0	6	0	0	0	7.77	7.77	5.38
Stokes B.	9	24.0	110	5	4	3.75	15	9	0	1	31	2	0	.651	1	2	0	1	0	0	0	0	4.88	4.88	4.35
Walker T.	8	20.0	83	20	0	3.70	16	7	0	0	18	0	3	.683	3	0	0	1	3	10	12	0	4.95	4.95	2.71
Orvella C.	5	24.3	130	22	0	4.12	17	20	0	3	36	6	3	.631	4	1	0	1	5	0	3	1	8.51	7.40	7.91
Salas J.	3	10.0	48	8	0	3.85	8	3	0	0	13	1	0	.611	0	0	0	0	0	0	1	1	6.30	5.40	3.86
Childers J.	2	7.7	40	5	0	4.05	5	4	0	0	12	1	2	.533	1	0	0	0	1	0	0	0	7.04	4.70	5.22
Dunn S.	1	7.7	45	7	0	3.60	4	4	0	2	17	2	1	.545	0	0	0	1	0	0	1	2	11.74	11.74	7.96
Colome J.	0	0.3	1	1	0	4.00	0	1	0	0	0	0	0	0.000	0	0	0	0	0	0	0	0	27.00	27.00	12.26

Batted Ball Pitching Stats are listed after fielding stats

Fielding Stats

Name	POS	INN	SBA/G	CS%	ERA	WP+PB/G	PO	A	TE	FE
Hall, T.	C	494.0	0.75	20%	5.03	0.437	312	20	1	2
Navarro, D.	C	458.7	0.98	36%	5.32	0.608	330	34	6	1
Paul, J.	C	400.3	1.17	17%	4.61	0.427	303	22	0	0
Riggans, S.	C	67.3	0.40	0%	4.28	0.535	56	4	0	0

Name	POS	Inn	PO	A	TE	FE	FPct	RF	DPS	DPT
Lee, T.	1B	864.7	852	58	0	2	.998	9.47	8	0
Wigginton, T.	1B	329.7	300	28	0	1	.997	8.95	3	2
Norton, G.	1B	172.0	154	9	0	1	.994	8.53	1	0
Witt, K.	1B	37.0	28	1	0	2	.935	7.05	0	0
Branyan, R.	1B	9.0	8	0	0	0	1.000	8.00	0	0
Perez, T.	1B	8.0	8	0	0	0	1.000	9.00	0	0
Cantu, J.	2B	898.7	210	252	2	11	.973	4.63	24	37
Wigginton, T.	2B	328.3	66	115	0	0	1.000	4.96	9	23
Perez, T.	2B	161.3	27	58	0	1	.988	4.74	7	6
Green, N.	2B	32.0	7	8	0	0	1.000	4.22	2	1
Lugo, J.	SS	620.3	114	201	9	5	.957	4.57	25	15
Zobrist, B.	SS	440.7	86	147	4	5	.963	4.76	18	13
Perez, T.	SS	287.3	47	96	2	3	.966	4.48	10	12
Green, N.	SS	67.0	10	21	0	0	1.000	4.16	4	2
Ordaz, L.	SS	5.0	1	1	0	0	1.000	3.60	0	0
Huff, A.	3B	479.7	38	109	1	2	.980	2.76	12	1
Upton, B.	3B	412.7	38	88	7	5	.906	2.75	6	1
Wigginton, T.	3B	274.3	16	63	1	4	.940	2.59	7	1
Perez, T.	3B	162.3	15	37	1	1	.963	2.88	4	0
Burroughs, S.	3B	57.0	6	20	1	0	.963	4.11	3	0
Branyan, R.	3B	33.3	1	6	1	2	.700	1.89	1	0
Hall, T.	3B	1.0	0	0	0	0	0.000	0.00	0	0

Name	POS	Inn	PO	A	TE	FE	FPct	RF	DPS	DPT
Crawford, C.	LF	1252.0	302	9	1	2	.990	2.24	0	0
Hollins, D.	LF	102.0	27	1	0	2	.933	2.47	2	0
Wigginton, T.	LF	39.0	9	0	0	2	.818	2.08	0	0
Norton, G.	LF	17.0	2	1	0	0	1.000	1.59	0	0
Branyan, R.	LF	7.0	3	0	0	0	1.000	3.86	0	0
Perez, T.	LF	2.0	0	0	0	0	0.000	0.00	0	0
Paul, J.	LF	1.0	0	0	0	0	0.000	0.00	0	0
Baldelli, R.	CF	749.3	228	6	0	5	.979	2.81	6	0
Gathright, J.	CF	438.0	155	2	1	0	.994	3.23	4	0
Hollins, D.	CF	216.0	55	0	0	0	1.000	2.29	0	0
Crawford, C.	CF	9.0	2	1	0	0	1.000	3.00	0	0
Young, D.	CF	8.0	4	0	0	0	1.000	4.50	0	0
Hollins, D.	RF	463.7	134	4	0	2	.986	2.68	0	0
Branyan, R.	RF	357.3	86	5	1	2	.968	2.29	0	0
Young, D.	RF	252.3	50	4	0	1	.982	1.93	0	0
Norton, G.	RF	207.3	40	0	0	2	.952	1.74	0	0
Gomes, J.	RF	60.0	19	0	0	0	1.000	2.85	0	0
Wigginton, T.	RF	45.7	10	2	0	0	1.000	2.36	0	0
Perez, T.	RF	28.0	11	0	0	0	1.000	3.54	0	0
Green, N.	RF	6.0	1	0	0	0	1.000	1.50	0	0

Batted Ball Batting Stats

Player	PA	% of PA		% of Batted Balls					Runs Per Event				Total Runs vs. Avg.				
		K%	BB%	GB%	LD%	FB%	IF/F	HR/OF	NIP	GB	LD	OF	NIP	GB	LD	FB	Tot
Baldelli R.	387	18	5	51	16	34	.20	.16	-.01	.12	.47	.31	-6	13	0	6	13
Norton G.	335	21	11	38	19	42	.05	.19	.05	.04	.42	.31	1	-1	-0	13	12
Crawford C.	653	13	6	52	18	30	.09	.13	.04	.11	.33	.23	-4	19	-5	2	12
Lugo J.	322	15	9	50	18	31	.05	.17	.07	.09	.33	.28	1	7	-3	5	9
Wigginton T.	486	20	8	40	19	41	.18	.21	.02	.04	.38	.32	-4	-1	-1	15	9
Young D.	131	18	3	47	26	27	.04	.11	-.05	.04	.42	.28	-3	-0	4	2	3
Huff A.	256	10	9	48	18	34	.11	.11	.11	.04	.44	.17	2	-0	2	-2	3
Branyan R.	193	32	11	29	19	53	.04	.22	.00	-.03	.36	.31	-2	-3	-3	9	-0
Gomes J.	461	25	15	29	17	54	.11	.13	.05	.03	.43	.20	4	-5	-5	5	-1
Paul J.	165	24	9	48	22	30	.09	.03	.01	.10	.42	.06	-1	3	1	-6	-4
Hollins D.	355	18	5	41	19	40	.13	.14	-.01	.03	.36	.19	-5	-1	-1	1	-7
Navarro D.	216	15	10	36	23	41	.12	.07	.07	-.02	.37	.08	1	-4	2	-5	-7
Hall T.	234	7	4	35	16	50	.20	.10	.06	-.03	.36	.13	-2	-5	-1	-1	-8
Upton B.	189	21	7	54	19	27	.14	.03	.01	.08	.34	.02	-2	3	-2	-8	-9
Zobrist B.	198	13	5	47	22	30	.15	.05	.01	.02	.27	.08	-2	-0	-1	-6	-10
Lee T.	388	19	11	46	20	34	.15	.13	.06	.02	.33	.16	2	-2	-4	-6	-10
Gathright J.	182	16	13	61	19	19	.19	.00	.09	.02	.31	.01	2	-1	-4	-8	-10
Cantu J.	448	20	6	42	20	38	.05	.11	-.00	.04	.33	.16	-6	-1	-3	-0	-11
Perez T.	254	17	2	40	14	46	.19	.03	-.07	.06	.39	.01	-7	2	-3	-12	-20
MLB Average		*17*	*9*	*44*	*20*	*37*	*.11*	*.11*	*.05*	*.04*	*.39*	*.19*	-	-	-	-	-

Batted Ball Pitching Stats

Player	PA	% of PA		% of Batted Balls					Runs Per Event				Total Runs vs. Avg.				
		K%	BB%	GB%	LD%	FB%	IF/F	HR/OF	NIP	GB	LD	OF	NIP	GB	LD	FB	Tot
Lugo R.	363	13	12	44	16	40	.12	.04	.10	.04	.36	.08	4	-1	-4	-9	-10
Hendrickson M.	377	14	10	48	11	41	.13	.09	.08	.05	.36	.14	2	3	-10	-4	-9
Kazmir S.	610	27	9	42	19	39	.09	.10	.00	.10	.38	.19	-8	8	-6	-2	-7
Miceli D.	142	13	15	42	13	44	.16	.08	.13	.07	.47	.07	3	1	-2	-4	-2
Harville C.	184	16	12	53	19	27	.14	.17	.08	.06	.32	.24	2	1	-2	-1	-0
Howell J.	187	18	9	45	26	29	.10	.08	.04	.07	.41	.11	-0	2	4	-4	1
Switzer J.	157	11	13	49	14	37	.12	.11	.13	.05	.53	.15	3	1	-0	-2	2
Stokes B.	110	14	9	40	15	45	.18	.06	.07	.15	.31	.18	0	4	-2	0	2
Jackson E.	174	16	15	52	17	31	.11	.06	.11	.07	.57	.11	4	1	2	-4	2
Corcoran T.	396	15	13	40	23	37	.10	.10	.10	.02	.41	.17	6	-3	4	-3	5
Waechter D.	249	10	10	33	23	44	.12	.07	.11	.10	.44	.07	2	4	6	-6	5
Shields J.	540	19	8	43	23	34	.09	.15	.02	.05	.42	.21	-4	1	8	1	5
Camp S.	328	16	8	57	18	24	.13	.15	.04	.09	.42	.24	-1	9	1	-2	6
Fossum C.	594	15	13	46	21	33	.07	.13	.10	.06	.31	.22	8	3	-5	2	8
Meadows B.	312	11	5	38	18	44	.07	.13	.03	.08	.41	.20	-3	4	2	7	10
Hammel J.	208	15	11	44	19	38	.16	.14	.07	.11	.53	.21	1	4	4	0	10
Harper T.	196	16	8	37	25	38	.05	.12	.03	.11	.46	.22	-1	3	6	3	10
Orvella C.	130	13	18	36	22	41	.06	.18	.15	.07	.47	.30	4	0	2	4	10
McClung S.	489	12	15	37	20	43	.13	.11	.14	.07	.43	.13	11	3	4	-6	11
Seo J.	411	9	8	32	24	44	.12	.13	.10	.06	.43	.20	2	-0	11	6	19
MLB Average		*17*	*9*	*44*	*20*	*37*	*.11*	*.11*	*.05*	*.04*	*.39*	*.19*	-	-	-	-	-

Texas Rangers

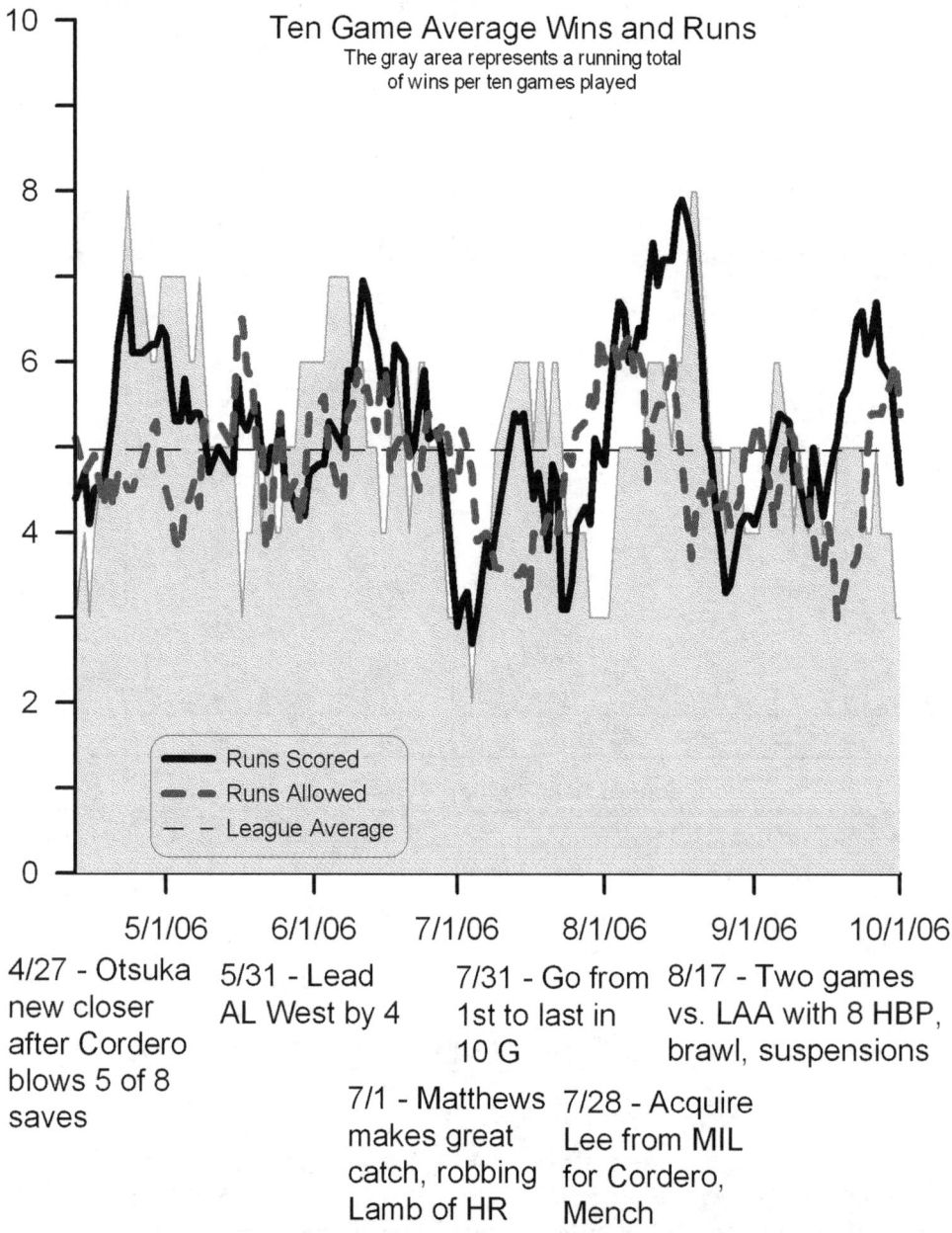

Ten Game Average Wins and Runs
The gray area represents a running total
of wins per ten games played

Legend:
— Runs Scored
- - Runs Allowed
– – League Average

4/27 - Otsuka new closer after Cordero blows 5 of 8 saves

5/31 - Lead AL West by 4

7/1 - Matthews makes great catch, robbing Lamb of HR

7/31 - Go from 1st to last in 10 G

7/28 - Acquire Lee from MIL for Cordero, Mench

8/17 - Two games vs. LAA with 8 HBP, brawl, suspensions

Team Batting and Pitching/Fielding Stats by Month						
	April	May	June	July	Aug	Sept/Oct
Wins	13	15	13	11	17	11
Losses	12	13	14	15	12	16
OBP	.348	.349	.337	.329	.335	.333
SLG	.459	.459	.435	.429	.461	.431
FIP	4.66	4.15	4.25	4.69	4.38	4.64
DER	.676	.694	.670	.689	.680	.679

Batting Stats

Player	RC	Runs	RBI	PA	Outs	P/PA	H	2B	3B	HR	TB	K	BB	IBB	HBP	SH	SF	SB	CS	GDP	BA	OBP	SLG	GPA
Young M.	116	93	103	748	504	3.75	217	52	3	14	317	96	48	0	1	0	8	7	3	27	.314	.356	.459	.261
Teixeira M.	110	99	110	727	468	3.97	177	45	1	33	323	128	89	12	4	0	6	2	0	17	.282	.371	.514	.281
Matthews Jr. G.	105	102	79	690	441	3.71	194	44	6	19	307	99	58	5	4	0	8	10	7	8	.313	.371	.495	.276
Blalock H.	84	76	89	646	449	3.61	157	26	3	16	237	98	51	6	2	0	2	1	0	15	.266	.325	.401	.234
DeRosa M.	76	78	74	572	383	3.73	154	40	2	13	237	102	44	1	6	0	2	4	4	13	.296	.357	.456	.261
Kinsler I.	63	65	55	474	318	3.90	121	27	4	14	192	64	40	1	3	1	7	11	4	12	.286	.347	.454	.256
Mench K.	47	36	50	349	233	3.56	91	18	1	12	147	42	23	5	4	0	2	1	0	4	.284	.338	.459	.254
Wilkerson B.	38	56	44	365	257	4.19	71	15	2	15	135	116	37	1	3	2	3	3	2	6	.222	.306	.422	.231
Lee C.	37	42	35	260	169	3.51	76	19	1	9	124	26	20	2	0	0	4	7	0	9	.322	.369	.525	.283
Barajas R.	35	49	41	371	265	3.61	88	20	0	11	141	51	17	0	4	5	1	0	0	9	.256	.298	.410	.225
Laird G.	23	46	22	260	179	3.62	72	20	1	7	115	54	12	0	2	1	2	3	1	7	.296	.332	.473	.254
Nevin P.	21	26	31	199	147	3.99	38	8	0	9	73	39	21	0	2	0	0	0	0	9	.216	.307	.415	.230
Cruz N.	17	15	22	138	102	3.92	29	3	0	6	50	32	7	0	0	0	1	1	0	1	.223	.261	.385	.203
Stairs M.	9	6	11	88	65	3.93	17	4	0	3	30	22	6	1	1	0	0	0	0	1	.210	.273	.370	.205
Jimenez D.	7	7	8	68	47	4.15	12	3	0	1	18	6	10	0	0	1	0	0	0	2	.211	.328	.316	.215
Botts J.	6	8	6	60	39	4.22	11	4	0	1	18	18	8	1	0	0	2	0	0	0	.220	.317	.360	.221
Hairston J.	4	17	6	100	76	3.70	18	3	1	0	23	20	9	0	1	2	0	2	2	4	.205	.286	.261	.184
Arias J.	2	4	1	12	6	3.33	6	1	0	0	7	0	1	0	0	0	0	0	1	0	.545	.583	.636	.401
Ojeda M.	2	0	4	14	9	3.71	4	2	0	0	6	3	0	0	0	0	0	0	0	0	.308	.308	.462	.241
Young E.	2	1	2	12	9	3.50	2	1	1	0	5	1	1	0	0	1	0	0	0	1	.200	.273	.500	.235
Guzman F.	1	1	0	9	5	4.44	2	0	0	0	2	1	1	0	1	0	0	0	0	0	.286	.444	.286	.258
Meyer D.	1	1	0	15	11	3.33	3	0	0	0	3	8	0	0	0	1	0	0	0	0	.214	.214	.214	.143
Brown A.	0	6	2	40	31	3.85	7	1	0	0	8	9	2	0	0	1	1	1	0	2	.194	.231	.222	.151
Hyzdu A.	0	0	0	4	3	3.75	1	0	0	0	1	2	0	0	0	0	0	0	0	0	.250	.250	.250	.166
Rheinecker J.	0	0	0	1	0	0.00	0	0	0	0	0	0	0	0	1	0	0	0	0	0	.000	1.000	.000	.428
Padilla V.	-0	0	0	2	1	2.50	0	0	0	0	0	1	0	0	0	1	0	0	0	0	.000	.000	.000	.000
Tejeda R.	-0	0	0	3	2	2.00	0	0	0	0	0	1	0	0	0	1	0	0	0	0	.000	.000	.000	.000
Millwood K.	-0	0	0	6	5	2.83	0	0	0	0	0	3	0	0	0	1	0	0	0	0	.000	.000	.000	.000
Nix L.	-1	1	4	34	29	3.88	3	1	0	0	4	17	0	0	1	0	1	0	0	0	.094	.118	.125	.080
Koronka J.	-1	0	0	6	7	3.33	0	0	0	0	0	2	0	0	0	0	0	0	0	1	.000	.000	.000	.000

Italicized stats have been adjusted for home park.

Batted Ball Batting Stats are listed after fielding stats

Pitching Stats

Player	PRC	IP	BFP	G	GS	P/PA	K	BB	IBB	HBP	H	HR	DP	DER	SB	CS	PO	W	L	Sv	Op	Hld	RA	ERA	FIP
Millwood K.	88	215.0	907	34	34	3.64	157	53	4	4	228	23	23	.687	10	3	0	16	12	0	0	0	4.77	4.52	3.93
Padilla V.	82	200.0	872	33	33	3.76	156	70	2	17	206	21	22	.686	8	3	2	15	10	0	0	0	4.86	4.50	4.34
Otsuka A.	42	59.7	232	63	0	3.77	47	11	0	0	53	3	11	.696	2	2	0	2	4	32	36	7	2.56	2.11	2.89
Koronka J.	38	125.0	554	23	23	3.67	61	47	2	5	145	17	15	.693	9	3	2	7	7	0	0	0	5.76	5.69	5.25
Bauer R.	32	71.0	302	58	1	3.78	35	25	0	4	73	4	15	.684	4	2	0	3	1	2	5	7	3.93	3.55	4.23
Benoit J.	31	79.7	347	56	0	4.18	85	38	4	3	68	5	4	.699	1	0	0	1	1	0	2	7	5.54	4.86	3.34
Littleton W.	30	36.3	138	33	0	3.48	17	13	0	2	23	2	9	.788	1	1	0	2	1	1	1	7	1.73	1.73	4.28
Tejeda R.	28	73.7	329	14	14	3.83	40	32	1	3	83	10	8	.689	4	3	0	5	5	0	0	0	4.89	4.28	5.33
Mahay R.	25	57.0	246	62	0	4.04	56	28	2	0	54	7	8	.677	2	2	1	1	3	0	1	9	4.74	3.95	4.26
Eaton A.	24	65.0	291	13	13	3.88	43	24	0	4	78	11	5	.670	2	5	0	7	4	0	0	0	5.26	5.12	5.43
Loe K.	22	78.3	358	15	15	3.60	34	22	0	1	105	10	8	.663	5	0	0	3	6	0	0	0	6.20	5.86	4.94
Cordero F.	21	48.7	210	49	0	4.04	54	16	1	3	49	5	2	.659	3	2	0	7	4	6	15	15	4.99	4.81	3.49
Rheinecker J	20	70.7	322	21	13	3.56	28	19	0	3	104	6	11	.628	2	5	1	4	6	0	0	1	5.86	5.86	4.51
Wilson C.	20	44.3	191	44	0	3.90	43	18	1	5	39	7	6	.703	5	3	1	2	4	1	2	7	4.67	4.06	4.86
Feldman S.	19	41.3	175	36	0	3.69	30	10	0	4	42	4	8	.685	2	1	0	0	2	0	1	7	4.14	3.92	4.09
Rupe J.	15	29.0	126	16	0	3.59	14	9	0	1	33	2	5	.680	1	0	0	0	1	0	1	1	3.41	3.41	4.23
Corey B.	12	17.3	75	16	0	3.83	13	8	0	0	15	0	1	.685	0	0	0	1	1	0	0	0	2.60	2.60	3.15
Wasdin J.	10	30.0	141	9	5	3.81	16	13	0	4	33	6	1	.716	2	1	0	2	2	0	0	0	5.70	5.10	6.50
Volquez E.	7	33.3	164	8	8	3.97	15	17	0	1	52	7	4	.637	4	1	0	1	6	0	0	0	7.56	7.29	6.71
Alfonseca A.	5	16.0	74	19	0	3.69	5	7	0	0	23	3	3	.661	0	1	0	0	0	0	0	8	5.63	5.63	6.39
Masset N.	4	8.7	36	8	0	3.47	4	2	0	2	9	0	2	.679	0	0	0	0	0	0	0	0	4.15	4.15	3.72
Francisco F.	3	7.3	32	8	0	3.66	6	2	0	0	8	2	0	.682	0	1	0	0	1	0	0	2	4.91	4.91	5.99
Castro F.	3	8.3	37	4	0	3.73	5	7	0	0	6	0	3	.680	0	0	0	0	0	0	0	0	5.40	4.32	4.58
Wells K.	2	8.0	40	2	2	3.85	4	3	0	0	15	0	3	.515	0	1	0	1	0	0	0	0	6.75	5.63	3.39
Shouse B.	2	4.3	20	6	0	3.30	3	1	1	0	6	1	1	.600	0	0	0	0	0	0	1	1	4.15	4.15	4.88
Dickey R.	0	3.3	18	1	1	3.39	1	1	0	0	8	6	0	.800	0	0	0	0	1	0	0	0	18.90	18.90	26.96

Batted Ball Pitching Stats are listed after fielding stats

Fielding Stats

Name	POS	INN	SBA/G	CS%	ERA	WP+PB/G	PO	A	TE	FE
Barajas, R.	C	825.0	0.58	28%	4.73	0.262	591	35	10	0
Laird, G.	C	578.3	0.68	43%	4.39	0.311	392	30	5	0
Ojeda, M.	C	28.0	1.29	0%	5.46	0.321	21	2	0	0

Name	POS	Inn	PO	A	TE	FE	FPct	RF	DPS	DPT
Teixeira, M.	1B	1399.0	1481	88	0	3	.997	10.09	15	3
Barajas, R.	1B	12.0	14	1	0	0	1.000	11.25	0	0
DeRosa, M.	1B	9.0	4	1	0	0	1.000	5.00	0	0
Nevin, P.	1B	8.3	8	0	0	0	1.000	8.64	0	0
Stairs, M.	1B	3.0	2	0	0	0	1.000	6.00	0	0
Kinsler, I.	2B	1032.0	247	393	7	11	.973	5.58	44	48
DeRosa, M.	2B	222.7	50	86	0	1	.993	5.50	6	11
Jimenez, D.	2B	130.7	35	33	1	3	.944	4.68	6	8
Meyer, D.	2B	28.0	8	6	0	0	1.000	4.50	0	1
Hairston, J.	2B	9.0	2	2	0	1	.800	4.00	0	1
Young, E.	2B	9.0	2	6	0	0	1.000	8.00	2	0
Young, M.	SS	1356.0	241	493	5	9	.981	4.87	59	52
DeRosa, M.	SS	42.0	9	19	0	0	1.000	6.00	0	5
Arias, J.	SS	20.0	6	9	0	0	1.000	6.75	0	2
Hairston, J.	SS	12.0	4	6	0	0	1.000	7.50	1	2
Meyer, D.	SS	1.0	0	0	0	1	0.000	0.00	0	0
Blalock, H.	3B	1062.0	72	237	5	7	.963	2.62	19	0
DeRosa, M.	3B	342.7	19	82	1	2	.971	2.65	7	0
Jimenez, D.	3B	10.0	0	1	0	0	1.000	0.90	0	0
Hairston, J.	3B	8.0	1	1	0	0	1.000	2.25	0	0
Arias, J.	3B	8.0	1	4	0	0	1.000	5.63	0	0

Name	POS	Inn	PO	A	TE	FE	FPct	RF	DPS	DPT
Wilkerson, B.	LF	664.3	139	7	0	1	.993	1.98	6	0
Lee, C.	LF	424.0	82	1	0	2	.976	1.76	0	0
Hairston, J.	LF	141.3	31	5	0	0	1.000	2.29	2	0
Mench, K.	LF	130.7	16	1	0	1	.944	1.17	0	0
DeRosa, M.	LF	37.0	7	1	0	0	1.000	1.95	0	0
Brown, A.	LF	13.0	0	0	0	0	0.000	0.00	0	0
Young, E.	LF	9.0	4	0	0	0	1.000	4.00	0	0
Guzman, F.	LF	8.0	1	0	0	0	1.000	1.13	0	0
Cruz, N.	LF	3.0	0	0	0	0	0.000	0.00	0	0
Botts, J.	LF	1.0	1	0	0	0	1.000	9.00	0	0
Matthews Jr., G.	CF	1227.0	331	8	0	7	.980	2.49	4	0
Nix, L.	CF	78.3	21	2	0	0	1.000	2.64	4	0
Brown, A.	CF	60.0	24	1	1	0	.962	3.75	0	0
Hairston, J.	CF	51.0	16	3	0	0	1.000	3.35	2	0
Guzman, F.	CF	11.0	4	0	0	0	1.000	3.27	0	0
Cruz, N.	CF	3.0	0	0	0	0	0.000	0.00	0	0
Wilkerson, B.	CF	1.0	0	0	0	0	0.000	0.00	0	0
DeRosa, M.	RF	512.0	125	4	0	1	.992	2.27	2	0
Mench, K.	RF	488.7	112	2	0	0	1.000	2.10	2	0
Cruz, N.	RF	307.3	69	4	0	0	1.000	2.14	2	0
Hairston, J.	RF	31.7	6	0	0	0	1.000	1.71	0	0
Matthews Jr., G.	RF	26.0	9	0	0	0	1.000	3.12	0	0
Wilkerson, B.	RF	21.0	4	0	0	0	1.000	1.71	0	0
Brown, A.	RF	20.7	7	2	0	0	1.000	3.92	2	0
Hyzdu, A.	RF	9.0	3	0	0	0	1.000	3.00	0	0
Stairs, M.	RF	8.0	1	0	0	0	1.000	1.13	0	0
Meyer, D.	RF	4.0	0	0	0	0	0.000	0.00	0	0
Laird, G.	RF	2.0	0	0	0	0	0.000	0.00	0	0
Guzman, F.	RF	1.0	0	0	0	0	0.000	0.00	0	0

Batted Ball Batting Stats

Player	PA	% of PA		% of Batted Balls					Runs Per Event				Total Runs vs. Avg.				
		K%	BB%	GB%	LD%	FB%	IF/F	HR/OF	NIP	GB	LD	OF	NIP	GB	LD	FB	Tot
Teixeira M.	727	18	13	39	20	41	.12	.16	.08	.03	.46	.25	8	-4	6	13	24
Matthews Jr. G.	690	14	9	51	19	30	.09	.11	.06	.08	.49	.20	1	13	10	-3	21
Young M.	748	13	7	48	25	27	.04	.08	.04	.07	.36	.15	-4	9	13	-8	10
DeRosa M.	572	18	9	49	23	29	.12	.12	.04	.06	.43	.23	-2	4	9	-1	10
Lee C.	260	10	8	40	21	39	.14	.13	.09	.07	.39	.23	0	2	4	4	10
Mench K.	349	12	8	41	18	41	.17	.12	.07	.06	.36	.23	-0	2	-2	5	4
Kinsler I.	474	14	9	35	21	44	.14	.10	.07	.06	.37	.16	1	2	1	-1	4
Laird G.	260	21	5	34	19	46	.14	.10	-.02	.05	.47	.21	-5	3	2	3	3
Cruz N.	138	23	5	46	12	42	.12	.14	-.03	.12	.32	.18	-3	3	-4	0	-3
Nevin P.	199	20	12	45	22	34	.13	.20	.06	-.04	.35	.26	1	-5	-1	1	-4
Wilkerson B.	365	32	11	35	15	50	.06	.16	.00	.04	.40	.27	-4	-2	-8	9	-5
Hairston J.	100	20	10	49	12	39	.19	.00	.04	.02	.57	.03	-0	-1	-1	-4	-6
Barajas R.	371	14	6	31	17	51	.16	.09	.02	.04	.38	.15	-3	-2	-1	0	-6
Blalock H.	646	15	8	42	21	37	.10	.08	.05	.03	.38	.13	-1	-3	4	-8	-8
MLB Average		*17*	*9*	*44*	*20*	*37*	*.11*	*.11*	*.05*	*.04*	*.39*	*.19*	-	-	-	-	-

Batted Ball Pitching Stats

Player	PA	% of PA		% of Batted Balls					Runs Per Event				Total Runs vs. Avg.				
		K%	BB%	GB%	LD%	FB%	IF/F	HR/OF	NIP	GB	LD	OF	NIP	GB	LD	FB	Tot
Benoit J.	347	24	12	37	19	44	.13	.06	.04	.06	.35	.10	-0	-0	-5	-7	-13
Otsuka A.	232	20	5	52	19	28	.16	.07	-.03	.05	.32	.08	-5	2	-2	-8	-12
Millwood K.	907	17	6	45	21	34	.08	.10	.01	.02	.38	.20	-10	-7	5	2	-11
Littleton W.	138	12	11	71	12	17	.11	.13	.10	-.01	.29	.09	1	-3	-4	-5	-10
Bauer R.	302	12	10	53	17	30	.17	.07	.10	.06	.40	.10	2	3	-0	-8	-4
Feldman S.	175	17	8	59	22	19	.08	.18	.03	.01	.35	.29	-1	-1	0	-1	-3
Cordero F.	210	26	9	43	21	36	.04	.11	.01	.08	.34	.19	-2	2	-2	-0	-3
Padilla V.	872	18	10	44	22	34	.09	.10	.05	.05	.38	.17	1	0	3	-7	-3
Rupe J.	126	11	8	66	13	21	.05	.10	.08	.05	.33	.22	0	1	-3	-1	-2
Wilson C.	191	23	12	49	21	30	.14	.19	.05	.01	.36	.33	1	-2	-1	1	-1
Mahay R.	246	23	11	41	21	38	.05	.12	.04	-.01	.49	.19	0	-4	3	-0	-1
Tejeda R.	329	12	11	37	18	45	.11	.10	.10	.08	.43	.12	3	3	1	-4	3
Wasdin J.	141	11	12	40	18	43	.17	.16	.12	.06	.32	.25	2	1	-2	3	4
Eaton A.	291	15	10	37	24	38	.12	.12	.07	.06	.38	.22	1	0	4	2	7
Koronka J.	554	11	9	42	19	39	.08	.11	.10	.04	.35	.20	4	0	-1	6	8
Rheinecker J.	322	9	7	59	19	22	.14	.12	.09	.06	.43	.24	0	6	5	-2	8
Loe K.	358	9	6	51	19	30	.06	.11	.07	.05	.43	.21	-1	2	5	2	8
Volquez E.	164	9	11	43	22	35	.11	.17	.14	.11	.41	.18	2	4	3	-0	9
MLB Average		*17*	*9*	*44*	*20*	*37*	*.11*	*.11*	*.05*	*.04*	*.39*	*.19*	-	-	-	-	-

Toronto Blue Jays

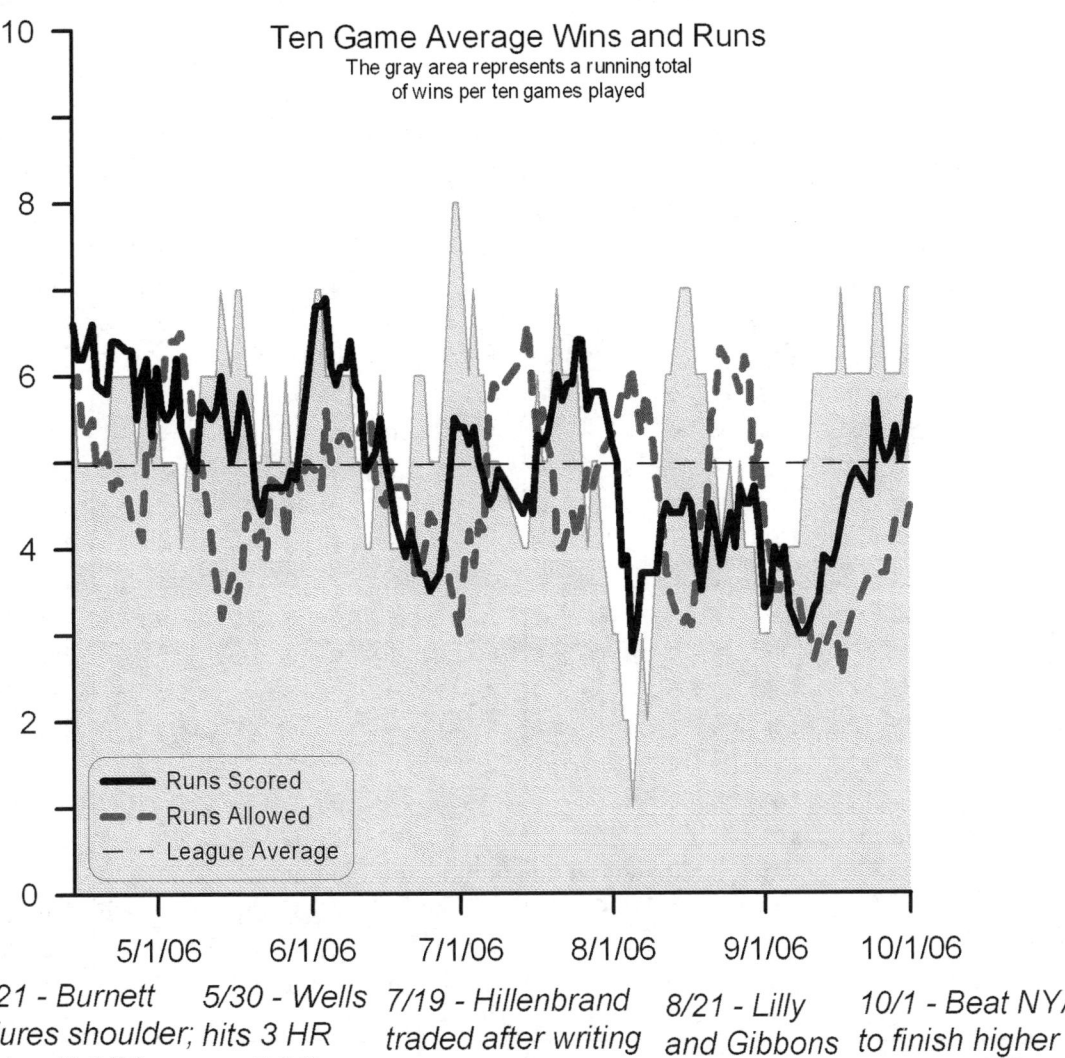

Ten Game Average Wins and Runs
The gray area represents a running total
of wins per ten games played

- Runs Scored
- Runs Allowed
- League Average

4/21 - Burnett injures shoulder; out until 6/22

5/30 - Wells hits 3 HR vs. BOS

7/19 - Hillenbrand traded after writing comments on clubhouse board

8/21 - Lilly and Gibbons argue in clubhouse

10/1 - Beat NYA to finish higher than 3rd for first time since 1993

Team Batting and Pitching/Fielding Stats by Month						
	April	May	June	July	Aug	Sept/Oct
Wins	12	17	16	12	12	18
Losses	11	12	11	14	17	10
OBP	.364	.363	.369	.346	.305	.344
SLG	.493	.501	.469	.463	.404	.451
FIP	5.59	4.79	3.80	4.12	4.55	3.96
DER	.702	.712	.689	.665	.703	.704

Batting Stats

Player	RC	Runs	RBI	PA	Outs	P/PA	H	2B	3B	HR	TB	K	BB	IBB	HBP	SH	SF	SB	CS	GDP	BA	OBP	SLG	GPA
Wells V.	109	91	106	677	443	3.39	185	40	5	32	331	90	54	0	3	0	9	17	4	13	.303	.357	.542	.287
Overbay L.	91	82	92	640	422	3.57	181	46	1	22	295	96	55	7	2	0	2	5	3	19	.312	.372	.508	.285
Glaus T.	86	105	104	634	431	4.21	136	27	0	38	277	134	86	6	3	0	5	3	2	25	.252	.355	.513	.279
Rios A.	85	68	82	498	330	3.90	136	33	6	17	232	89	35	1	3	0	10	15	6	10	.302	.349	.516	.277
Johnson R.	78	86	49	517	325	3.82	147	34	2	12	221	81	33	4	21	1	1	8	2	9	.319	.390	.479	.286
Catalanotto F.	74	56	56	499	320	3.96	131	36	2	7	192	37	52	0	4	2	4	1	3	11	.300	.376	.439	.270
Hill A.	70	70	50	606	404	3.73	159	28	3	6	211	66	42	5	9	4	5	5	2	15	.291	.349	.386	.245
Molina B.	59	44	57	458	326	3.64	123	20	1	19	202	47	19	1	4	0	2	1	1	15	.284	.319	.467	.252
Zaun G.	42	39	40	339	223	4.19	79	19	0	12	134	42	41	3	3	0	5	0	2	10	.272	.363	.462	.270
Hillenbrand S.	39	40	39	319	224	3.47	89	15	1	12	142	40	14	2	6	0	3	1	2	15	.301	.342	.480	.265
Hinske E.	30	35	29	224	152	3.96	52	9	2	12	101	49	27	2	0	0	0	1	1	6	.264	.353	.513	.278
Adams R.	23	31	28	280	203	3.87	55	14	1	3	80	41	22	0	1	3	3	1	2	5	.219	.282	.319	.200
McDonald J.	20	35	23	286	212	3.62	58	7	3	3	80	41	16	0	2	6	2	7	2	8	.223	.271	.308	.193
Lind A.	14	8	8	65	38	4.03	22	8	0	2	36	12	5	0	0	0	0	0	0	0	.367	.415	.600	.326
Hattig J.	5	2	3	29	17	4.31	8	1	0	0	9	8	5	0	0	0	0	0	0	1	.333	.448	.375	.286
Phillips J.	3	4	6	51	39	2.98	12	6	0	0	18	5	1	0	1	0	1	0	1	2	.250	.275	.375	.210
Alfonzo E.	1	4	4	43	32	3.77	6	1	0	0	7	1	5	0	1	0	0	0	0	1	.162	.279	.189	.167
Mottola C.	0	3	0	16	12	2.88	4	2	0	0	6	3	0	0	0	0	0	0	0	0	.250	.250	.375	.200
Taubenheim T.	0	0	0	3	2	4.00	1	0	0	0	1	2	0	0	0	0	0	0	0	0	.333	.333	.333	.226
Barker K.	0	3	1	18	13	3.94	4	1	0	1	8	10	1	0	0	0	0	0	0	0	.235	.278	.471	.235
Rosario F.	-0	0	0	1	1	3.00	0	0	0	0	0	0	0	0	0	0	0	0	0	0	.000	.000	.000	.000
Janssen R.	-0	0	0	1	1	3.00	0	0	0	0	0	1	0	0	0	0	0	0	0	0	.000	.000	.000	.000
Towers J.	-0	1	0	5	4	3.00	1	0	0	0	1	1	0	0	0	0	0	0	0	0	.200	.200	.200	.136
Burnett A.	-0	0	0	3	3	3.33	0	0	0	0	0	1	0	0	0	0	0	0	0	0	.000	.000	.000	.000
Lilly T.	-0	0	0	3	3	3.00	0	0	0	0	0	1	0	0	0	0	0	0	0	0	.000	.000	.000	.000
Halladay R.	-0	0	0	3	3	3.33	0	0	0	0	0	2	0	0	0	0	0	0	0	0	.000	.000	.000	.000
Figueroa L.	-0	1	0	9	8	3.00	1	1	0	0	2	2	0	0	0	0	0	0	0	0	.111	.111	.222	.102
Roberts R.	-0	1	1	14	13	3.57	1	0	0	1	4	4	1	0	0	0	0	0	0	1	.077	.143	.308	.137

Italicized stats have been adjusted for home park.

Batted Ball Batting Stats

Player	PA	% of PA		% of Batted Balls			IF/F	HR/OF	Runs Per Event				Total Runs vs. Avg.				
		K%	BB%	GB%	LD%	FB%			NIP	GB	LD	OF	NIP	GB	LD	FB	Tot
Wells V.	677	13	8	42	18	40	.12	.16	.06	.08	.44	.24	0	7	6	12	25
Overbay L.	640	15	9	46	22	32	.05	.14	.06	.04	.39	.28	0	-1	7	13	19
Johnson R.	517	16	10	47	20	33	.09	.11	.07	.08	.45	.21	3	9	4	-0	16
Glaus T.	634	21	14	34	17	49	.11	.20	.07	.03	.38	.28	7	-5	-9	21	14
Rios A.	498	18	8	37	22	42	.05	.12	.02	.04	.42	.23	-4	-1	6	12	13
Catalanotto F.	499	7	11	48	19	34	.09	.05	.16	.02	.43	.15	8	-4	5	-3	6
Hinske E.	224	22	12	41	14	45	.03	.18	.05	-.01	.52	.30	1	-4	-1	10	5
Zaun G.	339	12	13	38	20	42	.08	.12	.12	-.01	.37	.20	6	-6	0	4	4
Hillenbrand S.	319	13	6	46	19	36	.08	.13	.04	.06	.37	.21	-2	2	0	3	4
Molina B.	458	10	5	39	23	38	.05	.14	.04	-.02	.34	.22	-4	-10	6	10	2
Hill A.	606	11	8	46	19	35	.07	.04	.09	.06	.37	.10	2	4	1	-12	-4
Adams R.	280	15	8	36	20	44	.09	.04	.05	.01	.41	.03	-0	-4	1	-11	-14
McDonald J.	286	14	6	48	18	34	.11	.05	.03	.01	.37	.03	-2	-2	-1	-11	-17
MLB Average		17	9	44	20	37	.11	.11	.05	.04	.39	.19	-	-	-	-	-

Pitching Stats

Player	PRC	IP	BFP	G	GS	P/PA	K	BB	IBB	HBP	H	HR	DP	DER	SB	CS	PO	W	L	Sv	Op	Hld	RA	ERA	FIP
Halladay R.	118	220.0	876	32	32	3.48	132	34	5	5	208	19	29	.716	20	5	0	16	5	0	0	0	3.35	3.19	3.65
Ryan B.	82	72.3	270	65	0	4.07	86	20	1	0	42	3	9	.739	7	3	2	2	2	38	42	1	1.49	1.37	2.21
Lilly T.	76	181.7	797	32	32	3.99	160	81	6	4	179	28	16	.695	14	3	2	15	13	0	0	0	4.86	4.31	4.81
Burnett A.	62	135.7	577	21	21	3.76	118	39	3	8	138	14	18	.671	18	4	1	10	8	0	0	0	4.44	3.98	3.84
Downs S.	34	77.0	327	59	5	3.97	61	30	6	2	73	9	10	.707	1	1	0	6	2	1	4	6	4.44	4.09	4.21
Speier J.	33	51.3	222	58	0	3.89	55	21	3	1	47	5	2	.686	9	1	1	2	0	0	3	25	3.16	2.98	3.50
Marcum S.	31	78.3	357	21	14	4.03	65	38	3	4	87	14	7	.686	2	1	0	3	4	0	0	0	5.06	5.06	5.42
Chacin G.	30	87.3	384	17	17	3.81	47	38	2	6	90	19	14	.730	5	0	0	9	4	0	0	0	5.26	5.05	6.46
Janssen R.	30	94.0	407	19	17	3.76	44	21	3	7	103	12	10	.697	2	3	2	6	10	0	0	0	5.55	5.07	4.78
Tallet B.	26	54.3	229	44	1	3.92	37	31	4	3	45	5	5	.732	4	4	3	3	0	0	0	5	3.98	3.81	4.75
Frasor J.	24	50.0	215	51	0	4.32	51	17	1	2	47	8	1	.701	4	1	0	3	2	0	1	12	4.32	4.32	4.38
League B.	22	42.7	173	33	0	3.33	29	9	2	3	34	3	7	.736	1	1	0	1	2	1	4	12	3.59	2.53	3.52
Taubenheim T.	12	35.0	167	12	7	3.74	26	18	0	4	40	5	1	.684	3	0	0	1	5	0	0	0	5.66	4.89	5.52
Towers J.	11	62.0	295	15	12	3.37	35	17	3	3	93	17	6	.655	12	2	0	2	10	0	0	0	9.00	8.42	6.52
Schoeneweis S	10	37.3	161	55	0	3.50	18	16	5	1	39	3	6	.691	4	1	0	2	2	1	3	18	6.51	6.51	4.31
Accardo J.	8	28.7	127	27	0	3.87	14	9	2	0	38	5	4	.667	5	1	0	1	1	0	2	2	5.97	5.97	5.29
Walker P.	8	30.0	138	23	0	3.56	27	13	2	0	37	5	3	.656	3	0	0	1	1	1	1	3	7.20	5.40	4.73
Romero D.	8	16.3	71	7	0	3.73	10	6	1	1	19	1	3	.660	5	0	0	1	0	0	0	0	3.86	3.86	3.94
Chulk V.	8	24.0	107	20	0	3.61	18	5	0	2	29	4	2	.667	0	0	0	1	0	0	1	1	6.00	5.25	4.80
Rosario F.	7	23.0	108	17	1	4.11	21	16	2	1	24	4	2	.697	8	0	0	1	2	0	0	1	6.65	6.65	5.65
McGowan D.	5	27.3	143	16	3	3.90	22	25	2	2	35	2	2	.609	3	1	0	1	2	0	1	1	8.89	7.24	5.35

Batted Ball Pitching Stats

Player	PA	% of PA		% of Batted Balls			IF/F	HR/OF	Runs Per Event				Total Runs vs. Avg.				
		K%	BB%	GB%	LD%	FB%			NIP	GB	LD	OF	NIP	GB	LD	FB	Tot
Halladay R.	876	15	4	57	21	22	.14	.14	-.01	.00	.35	.24	-13	-9	1	-8	-30
Ryan R.	270	32	7	37	20	43	.07	.05	-.03	.06	.22	.01	-6	0	-8	-12	-25
League B.	173	17	7	73	13	14	.06	.18	.02	.00	.30	.26	-1	-1	-5	-3	-10
Burnett A.	577	20	8	50	20	29	.13	.13	.02	.06	.32	.28	-5	3	-6	3	-5
Downs S.	327	19	10	56	18	26	.10	.16	.04	.01	.40	.30	-0	-3	-1	2	-3
Speier J.	222	25	10	30	20	50	.10	.08	.02	.11	.37	.14	-2	2	-2	-1	-3
Frasor J.	215	24	9	43	23	34	.04	.15	.01	.06	.29	.21	-2	1	-2	0	-3
Tallet B.	229	16	15	41	18	41	.09	.05	.11	.00	.50	.08	4	-3	2	-5	-2
Schoeneweis S.	161	11	11	57	16	28	.15	.11	.11	.04	.36	.22	2	0	-2	-1	-1
Chulk V.	107	17	7	43	22	35	.18	.17	.02	.12	.26	.22	-1	3	-1	0	1
Rosario F.	108	19	16	32	26	41	.21	.18	.09	-.03	.36	.29	2	-2	0	1	2
Janssen R.	407	11	7	53	16	31	.12	.13	.07	.04	.39	.24	-1	2	-2	3	2
Lilly T.	797	20	11	38	19	43	.14	.14	.05	.03	.43	.21	1	-4	1	5	2
Walker P.	138	20	9	46	24	29	.07	.12	.04	.05	.44	.24	-0	0	3	0	2
Taubenheim T.	167	16	13	45	17	38	.16	.14	.10	.08	.48	.20	2	2	0	-1	4
Accardo J.	127	11	7	44	27	29	.07	.14	.07	-.00	.43	.28	-0	-2	5	2	5
McGowan D.	143	15	19	43	26	31	.07	.07	.14	.04	.40	.22	5	-0	2	-0	6
Marcum S.	357	18	12	36	18	46	.10	.13	.07	.06	.51	.18	2	0	3	3	8
Chacin G.	384	12	11	35	21	44	.10	.17	.11	.03	.37	.23	5	-2	1	8	11
Towers J.	295	12	7	39	21	40	.06	.18	.05	.08	.46	.24	-1	4	6	8	17
MLB Average		17	9	44	20	37	.11	.11	.05	.04	.39	.19	-	-	-	-	-

Fielding Stats

Name	POS	INN	SBA/G	CS%	ERA	WP+PB/G	PO	A	TE	FE
Molina, B.	C	842.0	0.87	16%	4.40	0.428	615	47	1	1
Zaun, G.	C	541.3	1.11	18%	4.34	0.432	438	31	2	1
Phillips, J.	C	45.0	1.40	0%	4.20	0.400	41	1	0	0

Name	POS	Inn	PO	A	TE	FE	FPct	RF	DPS	DPT
Overbay, L.	1B	1233.0	1355	94	1	7	.994	10.58	12	6
Hillenbrand, S.	1B	144.3	136	12	1	1	.987	9.23	2	0
Phillips, J.	1B	25.0	23	0	0	1	.958	8.28	0	0
Hinske, E.	1B	14.0	15	0	0	0	1.000	9.64	0	0
Barker, K.	1B	12.0	13	0	0	0	1.000	9.75	0	0
Hill, A.	2B	914.3	174	345	4	3	.987	5.11	41	52
Adams, R.	2B	324.7	58	99	1	1	.987	4.35	6	11
Alfonzo, E.	2B	99.0	14	31	0	0	1.000	4.09	2	2
McDonald, J.	2B	43.7	11	15	0	0	1.000	5.36	3	1
Roberts, R.	2B	31.7	8	11	0	0	1.000	5.40	0	2
Figueroa, L.	2B	15.0	4	5	0	1	.900	5.40	1	1
McDonald, J.	SS	661.7	106	232	8	6	.960	4.60	19	33
Hill, A.	SS	428.3	60	129	7	5	.940	3.97	9	8
Adams, R.	SS	271.0	41	87	9	1	.928	4.25	9	8
Glaus, T.	SS	55.3	5	18	0	0	1.000	3.74	2	0
Figueroa, L.	SS	12.0	2	2	0	0	1.000	3.00	0	0
Glaus, T.	3B	1175.0	95	271	8	6	.963	2.80	36	1
Hillenbrand, S.	3B	122.3	6	18	2	3	.828	1.77	2	0
Hinske, E.	3B	64.0	3	14	0	0	1.000	2.39	1	0
Hattig, J.	3B	63.0	4	14	0	0	1.000	2.57	1	0
McDonald, J.	3B	4.0	0	0	0	0	0.000	0.00	0	0

Name	POS	Inn	PO	A	TE	FE	FPct	RF	DPS	DPT
Catalanotto, F.	LF	760.0	140	9	0	0	1.000	1.76	6	0
Johnson, R.	LF	635.3	129	7	0	1	.993	1.93	0	0
Lind, A.	LF	17.0	4	0	0	0	1.000	2.12	0	0
Mottola, C.	LF	15.0	2	0	0	0	1.000	1.20	0	0
Hinske, E.	LF	1.0	0	0	0	0	0.000	0.00	0	0
Wells, V.	CF	1290.0	332	4	2	2	.988	2.34	6	0
Johnson, R.	CF	106.0	20	2	0	0	1.000	1.87	2	0
Rios, A.	CF	32.0	6	1	0	0	1.000	1.97	0	0
Rios, A.	RF	953.0	218	7	0	1	.996	2.12	4	0
Johnson, R.	RF	242.3	64	3	0	0	1.000	2.49	2	0
Hinske, E.	RF	214.0	41	2	0	0	1.000	1.81	2	0
Barker, K.	RF	8.0	1	0	1	0	.500	1.13	0	0
Catalanotto, F.	RF	8.0	3	0	1	0	.750	3.38	0	0
Mottola, C.	RF	3.0	1	0	0	0	1.000	3.00	0	0

Washington Nationals

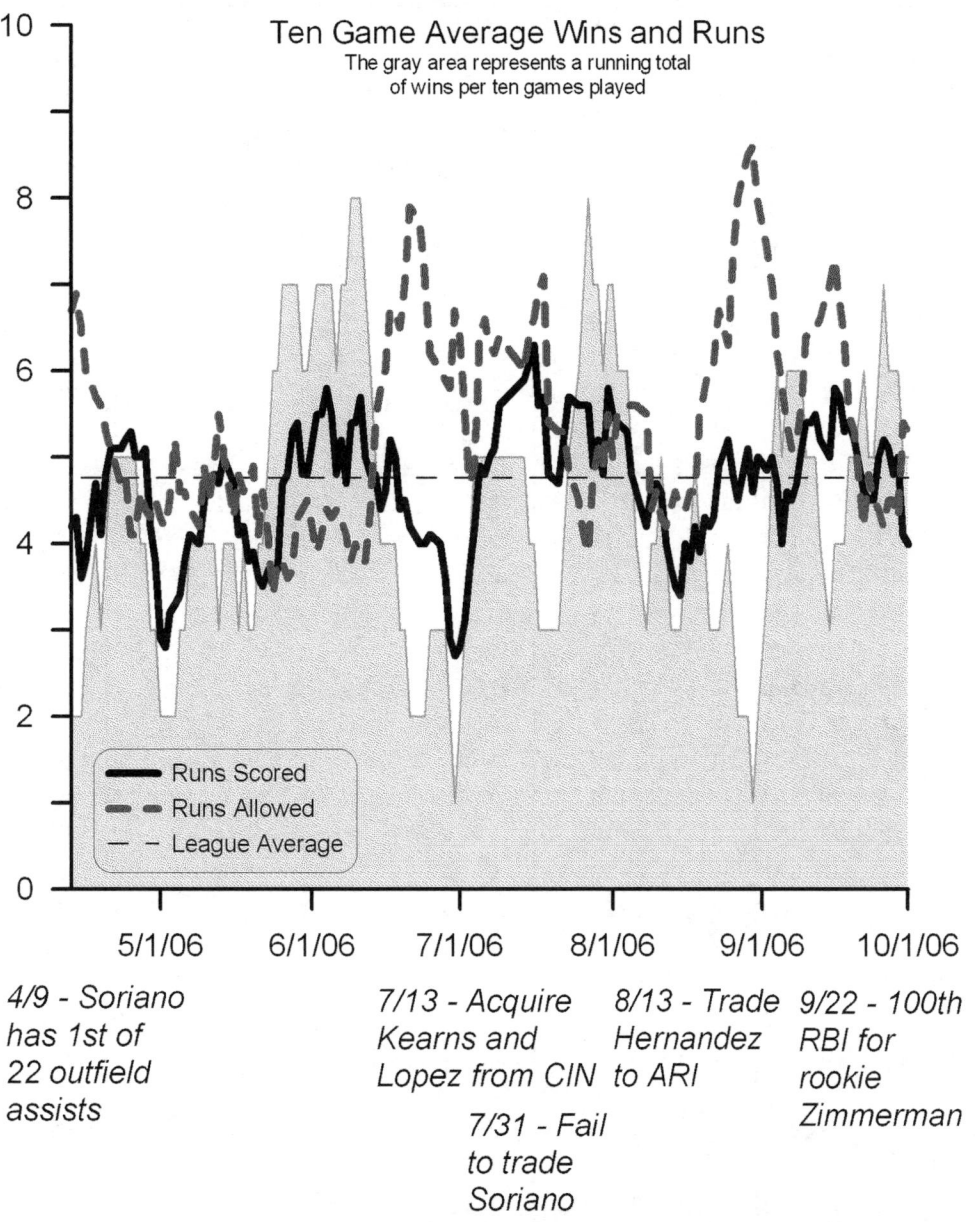

Ten Game Average Wins and Runs
The gray area represents a running total
of wins per ten games played

- —— Runs Scored
- – – Runs Allowed
- — – League Average

5/1/06 6/1/06 7/1/06 8/1/06 9/1/06 10/1/06

*4/9 - Soriano
has 1st of
22 outfield
assists*

*7/13 - Acquire
Kearns and
Lopez from CIN*

*8/13 - Trade
Hernandez
to ARI*

*9/22 - 100th
RBI for
rookie
Zimmerman*

*7/31 - Fail
to trade
Soriano*

Team Batting and Pitching/Fielding Stats by Month						
	April	May	June	July	Aug	Sept/Oct
Wins	8	14	11	14	9	15
Losses	17	15	16	11	18	14
OBP	.338	.312	.327	.378	.338	.339
SLG	.413	.425	.384	.466	.428	.395
FIP	4.91	4.43	4.70	5.02	4.80	5.13
DER	.715	.706	.668	.680	.678	.716

Batting Stats

Player	RC	Runs	RBI	PA	Outs	P/PA	H	2B	3B	HR	TB	K	BB	IBB	HBP	SH	SF	SB	CS	GDP	BA	OBP	SLG	GPA
Soriano A.	121	119	95	728	488	3.90	179	41	2	46	362	160	67	16	9	2	3	41	17	3	.277	.351	.560	.310
Johnson N.	110	100	77	628	370	4.29	145	46	0	23	260	99	110	15	13	2	3	10	3	12	.290	.428	.520	.336
Zimmerman R.	108	84	110	682	461	3.88	176	47	3	20	289	120	61	7	2	1	4	11	8	15	.287	.351	.471	.287
Vidro J.	63	52	47	511	345	3.47	134	26	1	7	183	48	41	3	3	0	4	1	0	16	.289	.348	.395	.266
Schneider B.	47	30	55	455	321	3.63	105	18	0	4	135	67	38	10	2	2	3	2	2	14	.256	.320	.329	.235
Lopez F.	39	43	22	320	207	4.19	77	13	2	2	100	60	34	0	2	8	2	21	6	4	.281	.362	.365	.264
Church R.	38	22	35	230	147	4.00	54	17	1	10	103	60	26	0	3	3	2	6	1	4	.276	.366	.526	.308
Kearns A.	37	33	36	261	166	4.07	53	12	1	8	91	50	41	2	5	1	2	2	3	4	.250	.381	.429	.290
Clayton R.	34	36	27	338	234	3.46	82	22	1	0	106	53	19	3	4	5	5	8	3	8	.269	.315	.348	.238
Anderson M.	30	31	23	239	161	4.13	59	13	2	5	91	41	18	1	1	3	2	2	4	1	.274	.331	.423	.265
Guillen J.	25	28	40	268	197	3.60	52	15	1	9	96	48	15	4	7	0	5	1	0	8	.216	.276	.398	.233
Ward D.	20	15	19	123	78	4.02	32	9	0	6	59	21	14	1	2	0	3	0	1	5	.308	.390	.567	.330
Byrd M.	19	28	18	228	162	4.15	44	8	1	5	69	47	22	1	6	1	2	3	3	6	.223	.317	.350	.239
Escobar A.	17	14	18	99	59	3.93	31	3	2	4	50	18	8	0	0	0	4	2	0	3	.356	.394	.575	.334
Jackson D.	13	16	10	135	97	4.19	23	6	1	4	43	39	12	0	4	3	0	1	3	1	.198	.295	.371	.235
Fick R.	12	14	9	141	99	3.79	34	4	0	2	44	24	10	1	1	2	0	1	1	4	.266	.324	.344	.241
Logan N.	11	13	8	99	64	3.70	27	3	1	1	35	20	6	1	0	1	2	2	1	0	.300	.337	.389	.259
Castro B.	11	18	10	120	89	3.60	25	1	3	0	32	18	9	0	0	1	0	7	2	2	.227	.286	.291	.209
LeCroy M.	10	5	9	80	53	3.76	16	3	0	2	25	17	11	0	1	0	1	0	0	2	.239	.350	.373	.261
Harper B.	7	6	6	47	30	3.68	12	3	0	2	21	4	4	0	1	0	1	0	0	1	.293	.362	.512	.302
Hernandez L.	5	6	6	55	33	2.71	12	4	0	1	19	3	1	0	0	9	0	0	0	0	.267	.283	.422	.242
Harris B.	4	3	2	36	25	3.39	8	2	0	0	10	3	3	0	1	0	0	0	0	1	.250	.333	.313	.237
Vento M.	3	3	1	22	13	3.86	5	1	0	0	6	5	4	1	0	0	0	0	0	0	.278	.409	.333	.278
Gonzalez W.	2	3	2	38	27	3.47	8	0	0	0	8	5	2	0	0	0	1	0	0	0	.229	.263	.229	.183
Mateo H.	2	5	3	29	23	3.83	4	2	0	1	9	3	2	0	0	1	0	0	0	1	.154	.214	.346	.190
Lombard G.	2	2	1	26	18	4.27	3	0	0	1	6	10	5	0	0	0	0	2	0	0	.143	.308	.286	.218
Wagner R.	1	0	0	3	2	5.00	1	0	0	0	1	1	0	0	0	0	0	0	0	0	.333	.333	.333	.243
Watson B.	1	0	0	29	25	3.66	5	0	0	0	5	3	1	0	0	0	0	0	2	0	.179	.207	.179	.143
Hughes T.	1	0	0	1	0	1.00	1	0	0	0	1	0	0	0	0	0	0	0	0	0	1.000	1.000	1.000	.728
Matos L.	1	2	0	15	12	3.20	3	2	0	0	5	2	0	0	0	0	0	0	0	0	.200	.200	.333	.180
Perez B.	0	0	0	7	3	3.14	3	0	0	0	3	2	1	0	0	0	0	0	0	0	.500	.571	.500	.397
Corcoran R.	0	0	0	2	1	4.50	0	0	0	0	0	1	1	0	0	0	0	0	0	0	.000	.500	.000	.234
Traber B.	0	1	1	16	12	4.38	1	0	0	0	1	8	1	0	0	2	0	0	0	0	.077	.143	.077	.087
Patterson J.	0	0	0	10	6	2.20	2	0	0	0	2	1	0	0	0	2	0	0	0	0	.250	.250	.250	.182
Astacio P.	0	2	0	34	20	2.21	5	0	0	0	5	8	0	0	2	7	0	0	0	0	.200	.259	.200	.173
Stanton M.	-0	0	0	1	1	1.00	0	0	0	0	0	0	0	0	0	0	0	0	0	0	.000	.000	.000	.000
Rodriguez F.	-0	0	0	1	1	1.00	0	0	0	0	0	0	0	0	0	0	0	0	0	0	.000	.000	.000	.000
Bowie M.	-0	0	0	1	1	4.00	0	0	0	0	0	0	0	0	0	0	0	0	0	0	.000	.000	.000	.000
Bray B.	-0	0	0	1	1	5.00	0	0	0	0	0	1	0	0	0	0	0	0	0	0	.000	.000	.000	.000
Dorta M.	-0	3	0	20	17	3.95	4	1	0	0	5	2	1	0	0	0	0	0	2	0	.211	.250	.263	.185
Eischen J.	-0	0	0	3	2	3.67	0	0	0	0	0	2	0	0	0	1	0	0	0	0	.000	.000	.000	.000
Cordero C.	-0	0	0	2	2	4.50	0	0	0	0	0	1	0	0	0	0	0	0	0	0	.000	.000	.000	.000
Schroder C.	-0	0	0	2	2	4.00	0	0	0	0	0	1	0	0	0	0	0	0	0	0	.000	.000	.000	.000
Hill S.	-0	1	0	8	5	3.25	1	0	0	0	1	4	0	0	0	2	0	0	0	0	.167	.167	.167	.121

Italicized stats have been adjusted for home park.

Batting Stats continue on next page

Pitching Stats

Player	PRC	IP	BFP	G	GS	P/PA	K	BB	IBB	HBP	H	HR	DP	DER	SB	CS	PO	W	L	Sv	Op	Hld	RA	ERA	FIP
Ortiz R.	55	190.7	871	33	33	3.60	104	64	14	18	230	31	18	.679	6	4	1	11	16	0	0	0	5.99	5.57	5.31
Armas Jr. T.	49	154.0	693	30	30	4.00	97	64	7	13	167	19	18	.690	11	2	0	9	12	0	0	0	5.61	5.03	4.93
Rauch J.	49	91.3	383	85	0	4.16	86	36	6	2	78	13	5	.728	8	4	0	4	5	2	5	18	3.65	3.35	4.24
Hernandez L.	45	146.7	661	24	24	3.68	89	52	4	2	176	22	14	.671	12	1	1	9	8	0	0	0	5.77	5.34	4.98
Cordero C.	42	73.3	307	68	0	3.93	69	22	5	3	59	13	1	.755	3	1	0	7	4	29	33	0	3.31	3.19	4.46
O'Connor M.	35	105.0	454	21	20	3.70	59	45	5	7	96	15	9	.744	17	1	0	3	8	0	0	0	5.23	4.80	5.29
Rivera S.	26	60.3	278	54	0	3.67	41	32	6	4	59	4	4	.695	4	0	0	3	0	1	3	9	4.18	3.43	4.21
Majewski G.	25	55.3	237	46	0	3.95	34	25	1	1	49	4	7	.728	2	1	0	3	2	0	5	6	3.90	3.58	4.28
Astacio P.	23	90.3	407	17	17	3.56	42	31	3	1	109	14	8	.693	4	1	0	5	5	0	0	0	6.38	5.98	5.27
Bowie M.	19	19.7	75	15	0	4.05	11	7	0	0	11	1	2	.804	0	0	0	0	1	0	0	5	1.37	1.37	3.83
Stanton M.	18	44.3	196	56	0	3.73	30	21	11	1	47	1	4	.678	4	3	2	3	5	0	3	10	4.47	4.47	2.90
Patterson J.	18	40.7	170	8	8	3.84	42	9	1	3	36	4	1	.696	8	0	0	1	2	0	0	0	4.65	4.43	3.24
Bergmann J.	18	64.7	303	29	6	3.83	54	27	6	6	81	12	4	.657	1	1	0	0	2	0	0	1	6.82	6.68	5.21
Hill S.	12	36.7	163	6	6	3.53	16	12	2	3	43	2	3	.677	2	1	0	1	3	0	0	0	4.91	4.66	4.12
Traber B.	11	43.3	202	15	8	3.52	25	14	2	8	53	5	5	.653	3	2	1	4	3	0	0	2	6.85	6.44	4.95
Bray B.	10	23.0	100	19	0	3.36	16	9	2	1	24	2	4	.667	1	1	0	1	1	0	0	1	4.30	3.91	4.00
Day Z.	9	26.7	119	5	5	3.70	13	11	1	2	29	2	3	.681	6	1	0	1	3	0	0	0	5.06	4.73	4.57
Perez B.	9	21.0	87	8	3	3.71	9	13	2	0	16	3	2	.790	4	2	0	2	1	0	0	0	3.86	3.86	5.79
Wagner R.	9	30.7	141	26	0	3.67	20	15	3	2	36	3	4	.663	3	0	0	3	3	0	2	3	6.16	4.70	4.55
Schroder C.	9	28.3	127	21	0	4.06	39	15	3	5	23	7	2	.721	2	0	0	0	2	0	1	1	6.67	6.35	5.48
Rodriguez F.	6	29.3	139	31	0	3.97	15	16	3	4	32	5	0	.717	2	1	0	1	1	0	0	3	7.67	7.67	6.15
Booker C.	4	7.3	27	10	0	4.11	7	1	0	0	5	1	1	.778	1	0	0	0	0	0	0	2	3.68	3.68	3.49
Hughes T.	3	11.3	54	8	0	3.46	4	6	1	3	13	2	2	.718	0	0	0	0	0	0	0	0	6.35	6.35	6.92
Eischen J.	2	14.7	83	22	0	3.82	18	19	5	1	18	2	0	.628	3	0	0	0	1	0	1	0	11.05	8.59	5.60
Drese R.	2	8.7	41	2	2	3.93	5	8	0	0	9	0	1	.643	1	2	1	0	2	0	0	0	8.31	5.19	4.83
Campbell B.	1	4.3	19	4	0	4.42	4	2	0	1	4	1	1	.727	1	1	0	0	0	0	0	0	10.38	10.38	6.45
Corcoran R.	1	5.7	34	6	0	3.82	6	4	0	0	12	1	0	.435	1	0	0	0	1	0	0	0	12.71	11.12	5.51
Ramirez S.	1	3.3	18	4	0	3.33	1	2	0	0	6	1	0	.643	0	0	0	0	0	0	0	1	8.10	8.10	8.32
Gryboski K.	0	5.7	35	6	0	3.74	4	2	0	1	14	3	0	.520	0	0	0	0	0	0	1	0	17.47	14.29	10.28

Batted Ball Pitching Stats are listed after fielding stats

Batting Stats (cont.)

Player	RC	Runs	RBI	PA	Outs	P/PA	H	2B	3B	HR	TB	K	BB	IBB	HBP	SH	SF	SB	CS	GDP	BA	OBP	SLG	GPA
Majewski G.	-0	0	0	4	3	2.50	0	0	0	0	0	1	0	0	0	1	0	0	0	0	.000	.000	.000	.000
Drese R.	-0	0	0	3	3	4.00	0	0	0	0	0	1	0	0	0	0	0	0	0	0	.000	.000	.000	.000
Rivera S.	-0	0	0	4	4	5.25	0	0	0	0	0	2	0	0	0	0	0	0	0	0	.000	.000	.000	.000
Rauch J.	-0	0	0	4	4	5.00	0	0	0	0	0	3	0	0	0	0	0	0	0	0	.000	.000	.000	.000
Bergmann J.	-0	0	0	11	8	2.82	0	0	0	0	0	2	1	0	0	2	0	0	0	0	.000	.111	.000	.052
Ortiz R.	-1	5	3	66	51	3.48	6	0	0	1	9	26	3	0	0	7	0	0	0	1	.107	.153	.161	.113
Day Z.	-1	0	0	8	8	3.88	0	0	0	0	0	2	0	0	0	1	0	0	0	1	.000	.000	.000	.000
O'Connor M.	-1	2	1	33	29	3.39	2	0	0	0	2	18	1	0	0	1	0	0	0	0	.065	.094	.065	.061
Armas Jr. T.	-2	1	1	56	49	3.46	3	0	0	0	3	21	1	0	0	5	0	0	0	2	.060	.078	.060	.052

Batted Ball Batting Stats are listed after fielding stats

Fielding Stats

Name	POS	INN	SBA/G	CS%	ERA	WP+PB/G	PO	A	TE	FE
Schneider, B.	C	990.3	0.72	27%	5.28	0.300	695	52	4	0
Fick, R.	C	164.0	0.99	6%	4.55	0.549	104	7	1	0
Harper, B.	C	104.0	0.78	0%	5.71	0.087	77	1	1	0
Gonzalez, W.	C	90.0	0.90	33%	3.30	1.000	62	8	2	0
LeCroy, M.	C	88.0	2.05	0%	4.09	0.409	60	1	2	0

Name	POS	Inn	PO	A	TE	FE	FPct	RF	DPS	DPT
Johnson, N.	1B	1252.0	1159	93	7	5	.988	9.00	16	1
Vidro, J.	1B	61.0	54	3	0	0	1.000	8.41	0	0
Fick, R.	1B	59.0	57	5	0	0	1.000	9.46	0	0
Ward, D.	1B	34.0	29	1	0	1	.968	7.94	0	0
LeCroy, M.	1B	22.0	19	1	0	1	.952	8.18	0	0
Anderson, M.	1B	5.0	2	0	0	0	1.000	3.60	0	0
Schneider, B.	1B	3.0	1	0	0	0	1.000	3.00	0	0
Vidro, J.	2B	901.7	224	250	1	4	.990	4.73	18	31
Anderson, M.	2B	231.3	51	71	3	2	.961	4.75	5	9
Castro, B.	2B	228.0	65	58	0	2	.984	4.86	5	6
Jackson, D.	2B	53.3	9	18	0	0	1.000	4.56	1	2
Harris, B.	2B	22.0	5	4	0	0	1.000	3.68	0	0
Clayton, R.	SS	720.3	110	240	3	8	.970	4.37	19	19
Lopez, F.	SS	601.3	89	162	5	9	.947	3.76	15	16
Jackson, D.	SS	57.3	8	12	2	1	.833	3.14	1	0
Harris, B.	SS	26.3	5	7	1	0	.923	4.10	0	1
Dorta, M.	SS	16.0	1	9	1	0	.909	5.63	0	0
Mateo, H.	SS	15.0	4	3	1	0	.875	4.20	0	1
Zimmerman, R.	3B	1368.0	152	260	9	6	.965	2.71	26	2
Jackson, D.	3B	21.0	1	5	2	2	.600	2.57	1	0
Harris, B.	3B	20.0	1	5	0	0	1.000	2.70	0	0
Dorta, M.	3B	17.0	0	3	0	0	1.000	1.59	0	0
Mateo, H.	3B	10.0	0	1	0	0	1.000	0.90	0	0

Name	POS	Inn	PO	A	TE	FE	FPct	RF	DPS	DPT
Soriano, A.	LF	1373.0	326	22	2	9	.969	2.28	18	0
Lombard, G.	LF	24.0	8	0	0	0	1.000	3.00	0	0
Ward, D.	LF	14.0	5	0	0	0	1.000	3.21	0	0
Jackson, D.	LF	7.0	0	0	0	0	0.000	0.00	0	0
Byrd, M.	LF	6.7	2	0	0	0	1.000	2.70	0	0
Castro, B.	LF	4.0	0	0	0	0	0.000	0.00	0	0
Church, R.	LF	4.0	2	1	0	0	1.000	6.75	0	0
Matos, L.	LF	3.0	2	0	0	0	1.000	6.00	0	0
Byrd, M.	CF	393.3	125	1	0	1	.992	2.88	0	0
Church, R.	CF	369.7	122	1	0	2	.984	2.99	2	0
Logan, N.	CF	220.0	59	0	0	1	.983	2.41	0	0
Escobar, A.	CF	174.7	61	1	1	0	.984	3.19	0	0
Jackson, D.	CF	141.7	44	0	1	1	.957	2.80	0	0
Watson, B.	CF	56.7	17	0	0	0	1.000	2.70	0	0
Anderson, M.	CF	41.0	16	1	0	1	.944	3.73	2	0
Kearns, A.	CF	29.0	8	1	0	0	1.000	2.79	0	0
Matos, L.	CF	9.3	2	1	0	0	1.000	2.89	0	0
Mateo, H.	CF	1.0	0	0	0	0	0.000	0.00	0	0
Guillen, J.	RF	537.7	163	3	0	2	.988	2.78	0	0
Kearns, A.	RF	482.3	139	2	3	2	.966	2.63	2	0
Church, R.	RF	97.0	20	0	0	0	1.000	1.86	0	0
Byrd, M.	RF	83.0	23	0	0	0	.958	2.49	0	0
Anderson, M.	RF	69.0	14	1	1	1	.882	1.96	2	0
Ward, D.	RF	66.0	13	0	0	0	1.000	1.77	0	0
Vento, M.	RF	49.0	13	0	0	0	1.000	2.39	0	0
Fick, R.	RF	32.0	4	0	0	0	1.000	1.13	0	0
Lombard, G.	RF	16.0	5	1	0	1	.857	3.38	0	0
Jackson, D.	RF	2.3	0	0	0	0	0.000	0.00	0	0
Escobar, A.	RF	2.0	1	0	0	0	1.000	4.50	0	0

Batted Ball Batting Stats

Player	PA	% of PA		% of Batted Balls					Runs Per Event				Total Runs vs. Avg.				
		K%	BB%	GB%	LD%	FB%	IF/F	HR/OF	NIP	GB	LD	OF	NIP	GB	LD	FB	Tot
Johnson N.	628	16	20	42	22	36	.09	.17	.14	.02	.42	.32	23	-7	3	14	34
Soriano A.	728	22	10	29	20	51	.08	.19	.03	.08	.39	.29	-2	1	-3	35	32
Zimmerman R.	682	18	9	42	22	36	.13	.11	.04	.05	.46	.18	-1	5	11	-5	10
Church R.	230	26	13	39	18	43	.07	.16	.04	.02	.56	.32	0	-2	1	7	7
Ward D.	123	17	13	34	19	48	.07	.13	.09	.03	.46	.27	2	-1	1	5	6
Kearns A.	261	19	18	40	17	42	.04	.11	.11	.05	.50	.15	7	-0	-0	-2	4
Anderson M.	239	17	8	40	24	36	.13	.07	.03	.05	.46	.10	-1	0	6	-6	-1
Jackson D.	135	29	12	34	19	47	.06	.12	.02	.05	.39	.18	-1	-1	-2	-0	-4
Byrd M.	228	21	12	45	21	34	.10	.09	.06	.03	.33	.18	1	-2	-2	-2	-4
Vidro J.	511	9	9	46	22	32	.08	.05	.11	.02	.41	.08	3	-4	9	-13	-5
Lopez F.	320	19	11	50	21	28	.00	.03	.06	.06	.35	.11	1	2	-2	-7	-5
Fick R.	141	17	8	34	18	48	.08	.04	.03	-.01	.36	.11	-1	-2	-1	-1	-5
Castro B.	120	15	8	63	18	18	.13	.00	.04	.02	.32	-.01	-1	1	-1	-6	-7
Guillen J.	268	18	8	41	14	45	.07	.08	.03	-.03	.49	.15	-1	-6	-1	0	-9
Clayton R.	338	16	7	52	20	28	.08	.00	.03	.04	.41	.05	-3	1	2	-12	-11
Schneider B.	455	15	9	47	23	30	.13	.04	.06	-.00	.38	.09	0	-7	5	-13	-14
MLB Average		*17*	*9*	*44*	*20*	*37*	*.11*	*.11*	*.05*	*.04*	*.39*	*.19*	-	-	-	-	-

Batted Ball Pitching Stats

Player	PA	% of PA		% of Batted Balls					Runs Per Event				Total Runs vs. Avg.				
		K%	BB%	GB%	LD%	FB%	IF/F	HR/OF	NIP	GB	LD	OF	NIP	GB	LD	FB	Tot
Rauch J.	383	22	10	30	21	49	.17	.13	.03	.09	.36	.13	-2	1	-2	-5	-7
Cordero C.	307	22	8	35	13	52	.11	.13	.01	.06	.34	.22	-3	-0	-8	6	-6
Majewski G.	237	14	11	53	17	29	.06	.06	.09	.01	.35	.19	2	-3	-2	-2	-5
Patterson J.	170	25	7	30	16	54	.10	.04	-.01	.15	.36	.11	-3	2	-3	-0	-4
Rivera S.	278	15	13	46	19	35	.07	.06	.10	.07	.44	.04	4	2	1	-10	-3
Stanton M.	196	15	11	42	19	39	.16	.02	.08	.06	.41	.10	2	1	0	-5	-2
O'Connor M.	454	13	11	36	18	46	.14	.11	.10	.06	.36	.14	5	1	-4	-3	-2
Day S.	119	11	11	52	26	22	.15	.12	.12	.06	.19	.20	1	2	-2	-2	-1
Bray B.	100	16	10	49	19	32	.13	.10	.06	.06	.33	.20	0	1	-1	-1	-0
Hill S.	163	10	9	50	19	31	.05	.05	.11	.02	.47	.15	1	-1	2	-2	1
Wagner R.	141	14	12	61	18	20	.15	.18	.10	.08	.34	.31	2	2	-2	-1	1
Schroder C.	127	31	16	30	13	57	.21	.23	.04	.13	.26	.37	1	1	-5	5	1
Rodriguez F.	139	11	14	36	24	41	.15	.11	.15	.04	.44	.18	3	-1	3	-0	5
Armas Jr. T.	693	14	11	39	22	40	.09	.10	.09	.04	.37	.17	6	-2	3	-1	6
Traber B.	202	12	11	45	19	36	.09	.10	.10	.07	.41	.22	2	1	1	2	6
Astacio P.	407	10	8	37	18	46	.10	.11	.09	.09	.37	.19	1	4	-2	6	9
Hernandez L.	661	13	8	38	19	43	.10	.10	.06	.08	.38	.20	-0	6	-0	8	13
Bergmann J.	303	18	11	32	24	45	.14	.15	.06	.05	.47	.27	1	-1	6	7	14
Ortiz R.	871	12	9	41	20	39	.09	.13	.09	.06	.41	.20	5	3	6	8	23
MLB Average		*17*	*9*	*44*	*20*	*37*	*.11*	*.11*	*.05*	*.04*	*.39*	*.19*	-	-	-	-	-

Win Statistics

You'll find an assortment of statistics related to wins in this appendix. Win-based stats assign responsibility for a team's wins and losses to specific players. In the *THT Annual*, we have used two win-based stats, Win Shares and Win Probability Added, and key stats associated with both systems are listed here.

In the Win Shares section, you'll find each player's Win Shares (WS), Win Shares Percentage (similar to a team's winning percentage, lableled WS%), Win Shares Above Bench (Win Shares contributed above a bench player's level, labeled WSAB)and Net Win Shares Value (WS$, as explained in "Net Win Shares Value 2006"). All of these stats are defined in our Glossary, as well as the article "Net Win Shares Value, 2006" in our Analysis section.

Win Probability Added (WPA) stats are also discussed in the Analysis section, in the article "WPA in the USA." Here we've listed each player's batting and pitching WPA, as well as the Leverage Index of all pitchers.

The WPA stats are contributed by David Appelman of FanGraphs (www.fangraphs.com), based on tables supplied by Tom M. Tango.

We have listed win-based stats for all players with at least four expected Win Shares in 2006. You can download a complete list of win stats for all players who appeared in major league games last year at http://www.hardballtimes.com/THT2007Annual/. The user name is "tht07" and the password is "verlander." This is a service to book purchasers only.

Player	WS	WS%	WSAB	WS$	bWPA	pWPA	pLI
Arizona Diamondbacks							
Batista, M.	9	.503	4.7	$1,417	-1.0	-0.3	0.97
Byrnes, E.	16	.489	4.1	$2,348	-0.4	-	-
Clark, T.	0	.000	-2.7	($2,636)	-1.0	-	-
Counsell, C.	9	.406	1.2	$174	-1.0	-	-
Cruz, J.	5	.587	3.3	$2,482	-0.8	0.8	0.94
DaVanon, J.	8	.607	3.5	$2,701	0.6	-	-
Drew, S.	6	.481	2.1	$1,767	-0.2	-	-
Easley, D.	5	.432	0.9	$552	-0.5	-	-
Estrada, J.	14	.575	5.5	$2,791	-0.9	-	-
Gonzalez, E.	3	.322	0.4	$317	-0.2	-1.2	0.95
Gonzalez, L.	14	.387	1.4	($5,331)	0.3	-	-
Green, S.	9	.356	0.4	($4,514)	0.1	-	-
Hudson, O.	19	.533	7.0	$3,706	1.3	-	-
Jackson, C.	12	.400	1.8	$1,520	1.4	-	-
Julio, J.	5	.582	2.4	$214	-	0.7	1.52
Lyon, B.	6	.566	2.6	$1,674	0.1	0.5	1.53
Medders, B.	6	.665	2.7	$2,230	-0.1	0.5	0.92
Quentin, C.	6	.572	2.8	$2,313	-0.5	-	-
Snyder, C.	7	.581	3.1	$2,576	-0.3	-	-
Tracy, C.	14	.391	1.6	$1,042	-0.6	-	-
Valverde, J.	3	.311	-0.5	($470)	-	-0.3	1.44
Vargas, C.	7	.483	3.0	$1,518	-1.0	-0.4	0.95
Vizcaino, L.	7	.743	3.4	$1,319	-	1.1	1.36
Webb, B.	22	1.089	16.5	$11,412	-1.0	3.7	0.96
Atlanta Braves							
Betemit, W.	8	.703	3.6	$2,985	-0.7	-	-
Cormier, L.	2	.247	-0.5	($462)	-0.3	0.3	0.89
Diaz, M.	7	.408	1.5	$1,261	-0.3	-	-
Francoeur, J.	16	.426	3.2	$2,636	0.1	-	-
Giles, M.	16	.481	4.7	$219	2.1	-	-

Player	WS	WS%	WSAB	WS$	bWPA	pWPA	pLI
Hudson, T.	7	.372	2.2	($1,692)	-1.3	0.1	0.95
James, C.	8	.770	5.0	$4,186	-0.9	1.6	0.93
Jones, A.	25	.692	12.2	$2,930	3.9	-	-
Jones, C.	21	.826	12.6	$3,629	1.1	-	-
Langerhans, R.	9	.436	1.4	$1,126	-1.5	-	-
LaRoche, A.	17	.558	6.1	$4,975	1.2	-	-
McBride, M.	4	.530	1.9	$1,606	-	0.7	0.83
McCann, B.	23	.855	14.1	$11,768	2.5	-	-
Orr, P.	2	.244	-0.9	($784)	-0.3	-	-
Paronto, C.	5	.678	2.3	$1,860	-0.0	-1.0	0.86
Pratt, T.	2	.233	-1.2	($1,340)	-0.8	-	-
Ray, K.	3	.311	0.2	$162	-0.0	-0.1	0.79
Renteria, E.	19	.528	6.1	$74	1.4	-	-
Smoltz, J.	17	.854	12.2	$4,013	-1.4	3.3	1.04
Sosa, J.	1	.116	-1.3	($2,459)	-0.4	-3.1	1.08
Thorman, S.	2	.282	-0.3	($288)	-0.6	-	-
Villarreal, O.	8	.715	3.8	$3,003	-0.3	0.5	0.83
Yates, T.	4	.528	1.1	$897	-	-1.3	1.01
Baltimore Orioles							
Bedard, E.	16	.757	10.9	$7,902	-0.1	1.3	0.99
Benson, K.	9	.451	4.2	($1,211)	-0.1	0.4	0.97
Britton, C.	5	.691	2.3	$1,936	-	0.2	0.82
Cabrera, D.	8	.502	4.3	$3,526	-0.1	-0.5	1.05
Chen, B.	-1	-.085	-5.2	($8,001)	-0.0	-2.1	0.62
Conine, J.	7	.307	-1.2	($1,622)	-1.2	-	-
Fahey, B.	4	.265	-1.6	($1,323)	-1.4	-	-
Gibbons, J.	9	.531	3.4	($1,243)	0.1	-	-
Gomez, C.	5	.649	2.0	$1,657	0.1	-	-
Hawkins, L.	4	.455	1.6	($1,004)	-	0.9	1.22
Hernandez, R.	22	.753	12.2	$8,079	-0.3	-	-
Loewen, A.	4	.328	1.2	$1,023	-0.0	-0.8	1.03

Player	WS	WS%	WSAB	WS$	bWPA	pWPA	pLI
Lopez, J.	6	.474	1.5	($2,439)	-1.1	-	-
Lopez, R.	4	.196	-0.9	($742)	-0.1	-1.9	0.96
Markakis, N.	13	.447	2.9	$2,382	0.7	-	-
Matos, L.	0	.000	-2.9	($3,659)	-1.1	-	-
Millar, K.	13	.523	4.7	$2,881	0.5	-	-
Mora, M.	17	.467	4.7	($503)	1.8	-	-
Newhan, D.	0	.000	-2.3	($2,183)	-1.4	-	-
Patterson, C.	14	.524	5.0	$1,540	-0.5	-	-
Ray, C.	12	.824	6.8	$5,683	-	3.0	1.91
Roberts, B.	14	.433	2.7	($666)	0.0	-	-
Tejada, M.	23	.633	10.3	$1,899	1.3	-	-
Williams, T.	2	.238	-0.5	($914)	-	-1.5	1.28

Boston Red Sox

Player	WS	WS%	WSAB	WS$	bWPA	pWPA	pLI
Beckett, J.	12	.540	6.1	$896	0.2	0.0	0.93
Clement, M.	1	.140	-1.0	($6,098)	0.0	-1.2	0.87
Cora, A.	5	.350	0.2	($482)	-1.2	-	-
Crisp, C.	10	.420	1.4	($1,686)	-1.4	-	-
Delcarmen, M.	3	.382	0.1	$111	-	-0.2	1.00
Gonzalez, A.	9	.385	0.7	($926)	-1.8	-	-
Kapler, G.	2	.249	-0.3	($513)	-0.7	-	-
Lester, J.	5	.563	3.0	$2,516	-0.1	0.1	1.18
Loretta, M.	16	.446	3.6	$1,489	0.9	-	-
Lowell, M.	18	.537	6.3	$310	0.4	-	-
Mirabelli, D.	2	.208	-1.3	($1,658)	-0.7	-	-
Nixon, T.	10	.421	2.3	($1,644)	-0.6	-	-
Ortiz, D.	29	1.078	20.0	$12,865	8.0	-	-
Papelbon, J.	18	1.171	12.5	$10,382	-	5.2	2.02
Pena, W.	8	.504	2.4	$1,012	0.3	-	-
Ramirez, M.	29	1.007	18.9	$5,064	4.0	-	-
Schilling, C.	16	.729	11.1	$1,972	-0.0	1.3	1.01
Tavarez, J.	6	.487	1.6	($253)	-	-0.8	0.95
Timlin, M.	6	.507	1.5	($579)	-	-0.2	1.93
Varitek, J.	8	.366	0.1	($5,454)	0.0	-	-
Wakefield, T.	7	.461	3.3	$619	-0.1	-0.1	0.85
Youkilis, K.	22	.627	10.2	$8,425	1.9	-	-

Chicago Cubs

Player	WS	WS%	WSAB	WS$	bWPA	pWPA	pLI
Barrett, M.	14	.615	5.8	$2,500	0.4	-	-
Blanco, H.	6	.414	0.8	$3	-1.0	-	-
Bynum, F.	3	.397	0.3	$277	-0.6	-	-
Cedeno, R.	4	.126	-7.3	($6,099)	-4.7	-	-
Dempster, R.	4	.275	-0.6	($2,798)	-0.1	-3.1	1.77
Eyre, S.	5	.576	2.1	$97	-0.0	0.6	1.01
Hill, R.	5	.578	3.1	$2,614	-0.5	0.3	0.88
Howry, B.	9	.770	5.1	$2,682	0.0	1.1	1.42
Jones, J.	17	.538	5.9	$2,954	2.1	-	-
Lee, D.	5	.457	1.0	($6,438)	0.3	-	-
Mabry, J.	3	.244	-1.2	($1,462)	-1.9	-	-

Player	WS	WS%	WSAB	WS$	bWPA	pWPA	pLI
Maddux, G.	5	.423	2.7	($1,011)	-0.7	-0.9	0.89
Marshall, S.	2	.183	-0.8	($685)	-0.9	-0.3	1.00
Murton, M.	13	.469	3.7	$3,070	1.3	-	-
Nevin, P.	5	.479	1.6	($1,583)	0.3	-	-
Novoa, R.	4	.451	0.8	$616	-0.0	-0.1	0.69
Ohman, W.	5	.617	2.0	$1,359	0.0	1.2	0.57
Pagan, A.	4	.402	0.4	$345	-0.0	-	-
Perez, N.	3	.223	-1.5	($2,200)	-1.5	-	-
Pierre, J.	16	.399	2.5	($3,671)	-1.1	-	-
Ramirez, A.	23	.639	10.3	$2,667	2.3	-	-
Theriot, R.	7	.825	3.9	$3,248	1.3	-	-
Walker, T.	6	.315	-0.9	($1,605)	-0.3	-	-
Zambrano, C.	19	1.037	14.4	$5,476	-0.3	1.9	0.94

Chicago White Sox

Player	WS	WS%	WSAB	WS$	bWPA	pWPA	pLI
Anderson, B.	5	.221	-3.2	($2,640)	-1.5	-	-
Buehrle, M.	10	.453	4.4	($4,212)	-0.1	-1.0	0.91
Cintron, A.	6	.376	0.0	($1,313)	0.3	-	-
Contreras, J.	14	.659	8.5	$2,644	-0.2	0.6	0.98
Cotts, N.	2	.252	-0.6	($569)	-	-0.5	0.92
Crede, J.	20	.631	9.1	$5,067	-0.0	-	-
Dye, J.	26	.798	15.0	$9,846	5.1	-	-
Garcia, F.	15	.640	8.8	$2,342	-0.1	0.3	0.87
Garland, J.	15	.654	9.5	$838	-0.0	0.8	0.88
Gload, R.	4	.452	1.4	$1,111	0.0	-	-
Iguchi, T.	18	.546	6.8	$4,481	0.6	-	-
Jenks, B.	9	.574	3.8	$3,155	-	2.7	2.13
Konerko, P.	23	.689	10.9	$2,356	2.1	-	-
Mackowiak, R.	6	.382	1.0	($1,231)	-0.4	-	-
McCarthy, B.	5	.459	1.5	$1,248	-0.0	0.2	0.95
Ozuna, P.	5	.474	1.8	$1,340	0.7	-	-
Pierzynski, A.	13	.447	3.2	($1,196)	-0.2	-	-
Podsednik, S.	9	.293	-1.8	($3,317)	-0.9	-	-
Thome, J.	26	1.090	17.6	$6,549	3.3	-	-
Thornton, M.	7	.839	3.9	$3,257	-	1.1	1.35
Uribe, J.	11	.404	1.5	($1,752)	-1.6	-	-
Vazquez, J.	11	.504	5.8	($1,582)	0.0	-0.8	0.97

Cincinnati Reds

Player	WS	WS%	WSAB	WS$	bWPA	pWPA	pLI
Arroyo, B.	21	1.028	15.5	$10,068	-1.3	3.0	0.91
Aurilia, R.	16	.617	6.7	$4,992	1.3	-	-
Clayton, R.	1	.111	-2.2	($1,960)	-0.3	-	-
Coffey, T.	8	.663	4.1	$3,429	-	0.9	1.67
Dunn, A.	20	.541	7.4	($1,443)	1.2	-	-
Encarnacion, E.	14	.553	4.9	$4,111	1.9	-	-
Freel, R.	13	.464	3.1	$1,513	0.1	-	-
Griffey Jr., K.	10	.397	1.4	($5,790)	1.8	-	-
Harang, A.	17	.835	11.7	$7,590	-1.4	2.1	1.02
Hatteberg, S.	15	.510	4.4	$3,422	0.0	-	-

Player	WS	WS%	WSAB	WS$	bWPA	pWPA	pLI
Kearns, A.	10	.497	2.9	$1,489	-0.3	-	-
LaRue, J.	5	.388	0.9	($2,995)	-0.8	-	-
Lopez, F.	9	.427	2.1	$374	0.3	-	-
Milton, E.	7	.537	3.7	($2,365)	-0.7	-0.2	0.93
Phillips, B.	14	.433	2.9	$2,447	-0.1	-	-
Ramirez, E.	3	.321	0.6	$500	-0.3	-1.7	0.93
Ross, D.	13	.797	7.8	$6,290	0.9	-	-
Valentin, J.	3	.290	-0.8	($1,514)	-0.2	-	-
Weathers, D.	9	.726	4.4	$2,978	-0.0	1.6	1.52

Cleveland Indians

Player	WS	WS%	WSAB	WS$	bWPA	pWPA	pLI
Belliard, R.	9	.442	1.5	($56)	0.0	-	-
Betancourt, R.	4	.489	1.6	$1,312	-	1.0	1.36
Blake, C.	11	.457	2.5	($799)	-0.5	-	-
Boone, A.	7	.328	-0.6	($2,425)	-1.6	-	-
Broussard, B.	9	.588	3.6	$1,428	-0.2	-	-
Byrd, P.	6	.309	1.0	($3,030)	-0.1	-1.9	0.95
Cabrera, F.	2	.243	-0.5	($452)	-	-0.7	0.79
Carmona, F.	1	.100	-2.1	($1,786)	-	-2.2	1.27
Choo, S.	4	.449	1.3	$1,059	0.6	-	-
Davis, J.	4	.538	1.1	$868	-	-0.7	0.82
Garko, R.	6	.546	1.8	$1,483	0.6	-	-
Gutierrez, F.	1	.128	-1.5	($1,266)	-0.8	-	-
Hafner, T.	25	1.123	17.2	$12,012	4.4	-	-
Hollandsworth, T.	4	.468	0.5	$215	-0.9	-	-
Inglett, J.	5	.414	1.1	$881	0.2	-	-
Johnson, J.	1	.121	-1.4	($2,374)	-	-1.5	0.91
Lee, C.	10	.460	4.6	$3,775	-0.0	-0.4	0.95
Luna, H.	2	.276	-0.4	($324)	-0.3	-	-
Marte, A.	4	.400	0.5	$449	-0.4	-	-
Martinez, V.	19	.550	6.6	$4,785	-0.2	-	-
Michaels, J.	9	.314	-1.4	($2,392)	0.2	-	-
Peralta, J.	14	.415	2.5	$1,645	-0.8	-	-
Sabathia, C.	14	.666	9.1	$559	-0.0	2.6	0.98
Sizemore, G.	25	.638	11.8	$9,478	3.6	-	-
Sowers, J.	7	.739	4.4	$3,679	-	1.0	0.98
Westbrook, J.	13	.569	7.0	$1,674	0.0	0.9	0.97

Colorado Rockies

Player	WS	WS%	WSAB	WS$	bWPA	pWPA	pLI
Atkins, G.	26	.687	12.7	$10,525	3.5	-	-
Barmes, C.	5	.171	-4.7	($3,881)	-1.8	-	-
Carroll, J.	13	.456	3.0	$2,140	-1.5	-	-
Cook, A.	11	.597	6.2	$4,262	-1.6	1.2	0.94
Fogg, J.	5	.345	1.1	$747	-0.8	-0.5	0.96
Francis, J.	13	.774	8.7	$7,258	-0.8	0.9	0.96
Freeman, C.	3	.296	-0.0	($4)	-0.5	-	-
Fuentes, B.	10	.719	4.8	$2,232	-	1.1	1.87
Gonzalez, L.	1	.117	-1.8	($1,526)	-0.9	-	-
Hawpe, B.	17	.537	6.0	$4,956	2.3	-	-

Player	WS	WS%	WSAB	WS$	bWPA	pWPA	pLI
Helton, T.	23	.654	10.8	($322)	4.1	-	-
Holliday, M.	22	.606	9.5	$7,744	2.5	-	-
Jennings, J.	14	.763	9.5	$3,484	-1.1	1.4	0.98
Kim, B.	4	.300	0.5	($93)	-0.9	-2.2	1.01
Martin, T.	3	.391	0.3	$90	0.0	0.3	0.69
Mesa, J.	5	.459	1.8	$512	-0.0	-0.4	1.29
Ramirez, R.	7	.814	3.7	$3,082	-0.0	0.4	0.82
Spilborghs, R.	3	.308	0.1	$65	-1.1	-	-
Sullivan, C.	7	.294	-0.7	($630)	-2.6	-	-
Torrealba, Y.	6	.446	0.9	$178	-0.1	-	-

Detroit Tigers

Player	WS	WS%	WSAB	WS$	bWPA	pWPA	pLI
Bonderman, J.	14	.606	8.1	$4,636	-0.2	2.4	1.01
Casey, S.	4	.375	0.1	($1,986)	-0.6	-	-
Granderson, C.	20	.555	7.7	$6,410	0.7	-	-
Grilli, J.	3	.381	0.8	$617	-	-0.6	0.70
Guillen, C.	26	.775	14.1	$9,030	2.9	-	-
Infante, O.	4	.317	-0.0	($75)	-1.2	-	-
Inge, B.	18	.536	6.2	$2,323	-0.1	-	-
Jones, T.	7	.486	1.8	($1,758)	-	1.1	1.99
Ledezma, W.	4	.538	1.7	$1,362	-	-0.1	0.99
Miner, Z.	4	.390	1.7	$1,378	0.0	-0.6	0.90
Monroe, C.	14	.467	3.6	$400	1.3	-	-
Ordonez, M.	20	.581	7.8	($2,583)	1.2	-	-
Polanco, P.	13	.496	4.1	$1,000	-0.1	-	-
Robertson, N.	14	.619	8.3	$6,821	-0.1	3.0	1.04
Rodney, F.	7	.606	3.2	$2,580	0.0	1.2	1.55
Rodriguez, I.	25	.813	13.8	$5,376	-1.3	-	-
Rogers, K.	15	.677	9.2	$3,282	-0.0	0.8	0.89
Shelton, C.	9	.396	0.7	$528	-0.9	-	-
Thames, M.	12	.648	6.1	$5,022	1.1	-	-
Verlander, J.	15	.749	10.4	$8,003	-0.0	2.3	0.93
Wilson, V.	5	.531	2.2	$1,408	-0.1	-	-
Young, D.	2	.270	-0.6	($4,922)	-1.1	-	-
Zumaya, J.	12	.944	7.5	$6,269	-	3.7	1.60

Florida Marlins

Player	WS	WS%	WSAB	WS$	bWPA	pWPA	pLI
Abercrombie, R.	4	.254	-1.9	($1,611)	-1.6	-	-
Amezaga, A.	4	.194	-2.7	($2,268)	-1.7	-	-
Borchard, J.	4	.297	-0.4	($351)	-0.8	-	-
Borowski, J.	8	.518	2.4	$1,967	-	1.0	1.83
Cabrera, M.	34	.924	20.7	$17,121	4.3	-	-
Helms, W.	10	.667	4.9	$3,773	2.1	-	-
Herges, M.	3	.316	-0.6	($783)	-	-1.5	0.95
Hermida, J.	7	.363	-0.0	($11)	-1.1	-	-
Jacobs, M.	13	.465	3.0	$2,525	0.7	-	-
Johnson, J.	12	.856	8.9	$7,385	-0.8	1.6	1.06
Messenger, R.	0	.000	-2.4	($2,008)	-0.0	-1.7	0.84
Moehler, B.	-2	-.184	-4.9	($4,714)	-0.4	-2.5	0.90

Player	WS	WS%	WSAB	WS$	bWPA	pWPA	pLI
Nolasco, R.	5	.408	1.6	$1,314	-0.6	-0.1	0.96
Olivo, M.	14	.555	5.2	$3,937	-0.7	-	-
Olsen, S.	10	.640	6.5	$5,437	-0.4	1.0	1.07
Ramirez, H.	25	.663	11.7	$9,744	2.0	-	-
Ross, C.	5	.327	-0.5	($380)	-0.9	-	-
Sanchez, A.	11	1.100	8.3	$6,872	-0.9	3.1	1.11
Tankersley, T.	5	.694	2.3	$1,900	-0.0	1.2	1.65
Treanor, M.	5	.472	1.6	$1,367	-0.2	-	-
Uggla, D.	22	.597	9.3	$7,780	0.2	-	-
Willingham, J.	15	.486	4.1	$3,428	1.1	-	-
Willis, D.	14	.719	9.6	$3,748	-0.6	1.5	1.07

Houston Astros

Player	WS	WS%	WSAB	WS$	bWPA	pWPA	pLI
Ausmus, B.	8	.281	-1.5	($3,375)	-2.7	-	-
Berkman, L.	34	.962	21.4	$9,657	5.4	-	-
Biggio, C.	11	.340	-0.1	($2,174)	-2.1	-	-
Borkowski, D.	3	.370	0.6	$471	-0.3	0.5	0.68
Bruntlett, E.	3	.400	0.8	$630	0.3	-	-
Buchholz, T.	0	.000	-2.7	($2,269)	-0.5	-0.9	0.92
Burke, C.	10	.441	2.3	$1,936	-0.0	-	-
Clemens, R.	12	1.212	9.2	($4,750)	-0.5	2.8	1.01
Ensberg, M.	17	.626	7.3	$2,375	0.4	-	-
Everett, A.	12	.372	1.0	($791)	-3.3	-	-
Huff, A.	5	.352	-0.4	($3,949)	0.1	-	-
Lamb, M.	9	.396	1.4	($282)	-0.4	-	-
Lane, J.	7	.364	0.6	$371	-1.4	-	-
Lidge, B.	4	.254	-1.5	($5,093)	-	-0.8	1.92
Miller, T.	5	.701	2.9	$1,375	-	1.3	0.86
Munson, E.	2	.235	-1.3	($1,088)	-1.3	-	-
Nieve, F.	5	.489	2.0	$1,628	-0.3	0.7	0.80
Oswalt, R.	21	1.131	16.4	$2,375	-1.3	4.1	1.00
Pettitte, A.	12	.643	7.6	($3,549)	-0.7	0.2	1.05
Qualls, C.	9	.707	4.2	$3,459	-	1.6	1.45
Rodriguez, W.	1	.084	-1.8	($1,490)	-0.5	-1.9	0.91
Scott, L.	12	.875	7.1	$5,885	1.7	-	-
Springer, R.	5	.668	2.4	$1,720	-	0.1	0.68
Taveras, W.	13	.407	2.3	$1,867	-0.5	-	-
Wheeler, D.	10	.846	5.6	$4,027	-	2.4	1.62
Wilson, P.	7	.302	-1.5	($2,899)	-0.4	-	-

Kansas City Royals

Player	WS	WS%	WSAB	WS$	bWPA	pWPA	pLI
Affeldt, J.	2	.236	-1.3	($1,538)	-0.0	-1.0	0.79
Bako, P.	0	.000	-2.8	($2,542)	-1.1	-	-
Berroa, A.	1	.037	-8.2	($8,571)	-3.3	-	-
Brown, E.	15	.489	4.3	$2,053	0.3	-	-
Buck, J.	10	.455	1.8	$1,508	-0.7	-	-
Burgos, A.	3	.210	-2.4	($1,985)	-	-2.3	1.63
Costa, S.	3	.229	-1.1	($945)	-0.6	-	-
DeJesus, D.	15	.535	5.6	$4,494	1.1	-	-

Player	WS	WS%	WSAB	WS$	bWPA	pWPA	pLI
Dessens, E.	4	.479	1.4	$598	-	-1.4	1.49
Elarton, S.	5	.402	1.4	($935)	0.0	-1.1	0.95
Gathright, J.	5	.357	0.6	$468	-0.1	-	-
German, E.	12	.748	6.4	$5,317	2.0	-	-
Gobble, J.	4	.353	0.3	$246	0.0	-1.9	0.88
Graffanino, T.	6	.471	1.3	$616	-0.0	-	-
Grudzielanek, M.	13	.433	2.7	$147	-1.4	-	-
Hernandez, R.	1	.085	-1.8	($2,466)	-	-1.7	0.97
Hudson, L.	5	.448	2.6	$2,151	-	0.6	1.07
Mientkiewicz, D.	9	.482	2.1	$905	-0.6	-	-
Nelson, J.	4	.544	1.5	$1,248	-	1.2	1.28
Peralta, J.	5	.487	1.7	$1,454	-	0.2	0.88
Perez, O.	0	.000	-1.8	($4,237)	-	-1.0	1.10
Redman, M.	6	.333	1.9	($837)	-0.0	-0.7	0.96
Sanders, R.	6	.338	-0.2	($2,827)	-0.9	-	-
Shealy, R.	6	.540	2.2	$1,861	1.0	-	-
Sisco, A.	0	.000	-3.0	($2,474)	-	-1.9	0.90
Stairs, M.	6	.573	2.2	$1,445	0.4	-	-
Sweeney, M.	5	.527	2.0	($4,474)	1.0	-	-
Teahen, M.	19	.823	11.2	$9,299	2.9	-	-
Wellemeyer, T.	5	.697	2.1	$1,698	-0.0	-0.1	0.85
Wood, M.	1	.128	-1.5	($1,210)	-0.1	-0.7	0.83

Los Angeles Angels of Anaheim

Player	WS	WS%	WSAB	WS$	bWPA	pWPA	pLI
Anderson, G.	14	.484	4.0	($2,610)	-1.1	-	-
Cabrera, O.	19	.528	6.2	$1,089	0.8	-	-
Carrasco, H.	9	.732	4.6	$2,567	-	1.2	0.60
Donnelly, B.	5	.595	2.4	$1,370	-	0.7	0.92
Escobar, K.	13	.635	8.0	$3,013	-0.1	1.4	1.01
Figgins, C.	17	.470	4.3	$1,578	-0.6	-	-
Gregg, K.	4	.426	1.1	$873	-0.1	-0.6	0.52
Guerrero, V.	25	.737	13.4	$3,568	3.2	-	-
Izturis, M.	12	.564	4.7	$3,928	0.2	-	-
Kendrick, H.	7	.459	1.4	$1,163	0.2	-	-
Kennedy, A.	15	.538	5.0	$2,400	-0.1	-	-
Lackey, J.	17	.725	10.9	$5,924	-0.2	1.4	0.99
Molina, J.	5	.358	0.3	($307)	-1.0	-	-
Morales, K.	2	.171	-1.7	($1,642)	-1.6	-	-
Napoli, M.	11	.615	4.9	$4,095	0.7	-	-
Quinlan, R.	8	.592	3.2	$2,648	0.1	-	-
Rivera, J.	18	.704	9.6	$7,030	0.4	-	-
Rodriguez, F.	15	.914	9.0	$3,839	-	5.4	2.12
Salmon, T.	4	.408	0.4	$288	-0.9	-	-
Santana, E.	13	.590	7.8	$6,479	-0.1	0.7	0.95
Saunders, J.	4	.528	2.1	$1,732	-	0.7	0.96
Shields, S.	11	.805	6.4	$3,473	-0.0	2.0	1.66
Weaver, Jer.	14	1.061	11.1	$9,277	-	2.8	1.02
Weaver, Jef.	0	.000	-2.5	($4,728)	-0.0	-1.9	0.92

Los Angeles Dodgers

Player	WS	WS%	WSAB	WS$	bWPA	pWPA	pLI
Aybar, W.	4	.480	1.5	$1,220	-0.3	-	-
Baez, D.	4	.447	1.0	($940)	-	-0.8	1.62
Beimel, J.	7	.773	3.4	$2,831	-0.0	1.7	0.82
Betemit, W.	2	.188	-1.2	($1,045)	0.2	-	-
Billingsley, C.	6	.754	4.0	$3,355	-0.3	0.8	1.16
Broxton, J.	9	.845	5.2	$4,355	0.0	1.2	1.12
Cruz, J.	5	.340	-0.2	($1,640)	-1.2	-	-
Drew, J.	21	.657	10.3	$2,258	2.5	-	-
Ethier, A.	12	.496	3.9	$3,256	-0.9	-	-
Furcal, R.	27	.683	13.0	$5,835	0.3	-	-
Garciaparra, N.	18	.634	8.4	$3,747	1.3	-	-
Izturis, C.	1	.140	-1.0	($2,705)	-0.6	-	-
Kemp, M.	4	.440	0.4	$328	-0.1	-	-
Kent, J.	18	.699	9.2	$1,765	0.6	-	-
Lofton, K.	13	.465	3.4	$823	0.9	-	-
Lowe, D.	15	.799	10.1	$3,109	-1.4	3.2	1.08
Lugo, J.	1	.112	-2.5	($3,785)	-1.1	-	-
Martin, R.	16	.613	6.4	$5,326	0.8	-	-
Martinez, R.	5	.466	0.8	$435	0.4	-	-
Penny, B.	12	.738	7.5	$3,281	-0.7	1.1	0.95
Repko, J.	4	.476	1.6	$1,281	-0.4	-	-
Saenz, O.	7	.700	3.6	$2,635	0.5	-	-
Saito, T.	14	.994	9.4	$7,680	-	4.1	1.50
Sele, A.	5	.540	2.4	$1,879	-0.4	-0.2	1.13
Tomko, B.	5	.462	2.0	($214)	-0.3	-1.0	0.95

Milwaukee Brewers

Player	WS	WS%	WSAB	WS$	bWPA	pWPA	pLI
Bell, D.	5	.442	1.5	$306	0.3	-	-
Bush, D.	13	.709	8.8	$7,266	-0.6	0.4	0.88
Capellan, J.	5	.523	2.3	$1,931	-0.0	1.0	1.30
Capuano, C.	15	.777	10.0	$8,229	-1.2	1.2	0.98
Cirillo, J.	8	.522	2.4	$1,724	0.2	-	-
Clark, B.	8	.303	-1.0	($3,631)	-1.2	-	-
Davis, D.	7	.404	3.2	($476)	-1.3	-0.6	1.03
Fielder, P.	17	.473	4.6	$3,828	0.4	-	-
Graffanino, T.	7	.488	2.3	$1,374	0.3	-	-
Gross, G.	11	.827	6.8	$5,637	1.8	-	-
Hall, B.	21	.623	9.1	$7,523	1.9	-	-
Hardy, J.	2	.266	-0.3	($317)	-1.5	-	-
Hart, C.	6	.436	0.9	$790	-0.7	-	-
Jenkins, G.	17	.556	6.2	$895	3.2	-	-
Koskie, C.	10	.620	4.5	$936	0.4	-	-
Lee, C.	18	.758	9.6	$4,966	1.7	-	-
Mench, K.	0	.000	-2.4	($2,793)	-1.0	-	-
Miller, D.	9	.422	2.2	$173	-0.2	-	-
Ohka, T.	5	.598	2.8	($2,142)	-0.4	0.1	1.01
Rivera, M.	5	.557	1.6	$1,328	-0.3	-	-
Sheets, B.	7	.761	5.0	($5,637)	-0.7	1.9	1.00
Turnbow, D.	0	.000	-5.0	($4,490)	-0.0	-2.9	1.78
Weeks, R.	10	.443	2.5	$1,206	0.1	-	-

Minnesota Twins

Player	WS	WS%	WSAB	WS$	bWPA	pWPA	pLI
Baker, S.	0	.000	-1.9	($1,625)	-0.0	-1.1	0.95
Bartlett, J.	13	.616	5.3	$4,434	0.5	-	-
Batista, T.	5	.460	0.8	$115	-1.0	-	-
Bonser, B.	6	.549	3.7	$3,113	-0.0	0.6	1.00
Castillo, L.	17	.488	5.0	$1,085	-1.2	-	-
Castro, J.	2	.212	-1.2	($1,270)	-1.2	-	-
Crain, J.	7	.675	3.2	$2,657	-	-0.1	0.93
Cuddyer, M.	23	.668	11.4	$8,458	2.5	-	-
Eyre, W.	2	.283	-0.6	($480)	0.0	0.1	0.31
Ford, L.	3	.215	-2.1	($1,833)	-0.5	-	-
Guerrier, M.	5	.585	2.5	$2,071	-	0.3	0.51
Hunter, T.	18	.543	6.8	($354)	-0.9	-	-
Kubel, J.	1	.090	-2.5	($2,046)	-0.7	-	-
Liriano, F.	16	1.188	12.5	$10,376	-0.0	3.0	0.84
Mauer, J.	31	.975	19.7	$16,334	2.4	-	-
Morneau, J.	27	.751	14.9	$12,348	4.5	-	-
Nathan, J.	17	1.143	11.9	$6,248	-0.0	5.2	1.62
Punto, N.	12	.423	1.7	$1,028	-1.1	-	-
Radke, B.	10	.572	5.5	($364)	-0.1	-0.1	0.90
Redmond, M.	6	.584	2.7	$1,906	0.2	-	-
Reyes, D.	9	1.264	6.4	$5,205	-	1.5	0.90
Rincon, J.	8	.736	3.9	$2,874	-	2.4	1.08
Rodriguez, L.	0	.000	-2.1	($1,734)	-1.0	-	-
Santana, J.	25	.994	18.6	$6,619	-0.1	4.2	0.97
Silva, C.	3	.153	-2.2	($4,843)	-0.1	-1.6	0.86
Stewart, S.	5	.520	1.3	($2,469)	0.2	-	-
Tyner, J.	6	.487	2.2	$1,872	0.6	-	-
White, R.	1	.062	-4.7	($5,176)	-1.2	-	-

New York Yankees

Player	WS	WS%	WSAB	WS$	bWPA	pWPA	pLI
Abreu, B.	11	.855	7.1	$3,338	2.0	-	-
Cabrera, M.	13	.462	3.7	$3,089	0.8	-	-
Cairo, M.	5	.374	0.3	($160)	-1.5	-	-
Cano, R.	18	.668	8.3	$6,866	0.8	-	-
Damon, J.	22	.650	10.0	$1,046	1.7	-	-
Farnsworth, K.	4	.373	0.7	($2,300)	-	0.7	1.50
Giambi, J.	23	.886	14.2	$1,103	4.2	-	-
Jeter, D.	33	.891	19.7	$4,545	6.0	-	-
Johnson, R.	9	.405	3.2	($6,341)	-0.1	-1.8	0.92
Matsui, H.	6	.607	3.1	($4,642)	-0.3	-	-
Mussina, M.	15	.704	9.7	($2,590)	-0.1	1.6	0.85
Phillips, A.	1	.070	-3.7	($3,109)	-1.3	-	-
Posada, J.	24	.836	13.6	$3,774	2.2	-	-
Proctor, S.	9	.597	4.3	$3,557	-	1.0	1.24

Player	WS	WS%	WSAB	WS$	bWPA	pWPA	pLI
Rivera, M.	14	.904	8.3	$1,081	-0.0	3.4	1.83
Rodriguez, A.	25	.706	12.4	($4,356)	1.1	-	-
Sheffield, G.	3	.373	0.8	($6,601)	-0.3	-	-
Villone, R.	3	.299	-0.5	($1,516)	-	-0.0	0.74
Wang, C.	17	.717	11.7	$9,689	-0.1	2.5	1.06
Williams, B.	8	.352	0.7	($113)	-0.2	-	-
Wright, J.	8	.523	3.9	($1,184)	-0.1	0.1	0.98

New York Mets

Player	WS	WS%	WSAB	WS$	bWPA	pWPA	pLI
Beltran, C.	38	1.132	26.5	$14,495	4.9	-	-
Bradford, C.	7	.840	3.8	$2,509	-	1.2	1.01
Castro, R.	2	.248	-0.2	($695)	-0.7	-	-
Chavez, E.	14	.646	6.6	$5,432	0.8	-	-
Delgado, C.	24	.705	12.1	$2,481	2.8	-	-
Feliciano, P.	8	.999	5.5	$4,419	-0.0	0.8	0.82
Floyd, C.	9	.433	2.2	($1,683)	-0.4	-	-
Franco, J.	3	.339	0.3	($140)	-0.8	-	-
Glavine, T.	13	.759	8.9	$3,263	-0.7	0.9	1.06
Green, S.	2	.285	-0.6	($1,866)	-0.5	-	-
Heilman, A.	8	.635	3.4	$2,764	-	1.8	1.50
Hernandez, O.	6	.591	3.5	$1,222	-0.6	0.7	0.96
Lo Duca, P.	17	.571	6.4	$1,730	0.7	-	-
Maine, J.	5	.643	3.2	$2,636	-0.4	0.3	0.89
Martinez, P.	5	.439	2.3	($6,399)	-0.9	0.9	1.02
Matsui, K.	0	.000	-2.7	($4,614)	-2.0	-	-
Milledge, L.	4	.386	0.7	$544	0.2	-	-
Nady, X.	8	.490	2.2	$1,783	-0.1	-	-
Oliver, D.	6	.673	3.4	$2,657	-0.1	0.9	0.58
Reyes, J.	29	.762	16.1	$13,344	1.7	-	-
Sanchez, D.	6	.816	4.0	$3,219	0.0	2.1	1.49
Trachsel, S.	6	.422	2.9	$1,180	-0.9	-0.3	1.01
Valentin, J.	16	.677	7.4	$5,801	1.2	-	-
Wagner, B.	12	.749	6.7	($229)	-	3.9	1.88
Woodward, C.	2	.143	-2.4	($2,517)	-1.2	-	-
Wright, D.	32	.874	18.9	$15,695	4.2	-	-

Oakland Athletics

Player	WS	WS%	WSAB	WS$	bWPA	pWPA	pLI
Blanton, J.	10	.477	5.2	$4,332	-0.1	-0.5	0.97
Bradley, M.	13	.610	6.0	$2,174	1.9	-	-
Calero, K.	7	.768	3.4	$2,287	-	1.6	1.35
Chavez, E.	17	.558	6.8	$384	1.1	-	-
Crosby, B.	8	.377	0.4	($153)	-0.7	-	-
Duchscherer, J.	8	.838	4.3	$3,597	-	2.8	1.38
Ellis, M.	14	.521	4.3	$1,537	-1.6	-	-
Gaudin, C.	7	.799	3.8	$3,125	-	1.3	0.78
Halsey, B.	5	.430	0.9	$699	-	0.3	1.02
Haren, D.	15	.620	8.7	$7,062	-0.2	2.5	0.94
Johnson, D.	5	.280	-1.4	($1,183)	-0.1	-	-
Kendall, J.	23	.696	12.0	$3,413	-1.0	-	-

Player	WS	WS%	WSAB	WS$	bWPA	pWPA	pLI
Kielty, B.	8	.511	3.1	$955	0.5	-	-
Kotsay, M.	12	.412	1.7	($2,420)	-0.4	-	-
Loaiza, E.	7	.416	2.7	($988)	-0.1	-1.3	0.98
Payton, J.	15	.480	4.6	$1,761	1.8	-	-
Saarloos, K.	6	.445	2.6	$2,096	-	-0.3	0.95
Scutaro, M.	11	.476	3.1	$2,541	-1.4	-	-
Street, H.	12	.755	6.4	$5,320	-	1.5	2.11
Swisher, N.	22	.619	9.2	$7,668	2.0	-	-
Thomas, F.	22	1.020	14.3	$11,839	3.2	-	-
Zito, B.	18	.755	11.7	$1,087	-0.1	2.6	1.04

Philadelphia Phillies

Player	WS	WS%	WSAB	WS$	bWPA	pWPA	pLI
Abreu, B.	17	.723	9.0	$2,798	2.7	-	-
Bell, D.	8	.398	1.0	($756)	-2.0	-	-
Burrell, P.	17	.573	6.3	($4,735)	1.2	-	-
Coste, C.	8	.688	4.3	$3,576	0.2	-	-
Dellucci, D.	8	.520	3.1	$2,198	0.6	-	-
Fasano, S.	3	.351	-0.4	($371)	-1.3	-	-
Fultz, A.	4	.444	0.9	($144)	-0.1	-0.1	0.81
Geary, G.	10	.836	5.8	$4,834	0.0	1.1	0.88
Gordon, T.	8	.609	3.6	$632	-	1.6	2.10
Hamels, C.	8	.716	5.0	$4,173	-0.4	1.1	0.83
Howard, R.	31	.813	17.6	$14,642	8.2	-	-
Lidle, C.	5	.453	2.5	$879	-0.3	-0.6	1.00
Lieber, J.	5	.348	1.4	($2,982)	-0.9	-0.0	0.99
Lieberthal, M.	6	.475	1.8	($2,615)	-0.2	-	-
Madson, R.	4	.309	0.3	$166	-0.4	-1.0	1.15
Myers, B.	11	.649	7.2	$2,868	-1.6	2.2	1.04
Nunez, A.	3	.152	-3.9	($3,732)	-2.1	-	-
Rhodes, A.	2	.253	-0.8	($3,255)	-	-0.1	1.52
Rollins, J.	26	.648	11.9	$4,942	2.3	-	-
Rowand, A.	9	.372	0.4	($2,788)	0.6	-	-
Utley, C.	28	.711	14.3	$11,708	4.1	-	-
Victorino, S.	12	.495	3.5	$2,909	-0.8	-	-

Pittsburgh Pirates

Player	WS	WS%	WSAB	WS$	bWPA	pWPA	pLI
Bautista, J.	11	.433	1.8	$1,485	-0.6	-	-
Bay, J.	24	.643	10.8	$8,294	1.6	-	-
Burnitz, J.	5	.274	-1.0	($4,111)	-1.6	-	-
Capps, M.	8	.679	4.3	$3,558	-0.0	0.0	1.02
Casey, S.	6	.460	1.8	($1,047)	-0.3	-	-
Castillo, J.	7	.224	-3.7	($3,105)	-2.9	-	-
Doumit, R.	2	.216	-0.7	($564)	-0.9	-	-
Duffy, C.	6	.321	-0.0	($27)	-1.0	-	-
Duke, Z.	10	.539	5.9	$4,866	-0.6	-0.7	1.00
Gonzalez, M.	9	.847	5.3	$4,421	-0.0	2.5	1.83
Grabow, J.	5	.551	1.9	$1,529	-0.0	0.5	0.78
Maholm, P.	6	.390	2.3	$1,883	-0.9	-0.6	1.04
Marte, D.	4	.489	0.8	($1,326)	-0.0	-0.7	1.18

Player	WS	WS%	WSAB	WS$	bWPA	pWPA	pLI
McLouth, N.	3	.193	-2.5	($2,092)	-1.4	-	-
Nady, X.	5	.412	0.8	$616	-0.3	-	-
Paulino, R.	16	.600	6.8	$5,666	-1.1	-	-
Randa, J.	3	.254	-1.2	($3,097)	-1.1	-	-
Sanchez, F.	24	.706	12.3	$10,249	1.7	-	-
Santos, V.	0	.000	-1.9	($1,797)	-0.3	-0.9	0.93
Snell, I.	7	.434	3.5	$2,918	-1.2	0.1	1.01
Torres, S.	8	.554	3.1	$1,299	-0.0	2.9	1.57
Wilson, C.	9	.585	3.6	$737	0.3	-	-
Wilson, J.	11	.346	-0.0	($4,682)	-1.7	-	-

San Diego Padres

Player	WS	WS%	WSAB	WS$	bWPA	pWPA	pLI
Bard, J.	11	.766	5.8	$4,767	2.2	-	-
Barfield, J.	18	.550	6.1	$5,117	-0.4	-	-
Bellhorn, M.	4	.258	-1.5	($1,535)	-1.5	-	-
Blum, G.	6	.361	0.1	($63)	-1.8	-	-
Cameron, M.	28	.801	16.1	$9,587	0.5	-	-
Castilla, V.	1	.066	-3.9	($4,740)	-1.0	-	-
Giles, B.	23	.583	8.9	$3,184	1.1	-	-
Gonzalez, A.	17	.479	5.0	$4,177	0.3	-	-
Greene, K.	13	.500	3.6	$2,882	-0.9	-	-
Hensley, C.	10	.594	6.0	$4,986	-0.8	1.5	0.99
Hoffman, T.	11	.788	6.1	$2,717	-	4.0	2.08
Johnson, B.	3	.394	-0.0	($24)	-0.7	-	-
Linebrink, S.	8	.625	3.7	$1,994	-0.0	2.5	1.90
Meredith, C.	9	1.259	6.5	$5,428	-0.0	3.1	1.40
Park, C.	4	.338	1.1	($7,496)	-0.4	-0.1	0.97
Peavy, J.	12	.681	7.6	$3,991	-0.3	1.6	0.90
Piazza, M.	12	.517	3.9	$2,706	1.0	-	-
Roberts, D.	20	.646	9.6	$5,955	-1.2	-	-
Sweeney, B.	5	.709	2.1	$1,763	-0.1	0.1	0.45
Thompson, M.	1	.123	-0.5	($426)	-0.4	-0.8	0.99
Walker, T.	5	.638	2.2	$1,507	0.1	-	-
Williams, W.	10	.826	7.1	$3,266	-0.6	0.7	0.96
Young, C.	12	.770	8.3	$6,693	-1.0	3.1	0.98
Young, E.	0	.000	-2.6	($2,377)	-1.3	-	-

Seattle Mariners

Player	WS	WS%	WSAB	WS$	bWPA	pWPA	pLI
Beltre, A.	19	.530	6.5	($1,815)	0.3	-	-
Betancourt, Y.	12	.373	1.0	$853	-2.1	-	-
Bloomquist, W.	4	.258	-1.0	($1,120)	-0.2	-	-
Broussard, B.	2	.273	-0.7	($1,356)	0.0	-	-
Everett, C.	1	.075	-3.4	($4,561)	-0.9	-	-
Hernandez, F.	9	.435	4.1	$3,386	-0.1	0.4	0.96
Ibanez, R.	27	.734	14.2	$9,209	1.6	-	-
Johjima, K.	22	.754	12.0	$7,058	-0.2	-	-
Lopez, J.	16	.463	3.5	$2,932	-2.5	-	-
Mateo, J.	4	.548	2.0	$1,310	-	-0.9	1.20
Meche, G.	9	.446	4.0	($231)	-0.1	-0.2	1.01
Moyer, J.	8	.463	3.5	$546	0.1	0.2	0.94
Pineiro, J.	0	.000	-4.5	($10,015)	0.1	-2.1	0.93
Putz, J.	15	.872	9.3	$7,616	-	4.3	1.71
Reed, J.	0	.000	-4.1	($3,498)	-2.0	-	-
Sexson, R.	20	.575	8.2	($402)	0.4	-	-
Soriano, R.	8	.866	4.3	$3,471	-	2.5	1.27
Suzuki, I.	24	.618	10.6	$1,852	1.5	-	-
Washburn, J.	8	.396	2.9	($1,691)	-0.0	0.0	1.03
Woods, J.	7	.550	2.3	$1,880	-	0.6	0.70

San Francisco Giants

Player	WS	WS%	WSAB	WS$	bWPA	pWPA	pLI
Alfonzo, E.	10	.571	3.9	$3,271	-0.8	-	-
Alou, M.	15	.731	7.7	$3,130	1.8	-	-
Benitez, A.	5	.589	1.8	($3,535)	-	-0.8	2.07
Bonds, B.	27	1.028	17.8	$4,661	4.7	-	-
Cain, M.	12	.724	7.8	$6,494	-1.2	1.0	0.99
Correia, K.	6	.718	3.2	$2,651	-0.1	1.2	0.66
Durham, R.	21	.686	10.4	$4,845	2.9	-	-
Feliz, P.	13	.361	0.9	($3,103)	-1.6	-	-
Finley, S.	11	.416	1.6	($2,499)	-1.0	-	-
Greene, T.	5	.537	2.0	$1,431	-1.0	-	-
Hennessey, B.	6	.661	3.6	$2,960	-0.5	-0.4	1.00
Hillenbrand, S.	2	.147	-2.2	($4,650)	-1.4	-	-
Kline, S.	5	.690	2.3	$408	-	0.8	1.19
Lowry, N.	7	.509	3.5	$2,572	-0.6	0.9	1.04
Matheny, M.	3	.301	-0.7	($2,246)	-0.4	-	-
Morris, M.	8	.447	3.8	$129	-0.8	-1.1	0.90
Niekro, L.	3	.259	-1.1	($949)	-0.3	-	-
Schmidt, J.	16	.860	11.2	$3,457	-1.1	2.5	1.12
Sweeney, M.	5	.324	0.1	($187)	0.3	-	-
Vizcaino, J.	1	.135	-1.8	($1,915)	-0.9	-	-
Vizquel, O.	19	.530	6.3	$3,276	0.2	-	-
Winn, R.	14	.408	2.1	($1,355)	-1.0	-	-
Wright, J.	4	.293	1.0	$742	-0.7	-1.0	0.84

St. Louis Cardinals

Player	WS	WS%	WSAB	WS$	bWPA	pWPA	pLI
Belliard, R.	2	.170	-2.4	($2,807)	-2.1	-	-
Bennett, G.	2	.207	-1.0	($1,063)	0.0	-	-
Carpenter, C.	19	.994	14.7	$9,561	-1.1	3.4	1.02
Duncan, C.	11	.660	4.8	$4,011	0.7	-	-
Eckstein, D.	12	.402	1.4	($573)	-1.3	-	-
Edmonds, J.	12	.532	4.5	($3,121)	-0.3	-	-
Encarnacion, J.	16	.484	4.4	$1,846	-0.6	-	-
Hancock, J.	5	.529	1.8	$1,483	-0.2	0.3	0.60
Isringhausen, J.	6	.464	1.5	($3,602)	-	-0.5	2.34
Looper, B.	8	.826	4.9	$2,243	-0.1	0.7	1.14
Luna, H.	7	.514	2.2	$1,836	-1.2	-	-
Marquis, J.	1	.062	-2.7	($7,347)	-0.5	-1.7	0.88
Miles, A.	10	.385	0.5	$410	-0.6	-	-

Player	WS	WS%	WSAB	WS$	bWPA	pWPA	pLI
Molina, Y.	9	.344	0.0	($32)	-1.7	-	-
Mulder, M.	0	.000	-2.5	($9,907)	-0.1	-1.9	1.01
Pujols, A.	39	1.124	26.5	$7,612	9.2	-	-
Reyes, A.	2	.266	0.5	$424	-0.5	0.1	0.96
Rodriguez, J.	6	.555	2.3	$1,872	-0.4	-	-
Rolen, S.	22	.670	11.0	$2,433	0.6	-	-
Spiezio, S.	12	.720	6.3	$5,269	2.0	-	-
Suppan, J.	12	.735	8.3	$4,797	-0.6	1.1	1.02
Taguchi, S.	6	.301	-0.9	($1,212)	-0.7	-	-
Wainwright, A.	8	.773	4.7	$3,945	0.0	1.9	1.20

Tampa Bay Devil Rays

Player	WS	WS%	WSAB	WS$	bWPA	pWPA	pLI
Baldelli, R.	14	.699	7.2	$4,243	1.0	-	-
Branyan, R.	3	.294	-0.1	($351)	0.2	-	-
Camp, S.	5	.469	1.5	$1,250	-	0.7	1.19
Cantu, J.	5	.214	-3.5	($2,908)	-1.8	-	-
Corcoran, T.	5	.506	3.0	$2,498	-0.1	-0.5	1.00
Crawford, C.	23	.682	11.6	$7,239	1.2	-	-
Fossum, C.	4	.285	0.9	($1,030)	-0.1	-1.1	1.01
Gathright, J.	2	.200	-1.4	($1,193)	-0.8	-	-
Gomes, J.	7	.390	0.7	$578	-1.4	-	-
Hall, T.	5	.403	0.8	($954)	-1.5	-	-
Hendrickson, M.	7	.728	4.3	$2,604	-	1.1	1.20
Hollins, D.	4	.210	-3.0	($2,547)	-1.9	-	-
Huff, A.	5	.381	0.3	($3,048)	0.1	-	-
Kazmir, S.	14	.896	10.2	$8,441	-0.1	2.2	1.06
Lee, T.	3	.144	-4.4	($4,885)	-1.7	-	-
Lugo, J.	12	.721	6.7	$2,406	0.3	-	-
Lugo, R.	7	.664	3.0	$2,460	-	0.0	0.65
McClung, S.	1	.082	-2.0	($1,645)	-0.1	-2.1	1.27
Meadows, B.	3	.292	-0.5	($561)	-	-0.1	1.13
Navarro, D.	2	.175	-1.5	($1,278)	-0.7	-	-
Norton, G.	10	.644	4.8	$4,032	0.2	-	-
Paul, J.	3	.329	0.2	$32	-0.6	-	-
Perez, T.	0	.000	-5.3	($4,654)	-1.9	-	-
Seo, J.	3	.307	0.6	$477	-0.0	-0.6	1.06
Shields, J.	7	.512	3.3	$2,728	-0.1	-0.5	1.09
Upton, B.	2	.198	-1.5	($1,245)	-1.6	-	-
Wigginton, T.	14	.545	4.6	$3,442	1.6	-	-
Zobrist, B.	1	.094	-2.5	($2,052)	-1.5	-	-

Texas Rangers

Player	WS	WS%	WSAB	WS$	bWPA	pWPA	pLI
Barajas, R.	7	.344	-0.3	($3,284)	-1.4	-	-
Bauer, R.	6	.618	2.9	$2,364	-	1.1	0.85
Benoit, J.	4	.392	0.2	($286)	-	-0.5	0.77
Blalock, H.	13	.399	1.4	($1,661)	0.4	-	-
Cordero, F.	5	.537	1.8	$177	-	-1.5	1.69
Cruz, N.	3	.396	0.3	$226	-0.8	-	-
DeRosa, M.	14	.459	3.8	$2,783	-0.1	-	-

Player	WS	WS%	WSAB	WS$	bWPA	pWPA	pLI
Kinsler, I.	12	.467	3.5	$2,923	-0.1	-	-
Koronka, J.	4	.293	0.6	$506	-0.3	-0.3	0.92
Laird, G.	6	.422	0.7	$560	-0.7	-	-
Lee, C.	7	.534	2.1	$81	0.8	-	-
Loe, K.	2	.238	-0.2	($197)	-	-1.1	1.02
Mahay, R.	4	.536	1.1	$94	-	-0.4	0.83
Matthews Jr., G.	22	.617	9.2	$5,493	1.6	-	-
Mench, K.	8	.446	1.7	($407)	0.5	-	-
Millwood, K.	13	.558	7.7	$1,024	-0.1	0.9	0.93
Nevin, P.	2	.257	-0.8	($2,845)	-0.0	-	-
Otsuka, A.	11	.820	6.4	$4,529	-	1.3	1.79
Padilla, V.	13	.604	7.3	$1,737	-0.1	-0.2	1.00
Rheinecker, J.	2	.261	0.3	$233	0.0	-0.3	1.06
Teixeira, M.	21	.550	8.1	$318	1.2	-	-
Tejeda, R.	5	.624	2.6	$2,122	-0.1	0.3	1.02
Wilkerson, B.	5	.263	-1.3	($4,882)	0.0	-	-
Young, M.	26	.673	12.7	$7,754	2.5	-	-

Toronto Blue Jays

Player	WS	WS%	WSAB	WS$	bWPA	pWPA	pLI
Adams, R.	3	.197	-2.6	($2,189)	-1.8	-	-
Burnett, A.	10	.682	6.1	$3,986	-0.2	0.1	0.96
Catalanotto, F.	14	.558	5.7	$3,352	2.2	-	-
Chacin, G.	5	.534	2.7	$2,218	-	0.0	1.01
Downs, S.	6	.589	2.7	$1,827	-	-0.0	0.79
Glaus, T.	16	.475	4.5	($1,240)	-0.8	-	-
Halladay, R.	21	.886	15.3	$5,606	-0.2	3.2	0.97
Hill, A.	14	.419	2.1	$1,744	0.4	-	-
Hillenbrand, S.	5	.346	-0.0	($3,013)	-1.1	w-	-
Hinske, E.	5	.459	1.7	($1,587)	-0.6	-	-
Janssen, R.	4	.395	1.3	$1,102	-0.0	-0.7	0.93
Johnson, R.	18	.659	8.0	$5,490	0.2	-	-
Lilly, T.	12	.612	6.8	$1,770	-0.0	0.4	0.95
Marcum, S.	4	.476	1.5	$1,243	-	-0.0	0.90
McDonald, J.	1	.061	-4.2	($3,707)	-1.6	-	-
Molina, B.	12	.500	3.2	$1,123	0.7	-	-
Overbay, L.	17	.501	5.5	$2,227	2.0	-	-
Rios, A.	19	.715	10.0	$8,268	1.9	-	-
Ryan, B.	17	1.057	11.2	$7,194	-	4.7	1.89
Speier, J.	6	.742	3.2	$1,549	-	0.5	1.52
Wells, V.	25	.698	12.9	$6,405	2.2	-	-
Zaun, G.	8	.465	2.4	$1,626	-0.3	-	-

Washington Nationals

Player	WS	WS%	WSAB	WS$	bWPA	pWPA	pLI
Anderson, M.	5	.419	1.1	$653	0.1	-	-
Armas Jr., T.	3	.226	-0.5	($1,444)	-1.1	-0.8	1.00
Astacio, P.	0	.000	-3.1	($2,838)	-0.5	-1.3	1.00
Bergmann, J.	0	.000	-2.8	($2,324)	-0.3	-1.3	0.74
Byrd, M.	3	.241	-1.5	($1,733)	-1.2	-	-
Church, R.	10	.803	5.5	$4,518	1.1	-	-

Player	WS	WS%	WSAB	WS$	bWPA	pWPA	pLI
Clayton, R.	6	.325	-0.9	($980)	-2.0	-	-
Cordero, C.	10	.702	5.0	$3,947	-0.0	2.3	1.99
Fick, R.	1	.135	-1.2	($1,297)	-0.1	-	-
Guillen, J.	4	.277	-1.1	($2,992)	-1.2	-	-
Hernandez, L.	4	.319	1.3	($1,884)	-0.2	-1.0	0.98
Jackson, D.	2	.272	-0.9	($998)	-0.9	-	-
Johnson, N.	26	.770	14.2	$8,763	3.0	-	-
Kearns, A.	8	.573	3.3	$2,121	0.1	-	-
Lopez, F.	7	.413	1.0	($268)	0.0	-	-

Player	WS	WS%	WSAB	WS$	bWPA	pWPA	pLI
Majewski, G.	4	.533	1.9	$1,550	-0.1	-0.7	1.15
O'Connor, M.	2	.216	0.0	$19	-0.6	-0.1	1.06
Ortiz, R.	2	.121	-2.1	($4,068)	-1.2	-1.5	1.01
Rauch, J.	8	.645	3.3	$2,760	-0.0	0.5	0.99
Rivera, S.	5	.632	1.9	$1,570	-0.1	0.6	0.83
Schneider, B.	9	.359	0.3	($2,275)	0.3	-	-
Soriano, A.	30	.777	16.0	$3,113	2.1	-	-
Vidro, J.	11	.406	1.9	($2,251)	-1.2	-	-
Zimmerman, R.	25	.681	12.0	$9,983	3.8	-	-

Playing Time Constellations

In our stats, you can find the number of games each player played at each position. What you can't find, however, is a sense of time. You can't see that Nick Markakis took over right field for Baltimore in the second half of the year, or that Ichiro Suzuki moved to center field full time for Seattle in the last two months of the season.

With Playing Time Constellations, you can.

The graphs on the following pages are the best source of who played where, and when. You'll find positions listed in the vertical axis and players listed in the horizontal axis. Upward trajectory indicates increased playing time; downward trajectory indicates decreased playing time.

Each dot represents a month's worth of playing time for that player at that position. In each cell, the plot moves from left to right, from April to September. A dot is displayed only if the player appeared at that position that month. Cells are 150 PA tall, and each team is represented by players with at least 100 appearances last year (somewhat higher for the

Rockies, Dodgers, and Devil Rays). Players with asterisks finished the year with another team.

Below you can see the Texas Rangers' constellation. Notice how Mark DeRosa moved from 2B to RF to 3B, where he took over for Hank Blalock? Blalock moved to DH, Kinsler took over 2B when he returned from the disabled list and Cruz manned RF when DeRosa moved to 3B. In a nutshell, that is how Texas managed to keep DeRosa's bat in the lineup.

The constellations were contributed by John Burnson, publisher of *Heater Magazine*. *Heater* is an electronic baseball magazine, published twice a week during the season, and providing the very best in fantasy baseball coverage and statistics. THT's Dave Studenmund and David Gassko both contribute regularly to *Heater*. Really, these graphs are only a small sample of what you can receive with a one-year subscription. To learn more (and subscribe), visit the *Heater Magazine* website (http://www.heatermagazine.com/). John is also the creator of the *2007 Graphical Player*.

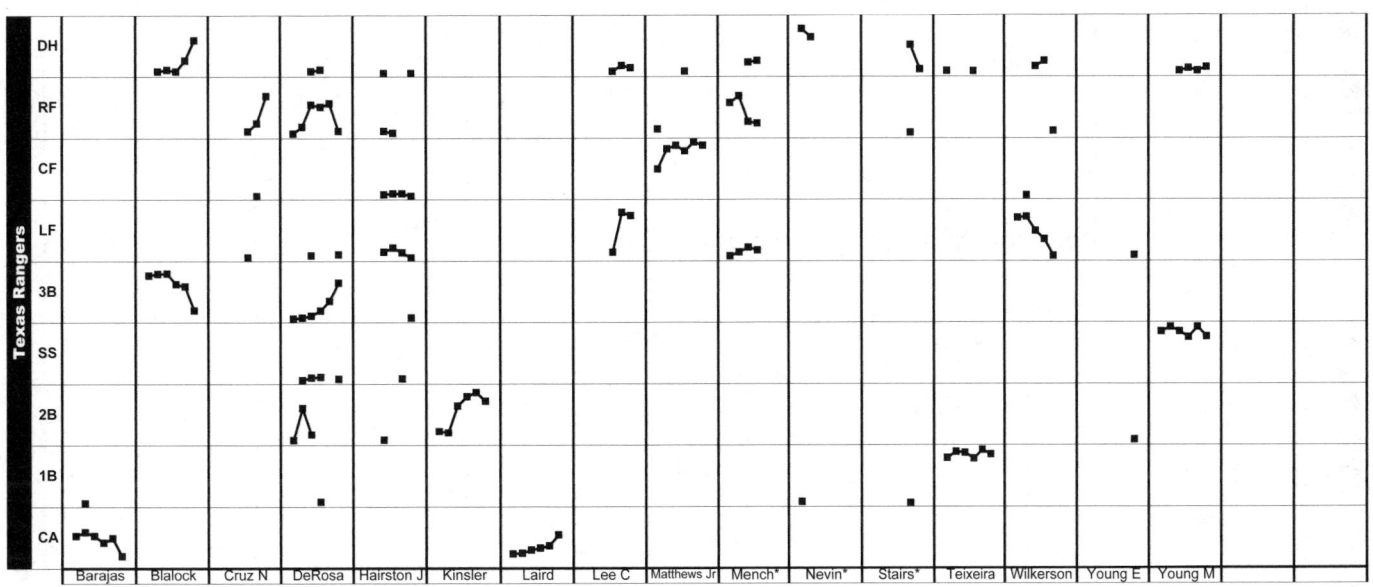

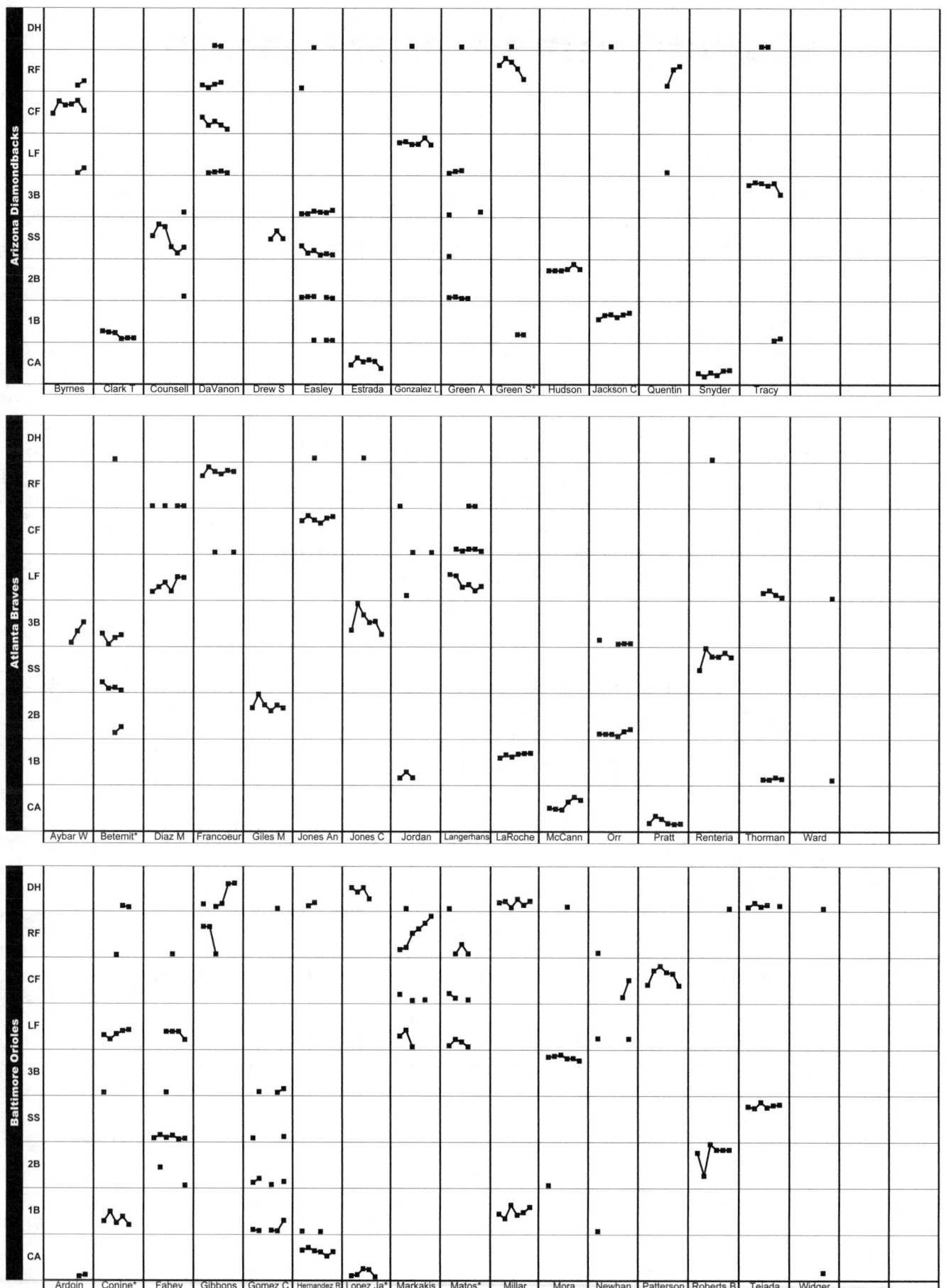

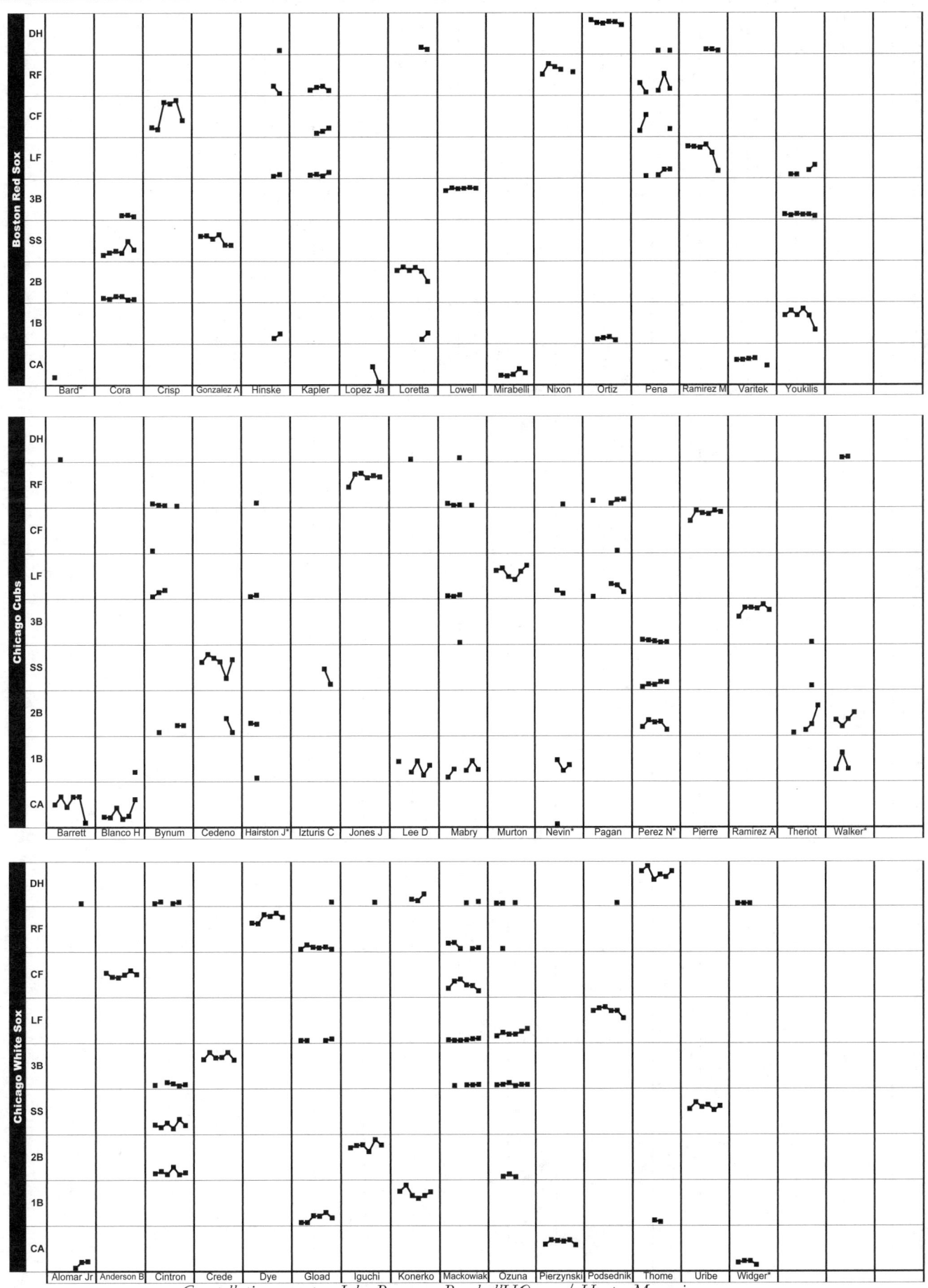

Constellations courtesy John Burnson; BaseballHQ.com / Heater Magazine

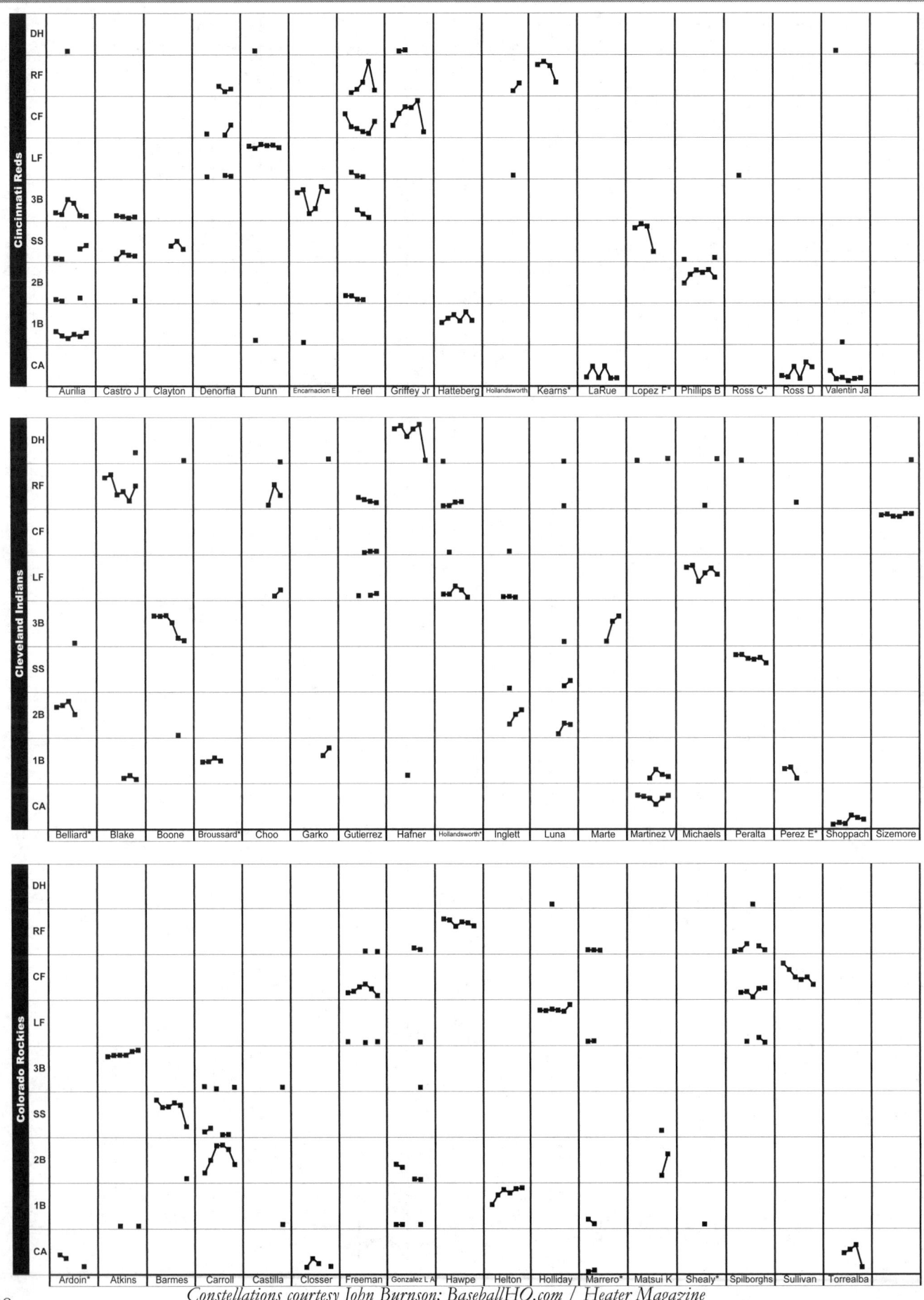

Constellations courtesy John Burnson; BaseballHQ.com / Heater Magazine

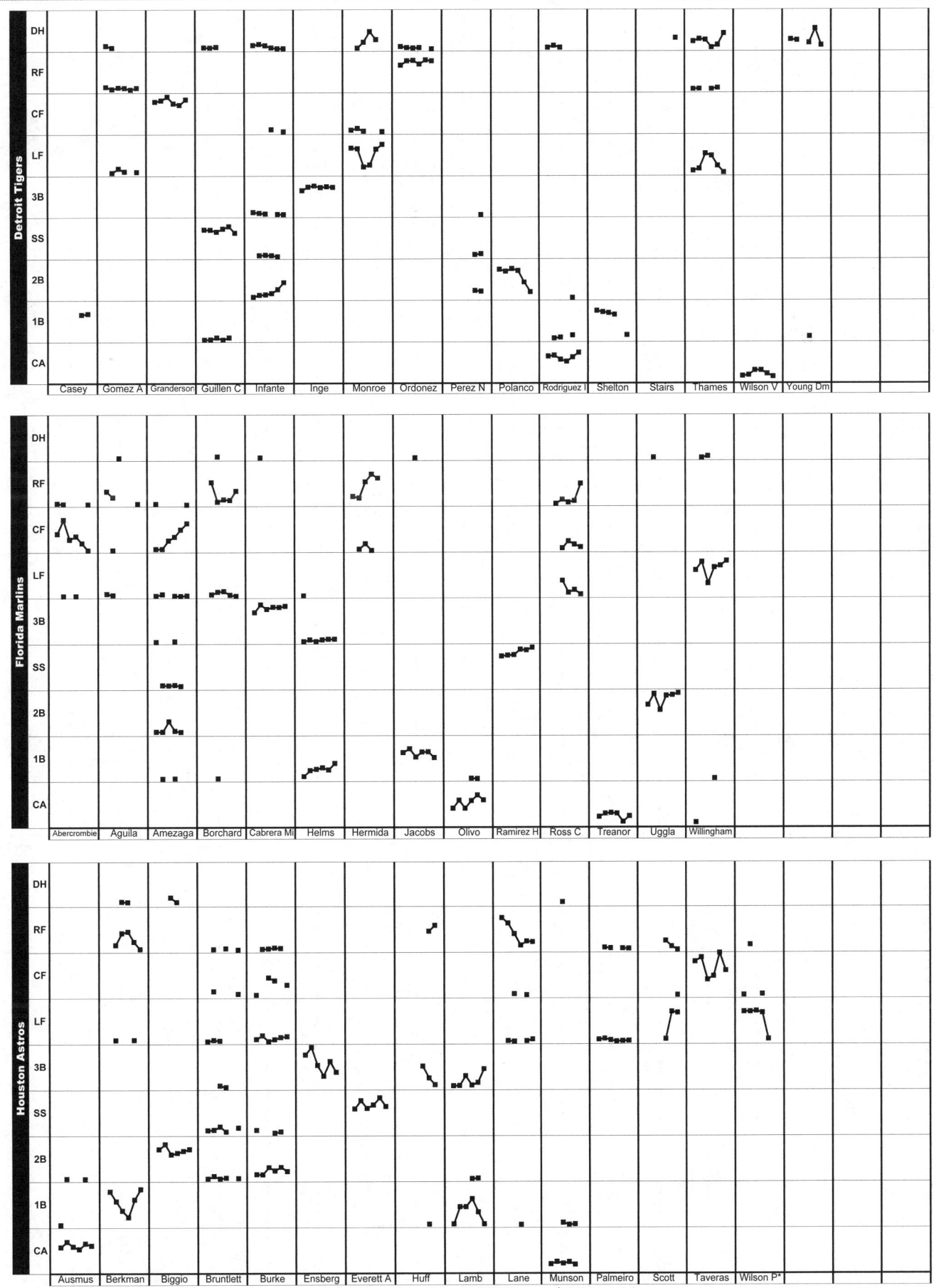

Constellations courtesy John Burnson; BaseballHQ.com / Heater Magazine

Playing Time Constellations

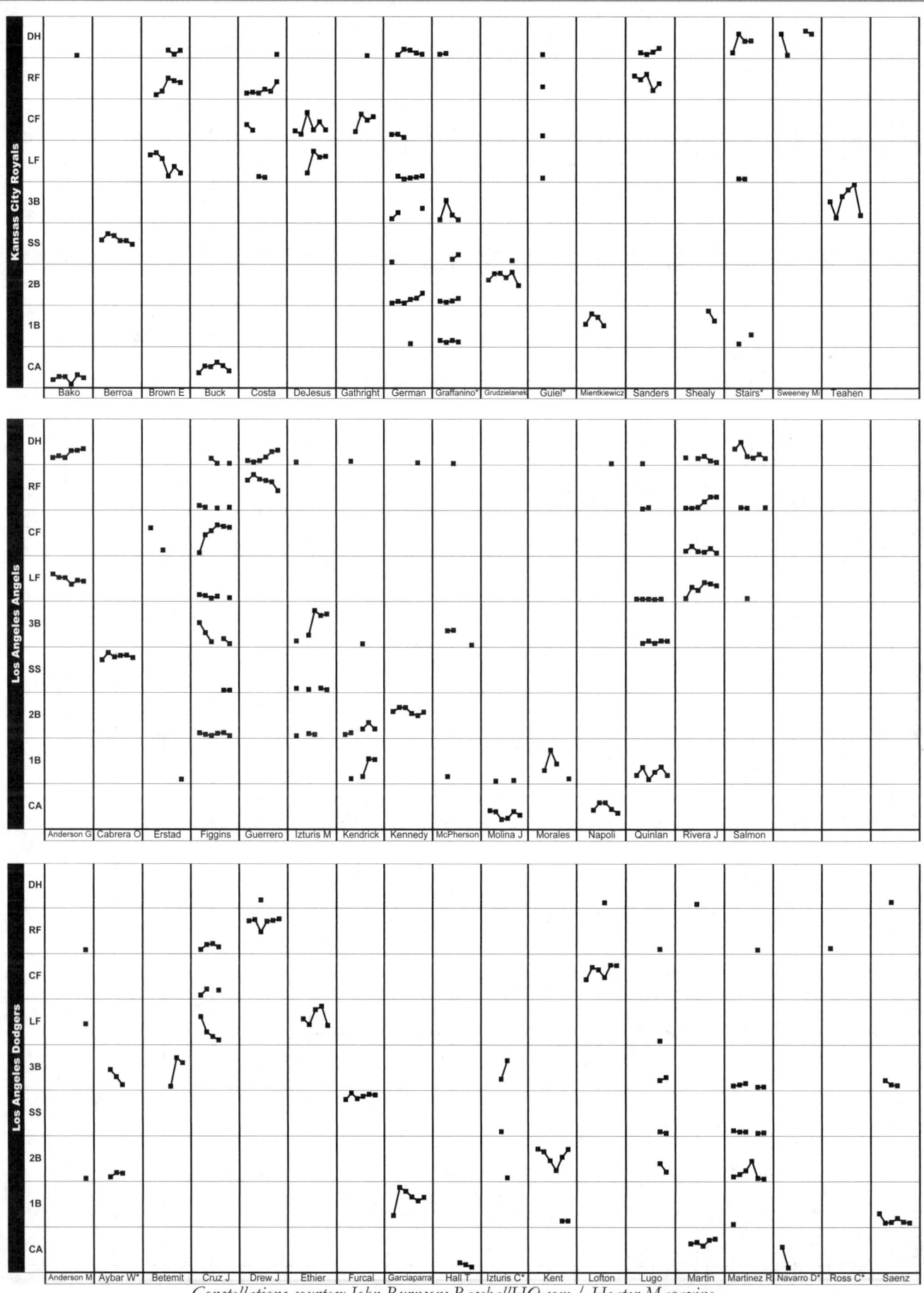

Constellations courtesy John Burnson; BaseballHQ.com / Heater Magazine

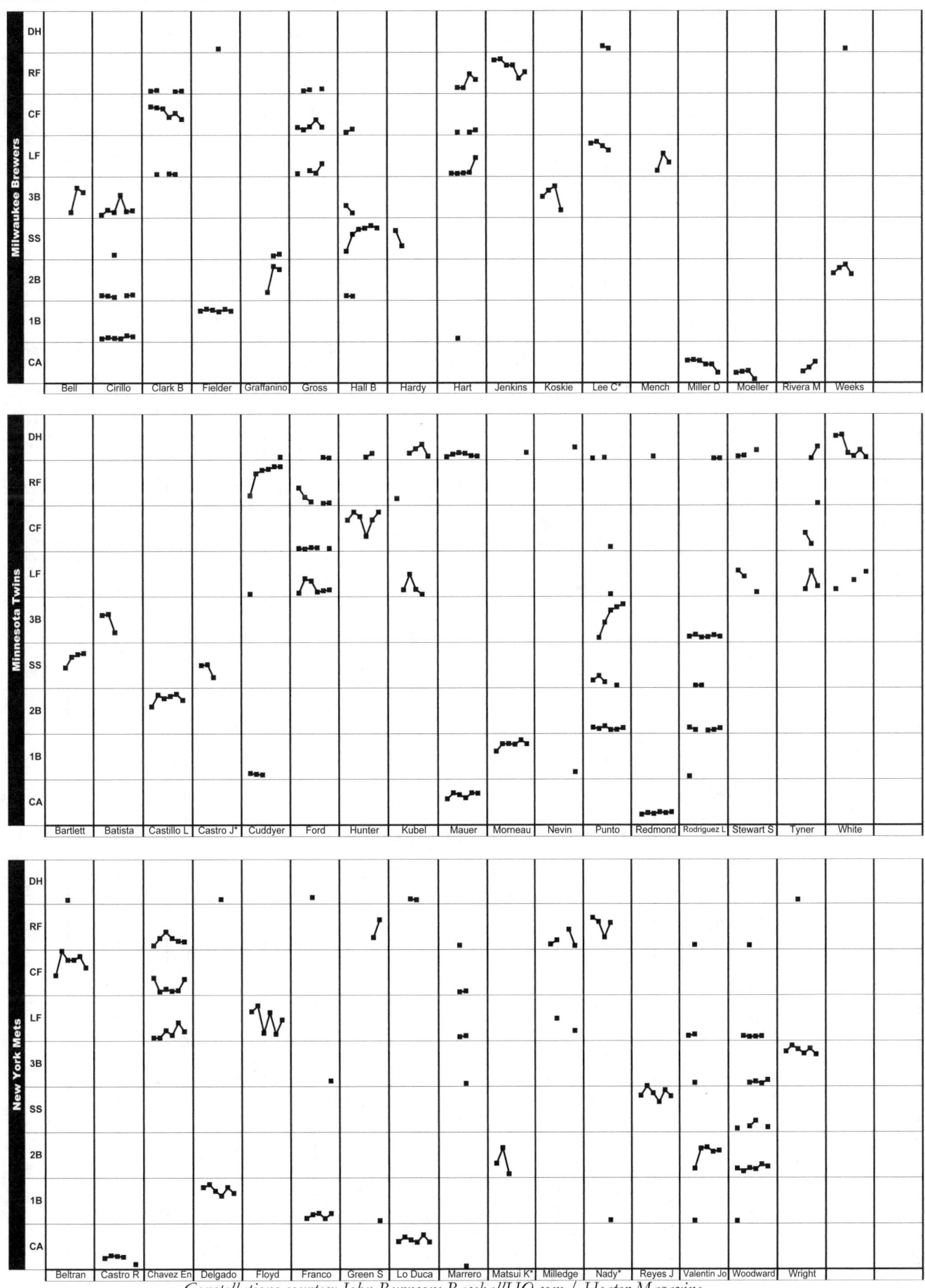

Constellations courtesy John Burnson; BaseballHQ.com / Heater Magazine

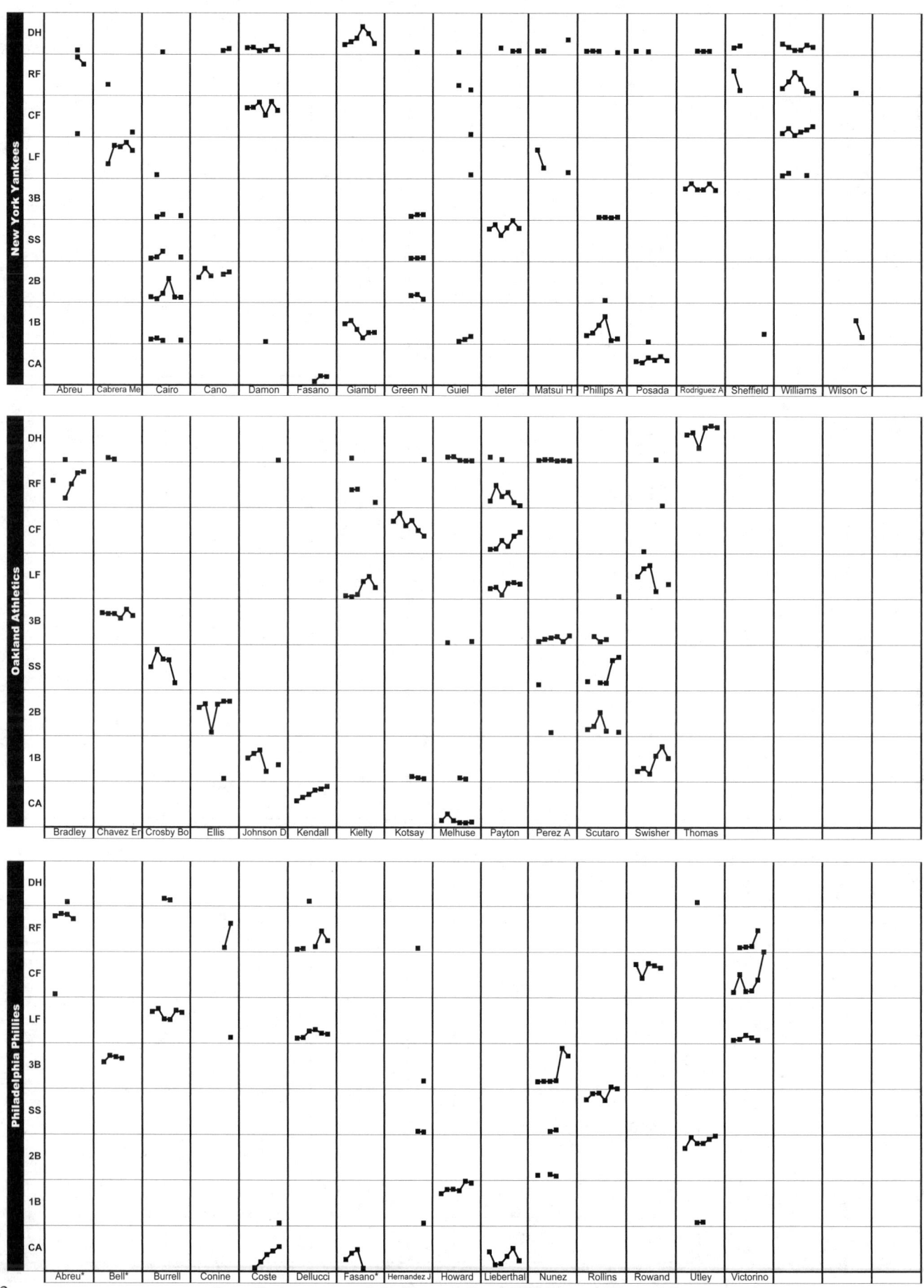

Constellations courtesy John Burnson; BaseballHQ.com / Heater Magazine

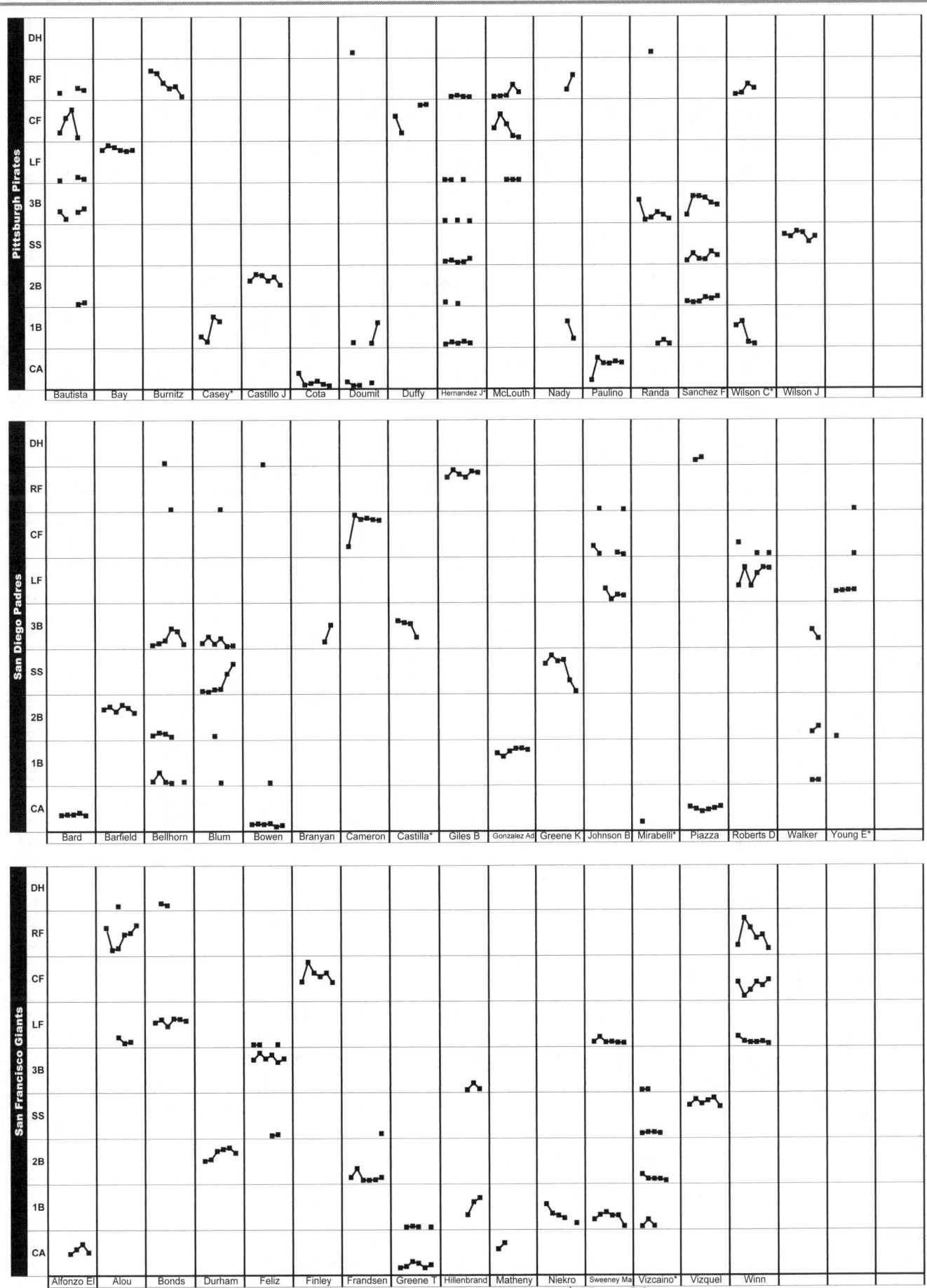

Constellations courtesy John Burnson; BaseballHQ.com / Heater Magazine

Playing Time Constellations

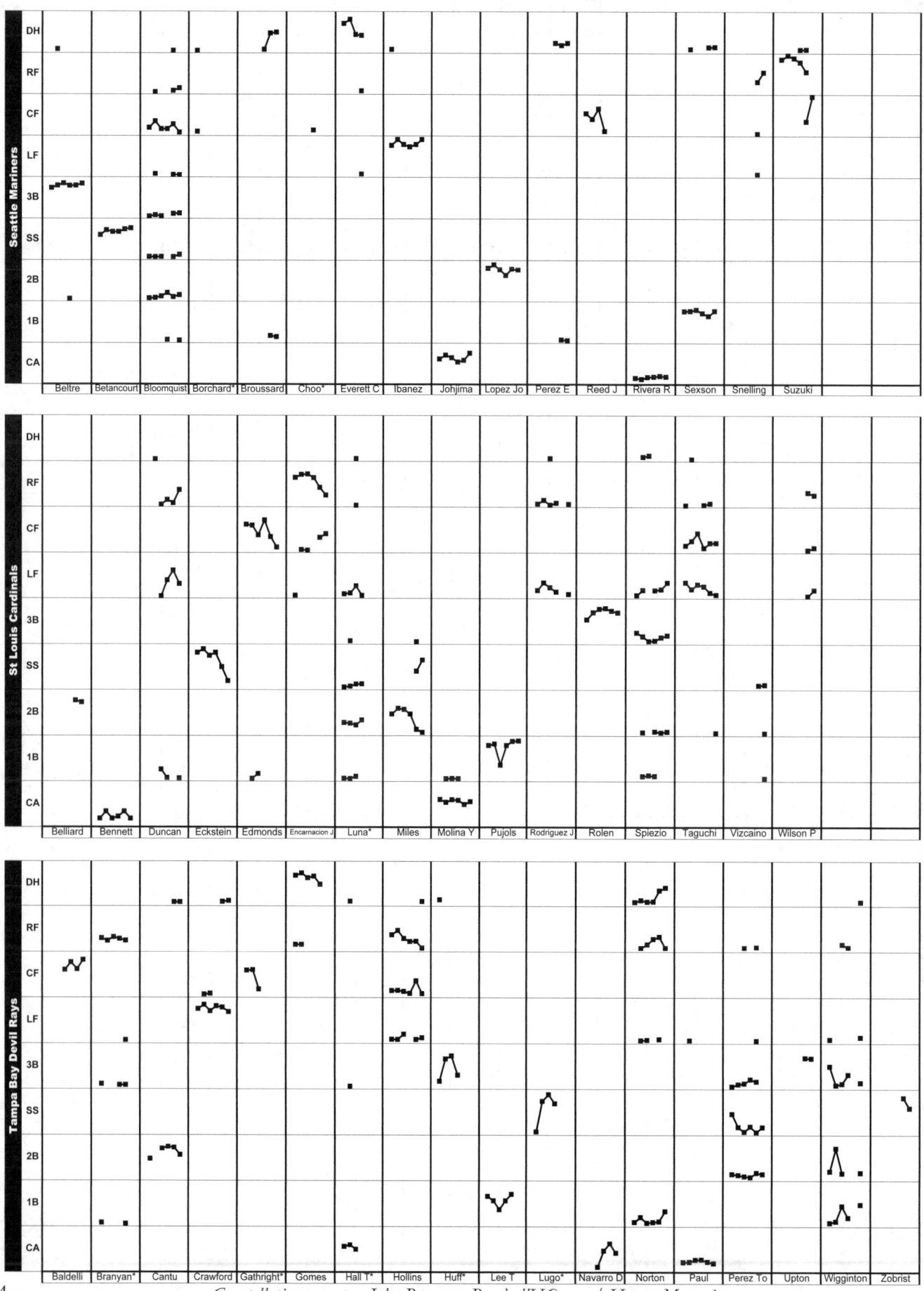

Seattle Mariners

| | Beltre | Betancourt | Bloomquist | Borchard* | Broussard | Choo* | Everett C | Ibanez | Johjima | Lopez Jo | Perez E | Reed J | Rivera R | Sexson | Snelling | Suzuki |

St Louis Cardinals

| | Belliard | Bennett | Duncan | Eckstein | Edmonds | Encarnacion J | Luna* | Miles | Molina Y | Pujols | Rodriguez J | Rolen | Spiezio | Taguchi | Vizcaino | Wilson P |

Tampa Bay Devil Rays

| | Baldelli | Branyan* | Cantu | Crawford | Gathright* | Gomes | Hall T* | Hollins | Huff* | Lee T | Lugo* | Navarro D | Norton | Paul | Perez To | Upton | Wigginton | Zobrist |

Constellations courtesy John Burnson; BaseballHQ.com / Heater Magazine

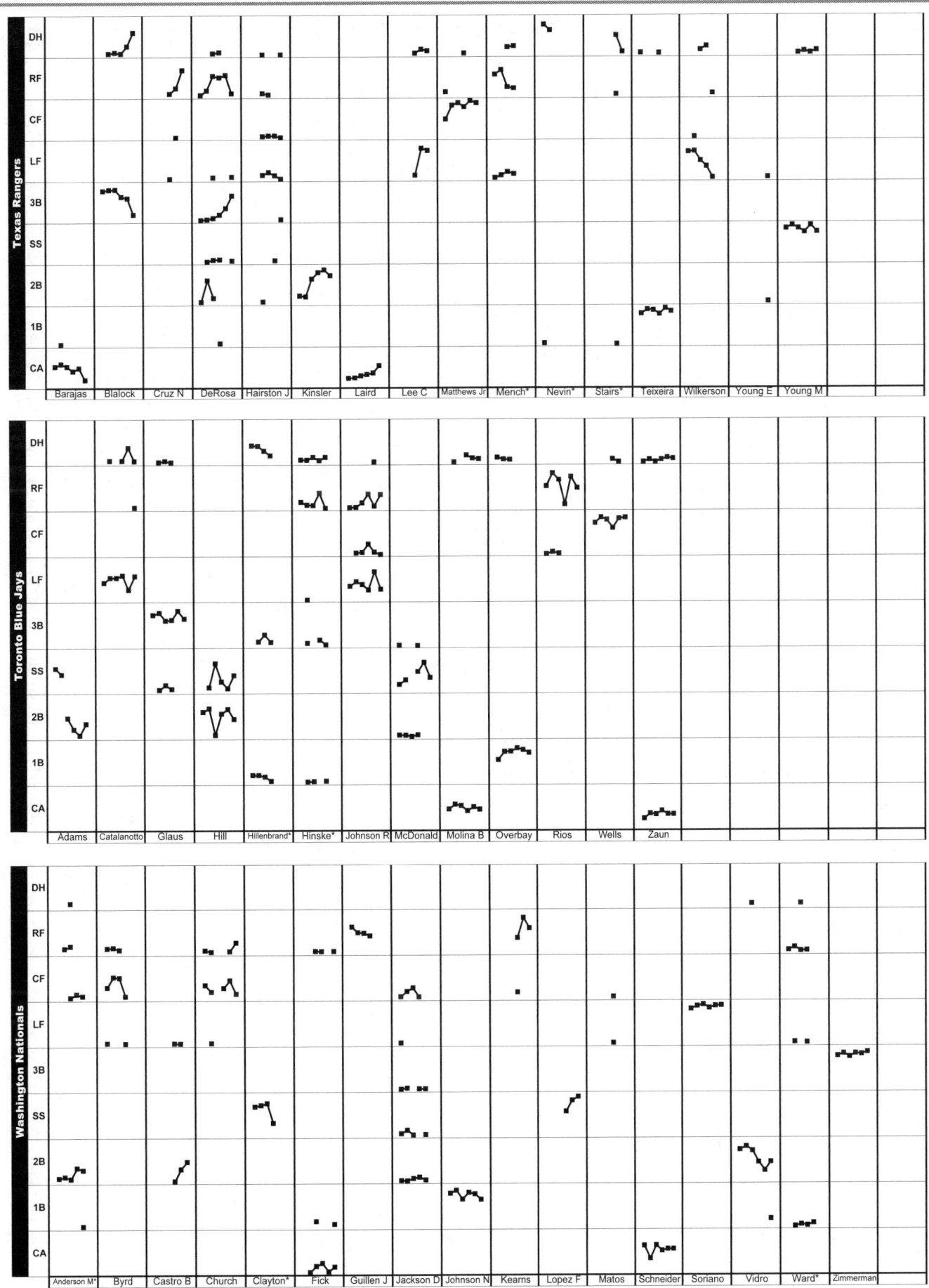

Constellations courtesy John Burnson; BaseballHQ.com / Heater Magazine

What's What: The THT Glossary

A: Assists. The number of times a fielder makes a throw that results in an out.

AB: At-Bats

AB/RSP: At-Bats with Runners in Scoring Position (second and/or third base)

BA: Batting Average; Hits divided by At-Bats

BA/RSP Batting Average with Runners in Scoring Position (second and/or third base)

BABIP Batting Average on Balls in Play. This is a measure of the number of batted balls that safely fall in for hits (not including home runs). The exact formula we use is (H-HR)/(AB-K-HR). This is similar to DER, but from the batter's perspective.

BB: Bases on Balls, otherwise known as walks

BB/G: Walks Allowed per Games pitched. This stat is based on the number of walks allowed divided by total number of batters faced, times the average number of batters per game in that specific league (generally around 38 batters a game).

BFP: Batters Faced by Pitcher; the pitching equivalent of Plate Appearances for batters

CS: Caught Stealing

CWS: Career Win Shares

DER Defense Efficiency Ratio. The percent of times a batted ball is turned into an out by the team's fielders, not including home runs. The exact formula we use is (BFP-H-K-BB-HBP-0.6*E)/(BFP-HR-K-BB-HBP). This is similar to BABIP, but from the defensive team's perspective.

DP: Double Plays

DPS: Double Plays Started, in which the fielder typically gets only an assist

DPT: Double Plays Turned, in which the fielder records both an assist and a putout

ERA: Earned Run Average. Number of earned runs allowed divided by innings pitched multiplied by nine.

ERA+: ERA measured against the league average and adjusted for ballpark factors. An ERA+ over 100 is better than average, less than 100 is below average.

ExpWS: Expected Win Shares. See the Win Shares section for a fuller discussion.

FE: Fielding Errors, as opposed to Throwing Errors (TE)

FIP: Fielding Independent Pitching, a measure of all those things for which a pitcher is specifically responsible. The formula is (HR*13+(BB+HBP)*3-K*2)/IP, plus a league-specific factor (usually around 3.2) to round out the number to an equivalent ERA number. FIP helps you understand how well a pitcher pitched, regardless of how well his fielders fielded. FIP was invented by Tom M. Tango.

FPct: Fielding Percentage, or the number of fielding chances handled without an error. The formula is (A+PO)/(A+PO+E).

G: Games played

GB%: The percent of batted balls that are grounders. GB% is a better way to measure groundball tendencies than the more common Ground ball/Fly ball ratio (G/F), because ratios don't follow normal scales (a G/F ratio of 2 doesn't equal twice as many groundballs than 1) and definitions of fly balls can be inconsistent.

GIDP (or GDP): The number of times a batter Grounded Into Double Plays

GPA: Gross Production Average, a variation of OPS, but more accurate and easier to interpret. The exact formula is (OBP*1.8+SLG)/4, adjusted for ballpark. The scale of GPA is similar to BA: .200 is lousy, .265 is around average and .300 is a star.

GS: Games Started, a pitching stat.

Holds: A bullpen stat. According to MLB.com, *A relief pitcher is credited with a hold any time he enters a game in a save situation, records at least one out and leaves the game never having relinquished the lead. A pitcher cannot finish the game and receive credit for a hold, nor can he earn a hold and a save in the same game.*

HRA: Home Runs Allowed, also a pitching stat

HR/Fly or HR/F: Home Runs as a percent of outfield Fly balls. Research has shown that about 11% of outfield flies are hit for home runs.

HR/G: Home Runs Allowed per Games pitched. This stat is based on the number of home runs allowed divided by total number of batters faced, times the average number of batters per game in that specific league (generally around 38 batters a game).

IBB: Intentional Base on Balls.

IF/Fly or IF/F: The percent of fly balls that are infield flies.

ISO: Isolated Power, which measures the "true power" of a batter. The formula is SLG-BA.

K: Strikeouts

K/G: Strikeouts per games pitched. This stat is based on the number of strikeouts divided by total number of batters faced, times the average number of batters per game in that specific league (generally around 38 batters a game).

L: Losses

LD%: Line Drive Percentage. Baseball Info Solutions tracks the trajectory of each batted ball and categorizes it as a ground ball, fly ball or line drive. LD% is the percent of batted balls that are line drives. Line drives are not necessarily the hardest hit balls, but they do fall for a hit around 75% of the time.

LOB and LOB%: LOB stands for Left On Base. It is the number of runners that are left on base at the end of an inning. LOB% is slightly different; it is the percentage of base runners allowed that didn't score a run. LOB% is used to track a pitcher's luck or effectiveness (depending on your point of view). The exact formula is (H+BB+HBP-R)/(H+BB+HBP-(1.4*HR)).

Net Stolen Bases: The effective impact of a player's stolen bases. For batters, the formula is SB-(2*CS) because being caught stealing hurts twice as much as a stolen base helps. For pitchers, the formula is (SB+balks)-2*(CS+pickoffs).

Net Win Shares Value: A dollar figure that represents the relative value of a player's contract, given how much the player contributed. See the article of the same name for more information.

OBP: On Base Percentage, the proportion of plate appearances in which a batter reached base successfully, including hits, walks and hit by pitches.

Op: Save Opportunities

OPS: On Base plus Slugging Percentage, a crude but quick measure of a batter's true contribution to his team's offense. See GPA for a better approach.

OPS+: OPS measured against the league average, and adjusted for ballpark factors. An OPS+ over 100 is better than average, less than 100 is below average.

Outs: Outs. Not just outs at bat, by the way, but also outs when caught stealing. Two outs are included when hitting into a double play.

P/PA: Pitches per Plate Appearance.

PA: Plate Appearances, or AB+BB+HBP+SF+SH.

PO: Putouts, the number of times a fielder recorded an out in the field. First basemen and catchers get lots of these. From a pitching perspective, PO stands for pickoffs—the number of times a pitcher picks a base runner off a base.

POS: Position played in the field

PRC: Pitching Runs Created, a new stat developed by THT's David Gassko. PRC measures the impact of a pitcher by putting his production on the same scale as a batter's Runs Created. PRC is calculated by inserting the number of runs allowed by a pitcher into a league-average context, and then using the Pythagorean Formula to estimate how many wins that pitcher/team would achieve. That win total is then converted into the number of offensive runs it would take to achieve the same number of wins. The impact of fielders is separated in the process.

Pythagorean Formula: A formula for converting a team's Run Differential into a projected win-loss record. The formula is RS^2/(RS^2+RA^2). Teams' actual win-loss records tend to mirror their Pythagorean records, and variances can usually be attributed to luck.

You can improve the accuracy of the Pythagorean formula by using a different exponent (the 2 in the formula). In particular, a sabermetrician named US Patriot discovered that the best exponent can be calculated this way: (RS/G+RA/G)^.285, where RS/G is Runs Scored per Game and RA/G is Runs Allowed per Game. This is called the **PythagenPat formula**.

PWins: Pythagorean Wins. See the previous entry.

R: Runs Scored and/or Allowed.

R/G: Runs Scored Per Game. Literally, R divided by games played.

RA: Runs Allowed or Runs Allowed Per Nine Innings. Just like ERA, but with unearned runs, too.

RBI: Runs Batted In

RC: Runs Created. Invented by Bill James, RC is a very good measure of the number of runs a batter truly contributed to his team's offense. The basic formula for RC is OBP*TB, but it has evolved into over 14 different versions. We use the most complicated version, which includes the impact of hitting well with runners in scoring position, and we adjust for ballpark impact.

RCAA: Runs Created Above Average. A stat invented and tracked by Lee Sinins, the author of the *Sabermetric Baseball Encyclopedia*. Lee calculates each player's Runs Created and then compares it to the league average, given that player's number of plate appearances.

RF: Range Factor, a measure of the total chances fielded in a player's playing time. The formula we use is 9*(PO+A)/Innings in Field.

RISP: Runners In Scoring Position

RS: Runs Scored

RSAA: Runs Saved Above Average. This stat, which is also tracked and reported by Lee Sinins, is a measure of a pitcher's effectiveness and contribution.

Run Differential: Runs Scored minus Runs Allowed

SB: Stolen Bases

SB%: The percent of time a runner stole a base successfully. The formula is SB/SBA.

SBA: Stolen Bases Attempted.

SBA/G: Stolen Base Attempts per nine innings played.

ShO: Shutouts

Situational Hitting: The portion of Bill James's Runs Created formula that includes the impact of a batter's batting average with runners in scoring position and the number of home runs with runners on. It is an estimate of the number of runs a player created, compared to his overall Runs Created, by hitting with runners on base.

SLG and SLGA: Slugging Percentage. Total Bases divided by At-Bats. SLGA stands for Slugging Percentage Against. It represents SLG from the pitcher's perspective.

SO: Strikeouts

Sv: Saves. According to MLB.com, *A pitcher is credited with a save when he finishes a game won by his club, is not the winning pitcher, and either (a) enters the game with a lead of no more than three runs and pitches for at least one inning, (b) enters the game with the potential tying run either on base, or at bat, or on deck, or (c) pitches effectively for at least three innings.*

Sv%: Saves divided by Save Opportunities

TB: Total Bases, calculated as 1B+2B*2+3B*3+HR*4

TBA: Total Bases Allowed. A pitching stat.

TE: Throwing Errors, as opposed to Fielding Errors (FE)

UER: Unearned Runs

UERA: Unearned Run Average, or the number of unearned runs allowed for each nine innings pitched.

W: Wins

WHIP: Walks and Hits Per Inning Pitched, a variant of OBP for pitchers. This is a popular stat in rotisserie baseball circles.

wOBA: Like GPA, wOBA (weighted On Base Average) is an improvement over OPS Introduced this year in *The Book*, it captures all of a batter's contributions in a single "rate metric" that is engineered to resemble the scale of OBP.

WPA: Win Probability Added. A system in which each player is given credit toward helping his team win, based on play-by-play data and the impact each specific play has on the team's probability of winning. See "WPA in the USA" for more information.

WP+PB/G: Wild Pitches and Passed Balls per Nine Innings played. A fielding stat for catchers.

Win Shares Definitions

WS: Win Shares. Invented by Bill James. Win Shares is a very complicated statistic that takes all the contributions a player made toward his team's wins and distills them into a single number that represents the number of wins he contributed to the team, times three.

There are three subcategories of Win Shares: batting, pitching and fielding.

We have tweaked James' original formula in two ways:

1) We allow players to accumulate negative Win Shares. Adding an artificial "floor" at zero (which the original formula does) has unfortunate repercussions for all player's totals.

2) We have somewhat de-emphasized the portion of Win Shares that credits relief pitchers. We feel this is appropriate in today's "save-happy" environment.

CWS: Career Win Shares. Each player's career Win Shares includes Bill James's totals through 2003 and our totals for the last three years.

WSAge: The average age of a team, weighted by each player's total Win Shares contribution.

NetWSValue: A dollar figure that represents the relative value of a player's contract, given how much the player contributed. See the article of the same name for more information.

ExpWS: Expected Win Shares. This figure represents a player's average baseline, or the number of Win Shares he would have contributed if he were an average player. To calculate this, we count each player's plate appearances, innings in the field, innings pitched and relief innings pitched.

WSAB: Win Shares Above Bench. WSAB is a refined approach to Win Shares, in which each player's total Win Shares are compared to the Win Shares an average bench player would have received.

Our research indicates that this is an important adjustment to Win Shares, because it gives greater context to the Win Shares totals. The impact is similar to adding "Loss Shares" for each player.

The bench player is defined as 70% of Expected Win Shares for all players except starting pitchers, for whom it is 50% of Expected Win Shares.

WSP: Win Shares Percentage is a rate stat, calculated as WS/(2*ExpWS). WSP is similar to winning percentage in that .500 is average, but WSP ranges above 1.000 and below .000.

Who's Who

Carolina Bolado is a Miami native (Go Marlins!) who graduated from the University of Chicago (Go White Sox!) and now lives in New Jersey, where she is a food writer by day and THT copy editor by night. When not watching baseball, she spends her time swimming, cooking, reading Jane Austen and watching an unhealthy amount of *Law & Order*.

A graduate of Michigan State University, **Brian Borawski** is a CPA and works for a Detroit-area real estate developer. A lifelong Tigers fan, Brian writes about his favorite team at Tiger Blog (www.tigerblog. net). In 2004, Brian became a member of SABR, and is currently on the Business of Baseball committee.

John Brattain has been tilting at MLB's windmills and raging against the baseball machine online for close to a decade. He's grateful to his wife Kelly (AKA Shego) and his beautiful daughters Belinda and Kataryna for their patience. A special shout out to baseball historian extraordinaire Steve Treder for his help on the Federal League chapter and the Hardball Times' overworked editors in general. He is grateful to the God he worships for caffeine.

John Burnson is a writer for BaseballHQ.com, the author of the *2007 Graphical Player*, and the publisher of *Heater*, a weekly PDF magazine of baseball stats with commentary (www.heatermagazine.com).

Chris Constancio lives in the Midwest and crunches numbers for a living. He does more of the same in his spare time when writing about player development for The Hardball Times and maintaining a database of minor league statistics at FirstInning (www.FirstInning.com).

John Dewan has consistently broken new ground in the area of sports statistical analysis, first as one of the founders and former CEO of STATS, Inc. and now as the owner of Baseball Info Solutions. He is also the co-publisher of ACTA Publications and the author of last year's ground-breaking book on defense in baseball, *The Fielding Bible*. As a noted sports expert, he is heard weekly on WSCR, "The Score," an all-sports radio station in Chicago, where he lives with his wife and two children.

Bryan Donovan is a lifelong A's fan and baseball stats buff currently residing in Portland, Oregon. He works as a quality engineer at Sun Microsystems, Inc., where he develops web applications that report and analyze manufacturing quality data.

David Gassko has consulted for major league baseball teams, and is a student in his spare time. He can generally be found watching Mexican League games on Univision or cursing at his laptop. A lifelong resident of Massachusetts, he is also a Red Sox fan with all the issues that generally accompany such an unfortunate rooting interest.

Vince Gennaro is the author of *Diamond Dollars: The Economics of Winning in Baseball* (Maple Street Press). He is currently a consultant for a wide range of clients, including an MLB team. Over his 30-year business career, he served as a CEO of a public company, was President of a billion dollar division of Pepsico and an owner of a women's pro basketball team. His innovative analytical work on the business of baseball has been featured in *The Sporting News* and *The New York Times*, and he has written for *The Hardball Times, Boston Baseball* and the *Red Sox Annual*. He has an MBA from the University of Chicago and lives in Purchase, NY.

Aaron Gleeman is co-founder of The Hardball Times, a Senior Baseball Editor at RotoWorld.com and NBCSports.com, and can also be found writing at FoxSports.com and USAToday.com. He blogs about the Minnesota Twins and far less interesting topics every day at AaronGleeman.com.

Brian Gunn is an occasional contributor to The Hardball Times, a full-time screenwriter living in Los Angeles, and, on account of the lucky shirt he wore throughout the playoffs, the man most responsible for the Cardinals' world championship in 2006.

Ben Jacobs is a die-hard Boston Red Sox fan who lived in New York for seven years before finally escaping Yankee country. He now works as a sports copy editor for the *Tallahassee Democrat*.

Rich Lederer is President and Chief Investment Officer of Lederer & Associates, a Registered Investment Adviser in Long Beach, California. He is also the co-founder and lead writer for Baseball Analysts (www.baseballanalysts.com). A Bill James devotee, Rich owns all of the Baseball Abstracts (including the self-published books) and reviewed each of them in the popular Abstracts From The Abstracts series. He is married with two adult children and has more time than ever to write about baseball.

Will Leitch is the editor of Deadspin (www.deadspin.com) and the author of two books, *Life As A Loser* and *Catch*.

Larry Mahnken is a guy who likes baseball. He writes sometimes, and lives in York, PA. They actually paid him money for this! Suckers!

Rob Neyer joined ESPN.com in 1996, and since then he's written more words for that website than anyone. The author or co-author of five books, including *Rob Neyer's Big Book of Baseball Blunders* (2006), Rob lives in Portland, Oregon, with his wife and son.

Greg Rybarczyk served 7 years as an officer in the U.S. Navy, and spent the last 9 years as a reliability engineer, design engineer and Six Sigma "Black Belt" and "Master Black Belt" for two major U.S. & global corporations. He was inspired to create Hit Tracker, the new method for accurately estimating home run distances, by a Manny Ramirez home run over the Green Monster at Fenway Park on April 19, 2005, whose distance no one could estimate. Greg lives in the Portland, OR area with his wife and two children.

Jeff Sackmann is the creator of MinorLeagueSplits (www.minorleaguesplits.com), the only source for comprehensive split and situational stats for every active minor leaguer. He is a long-time Brewers fan and blogs about them at BrewCrew Ball (www.brewcrewball.com). Jeff lives in New York City, where he writes music, plays a lot of tennis, and earns his keep helping people get into business school.

Dave Studenmund has no idea how he wound up doing this stuff.

Mac Thomason has been a Braves fan since the early eighties, to the despair of his Mets-leaning family. He resides in Tuscaloosa, Alabama, where he is a librarian and doctoral student. He writes about the Braves at Braves Journal (www.bravesjournal.com).

Steve Treder has presented papers to the Cooperstown Symposium on Baseball and American Culture, and to the SABR Annual Convention. His articles have been published in *Nine: A Journal of Baseball History and Culture*, as well as in *The National Pastime*. A lifelong San Francisco Giants' fan, he is Vice President for Strategic Development for Western Management Group, a compensation consulting firm headquartered in Los Gatos, California.

Bryan Tsao has previously served as an editor for the *UCSD Guardian* and and an intern editor/writer for the *Taiwan News*. A graduate of the Cognitive Science department of the University of California, San Diego, he is currently pursuing a Masters in Information Management Systems from UC Berkeley. In between going to Oakland A's games, he also works as a User Experience Researcher for Bolt | Peters, a user experience consulting firm in San Francisco.

John Walsh is a research physicist at the Istituto Nazionale di Fisica Nucleare in Pisa, Italy. Despite living four thousand miles from Fenway Park, he remains an avid Red Sox fan. He would like to thank his wife, Giuliana, and two kids, Anna and Paolo. And mlb.tv.

Jon Weisman writes about the Dodgers at Dodger Thoughts (www.dodgerthoughts.com) and about baseball at SportsIllustrated.com. In his non-spare time, he is a features editor at *Variety*.